T0331706

Kernel Methods for Pattern Analysis

Pattern Analysis is the process of finding general relations in a set of data, and forms the core of many disciplines, from neural networks to so-called syntactical pattern recognition, from statistical pattern recognition to machine learning and data mining. Applications of pattern analysis range from bioinformatics to document retrieval.

The kernel methodology described here provides a powerful and unified framework for all of these disciplines, motivating algorithms that can act on general types of data (e.g. strings, vectors, text, etc.) and look for general types of relations (e.g. rankings, classifications, regressions, clusters, etc.). This book fulfils two major roles. Firstly it provides practitioners with a large toolkit of algorithms, kernels and solutions ready to be implemented, many given as Matlab code suitable for many pattern analysis tasks in fields such as bioinformatics, text analysis, and image analysis. Secondly it furnishes students and researchers with an easy introduction to the rapidly expanding field of kernel-based pattern analysis, demonstrating with examples how to handcraft an algorithm or a kernel for a new specific application, while covering the required conceptual and mathematical tools necessary to do so.

The book is in three parts. The first provides the conceptual foundations of the field, both by giving an extended introductory example and by covering the main theoretical underpinnings of the approach. The second part contains a number of kernel-based algorithms, from the simplest to sophisticated systems such as kernel partial least squares, canonical correlation analysis, support vector machines, principal components analysis, etc. The final part describes a number of kernel functions, from basic examples to advanced recursive kernels, kernels derived from generative models such as HMMs and string matching kernels based on dynamic programming, as well as special kernels designed to handle text documents.

All those involved in pattern recognition, machine learning, neural networks and their applications, from computational biology to text analysis will welcome this account.

Kernel Methods for Pattern Analysis

John Shawe-Taylor
University of Southampton

Nello Cristianini
University of California at Davis

CAMBRIDGE
UNIVERSITY PRESS

CAMBRIDGE
UNIVERSITY PRESS

University Printing House, Cambridge CB2 8BS, United Kingdom

Published in the United States of America by Cambridge University Press, New York

Cambridge University Press is part of the University of Cambridge.

It furthers the University's mission by disseminating knowledge in the pursuit of education, learning and research at the highest international levels of excellence.

www.cambridge.org
Information on this title: www.cambridge.org/9780521813976

© Cambridge University Press 2004

First published 2004
6th printing 2012

A catalogue record for this publication is available from the British Library

Library of Congress Cataloguing in Publication data available

Shawe-Taylor, John.
Kernel methods for pattern analysis / John Shawe-Taylor, Nello Cristianini.
p.   cm.
Includes bibliographical references and index.
ISBN 0 521 81397 2 (hardback)
1. Machine learning.   2. Algorithms.   3. Kernel functions.   4. Pattern perception – Data processing.   I. Cristianini, Nello.   II. Title.
Q325.5.S475 2004
006.3'1 – dc22   2003069590

ISBN 978-0-521-81397-6 Hardback

Contents

Code fragments

Preface

The study of patterns in data is as old as science. Consider, for example, the astronomical breakthroughs of Johannes Kepler formulated in his three famous laws of planetary motion. They can be viewed as relations that he detected in a large set of observational data compiled by Tycho Brahe.

Equally the wish to automate the search for patterns is at least as old as computing. The problem has been attacked using methods of statistics, machine learning, data mining and many other branches of science and engineering.

Pattern analysis deals with the problem of (automatically) detecting and characterising relations in data. Most statistical and machine learning methods of pattern analysis assume that the data is in vectorial form and that the relations can be expressed as classification rules, regression functions or cluster structures; these approaches often go under the general heading of 'statistical pattern recognition'. 'Syntactical' or 'structural pattern recognition' represents an alternative approach that aims to detect rules among, for example, strings, often in the form of grammars or equivalent abstractions.

The evolution of automated algorithms for pattern analysis has undergone three revolutions. In the 1960s efficient algorithms for detecting linear relations within sets of vectors were introduced. Their computational and statistical behaviour was also analysed. The Perceptron algorithm introduced in 1957 is one example. The question of how to detect nonlinear relations was posed as a major research goal at that time. Despite this developing algorithms with the same level of efficiency and statistical guarantees has proven an elusive target.

In the mid 1980s the field of pattern analysis underwent a 'nonlinear revolution' with the almost simultaneous introduction of backpropagation multilayer neural networks and efficient decision tree learning algorithms. These approaches for the first time made it possible to detect nonlinear patterns, albeit with heuristic algorithms and incomplete statistical analysis. The impact of the nonlinear revolution cannot be overemphasised: entire fields such as data mining and bioinformatics were enabled by it. These nonlinear algorithms, however, were based on gradient descent or greedy heuristics and so suffered from local minima. Since their statistical behaviour was not well understood, they also frequently suffered from overfitting.

A third stage in the evolution of pattern analysis algorithms took place in the mid-1990s with the emergence of a new approach to pattern analysis known as kernel-based learning methods that finally enabled researchers to analyse nonlinear relations with the efficiency that had previously been reserved for linear algorithms. Furthermore advances in their statistical analysis made it possible to do so in high-dimensional feature spaces while avoiding the dangers of overfitting. From all points of view, computational, statistical and conceptual, the nonlinear pattern analysis algorithms developed in this third generation are as efficient and as well founded as linear ones. The problems of local minima and overfitting that were typical of neural networks and decision trees have been overcome. At the same time, these methods have been proven very effective on non vectorial data, in this way creating a connection with other branches of pattern analysis.

Kernel-based learning first appeared in the form of support vector machines, a classification algorithm that overcame the computational and statistical difficulties alluded to above. Soon, however, kernel-based algorithms able to solve tasks other than classification were developed, making it increasingly clear that the approach represented a revolution in pattern analysis. Here was a whole new set of tools and techniques motivated by rigorous theoretical analyses and built with guarantees of computational efficiency.

Furthermore, the approach is able to bridge the gaps that existed between the different subdisciplines of pattern recognition. It provides a unified framework to reason about and operate on data of all types be they vectorial, strings, or more complex objects, while enabling the analysis of a wide variety of patterns, including correlations, rankings, clusterings, etc.

This book presents an overview of this new approach. We have attempted to condense into its chapters an intense decade of research generated by a new and thriving research community. Together its researchers have created a class of methods for pattern analysis, which has become an important part of the practitioner's toolkit.

The algorithms presented in this book can identify a wide variety of relations, ranging from the traditional tasks of classification and regression, through more specialised problems such as ranking and clustering, to advanced techniques including principal components analysis and canonical correlation analysis. Furthermore, each of the pattern analysis tasks can be applied in conjunction with each of the bank of kernels developed in the final part of the book. This means that the analysis can be applied to a wide variety of data, ranging from standard vectorial types through more complex objects such as images and text documents, to advanced datatypes associated with biosequences, graphs and grammars.

Kernel-based analysis is a powerful new tool for mathematicians, scientists and engineers. It provides a surprisingly rich way to interpolate between pattern analysis, signal processing, syntactical pattern recognition and pattern recognition methods from splines to neural networks. In short, it provides a new viewpoint whose full potential we are still far from understanding.

The authors have played their part in the development of kernel-based learning algorithms, providing a number of contributions to the theory, implementation, application and popularisation of the methodology. Their book, *An Introduction to Support Vector Machines*, has been used as a textbook in a number of universities, as well as a research reference book. The authors also assisted in the organisation of a European Commission funded Working Group in 'Neural and Computational Learning (NeuroCOLT)' that played an important role in defining the new research agenda as well as in the project 'Kernel Methods for Images and Text (KerMIT)' that has seen its application in the domain of document analysis.

The authors would like to thank the many people who have contributed to this book through discussion, suggestions and in many cases highly detailed and enlightening feedback. Particularly thanks are owing to Gert Lanckriet, Michinari Momma, Kristin Bennett, Tijl DeBie, Roman Rosipal, Christina Leslie, Craig Saunders, Bernhard Schölkopf, Nicolò Cesa-Bianchi, Peter Bartlett, Colin Campbell, William Noble, Prabir Burman, Jean-Philippe Vert, Michael Jordan, Manju Pai, Andrea Frome, Chris Watkins, Juho Rousu, Thore Graepel, Ralf Herbrich, and David Hardoon. They would also like to thank the European Commission and the UK funding council EPSRC for supporting their research into the development of kernel-based learning methods.

Nello Cristianini is Assistant Professor of Statistics at University of California in Davis. Nello would like to thank UC Berkeley Computer Science Department and Mike Jordan for hosting him during 2001–2002, when Nello was a Visiting Lecturer there. He would also like to thank MIT CBLC and Tommy Poggio for hosting him during the summer of 2002, as well as the Department of Statistics at UC Davis, which has provided him with an ideal environment for this work. Much of the structure of the book is based on courses taught by Nello at UC Berkeley, at UC Davis and tutorials given in a number of conferences.

John Shawe-Taylor is professor of computing science at the University of Southampton. John would like to thank colleagues in the Computer Science Department of Royal Holloway, University of London, where he was employed during most of the writing of the book.

Part I

Basic concepts

1

Pattern analysis

Pattern analysis deals with the automatic detection of patterns in data, and plays a central role in many modern artificial intelligence and computer science problems. By patterns we understand any relations, regularities or structure inherent in some source of data. By detecting significant patterns in the available data, a system can expect to make predictions about new data coming from the same source. In this sense the system has acquired generalisation power by '*learning*' something about the source generating the data. There are many important problems that can only be solved using this approach, problems ranging from bioinformatics to text categorization, from image analysis to web retrieval. In recent years, pattern analysis has become a standard software engineering approach, and is present in many commercial products.

Early approaches were efficient in finding linear relations, while nonlinear patterns were dealt with in a less principled way. The methods described in this book combine the theoretically well-founded approach previously limited to linear systems, with the flexibility and applicability typical of nonlinear methods, hence forming a remarkably powerful and robust class of pattern analysis techniques.

There has been a distinction drawn between statistical and syntactical pattern recognition, the former dealing essentially with vectors under statistical assumptions about their distribution, and the latter dealing with structured objects such as sequences or formal languages, and relying much less on statistical analysis. The approach presented in this book reconciles these two directions, in that it is capable of dealing with general types of data such as sequences, while at the same time addressing issues typical of statistical pattern analysis such as learning from finite samples.

1.1 Patterns in data

1.1.1 Data

This book deals with data and ways to exploit it through the identification of valuable knowledge. By data we mean the output of any observation, measurement or recording apparatus. This therefore includes images in digital format; vectors describing the state of a physical system; sequences of DNA; pieces of text; time series; records of commercial transactions, etc. By knowledge we mean something more abstract, at the level of relations between and patterns within the data. Such knowledge can enable us to make predictions about the source of the data or draw inferences about the relationships inherent in the data.

Many of the most interesting problems in AI and computer science in general are extremely complex often making it difficult or even impossible to specify an explicitly programmed solution. As an example consider the problem of recognising genes in a DNA sequence. We do not know how to specify a program to pick out the subsequences of, say, human DNA that represent genes. Similarly we are not able directly to program a computer to recognise a face in a photo. Learning systems offer an alternative methodology for tackling these problems. By exploiting the knowledge extracted from a sample of data, they are often capable of adapting themselves to infer a solution to such tasks. We will call this alternative approach to software design the *learning methodology*. It is also referred to as the *data driven* or *data based* approach, in contrast to the *theory driven* approach that gives rise to precise specifications of the required algorithms.

The range of problems that have been shown to be amenable to the learning methodology has grown very rapidly in recent years. Examples include text categorization; email filtering; gene detection; protein homology detection; web retrieval; image classification; handwriting recognition; prediction of loan defaulting; determining properties of molecules, etc. These tasks are very hard or in some cases impossible to solve using a standard approach, but have all been shown to be tractable with the learning methodology. Solving these problems is not just of interest to researchers. For example, being able to predict important properties of a molecule from its structure could save millions of dollars to pharmaceutical companies that would normally have to test candidate drugs in expensive experiments, while being able to identify a combination of biomarker proteins that have high predictive power could result in an early cancer diagnosis test, potentially saving many lives.

In general, the field of pattern analysis studies systems that use the learning methodology to discover *patterns in data*. The patterns that are sought include many different types such as classification, regression, cluster analysis (sometimes referred to together as *statistical pattern recognition*), feature extraction, grammatical inference and parsing (sometimes referred to as *syntactical pattern recognition*). In this book we will draw concepts from all of these fields and at the same time use examples and case studies from some of the applications areas mentioned above: bioinformatics, machine vision, information retrieval, and text categorization.

It is worth stressing that while traditional statistics dealt mainly with data in vector form in what is known as *multivariate statistics*, the data for many of the important applications mentioned above are non-vectorial. We should also mention that pattern analysis in computer science has focussed mainly on classification and regression, to the extent that pattern analysis is synonymous with classification in the neural network literature. It is partly to avoid confusion between this more limited focus and our general setting that we have introduced the term *pattern analysis*.

1.1.2 Patterns

Imagine a dataset containing thousands of observations of planetary positions in the solar system, for example daily records of the positions of each of the nine planets. It is obvious that the position of a planet on a given day is not independent of the position of the same planet in the preceding days: it can actually be predicted rather accurately based on knowledge of these positions. The dataset therefore contains a certain amount of redundancy, that is information that can be reconstructed from other parts of the data, and hence that is not strictly necessary. In such cases the dataset is said to be *redundant*: simple laws can be extracted from the data and used to reconstruct the position of each planet on each day. The rules that govern the position of the planets are known as Kepler's laws. Johannes Kepler discovered his three laws in the seventeenth century by analysing the planetary positions recorded by Tycho Brahe in the preceding decades.

Kepler's discovery can be viewed as an early example of pattern analysis, or data-driven analysis. By assuming that the laws are invariant, they can be used to make predictions about the outcome of future observations. The laws correspond to regularities present in the planetary data and by inference therefore in the planetary motion itself. They state that the planets move in ellipses with the sun at one focus; that equal areas are swept in equal times by the line joining the planet to the sun; and that the period P (the time

	D	P	D²	P³
Mercury	0.24	0.39	0.058	0.059
Venus	0.62	0.72	0.38	0.39
Earth	1.00	1.00	1.00	1.00
Mars	1.88	1.53	3.53	3.58
Jupiter	11.90	5.31	142.00	141.00
Saturn	29.30	9.55	870.00	871.00

Table 1.1. *An example of a pattern in data: the quantity D^2/P^3 remains invariant for all the planets. This means that we could compress the data by simply listing one column or that we can predict one of the values for new previously unknown planets, as happened with the discovery of the outer planets.*

of one revolution around the sun) and the average distance D from the sun are related by the equation $P^3 = D^2$ for each planet.

Example 1.1 From Table 1.1 we can observe two potential properties of redundant datasets: on the one hand they are *compressible* in that we could construct the table from just one column of data with the help of Kepler's third law, while on the other hand they are *predictable* in that we can, for example, infer from the law the distances of newly discovered planets once we have measured their period. The predictive power is a direct consequence of the presence of the possibly hidden relations in the data. It is these relations once discovered that enable us to predict and therefore manipulate new data more effectively.   ∎

Typically we anticipate predicting one feature as a function of the remaining features: for example the distance as a function of the period. For us to be able to do this, the relation must be invertible, so that the desired feature can be expressed as a function of the other values. Indeed we will seek relations that have such an explicit form whenever this is our intention. Other more general relations can also exist within data, can be detected and can be exploited. For example, if we find a general relation that is expressed as an invariant function f that satisfies

$$f(\mathbf{x}) = 0, \tag{1.1}$$

where $\mathbf{x}$ is a data item, we can use it to identify novel or faulty data items for which the relation fails, that is for which $f(\mathbf{x}) \neq 0$. In such cases it is, however, harder to realise the potential for compressibility since it would require us to define a lower-dimensional coordinate system on the manifold defined by equation (1.1).

Kepler's laws are accurate and hold for all planets of a given solar system. We refer to such relations as *exact*. The examples that we gave above included problems such as loan defaulting, that is the prediction of which borrowers will fail to repay their loans based on information available at the time the loan is processed. It is clear that we cannot hope to find an exact prediction in this case since there will be factors beyond those available to the system, which may prove crucial. For example, the borrower may lose his job soon after taking out the loan and hence find himself unable to fulfil the repayments. In such cases the most the system can hope to do is find relations that hold with a certain probability. Learning systems have succeeded in finding such relations. The two properties of compressibility and predictability are again in evidence. We can specify the relation that holds for much of the data and then simply append a list of the exceptional cases. Provided the description of the relation is succinct and there are not too many exceptions, this will result in a reduction in the size of the dataset. Similarly, we can use the relation to make predictions, for example whether the borrower will repay his or her loan. Since the relation holds with a certain probability we will have a good chance that the prediction will be fulfilled. We will call relations that hold with a certain probability *statistical*.

Predicting properties of a substance based on its molecular structure is hindered by a further problem. In this case, for properties such as boiling point that take real number values, the relations sought will necessarily have to be approximate in the sense that we cannot expect an exact prediction. Typically we may hope that the expected error in the prediction will be small, or that with high probability the true value will be within a certain margin of the prediction, but our search for patterns must necessarily seek a relation that is approximate. One could claim that Kepler's laws are approximate if for no other reason because they fail to take general relativity into account. In the cases of interest to learning systems, however, the approximations will be much looser than those affecting Kepler's laws. Relations that involve some inaccuracy in the values accepted are known as *approximate*. For approximate relations we can still talk about prediction, though we must qualify the accuracy of the estimate and quite possibly the probability with which it applies. Compressibility can again be demonstrated if we accept that specifying the error corrections between the value output by the rule and the true value, take less space if they are small.

The relations that make a dataset redundant, that is the laws that we extract by mining it, are called *patterns* throughout this book. Patterns can be deterministic relations like Kepler's exact laws. As indicated above other relations are approximate or only holds with a certain probability. We are interested in situations where exact laws, especially ones that can be described as simply as Kepler's, may not exist. For this reason we will understand a *pattern* to be any relation present in the data, whether it be exact, approximate or statistical.

Example 1.2 Consider the following artificial example, describing some observations of planetary positions in a two dimensional orthogonal coordinate system. Note that this is certainly not what Kepler had in Tycho's data.

x	y	x^2	y^2	xy
0.8415	0.5403	0.7081	0.2919	0.4546
0.9093	−0.4161	0.8268	0.1732	−0.3784
0.1411	−0.99	0.0199	0.9801	−0.1397
−0.7568	−0.6536	0.5728	0.4272	0.4947
−0.9589	0.2837	0.9195	0.0805	−0.272
−0.2794	0.9602	0.0781	0.9219	−0.2683
0.657	0.7539	0.4316	0.5684	0.4953
0.9894	−0.1455	0.9788	0.0212	−0.144
0.4121	−0.9111	0.1698	0.8302	−0.3755
−0.544	−0.8391	0.296	0.704	0.4565

The upper plot of Figure 1.1 shows the data in the (x, y) plane. We can make many assumptions about the law underlying such positions. However if we consider the quantity $c_1 x^2 + c_2 y^2 + c_3 xy + c_4 x + c_5 y + c_6$ we will see that it is constant for some choice of the parameters, indeed as shown in the lower plot of Figure 1.1 we obtain a linear relation with just two features, x^2 and y^2. This would not generally be the case if the data were random, or even if the trajectory was following a curve different from a quadratic. In fact this invariance in the data means that the planet follows an elliptic trajectory. By changing the coordinate system the relation has become linear. ∎

In the example we saw how applying a change of coordinates to the data leads to the representation of a pattern changing. Using the initial coordinate system the pattern was expressed as a quadratic form, while in the coordinate system using monomials it appeared as a linear function. The possibility of transforming the representation of a pattern by changing the coordinate system in which the data is described will be a recurrent theme in this book.

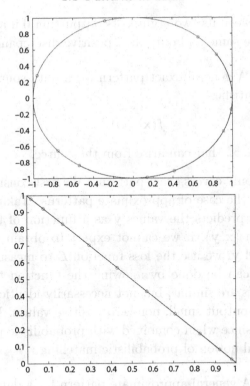

Fig. 1.1. The artificial planetary data lying on an ellipse in two dimensions and the same data represented using the features x^2 and y^2 showing a linear relation

The pattern in the example had the form of a function f that satisfied

$$f(\mathbf{x}) = 0,$$

for all the data points $\mathbf{x}$. We can also express the pattern described by Kepler's third law in this form

$$f(D, P) = D^2 - P^3 = 0.$$

Alternatively

$$g(D, P) = 2 \log D - 3 \log P = 0.$$

Similarly, if we have a function g that for each data item $(\mathbf{x}, \mathbf{y})$ predicts some output values $\mathbf{y}$ as a function of the input features $\mathbf{x}$, we can express the pattern in the form

$$f(\mathbf{x}, \mathbf{y}) = \mathcal{L}(g(\mathbf{x}), \mathbf{y}) = 0,$$

where $\mathcal{L} : Y \times Y \to \mathbb{R}^+$ is a so-called *loss function* that measures the disagreement between its two arguments outputting 0 if and only if the two arguments are the same and outputs a positive discrepancy if they differ.

Definition 1.3 A general exact pattern for a data source is a non-trivial function f that satisfies

$$f(\mathbf{x}) = 0,$$

for all of the data, $\mathbf{x}$, that can arise from the source. ∎

The definition only covers exact patterns. We first consider the relaxation required to cover the case of approximate patterns. Taking the example of a function g that predicts the values $\mathbf{y}$ as a function of the input features $\mathbf{x}$ for a data item $(\mathbf{x}, \mathbf{y})$, if we cannot expect to obtain an exact equality between $g(\mathbf{x})$ and $\mathbf{y}$, we use the loss function $\mathcal{L}$ to measure the amount of mismatch. This can be done by allowing the function to output 0 when the two arguments are similar, but not necessarily identical, or by allowing the function f to output small, non-zero positive values. We will adopt the second approach since when combined with probabilistic patterns it gives a distinct and useful notion of probabilistic matching.

Definition 1.4 A general approximate pattern for a data source is a non-trivial function f that satisfies

$$f(\mathbf{x}) \approx 0$$

for all of the data $\mathbf{x}$, that can arise from the source. ∎

We have deliberately left vague what approximately equal to zero might mean in a particular context.

Finally, we consider statistical patterns. In this case there is a probability distribution that generates the data. In many cases the individual data items can be assumed to be generate independently and identically, a case often referred to as independently and identically distributed or i.i.d. for short. We will use the symbol $\mathbb{E}$ to denote the *expectation* of some quantity under a distribution. If we wish to indicate the distribution over which the expectation is taken we add either the distribution or the variable as an index.

Note that our definitions of patterns hold for each individual data item in the case of exact and approximate patterns, but for the case of a statistical pattern we will consider the expectation of a function according to the underlying distribution. In this case we require the pattern function to be positive to ensure that a small expectation arises from small function values and not through the averaging of large positive and negative outputs. This can always be achieved by taking the absolute value of a pattern function that can output negative values.

Definition 1.5 A general statistical pattern for a data source generated i.i.d. according to a distribution $\mathcal{D}$ is a non-trivial non-negative function f that satisfies

$$\mathbb{E}_{\mathcal{D}}f(\mathbf{x}) = \mathbb{E}_{\mathbf{x}}f(\mathbf{x}) \approx 0.$$

∎

If the distribution does not satisfy the i.i.d. requirement this is usually as a result of dependencies between data items generated in sequence or because of slow changes in the underlying distribution. A typical example of the first case is time series data. In this case we can usually assume that the source generating the data is ergodic, that is, the dependency decays over time to a probability that is i.i.d. It is possible to develop an analysis that approximates i.i.d. for this type of data. Handling changes in the underlying distribution has also been analysed theoretically but will also be beyond the scope of this book.

Remark 1.6 [Information theory] It is worth mentioning how the patterns we are considering and the corresponding compressibility are related to the traditional study of statistical information theory. Information theory defines the entropy of a (not necessarily i.i.d.) source of data and limits the compressibility of the data as a function of its entropy. For the i.i.d. case it relies on knowledge of the exact probabilities of the finite set of possible items.

Algorithmic information theory provides a more general framework for defining redundancies and regularities in datasets, and for connecting them with the compressibility of the data. The framework considers all computable functions, something that for finite sets of data becomes too rich a class. For in general we do not have access to all of the data and certainly not an exact knowledge of the distribution that generates it. ∎

Our information about the data source must rather be gleaned from a finite set of observations generated according to the same underlying distribution. Using only this information a pattern analysis algorithm must be able to identify patterns. Hence, we give the following general definition of a pattern analysis algorithm.

Definition 1.7 [Pattern analysis algorithm] A *Pattern analysis algorithm* takes as input a finite set of examples from the source of data to be analysed. Its output is either an indication that no patterns were detectable in the data, or a positive pattern function f that the algorithm asserts satisfies

$$\mathbb{E}f(\mathbf{x}) \approx 0,$$

where the expectation is with respect to the data generated by the source. We refer to input data examples as the training instances, the training examples or the training data and to the pattern function f as the hypothesis returned by the algorithm. The value of the expectation is known as the generalisation error.   ∎

Note that the form of the pattern function is determined by the particular algorithm, though of course the particular function chosen will depend on the sample of data given to the algorithm.

It is now time to examine in more detail the properties that we would like a pattern analysis algorithm to possess.

1.2 Pattern analysis algorithms

Identifying patterns in a finite set of data presents very different and distinctive challenges. We will identify three key features that a pattern analysis algorithm will be required to exhibit before we will consider it to be effective.

Computational efficiency Since we are interested in practical solutions to real-world problems, pattern analysis algorithms must be able to handle very large datasets. Hence, it is not sufficient for an algorithm to work well on small toy examples; we require that its performance should scale to large datasets. The study of the computational complexity or scalability of algorithms identifies *efficient algorithms* as those whose resource requirements scale polynomially with the size of the input. This means that we can bound the number of steps and memory that the algorithm requires as a polynomial function of the size of the dataset and other relevant parameters such as the number of features, accuracy required, etc. Many algorithms used in pattern analysis fail to satisfy this apparently benign criterion, indeed there are some for which there is no guarantee that a solution will be found at all. *For the purposes of this book we will require all algorithms to be computationally efficient and furthermore that the degree of any polynomial involved should render the algorithm practical for large datasets.*

Robustness The second challenge that an effective pattern analysis algorithm must address is the fact that in real-life applications data is often corrupted by noise. By noise we mean that the values of the features for individual data items may be affected by measurement inaccuracies or even miscodings, for example through human error. This is closely related to the notion of approximate patterns discussed above, since even if the underlying relation is exact, once noise has been introduced it will necessarily become approximate and quite possibly statistical. *For our purposes we will require that the algorithms will be able to handle noisy data and identify approximate patterns.* They should therefore tolerate a small amount of noise in the sense that it will not affect their output too much. We describe an algorithm with this property as *robust*.

Statistical stability The third property is perhaps the most fundamental, namely that the patterns the algorithm identifies really are genuine patterns of the data source and not just an accidental relation occurring in the finite training set. We can view this property as the *statistical* robustness of the output in the sense that if we rerun the algorithm on a new sample from the same source it should identify a similar pattern. Hence, the output of the algorithm should not be sensitive to the particular dataset, just to the underlying source of the data. For this reason we will describe an algorithm with this property as *statistically stable* or *stable* for short. A relation identified by such an algorithm as a pattern of the underlying source is also referred to as *stable, significant* or *invariant*. *Again for our purposes we will aim to demonstrate that our algorithms are statistically stable.*

Remark 1.8 [Robustness and stability] There is some overlap between robustness and statistical stability in that they both measure sensitivity of the pattern function to the sampling process. The difference is that robustness emphasise the effect of the sampling on the pattern function itself, while statistical stability measures how reliably the particular pattern function will process unseen examples. We have chosen to separate them as they lead to different considerations in the design of pattern analysis algorithms. ∎

To summarise: a pattern analysis algorithm should possess three properties: efficiency, robustness and statistical stability. We will now examine the third property in a little more detail.

1.2.1 Statistical stability of patterns

Proving statistical stability Above we have seen how discovering patterns in data can enable us to make predictions and hence how a stable pattern analysis algorithm can extend the usefulness of the data by learning general properties from the analysis of particular observations. When a learned pattern makes correct predictions about future observations we say that it has *generalised,* as this implies that the pattern has more general applicability. We will also refer to the accuracy of these future predictions as the *quality of the generalization.* This property of an observed relation is, however, a delicate one. Not all the relations found in a given set of data can be assumed to be invariant or stable. It may be the case that a relation has arisen by chance in the particular set of data. Hence, at the heart of pattern analysis is the problem of assessing the reliability of relations and distinguishing them from ephemeral coincidences. How can we be sure we have not been misled by a particular relation we have observed in the given dataset? After all it is always possible to find some relation between any finite set of numbers, even random ones, provided we are prepared to allow arbitrarily complex relations.

Conversely, the possibility of false patterns means there will always be limits to the level of assurance that we are able to give about a pattern's stability.

Example 1.9 Suppose all of the phone numbers stored in your friend's mobile phone are even. If (s)he has stored 20 numbers the probability of this occurring by chance is approximately 10^{-6}, but you probably shouldn't conclude that you would cease to be friends if your phone number were changed to an odd number (of course if in doubt, changing your phone number might be a way of putting your friendship to the test). ∎

Pattern analysis and hypothesis testing The pattern analysis algorithm similarly identifies a stable pattern with a proviso that there is a small probability that it could be the result of a misleading dataset. The status of this assertion is identical to that of a statistical test for a property P. The null hypothesis of the test states that P does not hold. The test then bounds the probability that the observed data could have arisen if the null hypothesis is true. If this probability is some small number p, then we conclude that the property does hold subject to the caveat that there is a probability p we were misled by the data. The number p is the so-called *significance* with which the assertion is made. In pattern analysis this probability is referred to as the *confidence parameter* and it is usually denoted with the symbol δ.

If we were testing for the presence of just one pattern we could apply the methodology of a statistical test. Learning theory provides a framework for testing for the presence of one of a set of patterns in a dataset. This at first sight appears a difficult task. For example if we applied the same test for n hypotheses $P_1, \ldots, P_n$, and found that for one of the hypotheses, say P^*, a significance of p is measured, we can only assert the hypothesis with significance np. This is because the data could have misled us about any one of the hypotheses, so that even if none were true there is still a probability p for each hypothesis that it could have appeared significant, giving in the worst case a probability of np that one of the hypotheses appears significant at level p. It is therefore remarkable that learning theory enables us to improve on this worst case estimate in order to test very large numbers (in some cases infinitely many) of hypotheses and still obtain significant results.

Without restrictions on the set of possible relations, proving that a certain pattern is stable is impossible. Hence, to ensure stable pattern analysis we will have to restrict the set of possible relations. At the same time we must make assumptions about the way in which the data is generated by the source. For example we have assumed that there is a fixed distribution and that the data is generated i.i.d. Some statistical tests make the further assumption that the data distribution is Gaussian making it possible to make stronger assertions, but ones that no longer hold if the distribution fails to be Gaussian.

Overfitting At a general level the task of a learning theory is to derive results which enable testing of as wide as possible a range of hypotheses, while making as few assumptions as possible. This is inevitably a trade-off. If we make too restrictive assumptions there will be a misfit with the source and hence unreliable results or no detected patterns. This may be because for example the data is not generated in the manner we assumed; say a test that assumes a Gaussian distribution is used for non-Gaussian data or because we have been too miserly in our provision of hypotheses and failed to include any of the patterns exhibited by the source. In these cases we say that we have *underfit* the data. Alternatively, we may make too few assumptions either by assuming too much flexibility for the way in which the data is generated (say that there are interactions between neighbouring examples) or by allowing too rich a set of hypotheses making it likely that there will be a chance fit with one of them. This is called *overfitting* the data.

In general it makes sense to use all of the known facts about the data, though in many cases this may mean eliciting domain knowledge from experts. In the next section we describe one approach that can be used to incorporate knowledge about the particular application domain.

1.2.2 Detecting patterns by recoding

As we have outlined above if we are to avoid overfitting we must necessarily bias the learning machine towards some subset of all the possible relations that could be found in the data. It is only in this way that the probability of obtaining a chance match on the dataset can be controlled. This raises the question of how the particular set of patterns should be chosen. This will clearly depend on the problem being tackled and with it the dataset being analysed. The obvious way to address this problem is to attempt to elicit knowledge about the types of patterns that might be expected. These could then form the basis for a matching algorithm.

There are two difficulties with this approach. The first is that eliciting possible patterns from domain experts is not easy, and the second is that it would mean designing specialist algorithms for each problem.

An alternative approach that will be exploited throughout this book follows from the observation that *regularities can be translated*. By this we mean that they can be rewritten into different regularities by changing the representation of the data. We have already observed this fact in the example of the planetary ellipses. By representing the data as a feature vector of monomials of degree two, the ellipse became a linear rather than a quadratic pattern. Similarly, with Kepler's third law the pattern becomes linear if we include $\log D$ and $\log P$ as features.

Example 1.10 The most convincing example of how the choice of representation can make the difference between learnable and non-learnable patterns is given by cryptography, where explicit efforts are made to find representations of the data that appear random, unless the right representation, as revealed by the key, is known. In this sense, pattern analysis has the opposite task of finding representations in which the patterns in the data are made sufficiently explicit that they can be discovered automatically. ∎

It is this viewpoint that suggests the alternative strategy alluded to above. Rather than devising a different algorithm for each problem, we fix on a standard set of algorithms and then transform the particular dataset into a representation suitable for analysis using those standard algorithms. The advantage of this approach is that we no longer have to devise a new algorithm for each new problem, but instead we must search for a recoding of the data into a representation that is suited to the chosen algorithms. For the algorithms that we will describe this turns out to be a more natural task in which we can reasonably expect a domain expert to assist. A further advantage of the approach is that much of the efficiency, robustness and stability analysis can be undertaken in the general setting, so that the algorithms come already certified with the three required properties.

The particular choice we fix on is the use of patterns that are determined by linear functions in a suitably chosen feature space. Recoding therefore involves selecting a feature space for the linear functions. The use of linear functions has the further advantage that it becomes possible to specify the feature space in an indirect but very natural way through a so-called *kernel function*. The kernel technique introduced in the next chapter makes it possible to work directly with objects such as biosequences, images, text data, etc. It also enables us to use feature spaces whose dimensionality is more than polynomial in the relevant parameters of the system, even though the computational cost remains polynomial. This ensures that even though we are using linear functions the flexibility they afford can be arbitrarily extended.

Our approach is therefore to design a set of efficient pattern analysis algorithms for patterns specified by linear functions in a kernel-defined feature space. Pattern analysis is then a two-stage process. First we must recode the data in a particular application so that the patterns become representable with linear functions. Subsequently, we can apply one of the standard linear pattern analysis algorithms to the transformed data. The resulting class of pattern analysis algorithms will be referred to as *kernel methods*.

1.3 Exploiting patterns

We wish to design pattern analysis algorithms with a view to using them to make predictions on new previously unseen data. For the purposes of benchmarking particular algorithms the unseen data usually comes in the form of a set of data examples from the same source. This set is usually referred to as the *test set*. The performance of the pattern function on random data from the source is then estimated by averaging its performance on the test set. In a real-world application the resulting pattern function would of course be applied continuously to novel data as they are received by the system. Hence, for example in the problem of detecting loan defaulters, the pattern function returned by the pattern analysis algorithm would be used to screen loan applications as they are received by the bank.

We understand by pattern analysis this process in all its various forms and applications, regarding it as synonymous with Machine Learning, at other times as Data Mining, Pattern Recognition or Pattern Matching; in many cases the name just depends on the application domain, type of pattern being sought or professional background of the algorithm designer. By drawing these different approaches together into a unified framework many correspondences and analogies will be made explicit, making it possible to extend the range of pattern types and application domains in a relatively seamless fashion.

The emerging importance of this approach cannot be over-emphasised. It is not an exaggeration to say that it has become a standard software engineering strategy, in many cases being the only known method for solving a particular problem. The entire Genome Project, for example, relies on pattern analysis techniques, as do many web applications, optical character recognition (OCR) systems, marketing analysis techniques, and so on. The use of such techniques is already very extensive, and with the increase in the availability of digital information expected in the next years, it is clear that it is destined to grow even further.

1.3.1 The overall strategy

All the conceptual issues discussed in the previous sections have arisen out of practical considerations in application domains. We have seen that we must incorporate some prior insights about the regularities in the source generating the data in order to be able to reliably detect them. The question therefore arises as to what assumptions best capture that prior knowledge and/or expectations. How should we model the data generation process and how can we ensure we are searching the right class of relations? In other words, how should we insert domain knowledge into the system, while still ensuring that the desiderata of efficiency, robustness and stability can be delivered by the resulting algorithm? There are many different approaches to these problems, from the inferring of logical rules to the training of neural networks; from standard statistical methods to fuzzy logic. They all have shown impressive results for particular types of patterns in particular domains.

What we will present, however, is a *novel, principled and unified* approach to pattern analysis, based on statistical methods that ensure stability and robustness, optimization techniques that ensure computational efficiency and enables a straightforward incorporation of domain knowledge. Such algorithms will offer many advantages: from the firm theoretical underpinnings of their computational and generalization properties, to the software engineering advantages offered by the modularity that decouples the inference algorithm from the incorporation of prior knowledge into the kernel.

We will provide examples from the fields of bioinformatics, document analysis, and image recognition. While highlighting the applicability of the methods, these examples should not obscure the fact that the techniques and theory we will describe are entirely general, and can in principle be applied to any type of data. This flexibility is one of the major advantages of kernel methods.

1.3.2 Common pattern analysis tasks

When discussing what constitutes a pattern in data, we drew attention to the fact that the aim of pattern analysis is frequently to predict one feature of the data as a function of the other feature values. It is therefore to be expected that many pattern analysis tasks isolate one feature that it is their intention to predict. Hence, the training data comes in the form

$$(\mathbf{x}, y),$$

where y is the value of the feature that the system aims to predict, and $\mathbf{x}$ is a vector containing the remaining feature values. The vector $\mathbf{x}$ is known as the *input*, while y is referred to as the *target output* or *label*. The test data will only have inputs since the aim is to predict the corresponding output values.

Supervised tasks The pattern analysis tasks that have this form are referred to as *supervised*, since each input has an associated label. For this type of task a pattern is sought in the form

$$f(\mathbf{x}, y) = \mathcal{L}(y, g(\mathbf{x})),$$

where g is referred to as the *prediction function* and $\mathcal{L}$ is known as a *loss function*. Since it measures the discrepancy between the output of the prediction function and the correct value y, we may expect the loss to be close to zero when a pattern is detected. When new data is presented the target output is not available and the pattern function is used to predict the value of y for the given input $\mathbf{x}$ using the function $g(\mathbf{x})$. The prediction that $f(\mathbf{x}, y) = 0$ implies that the discrepancy between $g(\mathbf{x})$ and y is small.

Different supervised pattern analysis tasks are distinguished by the type of the feature y that we aim to predict. *Binary classification*, refering to the case when $y \in \{-1, 1\}$, is used to indicate that the input vector belongs to a chosen category ($y = +1$), or not ($y = -1$). In this case we use the so-called discrete loss function that returns 1 if its two arguments differ and 0 otherwise. Hence, in this case the generalisation error is just the probability that a randomly drawn test example is misclassified. If the training data is labelled as belonging to one of N classes and the system must learn to assign new data points to their class, then y is chosen from the set $\{1, 2, \ldots, N\}$ and the task is referred to as *multiclass classification*. *Regression* refers to the case of supervised pattern analysis in which the unknown feature is real-valued, that is $y \in \mathbb{R}$. The term regression is also used to describe the case when $\mathbf{y}$ is vector valued, $\mathbf{y} \in \mathbb{R}^n$, for some $n \in \mathbb{N}$, though this can also be reduced to n separate regression tasks each with one-dimensional output but with potentially a loss of useful information. Another variant of regression is time-series analysis. In this case each example consists of a series of observations and the special feature is the value of the next observation in the series. Hence, the aim of pattern analysis is to make a forecast based on previous values of relevant features.

Semisupervised tasks In some tasks the distinguished feature or label is only partially known. For example in the case of *ranking* we may only have available the relative ordering of the the examples in the training set, while our aim is to enable a similar ordering of novel data. For this problem an underlying value function is often assumed and inference about its value for the training data is made during the training process. New data is then assessed by its value function output. Another situation in which only partial information is available about the labels is the case of *transduction*. Here only some of the data comes with the value of the label instantiated. The task may be simply to predict the label for the unlabelled data. This corresponds to being given the test data during the training phase.

Alternatively, the aim may be to make use of the unlabelled data to improve the ability of the pattern function learned to predict the labels of new data. A final variant on partial label information is the *query scenario* in which the algorithm can ask for an unknown label, but pays a cost for extracting this information. The aim here is to minimise a combination of the generalization error and querying cost.

Unsupervised tasks In contrast to supervised learning some tasks do not have a label that is only available for the training examples and must be predicted for the test data. In this case all of the features are available in both training and test data. Pattern analysis tasks that have this form are referred to as *unsupervised*. The information or pattern needs to be extracted without the highlighted 'external' information provided by the label. *Clustering* is one of the tasks that falls into this category. The aim here is to find a natural division of the data into homogeneous groups. We might represent each cluster by a centroid or prototype and measure the quality of the pattern by the expected distance of a new data point to its nearest prototype.

Anomaly or novelty-detection is the task of detecting new data points that deviate from the normal. Here, the exceptional or anomalous data are not available in the training phase and are assumed not to have been generated by the same source as the rest of the data. The task is tackled by finding a pattern function that outputs a low expected value for examples generated by the data source. If the output generated by a new example deviates significantly from its expected value, we identify it as exceptional in the sense that such a value would be very unlikely for the standard data. Novelty-detection arises in a number of different applications. For example engine monitoring attempts to detect abnormal engine conditions that may indicate the onset of some malfunction.

There are further unsupervised tasks that attempt to find low-dimensional representations of the data. Here the aim is to find a projection function P_V that maps X into a subspace V of a given fixed dimension k

$$P_V : X \longrightarrow V \subseteq X,$$

such that the expected value of the residual

$$f(\mathbf{x}) = \|P_V(\mathbf{x}) - \mathbf{x}\|^2$$

is small, or in other words such that f is a pattern function. The kernel principal components analysis (PCA) falls into this category.

A related method known as kernel canonical correlation analysis (CCA) considers data that has separate representations included in each input, for example $\mathbf{x} = (\mathbf{x}^A, \mathbf{x}^B)$ for the case when there are two representations. CCA now seeks a common low-dimensional representation described by two projections P_V^A and P_V^B such that the residual

$$f(\mathbf{x}) = \left\| P_V^A(\mathbf{x}^A) - P_V^B(\mathbf{x}^B) \right\|^2$$

is small. The advantage of this method becomes apparent when the two representations are very distinct but our prior knowledge of the data assures us that the patterns of interest are detectable in both. In such cases the projections are likely to pick out dimensions that retain the information of interest, while discarding aspects that distinguish the two representations and are hence irrelevant to the analysis.

Assumptions and notation We will mostly make the statistical assumption that the sample of data is drawn i.i.d. and we will look for statistical patterns in the data, hence also handling approximate patterns and noise. As explained above this necessarily implies that the patterns are only identified with high probability. In later chapters we will define the corresponding notions of generalization error.

Now we introduce some of the basic notation. We denote the input space by X and for supervised tasks use Y to denote the target output domain. The space X is often a subset of $\mathbb{R}^n$, but can also be a general set. Note that if X is a vector space, the input vectors are given as column vectors. If we wish to form a row vector for an instance $\mathbf{x}$, we can take the transpose $\mathbf{x}'$. For a supervised task the *training set* is usually denoted by

$$S = \{(\mathbf{x}_1, y_1), \ldots, (\mathbf{x}_\ell, y_\ell)\} \subseteq (X \times Y)^\ell,$$

where ℓ is the number of training examples. For unsupervised tasks this simplifies to

$$S = \{\mathbf{x}_1, \ldots, \mathbf{x}_\ell\} \subseteq X^\ell.$$

1.4 Summary

- Patterns are regularities that characterise the data coming from a particular source. They can be exact, approximate or statistical. We have chosen to represent patterns by a positive pattern function f that has small expected value for data from the source.
- A pattern analysis algorithm takes a finite sample of data from the source and outputs a detected regularity or pattern function.
- Pattern analysis algorithms are expected to exhibit three key properties: efficiency, robustness and stability.

Computational efficiency implies that the performance of the algorithm scales to large datasets.

Robustness refers to the insensitivity of the algorithm to noise in the training examples.

Statistical stability implies that the detected regularities should indeed be patterns of the underlying source. They therefore enable prediction on unseen data.

- Recoding, by for example a change of coordinates, maintains the presence of regularities in the data, but changes their representation. Some representations make regularities easier to detect than others and fixing on one form enables a standard set of algorithms and analysis to be used.
- We have chosen to recode relations as linear patterns through the use of kernels that allow arbitrary complexity to be introduced by a natural incorporation of domain knowledge.
- The standard scenarios in which we want to exploit patterns in data include binary and multiclass classification, regression, novelty-detection, clustering, and dimensionality reduction.

1.5 Further reading and advanced topics

Pattern analysis (or recognition, detection, discovery) has been studied in many different contexts, from statistics to signal processing, to the various flavours of artificial intelligence. Furthermore, many relevant ideas have been developed in the neighboring fields of information theory, machine vision, data-bases, and so on. In a way, pattern analysis has always been a constant theme of computer science, since the pioneering days. The references [39], [40], [46], [14], [110], [38], [45] are textbooks covering the topic from some of these different fields.

There are several important stages that can be identified in the evolution of pattern analysis algorithms. Efficient algorithms for detecting linear relations were already used in the 1950s and 1960s, and their computational and statistical behaviour was well understood [111], [44]. The step to handling nonlinear relations was seen as a major research goal at that time. The development of nonlinear algorithms that maintain the same level of efficiency and stability has proven an elusive goal. In the mid 80s the field of pattern analysis underwent a *nonlinear revolution*, with the almost simultaneous introduction of both backpropagation networks and decision trees [19], [109], [57]. Although based on simple heuristics and lacking a firm theoretical foundation, these approaches were the first to make a step towards the efficient and reliable detection of nonlinear patterns. The impact of that revolution cannot be overemphasized: entire fields such as data-mining and bioinformatics became possible as a result of it. In the mid 90s, the introduction of kernel-based learning methods [143], [16], [32], [120] has finally enabled researchers to deal with nonlinear relations, while retaining the guarantees and understanding that have been developed for linear algorithms over decades of research.

From all points of view, computational, statistical, and conceptual, the nonlinear pattern analysis algorithms developed in this third wave are as efficient and as well-founded as their linear counterparts. The drawbacks of local minima and incomplete statistical analysis that is typical of neural networks and decision trees have been circumvented, while their flexibility has been shown to be sufficient for a wide range of successful applications. In 1973 Duda and Hart defined statistical pattern recognition in the context of classification in their classical book, now available in a new edition [40]. Other important references include [137], [46]. Algorithmic information theory defines random data as data not containing any pattern, and provides many insights for thinking about regularities and relations in data. Introduced by Chaitin [22], it is discussed in the introductory text by Li and Vitanyi [91]. A classic introduction to Shannon's information theory can be found in Cover and Thomas [29].

The statistical study of pattern recognition can be divided into two main (but strongly interacting) directions of research. The earlier one is that presented by Duda and Hart [40], based on Bayesian statistics, and also to be found in the recent book [53]. The more recent method based on empirical processes, has been pioneered by Vapnik and Chervonenkis's work since the 1960s, [141], and has recently been greatly extended by several authors. Easy introductions can be found in [76], [5], [141]. The most recent (and most effective) methods are based on the notions of sharp concentration [38], [17] and notions of Rademacher complexity [9], [80], [134], [135].

The second direction will be the one followed in this book for its simplicity, elegance and effectiveness. Other discussions of pattern recognition via specific algorithms can be found in the following books: [14] and [110] for neural networks; [109] and [19] for decision trees, [32], and [102] for a general introduction to the field of machine learning from the perspective of artificial intelligence.

More information about Kepler's laws and the process by which he arrived at them can be found in a book by Arthur Koestler [78].

For constantly updated pointers to online literature and free software see the book's companion website: www.kernel-methods.net

2

Kernel methods: an overview

In Chapter 1 we gave a general overview to pattern analysis. We identified three properties that we expect of a pattern analysis algorithm: computational efficiency, robustness and statistical stability. Motivated by the observation that recoding the data can increase the ease with which patterns can be identified, we will now outline the kernel methods approach to be adopted in this book. This approach to pattern analysis first embeds the data in a suitable feature space, and then uses algorithms based on linear algebra, geometry and statistics to discover patterns in the embedded data.

The current chapter will elucidate the different components of the approach by working through a simple example task in detail. The aim is to demonstrate all of the key components and hence provide a framework for the material covered in later chapters.

Any kernel methods solution comprises two parts: a module that performs the mapping into the embedding or feature space and a learning algorithm designed to discover linear patterns in that space. There are two main reasons why this approach should work. First of all, detecting linear relations has been the focus of much research in statistics and machine learning for decades, and the resulting algorithms are both well understood and efficient. Secondly, we will see that there is a computational shortcut which makes it possible to represent linear patterns efficiently in high-dimensional spaces to ensure adequate representational power. The shortcut is what we call a kernel function.

25

2.1 The overall picture

This book will describe an approach to pattern analysis that can deal effectively with the problems described in Chapter 1 one that can detect stable patterns robustly and efficiently from a finite data sample. The strategy adopted is to embed the data into a space where the patterns can be discovered as linear relations. This will be done in a *modular* fashion. Two distinct components will perform the two steps. The initial mapping component is defined implicitly by a so-called *kernel function*. This component will depend on the specific data type and domain knowledge concerning the patterns that are to be expected in the particular data source. The pattern analysis algorithm component is general purpose, and robust. Furthermore, it typically comes with a statistical analysis of its stability. The algorithm is also *efficient*, requiring an amount of computational resources that is polynomial in the size and number of data items even when the dimension of the embedding space grows exponentially.

The strategy suggests *a software engineering approach* to learning systems' design through the breakdown of the task into subcomponents and the reuse of key modules.

In this chapter, through the example of least squares linear regression, we will introduce all of the main ingredients of kernel methods. Though this example means that we will have restricted ourselves to the particular task of supervised regression, four key aspects of the approach will be highlighted.

(i) Data items are embedded into a vector space called the feature space.

(ii) Linear relations are sought among the images of the data items in the feature space.

(iii) The algorithms are implemented in such a way that the coordinates of the embedded points are not needed, only their pairwise inner products.

(iv) The pairwise inner products can be computed efficiently directly from the original data items using a kernel function.

These stages are illustrated in Figure 2.1.

These four observations will imply that, despite restricting ourselves to algorithms that optimise linear functions, our approach will enable the development of a rich toolbox of efficient and well-founded methods for discovering nonlinear relations in data through the use of nonlinear embedding mappings. Before delving into an extended example we give a general definition of a linear pattern.

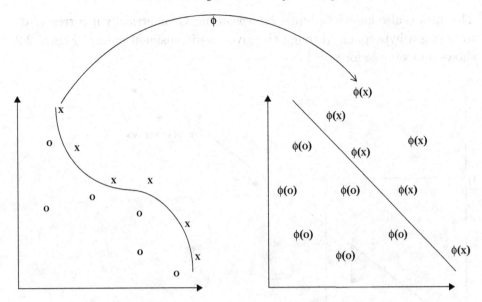

Fig. 2.1. The function ϕ embeds the data into a feature space where the nonlinear pattern now appears linear. The kernel computes inner products in the feature space directly from the inputs.

Definition 2.1 [Linear pattern] A linear pattern is a pattern function drawn from a set of patterns based on a linear function class. ∎

2.2 Linear regression in a feature space

2.2.1 Primal linear regression

Consider the problem of finding a homogeneous real-valued linear function

$$g(\mathbf{x}) = \langle \mathbf{w}, \mathbf{x} \rangle = \mathbf{w}'\mathbf{x} = \sum_{i=1}^{n} w_i x_i,$$

that best interpolates a given training set $S = \{(\mathbf{x}_1, y_1), \ldots, (\mathbf{x}_\ell, y_\ell)\}$ of points $\mathbf{x}_i$ from $X \subseteq \mathbb{R}^n$ with corresponding labels y_i in $Y \subseteq \mathbb{R}$. Here, we use the notation $\mathbf{x} = (x_1, x_2, \ldots, x_n)$ for the n-dimensional input vectors, while $\mathbf{w}'$ denotes the transpose of the vector $\mathbf{w} \in \mathbb{R}^n$. This is naturally one of the simplest relations one might find in the source $X \times Y$, namely a linear function g of the features $\mathbf{x}$ matching the corresponding label y, creating a pattern function that should be approximately equal to zero

$$f((\mathbf{x}, y)) = |y - g(\mathbf{x})| = |y - \langle \mathbf{w}, \mathbf{x} \rangle| \approx 0.$$

This task is also known as *linear interpolation*. Geometrically it corresponds to fitting a hyperplane through the given n-dimensional points. Figure 2.2 shows an example for $n = 1$.

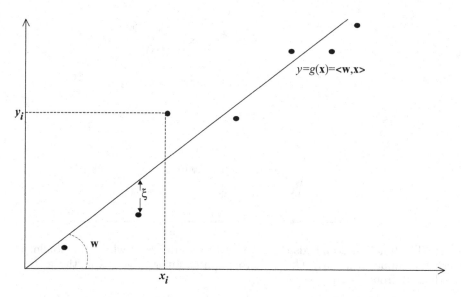

Fig. 2.2. A one-dimensional linear regression problem.

In the exact case, when the data has been generated in the form $(\mathbf{x}, g(\mathbf{x}))$, where $g(\mathbf{x}) = \langle \mathbf{w}, \mathbf{x} \rangle$ and there are exactly $\ell = n$ linearly independent points, it is possible to find the parameters $\mathbf{w}$ by solving the system of linear equations

$$\mathbf{Xw} = \mathbf{y},$$

where we have used $\mathbf{X}$ to denote the matrix whose rows are the row vectors $\mathbf{x}'_1, \ldots, \mathbf{x}'_\ell$ and $\mathbf{y}$ to denote the vector $(y_1, \ldots, y_\ell)'$.

Remark 2.2 [Row versus column vectors] Note that our inputs are column vectors but they are stored in the matrix $\mathbf{X}$ as row vectors. We adopt this convention to be consistent with the typical representation of data in an input file and in our Matlab code, while preserving the standard vector representation. ∎

If there are less points than dimensions, there are many possible $\mathbf{w}$ that describe the data exactly, and a criterion is needed to choose between them. In this situation we will favour the vector $\mathbf{w}$ with minimum norm. If there are more points than dimensions and there is noise in the generation process, then we should not expect there to be an exact pattern, so that an approximation criterion is needed. In this situation we will select the pattern with smallest error. In general, if we deal with noisy small datasets, a mix of the two strategies is needed: find a vector $\mathbf{w}$ that has both small norm and small error.

The distance shown as ξ in the figure is the error of the linear function on the particular training example, $\xi = (y - g(\mathbf{x}))$. This value is the output of the putative pattern function

$$f((\mathbf{x}, y)) = |y - g(\mathbf{x})| = |\xi|.$$

We would like to find a function for which all of these training errors are small. The sum of the squares of these errors is the most commonly chosen measure of the collective discrepancy between the training data and a particular function

$$\mathcal{L}(g, S) = \mathcal{L}(\mathbf{w}, S) = \sum_{i=1}^{\ell}(y_i - g(\mathbf{x}_i))^2 = \sum_{i=1}^{\ell}\xi_i^2 = \sum_{i=1}^{\ell}\mathcal{L}(g, (\mathbf{x}_i, y_i)),$$

where we have used the same notation $\mathcal{L}(g, (\mathbf{x}_i, y_i)) = \xi_i^2$ to denote the squared error or *loss* of g on example $(\mathbf{x}_i, y_i)$ and $\mathcal{L}(f, S)$ to denote the collective loss of a function f on the training set S. The learning problem now becomes that of choosing the vector $\mathbf{w} \in W$ that minimises the collective loss. This is a well-studied problem that is applied in virtually every discipline. It was introduced by Gauss and is known as *least squares approximation*.

Using the notation above, the vector of output discrepancies can be written as

$$\xi = \mathbf{y} - \mathbf{X}\mathbf{w}.$$

Hence, the loss function can be written as

$$\mathcal{L}(\mathbf{w}, S) = \|\xi\|_2^2 = (\mathbf{y} - \mathbf{X}\mathbf{w})'(\mathbf{y} - \mathbf{X}\mathbf{w}). \tag{2.1}$$

Note that we again use $\mathbf{X}'$ to denote the transpose of $\mathbf{X}$. We can seek the optimal $\mathbf{w}$ by taking the derivatives of the loss with respect to the parameters $\mathbf{w}$ and setting them equal to the zero vector

$$\frac{\partial \mathcal{L}(\mathbf{w}, S)}{\partial \mathbf{w}} = -2\mathbf{X}'\mathbf{y} + 2\mathbf{X}'\mathbf{X}\mathbf{w} = \mathbf{0},$$

hence obtaining the so-called 'normal equations'

$$\mathbf{X}'\mathbf{X}\mathbf{w} = \mathbf{X}'\mathbf{y}. \tag{2.2}$$

If the inverse of $\mathbf{X}'\mathbf{X}$ exists, the solution of the least squares problem can be expressed as

$$\mathbf{w} = (\mathbf{X}'\mathbf{X})^{-1}\mathbf{X}'\mathbf{y}.$$

Hence, to minimise the squared loss of a linear interpolant, one needs to maintain as many parameters as dimensions, while solving an $n \times n$ system of linear equations is an operation that has cubic cost in n.

This cost refers to the number of operations and is generally expressed as a complexity of $O\left(n^3\right)$, meaning that the number of operations $t\left(n\right)$ required for the computation can be bounded by

$$t\left(n\right) \leq Cn^3$$

for some constant C.

The predicted output on a new data point can now be computed using the prediction function

$$g(\mathbf{x}) = \langle \mathbf{w}, \mathbf{x} \rangle.$$

Remark 2.3 [Dual representation] Notice that if the inverse of $\mathbf{X}'\mathbf{X}$ exists we can express $\mathbf{w}$ in the following way

$$\mathbf{w} = (\mathbf{X}'\mathbf{X})^{-1}\mathbf{X}'\mathbf{y} = \mathbf{X}'\mathbf{X}(\mathbf{X}'\mathbf{X})^{-2}\mathbf{X}'\mathbf{y} = \mathbf{X}'\boldsymbol{\alpha},$$

making it a linear combination of the training points, $\mathbf{w} = \sum_{i=1}^{\ell} \alpha_i \mathbf{x}_i$. ∎

Remark 2.4 [Pseudo-inverse] If $\mathbf{X}'\mathbf{X}$ is singular, the pseudo-inverse can be used. This finds the $\mathbf{w}$ that satisfies equation (2.2) with minimal norm. Alternatively we can trade off the size of the norm against the loss. This is the approach known as ridge regression that we will describe below. ∎

As mentioned Remark 2.4 there are situations where fitting the data exactly may not be possible. Either there is not enough data to ensure that the matrix $\mathbf{X}'\mathbf{X}$ is invertible, or there may be noise in the data making it unwise to try to match the target output exactly. We described this situation in Chapter 1 as seeking an approximate pattern with algorithms that are robust. Problems that suffer from this difficulty are known as *ill-posed*, since there is not enough information in the data to precisely specify the solution. In these situations an approach that is frequently adopted is to restrict the choice of functions in some way. Such a restriction or bias is referred to as *regularisation*. Perhaps the simplest regulariser is to favour functions that have small norms. For the case of least squares regression, this gives the well-known optimisation criterion of ridge regression.

Computation 2.5 [Ridge regression] Ridge regression corresponds to solving the optimisation

$$\min_{\mathbf{w}} \mathcal{L}_\lambda(\mathbf{w}, S) = \min_{\mathbf{w}} \lambda \|\mathbf{w}\|^2 + \sum_{i=1}^{\ell} (y_i - g(\mathbf{x}_i))^2, \qquad (2.3)$$

where λ is a positive number that defines the relative trade-off between norm and loss and hence controls the degree of regularisation. The learning problem is reduced to solving an optimisation problem over $\mathbb{R}^n$. ∎

2.2.2 Ridge regression: primal and dual

Again taking the derivative of the cost function with respect to the parameters we obtain the equations

$$\mathbf{X}'\mathbf{X}\mathbf{w} + \lambda \mathbf{w} = \left(\mathbf{X}'\mathbf{X} + \lambda \mathbf{I}_n\right)\mathbf{w} = \mathbf{X}'\mathbf{y}, \qquad (2.4)$$

where $\mathbf{I}_n$ is the $n \times n$ identity matrix. In this case the matrix $(\mathbf{X}'\mathbf{X} + \lambda \mathbf{I}_n)$ is always invertible if $\lambda > 0$, so that the solution is given by

$$\mathbf{w} = \left(\mathbf{X}'\mathbf{X} + \lambda \mathbf{I}_n\right)^{-1} \mathbf{X}'\mathbf{y}. \qquad (2.5)$$

Solving this equation for $\mathbf{w}$ involves solving a system of linear equations with n unknowns and n equations. The complexity of this task is $O(n^3)$. The resulting prediction function is given by

$$g(\mathbf{x}) = \langle \mathbf{w}, \mathbf{x} \rangle = \mathbf{y}'\mathbf{X} \left(\mathbf{X}'\mathbf{X} + \lambda \mathbf{I}_n\right)^{-1} \mathbf{x}.$$

Alternatively, we can rewrite equation (2.4) in terms of $\mathbf{w}$ (similarly to Remark 2.3) to obtain

$$\mathbf{w} = \lambda^{-1}\mathbf{X}' \left(\mathbf{y} - \mathbf{X}\mathbf{w}\right) = \mathbf{X}'\boldsymbol{\alpha},$$

showing that again $\mathbf{w}$ can be written as a linear combination of the training points, $\mathbf{w} = \sum_{i=1}^{\ell} \alpha_i \mathbf{x}_i$ with $\boldsymbol{\alpha} = \lambda^{-1}\left(\mathbf{y} - \mathbf{X}\mathbf{w}\right)$. Hence, we have

$$\begin{aligned}
\boldsymbol{\alpha} &= \lambda^{-1}\left(\mathbf{y} - \mathbf{X}\mathbf{w}\right) \\
&\Rightarrow \lambda\boldsymbol{\alpha} = \left(\mathbf{y} - \mathbf{X}\mathbf{X}'\boldsymbol{\alpha}\right) \\
&\Rightarrow \left(\mathbf{X}\mathbf{X}' + \lambda \mathbf{I}_\ell\right)\boldsymbol{\alpha} = \mathbf{y} \\
&\Rightarrow \boldsymbol{\alpha} = \left(\mathbf{G} + \lambda \mathbf{I}_\ell\right)^{-1}\mathbf{y}, \qquad (2.6)
\end{aligned}$$

where $\mathbf{G} = \mathbf{XX}'$ or, component-wise, $\mathbf{G}_{ij} = \langle \mathbf{x}_i, \mathbf{x}_j \rangle$. Solving for $\boldsymbol{\alpha}$ involves solving ℓ linear equations with ℓ unknowns, a task of complexity $O(\ell^3)$. The resulting prediction function is given by

$$g(\mathbf{x}) = \langle \mathbf{w}, \mathbf{x} \rangle = \left\langle \sum_{i=1}^{\ell} \alpha_i \mathbf{x}_i, \mathbf{x} \right\rangle = \sum_{i=1}^{\ell} \alpha_i \langle \mathbf{x}_i, \mathbf{x} \rangle = \mathbf{y}' \left(\mathbf{G} + \lambda \mathbf{I}_\ell \right)^{-1} \mathbf{k},$$

where $k_i = \langle \mathbf{x}_i, \mathbf{x} \rangle$. We have thus found two distinct methods for solving the ridge regression optimisation of equation (2.3). The first given in equation (2.5) computes the weight vector explicitly and is known as the *primal solution*, while equation (2.6) gives the solution as a linear combination of the training examples and is known as the *dual solution*. The parameters $\boldsymbol{\alpha}$ are known as the *dual variables*.

The crucial observation about the dual solution of equation (2.6) is that the information from the training examples is given by the inner products between pairs of training points in the matrix $\mathbf{G} = \mathbf{XX}'$. Similarly, the information about a novel example $\mathbf{x}$ required by the predictive function is just the inner products between the training points and the new example $\mathbf{x}$.

The matrix $\mathbf{G}$ is referred to as the *Gram matrix*. The Gram matrix and the matrix $(\mathbf{G} + \lambda \mathbf{I}_\ell)$ have dimensions $\ell \times \ell$. If the dimension n of the feature space is larger than the number ℓ of training examples, it becomes more efficient to solve equation (2.6) rather than the primal equation (2.5) involving the matrix $(\mathbf{X}'\mathbf{X} + \lambda \mathbf{I}_n)$ of dimension $n \times n$. Evaluation of the predictive function in this setting is, however, always more costly since the primal involves $O(n)$ operations, while the complexity of the dual is $O(n\ell)$. Despite this we will later see that the dual solution can offer enormous advantages.

Hence one of the key findings of this section is that the ridge regression algorithm can be solved in a form that only requires inner products between data points.

Remark 2.6 [Primal-dual] The primal-dual dynamic described above recurs throughout the book. It also plays an important role in optimisation, text analysis, and so on. ∎

Remark 2.7 [Statistical stability] Though we have addressed the question of efficiency of the ridge regression algorithm, we have not attempted to analyse explicitly its robustness or stability. These issues will be considered in later chapters. ∎

2.2.3 Kernel-defined nonlinear feature mappings

The ridge regression method presented in the previous subsection addresses the problem of identifying linear relations between one selected variable and the remaining features, where the relation is assumed to be functional. The resulting predictive function can be used to estimate the value of the selected variable given the values of the other features. Often, however, the relations that are sought are nonlinear, that is the selected variable can only be accurately estimated as a nonlinear function of the remaining features. Following our overall strategy we will map the remaining features of the data into a new feature space in such a way that the sought relations can be represented in a linear form and hence the ridge regression algorithm described above will be able to detect them.

We will consider an embedding map

$$\phi : \mathbf{x} \in \mathbb{R}^n \longmapsto \phi(\mathbf{x}) \in F \subseteq \mathbb{R}^N.$$

The choice of the map ϕ aims to convert the nonlinear relations into linear ones. Hence, the map reflects our expectations about the relation $y = g(\mathbf{x})$ to be learned. The effect of ϕ is to recode our dataset S as $\widehat{S} = \{(\phi(\mathbf{x}_1), y_1), ..., (\phi(\mathbf{x}_\ell), y_\ell)\}$. We can now proceed as above looking for a relation of the form

$$f((\mathbf{x}, y)) = |y - g(\mathbf{x})| = |y - \langle \mathbf{w}, \phi(\mathbf{x}) \rangle| = |\xi|.$$

Although the primal method could be used, problems will arise if N is very large making the solution of the $N \times N$ system of equation (2.5) very expensive. If, on the other hand, we consider the dual solution, we have shown that all the information the algorithm needs is the inner products between data points $\langle \phi(\mathbf{x}), \phi(\mathbf{z}) \rangle$ in the feature space F. In particular the predictive function $g(\mathbf{x}) = \mathbf{y}'(\mathbf{G} + \lambda\mathbf{I}_\ell)^{-1}\mathbf{k}$ involves the Gram matrix $\mathbf{G} = \mathbf{X}\mathbf{X}'$ with entries

$$\mathbf{G}_{ij} = \langle \phi(\mathbf{x}_i), \phi(\mathbf{x}_j) \rangle, \tag{2.7}$$

where the rows of $\mathbf{X}$ are now the feature vectors $\phi(\mathbf{x}_1)', \ldots, \phi(\mathbf{x}_\ell)'$, and the vector $\mathbf{k}$ contains the values

$$k_i = \langle \phi(\mathbf{x}_i), \phi(\mathbf{x}) \rangle. \tag{2.8}$$

When the value of N is very large, it is worth taking advantage of the dual solution to avoid solving the large $N \times N$ system. Making the optimistic assumption that the complexity of evaluating ϕ is $O(N)$, the complexity of evaluating the inner products of equations (2.7) and (2.8) is still $O(N)$

making the overall complexity of computing the vector $\boldsymbol{\alpha}$ equal to

$$O(\ell^3 + \ell^2 N), \tag{2.9}$$

while that of evaluating g on a new example is

$$O(\ell N). \tag{2.10}$$

We have seen that in the dual solution we make use of inner products in the feature space. In the above analysis we assumed that the complexity of evaluating each inner product was proportional to the dimension of the feature space. The inner products can, however, sometimes be computed more efficiently as a direct function of the input features, without explicitly computing the mapping ϕ. In other words the feature-vector representation step can be by-passed. A function that performs this direct computation is known as a *kernel function*.

Definition 2.8 [Kernel function] A *kernel* is a function κ that for all $\mathbf{x}, \mathbf{z} \in X$ satisfies

$$\kappa(\mathbf{x}, \mathbf{z}) = \langle \phi(\mathbf{x}), \phi(\mathbf{z}) \rangle,$$

where ϕ is a mapping from X to an (inner product) feature space F

$$\phi : \mathbf{x} \longmapsto \phi(\mathbf{x}) \in F.$$

■

Kernel functions will be an important theme throughout this book. We will examine their properties, the algorithms that can take advantage of them, and their use in general pattern analysis applications. We will see that they make possible the use of feature spaces with an exponential or even infinite number of dimensions, something that would seem impossible if we wish to satisfy the efficiency requirements given in Chapter 1. Our aim in this chapter is to give examples to illustrate the key ideas underlying the proposed approach. We therefore now give an example of a kernel function whose complexity is less than the dimension of its corresponding feature space F, hence demonstrating that the complexity of applying ridge regression using the kernel improves on the estimates given in expressions (2.9) and (2.10) involving the dimension N of F.

Example 2.9 Consider a two-dimensional input space $X \subseteq \mathbb{R}^2$ together with the feature map

$$\phi : \mathbf{x} = (x_1, x_2) \longmapsto \phi(\mathbf{x}) = (x_1^2, x_2^2, \sqrt{2}x_1 x_2) \in F = \mathbb{R}^3.$$

The hypothesis space of linear functions in F would then be

$$g(\mathbf{x}) = w_{11}x_1^2 + w_{22}x_2^2 + w_{12}\sqrt{2}x_1x_2$$

The feature map takes the data from a two-dimensional to a three-dimensional space in a way that linear relations in the feature space correspond to quadratic relations in the input space. The composition of the feature map with the inner product in the feature space can be evaluated as follows

$$
\begin{aligned}
\langle \phi(\mathbf{x}), \phi(\mathbf{z}) \rangle &= \left\langle (x_1^2, x_2^2, \sqrt{2}x_1x_2), (z_1^2, z_2^2, \sqrt{2}z_1z_2) \right\rangle \\
&= x_1^2z_1^2 + x_2^2z_2^2 + 2x_1x_2z_1z_2 \\
&= (x_1z_1 + x_2z_2)^2 = \langle \mathbf{x}, \mathbf{z} \rangle^2 .
\end{aligned}
$$

Hence, the function

$$\kappa(\mathbf{x}, \mathbf{z}) = \langle \mathbf{x}, \mathbf{z} \rangle^2$$

is a kernel function with F its corresponding feature space. This means that we can compute the inner product between the projections of two points into the feature space without explicitly evaluating their coordinates. Note that the same kernel computes the inner product corresponding to the four-dimensional feature map

$$\phi : \mathbf{x} = (x_1, x_2) \longmapsto \phi(\mathbf{x}) = (x_1^2, x_2^2, x_1x_2, x_2x_1) \in F = \mathbb{R}^4,$$

showing that the feature space is not uniquely determined by the kernel function. ∎

Example 2.10 The previous example can readily be generalised to higher dimensional input spaces. Consider an n-dimensional space $X \subseteq \mathbb{R}^n$; then the function

$$\kappa(\mathbf{x}, \mathbf{z}) = \langle \mathbf{x}, \mathbf{z} \rangle^2$$

is a kernel function corresponding to the feature map

$$\phi : \mathbf{x} \longmapsto \phi(\mathbf{x}) = (x_ix_j)_{i,j=1}^n \in F = \mathbb{R}^{n^2},$$

since we have that

$$
\begin{aligned}
\langle \phi(\mathbf{x}), \phi(\mathbf{z}) \rangle &= \left\langle (x_ix_j)_{i,j=1}^n, (z_iz_j)_{i,j=1}^n \right\rangle \\
&= \sum_{i,j=1}^n x_ix_jz_iz_j = \sum_{i=1}^n x_iz_i \sum_{j=1}^n x_jz_j \\
&= \langle \mathbf{x}, \mathbf{z} \rangle^2 .
\end{aligned}
$$

If we now use this kernel in the dual form of the ridge regression algorithm, the complexity of the computation of the vector $\boldsymbol{\alpha}$ is $O(n\ell^2 + \ell^3)$ as opposed to a complexity of $O(n^2\ell^2 + \ell^3)$ predicted in the expressions (2.9) and (2.10). If we were analysing 1000 images each with 256 pixels this would roughly correspond to a 50-fold reduction in the computation time. Similarly, the time to evaluate the predictive function would be reduced by a factor of 256.   ∎

The example illustrates our second key finding that kernel functions can improve the computational complexity of computing inner products in a feature space, hence rendering algorithms efficient in very high-dimensional feature spaces.

The example of dual ridge regression and the polynomial kernel of degree 2 have demonstrated how a linear pattern analysis algorithm can be efficiently applied in a high-dimensional feature space by using an appropriate kernel function together with the dual form of the algorithm. In the next remark we emphasise an observation arising from this example as it provides the basis for the approach adopted in this book.

Remark 2.11 [Modularity] There was no need to change the underlying algorithm to accommodate the particular choice of kernel function. Clearly, we could use any suitable kernel for the data being considered. Similarly, if we wish to undertake a different type of pattern analysis we could substitute a different algorithm while retaining the chosen kernel. This illustrates the modularity of the approach that makes it possible to consider the algorithmic design and analysis separately from that of the kernel functions. This modularity will also become apparent in the structure of the book.   ∎

Hence, some chapters of the book are devoted to the theory and practice of designing kernels for data analysis. Other chapters will be devoted to the development of algorithms for some of the specific data analysis tasks described in Chapter 1.

2.3 Other examples

The previous section illustrated how the kernel methods approach can implement nonlinear regression through the use of a kernel-defined feature space. The aim was to show how the key components of the kernel methods approach fit together in one particular example. In this section we will briefly describe how kernel methods can be used to solve many of the tasks outlined in Chapter 1, before going on to give an overview of the different kernels we will be considering. This will lead naturally to a road map for the rest of the book.

2.3.1 Algorithms

Part II of the book will be concerned with algorithms. Our aim now is to indicate the range of tasks that can be addressed.

Classification Consider now the supervised classification task. Given a set

$$S = \{(\mathbf{x}_1, y_1), \ldots, (\mathbf{x}_\ell, y_\ell)\}$$

of points $\mathbf{x}_i$ from $X \subseteq \mathbb{R}^n$ with labels y_i from $Y = \{-1, +1\}$, find a prediction function $g(\mathbf{x}) = \text{sign}(\langle \mathbf{w}, \mathbf{x} \rangle - b)$ such that

$$\mathbb{E}[0.5\,|g(\mathbf{x}) - y|]$$

is small, where we will use the convention that $\text{sign}(0) = 1$. Note that the 0.5 is included to make the loss the discrete loss and the value of the expectation the probability that a randomly drawn example $\mathbf{x}$ is misclassified by g.

Since g is a thresholded linear function, this can be regarded as learning a hyperplane defined by the equation $\langle \mathbf{w}, \mathbf{x} \rangle = b$ separating the data according to their labels, see Figure 2.3. Recall that a hyperplane is an affine subspace of dimension $n-1$ which divides the space into two half spaces corresponding to the inputs of the two distinct classes. For example in Figure 2.3 the hyperplane is the dark line, with the positive region above and the negative region below. The vector $\mathbf{w}$ defines a direction perpendicular to the hyperplane, while varying the value of b moves the hyperplane parallel to itself. A representation involving $n+1$ free parameters therefore can describe all possible hyperplanes in $\mathbb{R}^n$.

Both statisticians and neural network researchers have frequently used this simple kind of classifier, calling them respectively *linear discriminants* and *perceptrons*. The theory of linear discriminants was developed by Fisher in 1936, while neural network researchers studied perceptrons in the early 1960s, mainly due to the work of Rosenblatt. We will refer to the quantity $\mathbf{w}$ as the *weight vector*, a term borrowed from the neural networks literature.

There are many different algorithms for selecting the weight vector $\mathbf{w}$, many of which can be implemented in dual form. We will describe the perceptron algorithm and support vector machine algorithms in Chapter 7.

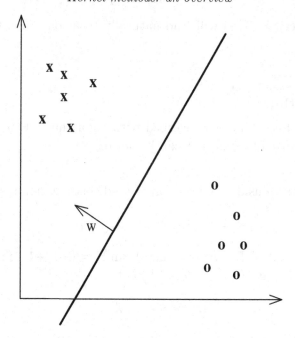

Fig. 2.3. A linear function for classification creates a separating hyperplane.

Principal components analysis Detecting regularities in an unlabelled set $S = \{\mathbf{x}_1, \ldots, \mathbf{x}_\ell\}$ of points from $X \subseteq \mathbb{R}^n$ is referred to as unsupervised learning. As mentioned in Chapter 1, one such task is finding a low-dimensional representation of the data such that the expected residual is as small as possible. Relations between features are important because they reduce the effective dimensionality of the data, causing it to lie on a lower dimensional surface. This may make it possible to recode the data in a more efficient way using fewer coordinates. The aim is to find a smaller set of variables defined by functions of the original features in such a way that the data can be approximately reconstructed from the new coordinates.

Despite the difficulties encountered if more general functions are considered, a good understanding exists of the special case when the relations are assumed to be linear. This subcase is attractive because it leads to analytical solutions and simple computations. For linear functions the problem is equivalent to projecting the data onto a lower-dimensional linear subspace in such a way that the distance between a vector and its projection is not too large. The problem of minimising the average squared distance between vectors and their projections is equivalent to projecting the data onto the space spanned by the first k eigenvectors of the matrix $\mathbf{X}'\mathbf{X}$

$$\mathbf{X}'\mathbf{X}\mathbf{v}_i = \lambda_i \mathbf{v}_i$$

and hence the coordinates of a new vector $\mathbf{x}$ in the new space can be obtained by considering its projection onto the eigenvectors $\langle \mathbf{x}, \mathbf{v}_i \rangle$, $i = 1, \ldots, k$. This technique is known as principal components analysis (PCA).

The algorithm can be rendered nonlinear by first embedding the data into a feature space and then consider projections in that space. Once again we will see that kernels can be used to define the feature space, since the algorithm can be rewritten in a form that only requires inner products between inputs. Hence, we can detect nonlinear relations between variables in the data by embedding the data into a kernel-induced feature space, where linear relations can be found by means of PCA in that space. This approach is known as *kernel PCA* and will be described in detail in Chapter 6.

Remark 2.12 [Low-rank approximation] Of course some information about linear relations in the data is already implicit in the rank of the data matrix. The rank corresponds to the number of non-zero eigenvalues of the matrix $\mathbf{X}'\mathbf{X}$ and is the dimensionality of the subspace in which the data lie. The rank can also be computed using only inner products, since the eigenvalues of the inner product matrix are equal to those of the covariance matrix. We can think of PCA as finding a low-rank approximation, where the quality of the approximation depends on how close the data is to lying in a subspace of the given dimensionality. ∎

Clustering Finally, we mention finding clusters in a training set $S = \{\mathbf{x}_1, \ldots, \mathbf{x}_\ell\}$ of points from $X \subseteq \mathbb{R}^n$. One method of defining clusters is to identify a fixed number of centres or prototypes and assign points to the cluster defined by the closest centre. Identifying clusters by a set of prototypes divides the space into what is known as a Voronoi partitioning.

The aim is to minimise the expected squared distance of a point from its cluster centre. If we fix the number of centres to be k, a classic procedure is known as k-means and is a widely used heuristic for clustering data. The k-means procedure must have some method for measuring the distance between two points. Once again this distance can always be computed using only inner product information through the equality

$$\|\mathbf{x} - \mathbf{z}\|^2 = \langle \mathbf{x}, \mathbf{x} \rangle + \langle \mathbf{z}, \mathbf{z} \rangle - 2\langle \mathbf{x}, \mathbf{z} \rangle.$$

This distance, together with a dual representation of the mean of a given set of points, implies the k-means procedure can be implemented in a kernel-defined feature space. This procedure is not, however, a typical example of a kernel method since it fails to meet our requirement of efficiency. This is because the optimisation criterion is not convex and hence we cannot guarantee that the procedure will converge to the optimal arrangement. A number of clustering methods will be described in Chapter 8.

2.3.2 Kernels

Part III of the book will be devoted to the design of a whole range of kernel functions. The approach we have outlined in this chapter shows how a number of useful tasks can be accomplished in high-dimensional feature spaces defined implicitly by a kernel function. So far we have only seen how to construct very simple polynomial kernels. Clearly, for the approach to be useful, we would like to have a range of potential kernels together with machinery to tailor their construction to the specifics of a given data domain. If the inputs are elements of a vector space such as $\mathbb{R}^n$ there is a natural inner product that is referred to as the *linear kernel* by analogy with the polynomial construction. Using this kernel corresponds to running the original algorithm in the input space. As we have seen above, at the cost of a few extra operations, the polynomial construction can convert the linear kernel into an inner product in a vastly expanded feature space. This example illustrates a general principle we will develop by showing how more complex kernels can be created from simpler ones in a number of different ways. Kernels can even be constructed that correspond to infinite-dimensional feature spaces at the cost of only a few extra operations in the kernel evaluations.

An example of creating a new kernel from an existing one is provided by normalising a kernel. Given a kernel $\kappa(\mathbf{x}, \mathbf{z})$ that corresponds to the feature mapping ϕ, the *normalised kernel* $\kappa(\mathbf{x}, \mathbf{z})$ corresponds to the feature map

$$\mathbf{x} \longmapsto \phi(\mathbf{x}) \longmapsto \frac{\phi(\mathbf{x})}{\|\phi(\mathbf{x})\|}.$$

Hence, we will show in Chapter 5 that we can express the kernel $\hat{\kappa}$ in terms of κ as follows

$$\hat{\kappa}(\mathbf{x}, \mathbf{z}) = \left\langle \frac{\phi(\mathbf{x})}{\|\phi(\mathbf{x})\|}, \frac{\phi(\mathbf{z})}{\|\phi(\mathbf{z})\|} \right\rangle = \frac{\kappa(\mathbf{x}, \mathbf{z})}{\sqrt{\kappa(\mathbf{x}, \mathbf{x})\kappa(\mathbf{z}, \mathbf{z})}}.$$

These constructions will not, however, in themselves extend the range of data types that can be processed. We will therefore also develop kernels that correspond to mapping inputs that are not vectors into an appropriate feature space. As an example, consider the input space consisting of all subsets of a fixed set D. Consider the kernel function of two subsets A_1 and A_2 of D defined by

$$\kappa\left(A_1, A_2\right) = 2^{|A_1 \cap A_2|},$$

that is the number of common subsets A_1 and A_2 share. This kernel corresponds to a feature map ϕ to the vector space of dimension $2^{|D|}$ indexed by all subsets of D, where the image of a set A is the vector with

$$\phi\left(A\right)_U = \begin{cases} 1; & \text{if } U \subseteq A, \\ 0; & \text{otherwise.} \end{cases}$$

This example is defined over a general set and yet we have seen that it fulfills the conditions for being a valid kernel, namely that it corresponds to an inner product in a feature space. Developing this approach, we will show how kernels can be constructed from different types of input spaces in a way that reflects their structure even though they are not in themselves vector spaces. These kernels will be needed for many important applications such as text analysis and bioinformatics. In fact, the range of valid kernels is very large: some are given in closed form; others can only be computed by means of a recursion or other algorithm; in some cases the actual feature mapping corresponding to a given kernel function is not known, only a guarantee that the data can be embedded in some feature space that gives rise to the chosen kernel. In short, provided the function can be evaluated efficiently and it corresponds to computing the inner product of suitable images of its two arguments, it constitutes a potentially useful kernel.

Selecting the best kernel from among this extensive range of possibilities becomes the most critical stage in applying kernel-based algorithms in practice. The selection of the kernel can be shown to correspond in a very tight sense to the encoding of our prior knowledge about the data and the types of patterns we can expect to identify. This relationship will be explored by examining how kernels can be derived from probabilistic models of the process generating the data.

In Chapter 3 the techniques for creating and adapting kernels will be presented, hence laying the foundations for the later examples of practical kernel based applications. It is possible to construct complex kernel functions from simpler kernels, from explicit features, from similarity measures or from other types of prior knowledge. In short, we will see how it will be possible to treat the kernel part of the algorithm in a modular fashion, constructing it from simple components and then modifying it by means of a set of well-defined operations.

2.4 The modularity of kernel methods

The procedures outlined in the previous sections will be generalised and analysed in subsequent chapters, but a consistent trend will emerge. An algorithmic procedure is adapted to use only inner products between inputs. The method can then be combined with a kernel function that calculates the inner product between the images of two inputs in a feature space, hence making it possible to implement the algorithm in a high-dimensional space.

The modularity of kernel methods shows itself in the reusability of the learning algorithm. The same algorithm can work with any kernel and hence for any data domain. The kernel component is data specific, but can be combined with different algorithms to solve the full range of tasks that we will consider. All this leads to a very natural and elegant approach to learning systems design, where modules are combined together to obtain complex learning systems. Figure 2.4 shows the stages involved in the implementation of kernel pattern analysis. The data is processed using a kernel to create a kernel matrix, which in turn is processed by a pattern analysis algorithm to producce a pattern function. This function is used to process unseen examples. This book will follow a corresponding modular structure

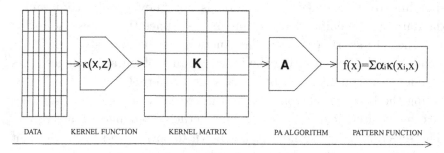

Fig. 2.4. The stages involved in the application of kernel methods.

developing each of the aspects of the approach independently.

From a computational point of view kernel methods have two important properties. First of all, they enable access to very high-dimensional and correspondingly flexible feature spaces at low computational cost both in space and time, and yet secondly, despite the complexity of the resulting function classes, virtually all of the algorithms presented in this book solve convex optimisation problems and hence do not suffer from local minima. In Chapter 7 we will see that optimisation theory also confers other advantages on the resulting algorithms. In particular duality will become a central theme throughout this book, arising within optimisation, text representation, and algorithm design.

Finally, the algorithms presented in this book have a firm statistical foundation that ensures they remain resistant to overfitting. Chapter 4 will give a unified analysis that makes it possible to view the algorithms as special cases of a single framework for analysing generalisation.

2.5 Roadmap of the book

The first two chapters of the book have provided the motivation for pattern analysis tasks and an overview of the kernel methods approach to learning systems design. We have described how at the top level they involve a two-stage process: the data is implicitly embedded into a feature space through the use of a kernel function, and subsequently linear patterns are sought in the feature space using algorithms expressed in a dual form. The resulting systems are modular: any kernel can be combined with any algorithm and vice versa. The structure of the book reflects that modularity, addressing in three main parts general design principles, specific algorithms and specific kernels.

Part I covers **foundations** and presents the general principles and properties of kernel functions and kernel-based algorithms. Chapter 3 presents the theory of kernel functions including their characterisations and properties. It covers methods for combining kernels and for adapting them in order to modify the geometry of the feature space. The chapter lays the groundwork necessary for the introduction of specific examples of kernels in Part III. Chapter 4 develops the framework for understanding how their statistical stability can be controlled. Again it sets the scene for Part II, where specific algorithms for dimension reduction, novelty-detection, classification, ranking, clustering, and regression are examined.

Part II develops specific **algorithms**. Chapter 5 starts to develop the tools for analysing data in a kernel-defined feature space. After covering a number of basic techniques, it shows how they can be used to create a simple novelty-detection algorithm. Further analysis of the structure of the data in the feature space including implementation of Gram–Schmidt orthonormalisation, leads eventually to a dual version of the Fisher discriminant. Chapter 6 is devoted to discovering patterns using eigenanalysis. The techniques developed include principal components analysis, maximal covariance, and canonical correlation analysis. The application of the patterns in classification leads to an alternative formulation of the Fisher discriminant, while their use in regression gives rise to the partial least squares algorithm. Chapter 7 considers algorithms resulting from optimisation problems and includes sophisticated novelty detectors, the support vector machine, ridge regression, and support vector regression. On-line algorithms for classification and regression are also introduced. Finally, Chapter 8 considers ranking and shows how both batch and on-line kernel based algorithms can be created to solve this task. It then considers clustering in kernel-defined feature spaces showing how the classical k-means algorithm can be implemented in such feature spaces as well as spectral clustering methods. Finally, the problem of data visualisation is formalised and solved also using spectral methods. Appendix C contains an index of the pattern analysis methods covered in Part II.

Part III is concerned with **kernels.** Chapter 9 develops a number of techniques for creating kernels leading to the introduction of ANOVA kernels, kernels defined over graphs, kernels on sets and randomised kernels. Chapter 10 considers kernels based on the vector space model of text, with emphasis on the refinements aimed at taking account of the semantics. Chapter 11 treats kernels for strings of symbols, trees, and general structured data. Finally Chapter 12 examines how kernels can be created from generative models of data either using the probability of co-occurrence or through the Fisher kernel construction. Appendix D contains an index of the kernels described in Part III.

We conclude this roadmap with a specific mention of some of the questions that will be addressed as the themes are developed through the chapters (referenced in brackets):

- Which functions are valid kernels and what are their properties? (Chapter 3)
- How can we guarantee the statistical stability of patterns? (Chapter. 4)
- What algorithms can be kernelised? (Chapter 5, 6, 7 and 8)
- Which problems can be tackled effectively using kernel methods? (Chapters 9 and 10)
- How can we develop kernels attuned to particular applications? (Chapters 10, 11 and 12)

2.6 Summary

- Linear patterns can often be detected efficiently by well-known techniques such as least squares regression.

- Mapping the data via a nonlinear function into a suitable feature space enables the use of the same tools for discovering nonlinear patterns.
- Kernels can make it feasible to use high-dimensional feature spaces by avoiding the explicit computation of the feature mapping.
- The proposed approach is modular in the sense that any kernel will work with any kernel-based algorithm.
- Although linear functions require vector inputs, the use of kernels enables the approach to be applied to other types of data.

2.7 Further reading and advanced topics

The method of least squares for linear regression was (re)invented and made famous by Carl F. Gauss (1777–1855) in the late eighteenth century, by using it to predict the position of an asteroid that had been observed by the astronomer Giuseppe Piazzi for several days and then 'lost'. Before Gauss (who published it in *Theoria motus corporum coelestium*, 1809), it had been independently discovered by Legendre (but published only in 1812, in *Nouvelle Methods pour la determination des orbites des cometes*). It is now a cornerstone of function approximation in all disciplines.

The Widrow–Hoff algorithm is described in [160]. The ridge regression algorithm was published by Hoerl and Kennard [58], and subsequently discovered to be a special case of the regularisation theory of [138] for the solution of ill-posed problems. The dual form of ridge regression was studied by Saunders *et al.*, [115], which gives a formulation similar to that presented here. An equivalent heuristic was widely used in the neural networks literature under the name of weight decay. The combination of ridge regression and kernels has also been explored in the literature of Gaussian Processes [161] and in the literature on regularization networks [107] and RKHSs: [155], see also [131].

The linear Fisher discriminant dates back to 1936 [44], and its use with kernels to the works in [11] and [100], see also [123]. The perceptron algorithm dates back to 1957 by Rosenblatt [111], and its kernelization is a well-known folk algorithm, closely related to the work in [1].

The theory of linear discriminants dates back to the 1930s, when Fisher [44] proposed a procedure for classification of multivariate data by means of a hyperplane. In the field of artificial intelligence, attention was drawn to this problem by the work of Frank Rosenblatt [111], who starting from 1956 introduced the perceptron learning rule. Minsky and Papert's famous book Perceptrons [101] analysed the computational limitations of linear learning machines. The classical book by Duda and Hart (recently reprinted in a new edition [40]) provides a survey of the state-of-the-art in the field. Also useful is [14] which includes a description of a class of generalised learning machines.

The idea of using kernel functions as inner products in a feature space was introduced into machine learning in 1964 by the work of Aizermann, Bravermann and Rozoener [1] on the method of potential functions and this work is mentioned in a footnote of the very popular first edition of Duda and Hart's book on pattern classification [39]. Through this route it came to the attention of the authors of [16], who combined it with large margin hyperplanes, leading to support vector machines and the (re)introduction of the notion of a kernel into the mainstream of the machine learning literature.

The use of kernels for function approximation however dates back to Aronszain [6], as does the development of much of their theory [155].

An early survey of the modern usage of kernel methods in pattern analysis can be found in [20], and more accounts in the books by [32] and [120]. The book [141] describes SVMs, albeit with not much emphasis on kernels. Other books in the area include: [131], [68], [55].

A further realization of the possibilities opened up by the concept of the kernel function is represented by the development of kernel PCA by [121] that will be discussed in Chapter 6. That work made the point that much more complex relations than just linear classifications can be inferred using kernel functions.

Clustering will be discussed in more detail in Chapter 8, so pointers to the relevant literature can be found in Section 8.5.

For constantly updated pointers to online literature and free software see the book's companion website: www.kernel-methods.net

3

Properties of kernels

As we have seen in Chapter 2, the use of kernel functions provides a powerful and principled way of detecting nonlinear relations using well-understood linear algorithms in an appropriate feature space. The approach decouples the design of the algorithm from the specification of the feature space. This inherent modularity not only increases the flexibility of the approach, it also makes both the learning algorithms and the kernel design more amenable to formal analysis. Regardless of which pattern analysis algorithm is being used, the theoretical properties of a given kernel remain the same. It is the purpose of this chapter to introduce the properties that characterise kernel functions.

We present the fundamental properties of kernels, thus formalising the intuitive concepts introduced in Chapter 2. We provide a characterization of kernel functions, derive their properties, and discuss methods for designing them. We will also discuss the role of prior knowledge in kernel-based learning machines, showing that a universal machine is not possible, and that kernels must be chosen for the problem at hand with a view to capturing our prior belief of the relatedness of different examples. We also give a framework for quantifying the match between a kernel and a learning task.

Given a kernel and a training set, we can form the matrix known as the kernel, or Gram matrix: the matrix containing the evaluation of the kernel function on all pairs of data points. This matrix acts as an information bottleneck, as all the information available to a kernel algorithm, be it about the distribution, the model or the noise, must be extracted from that matrix. It is therefore not surprising that the kernel matrix plays a central role in the development of this chapter.

47

3.1 Inner products and positive semi-definite matrices

Chapter 2 showed how data can be embedded in a high-dimensional feature space where linear pattern analysis can be performed giving rise to non-linear pattern analysis in the input space. The use of kernels enables this technique to be applied without paying the computational penalty implicit in the number of dimensions, since it is possible to evaluate the inner product between the images of two inputs in a feature space without explicitly computing their coordinates.

These observations imply that we can apply pattern analysis algorithms to the image of the training data in the feature space through indirect evaluation of the inner products. As defined in Chapter 2, a function that returns the inner product between the images of two inputs in some feature space is known as a *kernel function*.

This section reviews the notion and properties of inner products that will play a central role in this book. We will relate them to the positive semi-definiteness of the Gram matrix and general properties of positive semi-definite symmetric functions.

3.1.1 Hilbert spaces

First we recall what is meant by a linear function. Given a vector space X over the reals, a function

$$f : X \longrightarrow \mathbb{R}$$

is linear if $f(\alpha \mathbf{x}) = \alpha f(\mathbf{x})$ and $f(\mathbf{x} + \mathbf{z}) = f(\mathbf{x}) + f(\mathbf{z})$ for all $\mathbf{x}, \mathbf{z} \in X$ and $\alpha \in \mathbb{R}$.

Inner product space A vector space X over the reals $\mathbb{R}$ is an *inner product space* if there exists a real-valued symmetric bilinear (linear in each argument) map $\langle \cdot, \cdot \rangle$, that satisfies

$$\langle \mathbf{x}, \mathbf{x} \rangle \geq 0.$$

The bilinear map is known as the inner, dot or scalar product. Furthermore we will say the inner product is *strict* if

$$\langle \mathbf{x}, \mathbf{x} \rangle = 0 \text{ if and only if } \mathbf{x} = \mathbf{0}.$$

Given a strict inner product space we can define a norm on the space X by

$$\|\mathbf{x}\|_2 = \sqrt{\langle \mathbf{x}, \mathbf{x} \rangle}.$$

The associated metric or distance between two vectors $\mathbf{x}$ and $\mathbf{z}$ is defined as $d(\mathbf{x}, \mathbf{z}) = \|\mathbf{x} - \mathbf{z}\|_2$. For the vector space $\mathbb{R}^n$ the standard inner product is given by

$$\langle \mathbf{x}, \mathbf{z} \rangle = \sum_{i=1}^{n} x_i z_i.$$

Furthermore, if the inner product is not strict, those points $\mathbf{x}$ for which $\|\mathbf{x}\| = 0$ form a linear subspace since Proposition 3.5 below shows $\langle \mathbf{x}, \mathbf{y} \rangle^2 \leq \|\mathbf{x}\|^2 \|\mathbf{y}\|^2 = 0$, and hence if also $\|\mathbf{z}\| = 0$ we have for all $a, b \in \mathbb{R}$

$$\|a\mathbf{x} + b\mathbf{z}\|^2 = \langle a\mathbf{x} + b\mathbf{z}, a\mathbf{x} + b\mathbf{z} \rangle = a^2 \|\mathbf{x}\|^2 + 2ab \langle \mathbf{x}, \mathbf{z} \rangle + b^2 \|\mathbf{z}\|^2 = 0.$$

This means that we can always convert a non-strict inner product to a strict one by taking the quotient space with respect to this subspace.

A vector space with a metric is known as a *metric space*, so that a strict inner product space is also a metric space. A metric space has a derived topology with a sub-basis given by the set of open balls.

A strict inner product space is sometimes referred to as a Hilbert space, though most researchers require the additional properties of completeness and separability, as well as sometimes requiring that the dimension be infinite. We give a formal definition.

Definition 3.1 A *Hilbert Space* $\mathcal{F}$ is a strict inner product space with the additional properties that it is *separable* and *complete*. Completeness refers to the property that every Cauchy sequence $\{h_n\}_{n \geq 1}$ of elements of $\mathcal{F}$ converges to a element $h \in \mathcal{F}$, where a Cauchy sequence is one satisfying the property that

$$\sup_{m > n} \|h_n - h_m\| \to 0, \text{ as } n \to \infty.$$

A space $\mathcal{F}$ is separable if there is a countable set of elements $h_1, \ldots, h_i \ldots$ of $\mathcal{F}$ such that for all $h \in \mathcal{F}$ and $\epsilon > 0$ there exists such that

$$\|h_i - h\| < \epsilon.$$

     ■

Example 3.2 Let X be the set of all countable sequences of real numbers $\mathbf{x} = (x_1, x_2, \ldots, x_n, \ldots)$, such that the sum

$$\sum_{i=1}^{\infty} x_i^2 < \infty,$$

with the inner product between two sequences $\mathbf{x}$ and $\mathbf{y}$ defined by

$$\langle \mathbf{x}, \mathbf{y} \rangle = \sum_{i=1}^{\infty} x_i y_i.$$

This is the space known as ℓ^2. ∎

The reason for the importance of the properties of completeness and separability is that together they ensure that non-trivial Hilbert spaces are either isometrically isomorphic to $\mathbb{R}^n$ for some finite n or to the space ℓ^2 introduced in Example 3.2. For our purposes we therefore require that the feature space be a complete, separable inner product space, as this will imply that it can be given a coordinate system. Since we will be using the dual representation there will, however, be no need to actually construct the feature vectors.

This fact may seem strange at first since we are learning a linear function represented by a weight vector in this space. But as discussed in Chapter 2 the weight vector is a linear combination of the feature vectors of the training points. Generally, all elements of a Hilbert space are also linear functions in that space via the inner product. For a point $\mathbf{z}$ the corresponding function $f_{\mathbf{z}}$ is given by

$$f_{\mathbf{z}}(\mathbf{x}) = \langle \mathbf{x}, \mathbf{z} \rangle.$$

Finding the weight vector is therefore equivalent to identifying an appropriate element of the feature space.

We give two more examples of inner product spaces.

Example 3.3 Let $X = \mathbb{R}^n$, $\mathbf{x} = (x_1, \ldots, x_n)'$, $\mathbf{z} = (z_1, \ldots, z_n)'$. Let λ_i be fixed positive numbers, for $i = 1, \ldots, n$. The following defines a valid inner product on X

$$\langle \mathbf{x}, \mathbf{z} \rangle = \sum_{i=1}^{n} \lambda_i x_i z_i = \mathbf{x}' \mathbf{\Lambda} \mathbf{z},$$

where $\mathbf{\Lambda}$ is the $n \times n$ diagonal matrix with entries $\mathbf{\Lambda}_{ii} = \lambda_i$. ∎

Example 3.4 Let $\mathcal{F} = L_2(X)$ be the vector space of square integrable functions on a compact subset X of $\mathbb{R}^n$ with the obvious definitions of addition and scalar multiplication, that is

$$L_2(X) = \left\{ f : \int_X f(x)^2 \, dx < \infty \right\}.$$

For $f, g \in X$, define the inner product by

$$\langle f, g \rangle = \int_X f(x)g(x)dx.$$

∎

Proposition 3.5 (Cauchy–Schwarz inequality) *In an inner product space*

$$\langle \mathbf{x}, \mathbf{z} \rangle^2 \leq \|\mathbf{x}\|^2 \|\mathbf{z}\|^2.$$

and the equality sign holds in a strict inner product space if and only if $\mathbf{x}$ *and* $\mathbf{z}$ *are rescalings of the same vector.*

Proof Consider an abitrary $\epsilon > 0$ and the following norm

$$
\begin{aligned}
0 \; \leq \; & \|(\|\mathbf{z}\| + \epsilon)\mathbf{x} \pm \mathbf{z}(\|\mathbf{x}\| + \epsilon)\|^2 \\
= \; & \langle(\|\mathbf{z}\| + \epsilon)\mathbf{x} \pm \mathbf{z}(\|\mathbf{x}\| + \epsilon), (\|\mathbf{z}\| + \epsilon)\mathbf{x} \pm \mathbf{z}(\|\mathbf{x}\| + \epsilon)\rangle \\
= \; & (\|\mathbf{z}\| + \epsilon)^2 \|\mathbf{x}\|^2 + \|\mathbf{z}\|^2(\|\mathbf{x}\| + \epsilon)^2 \pm 2\langle(\|\mathbf{z}\| + \epsilon)\mathbf{x}, \mathbf{z}(\|\mathbf{x}\| + \epsilon)\rangle \\
\leq \; & 2(\|\mathbf{z}\| + \epsilon)^2(\|\mathbf{x}\| + \epsilon)^2 \pm 2(\|\mathbf{z}\| + \epsilon)(\|\mathbf{x}\| + \epsilon)\langle\mathbf{x}, \mathbf{z}\rangle,
\end{aligned}
$$

implying that

$$\mp\langle\mathbf{x}, \mathbf{z}\rangle \leq (\|\mathbf{x}\| + \epsilon)(\|\mathbf{z}\| + \epsilon).$$

Letting $\epsilon \to 0$ gives the first result. In a strict inner product space equality implies

$$\mathbf{x}\|\mathbf{z}\| \pm \mathbf{z}\|\mathbf{x}\| = \mathbf{0},$$

making $\mathbf{x}$ and $\mathbf{z}$ rescalings as required. □

Angles, distances and dimensionality The *angle* θ between two vectors $\mathbf{x}$ and $\mathbf{z}$ of a strict inner product space is defined by

$$\cos\theta = \frac{\langle\mathbf{x}, \mathbf{z}\rangle}{\|\mathbf{x}\|\|\mathbf{z}\|}$$

If $\theta = 0$ the cosine is 1 and $\langle\mathbf{x}, \mathbf{z}\rangle = \|\mathbf{x}\|\|\mathbf{z}\|$, and $\mathbf{x}$ and $\mathbf{z}$ are said to be *parallel*. If $\theta = \frac{\pi}{2}$, the cosine is 0, $\langle\mathbf{x}, \mathbf{z}\rangle = 0$ and the vectors are said to be *orthogonal*.

A set $S = \{\mathbf{x}_1, \ldots, \mathbf{x}_\ell\}$ of vectors from X is called *orthonormal* if $\langle\mathbf{x}_i, \mathbf{x}_j\rangle =$

δ_{ij}, where δ_{ij} is the Kronecker delta satisfying $\delta_{ij} = 1$ if $i = j$, and 0 otherwise. For an orthonormal set S, and a vector $\mathbf{z} \in X$, the expression

$$\sum_{i=1}^{\ell} \langle \mathbf{x}_i, \mathbf{z} \rangle \, \mathbf{x}_i$$

is said to be a *Fourier series* for $\mathbf{z}$. If the Fourier series for $\mathbf{z}$ equals $\mathbf{z}$ for all $\mathbf{z}$, then the set S is also a basis. Since a Hilbert space is either equivalent to $\mathbb{R}^n$ or to L_2, it will always be possible to find an orthonormal basis, indeed this basis can be used to define the isomorphism with either $\mathbb{R}^n$ or L_2.

The *rank* of a general $n \times m$ matrix $\mathbf{X}$ is the dimension of the space spanned by its columns also known as the column space. Hence, the rank of $\mathbf{X}$ is the smallest r for which we can express

$$\mathbf{X} = \mathbf{RS},$$

where $\mathbf{R}$ is an $n \times r$ matrix whose linearly independent columns form a basis for the column space of $\mathbf{X}$, while the columns of the $r \times m$ matrix $\mathbf{S}$ express the columns of $\mathbf{X}$ in that basis. Note that we have

$$\mathbf{X}' = \mathbf{S}'\mathbf{R}',$$

and since $\mathbf{S}'$ is $m \times r$, the rank of $\mathbf{X}'$ is less than or equal to the rank of $\mathbf{X}$. By symmetry the two ranks are equal, implying that the dimension of the space spanned by the rows of $\mathbf{X}$ is also equal to its rank.

An $n \times m$ matrix is *full rank* if its rank is equal to $\min(n, m)$.

3.1.2 Gram matrix

Given a set of vectors, $S = \{\mathbf{x}_1, \ldots, \mathbf{x}_\ell\}$ the *Gram matrix* is defined as the $\ell \times \ell$ matrix $\mathbf{G}$ whose entries are $\mathbf{G}_{ij} = \langle \mathbf{x}_i, \mathbf{x}_j \rangle$. If we are using a kernel function κ to evaluate the inner products in a feature space with feature map ϕ, the associated Gram matrix has entries

$$\mathbf{G}_{ij} = \langle \phi(\mathbf{x}_i), \phi(\mathbf{x}_j) \rangle = \kappa(\mathbf{x}_i, \mathbf{x}_j).$$

In this case the matrix is often referred to as the *kernel matrix*. We will use a standard notation for displaying kernel matrices as:

K	1	2	$\cdots$	ℓ
1	$\kappa(\mathbf{x}_1, \mathbf{x}_1)$	$\kappa(\mathbf{x}_1, \mathbf{x}_2)$	$\cdots$	$\kappa(\mathbf{x}_1, \mathbf{x}_\ell)$
2	$\kappa(\mathbf{x}_2, \mathbf{x}_1)$	$\kappa(\mathbf{x}_2, \mathbf{x}_2)$	$\cdots$	$\kappa(\mathbf{x}_2, \mathbf{x}_\ell)$
$\vdots$	$\vdots$	$\vdots$	$\ddots$	$\vdots$
ℓ	$\kappa(\mathbf{x}_\ell, \mathbf{x}_1)$	$\kappa(\mathbf{x}_\ell, \mathbf{x}_2)$	$\cdots$	$\kappa(\mathbf{x}_\ell, \mathbf{x}_\ell)$

where the symbol $\mathbf{K}$ in the top left corner indicates that the table represents a kernel matrix – see the Appendix B for a summary of notations.

In Chapter 2, the Gram matrix has already been shown to play an important role in the dual form of some learning algorithms. The matrix is symmetric since $\mathbf{G}_{ij} = \mathbf{G}_{ji}$, that is $\mathbf{G}' = \mathbf{G}$. Furthermore, it contains all the information needed to compute the pairwise distances within the data set as shown above. In the Gram matrix there is of course some information that is lost when compared with the original set of vectors. For example the matrix loses information about the orientation of the original data set with respect to the origin, since the matrix of inner products is invariant to rotations about the origin. More importantly the representation loses information about any alignment between the points and the axes. This again follows from the fact that the Gram matrix is rotationally invariant in the sense that any rotation of the coordinate system will leave the matrix of inner products unchanged.

If we consider the dual form of the ridge regression algorithm described in Chapter 2, we will see that the only information received by the algorithm about the training set comes from the Gram or kernel matrix and the associated output values. This observation will characterise all of the kernel algorithms considered in this book. In other words all the information the pattern analysis algorithms can glean about the training data and chosen feature space is contained in the kernel matrix together with any labelling information.

In this sense we can view the matrix as an *information bottleneck* that must transmit enough information about the data for the algorithm to be able to perform its task. This view also reinforces the view that the kernel matrix is the central data type of all kernel-based algorithms. It is therefore natural to study the properties of these matrices, how they are created, how they can be adapted, and how well they are matched to the task being addressed.

Singular matrices and eigenvalues A matrix $\mathbf{A}$ is singular if there is a non-trivial linear combination of the columns of $\mathbf{A}$ that equals the vector $\mathbf{0}$. If we put the coefficients x_i of this combination into a (non-zero) vector $\mathbf{x}$, we have that

$$\mathbf{A}\mathbf{x} = \mathbf{0} = 0\mathbf{x}.$$

If an $n \times n$ matrix $\mathbf{A}$ is non-singular the columns are linearly independent and hence span a space of dimension n. Hence, we can find vectors $\mathbf{u}_i$ such that

$$\mathbf{A}\mathbf{u}_i = \mathbf{e}_i,$$

where $\mathbf{e}_i$ is the ith unit vector. Forming a matrix $\mathbf{U}$ with ith column equal to $\mathbf{u}_i$ we have

$$\mathbf{A}\mathbf{U} = \mathbf{I}$$

the identity matrix. Hence, $\mathbf{U} = \mathbf{A}^{-1}$ is the multiplicative inverse of $\mathbf{A}$.

Given a matrix $\mathbf{A}$, the real number λ and the vector $\mathbf{x}$ are an *eigenvalue* and corresponding *eigenvector* of $\mathbf{A}$ if

$$\mathbf{A}\mathbf{x} = \lambda\mathbf{x}.$$

It follows from the observation above about singular matrices that 0 is an eigenvalue of a matrix if and only if it is singular. Note that for an eigenvalue, eigenvector pair $\mathbf{x}$, λ, the quotient obeys

$$\frac{\mathbf{x}'\mathbf{A}\mathbf{x}}{\mathbf{x}'\mathbf{x}} = \lambda\frac{\mathbf{x}'\mathbf{x}}{\mathbf{x}'\mathbf{x}} = \lambda. \tag{3.1}$$

The quotient of equation (3.1) is known as the *Rayleigh quotient* and will form an important tool in the development of the algorithms of Chapter 6. Consider the optimisation problem

$$\max_{\mathbf{v}} \frac{\mathbf{v}'\mathbf{A}\mathbf{v}}{\mathbf{v}'\mathbf{v}} \tag{3.2}$$

and observe that the solution is invariant to rescaling. We can therefore impose the constraint that $\|\mathbf{v}\| = 1$ and solve using a Lagrange multiplier. We obtain for a symmetric matrix $\mathbf{A}$ the optimisation

$$\max_{\mathbf{v}} \left(\mathbf{v}'\mathbf{A}\mathbf{v} - \lambda \left(\mathbf{v}'\mathbf{v} - 1 \right) \right),$$

which on setting the derivatives with respect to $\mathbf{v}$ equal to zero gives

$$\mathbf{A}\mathbf{v} = \lambda\mathbf{v}.$$

We will always assume that an eigenvector is normalised.

Hence, the eigenvector of the largest eigenvalue is the solution of the optimisation (3.2) with the corresponding eigenvalue giving the value of the maximum. Since we are seeking the maximum over a compact set we are guaranteed a solution. A similar approach can also yield the minimum eigenvalue.

The *spectral norm* or *2-norm* of a matrix $\mathbf{A}$ is defined as

$$\max_{\mathbf{v}} \frac{\|\mathbf{A}\mathbf{v}\|}{\|\mathbf{v}\|} = \sqrt{\max_{\mathbf{v}} \frac{\mathbf{v}'\mathbf{A}'\mathbf{A}\mathbf{v}}{\mathbf{v}'\mathbf{v}}}. \tag{3.3}$$

Symmetric matrices and eigenvalues We say a square matrix $\mathbf{A}$ is *symmetric* if $\mathbf{A}' = \mathbf{A}$, that is the (i,j) entry equals the (j,i) entry for all i and j. A matrix is *diagonal* if its off-diagonal entries are all 0. A square matrix is *upper (lower) triangular* if its above (below) diagonal elements are all zero.

For symmetric matrices we have that eigenvectors corresponding to distinct eigenvalues are orthogonal, since if μ, $\mathbf{z}$ is a second eigenvalue, eigenvector pair with $\mu \neq \lambda$, we have that

$$
\begin{aligned}
\lambda \langle \mathbf{x}, \mathbf{z} \rangle &= \langle \mathbf{A}\mathbf{x}, \mathbf{z} \rangle \\
&= (\mathbf{A}\mathbf{x})' \mathbf{z} \\
&= \mathbf{x}' \mathbf{A}' \mathbf{z} \\
&= \mathbf{x}' \mathbf{A} \mathbf{z} \\
&= \mu \langle \mathbf{x}, \mathbf{z} \rangle,
\end{aligned}
$$

implying that $\langle \mathbf{x}, \mathbf{z} \rangle = \mathbf{x}'\mathbf{z} = 0$. This means that if $\mathbf{A}$ is an $n \times n$ symmetric matrix, it can have at most n distinct eigenvalues. Given an eigenvector–eigenvalue pair $\mathbf{x}$, λ of the matrix $\mathbf{A}$, the transformation

$$
\mathbf{A} \longmapsto \tilde{\mathbf{A}} = \mathbf{A} - \lambda \mathbf{x}\mathbf{x}',
$$

is known as *deflation*. Note that since $\mathbf{x}$ is normalised

$$
\tilde{\mathbf{A}}\mathbf{x} = \mathbf{A}\mathbf{x} - \lambda \mathbf{x}\mathbf{x}'\mathbf{x} = \mathbf{0},
$$

so that deflation leaves $\mathbf{x}$ an eigenvector but reduces the corresponding eigenvalue to zero. Since eigenvectors corresponding to distinct eigenvalues are orthogonal the remaining eigenvalues of $\mathbf{A}$ remain unchanged. By repeatedly finding the eigenvector corresponding to the largest positive (or smallest negative) eigenvalue and then deflating, we can always find an orthonormal set of n eigenvectors, where eigenvectors corresponding to an eigenvalue of 0 are added by extending the set of eigenvectors obtained by deflation to an orthonormal basis. If we form a matrix $\mathbf{V}$ with the (orthonormal) eigenvectors as columns and a diagonal matrix $\mathbf{\Lambda}$ with $\mathbf{\Lambda}_{ii} = \lambda_i$, $i = 1, \ldots, n$, the corresponding eigenvalues, we have $\mathbf{V}\mathbf{V}' = \mathbf{V}'\mathbf{V} = \mathbf{I}$, the identity matrix and

$$
\mathbf{A}\mathbf{V} = \mathbf{V}\mathbf{\Lambda}.
$$

This is often referred to as the *eigen-decomposition* of $\mathbf{A}$, while the set of eigenvalues $\lambda(\mathbf{A})$ are known as its *spectrum*. We generally assume that the eigenvalues appear in order of decreasing value

$$
\lambda_1 \geq \lambda_2 \geq \cdots \geq \lambda_n.
$$

Note that a matrix $\mathbf{V}$ with the property $\mathbf{VV'} = \mathbf{V'V} = \mathbf{I}$ is known as an *orthonormal or unitary matrix*.

The *principal minors* of a matrix are the submatrices obtained by selecting a subset of the rows and the same subset of columns. The corresponding minor contains the elements that lie on the intersections of the chosen rows and columns.

If the symmetric matrix $\mathbf{A}$ has k non-zero eigenvalues then we can express the eigen-decomposition as

$$\mathbf{A} = \mathbf{V}\mathbf{\Lambda}\mathbf{V'} = \mathbf{V}_k\mathbf{\Lambda}_k\mathbf{V'}_k,$$

where $\mathbf{V}_k$ and $\mathbf{\Lambda}_k$ are the matrices containing the k columns of $\mathbf{V}$ and the principal minor of $\mathbf{\Lambda}$ corresponding to non-zero eigenvalues. Hence, $\mathbf{A}$ has rank at most k. Given any vector $\mathbf{v}$ in the span of the columns of $\mathbf{V}_k$ we have

$$\mathbf{v} = \mathbf{V}_k\mathbf{u} = \mathbf{A}\mathbf{V}_k\mathbf{\Lambda}_k^{-1}\mathbf{u},$$

where $\mathbf{\Lambda}_k^{-1}$ is the diagonal matrix with inverse entries, so that the columns of $\mathbf{A}$ span the same k-dimensional space, implying the rank of a symmetric matrix $\mathbf{A}$ is equal to the number of non-zero eigenvalues.

For a matrix with all eigenvalues non-zero we can write

$$\mathbf{A}^{-1} = \mathbf{V}\mathbf{\Lambda}^{-1}\mathbf{V'},$$

as

$$\mathbf{V}\mathbf{\Lambda}^{-1}\mathbf{V'}\mathbf{V}\mathbf{\Lambda}\mathbf{V'} = \mathbf{I},$$

showing again that only full rank matrices are invertible.

For symmetric matrices the spectral norm can now be simply evaluated since the eigen-decomposition of $\mathbf{A'A} = \mathbf{A}^2$ is given by

$$\mathbf{A}^2 = \mathbf{V}\mathbf{\Lambda}\mathbf{V'}\mathbf{V}\mathbf{\Lambda}\mathbf{V'} = \mathbf{V}\mathbf{\Lambda}^2\mathbf{V'},$$

so that the spectrum of $\mathbf{A}^2$ is $\{\lambda^2 : \lambda \in \lambda(\mathbf{A})\}$. Hence, by (3.3) we have

$$\|\mathbf{A}\| = \max_{\lambda \in \lambda(\mathbf{A})} |\lambda|.$$

The Courant–Fisher Theorem gives a further characterisation of eigenvalues extending the characterisation of the largest eigenvalue given by the Raleigh quotient. It considers maximising or minimising the quotient in a subspace T of specified dimension, and then choosing the subspace either to minimise the maximum or maximise the minimum. The largest eigenvalue case corresponds to taking the dimension of T to be that of the whole space and hence maximising the quotient in the whole space.

Theorem 3.6 (Courant–Fisher) *If* $\mathbf{A} \in \mathbb{R}^{n \times n}$ *is symmetric, then for* $k = 1, \ldots, n$, *the kth eigenvalue* $\lambda_k(A)$ *of the matrix* A *satisfies*

$$\lambda_k(\mathbf{A}) = \max_{\dim(T)=k} \min_{0 \neq \mathbf{v} \in T} \frac{\mathbf{v}'\mathbf{A}\mathbf{v}}{\mathbf{v}'\mathbf{v}} = \min_{\dim(T)=n-k+1} \max_{0 \neq \mathbf{v} \in T} \frac{\mathbf{v}'\mathbf{A}\mathbf{v}}{\mathbf{v}'\mathbf{v}},$$

with the extrema achieved by the corresponding eigenvector.

Positive semi-definite matrices A symmetric matrix is *positive semi-definite*, if its eigenvalues are all non-negative. By Theorem 3.6 this holds if and only if

$$\mathbf{v}'\mathbf{A}\mathbf{v} \geq 0$$

for all vectors $\mathbf{v}$, since the minimal eigenvalue satisfies

$$\lambda_m(\mathbf{A}) = \min_{0 \neq \mathbf{v} \in \mathbb{R}^n} \frac{\mathbf{v}'\mathbf{A}\mathbf{v}}{\mathbf{v}'\mathbf{v}}.$$

Similarly a matrix is *positive definite*, if its eigenvalues are positive or equivalently

$$\mathbf{v}'\mathbf{A}\mathbf{v} > 0, \text{ for } \mathbf{v} \neq \mathbf{0}.$$

We now give two results concerning positive semi-definite matrices.

Proposition 3.7 *Gram and kernel matrices are positive semi-definite.*

Proof Considering the general case of a kernel matrix let

$$\mathbf{G}_{ij} = \kappa(\mathbf{x}_i, \mathbf{x}_j) = \langle \boldsymbol{\phi}(\mathbf{x}_i), \boldsymbol{\phi}(\mathbf{x}_j) \rangle, \text{ for } i, j = 1, \ldots, \ell.$$

For any vector $\mathbf{v}$ we have

$$\begin{aligned}
\mathbf{v}'\mathbf{G}\mathbf{v} &= \sum_{i,j=1}^{\ell} v_i v_j \mathbf{G}_{ij} = \sum_{i,j=1}^{\ell} v_i v_j \langle \boldsymbol{\phi}(\mathbf{x}_i), \boldsymbol{\phi}(\mathbf{x}_j) \rangle \\
&= \left\langle \sum_{i=1}^{\ell} v_i \boldsymbol{\phi}(\mathbf{x}_i), \sum_{j=1}^{\ell} v_j \boldsymbol{\phi}(\mathbf{x}_j) \right\rangle \\
&= \left\| \sum_{i=1}^{\ell} v_i \boldsymbol{\phi}(\mathbf{x}_i) \right\|^2 \geq 0,
\end{aligned}$$

as required.   □

Proposition 3.8 *A matrix* $\mathbf{A}$ *is positive semi-definite if and only if* $\mathbf{A} = \mathbf{B}'\mathbf{B}$ *for some real matrix* $\mathbf{B}$.

Proof Suppose $\mathbf{A} = \mathbf{B}'\mathbf{B}$, then for any vector $\mathbf{v}$ we have

$$\mathbf{v}'\mathbf{A}\mathbf{v} = \mathbf{v}'\mathbf{B}'\mathbf{B}\mathbf{v} = \|\mathbf{B}\mathbf{v}\|^2 \geq 0,$$

implying $\mathbf{A}$ is positive semi-definite.

Now suppose $\mathbf{A}$ is positive semi-definite. Let $\mathbf{A}\mathbf{V} = \mathbf{V}\mathbf{\Lambda}$ be the eigen-decomposition of $\mathbf{A}$ and set $\mathbf{B} = \sqrt{\mathbf{\Lambda}}\mathbf{V}'$, where $\sqrt{\mathbf{\Lambda}}$ is the diagonal matrix with entries $\left(\sqrt{\mathbf{\Lambda}}\right)_{ii} = \sqrt{\lambda_i}$. The matrix exists since the eigenvalues are non-negative. Then

$$\mathbf{B}'\mathbf{B} = \mathbf{V}\sqrt{\mathbf{\Lambda}}\sqrt{\mathbf{\Lambda}}\mathbf{V}' = \mathbf{V}\mathbf{\Lambda}\mathbf{V}' = \mathbf{A}\mathbf{V}\mathbf{V}' = \mathbf{A},$$

as required.   □

The choice of the matrix $\mathbf{B}$ in the proposition is not unique. For example the *Cholesky decomposition* of a positive semi-definite matrix $\mathbf{A}$ provides an alternative factorisation

$$\mathbf{A} = \mathbf{R}'\mathbf{R},$$

where the matrix $\mathbf{R}$ is upper-triangular with a non-negative diagonal. The Cholesky decomposition is the unique factorisation that has this property; see Chapter 5 for more details.

The next proposition gives another useful characterisation of positive (semi-) definiteness.

Proposition 3.9 *A matrix* $\mathbf{A}$ *is positive (semi-)definite if and only if all of its principal minors are positive (semi-)definite.*

Proof Consider a $k \times k$ minor $\mathbf{M}$ of $\mathbf{A}$. Clearly by inserting 0s in the positions of the rows that were not chosen for the minor $\mathbf{M}$ we can extend any vector $\mathbf{u} \in \mathbb{R}^k$ to a vector $\mathbf{v} \in \mathbb{R}^n$. Observe that for $\mathbf{A}$ positive semi-definite

$$\mathbf{u}'\mathbf{M}\mathbf{u} = \mathbf{v}'\mathbf{A}\mathbf{v} \geq 0,$$

with strict inequality if $\mathbf{A}$ is positive definite and $\mathbf{u} \neq \mathbf{0}$. Hence, if $\mathbf{A}$ is positive (semi-)definite so is $\mathbf{M}$. The reverse implication follows, since $\mathbf{A}$ is a principal minor of itself.   □

Note that each diagonal entry is a principal minor and so must be non-negative for a positive semi-definite matrix.

Determinant and trace The *determinant* $\det(\mathbf{A})$ of a square matrix $\mathbf{A}$ is the product of its eigenvalues. Hence, for a positive definite matrix the determinant will be strictly positive, while for singular matrices it will be zero.

If we consider the matrix as a linear transformation

$$\mathbf{x} \longmapsto \mathbf{A}\mathbf{x} = \mathbf{V}\mathbf{\Lambda}\mathbf{V}'\mathbf{x},$$

$\mathbf{V}'\mathbf{x}$ computes the projection of $\mathbf{x}$ onto the eigenvectors that form the columns of $\mathbf{V}$, multiplication by $\mathbf{\Lambda}$ rescales the projections, while the product with $\mathbf{V}$ recomputes the resulting vector. Hence the image of the unit sphere is an ellipse with its principal axes equal to the eigenvectors and with its lengths equal to the eigenvalues. The ratio of the volume of the image of the unit sphere to its pre-image is therefore equal to the absolute value of the determinant (the determinant is negative if the sphere has undergone a reflection). The same holds for any translation of a cube of any size aligned with the principal axes. Since we can approximate any shape arbitrarily closely with a collection of such cubes, it follows that the ratio of the volume of the image of any object to that of its pre-image is equal to the determinant. If we follow $\mathbf{A}$ with a second transformation $\mathbf{B}$ and consider the volume ratios, we conclude that $\det(\mathbf{AB}) = \det(\mathbf{A})\det(\mathbf{B})$.

The *trace* $\operatorname{tr}(\mathbf{A})$ of a $n \times n$ square matrix $\mathbf{A}$ is the sum of its diagonal entries

$$\operatorname{tr}(\mathbf{A}) = \sum_{i=1}^{n} \mathbf{A}_{ii}.$$

Since we have

$$\operatorname{tr}(\mathbf{AB}) = \sum_{i=1}^{n}\sum_{j=1}^{n} \mathbf{A}_{ij}\mathbf{B}_{ji} = \sum_{i=1}^{n}\sum_{j=1}^{n} \mathbf{B}_{ij}\mathbf{A}_{ji} = \operatorname{tr}(\mathbf{BA}),$$

the trace remains invariant under transformations of the form $\mathbf{A} \longrightarrow \mathbf{V}^{-1}\mathbf{A}\mathbf{V}$ for unitary $\mathbf{V}$ since

$$\operatorname{tr}(\mathbf{V}^{-1}\mathbf{A}\mathbf{V}) = \operatorname{tr}((\mathbf{A}\mathbf{V})\mathbf{V}^{-1}) = \operatorname{tr}(\mathbf{A}).$$

It follows by taking $\mathbf{V}$ from the eigen-decomposition of $\mathbf{A}$ that the trace of a matrix is equal to the sum of its eigenvalues.

3.2 Characterisation of kernels

Recall that a kernel function computes the inner product of the images under an embedding ϕ of two data points

$$\kappa(\mathbf{x}, \mathbf{z}) = \langle \phi(\mathbf{x}), \phi(\mathbf{z}) \rangle .$$

We have seen how forming a matrix of the pairwise evaluations of a kernel function on a set of inputs gives a positive semi-definite matrix. We also saw in Chapter 2 how a kernel function implicitly defines a feature space that in many cases we do not need to construct explicitly. This second observation suggests that we may also want to create kernels without explicitly constructing the feature space. Perhaps the structure of the data and our knowledge of the particular application suggest a way of comparing two inputs. The function that makes this comparison is a candidate for a kernel function.

A general characterisation So far we have only one way of verifying that the function is a kernel, that is to construct a feature space for which the function corresponds to first performing the feature mapping and then computing the inner product between the two images. For example we used this technique to show the polynomial function is a kernel and to show that the exponential of the cardinality of a set intersection is a kernel.

We will now introduce an alternative method of demonstrating that a candidate function is a kernel. This will provide one of the theoretical tools needed to create new kernels, and combine old kernels to form new ones.

One of the key observations is the relation with positive semi-definite matrices. As we saw above the kernel matrix formed by evaluating a kernel on all pairs of any set of inputs is positive semi-definite. This forms the basis of the following definition.

Definition 3.10 [Finitely positive semi-definite functions] A function

$$\kappa : X \times X \longrightarrow \mathbb{R}$$

satisfies the finitely positive semi-definite property if it is a symmetric function for which the matrices formed by restriction to any finite subset of the space X are positive semi-definite. ∎

Note that this definition does not require the set X to be a vector space. We will now demonstrate that the finitely positive semi-definite property characterises kernels. We will do this by explicitly constructing the feature space assuming only this property. We first state the result in the form of a theorem.

Theorem 3.11 (Characterisation of kernels) *A function*

$$\kappa : X \times X \longrightarrow \mathbb{R},$$

which is either continuous or has a countable domain, can be decomposed

$$\kappa(\mathbf{x}, \mathbf{z}) = \langle \phi(\mathbf{x}), \phi(\mathbf{z}) \rangle$$

into a feature map ϕ into a Hilbert space F applied to both its arguments followed by the evaluation of the inner product in F if and only if it satisfies the finitely positive semi-definite property.

Proof The 'only if' implication is simply the result of Proposition 3.7. We will now show the reverse implication. We therefore assume that κ satisfies the finitely positive semi-definite property and proceed to construct a feature mapping ϕ into a Hilbert space for which κ is the kernel.

There is one slightly unusual aspect of the construction in that the elements of the feature space will in fact be functions. They are, however, points in a vector space and will fulfil all the required properties. Recall our observation in Section 3.1.1 that learning a weight vector is equivalent to identifying an element of the feature space, in our case one of the functions. It is perhaps natural therefore that the feature space is actually the set of functions that we will be using in the learning problem

$$\mathcal{F} = \left\{ \sum_{i=1}^{\ell} \alpha_i \kappa(\mathbf{x}_i, \cdot) : \ell \in \mathbb{N}, \ \mathbf{x}_i \in X, \ \alpha_i \in \mathbb{R}, \ i = 1, \dots, \ell \right\}.$$

We have chosen to use a caligraphic $\mathcal{F}$ reserved for function spaces rather than the normal F of a feature space to emphasise that the elements are functions. We should, however, emphasise that this feature space is a set of points that are in fact functions. Note that we have used a $\cdot$ to indicate the position of the argument of the function. Clearly, the space is closed under multiplication by a scalar and addition of functions, where addition is defined by

$$f, g \in \mathcal{F} \implies (f + g)(\mathbf{x}) = f(\mathbf{x}) + g(\mathbf{x}).$$

Hence, $\mathcal{F}$ is a vector space. We now introduce an inner product on $\mathcal{F}$ as follows. Let $f, g \in \mathcal{F}$ be given by

$$f(\mathbf{x}) = \sum_{i=1}^{\ell} \alpha_i \kappa(\mathbf{x}_i, \mathbf{x}) \quad \text{and} \quad g(\mathbf{x}) = \sum_{i=1}^{n} \beta_i \kappa(\mathbf{z}_i, \mathbf{x})$$

then we define

$$\langle f, g \rangle = \sum_{i=1}^{\ell} \sum_{j=1}^{n} \alpha_i \beta_j \kappa(\mathbf{x}_i, \mathbf{z}_j) = \sum_{i=1}^{\ell} \alpha_i g(\mathbf{x}_i) = \sum_{j=1}^{n} \beta_j f(\mathbf{z}_j), \qquad (3.4)$$

where the second and third equalities follow from the definitions of f and g. It is clear from these equalities that $\langle f, g \rangle$ is real-valued, symmetric and bilinear and hence satisfies the properties of an inner product, provided

$$\langle f, f \rangle \geq 0 \text{ for all } f \in \mathcal{F}.$$

But this follows from the assumption that all kernel matrices are positive semi-definite, since

$$\langle f, f \rangle = \sum_{i=1}^{\ell} \sum_{j=1}^{\ell} \alpha_i \alpha_j \kappa(\mathbf{x}_i, \mathbf{x}_j) = \boldsymbol{\alpha}' \mathbf{K} \boldsymbol{\alpha} \geq 0,$$

where $\boldsymbol{\alpha}$ is the vector with entries α_i, $i = 1, \ldots, \ell$, and $\mathbf{K}$ is the kernel matrix constructed on $\mathbf{x}_1, \mathbf{x}_2, \ldots, \mathbf{x}_\ell$.

There is a further property that follows directly from the equations (3.4) if we take $g = \kappa(\mathbf{x}, \cdot)$

$$\langle f, \kappa(\mathbf{x}, \cdot) \rangle = \sum_{i=1}^{\ell} \alpha_i \kappa(\mathbf{x}_i, \mathbf{x}) = f(\mathbf{x}). \qquad (3.5)$$

This fact is known as the *reproducing property* of the kernel. It remains to show the two additional properties of completeness and separability. Separability will follow if the input space is countable or the kernel is continuous, but we omit the technical details of the proof of this fact. For completeness consider a fixed input $\mathbf{x}$ and a Cauchy sequence $(f_n)_{n=1}^{\infty}$. We have

$$(f_n(\mathbf{x}) - f_m(\mathbf{x}))^2 = \langle f_n - f_m, \kappa(\mathbf{x}, \cdot) \rangle^2 \leq \| f_n - f_m \|^2 \kappa(\mathbf{x}, \mathbf{x})$$

by the Cauchy–Schwarz inequality. Hence, $f_n(\mathbf{x})$ is a bounded Cauchy sequence of real numbers and hence has a limit. If we define the function

$$g(\mathbf{x}) = \lim_{n \to \infty} f_n(\mathbf{x}),$$

and include all such limit functions in $\mathcal{F}$ we obtain the Hilbert space F_κ associated with the kernel κ.

We have constructed the feature space, but must specify the image of an input $\mathbf{x}$ under the mapping ϕ

$$\phi : \mathbf{x} \in X \longmapsto \phi(\mathbf{x}) = \kappa(\mathbf{x}, \cdot) \in F_\kappa.$$

We can now evaluate the inner product between an element of F_κ and the image of an input $\mathbf{x}$ using equation (3.5)

$$\langle f, \phi(\mathbf{x}) \rangle = \langle f, \kappa(\mathbf{x}, \cdot) \rangle = f(\mathbf{x}).$$

This is precisely what we require, namely that the function f can indeed be represented as the linear function defined by an inner product (with itself) in the feature space F_κ. Furthermore the inner product is strict since if $\|f\| = 0$, then for all $\mathbf{x}$ we have that

$$|f(\mathbf{x})| = |\langle f, \phi(\mathbf{x}) \rangle| \le \|f\| \|\phi(\mathbf{x})\| = 0.$$

$\square$

Given a function κ that satisfies the finitely positive semi-definite property we will refer to the corresponding space F_κ as its *Reproducing Kernel Hilbert Space (RKHS)*. Similarly, we will use the notation $\langle \cdot, \cdot \rangle_{F_\kappa}$ for the corresponding inner product when we wish to emphasise its genesis.

Remark 3.12 [Reproducing property] We have shown how any kernel can be used to construct a Hilbert space in which the reproducing property holds. It is fairly straightforward to see that if a symmetric function $\kappa(\cdot, \cdot)$ satisfies the reproducing property in a Hilbert space F of functions

$$\langle \kappa(\mathbf{x}, \cdot), f(\cdot) \rangle_{\mathcal{F}} = f(\mathbf{x}), \text{ for } f \in \mathcal{F},$$

then κ satisfies the finitely positive semi-definite property, since

$$\sum_{i,j=1}^{\ell} \alpha_i \alpha_j \kappa(\mathbf{x}_i, \mathbf{x}_j) = \sum_{i,j=1}^{\ell} \alpha_i \alpha_j \langle \kappa(\mathbf{x}_i, \cdot), \kappa(\mathbf{x}_j, \cdot) \rangle_{\mathcal{F}}$$

$$= \left\langle \sum_{i=1}^{\ell} \alpha_i \kappa(\mathbf{x}_i, \cdot), \sum_{j=1}^{\ell} \alpha_j \kappa(\mathbf{x}_j, \cdot) \right\rangle_{\mathcal{F}}$$

$$= \left\| \sum_{i=1}^{\ell} \alpha_i \kappa(\mathbf{x}_i, \cdot) \right\|_{\mathcal{F}}^2 \ge 0.$$

$\blacksquare$

Mercer kernel We are now able to show Mercer's theorem as a consequence of the previous analysis. Mercer's theorem is usually used to construct a feature space for a valid kernel. Since we have already achieved this with the RKHS construction, we do not actually require Mercer's theorem itself. We include it for completeness and because it defines the feature space in terms of an explicit feature vector rather than using the function space of our RKHS construction. Recall the definition of the function space $L_2(X)$ from Example 3.4.

Theorem 3.13 (Mercer) *Let X be a compact subset of $\mathbb{R}^n$. Suppose κ is a continuous symmetric function such that the integral operator $T_\kappa : L_2(X) \to L_2(X)$*

$$(T_\kappa f)(\cdot) = \int_X \kappa(\cdot, \mathbf{x}) f(\mathbf{x}) d\mathbf{x},$$

is positive, that is

$$\int_{X \times X} \kappa(\mathbf{x}, \mathbf{z}) f(\mathbf{x}) f(\mathbf{z}) d\mathbf{x} d\mathbf{z} \geq 0,$$

for all $f \in L_2(X)$. Then we can expand $\kappa(\mathbf{x}, \mathbf{z})$ in a uniformly convergent series (on $X \times X$) in terms of functions ϕ_j, satisfying $\langle \phi_j, \phi_i \rangle = \delta_{ij}$

$$\kappa(\mathbf{x}, \mathbf{z}) = \sum_{j=1}^{\infty} \phi_j(\mathbf{x}) \phi_j(\mathbf{z}).$$

Furthermore, the series $\sum_{i=1}^{\infty} \|\phi_i\|_{L_2(X)}^2$ is convergent.

Proof The theorem will follow provided the positivity of the integral operator implies our condition that all finite submatrices are positive semi-definite. Suppose that there is a finite submatrix on the points $\mathbf{x}_1, \ldots, \mathbf{x}_\ell$ that is not positive semi-definite. Let the vector $\boldsymbol{\alpha}$ be such that

$$\sum_{i,j=1}^{\ell} \kappa(\mathbf{x}_i, \mathbf{x}_j) \alpha_i \alpha_j = \epsilon < 0,$$

and let

$$f_\sigma(\mathbf{x}) = \sum_{i=1}^{\ell} \alpha_i \frac{1}{(2\pi\sigma)^{d/2}} \exp\left(-\frac{\|\mathbf{x} - \mathbf{x}_i\|^2}{2\sigma^2}\right) \in L_2(X),$$

where d is the dimension of the space X. We have that

$$\lim_{\sigma \to 0} \int_{X \times X} \kappa(\mathbf{x}, \mathbf{z}) f_\sigma(\mathbf{x}) f_\sigma(\mathbf{z}) d\mathbf{x} d\mathbf{z} = \epsilon.$$

But then for some $\sigma > 0$ the integral will be less than 0 contradicting the positivity of the integral operator.

Now consider an orthonormal basis $\phi_i(\cdot)$, $i = 1, \ldots$ of F_κ the RKHS of the kernel κ. Then we have the Fourier series for $\kappa(\mathbf{x}, \cdot)$

$$\kappa(\mathbf{x}, \mathbf{z}) = \sum_{i=1}^{\infty} \langle \kappa(\mathbf{x}, \cdot), \phi_i(\cdot) \rangle \phi_i(\mathbf{z}) = \sum_{i=1}^{\infty} \phi_i(\mathbf{x}) \phi_i(\mathbf{z}),$$

as required.

Finally, to show that the series $\sum_{i=1}^{\infty} \|\phi_i\|_{L_2(X)}^2$ is convergent, using the compactness of X we obtain

$$\infty > \int_X \lim_{n \to \infty} \sum_{i=1}^{n} \phi_i(\mathbf{x}) \phi_i(\mathbf{x}) d\mathbf{x} = \lim_{n \to \infty} \int_X \sum_{i=1}^{n} \phi_i(\mathbf{x}) \phi_i(\mathbf{x}) d\mathbf{x}$$

$$= \lim_{n \to \infty} \sum_{i=1}^{n} \int_X \phi_i(\mathbf{x}) \phi_i(\mathbf{x}) d\mathbf{x} = \lim_{n \to \infty} \sum_{i=1}^{n} \|\phi_i\|_{L_2(X)}^2$$

$\square$

Example 3.14 Consider the kernel function $\kappa(\mathbf{x}, \mathbf{z}) = \kappa(\mathbf{x} - \mathbf{z})$. Such a kernel is said to be *translation invariant*, since the inner product of two inputs is unchanged if both are translated by the same vector. Consider the one-dimensional case in which κ is defined on the interval $[0, 2\pi]$ in such a way that $\kappa(u)$ can be extended to a continuous, symmetric, periodic function on $\mathbb{R}$. Such a function can be expanded in a uniformly convergent Fourier series

$$\kappa(u) = \sum_{n=0}^{\infty} a_n \cos(nu).$$

In this case we can expand $\kappa(x - z)$ as follows

$$\kappa(x - z) = a_0 + \sum_{n=1}^{\infty} a_n \sin(nx) \sin(nz) + \sum_{n=1}^{\infty} a_n \cos(nx) \cos(nz).$$

Provided the a_n are all positive this shows $\kappa(x, z)$ is the inner product in the feature space defined by the orthogonal features

$$\{\phi_i(x)\}_{i=0}^{\infty} = (1, \sin(x), \cos(x), \sin(2x), \cos(2x), \ldots, \sin(nx), \cos(nx), \ldots),$$

since the functions, 1, $\cos(nu)$ and $\sin(nu)$ form a set of orthogonal functions on the interval $[0, 2\pi]$. Hence, normalising them will provide a set of Mercer features. Note that the embedding is defined independently of the parameters a_n, which subsequently control the geometry of the feature space. ∎

Example 3.14 provides some useful insight into the role that the choice of kernel can play. The parameters a_n in the expansion of $\kappa(u)$ are its Fourier coefficients. If, for some n, we have $a_n = 0$, the corresponding features are removed from the feature space. Similarly, small values of a_n mean that the feature is given low weighting and so will have less influence on the choice of hyperplane. Hence, the choice of kernel can be seen as choosing a filter with a particular spectral characteristic, the effect of which is to control the influence of the different frequencies in determining the optimal separation.

Covariance kernels Mercer's theorem enables us to express a kernel as a sum over a set of functions of the product of their values on the two inputs

$$\kappa(\mathbf{x}, \mathbf{z}) = \sum_{j=1}^{\infty} \phi_j(\mathbf{x})\phi_j(\mathbf{z}).$$

This suggests a different view of kernels as a covariance function determined by a probability distribution over a function class. In general, given a distribution $q(f)$ over a function class $\mathcal{F}$, the covariance function is given by

$$\kappa_q(\mathbf{x}, \mathbf{z}) = \int_{\mathcal{F}} f(\mathbf{x})f(\mathbf{z})q(f)df.$$

We will refer to such a kernel as a *covariance kernel*. We can see that this is a kernel by considering the mapping

$$\phi : \mathbf{x} \longmapsto (f(\mathbf{x}))_{f \in \mathcal{F}}$$

into the space of functions on $\mathcal{F}$ with inner product given by

$$\langle a(\cdot), b(\cdot) \rangle = \int_{\mathcal{F}} a(f)\, b(f)\, q(f)\, df.$$

This definition is quite natural if we consider that the ideal kernel for learning a function f is given by

$$\kappa_f(\mathbf{x}, \mathbf{z}) = f(\mathbf{x})f(\mathbf{z}), \tag{3.6}$$

since the space $\mathcal{F} = \mathcal{F}_{\kappa_f}$ in this case contains functions of the form

$$\sum_{i=1}^{\ell} \alpha_i \kappa_f(\mathbf{x}_i, \cdot) = \sum_{i=1}^{\ell} \alpha_i f(\mathbf{x}_i) f(\cdot) = C f(\cdot).$$

So for the kernel κ_f, the corresponding $\mathcal{F}$ is one-dimensional, containing only multiples of f. We can therefore view κ_q as taking a combination of these simple kernels for all possible f weighted according to the prior distribution q. Any kernel derived in this way is a valid kernel, since it is easily verified that it satisfies the finitely positive semi-definite property

$$
\sum_{i=1}^{\ell}\sum_{j=1}^{\ell}\alpha_i\alpha_j\kappa_q(\mathbf{x}_i,\mathbf{x}_j) = \sum_{i=1}^{\ell}\sum_{j=1}^{\ell}\alpha_i\alpha_j\int_{\mathcal{F}}f(\mathbf{x}_i)f(\mathbf{x}_j)q(f)df
$$

$$
= \int_{\mathcal{F}}\sum_{i=1}^{\ell}\sum_{j=1}^{\ell}\alpha_i\alpha_jf(\mathbf{x}_i)f(\mathbf{x}_j)q(f)df
$$

$$
= \int_{\mathcal{F}}\left(\sum_{i=1}^{\ell}\alpha_if(\mathbf{x}_i)\right)^2 q(f)df \geq 0.
$$

Furthermore, if the underlying class $\mathcal{F}$ of functions are $\{-1,+1\}$-valued, the kernel κ_q will be normalised since

$$
\kappa_q(\mathbf{x},\mathbf{x}) = \int_{\mathcal{F}}f(\mathbf{x})f(\mathbf{x})q(f)df = \int_{\mathcal{F}}q(f)df = 1.
$$

We will now show that every kernel can be obtained as a covariance kernel in which the distribution has a particular form. Given a valid kernel κ, consider the Gaussian prior q that generates functions f according to

$$
f(\mathbf{x}) = \sum_{i=1}^{\infty}u_i\phi_i(\mathbf{x}),
$$

where ϕ_i are the orthonormal functions of Theorem 3.13 for the kernel κ, and u_i are generated according to the Gaussian distribution $\mathcal{N}(0,1)$ with mean 0 and standard deviation 1. Notice that this function will be in $L_2(X)$ with probability 1, since using the orthonormality of the ϕ_i we can bound its expected norm by

$$
\mathbb{E}\left[\|f\|_{L_2(X)}^2\right] = \mathbb{E}\left[\sum_{i=1}^{\infty}\sum_{j=1}^{\infty}u_iu_j\langle\phi_i,\phi_j\rangle_{L_2(X)}\right]
$$

$$
= \sum_{i=1}^{\infty}\sum_{j=1}^{\infty}\mathbb{E}[u_iu_j]\langle\phi_i,\phi_j\rangle_{L_2(X)}
$$

$$
= \sum_{i=1}^{\infty}\mathbb{E}[u_i^2]\|\phi_i\|_{L_2(X)}^2 = \sum_{i=1}^{\infty}\|\phi_i\|_{L_2(X)}^2 < \infty,
$$

where the final inequality follows from Theorem 3.13. Since the norm is a positive function it follows that the measure of functions not in $L_2(X)$ is 0, as otherwise the expectation would not be finite. But curiously the function will almost certainly not be in $\mathcal{F}_\kappa$ for infinite-dimensional feature spaces. We therefore take the distribution q to be defined over the space $L_2(X)$.

The covariance function κ_q is now equal to

$$
\begin{aligned}
\kappa_q(\mathbf{x}, \mathbf{z}) &= \int_{L_2(X)} f(\mathbf{x}) f(\mathbf{z}) q(f) df \\
&= \lim_{n \to \infty} \sum_{i,j=1}^{n} \phi_i(\mathbf{x}) \phi_j(\mathbf{z}) \int_{\mathbb{R}^n} u_i u_j \prod_{k=1}^{n} \left(\frac{1}{\sqrt{2\pi}} \exp(-u_k^2/2) du_k \right) \\
&= \lim_{n \to \infty} \sum_{i,j=1}^{n} \phi_i(\mathbf{x}) \phi_j(\mathbf{z}) \delta_{ij} = \sum_{i=1}^{\infty} \phi_i(\mathbf{x}) \phi_i(\mathbf{z}) \\
&= \kappa(\mathbf{x}, \mathbf{z}).
\end{aligned}
$$

3.3 The kernel matrix

Given a training set $S = \{\mathbf{x}_1, \ldots, \mathbf{x}_\ell\}$ and kernel function $\kappa(\cdot, \cdot)$, we introduced earlier the kernel or Gram matrix $\mathbf{K} = (\mathbf{K}_{ij})_{i,j=1}^{\ell}$ with entries

$$
\mathbf{K}_{ij} = \kappa(\mathbf{x}_i, \mathbf{x}_j), \text{ for } i, j = 1, \ldots, \ell.
$$

The last subsection was devoted to showing that the function κ is a valid kernel provided its kernel matrices are positive semi-definite for all training sets S, the so-called finitely positive semi-definite property. This fact enables us to manipulate kernels without necessarily considering the corresponding feature space. Provided we maintain the finitely positive semi-definite property we are guaranteed that we have a valid kernel, that is, that there exists a feature space for which it is the corresponding kernel function. Reasoning about the similarity measure implied by the kernel function may be more natural than performing an explicit construction of its feature space.

The intrinsic modularity of kernel machines also means that any kernel function can be used provided it produces symmetric, positive semi-definite kernel matrices, and any kernel algorithm can be applied, as long as it can accept as input such a matrix together with any necessary labelling information. In other words, the kernel matrix acts as an interface between the data input and learning modules.

Kernel matrix as information bottleneck In view of our characterisation of kernels in terms of the finitely positive semi-definite property, it becomes clear why the kernel matrix is perhaps the core ingredient in the theory of kernel methods. It contains all the information available in order to perform the learning step, with the sole exception of the output labels in the case of supervised learning. It is worth bearing in mind that it is only through the kernel matrix that the learning algorithm obtains information about the choice of feature space or model, and indeed the training data itself.

The finitely positive semi-definite property can also be used to justify intermediate processing steps designed to improve the representation of the data, and hence the overall performance of the system through manipulating the kernel matrix before it is passed to the learning machine. One simple example is the addition of a constant to the diagonal of the matrix. This has the effect of introducing a soft margin in classification or equivalently regularisation in regression, something that we have already seen in the ridge regression example. We will, however, describe more complex manipulations of the kernel matrix that correspond to more subtle tunings of the feature space.

In view of the fact that it is only through the kernel matrix that the learning algorithm receives information about the feature space and input data, it is perhaps not surprising that some properties of this matrix can be used to assess the generalization performance of a learning system. The properties vary according to the type of learning task and the subtlety of the analysis, but once again the kernel matrix plays a central role both in the derivation of generalisation bounds and in their evaluation in practical applications.

The kernel matrix is not only the central concept in the design and analysis of kernel machines, it can also be regarded as the central data structure in their implementation. As we have seen, the kernel matrix acts as an interface between the data input module and the learning algorithms. Furthermore, many model adaptation and selection methods are implemented by manipulating the kernel matrix as it is passed between these two modules. Its properties affect every part of the learning system from the computation, through the generalisation analysis, to the implementation details.

Remark 3.15 [Implementation issues] One small word of caution is perhaps worth mentioning on the implementation side. Memory constraints mean that it may not be possible to store the full kernel matrix in memory for very large datasets. In such cases it may be necessary to recompute the kernel function as entries are needed. This may have implications for both the choice of algorithm and the details of the implementation. ∎

Another important aspect of our characterisation of valid kernels in terms

of the finitely positive semi-definite property is that the same condition holds
for kernels defined over any kind of inputs. We did not require that the
inputs should be real vectors, so that the characterisation applies whatever
the type of the data, be it strings, discrete structures, images, time series,
and so on. Provided the kernel matrices corresponding to any finite training
set are positive semi-definite the kernel computes the inner product after
projecting pairs of inputs into some feature space. Figure 3.1 illustrates this
point with an embedding showing objects being mapped to feature vectors
by the mapping ϕ.

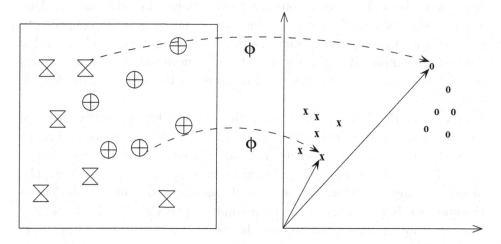

Fig. 3.1. The use of kernels enables the application of the algorithms to non-
vectorial data.

Remark 3.16 [Kernels and prior knowledge] The kernel contains all of the
information available to the learning machine about the relative positions
of the inputs in the feature space. Naturally, if structure is to be discovered
in the data set, the data must exhibit that structure through the kernel
matrix. If the kernel is too general and does not give enough importance
to specific types of similarity. In the language of our discussion of priors
this corresponds to giving weight to too many different classifications. The
kernel therefore views with the same weight any pair of inputs as similar or
dissimilar, and so the off-diagonal entries of the kernel matrix become very
small, while the diagonal entries are close to 1. The kernel can therefore only
represent the concept of identity. This leads to overfitting since we can easily
classify a training set correctly, but the kernel has no way of generalising to
new data. At the other extreme, if a kernel matrix is completely uniform,
then every input is similar to every other input. This corresponds to every

input being mapped to the same feature vector and leads to underfitting of the data since the only functions that can be represented easily are those which map all points to the same class. Geometrically the first situation corresponds to inputs being mapped to orthogonal points in the feature space, while in the second situation all points are merged into the same image. In both cases there are no non-trivial natural classes in the data, and hence no real structure that can be exploited for generalisation. ∎

Remark 3.17 [Kernels as oracles] It is possible to regard a kernel as defining a similarity measure between two data points. It can therefore be considered as an oracle, guessing the similarity of two inputs. If one uses normalised kernels, this can be thought of as the a priori probability of the inputs being in the same class minus the a priori probability of their being in different classes. In the case of a covariance kernel over a class of classification functions this is precisely the meaning of the kernel function under the prior distribution $q(f)$, since

$$\kappa_q(\mathbf{x}, \mathbf{z}) = \int_{\mathcal{F}} f(\mathbf{x}) f(\mathbf{z}) q(f) df = P_q\left(f(\mathbf{x}) = f(\mathbf{z})\right) - P_q\left(f(\mathbf{x}) \neq f(\mathbf{z})\right).$$

∎

Remark 3.18 [Priors over eigenfunctions] Notice that the kernel matrix can be decomposed as follows

$$\mathbf{K} = \sum_{i=1}^{\ell} \lambda_i \mathbf{v}_i \mathbf{v}_i',$$

where $\mathbf{v}_i$ are eigenvectors and λ_i are the corresponding eigenvalues. This decomposition is reminiscent of the form of a covariance kernel if we view each eigenvector $\mathbf{v}_i$ as a function over the set of examples and treat the eigenvalues as a (unnormalised) distribution over these functions. We can think of the eigenvectors as defining a feature space, though this is restricted to the training set in the form given above. Extending this to the eigenfunctions of the underlying integral operator

$$f(\cdot) \longmapsto \int_X \kappa(\mathbf{x}, \cdot) f(\mathbf{x}) dx$$

gives another construction for the feature space of Mercer's theorem. We can therefore think of a kernel as defining a prior over the eigenfunctions of the kernel operator. This connection will be developed further when we come to consider principle components analysis. In general, defining a good kernel involves incorporating the functions that are likely to arise in the particular application and excluding others.   ∎

Remark 3.19 [Hessian matrix] For supervised learning with a target vector of $\{+1, -1\}$ values $\mathbf{y}$, we will often consider the matrix $\mathbf{H}_{ij} = y_i y_j \mathbf{K}_{ij}$. This matrix is known as the *Hessian* for reasons to be clarified later. It can be defined as the Schur product (entrywise multiplication) of the matrix $\mathbf{yy}'$ and $\mathbf{K}$. If $\lambda, \mathbf{v}$ is an eigenvalue-eigenvector pair of $\mathbf{K}$ then $\lambda, \mathbf{u}$ is an eigenvalue-eigenvector pair of $\mathbf{H}$, where $u_i = v_i y_i$, for all i.   ∎

Selecting a kernel We have already seen in the covariance kernels how the choice of kernel amounts to encoding our prior expectation about the possible functions we may be expected to learn. Ideally we select the kernel based on our prior knowledge of the problem domain and restrict the learning to the task of selecting the particular pattern function in the feature space defined by the chosen kernel. Unfortunately, it is not always possible to make the right choice of kernel a priori. We are rather forced to consider a family of kernels defined in a way that again reflects our prior expectations, but which leaves open the choice of the particular kernel that will be used. The learning system must now solve two tasks, that of choosing a kernel from the family, and either subsequently or concurrently of selecting a pattern function in the feature space of the chosen kernel.

Many different approaches can be adopted for solving this two-part learning problem. The simplest examples of kernel families require only limited amount of additional information that can be estimated from the training data, frequently without using the label information in the case of a supervised learning task.

More elaborate methods that make use of the labelling information need a measure of 'goodness' to drive the kernel selection stage of the learning. This can be provided by introducing a notion of similarity between kernels and choosing the kernel that is closest to the ideal kernel described in equation (3.6) given by $\kappa(\mathbf{x}, \mathbf{z}) = y(\mathbf{x})y(\mathbf{z})$. A measure of matching between kernels or, in the case of the ideal kernel, between a kernel and a target should satisfy some basic properties: it should be symmetric, should be maximised when its arguments are equal, and should be minimised when applied to two independent kernels.

Furthermore, in practice the comparison with the ideal kernel will only be feasible when restricted to the kernel matrix on the training set rather than between complete functions, since the ideal kernel can only be computed on the training data. It should therefore be possible to justify that reliable estimates of the true similarity can be obtained using only the training set.

Cone of kernel matrices Positive semi-definite matrices form a *cone* in the vector space of $\ell \times \ell$ matrices, where by cone we mean a set closed under addition and under multiplication by non-negative scalars. This is important if we wish to optimise over such matrices, since it implies that they will be convex, an important property in ensuring the existence of efficient methods. The study of optimization over such sets is known as semi-definite programming (SDP). In view of the central role of the kernel matrix in the above discussion, it is perhaps not surprising that this recently developed field has started to play a role in kernel optimization algorithms.

We now introduce a measure of similarity between two kernels. First consider the *Frobenius inner product* between pairs of matrices with identical dimensions

$$\langle \mathbf{M}, \mathbf{N} \rangle = \mathbf{M} \cdot \mathbf{N} = \sum_{i,j=1}^{\ell} \mathbf{M}_{ij} \mathbf{N}_{ij} = \mathrm{tr}(\mathbf{M}'\mathbf{N}).$$

The corresponding matrix norm is known as the *Frobenius norm*. Furthermore if we consider $\mathrm{tr}(\mathbf{M}'\mathbf{N})$ as a function of $\mathbf{M}$, its gradient is of course $\mathbf{N}$.

Based on this inner product a simple measure of similarity between two kernel matrices $\mathbf{K}_1$ and $\mathbf{K}_2$ is the following:

Definition 3.20 The *alignment* $A(\mathbf{K}_1, \mathbf{K}_2)$ between two kernel matrices $\mathbf{K}_1$ and $\mathbf{K}_2$ is given by

$$A(\mathbf{K}_1, \mathbf{K}_2) = \frac{\langle \mathbf{K}_1, \mathbf{K}_2 \rangle}{\sqrt{\langle \mathbf{K}_1, \mathbf{K}_1 \rangle \langle \mathbf{K}_2, \mathbf{K}_2 \rangle}}$$

The alignment between a kernel $\mathbf{K}$ and a target $\mathbf{y}$ is simply $A(\mathbf{K}, \mathbf{yy}')$, as $\mathbf{yy}'$ is the ideal kernel for that target. For $\mathbf{y} \in \{-1, +1\}^{\ell}$ this becomes

$$A(\mathbf{K}, \mathbf{yy}') = \frac{\mathbf{y}'\mathbf{K}\mathbf{y}}{\ell \|\mathbf{K}\|}.$$

∎

Since the alignment can be viewed as the cosine of the angle between the matrices viewed as ℓ^2-dimensional vectors, it satisfies $-1 \le A(\mathbf{K}_1, \mathbf{K}_2) \le 1$.

The definition of alignment has not made use of the fact that the matrices we are considering are positive semi-definite. For such matrices the lower bound on alignment is in fact 0 as can be seen from the following proposition.

Proposition 3.21 *Let* $\mathbf{M}$ *be symmetric. Then* $\mathbf{M}$ *is positive semi-definite if and only if* $\langle \mathbf{M}, \mathbf{N} \rangle \geq 0$ *for every positive semi-definite* $\mathbf{N}$.

Proof Let $\lambda_1, \lambda_2, \ldots, \lambda_\ell$ be the eigenvalues of $\mathbf{M}$ with corresponding eigenvectors $\mathbf{v}_1, \mathbf{v}_2, \ldots, \mathbf{v}_\ell$. It follows that

$$\langle \mathbf{M}, \mathbf{N} \rangle = \left\langle \sum_{i=1}^{\ell} \lambda_i \mathbf{v}_i \mathbf{v}_i', \mathbf{N} \right\rangle = \sum_{i=1}^{\ell} \lambda_i \langle \mathbf{v}_i \mathbf{v}_i', \mathbf{N} \rangle = \sum_{i=1}^{\ell} \lambda_i \mathbf{v}_i' \mathbf{N} \mathbf{v}_i.$$

Note that $\mathbf{v}_i' \mathbf{N} \mathbf{v}_i \geq 0$ if $\mathbf{N}$ is positive semi-definite and we can choose $\mathbf{N}$ so that only one of these is non-zero. Furthermore, $\mathbf{M}$ is positive semi-definite if and only if $\lambda_i \geq 0$ for all i, and so $\langle \mathbf{M}, \mathbf{N} \rangle \geq 0$ for all positive semi-definite $\mathbf{N}$ if and only if $\mathbf{M}$ is positive semi-definite. $\qquad\square$

The alignment can also be considered as a Pearson correlation coefficient between the random variables $\mathbf{K}_1(\mathbf{x}, \mathbf{z})$ and $\mathbf{K}_2(\mathbf{x}, \mathbf{z})$ generated with a uniform distribution over the pairs $(\mathbf{x}_i, \mathbf{z}_j)$. It is also easily related to the distance between the normalised kernel matrices in the Frobenius norm

$$\left\| \frac{\mathbf{K}_1}{\|\mathbf{K}_1\|} - \frac{\mathbf{K}_2}{\|\mathbf{K}_2\|} \right\| = 2 - A(\mathbf{K}_1, \mathbf{K}_2)$$

3.4 Kernel construction

The characterization of kernel functions and kernel matrices given in the previous sections is not only useful for deciding whether a given candidate is a valid kernel. One of its main consequences is that it can be used to justify a series of rules for manipulating and combining simple kernels to obtain more complex and useful ones. In other words, such operations on one or more kernels can be shown to preserve the finitely positive semi-definiteness 'kernel' property. We will say that the class of kernel functions is *closed* under such operations. These will include operations on kernel functions and operations directly on the kernel matrix. As long as we can guarantee that the result of an operation will always be a positive semi-definite symmetric matrix, we will still be embedding the data in a feature space, albeit a feature space transformed by the chosen operation. We first consider the case of operations on the kernel function.

3.4.1 Operations on kernel functions

The following proposition can be viewed as showing that kernels satisfy a number of closure properties, allowing us to create more complicated kernels from simple building blocks.

Proposition 3.22 (Closure properties) *Let κ_1 and κ_2 be kernels over $X \times X$, $X \subseteq \mathbb{R}^n$, $a \in \mathbb{R}^+$, $f(\cdot)$ a real-valued function on X, $\phi\colon X \longrightarrow \mathbb{R}^N$ with κ_3 a kernel over $\mathbb{R}^N \times \mathbb{R}^N$, and $\mathbf{B}$ a symmetric positive semi-definite $n \times n$ matrix. Then the following functions are kernels:*

(i) $\kappa(\mathbf{x}, \mathbf{z}) = \kappa_1(\mathbf{x}, \mathbf{z}) + \kappa_2(\mathbf{x}, \mathbf{z})$,

(ii) $\kappa(\mathbf{x}, \mathbf{z}) = a\kappa_1(\mathbf{x}, \mathbf{z})$,

(iii) $\kappa(\mathbf{x}, \mathbf{z}) = \kappa_1(\mathbf{x}, \mathbf{z})\kappa_2(\mathbf{x}, \mathbf{z})$,

(iv) $\kappa(\mathbf{x}, \mathbf{z}) = f(\mathbf{x})f(\mathbf{z})$,

(v) $\kappa(\mathbf{x}, \mathbf{z}) = \kappa_3(\phi(\mathbf{x}), \phi(\mathbf{z}))$,

(vi) $\kappa(\mathbf{x}, \mathbf{z}) = \mathbf{x}'\mathbf{B}\mathbf{z}$.

Proof Let S a finite set of points $\{\mathbf{x}_1, \ldots, \mathbf{x}_\ell\}$, and let $\mathbf{K}_1$ and $\mathbf{K}_2$, be the corresponding kernel matrices obtained by restricting κ_1 and κ_2 to these points. Consider any vector $\boldsymbol{\alpha} \in \mathbb{R}^\ell$. Recall that a matrix $\mathbf{K}$ is positive semi-definite if and only if $\boldsymbol{\alpha}'\mathbf{K}\boldsymbol{\alpha} \geq 0$, for all $\boldsymbol{\alpha}$.

(i) We have

$$\boldsymbol{\alpha}'\left(\mathbf{K}_1 + \mathbf{K}_2\right)\boldsymbol{\alpha} = \boldsymbol{\alpha}'\mathbf{K}_1\boldsymbol{\alpha} + \boldsymbol{\alpha}'\mathbf{K}_2\boldsymbol{\alpha} \geq 0,$$

and so $\mathbf{K}_1 + \mathbf{K}_2$ is positive semi-definite and $\kappa_1 + \kappa_2$ a kernel function.

(ii) Similarly $\boldsymbol{\alpha}'a\mathbf{K}_1\boldsymbol{\alpha} = a\boldsymbol{\alpha}'\mathbf{K}_1\boldsymbol{\alpha} \geq 0$, verifying that $a\kappa_1$ is a kernel.

(iii) Let

$$\mathbf{K} = \mathbf{K}_1 \bigotimes \mathbf{K}_2$$

be the tensor product of the matrices $\mathbf{K}_1$ and $\mathbf{K}_2$ obtained by replacing each entry of $\mathbf{K}_1$ by $\mathbf{K}_2$ multiplied by that entry. The tensor product of two positive semi-definite matrices is itself positive semi-definite since the eigenvalues of the product are all pairs of products of the eigenvalues of the two components. The matrix corresponding to the function $\kappa_1\kappa_2$ is known as the *Schur product* $\mathbf{H}$ of $\mathbf{K}_1$ and $\mathbf{K}_2$ with entries the products of the corresponding entries in the two components. The matrix $\mathbf{H}$ is a principal submatrix of $\mathbf{K}$ defined by a set of columns and the same set of rows. Hence for any $\boldsymbol{\alpha} \in \mathbb{R}^\ell$, there is a corresponding $\boldsymbol{\alpha}_1 \in \mathbb{R}^{\ell^2}$, such that

$$\boldsymbol{\alpha}'\mathbf{H}\boldsymbol{\alpha} = \boldsymbol{\alpha}_1'\mathbf{K}\boldsymbol{\alpha}_1 \geq 0,$$

and so $\mathbf{H}$ is positive semi-definite as required.

(iv) Consider the 1-dimensional feature map

$$\phi : \mathbf{x} \longmapsto f(\mathbf{x}) \in \mathbb{R};$$

then $\kappa(\mathbf{x}, \mathbf{z})$ is the corresponding kernel.

(v) Since κ_3 is a kernel, the matrix obtained by restricting κ_3 to the points $\phi(\mathbf{x}_1), \dots, \phi(\mathbf{x}_\ell)$ is positive semi-definite as required.

(vi) Consider the diagonalisation of $\mathbf{B} = \mathbf{V}'\mathbf{\Lambda}\mathbf{V}$ by an orthogonal matrix $\mathbf{V}$, where $\mathbf{\Lambda}$ is the diagonal matrix containing the non-negative eigenvalues. Let $\sqrt{\mathbf{\Lambda}}$ be the diagonal matrix with the square roots of the eigenvalues and set $\mathbf{A} = \sqrt{\mathbf{\Lambda}}\mathbf{V}$. We therefore have

$$\kappa(\mathbf{x}, \mathbf{z}) = \mathbf{x}'\mathbf{B}\mathbf{z} = \mathbf{x}'\mathbf{V}'\mathbf{\Lambda}\mathbf{V}\mathbf{z} = \mathbf{x}'\mathbf{A}'\mathbf{A}\mathbf{z} = \langle \mathbf{A}\mathbf{x}, \mathbf{A}\mathbf{z} \rangle,$$

the inner product using the linear feature mapping $\mathbf{A}$.

□

Remark 3.23 [Schur product] The combination of kernels given in part (iii) is often referred to as the *Schur product*. We can decompose any kernel into the Schur product of its normalisation and the 1-dimensional kernel of part (iv) with $f(\mathbf{x}) = \sqrt{\kappa(\mathbf{x}, \mathbf{x})}$. ∎

The original motivation for introducing kernels was to search for nonlinear patterns by using linear functions in a feature space created using a nonlinear feature map. The last example of the proposition might therefore seem an irrelevance since it corresponds to a linear feature map. Despite this, such mappings can be useful in practice as they can rescale the geometry of the space, and hence change the relative weightings assigned to different linear functions. In Chapter 10 we will describe the use of such feature maps in applications to document analysis.

Proposition 3.24 *Let $\kappa_1(\mathbf{x}, \mathbf{z})$ be a kernel over $X \times X$, where $\mathbf{x}, \mathbf{z} \in X$, and $p(x)$ is a polynomial with positive coefficients. Then the following functions are also kernels:*

(i) $\kappa(\mathbf{x}, \mathbf{z}) = p(\kappa_1(\mathbf{x}, \mathbf{z}))$,

(ii) $\kappa(\mathbf{x}, \mathbf{z}) = \exp(\kappa_1(\mathbf{x}, \mathbf{z}))$,

(iii) $\kappa(\mathbf{x}, \mathbf{z}) = \exp(-\|\mathbf{x} - \mathbf{z}\|^2 / (2\sigma^2))$.

Proof We consider the three parts in turn:

(i) For a polynomial the result follows from parts (i), (ii), (iii) of Proposition 3.22 with part (iv) covering the constant term if we take $f(\cdot)$ to be a constant.

(ii) The exponential function can be arbitrarily closely approximated by polynomials with positive coefficients and hence is a limit of kernels. Since the finitely positive semi-definiteness property is closed under taking pointwise limits, the result follows.

(iii) By part (ii) we have that $\exp(\langle \mathbf{x}, \mathbf{z} \rangle / \sigma^2)$ is a kernel for $\sigma \in \mathbb{R}^+$. We now normalise this kernel (see Section 2.3.2) to obtain the kernel

$$\frac{\exp(\langle \mathbf{x}, \mathbf{z} \rangle / \sigma^2)}{\sqrt{\exp(\|\mathbf{x}\|^2 / \sigma^2) \exp(\|\mathbf{z}\|^2 / \sigma^2)}} = \exp\left(\frac{\langle \mathbf{x}, \mathbf{z} \rangle}{\sigma^2} - \frac{\langle \mathbf{x}, \mathbf{x} \rangle}{2\sigma^2} - \frac{\langle \mathbf{z}, \mathbf{z} \rangle}{2\sigma^2} \right)$$

$$= \exp\left(-\frac{\|\mathbf{x} - \mathbf{z}\|^2}{2\sigma^2} \right).$$

$\square$

Remark 3.25 [Gaussian kernel] The final kernel of Proposition 3.24 is known as the *Gaussian kernel*. These functions form the hidden units of a radial basis function network, and hence using this kernel will mean the hypotheses are radial basis function networks. It is therefore also referred to as the *RBF kernel*. We will discuss this kernel further in Chapter 9. ∎

Embeddings corresponding to kernel constructions Proposition 3.22 shows that we can create new kernels from existing kernels using a number of simple operations. Our approach has demonstrated that new functions are kernels by showing that they are finitely positive semi-definite. This is sufficient to verify that the function is a kernel and hence demonstrates that there exists a feature space map for which the function computes the corresponding inner product. Often this information provides sufficient insight for the user to sculpt an appropriate kernel for a particular application. It is, however, sometimes helpful to understand the effect of the kernel combination on the structure of the corresponding feature space.

The proof of part (iv) used a feature space construction, while part (ii) corresponds to a simple re-scaling of the feature vector by $\sqrt{a}$. For the addition of two kernels in part (i) the feature vector is the concatenation of the corresponding vectors

$$\phi(\mathbf{x}) = [\phi_1(\mathbf{x}), \phi_2(\mathbf{x})],$$

since

$$\kappa(\mathbf{x}, \mathbf{z}) = \langle \phi(\mathbf{x}), \phi(\mathbf{z}) \rangle = \langle [\phi_1(\mathbf{x}), \phi_2(\mathbf{x})], [\phi_1(\mathbf{z}), \phi_2(\mathbf{z})] \rangle \quad (3.7)$$
$$= \langle \phi_1(\mathbf{x}), \phi_1(\mathbf{z}) \rangle + \langle \phi_2(\mathbf{x}), \phi_2(\mathbf{z}) \rangle \quad (3.8)$$
$$= \kappa_1(\mathbf{x}, \mathbf{z}) + \kappa_2(\mathbf{x}, \mathbf{z}).$$

For the Hadamard construction of part (iii) the corresponding features are the products of all pairs of features one from the first feature space and one from the second. Thus, the (i, j)th feature is given by

$$\phi(\mathbf{x})_{ij} = \phi_1(\mathbf{x})_i \phi_2(\mathbf{x})_j \text{ for } i = 1, \ldots, N_1 \text{ and } j = 1, \ldots, N_2,$$

where N_i is the dimension of the feature space corresponding to ϕ_i, $i = 1, 2$. The inner product is now given by

$$\kappa(\mathbf{x}, \mathbf{z}) = \langle \phi(\mathbf{x}), \phi(\mathbf{z}) \rangle = \sum_{i=1}^{N_1} \sum_{j=1}^{N_2} \phi(\mathbf{x})_{ij} \phi(\mathbf{z})_{ij}$$

$$= \sum_{i=1}^{N_1} \phi_1(\mathbf{x})_i \phi_1(\mathbf{z})_i \sum_{j=1}^{N_2} \phi_2(\mathbf{x})_j \phi_2(\mathbf{z})_j \quad (3.9)$$

$$= \kappa_1(\mathbf{x}, \mathbf{z}) \kappa_2(\mathbf{x}, \mathbf{z}). \quad (3.10)$$

The definition of the feature space in this case appears to depend on the choice of coordinate system since it makes use of the specific embedding function. The fact that the new kernel can be expressed simply in terms of the base kernels shows that in fact it is invariant to this choice. For the case of an exponent of a single kernel

$$\kappa(\mathbf{x}, \mathbf{z}) = \kappa_1(\mathbf{x}, \mathbf{z})^s,$$

we obtain by induction that the corresponding feature space is indexed by all monomials of degree s

$$\phi_{\mathbf{i}}(\mathbf{x}) = \phi_1(\mathbf{x})_1^{i_1} \phi_1(\mathbf{x})_2^{i_2} \cdots \phi_1(\mathbf{x})_N^{i_N}, \quad (3.11)$$

where $\mathbf{i} = (i_1, \ldots, i_N) \in \mathbb{N}^N$ satisfies

$$\sum_{j=1}^{N} i_j = s.$$

Remark 3.26 [Feature weightings] It is important to observe that the monomial features do not all receive an equal weighting in this embedding. This is due to the fact that in this case there are repetitions in the expansion given in equation (3.11), that is, products of individual features which lead to the same function ϕ_i. For example, in the 2-dimensional degree-2 case, the inner product can be written as

$$
\begin{aligned}
\kappa\left(\mathbf{x}, \mathbf{z}\right) &= 2x_1 x_2 z_1 z_2 + x_1^2 z_1^2 + x_2^2 z_2^2 \\
&= \left\langle \left(\sqrt{2} x_1 x_2, x_1^2, x_2^2 \right), \left(\sqrt{2} z_1 z_2, z_1^2, z_2^2 \right) \right\rangle,
\end{aligned}
$$

where the repetition of the cross terms leads to a weighting factor of $\sqrt{2}$. ∎

Remark 3.27 [Features of the Gaussian kernel] Note that from the proofs of parts (ii) and (iii) of Proposition 3.24 the Gaussian kernel is a polynomial kernel of infinite degree. Hence, its features are all possible monomials of input features with no restriction placed on the degrees. The Taylor expansion of the exponential function

$$
\exp\left(x\right) = \sum_{i=0}^{\infty} \frac{1}{i!} x^i
$$

shows that the weighting of individual monomials falls off as $i!$ with increasing degree. ∎

3.4.2 Operations on kernel matrices

We can also transform the feature space by performing operations on the kernel matrix, provided that they leave it positive semi-definite and symmetric. This type of transformation raises the question of how to compute the kernel on new test points.

In some cases we may have already constructed the kernel matrix on both the training and test points so that the transformed kernel matrix contains all of the information that we will require. In other cases the transformation of the kernel matrix corresponds to a computable transformation in the feature space, hence enabling the computation of the kernel on test points.

In addition to these computational problems there is also the danger that by adapting the kernel based on the particular kernel matrix, we may have adjusted it in a way that is too dependent on the training set and does not perform well on new data.

For the present we will ignore these concerns and mention a number of different transformations that will prove useful in different contexts, where possible explaining the corresponding effect in the feature space. Detailed presentations of these methods will be given in Chapters 5 and 6.

Simple transformations There are a number of very simple transformations that have practical significance. For example adding a constant to all of the entries in the matrix corresponds to adding an extra constant feature, as follows from parts (i) and (iv) of Proposition 3.22. This effectively augments the class of functions with an adaptable offset, though this has a slightly different effect than introducing such an offset into the algorithm itself as is done with for example support vector machines.

Another simple operation is the addition of a constant to the diagonal. This corresponds to adding a new different feature for each input, hence enhancing the independence of all the inputs. This forces algorithms to create functions that depend on more of the training points. In the case of hard margin support vector machines this results in the so-called 2-norm soft margin algorithm, to be described in Chapter 7..

A further transformation that we have already encountered in Section 2.3.2 is that of normalising the data in the feature space. This transformation can be implemented for a complete kernel matrix with a short sequence of operations, to be described in Chapter 5.

Centering data Centering data in the feature space is a more complex transformation, but one that can again be performed by operations on the kernel matrix. The aim is to move the origin of the feature space to the centre of mass of the training examples. Furthermore, the choice of the centre of mass can be characterised as the origin for which the sum of the norms of the points is minimal. Since the sum of the norms is the trace of the kernel matrix this is also equal to the sum of its eigenvalues. It follows that this choice of origin minimises the sum of the eigenvalues of the corresponding kernel matrix. We describe how to perform this centering transformation on a kernel matrix in Chapter 5.

Subspace projection In high-dimensional feature spaces there is no a priori reason why the eigenvalues of the kernel matrix should decay. If each input vector is orthogonal to the remainder, the eigenvalues will be equal to the norms of the inputs. If the points are constrained in a low-dimensional subspace, the number of non-zero eigenvalues is equal to the subspace dimension. Since the sum of the eigenvalues will still be equal to the sum of the squared norms, the individual eigenvalues will be correspondingly larger.

Although it is unlikely that data will lie exactly in a low-dimensional subspace, it is not unusual that the data can be accurately approximated by projecting into a carefully chosen low-dimensional subspace. This means that the sum of the squares of the distances between the points and their approximations is small. We will see in Chapter 6 that in this case the first eigenvectors of the covariance matrix will be a basis of the subspace, while the sum of the remaining eigenvalues will be equal to the sum of the squared residuals. Since the eigenvalues of the covariance and kernel matrices are the same, this means that the kernel matrix can be well approximated by a low-rank matrix.

It may be that the subspace corresponds to the underlying structure of the data, and the residuals are the result of measurement or estimation noise. In this case, subspace projections give a better model of the data for which the corresponding kernel matrix is given by the low-rank approximation. Hence, forming a low-rank approximation of the kernel matrix can be an effective method of de-noising the data. In Chapter 10 we will also refer to this method of finding a more accurate model of the data as *semantic focussing*.

In Chapters 5 and 6 we will present in more detail methods for creating low-rank approximations, including projection into the subspace spanned by the first eigenvectors, as well as using the subspace obtained by performing a partial Gram–Schmidt orthonormalisation of the data points in the feature space, or equivalently taking a partial Cholesky decomposition of the kernel matrix. In both cases the projections and inner products of new test points can be evaluated using just the original kernel.

Whitening If a low-dimensional approximation fails to capture the data accurately enough, we may still find an eigen-decomposition useful in order to alter the scaling of the feature space by adjusting the size of the eigenvalues. One such technique, known as *whitening*, sets all of the eigenvalues to 1, hence creating a feature space in which the data distribution is spherically symmetric. Alternatively, values may be chosen to optimise some measure of fit of the kernel, such as the alignment.

Sculpting the feature space All these operations amount to moving the points in the feature space, by sculpting their inner product matrix. In some cases those modifications can be done in response to prior information as, for example, in the cases of adding a constant to the whole matrix, adding a constant to the diagonal and normalising the data. The second type of modification makes use of parameters estimated from the matrix itself as in the examples of centering the data, subspace projection and whitening. The final example of adjusting the eigenvalues to create a kernel that fits the data will usually make use of the corresponding labels or outputs.

We can view these operations as a first phase of learning in which the most appropriate feature space is selected for the data. As with many traditional learning algorithms, kernel methods improve their performance when data are preprocessed and the right features are selected. In the case of kernels it is also possible to view this process as selecting the right topology for the input space, that is, a topology which either correctly encodes our prior knowledge concerning the similarity between data points or learns the most appropriate topology from the training set.

Viewing kernels as defining a topology suggests that we should make use of prior knowledge about invariances in the input space. For example, small translations and rotations of hand written characters leave their label unchanged in a character recognition task, indicating that these transformed images, though distant in the original metric, should become close in the topology defined by the kernel.

Part III of the book will look at a number of methods for creating kernels for different data types, introducing prior knowledge into kernels, fitting a generative model to the data and creating a derived kernel, and so on. The aim of the current chapter has been to provide the framework on which these later chapters can build.

3.5 Summary

- Kernels compute the inner product of projections of two data points into a feature space.
- Kernel functions are characterised by the property that all finite kernel matrices are positive semi-definite.
- Mercer's theorem is an equivalent formulation of the finitely positive semi-definite property for vector spaces.
- The finitely positive semi-definite property suggests that kernel matrices form the core data structure for kernel methods technology.
- Complex kernels can be created by simple operations that combine simpler kernels.
- By manipulating kernel matrices one can tune the corresponding embedding of the data in the kernel-defined feature space.

3.6 Further reading and advanced topics

Jorgen P. Gram (1850–1916) was a Danish actuary, remembered for (re)discovering the famous orthonormalisation procedure that bears his name, and for studying the properties of the matrix $\mathbf{A}'\mathbf{A}$. The Gram matrix is a central concept in this book, and its many properties are well-known in linear algebra. In general, for properties of positive (semi-)definite matrices and general linear algebra, we recommend the excellent book of Carl Meyer [98], and for a discussion of the properties of the cone of PSD matrices, the collection [166].

The use of Mercer's theorem for interpreting kernels as inner products in a feature space was introduced into machine learning in 1964 by the work of Aizermann, Bravermann and Rozoener on the method of potential functions [1], but its possibilities did not begin to be fully understood until it was used in the article by Boser, Guyon and Vapnik that introduced the support vector method [16] (see also discussion in Section 2.7).

The mathematical theory of kernels is rather old: Mercer's theorem dates back to 1909 [97], and the study of reproducing kernel Hilbert spaces was developed by Aronszajn in the 1940s. This theory was used in approximation and regularisation theory, see for example the book of Wahba and her 1999 survey [155], [156]. The seed idea for polynomial kernels was contained in [106]. Reproducing kernels were extensively used in machine learning and neural networks by Poggio and Girosi from the early 1990s. [48]. Related results can be found in [99]. More references about the rich regularization literature can be found in section 4.6.

Chapter 1 of Wahba's book [155] gives a number of theoretical results on kernel functions and can be used as a reference. Closure properties are discussed in [54] and in [99]. Anova kernels were introduced by Burges and Vapnik [21]. The theory of positive definite functions was also developed in the context of covariance and correlation functions, so that classical work in statistics is closely related [156], [157].

The discussion about Reproducing Kernel Hilbert Spaces in this chapter draws on the paper of Haussler [54]. Our characterization of kernel functions, by means of the finitely positive semi-definite property, is based on a theorem of Saitoh [113]. This approach paves the way to the use of general kernels on general types of data, as suggested by [118] and developed by Watkins [158], [157] and Haussler [54]. These works have greatly extended the use of kernels, showing that they can in fact be defined on general objects, which do not need to be Euclidean spaces, allowing their use in a swathe of new real-world applications, on input spaces as diverse as biological sequences, text, and images.

The notion of kernel alignment was proposed by [33] in order to capture the idea of similarity of two kernel functions, and hence of the embedding they induce, and the information they extract from the data. A number of formal properties of such quantity are now known, many of which are discussed in the technical report, but two are most relevant here: its interpretation as the inner product in the cone of positive semi-definite matrices, and consequently its interpretation as a kernel between kernels, that is a higher order kernel function. Further papers on this theme include [72], [73]. This latest interpretation of alignment was further analysed in [104].

For constantly updated pointers to online literature and free software see the book's companion website: www.kernel-methods.net

4

Detecting stable patterns

As discussed in Chapter 1 perhaps the most important property of a pattern analysis algorithm is that it should identify statistically stable patterns. A stable relation is one that reflects some property of the source generating the data, and is therefore not a chance feature of the particular dataset. Proving that a given pattern is indeed significant is the concern of 'learning theory', a body of principles and methods that estimate the reliability of pattern functions under appropriate assumptions about the way in which the data was generated. The most common assumption is that the individual training examples are generated independently according to a fixed distribution, being the same distribution under which the expected value of the pattern function is small. Statistical analysis of the problem can therefore make use of the law of large numbers through the 'concentration' of certain random variables.

Concentration would be all that we need if we were only to consider one pattern function. Pattern analysis algorithms typically search for pattern functions over whole classes of functions, by choosing the function that best fits the particular training sample. We must therefore be able to prove stability not of a pre-defined pattern, but of one deliberately chosen for its fit to the data.

Clearly the more pattern functions at our disposal, the more likely that this choice could be a spurious pattern. The critical factor that controls how much our choice may have compromised the stability of the resulting pattern is the 'capacity' of the function class. The capacity will be related to tunable parameters of the algorithms for pattern analysis, hence making it possible to directly control the risk of overfitting the data. This will lead to close parallels with regularisation theory, so that we will control the capacity by using different forms of 'regularisation'.

4.1 Concentration inequalities

In Chapter 1 we introduced the idea of a statistically stable pattern function f as a non-negative function whose expected value on an example drawn randomly according to the data distribution $\mathcal{D}$ is small

$$\mathbb{E}_{\mathbf{x} \sim \mathcal{D}} f(\mathbf{x}) \approx 0.$$

Since we only have access to a finite sample of data, we will only be able to make assertions about this expected value subject to certain assumptions. It is in the nature of a theoretical model that it is built on a set of precepts that are assumed to hold for the phenomenon being modelled. Our basic assumptions are summarised in the following definition of our data model.

Definition 4.1 The model we adopt will make the assumption that the distribution $\mathcal{D}$ that provides the quality measure of the pattern is the same distribution that generated the examples in the finite sample used for training purposes. Furthermore, the model assumes that the individual training examples are independently and identically distributed (i.i.d.). We will denote the probability of an event A under distribution $\mathcal{D}$ by $P_{\mathcal{D}}(A)$. The model makes no assumptions about whether the examples include a label, are elements of $\mathbb{R}^n$, though some mild restrictions are placed on the generating distribution, albeit with no practical significance. ∎

We gave a definition of what was required of a pattern analysis algorithm in Definition 1.7, but for completeness we repeat it here with some embellishments.

Definition 4.2 A pattern analysis algorithm takes as input a finite set S of ℓ data items generated i.i.d. according to a fixed (but unknown) distribution $\mathcal{D}$ and a confidence parameter $\delta \in (0, 1)$. Its output is either an indication that no patterns were detectable, or a *pattern function* f that with probability $1 - \delta$ satisfies

$$\mathbb{E}_{\mathcal{D}} f(\mathbf{x}) \approx 0.$$

The value of the expectation is known as the *generalisation error* of the pattern function f. ∎

In any finite dataset, even if it comprises random numbers, it is always possible to find relations if we are prepared to create sufficiently complicated functions.

Example 4.3 Consider a set of ℓ people each with a credit card and mobile phone; we can find a degree $\ell - 1$ polynomial $g(t)$ that given a person's telephone number t computes that person's credit card number $c = g(t)$, making $|c - g(t)|$ look like a promising pattern function as far as the sample is concerned. This follows from the fact that a degree $\ell - 1$ polynomial can interpolate ℓ points. However, what is important in pattern analysis is to find relations that can be used to make predictions on unseen data, in other words relations, that capture some properties of the source generating the data. It is clear that $g(\cdot)$ will not provide a method of computing credit card numbers for people outside the initial set.   ∎

The aim of this chapter is to develop tools that enable us to distinguish between relations that are the effect of chance and those that are 'meaningful'. Intuitively, we would expect a statistically stable relation to be present in different randomly generated subsets of the dataset, in this way confirming that the relation is not just the property of the particular dataset.

Example 4.4 The relation found between card and phone numbers in Example 4.3 would almost certainly change if we were to generate a second dataset. If on the other hand we consider the function that returns 0 if the average height of the women in the group is less than the average height of the men and 1 otherwise, we would expect different subsets to usually return the same value of 0.   ∎

Another way to ensure that we have detected a significant relation is to check whether a similar relation could be learned from scrambled data: if we randomly reassign the height of all individuals in the sets of Example 4.4, will we still find a relation between height and gender? In this case the probability that this relation exists would be a half since there is equal chance of different heights being assigned to women as to men. We will refer to the process of randomly reassigning labels as *randomisation* of a labelled dataset. It is also sometimes referred to as *permutation testing*. We will see that checking for patterns in a randomised set can provide a lodestone for measuring the stability of a pattern function.

Randomisation should not be confused with the concept of a random variable. A *random variable* is any real-valued quantity whose value depends on some random generating process, while a *random vector* is such a vector-valued quantity. The starting point for the analysis presented in this chapter is the assumption that the data have been generated by a random process. Very little is assumed about this generating process, which can be thought of as the distribution governing the natural occurrence of the data. The only restricting assumption about the data generation is that individual examples are generated independently of one another. It is this property of the randomly-generated dataset that will ensure the stability of a significant pattern function in the original dataset, while the randomisation of the labels has the effect of deliberately removing any stable patterns.

Concentration of one random variable The first question we will consider is that of the stability of a fixed function of a finite dataset. In other words how different will the value of this same function be on another dataset generated by the same source? The key property that we will require of the relevant quantity or random variable is known as *concentration*. A random variable that is concentrated is very likely to assume values close to its expectation since values become exponentially unlikely away from the mean. For a concentrated quantity we will therefore be confident that it will assume very similar values on new datasets generated from the same source. This is the case, for example, for the function 'average height of the female individuals' used above. There are many results that assert the concentration of a random variable provided it exhibits certain properties. These results are often referred to as *concentration inqualities*. Here we present one of the best-known theorems that is usually attributed to McDiarmid.

Theorem 4.5 (McDiarmid) *Let* $X_1, \ldots, X_n$ *be independent random variables taking values in a set* A, *and assume that* $f : A^n \to \mathbb{R}$ *satisfies*

$$\sup_{x_1,\ldots,x_n,\, \hat{x}_i \in A} |f(x_1, \ldots, x_n) - f(x_1, \ldots, \hat{x}_i, x_{i+1}, \ldots, x_n)| \leq c_i, \quad 1 \leq i \leq n.$$

Then for all $\epsilon > 0$

$$P\left\{ f(X_1, \ldots, X_n) - \mathbb{E} f(X_1, \ldots, X_n) \geq \epsilon \right\} \leq \exp\left(\frac{-2\epsilon^2}{\sum_{i=1}^n c_i^2} \right)$$

The proof of this theorem is given in Appendix A.1.

Another well-used inequality that bounds the deviation from the mean for the special case of sums of random variables is Hoeffding's inequality. We quote it here as a simple special case of McDiarmid's inequality when

$$f(X_1, \ldots, X_n) = \sum_{i=1}^n X_i.$$

Theorem 4.6 (Hoeffding's inequality) *If* $X_1, \ldots, X_n$ *are independent random variables satisfying* $X_i \in [a_i, b_i]$, *and if we define the random variable*

$S_n = \sum_{i=1}^{n} X_i$, *then it follows that*

$$P\{|S_n - \mathbb{E}[S_n]| \geq \varepsilon\} \leq 2\exp\left(-\frac{2\varepsilon^2}{\sum_{i=1}^{n}(b_i - a_i)^2}\right).$$

Estimating univariate means As an example consider the average of a set of ℓ independent instances $r_1, r_2, \ldots, r_\ell$ of a random variable R given by a probability distribution P on the interval $[a, b]$. Taking $X_i = r_i/\ell$ it follows, in the notation of Hoeffding's Inequality, that

$$S_\ell = \frac{1}{\ell}\sum_{i=1}^{\ell} r_i = \hat{\mathbb{E}}[R],$$

where $\hat{\mathbb{E}}[R]$ denotes the sample average of the random variable R. Furthermore

$$\mathbb{E}[S_n] = \mathbb{E}\left[\frac{1}{\ell}\sum_{i=1}^{\ell} r_i\right] = \frac{1}{\ell}\sum_{i=1}^{\ell} \mathbb{E}[r_i] = \mathbb{E}[R],$$

so that an application of Hoeffding's Inequality gives

$$P\{|\hat{\mathbb{E}}[R] - \mathbb{E}[R]| \geq \varepsilon\} \leq 2\exp\left(-\frac{2\ell\varepsilon^2}{(b-a)^2}\right),$$

indicating an exponential decay of probability with the difference between observed sample average and the true average. Notice that the probability also decays exponentially with the size of the sample. If we consider Example 4.4, this bound shows that for moderately sized randomly chosen groups of women and men, the average height of the women will, with high probability, indeed be smaller than the average height of the men, since it is known that the true average heights do indeed differ significantly.

Estimating the centre of mass The example of the average of a random variable raises the question of how reliably we can estimate the average of a random vector $\phi(\mathbf{x})$, where ϕ is a mapping from the input space X into a feature space F corresponding to a kernel $\kappa(\cdot, \cdot)$. This is equivalent to asking how close the centre of mass of the projections of a training sample

$$S = \{\mathbf{x}_1, \mathbf{x}_2, \ldots, \mathbf{x}_\ell\}$$

will be to the true expectation

$$\mathbb{E}_{\mathbf{x}}[\phi(\mathbf{x})] = \int_X \phi(\mathbf{x})dP(\mathbf{x}).$$

We denote the centre of mass of the training sample by

$$\phi_S = \frac{1}{\ell}\sum_{i=1}^{\ell}\phi(\mathbf{x}_i).$$

We introduce the following real-valued function of the sample S as our measure of the accuracy of the estimate

$$g(S) = \|\phi_S - \mathbb{E}_\mathbf{x}[\phi(\mathbf{x})]\|.$$

We can apply McDiarmid's theorem to the random variable $g(S)$ by bounding the change in this quantity when $\mathbf{x}_i$ is replaced by $\hat{\mathbf{x}}_i$ to give $\hat{S}$

$$
\begin{aligned}
|g(S) - g(\hat{S})| &= \left|\|\phi_S - \mathbb{E}_\mathbf{x}[\phi(\mathbf{x})]\| - \|\phi_{S'} - \mathbb{E}_\mathbf{x}[\phi(\mathbf{x})]\|\right| \\
&\le \|\phi_S - \phi_{S'}\| = \frac{1}{\ell}\|\phi(\mathbf{x}_i) - \phi(\mathbf{x}_i')\| \le \frac{2R}{\ell},
\end{aligned}
$$

where $R = \sup_{\mathbf{x}\in X}\|\phi(\mathbf{x})\|$. Hence, applying McDiarmid's theorem with $c_i = 2R/\ell$, we obtain

$$P\{g(S) - \mathbb{E}_S[g(S)] \ge \epsilon\} \le \exp\left(-\frac{2\ell\epsilon^2}{4R^2}\right). \tag{4.1}$$

We are now at the equivalent point after the application of Hoeffding's inequality in the one-dimensional case. But in higher dimensions we no longer have a simple expression for $\mathbb{E}_S[g(S)]$. We need therefore to consider the more involved argument. We present a derivation bounding $\mathbb{E}_S[g(S)]$ that will be useful for the general theory we develop below. The derivation is not intended to be optimal as a bound for $\mathbb{E}_S[g(S)]$. An explanation of the individual steps is given below

$$
\begin{aligned}
\mathbb{E}_S[g(S)] &= \mathbb{E}_S\left[\|\phi_S - \mathbb{E}_\mathbf{x}[\phi(\mathbf{x})]\|\right] = \mathbb{E}_S\left[\|\phi_S - \mathbb{E}_{\tilde{S}}[\phi_{\tilde{S}}]\|\right] \\
&= \mathbb{E}_S\left[\|\mathbb{E}_{\tilde{S}}[\phi_S - \phi_{\tilde{S}}]\|\right] \le \mathbb{E}_{S\tilde{S}}\left[\|\phi_S - \phi_{\tilde{S}}\|\right] \\
&= \mathbb{E}_{\sigma S\tilde{S}}\left[\frac{1}{\ell}\left\|\sum_{i=1}^{\ell}\sigma_i\left(\phi(\mathbf{x}_i) - \phi(\tilde{\mathbf{x}}_i)\right)\right\|\right] \\
&= \mathbb{E}_{\sigma S\tilde{S}}\left[\frac{1}{\ell}\left\|\sum_{i=1}^{\ell}\sigma_i\phi(\mathbf{x}_i) - \sum_{i=1}^{\ell}\sigma_i\phi(\tilde{\mathbf{x}}_i)\right\|\right] \tag{4.2} \\
&\le 2\mathbb{E}_{S\sigma}\left[\frac{1}{\ell}\left\|\sum_{i=1}^{\ell}\sigma_i\phi(\mathbf{x}_i)\right\|\right] \tag{4.3} \\
&= \frac{2}{\ell}\mathbb{E}_{S\sigma}\left[\left(\left\langle\sum_{i=1}^{\ell}\sigma_i\phi(\mathbf{x}_i), \sum_{j=1}^{\ell}\sigma_j\phi(\mathbf{x}_j)\right\rangle\right)^{1/2}\right]
\end{aligned}
$$

$$\leq \frac{2}{\ell} \left(\mathbb{E}_{S\boldsymbol{\sigma}} \left[\sum_{i,j=1}^{\ell} \sigma_i \sigma_j \kappa(\mathbf{x}_i, \mathbf{x}_j) \right] \right)^{1/2}$$

$$= \frac{2}{\ell} \left(\mathbb{E}_S \left[\sum_{i=1}^{\ell} \kappa(\mathbf{x}_i, \mathbf{x}_i) \right] \right)^{1/2} \tag{4.4}$$

$$\leq \frac{2R}{\sqrt{\ell}}. \tag{4.5}$$

It is worth examining the stages in this derivation in some detail as they will form the template for the main learning analysis we will give below.

- The second equality introduces a second random sample $\tilde{S}$ of the same size drawn according to the same distribution. Hence the expectation of its centre of mass is indeed the true expectation of the random vector.
- The expectation over $\tilde{S}$ can now be moved outwards in two stages, the second of which follows from an application of the triangle inequality.
- The next equality makes use of the independence of the generation of the individual examples to introduce random exchanges of the corresponding points in the two samples. The random variables $\boldsymbol{\sigma} = \{\sigma_1, \ldots, \sigma_\ell\}$ assume values -1 and $+1$ independently with equal probability 0.5, hence either leave the effect of the examples $\mathbf{x}_i$ and $\tilde{\mathbf{x}}_i$ as it was or effectively interchange them. Since the points are generated independently such a swap gives an equally likely configuration, and averaging over all possible swaps leaves the overall expectation unchanged.
- The next steps split the sum and again make use of the triangle inequality together with the fact that the generation of S and $\tilde{S}$ is identical.
- The movement of the square root function through the expectation follows from Jensen's inequality and the concavity of the square root.
- The disappearance of the mixed terms $\sigma_i \sigma_j \kappa(\mathbf{x}_i, \mathbf{x}_j)$ for $i \neq j$ follows from the fact that the four possible combinations of -1 and $+1$ have equal probability with two of the four having the opposite sign and hence cancelling out.

Hence, setting the right-hand side of inequality (4.1) equal to δ, solving for ϵ, and combining with inequality (4.4) shows that with probability at least $1 - \delta$ over the choice of a random sample of ℓ points, we have

$$g(S) \leq \frac{R}{\sqrt{\ell}} \left(2 + \sqrt{2 \ln \frac{1}{\delta}} \right). \tag{4.6}$$

This shows that with high probability our sample does indeed give a good estimate of $\mathbb{E}[\phi(\mathbf{x})]$ in a way that does not depend on the dimension of the feature space. This example shows how concentration inequalities provide mechanisms for bounding the deviation of quantities of interest from their expected value, in the case considered this was the function g that measures the distance between the true mean of the random vector and its sample estimate. Figures 4.1 and 4.2 show two random samples drawn from a 2-dimensional Gaussian distribution centred at the origin. The sample means are shown with diamonds.

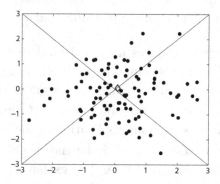

Fig. 4.1. The empirical centre of mass based on a random sample

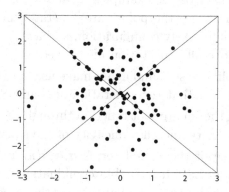

Fig. 4.2. The empirical centre of mass based on a second random sample.

Rademacher variables As mentioned above, the derivation of inequalities (4.2) to (4.4) will form a blueprint for the more general analysis described below. In particular the introduction of the random $\{-1, +1\}$ variables σ_i will play a key role. Such random numbers are known as Rademacher variables. They allow us to move from an expression involving two samples in equation (4.2) to twice an expression involving one sample modified by the Rademacher variables in formula (4.3).

The result motivates the use of samples as reliable estimators of the true quantities considered. For example, we have shown that the centre of mass of the training sample is indeed a good estimator for the true mean. In the next chapter we will use this result to motivate a simple novelty-detection algorithm that checks if a new datapoint is further from the true mean than the furthest training point. The chances of this happening for data generated from the same distribution can be shown to be small, hence when such points are found there is a high probability that they are outliers.

4.2 Capacity and regularisation: Rademacher theory

In the previous section we considered what were effectively fixed pattern functions, either chosen beforehand or else a fixed function of the data. The more usual pattern analysis scenario is, however, more complex, since the relation is chosen from a set of possible candidates taken from a function class. The dangers inherent in this situation were illustrated in the example involving phone numbers and credit cards. If we allow ourselves to choose from a large set of possibilities, we may find something that 'looks good' on the dataset at hand but does not reflect a property of the underlying process generating the data. The distance between the value of a certain function in two different random subsets does not only depend therefore on its being concentrated, but also on the richness of the class from which it was chosen. We will illustrate this point with another example.

Example 4.7 [Birthday paradox] Given a random set of N people, what is the probability that two of them have the same birthday? This probability depends of course on N and is surprisingly high even for small values of N. Assuming that the people have equal chance of being born on all days, the probability that a pair have the same birthday is 1 minus the probability that all N have different birthdays

$$
\begin{aligned}
P(\text{same birthday}) \;=&\; 1 - \prod_{i=1}^{N} \frac{365 - i + 1}{365} = 1 - \prod_{i=1}^{N}\left(1 - \frac{i-1}{365}\right) \\
\geq&\; 1 - \prod_{i=1}^{N} \exp\left(-\frac{i-1}{365}\right) = 1 - \exp\left(-\sum_{i=1}^{N} \frac{(i-1)}{365}\right) \\
=&\; 1 - \exp\left(-\frac{N(N-1)}{730}\right).
\end{aligned}
$$

It is well-known that this increases surprisingly quickly. For example taking $N = 28$ gives a probability greater than 0.645 that there are two people in the group that share a birthday. If on the other hand we consider a pre-fixed day, the probability that two people in the group have their birthday on that day is

$$P(\text{same birthday on a fixed day}) = \sum_{i=2}^{N} \binom{N}{i} \left(\frac{1}{365}\right)^{i} \left(\frac{364}{365}\right)^{N-i}.$$

If we evaluate this expression for $N = 28$ we obtain 0.0027. The difference between the two probabilities follows from the fact that in the one case we fix the day after choosing the set of people, while in the second case it is chosen beforehand. In the first case we have much more freedom, and hence it is more likely that we will find a pair of people fitting our hypothesis. We will expect to find a pair of people with the same birthday in a set of 28 people with more than even chance, so that no conclusions could be drawn from this observation about a relation between the group and that day. For a pre-fixed day the probability of two or more having a birthday on the same day would be less than 0.3%, a very unusual event. As a consequence, in the second case we would be justified in concluding that there is some connection between the chosen date and the way the group was selected, or in other words that we have detected a significant pattern.

Our observation shows that if we check for one property there is unlikely to be a spurious match, but if we allow a large number of properties such as the 365 different days there is a far higher chance of observing a match. In such cases we must be careful before drawing any conclusions. ∎

Uniform convergence and capacity What we require if we are to use a finite sample to make inferences involving a whole class of functions is that the difference between the sample and true performance should be small for every function in the class. This property will be referred to as *uniform convergence* over a class of functions. It implies that the concentration holds not just for one function but for all of the functions at the same time.

If a set is so rich that it always contains an element that fits any given random dataset, then the patterns found may not be significant and it is unlikely that the chosen function will fit a new dataset even if drawn from the same distribution. The example given in the previous section of finding a polynomial that maps phone numbers to credit card numbers is a case in point. The capability of a function class to fit different data is known as its *capacity*. Clearly the higher the capacity of the class the greater the risk of overfitting the particular training data and identifying a spurious pattern. The critical question is how one should measure the capacity of a function class. For the polynomial example the obvious choice is the degree of the polynomial, and keeping the degree smaller than the number of training examples would lessen the risk described above of finding a spurious relation between phone and credit card numbers. Learning theory has developed a number of more general measures that can be used for classes other than polynomials, one of the best known being the Vapnik–Chervonenkis dimension.

The approach we adopt here has already been hinted at in the previous section and rests on the intuition that we can measure the capacity of a class by its ability to fit random data. The definition makes use of the Rademacher variables introduced in the previous section and the measure is therefore known as the Rademacher complexity.

Definition 4.8 [Rademacher complexity] For a sample $S = \{\mathbf{x}_1, \ldots, \mathbf{x}_\ell\}$ generated by a distribution $\mathcal{D}$ on a set X and a real-valued function class $\mathcal{F}$ with domain X, the *empirical Rademacher complexity* of $\mathcal{F}$ is the random variable

$$\hat{R}_\ell(\mathcal{F}) = \mathbb{E}_\sigma \left[\sup_{f \in \mathcal{F}} \left| \frac{2}{\ell} \sum_{i=1}^\ell \sigma_i f(\mathbf{x}_i) \right| \ \middle| \ \mathbf{x}_1, \ldots, \mathbf{x}_\ell \right],$$

where $\boldsymbol{\sigma} = \{\sigma_1, \ldots, \sigma_\ell\}$ are independent uniform $\{\pm 1\}$-valued (Rademacher) random variables. The *Rademacher complexity* of $\mathcal{F}$ is

$$R_\ell(\mathcal{F}) = \mathbb{E}_S \left[\hat{R}_\ell(\mathcal{F}) \right] = \mathbb{E}_{S\sigma} \left[\sup_{f \in \mathcal{F}} \left| \frac{2}{\ell} \sum_{i=1}^\ell \sigma_i f(\mathbf{x}_i) \right| \right].$$

∎

The sup inside the expectation measures the best correlation that can be found between a function of the class and the random labels. It is important to stress that pattern detection is a probabilistic process, and there is therefore always the possibility of detecting a pattern in noise. The Rademacher complexity uses precisely the ability of the class to fit noise as its measure of capacity. Hence controlling this measure of capacity will intuitively guard against the identification of spurious patterns. We now give a result that formulates this insight as a precise bound on the error of pattern functions in terms of their empirical fit and the Rademacher complexity of the class.

Note that we denote the input space with Z in the theorem, so that in the case of supervised learning we would have $Z = X \times Y$. We use $\mathbb{E}_\mathcal{D}$ for the expectation with respect to the underlying distribution, while $\hat{\mathbb{E}}$ denotes the empirical expectation measured on a particular sample.

Theorem 4.9 *Fix $\delta \in (0,1)$ and let $\mathcal{F}$ be a class of functions mapping from Z to $[a, a+1]$. Let $(\mathbf{z}_i)_{i=1}^{\ell}$ be drawn independently according to a probability distribution $\mathcal{D}$. Then with probability at least $1 - \delta$ over random draws of samples of size ℓ, every $f \in \mathcal{F}$ satisfies*

$$
\begin{aligned}
\mathbb{E}_{\mathcal{D}}\left[f(\mathbf{z})\right] &\leq \hat{\mathbb{E}}\left[f(\mathbf{z})\right] + R_{\ell}(\mathcal{F}) + \sqrt{\frac{\ln(2/\delta)}{2\ell}} \\
&\leq \hat{\mathbb{E}}\left[f(\mathbf{z})\right] + \hat{R}_{\ell}(\mathcal{F}) + 3\sqrt{\frac{\ln(2/\delta)}{2\ell}}.
\end{aligned}
$$

Proof For a fixed $f \in \mathcal{F}$ we have

$$
\mathbb{E}_{\mathcal{D}}\left[f(\mathbf{z})\right] \leq \hat{\mathbb{E}}\left[f(\mathbf{z})\right] + \sup_{h \in \mathcal{F}}\left(\mathbb{E}_{\mathcal{D}}h - \hat{\mathbb{E}}h\right).
$$

We now apply McDiarmid's inequality bound to the second term on the right-hand side in terms of its expected value. Since the function takes values in the range $[a, a+1]$, replacing one example can change the value of the expression by at most $1/\ell$. Subsituting this value of c_i into McDiarmid's inequality, setting the right-hand side to be $\delta/2$, and solving for ϵ, we obtain that with probability greater than $1 - \delta/2$

$$
\sup_{h \in \mathcal{F}}\left(\mathbb{E}_{\mathcal{D}}h - \hat{\mathbb{E}}h\right) \leq \mathbb{E}_S\left[\sup_{h \in \mathcal{F}}\left(\mathbb{E}_{\mathcal{D}}h - \hat{\mathbb{E}}h\right)\right] + \sqrt{\frac{\ln(2/\delta)}{2\ell}}.
$$

giving

$$
\mathbb{E}_{\mathcal{D}}\left[f(\mathbf{z})\right] \leq \hat{\mathbb{E}}\left[f(\mathbf{z})\right] + \mathbb{E}_S\left[\sup_{h \in \mathcal{F}}\left(\mathbb{E}_{\mathcal{D}}h - \hat{\mathbb{E}}h\right)\right] + \sqrt{\frac{\ln(2/\delta)}{2\ell}}.
$$

We must now bound the middle term of the right-hand side. This is where we follow the technique applied in the previous section to bound the deviation of the mean of a random vector

$$
\begin{aligned}
\mathbb{E}_S\left[\sup_{h \in \mathcal{F}}\left(\mathbb{E}_{\mathcal{D}}h - \hat{\mathbb{E}}h\right)\right] &= \mathbb{E}_S\left[\sup_{h \in \mathcal{F}}\mathbb{E}_{\tilde{S}}\left[\frac{1}{\ell}\sum_{i=1}^{\ell}h(\tilde{\mathbf{z}}_i) - \frac{1}{\ell}\sum_{i=1}^{\ell}h(\mathbf{z}_i)\,\middle|\, S\right]\right] \\
&\leq \mathbb{E}_S\mathbb{E}_{\tilde{S}}\left[\sup_{h \in \mathcal{F}}\frac{1}{\ell}\sum_{i=1}^{\ell}\left(h(\tilde{\mathbf{z}}_i) - h(\mathbf{z}_i)\right)\right] \\
&= \mathbb{E}_{\sigma S\tilde{S}}\left[\sup_{h \in \mathcal{F}}\frac{1}{\ell}\sum_{i=1}^{\ell}\sigma_i\left(h(\tilde{\mathbf{z}}_i) - h(\mathbf{z}_i)\right)\right]
\end{aligned}
$$

$$\leq 2\mathbb{E}_{S_\sigma}\left[\sup_{h\in\mathcal{F}}\left|\frac{1}{\ell}\sum_{i=1}^{\ell}\sigma_i h(\mathbf{z}_i)\right|\right]$$

$$= R_\ell(\mathcal{F}).$$

Finally, with probability greater than $1-\delta/2$, we can bound the Rademacher complexity in terms of its empirical value by a further application of McDiarmid's theorem for which $c_i = 2/\ell$. The complete results follows. □

The only additional point to note about the proof is its use of the fact that the sup of an expectation is less than or equal to the expectation of the sup in order to obtain the second line from the first. This follows from the triangle inequality for the ℓ_∞ norm.

The theorem shows that modulo the small additional square root factor the difference between the empirical and true value of the functions or in our case with high probability the difference between the true and empirical error of the pattern function is bounded by the Rademacher complexity of the pattern function class. Indeed we do not even need to consider the full Rademacher complexity, but can instead use its empirical value on the given training set. In our applications of the theorem we will invariably make use of this empirical version of the bound.

In the next section we will complete our analysis of stability by computing the (empirical) Rademacher complexities of the kernel-based linear classes that are the chosen function classes for the majority of the methods presented in this book. We will also give an example of applying the theorem for a particular pattern analysis task.

4.3 Pattern stability for kernel-based classes

Clearly the results of the previous section can only be applied if we are able to bound the Rademacher complexities of the corresponding classes of pattern functions. As described in Chapter 1, it is frequently useful to decompose the pattern functions into an underlying class of functions whose outputs are fed into a so-called loss function. For example, for binary classification the function class $\mathcal{F}$ may be a set of real-valued functions that we convert to a binary value by thresholding at 0. Hence a function $g \in \mathcal{F}$ is converted to a binary output by applying the sign function to obtain a classification function h

$$h(\mathbf{x}) = \text{sgn}(g(\mathbf{x})) \in \{\pm 1\}.$$

We can therefore express the pattern function using the discrete loss function $\mathcal{L}$ given by

$$\mathcal{L}(\mathbf{x}, y) = \frac{1}{2}|h(\mathbf{x}) - y| = \begin{cases} 0, & \text{if } h(\mathbf{x}) = y; \\ 1, & \text{otherwise.} \end{cases}$$

Equivalently we can apply the *Heaviside function*, $\mathcal{H}(\cdot)$ that returns 1 if its argument is greater than 0 and zero otherwise as follows

$$\mathcal{L}(\mathbf{x}, y) = \mathcal{H}(-yg(\mathbf{x})).$$

Hence, the pattern function is $\mathcal{H} \circ f$, where $f(\mathbf{x}, y) = -yg(\mathbf{x})$. We use the notation $\hat{\mathcal{F}}$ to also denote the class

$$\hat{\mathcal{F}} = \{(\mathbf{x}, y) \mapsto -yg(\mathbf{x}) : g \in \mathcal{F}\}.$$

Using this loss implies that

$$\mathbb{E}_D[\mathcal{H}(-yg(\mathbf{x}))] = \mathbb{E}_D[\mathcal{H}(f(\mathbf{x}, y))] = P_D(y \neq h(\mathbf{x})).$$

This means we should consider the Rademacher complexity of the class

$$\mathcal{H} \circ \hat{\mathcal{F}} = \left\{\mathcal{H} \circ f : f \in \hat{\mathcal{F}}\right\}.$$

Since we will bound the complexity of such classes by assuming the loss function satisfies a Lipschitz condition, it is useful to introduce an auxiliary loss function $\mathcal{A}$ that has a better Lipschitz constant and satisfies

$$\mathcal{H}(f(\mathbf{x}, y)) \leq \mathcal{A}(f(\mathbf{x}, y)), \tag{4.7}$$

where the meaning of the Lipschitz condition is given in the following definition. A function $\mathcal{A}$ satisfying equation (4.7) will be known as a *dominating cost function*.

Definition 4.10 A loss function $\mathcal{A} : \mathbb{R} \to [0, 1]$ is Lipschitz with constant L if it satisfies

$$|\mathcal{A}(a) - \mathcal{A}(a')| \leq L|a - a'| \text{ for all } a, a' \in \mathbb{R}.$$

∎

We use the notation $(\cdot)_+$ for the function

$$(x)_+ = \begin{cases} x, & \text{if } x \geq 0; \\ 0, & \text{otherwise.} \end{cases}$$

The binary classification case described above is an example where such a function is needed, since the true loss is not a Lipschitz function at all. By taking $\mathcal{A}$ to be the *hinge loss* given by

$$\mathcal{A}(f(\mathbf{x}, y)) = (1 + f(\mathbf{x}, y))_+ = (1 - yg(\mathbf{x}))_+ ,$$

we get a Lipschitz constant of 1 with $\mathcal{A}$ dominating $\mathcal{H}$.

Since our underlying class will usually be linear functions in a kernel-defined feature space, we first turn our attention to bounding the Rademacher complexity of these functions. Given a training set S the class of functions that we will primarily be considering are linear functions with bounded norm

$$\left\{ \mathbf{x} \to \sum_{i=1}^{\ell} \alpha_i \kappa(\mathbf{x}_i, \mathbf{x}) : \boldsymbol{\alpha}' \mathbf{K} \boldsymbol{\alpha} \le B^2 \right\} \subseteq \{ \mathbf{x} \to \langle \mathbf{w}, \boldsymbol{\phi}(\mathbf{x}) \rangle : \|\mathbf{w}\| \le B \} = \mathcal{F}_B,$$

where ϕ is the feature mapping corresponding to the kernel κ and $\mathbf{K}$ is the kernel matrix on the sample S. Note that although the choice of functions appears to depend on S, the definition of $\mathcal{F}_B$ does not depend on the particular training set.

Remark 4.11 [The weight vector norm] Notice that for this class of functions, $f(\mathbf{x}) = \langle \mathbf{w}, \boldsymbol{\phi}(\mathbf{x}) \rangle = \left\langle \sum_{i=1}^{\ell} \alpha_i \boldsymbol{\phi}(\mathbf{x}_i), \boldsymbol{\phi}(\mathbf{x}) \right\rangle = \sum_{i=1}^{\ell} \alpha_i \kappa(\mathbf{x}_i, \mathbf{x})$, we have made use of the derivation

$$
\begin{aligned}
\|\mathbf{w}\|^2 &= \langle \mathbf{w}, \mathbf{w} \rangle = \left\langle \sum_{i=1}^{\ell} \alpha_i \boldsymbol{\phi}(\mathbf{x}_i), \sum_{j=1}^{\ell} \alpha_j \boldsymbol{\phi}(\mathbf{x}_j) \right\rangle \\
&= \sum_{i,j=1}^{\ell} \alpha_i \alpha_j \langle \boldsymbol{\phi}(\mathbf{x}_i), \boldsymbol{\phi}(\mathbf{x}_j) \rangle = \sum_{i,j=1}^{\ell} \alpha_i \alpha_j \kappa(\mathbf{x}_i, \mathbf{x}_j) \\
&= \boldsymbol{\alpha}' \mathbf{K} \boldsymbol{\alpha},
\end{aligned}
$$

in order to show that $\mathcal{F}_B$ is a superset of our class. We will further investigate the insights that can be made into the structure of the feature space using only information gleaned from the kernel matrix in the next chapter. ∎

The proof of the following theorem again uses part of the proof given in the first section showing the concentration of the mean of a random vector. Here we use the techniques of the last few lines of that proof.

Theorem 4.12 *If $\kappa : X \times X \to \mathbb{R}$ is a kernel, and $S = \{\mathbf{x}_1, \dots, \mathbf{x}_\ell\}$ is a sample of points from X, then the empirical Rademacher complexity of the* *class $\mathcal{F}_B$ satisfies*

$$\hat{R}_\ell(\mathcal{F}_B) \leq \frac{2B}{\ell} \sqrt{\sum_{i=1}^{\ell} \kappa(\mathbf{x}_i, \mathbf{x}_i)} = \frac{2B}{\ell} \sqrt{\operatorname{tr}(\mathbf{K})}$$

Proof The result follows from the following derivation

$$
\begin{aligned}
\hat{R}_\ell(\mathcal{F}_B) &= \mathbb{E}_\sigma \left[\sup_{f \in \mathcal{F}_B} \left| \frac{2}{\ell} \sum_{i=1}^{\ell} \sigma_i f(\mathbf{x}_i) \right| \right] \\
&= \mathbb{E}_\sigma \left[\sup_{\|\mathbf{w}\| \leq B} \left| \left\langle \mathbf{w}, \frac{2}{\ell} \sum_{i=1}^{\ell} \sigma_i \phi(\mathbf{x}_i) \right\rangle \right| \right] \\
&\leq \frac{2B}{\ell} \mathbb{E}_\sigma \left[\left\| \sum_{i=1}^{\ell} \sigma_i \phi(\mathbf{x}_i) \right\| \right] \\
&= \frac{2B}{\ell} \mathbb{E}_\sigma \left[\left(\left\langle \sum_{i=1}^{\ell} \sigma_i \phi(\mathbf{x}_i), \sum_{j=1}^{\ell} \sigma_j \phi(\mathbf{x}_j) \right\rangle \right)^{1/2} \right] \\
&\leq \frac{2B}{\ell} \left(\mathbb{E}_\sigma \left[\sum_{i,j=1}^{\ell} \sigma_i \sigma_j \kappa(\mathbf{x}_i, \mathbf{x}_j) \right] \right)^{1/2} \\
&= \frac{2B}{\ell} \left(\sum_{i=1}^{\ell} \kappa(\mathbf{x}_i, \mathbf{x}_i) \right)^{1/2}.
\end{aligned}
$$

$\square$

Note that in the proof the second line follows from the first by the linearity of the inner product, while to get the third we use the Cauchy–Schwarz inequality. The last three lines mimic the proof of the first section except that the sample is in this case fixed.

Remark 4.13 [Regularisation strategy] When we perform some kernel-based pattern analysis we typically compute a dual representation $\boldsymbol{\alpha}$ of the weight vector. We can compute the corresponding norm B as $\boldsymbol{\alpha}'\mathbf{K}\boldsymbol{\alpha}$ where $\mathbf{K}$ is the kernel matrix, and hence estimate the complexity of the corresponding function class. By controlling the size of $\boldsymbol{\alpha}'\mathbf{K}\boldsymbol{\alpha}$, we therefore control the capacity of the function class and hence improve the statistical stability of the pattern, a method known as *regularisation*. ∎

Properties of Rademacher complexity The final ingredient that will be required to apply the technique are the properties of the Rademacher complexity that allow it to be bounded in terms of properties of the loss function. The following theorem summarises some of the useful properties of the empirical Rademacher complexity, though the bounds also hold for the full complexity as well. We need one further definition.

Definition 4.14 Let F be a subset of a vector space. By $\operatorname{conv}(F)$ we denote the set of convex combinations of elements of F. ∎

Theorem 4.15 *Let $\mathcal{F}, \mathcal{F}_1, \ldots, \mathcal{F}_n$ and $\mathcal{G}$ be classes of real functions. Then:*

(i) *If $\mathcal{F} \subseteq \mathcal{G}$, then $\hat{R}_\ell(\mathcal{F}) \leq \hat{R}_\ell(\mathcal{G})$;*

(ii) *$\hat{R}_\ell(\mathcal{F}) = \hat{R}_\ell(\operatorname{conv} \mathcal{F})$;*

(iii) *For every $c \in \mathbb{R}$, $\hat{R}_\ell(c\mathcal{F}) = |c|\hat{R}_\ell(\mathcal{F})$;*

(iv) *If $A : \mathbb{R} \to \mathbb{R}$ is Lipschitz with constant L and satisfies $A(0) = 0$, then $\hat{R}_\ell(A \circ \mathcal{F}) \leq 2L\hat{R}_\ell(\mathcal{F})$;*

(v) *For any function h, $\hat{R}_\ell(\mathcal{F} + h) \leq \hat{R}_\ell(\mathcal{F}) + 2\sqrt{\hat{\mathbb{E}}[h^2]/\ell}$;*

(vi) *For any $1 \leq q < \infty$, let $\mathcal{L}_{\mathcal{F},h,q} = \{|f - h|^q \mid f \in \mathcal{F}\}$. If $\|f - h\|_\infty \leq 1$ for every $f \in \mathcal{F}$, then $\hat{R}_\ell(\mathcal{L}_{\mathcal{F},h,q}) \leq 2q\left(\hat{R}_\ell(\mathcal{F}) + 2\sqrt{\hat{\mathbb{E}}[h^2]/\ell}\right)$;*

(vii) *$\hat{R}_\ell(\sum_{i=1}^n \mathcal{F}_i) \leq \sum_{i=1}^n \hat{R}_\ell(\mathcal{F}_i)$.*

Though in many cases the results are surprising, with the exception of (iv) their proofs are all relatively straightforward applications of the definition of empirical Rademacher complexity. For example, the derivation of part (v) is as follows

$$
\begin{aligned}
\hat{R}_\ell(\mathcal{F} + h) &= \mathbb{E}_\sigma\left[\sup_{f \in \mathcal{F}} \left|\frac{2}{\ell}\sum_{i=1}^\ell \sigma_i\left(f(\mathbf{x}_i) + h(\mathbf{x}_i)\right)\right|\right] \\
&\leq \mathbb{E}_\sigma\left[\frac{2}{\ell}\sup_{f \in \mathcal{F}}\left|\sum_{i=1}^\ell \sigma_i f(\mathbf{x}_i)\right|\right] + \mathbb{E}_\sigma\left[\frac{2}{\ell}\left|\sum_{i=1}^\ell \sigma_i h(\mathbf{x}_i)\right|\right] \\
&\leq \hat{R}_\ell(\mathcal{F}) + \frac{2}{\ell}\left(\mathbb{E}_\sigma\left[\sum_{i,j=1}^\ell \sigma_i h(\mathbf{x}_i)\sigma_j h(\mathbf{x}_j)\right]\right)^{1/2} \\
&= \hat{R}_\ell(\mathcal{F}) + \frac{2}{\ell}\left(\sum_{i=1}^\ell h(\mathbf{x}_i)^2\right)^{1/2} \\
&= \hat{R}_\ell(\mathcal{F}) + \frac{2}{\ell}\left(\ell\hat{\mathbb{E}}[h^2]\right)^{1/2}.
\end{aligned}
$$

The proof of (iv) is discussed in Section 4.6.

Margin bound We are now in a position to give an example of an application of the bound. We will take the case of pattern analysis of a classification function. The results obtained here will be used in Chapter 7 where we describe algorithms that optimise the bounds we derive here based involving either the margin or the slack variables.

We need one definition before we can state the theorem. When using the Heaviside function to convert a real-valued function to a binary classification, the margin is the amount by which the real value is on the correct side of the threshold as formalised in the next definition.

Definition 4.16 For a function $g : X \to \mathbb{R}$, we define its *margin* on an example $(\mathbf{x}, y)$ to be $yg(\mathbf{x})$. The *functional margin* of a training set $S = \{(\mathbf{x}_1, y_1), \ldots, (\mathbf{x}_\ell, y_\ell)\}$, is defined to be

$$m(S, g) = \min_{1 \le i \le \ell} y_i g(\mathbf{x}_i).$$

Given a function g and a desired margin γ we denote by $\xi_i = \xi\left((\mathbf{x}_i, y_i), \gamma, g\right)$ the amount by which the function g fails to achieve margin γ for the example $(\mathbf{x}_i, y_i)$. This is also known as the example's *slack variable*

$$\xi_i = (\gamma - y_i g(\mathbf{x}_i))_+,$$

where $(x)_+ = x$ if $x \ge 0$ and 0 otherwise. ∎

Theorem 4.17 *Fix $\gamma > 0$ and let $\mathcal{F}$ be the class of functions mapping from $Z = X \times Y$ to $\mathbb{R}$ given by $f(\mathbf{x}, y) = -yg(\mathbf{x})$, where g is a linear function in a kernel-defined feature space with norm at most 1. Let*

$$S = \{(\mathbf{x}_1, y_1), \ldots, (\mathbf{x}_\ell, y_\ell)\}$$

be drawn independently according to a probability distribution $\mathcal{D}$ and fix $\delta \in (0, 1)$. Then with probability at least $1 - \delta$ over samples of size ℓ we have

$$
\begin{aligned}
P_{\mathcal{D}}\left(y \ne \operatorname{sgn}(g(\mathbf{x}))\right) &= \mathbb{E}_{\mathcal{D}}\left[\mathcal{H}(-yg(\mathbf{x}))\right] \\
&\le \frac{1}{\ell\gamma}\sum_{i=1}^{\ell}\xi_i + \frac{4}{\ell\gamma}\sqrt{\operatorname{tr}(\mathbf{K})} + 3\sqrt{\frac{\ln(2/\delta)}{2\ell}},
\end{aligned}
$$

where $\mathbf{K}$ is the kernel matrix for the training set and $\xi_i = \xi\left((\mathbf{x}_i, y_i), \gamma, g\right)$.

Proof Consider the loss function $\mathcal{A} : \mathbb{R} \to [0,1]$, given by

$$\mathcal{A}(a) = \begin{cases} 1, & \text{if } a > 0; \\ 1 + a/\gamma, & \text{if } -\gamma \leq a \leq 0; \\ 0, & \text{otherwise.} \end{cases}$$

By Theorem 4.9 and since the loss function $\mathcal{A} - 1$ dominates $\mathcal{H} - 1$, we have that

$$\mathbb{E}_{\mathcal{D}}\left[\mathcal{H}(f(\mathbf{x}, y)) - 1\right] \leq \mathbb{E}_{\mathcal{D}}\left[\mathcal{A}(f(\mathbf{x}, y)) - 1\right]$$

$$\leq \hat{\mathbb{E}}\left[\mathcal{A}(f(\mathbf{x}, y)) - 1\right] + \hat{R}_\ell((\mathcal{A} - 1) \circ \mathcal{F}) + 3\sqrt{\frac{\ln(2/\delta)}{2\ell}}.$$

But the function $\mathcal{A}(-y_i g(\mathbf{x}_i)) \leq \xi_i/\gamma$, for $i = 1, \ldots, \ell$, and so

$$\mathbb{E}_{\mathcal{D}}\left[\mathcal{H}(f(\mathbf{x}, y))\right] \leq \frac{1}{\ell\gamma} \sum_{i=1}^{\ell} \xi_i + \hat{R}_\ell((\mathcal{A} - 1) \circ \mathcal{F}) + 3\sqrt{\frac{\ln(2/\delta)}{2\ell}}.$$

Since $(\mathcal{A} - 1)(0) = 0$, we can apply part (iv) of Theorem 4.15 with $L = 1/\gamma$ to give $\hat{R}_\ell((\mathcal{A} - 1) \circ \mathcal{F}) \leq 2\hat{R}_\ell(\mathcal{F})/\gamma$. It remains to bound the empirical Rademacher complexity of the class $\mathcal{F}$

$$\hat{R}_\ell(\mathcal{F}) = \mathbb{E}_\sigma\left[\sup_{f \in \mathcal{F}} \left|\frac{2}{\ell} \sum_{i=1}^{\ell} \sigma_i f(\mathbf{x}_i, y_i)\right|\right] = \mathbb{E}_\sigma\left[\sup_{f \in \mathcal{F}_1} \left|\frac{2}{\ell} \sum_{i=1}^{\ell} \sigma_i y_i g(\mathbf{x}_i)\right|\right]$$

$$= \mathbb{E}_\sigma\left[\sup_{f \in \mathcal{F}_1} \left|\frac{2}{\ell} \sum_{i=1}^{\ell} \sigma_i g(\mathbf{x}_i)\right|\right] = \hat{R}_\ell(\mathcal{F}_1)$$

$$= \frac{2}{\ell} \sqrt{\operatorname{tr}(\mathbf{K})},$$

where we have used the fact that $g \in \mathcal{F}_1$ that is that the norm of the weight vector is bounded by 1, and that multiplying σ_i by a fixed y_i does not alter the expectation. This together with Theorem 4.12 gives the result. □

If the function g has margin γ, or in other words if it satisfies $m(S, g) \geq \gamma$, then the first term in the bound is zero since all the slack variables are zero in this case.

Remark 4.18 [Comparison with other bounds] This theorem mimics the well-known margin based bound on generalisation (see Section 4.6 for details), but has several advantages. Firstly, it does not involve additional $\log(\ell)$ factors in the second term and the constants are very tight. Furthermore it handles the case of slack variables without recourse to additional constructions. It also does not restrict the data to lie in a ball of some predefined radius, but rather uses the trace of the matrix in its place as an empirical estimate or effective radius. Of course if it is known that the support of the distribution is in a ball of radius R about the origin, then we have

$$\frac{4}{\ell\gamma}\sqrt{\mathrm{tr}(\mathbf{K})} \leq \frac{4}{\ell\gamma}\sqrt{\ell R^2} = 4\sqrt{\frac{R^2}{\ell\gamma^2}}.$$

Despite these advantages it suffers from requiring a square root factor of the ratio of the effective dimension and the training set size. For the classification case this can be avoided, but for more general pattern analysis tasks it is not clear that this can always be achieved. We do, however, feel that the approach succeeds in our aim of providing a unified and transparent framework for assessing stability across a wide range of different pattern analysis tasks.   ∎

As we consider different algorithms in later chapters we will indicate the factors that will affect the corresponding bound that guarantees their stability. Essentially this will involve specifying the relevant loss functions and estimating the corresponding Rademacher complexities.

4.4 A pragmatic approach

There exist many different methods for modelling learning algorithms and quantifying the reliability of their results. All involve some form of capacity control, in order to prevent the algorithm from fitting 'irrelevant' aspects of the data. The concepts outlined in this chapter have been chosen for their intuitive interpretability that can motivate the spirit of all the algorithms discussed in this book. However we will not seek to derive statistical bounds on the generalization of every algorithm, preferring the pragmatic strategy of using the theory to identify which parameters should be kept under control in order to control the algorithm's capacity. For detailed discussions of statistical bounds covering many of the algorithms, we refer the reader to the last section of this and the following chapters, which contain pointers to the relevant literature.

The relations we will deal with will be quite diverse ranging from correlations to classifications, from clusterings to rankings. For each of them, different performance measures can be appropriate, and different cost functions should be optimised in order to achieve best performance. In some cases we will see that we can estimate capacity by actually doing the randomisation ourselves, rather than relying on a priori bounds such as those given above. Such attempts to directly estimate the empirical Rademacher complexity are likely to lead to much better indications of the generalisation as they can take into account the structure of the data, rather than slightly uninformative measures such as the trace of the kernel matrix.

Our strategy will be to use cost functions that are 'concentrated', so that any individual pattern that has a good performance on the training sample will with high probability achieve a good performance on new data from the same distribution. For this same stability to apply across a class of pattern functions will depend on the size of the training set and the degree of control that is applied to the capacity of the class from which the pattern is chosen. In practice this trade-off between flexibility and generalisation will be achieved by controlling the parameters indicated by the theory. This will often lead to regularization techniques that penalise complex relations by controlling the norm of the linear functions that define them.

We will make no effort to eliminate every tunable component from our algorithms, as the current state-of-the-art in learning theory often does not give accurate enough estimates for this to be a reliable approach. We will rather emphasise the role of any parameters that can be tuned in the algorithms, leaving it for the practitioner to decide how best to set these parameters with the data at his or her disposal.

4.5 Summary

- The problem of determining the stability of patterns can be cast in a statistical framework.
- The stability of a fixed pattern in a finite sample can be reliably verified if it is statistically concentrated, something detectable using McDiarmid's inequality.
- When considering classes of pattern functions, the issue of the capacity of the class becomes crucial in ensuring that concentration applies simultaneously for all functions.
- The Rademacher complexity measures the capacity of a class. It assesses the 'richness' of the class by its ability to fit random noise. The difference between empirical and true estimation over the pattern class can be bounded in terms of its Rademacher complexity.
- Regularisation is a method of controlling capacity and hence ensuring that detected patterns are stable.
- There are natural methods for measuring and controlling the capacity of linear function classes in kernel-defined feature spaces.

4.6 Further reading and advanced topics

The modelling of learning algorithms with methods of empirical processes was pioneered by Vladimir Vapnik and Alexei Chervonenkis (VC) [144], [145] in the 1970s, and greatly extended in more recent years by a large number of other researchers. Their work emphasised the necessity to control the capacity of *a class* of functions, in order to avoid overfitting, and devised a measure of capacity known as VC dimension [142].

Their analysis does not, however, extend to generalisation bounds involving the margin or slack variables. The first papers to develop these bounds were [124] and [8]. The paper [124] developed the so-called luckiness framework for analysing generalisation based on fortuitous observations during training such as the size of the margin. The analysis of generalisation in terms of the slack variables in the soft margin support vector machine is given in [125]. A description of generalisation analysis for support vector machines based on these ideas is also contained in Chapter 4 of the book [32]. In this chapter we have, however, followed a somewhat different approach, still within a related general framework.

The original VC framework was specialised for the problem of classification, and later extended to cover regression problems and novelty-detection. Its extension to general classes of patterns in data is difficult. It is also well-known that traditional VC arguments provide rather loose bounds on the risk of overfitting. A number of new methodologies have been proposed in recent years to overcome some of these problems, mostly based on the notion of concentration inequalities [18], [17], and the use of Rademacher complexity: [80], [9], [82], [10], [80]. At an intuitive level we can think of Rademacher complexity as being an empirical estimate of the VC dimension. Despite the transparency of the results we have described, we have omitted a proof of part (iv) of Theorem 4.15. This is somewhat non-trivial and we refer the interested reader to [85] who in turn refer to [85]. The full proof of the result requires a further theorem proved by X. Fernique.

The analysis we presented in this chapter aims at covering all the types of patterns we are interested in, and therefore needs to be very general. What has remained unchanged during this evolution from VC to Rademacher-type of arguments, is the use of the notion of uniform convergence of the empirical means of a set of random variables to their expectations, although the methods for proving uniform convergence have become simpler and more refined. The rate of such uniform convergence is however still dictated by some measure of richness of such set.

The use of Rademacher Complexity for this purpose is due to [80]. Our discussion of Rademacher complexity for kernel function classes is based on the paper by Bartlett and Mendelson [10] and on the lectures given by Peter Bartlett at UC Berkeley in 2001. The discussion of concentration inequalities is based on Boucheron, Lugosi and Massart [17] and on the seminar notes of Gabor Lugosi.

More recently tighter bounds on generalisation of SVMs has been obtained using a theoretical linking of Bayesian and statistical learning [84]. Finally, notions of regularizations date back to [138], and certainly have been fully exploited by Wahba in similar contexts [155].

The books [38] and [4] also provide excellent coverage of theoretical foundations of inference and learning.

For constantly updated pointers to online literature and free software see the book's companion website: www.kernel-methods.net

Part II

Pattern analysis algorithms

5

Elementary algorithms in feature space

In this chapter we show how to evaluate a number of properties of a data set in a kernel-defined feature space. The quantities we consider are of interest in their own right in data analysis, but they will also form building blocks towards the design of complex pattern analysis systems. Furthermore, the computational methods we develop will play an important role in subsequent chapters.

The quantities include the distance between two points, the centre of mass, the projections of data onto particular directions, the rank, the variance and covariance of projections of a set of data points, all measured in the feature space. We will go on to consider the distance between the centres of mass of two sets of data.

Through the development of these methods we will arrive at a number of algorithmic solutions for certain problems. We give Matlab code for normalising the data, centering the data in feature space, and standardising the different coordinates. Finally, we develop two pattern analysis algorithms, the first is a novelty-detection algorithm that comes with a theoretical guarantee on performance, while the second is a first kernelised version of the Fisher discriminant algorithm. This important pattern analysis algorithm is somewhat similar to the ridge regression algorithm already previewed in Chapter 2, but tackles classification and takes account of more subtle structure of the data.

111

5.1 Means and distances

Given a finite subset $S = \{\mathbf{x}_1, \ldots, \mathbf{x}_\ell\}$ of an input space X, a kernel $\kappa(\mathbf{x}, \mathbf{z})$ and a feature map ϕ into a feature space F satisfying

$$\kappa(\mathbf{x}, \mathbf{z}) = \langle \phi(\mathbf{x}), \phi(\mathbf{z}) \rangle,$$

let $\phi(S) = \{\phi(\mathbf{x}_1), \ldots, \phi(\mathbf{x}_\ell)\}$ be the image of S under the map ϕ. Hence $\phi(S)$ is a subset of the inner product space F. In this chapter we continue our investigation of the information that can be obtained about $\phi(S)$ using only the inner product information contained in the kernel matrix $\mathbf{K}$ of kernel evaluations between all pairs of elements of S

$$\mathbf{K}_{ij} = \kappa(\mathbf{x}_i, \mathbf{x}_j), \quad i, j = 1, \ldots, \ell.$$

Working in a kernel-defined feature space means that we are not able to explicitly represent points. For example the image of an input point $\mathbf{x}$ is $\phi(\mathbf{x})$, but we do not have access to the components of this vector, only to the evaluation of inner products between this point and the images of other points. Despite this handicap there is a surprising amount of useful information that can be gleaned about $\phi(S)$.

Norm of feature vectors The simplest example already seen in Chapter 4 is the evaluation of the norm of $\phi(\mathbf{x})$ that is given by

$$\|\phi(\mathbf{x})\|_2 = \sqrt{\|\phi(\mathbf{x})\|^2} = \sqrt{\langle \phi(\mathbf{x}), \phi(\mathbf{x}) \rangle} = \sqrt{\kappa(\mathbf{x}, \mathbf{x})}.$$

Algorithm 5.1 [Normalisation] Using this observation we can now implement the normalisation transformation mentioned in Chapters 2 and 3 given by

$$\hat{\phi}(\mathbf{x}) = \frac{\phi(\mathbf{x})}{\|\phi(\mathbf{x})\|}.$$

For two data points the transformed kernel $\hat{\kappa}$ is given by

$$
\begin{aligned}
\hat{\kappa}(\mathbf{x}, \mathbf{z}) &= \left\langle \hat{\phi}(\mathbf{x}), \hat{\phi}(\mathbf{z}) \right\rangle = \left\langle \frac{\phi(\mathbf{x})}{\|\phi(\mathbf{x})\|}, \frac{\phi(\mathbf{z})}{\|\phi(\mathbf{z})\|} \right\rangle = \frac{\langle \phi(\mathbf{x}), \phi(\mathbf{z}) \rangle}{\|\phi(\mathbf{x})\|\|\phi(\mathbf{z})\|} \quad (5.1) \\
&= \frac{\kappa(\mathbf{x}, \mathbf{z})}{\sqrt{\kappa(\mathbf{x}, \mathbf{x})\kappa(\mathbf{z}, \mathbf{z})}}.
\end{aligned}
$$

The corresponding transformation of the kernel matrix can be implemented by the operations given in Code Fragment 5.1. ∎

```
% original kernel matrix stored in variable K
% output uses the same variable K
% D is a diagonal matrix storing the inverse of the norms
D = diag(1./sqrt(diag(K)));
K = D * K * D;
```

Code Fragment 5.1. Matlab code normalising a kernel matrix.

We can also evaluate the norms of linear combinations of images in the feature space. For example we have

$$\left\| \sum_{i=1}^{\ell} \alpha_i \phi(\mathbf{x}_i) \right\|^2 = \left\langle \sum_{i=1}^{\ell} \alpha_i \phi(\mathbf{x}_i), \sum_{j=1}^{\ell} \alpha_j \phi(\mathbf{x}_j) \right\rangle$$

$$= \sum_{i=1}^{\ell} \alpha_i \sum_{j=1}^{\ell} \alpha_j \left\langle \phi(\mathbf{x}_i), \phi(\mathbf{x}_j) \right\rangle$$

$$= \sum_{i,j=1}^{\ell} \alpha_i \alpha_j \kappa(\mathbf{x}_i, \mathbf{x}_j).$$

Distance between feature vectors A special case of the norm is the length of the line joining two images $\phi(\mathbf{x})$ and $\phi(\mathbf{z})$, which can be computed as

$$\| \phi(\mathbf{x}) - \phi(\mathbf{z}) \|^2 = \langle \phi(\mathbf{x}) - \phi(\mathbf{z}), \phi(\mathbf{x}) - \phi(\mathbf{z}) \rangle$$

$$= \langle \phi(\mathbf{x}), \phi(\mathbf{x}) \rangle - 2 \langle \phi(\mathbf{x}), \phi(\mathbf{z}) \rangle + \langle \phi(\mathbf{z}), \phi(\mathbf{z}) \rangle$$

$$= \kappa(\mathbf{x}, \mathbf{x}) - 2\kappa(\mathbf{x}, \mathbf{z}) + \kappa(\mathbf{z}, \mathbf{z}).$$

Norm and distance from the centre of mass As a more complex and useful example consider the centre of mass of the set $\phi(S)$. This is the vector

$$\phi_S = \frac{1}{\ell} \sum_{i=1}^{\ell} \phi(\mathbf{x}_i).$$

As with all points in the feature space we will not have an explicit vector representation of this point. However, in this case there may also not exist a point in X whose image under ϕ is ϕ_S. In other words, we are now considering points that potentially lie outside $\phi(X)$, that is the image of the input space X under the feature map ϕ.

Despite this apparent inaccessibility of the point ϕ_S, we can compute its norm using only evaluations of the kernel on the inputs

$$\|\phi_S\|_2^2 = \langle \phi_S, \phi_S \rangle = \left\langle \frac{1}{\ell} \sum_{i=1}^{\ell} \phi(\mathbf{x}_i), \frac{1}{\ell} \sum_{j=1}^{\ell} \phi(\mathbf{x}_j) \right\rangle$$

$$= \frac{1}{\ell^2} \sum_{i,j=1}^{\ell} \langle \phi(\mathbf{x}_i), \phi(\mathbf{x}_j) \rangle = \frac{1}{\ell^2} \sum_{i,j=1}^{\ell} \kappa(\mathbf{x}_i, \mathbf{x}_j).$$

Hence, the square of the norm of the centre of mass is equal to the average of the entries in the kernel matrix. Incidentally this implies that this sum is greater than or equal to zero, with equality if the centre of mass is at the origin of the coordinate system. Similarly, we can compute the distance of the image of a point $\mathbf{x}$ from the centre of mass ϕ_S

$$\|\phi(\mathbf{x}) - \phi_S\|^2 = \langle \phi(\mathbf{x}), \phi(\mathbf{x}) \rangle + \langle \phi_S, \phi_S \rangle - 2\langle \phi(\mathbf{x}), \phi_S \rangle$$

$$= \kappa(\mathbf{x}, \mathbf{x}) + \frac{1}{\ell^2} \sum_{i,j=1}^{\ell} \kappa(\mathbf{x}_i, \mathbf{x}_j) - \frac{2}{\ell} \sum_{i=1}^{\ell} \kappa(\mathbf{x}, \mathbf{x}_i). \quad (5.2)$$

Expected distance from the centre of mass Following the same approach it is also possible to express the expected squared distance of a point in a set from its mean

$$\frac{1}{\ell} \sum_{s=1}^{\ell} \|\phi(\mathbf{x}_s) - \phi_S\|^2 = \frac{1}{\ell} \sum_{s=1}^{\ell} \kappa(\mathbf{x}_s, \mathbf{x}_s) + \frac{1}{\ell^2} \sum_{i,j=1}^{\ell} \kappa(\mathbf{x}_i, \mathbf{x}_j)$$

$$- \frac{2}{\ell^2} \sum_{i,s=1}^{\ell} \kappa(\mathbf{x}_s, \mathbf{x}_i) \quad (5.3)$$

$$= \frac{1}{\ell} \sum_{s=1}^{\ell} \kappa(\mathbf{x}_s, \mathbf{x}_s) - \frac{1}{\ell^2} \sum_{i,j=1}^{\ell} \kappa(\mathbf{x}_i, \mathbf{x}_j). \quad (5.4)$$

Hence, the average squared distance of points to their centre of mass is the average of the diagonal entries of the kernel matrix minus the average of all the entries.

Properties of the centre of mass If we translate the origin of the feature space, the norms of the training points alter, but the left-hand side of equation (5.4) does not change. If the centre of mass is at the origin, then, as we observed above, the entries in the matrix will sum to zero. Hence, moving the origin to the centre of mass minimises the first term on the right-hand side of equation (5.4), corresponding to the sum of the squared norms of the points. This also implies the following proposition that will prove useful in Chapter 8.

Proposition 5.2 *The centre of mass ϕ_S of a set of points $\phi(S)$ solves the following optimisation problem*

$$\min_{\mu} \frac{1}{\ell} \sum_{s=1}^{\ell} \|\phi(\mathbf{x}_s) - \mu\|^2.$$

Proof Consider moving the origin to the point μ. The quantity to be optimised corresponds to the first term on the right-hand side of equation (5.4). Since the left-hand side does not depend on μ, the quantity will be minimised by minimising the second term on the right-hand side, something that is achieved by taking $\mu = \phi_S$. The result follows. $\square$

Centering data Since the first term on the right-hand side of equation (5.4) is the trace of the matrix divided by its size, moving the origin to the centre of mass also minimises the average eigenvalue. As announced in Chapter 3 we can perform this operation implicitly by transforming the kernel matrix. This follows from the fact that the new feature map is given by

$$\hat{\phi}(\mathbf{x}) = \phi(\mathbf{x}) - \phi_S = \phi(\mathbf{x}) - \frac{1}{\ell} \sum_{i=1}^{\ell} \phi(\mathbf{x}_i).$$

Hence, the kernel for the transformed space is

$$
\begin{aligned}
\hat{\kappa}(\mathbf{x}, \mathbf{z}) &= \left\langle \hat{\phi}(\mathbf{x}), \hat{\phi}(\mathbf{z}) \right\rangle = \left\langle \phi(\mathbf{x}) - \frac{1}{\ell} \sum_{i=1}^{\ell} \phi(\mathbf{x}_i), \phi(\mathbf{z}) - \frac{1}{\ell} \sum_{i=1}^{\ell} \phi(\mathbf{x}_i) \right\rangle \\
&= \kappa(\mathbf{x}, \mathbf{z}) - \frac{1}{\ell} \sum_{i=1}^{\ell} \kappa(\mathbf{x}, \mathbf{x}_i) - \frac{1}{\ell} \sum_{i=1}^{\ell} \kappa(\mathbf{z}, \mathbf{x}_i) + \frac{1}{\ell^2} \sum_{i,j=1}^{\ell} \kappa(\mathbf{x}_i, \mathbf{x}_j).
\end{aligned}
$$

Expressed as an operation on the kernel matrix this can be written as

$$\hat{\mathbf{K}} = \mathbf{K} - \frac{1}{\ell} \mathbf{j} \mathbf{j}' \mathbf{K} - \frac{1}{\ell} \mathbf{K} \mathbf{j} \mathbf{j}' + \frac{1}{\ell^2} \left(\mathbf{j}' \mathbf{K} \mathbf{j} \right) \mathbf{j} \mathbf{j}',$$

where $\mathbf{j}$ is the all 1s vector. We have the following algorithm.

Algorithm 5.3 [Centering data] We can centre the data in the feature space with the short sequence of operations given in Code Fragment 5.2. ∎

```
% original kernel matrix stored in variable K
% output uses the same variable K
% K is of dimension ell x ell
% D is a row vector storing the column averages of K
% E is the average of all the entries of K
ell = size(K,1);
D = sum(K) / ell;
E = sum(D) / ell;
J = ones(ell,1) * D;
K = K - J - J' + E * ones(ell, ell);
```

Code Fragment 5.2. Matlab code for centering a kernel matrix.

The stability of centering The example of centering raises the question of how reliably we can estimate the centre of mass from a training sample or in other words how close our sample centre will be to the true expectation

$$\mathbb{E}_{\mathbf{x}}[\phi(\mathbf{x})] = \int_X \phi(\mathbf{x})dP(\mathbf{x}).$$

Our analysis in Chapter 4 bounded the expected value of the quantity

$$g(S) = \|\phi_S - \mathbb{E}_{\mathbf{x}}[\phi(\mathbf{x})]\|.$$

There it was shown that with probability at least $1 - \delta$ over the choice of a random sample of ℓ points, we have

$$g(S) \leq \sqrt{\frac{2R^2}{\ell}}\left(\sqrt{2} + \sqrt{\ln\frac{1}{\delta}}\right), \tag{5.5}$$

assuring us that with high probability our sample does indeed give a good estimate of $\mathbb{E}_{\mathbf{x}}[\phi(\mathbf{x})]$ in a way that does not depend on the dimension of the feature space, where the support of the distribution is contained in a ball of radius R around the origin.

5.1.1 A simple algorithm for novelty-detection

Centering suggests a simple novelty-detection algorithm. If we consider the training set as a sample of points providing an estimate of the distances $d_1, \ldots, d_\ell$ from the point $\mathbb{E}_{\mathbf{x}}[\phi(\mathbf{x})]$, where

$$d_i = \|\phi(\mathbf{x}_i) - \mathbb{E}_{\mathbf{x}}[\phi(\mathbf{x})]\|,$$

we can bound the probability that a new random point $\mathbf{x}_{\ell+1}$ satisfies

$$d_{\ell+1} = \|\phi(\mathbf{x}_{\ell+1}) - \mathbb{E}_{\mathbf{x}}[\phi(\mathbf{x})]\| > \max_{1 \leq i \leq \ell} d_i,$$

with

$$P\left\{\|\phi(\mathbf{x}_{\ell+1}) - \mathbb{E}_{\mathbf{x}}[\phi(\mathbf{x})]\| > \max_{1 \le i \le \ell} d_i\right\} = P\left\{\max_{1 \le i \le \ell+1} d_i = d_{\ell+1} \neq \max_{1 \le i \le \ell} d_i\right\}$$

$$\le \frac{1}{\ell+1},$$

by the symmetry of the i.i.d. assumption. Though we cannot compute the distance to the point $\mathbb{E}_{\mathbf{x}}[\phi(\mathbf{x})]$, we can, by equation (5.2), compute

$$\|\phi(\mathbf{x}) - \phi_S\| = \sqrt{\kappa(\mathbf{x}, \mathbf{x}) + \frac{1}{\ell^2} \sum_{i,j=1}^{\ell} \kappa(\mathbf{x}_i, \mathbf{x}_j) - \frac{2}{\ell} \sum_{i=1}^{\ell} \kappa(\mathbf{x}, \mathbf{x}_i)}. \qquad (5.6)$$

Then we can with probability $1 - \delta$ estimate $\|\phi(\mathbf{x}_{\ell+1}) - \mathbb{E}_{\mathbf{x}}[\phi(\mathbf{x})]\|$ using the triangle inequality and (5.5)

$$\begin{aligned} d_{\ell+1} &= \|\phi(\mathbf{x}_{\ell+1}) - \mathbb{E}_{\mathbf{x}}[\phi(\mathbf{x})]\| \\ &\ge \|\phi(\mathbf{x}_{\ell+1}) - \phi_S\| - \|\phi_S - \mathbb{E}_{\mathbf{x}}[\phi(\mathbf{x})]\| \\ &\ge \|\phi(\mathbf{x}_{\ell+1}) - \phi_S\| - \sqrt{\frac{2R^2}{\ell}} \left(\sqrt{2} + \sqrt{\ln \frac{1}{\delta}}\right). \end{aligned}$$

Similarly, we have that for $i = 1, \ldots, \ell$

$$d_i = \|\phi(\mathbf{x}_i) - \mathbb{E}_{\mathbf{x}}[\phi(\mathbf{x})]\| \le \|\phi(\mathbf{x}_i) - \phi_S\| + \|\phi_S - \mathbb{E}_{\mathbf{x}}[\phi(\mathbf{x})]\|.$$

We now use the inequalities to provide a bound on the probability that a test point lies outside a ball centred on the empirical centre of mass. Effectively we choose its radius to ensure that with high probability it contains the ball of radius $\max_{1 \le i \le \ell} d_i$ with centre $\mathbb{E}_{\mathbf{x}}[\phi(\mathbf{x})]$. With probability $1 - \delta$ we have that

$$P\left\{\|\phi(\mathbf{x}_{\ell+1}) - \phi_S\| > \max_{1 \le i \le \ell} \|\phi(\mathbf{x}_i) - \phi_S\| + 2\sqrt{\frac{2R^2}{\ell}} \left(\sqrt{2} + \sqrt{\ln \frac{1}{\delta}}\right)\right\}$$

$$\le P\left\{\max_{1 \le i \le \ell+1} d_i = d_{\ell+1} \neq \max_{1 \le i \le \ell} d_i\right\} \le \frac{1}{\ell+1}. \qquad (5.7)$$

Using $\mathcal{H}(x)$ to denote the Heaviside function we have in the notation of Chapter 1 a pattern analysis algorithm that returns the pattern function

$$f(\mathbf{x})$$

$$= \mathcal{H}\left(\|\phi(\mathbf{x}) - \phi_S\| - \max_{1 \le i \le \ell} \|\phi(\mathbf{x}_i) - \phi_S\| - 2\sqrt{\frac{2R^2}{\ell}} \left(\sqrt{2} + \sqrt{\ln \frac{1}{\delta}}\right)\right),$$

since by inequality (5.7) with probability $1 - \delta$ the expectation is bounded by

$$\mathbb{E}_{\mathbf{x}}[f(\mathbf{x})] \leq 1/(\ell+1).$$

Hence, we can reject as anomalous data items satisfying $f(\mathbf{x}) = 1$, and reject authentic examples with probability at most $1/(\ell+1)$. This gives rise to the following novelty-detection algorithm.

Algorithm 5.4 [Simple novelty detection] An implementation of the simple novelty-detection algorithm is given in Code Fragment 5.3.   ∎

```
% K kernel matrix of training points
% inner products between ell training and t test points
%    stored in matrix Ktest of dimension (ell + 1) x t
%    last entry in each column is inner product with itself
% confidence parameter
delta = 0.01
% first compute distances of data to centre of mass
% D is a row vector storing the column averages of K
% E is the average of all the entries of K
ell = size(K,1);
D = sum(K) / ell;
E = sum(D) / ell;
traindist2 = diag(K) - 2 * D' + E * ones(ell, 1);
maxdist = sqrt(max(traindist2));
% compute the estimation error of empirical centre of mass
esterr = sqrt(2*max(diag(K))/ell)*(sqrt(2) + sqrt(log(1/delta)));
% compute resulting threshold
threshold = maxdist + 2 * esterr;
threshold = threshold * threshold;
% now compute distances of test data
t = size(Ktest,2);
Dtest = sum(Ktest(1:ell,:)) / ell;
testdist2 = Ktest(ell+1,:) - 2 * Dtest + E * ones(1, t);
% indices of novel test points are now
novelindices = find ( testdist2 > threshold )
```

Code Fragment 5.3. Matlab code for simple novelty detection algorithm.

The pattern function is unusual in that it is not always a thresholded linear function in the kernel-defined feature space, though by equation (5.2) if the feature space is normalised the function can be represented in the standard form. The algorithm considers a sphere containing the data centred on the centre of mass of the data sample. Figure 5.1 illustrates the spheres for data generated according to a spherical two-dimensional Gaussian distribution.

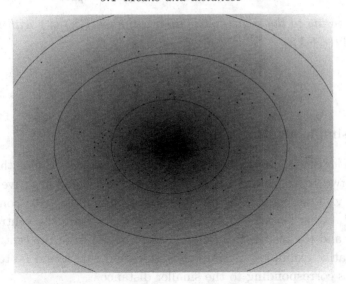

Fig. 5.1. Novelty detection spheres centred on the empirical centre of mass.

In Chapter 7 we will consider letting the centre of the hypersphere shift in order to reduce its radius. This approach results in a state-of-the-art method for novelty-detection.

Stability of novelty-detection The following proposition assesses the stability of the basic novelty-detection Algorithm 5.4.

Proposition 5.5 *Suppose that we wish to perform novelty-detection based on a training sample*

$$S = \{\mathbf{x}_1, \ldots, \mathbf{x}_\ell\},$$

using the feature space implicitly defined by the kernel $\kappa(\mathbf{x}, \mathbf{z})$; let $f(\mathbf{x})$ be given by

$$f(\mathbf{x})$$
$$= \mathcal{H}\left(\|\phi(\mathbf{x}) - \phi_S\| - \max_{1 \leq i \leq \ell} \|\phi(\mathbf{x}_i) - \phi_S\| - 2\sqrt{\frac{2R^2}{\ell}} \left(\sqrt{2} + \sqrt{\ln \frac{1}{\delta}} \right) \right)$$

where $\|\phi(\mathbf{x}) - \phi_S\|$ can be computed using equation (5.6). Then the function $f(\mathbf{x})$ is equivalent to identifying novel points that are further from the centre of mass in the feature space than any of the training points. Hence, with probability $1 - \delta$ over the random draw of the training set, any points drawn according to the same distribution will have $f(\mathbf{x}) = 1$ with probability less than $1/(\ell + 1)$.

5.1.2 A simple algorithm for classification

If we consider now the case of binary classification, we can divide the training set S into two sets S_+ and S_- containing the positive and negative examples respectively. One could now use the above methodology to compute the distance $d_+(\mathbf{x}) = \|\phi(\mathbf{x}) - \phi_{S_+}\|$ of a test point $\mathbf{x}$ from the centre of mass ϕ_{S_+} of S_+ and the distance $d_-(\mathbf{x}) = \|\phi(\mathbf{x}) - \phi_{S_-}\|$ from the centre of mass of the negative examples. A simple classification rule would be to assign $\mathbf{x}$ to the class corresponding to the smaller distance

$$h(\mathbf{x}) = \begin{cases} +1, & \text{if } d_-(\mathbf{x}) > d_+(\mathbf{x}); \\ -1, & \text{otherwise.} \end{cases}$$

We can express the function $h(\mathbf{x})$ in terms of the sign function

$$
\begin{aligned}
h(\mathbf{x}) &= \operatorname{sgn}\left(\|\phi(\mathbf{x}) - \bar{\phi}_{S_-}\|^2 - \|\phi(\mathbf{x}) - \bar{\phi}_{S_+}\|^2 \right) \\
&= \operatorname{sgn}\left(-\kappa(\mathbf{x}, \mathbf{x}) - \frac{1}{\ell_+^2} \sum_{i,j=1}^{\ell_+} \kappa(\mathbf{x}_i, \mathbf{x}_j) + \frac{2}{\ell_+} \sum_{i=1}^{\ell_+} \kappa(\mathbf{x}, \mathbf{x}_i) \right. \\
&\qquad \left. + \kappa(\mathbf{x}, \mathbf{x}) + \frac{1}{\ell_-^2} \sum_{i,j=\ell_++1}^{\ell_++\ell_-} \kappa(\mathbf{x}_i, \mathbf{x}_j) - \frac{2}{\ell_-} \sum_{i=\ell_++1}^{\ell_++\ell_-} \kappa(\mathbf{x}, \mathbf{x}_i) \right) \\
&= \operatorname{sgn}\left(\frac{1}{\ell_+} \sum_{i=1}^{\ell_+} \kappa(\mathbf{x}, \mathbf{x}_i) - \frac{1}{\ell_-} \sum_{i=\ell_++1}^{\ell} \kappa(\mathbf{x}, \mathbf{x}_i) - b \right),
\end{aligned}
$$

where we have assumed that the positive examples are indexed from 1 to ℓ_+ and the negative examples from $\ell_+ + 1$ to $\ell_+ + \ell_- = \ell$ and where b is a constant being half of the difference between the average entry of the positive examples kernel matrix and the average entry of the negative examples kernel matrix. This gives the following algorithm.

Algorithm 5.6 [Parzen based classifier] The simple Parzen based classifier algorithm is as follows:

input	Data $S = \{(\mathbf{x}_1, y_1), \dots, (\mathbf{x}_\ell, y_\ell)\}$.
process	$\alpha_i^+ = \ell_+^{-1}$ if $y_i = +1$, 0 otherwise.
2	$\alpha_i^- = \ell_-^{-1}$ if $y_i = -1$, 0 otherwise.
3	$b = 0.5 \left(\boldsymbol{\alpha}^{+\prime}\mathbf{K}\boldsymbol{\alpha}^+ - \boldsymbol{\alpha}^{-\prime}\mathbf{K}\boldsymbol{\alpha}^-\right)$
4	$\boldsymbol{\alpha} = \boldsymbol{\alpha}^+ - \boldsymbol{\alpha}^-$;
5	$h(\mathbf{x}) = \mathrm{sgn}\left(\sum_{i=1}^{\ell} \alpha_i \kappa(\mathbf{x}_i, \mathbf{x}) - b\right)$
output	Function h, dual variables $\boldsymbol{\alpha}$ and offset b.

If the origin of the feature space is equidistant from the two centres of mass, the offset b will be zero since the average entry of the kernel matrix is equal to the square of the norm of the centre of mass.

Note that $h(\mathbf{x})$ is a thresholded linear function in the feature space with weight vector given by

$$\mathbf{w} = \frac{1}{\ell_+} \sum_{i=1}^{\ell_+} \phi(\mathbf{x}_i) - \frac{1}{\ell_-} \sum_{i=\ell_++1}^{\ell} \phi(\mathbf{x}_i).$$

This function is the difference in likelihood of the Parzen window density estimator for positive and negative examples. The name derives from viewing the kernel $\kappa(\cdot, \cdot)$ as a Parzen window that can be used to estimate the input densities for the positive and negative empirical distributions. This is natural when for example considering the Gaussian kernel.

Remark 5.7 [On stability analysis] We will not present a stability bound for this classifier, though one could apply the novelty-detection argument for the case where a new example was outside the novelty-detection pattern function derived for its class. In this case we could assert with high confidence that it belonged to the other class.

Consideration of the distances to the centre of mass of a dataset has led to some simple algorithms for both novelty-detection and classification. They are, however, constrained by not being able to take into account information about the spread of the data. In Section 5.3 we will investigate how the variance of the data can also be estimated using only information contained in the kernel matrix. First, however, we turn our attention to projections.

5.2 Computing projections: Gram–Schmidt, QR and Cholesky

The basic classification function of the previous section had the form of a thresholded linear function

$$h(\mathbf{x}) = \text{sgn}\left(\langle \mathbf{w}, \phi(\mathbf{x}) \rangle\right),$$

where the weight vector $\mathbf{w}$ had the form

$$\mathbf{w} = \frac{1}{\ell_+} \sum_{i=1}^{\ell_+} \phi(\mathbf{x}_i) - \frac{1}{\ell_-} \sum_{i=\ell_+ + 1}^{\ell} \phi(\mathbf{x}_i).$$

Hence, the computation only requires knowledge of the inner product between two feature space vectors.

The projection $P_{\mathbf{w}}\left(\phi(\mathbf{x})\right)$ of a vector $\phi(\mathbf{x})$ onto the vector $\mathbf{w}$ is given as

$$P_{\mathbf{w}}\left(\phi(\mathbf{x})\right) = \frac{\langle \mathbf{w}, \phi(\mathbf{x}) \rangle}{\|\mathbf{w}\|^2} \mathbf{w}.$$

This example illustrates a general principle that also enables us to compute projections of vectors in the feature space. For example given a general vector

$$\mathbf{w} = \sum_{i=1}^{\ell} \alpha_i \phi(\mathbf{x}_i),$$

we can compute the norm of the projection $P_{\mathbf{w}}\left(\phi(\mathbf{x})\right)$ of the image of a point $\mathbf{x}$ onto the vector $\mathbf{w}$ as

$$\|P_{\mathbf{w}}\left(\phi(\mathbf{x})\right)\| = \frac{\langle \mathbf{w}, \phi(\mathbf{x}) \rangle}{\|\mathbf{w}\|} = \frac{\sum_{i=1}^{\ell} \alpha_i \kappa\left(\mathbf{x}_i, \mathbf{x}\right)}{\sqrt{\sum_{i,j=1}^{\ell} \alpha_i \alpha_j \kappa\left(\mathbf{x}_i, \mathbf{x}_j\right)}}.$$

Using Pythagoras's theorem allows us to compute the distance of the point from its projection as

$$
\begin{aligned}
\|P_{\mathbf{w}}\left(\phi(\mathbf{x})\right) - \phi(\mathbf{x})\|^2 &= \|\phi(\mathbf{x})\|^2 - \|P_{\mathbf{w}}\left(\phi(\mathbf{x})\right)\|^2 \\
&= \kappa\left(\mathbf{x}, \mathbf{x}\right) - \frac{\left(\sum_{i=1}^{\ell} \alpha_i \kappa\left(\mathbf{x}_i, \mathbf{x}\right)\right)^2}{\sum_{i,j=1}^{\ell} \alpha_i \alpha_j \kappa\left(\mathbf{x}_i, \mathbf{x}_j\right)}.
\end{aligned}
$$

If we have a set of orthonormal vectors $\mathbf{w}_1, \ldots, \mathbf{w}_k$ with corresponding dual representations given by $\boldsymbol{\alpha}^1, \ldots, \boldsymbol{\alpha}^k$, we can compute the orthogonal projection $P_V\left(\phi(\mathbf{x})\right)$ of a point $\phi(\mathbf{x})$ into the subspace V spanned by

$\mathbf{w}_1, \ldots, \mathbf{w}_k$ as

$$P_V\left(\phi(\mathbf{x})\right) = \left(\sum_{i=1}^{\ell} \alpha_i^j \kappa\left(\mathbf{x}_i, \mathbf{x}\right)\right)_{j=1}^{k},$$

where we have used the vectors $\mathbf{w}_1, \ldots, \mathbf{w}_k$ as a basis for V.

Definition 5.8 A *projection* is a mapping P satisfying

$$P\left(\phi(\mathbf{x})\right) = P^2\left(\phi(\mathbf{x})\right) \text{ and } \langle P\left(\phi(\mathbf{x})\right), \phi(\mathbf{x}) - P\left(\phi(\mathbf{x})\right)\rangle = 0,$$

with its dimension $\dim(P)$ given by the dimension of the image of P. The orthogonal projection to P is given by

$$P^{\perp}\left(\phi(\mathbf{x})\right) = \phi(\mathbf{x}) - P\left(\phi(\mathbf{x})\right)$$

and projects the data onto the orthogonal complement of the image of P, so that $\dim(P) + \dim\left(P^{\perp}\right) = N$, the dimension of the feature space. ∎

Remark 5.9 [Orthogonal projections] It is not hard to see that the orthogonal projection is indeed a projection, since

$$P^{\perp}\left(P^{\perp}\left(\phi(\mathbf{x})\right)\right) = P^{\perp}\left(\phi(\mathbf{x})\right) - P\left(P^{\perp}\left(\phi(\mathbf{x})\right)\right) = P^{\perp}\left(\phi(\mathbf{x})\right),$$

while

$$\left\langle P^{\perp}\left(\phi(\mathbf{x})\right), \phi(\mathbf{x}) - P^{\perp}\left(\phi(\mathbf{x})\right)\right\rangle$$
$$= \left\langle P^{\perp}\left(\phi(\mathbf{x})\right), \phi(\mathbf{x}) - \left(\phi(\mathbf{x}) - P\left(\phi(\mathbf{x})\right)\right)\right\rangle$$
$$= \langle\left(\phi(\mathbf{x}) - P\left(\phi(\mathbf{x})\right)\right), P\left(\phi(\mathbf{x})\right)\rangle = 0.$$

∎

Projections and deflations The projection $P_{\mathbf{w}}\left(\phi(\mathbf{x})\right)$ of $\phi(\mathbf{x})$ onto $\mathbf{w}$ introduced above are onto a 1-dimensional subspace defined by the vector $\mathbf{w}$. If we assume that $\mathbf{w}$ is normalised, $P_{\mathbf{w}}\left(\phi(\mathbf{x})\right)$ can also be expressed as

$$P_{\mathbf{w}}\left(\phi(\mathbf{x})\right) = \mathbf{w}\mathbf{w}'\phi(\mathbf{x}).$$

Hence, its orthogonal projection $P_{\mathbf{w}}^{\perp}\left(\phi(\mathbf{x})\right)$ can be expressed as

$$P_{\mathbf{w}}^{\perp}\left(\phi(\mathbf{x})\right) = \left(\mathbf{I} - \mathbf{w}\mathbf{w}'\right)\phi(\mathbf{x}).$$

If we have a data matrix $\mathbf{X}$ with rows $\phi(\mathbf{x}_i)$, $i = 1, \ldots, \ell$, then deflating the matrix $\mathbf{X}'\mathbf{X}$ with respect to one of its eigenvectors $\mathbf{w}$ is equivalent to projecting the data using $P_{\mathbf{w}}^{\perp}$. This follows from the observation that projecting the data creates the new data matrix

$$\tilde{\mathbf{X}} = \mathbf{X}\left(\mathbf{I} - \mathbf{ww}'\right)' = \mathbf{X}\left(\mathbf{I} - \mathbf{ww}'\right), \qquad (5.8)$$

so that

$$
\begin{aligned}
\tilde{\mathbf{X}}'\tilde{\mathbf{X}} &= \left(\mathbf{I} - \mathbf{ww}'\right)\mathbf{X}'\mathbf{X}\left(\mathbf{I} - \mathbf{ww}'\right) \\
&= \mathbf{X}'\mathbf{X} - \mathbf{ww}'\mathbf{X}'\mathbf{X} - \mathbf{X}'\mathbf{X}\mathbf{ww}' + \mathbf{ww}'\mathbf{X}'\mathbf{X}\mathbf{ww}' \\
&= \mathbf{X}'\mathbf{X} - \lambda\mathbf{ww}' - \lambda\mathbf{ww}' + \lambda\mathbf{ww}'\mathbf{ww}' \\
&= \mathbf{X}'\mathbf{X} - \lambda\mathbf{ww}',
\end{aligned}
$$

where λ is the eigenvalue corresponding to $\mathbf{w}$.

The actual spread of the data may not be spherical as is implicitly assumed in the novelty detector derived in the previous section. We may indeed observe that the data lies in a subspace of the feature space of lower dimensionality.

We now consider how to find an orthonormal basis for such a subspace. More generally we seek a subspace that fits the data in the sense that the distances between data items and their projections into the subspace are small. Again we would like to compute the projections of points into subspaces of the feature space implicitly using only information provided by the kernel.

Gram–Schmidt orthonormalisation We begin by considering a well-known method of deriving an orthonormal basis known as the *Gram–Schmidt* procedure. Given a sequence of linearly independent vectors the method creates the basis by orthogonalising each vector to all of the earlier vectors. Hence, if we are given the vectors

$$\phi\left(\mathbf{x}_1\right), \phi\left(\mathbf{x}_2\right), \ldots, \phi\left(\mathbf{x}_\ell\right),$$

the first basis vector is chosen to be

$$\mathbf{q}_1 = \frac{\phi\left(\mathbf{x}_1\right)}{\|\phi\left(\mathbf{x}_1\right)\|}.$$

The ith vector is then obtained by subtracting from $\phi\left(\mathbf{x}_i\right)$ multiples of $\mathbf{q}_1, \ldots, \mathbf{q}_{i-1}$ in order to ensure it becomes orthogonal to each of them

$$\phi\left(\mathbf{x}_i\right) \longrightarrow \phi\left(\mathbf{x}_i\right) - \sum_{j=1}^{i-1} \langle \mathbf{q}_j, \phi\left(\mathbf{x}_i\right)\rangle \mathbf{q}_j = \left(\mathbf{I} - \mathbf{Q}_{i-1}\mathbf{Q}'_{i-1}\right)\phi\left(\mathbf{x}_i\right),$$

where $\mathbf{Q}_i$ is the matrix whose i columns are the first i vectors $\mathbf{q}_1, \ldots, \mathbf{q}_i$. The matrix $\left(\mathbf{I} - \mathbf{Q}_i\mathbf{Q}'_i\right)$ is a projection matrix onto the orthogonal complement of the space spanned by the first i vectors $\mathbf{q}_1, \ldots, \mathbf{q}_i$. Finally, if we let

$$\nu_i = \left\| \left(\mathbf{I} - \mathbf{Q}_{i-1}\mathbf{Q}'_{i-1} \right) \phi\left(\mathbf{x}_i\right) \right\|,$$

the next basis vector is obtained by normalising the projection

$$\mathbf{q}_i = \nu_i^{-1} \left(\mathbf{I} - \mathbf{Q}_{i-1}\mathbf{Q}'_{i-1} \right) \phi\left(\mathbf{x}_i\right).$$

It follows that

$$
\begin{aligned}
\phi\left(\mathbf{x}_i\right) &= \mathbf{Q}_{i-1}\mathbf{Q}'_{i-1}\phi\left(\mathbf{x}_i\right) + \nu_i\mathbf{q}_i = \mathbf{Q}_i \begin{pmatrix} \mathbf{Q}'_{i-1}\phi\left(\mathbf{x}_i\right) \\ \nu_i \end{pmatrix} \\
&= \mathbf{Q} \begin{pmatrix} \mathbf{Q}'_{i-1}\phi\left(\mathbf{x}_i\right) \\ \nu_i \\ \mathbf{0}_{\ell-i} \end{pmatrix} = \mathbf{Q}\mathbf{r}_i,
\end{aligned}
$$

where $\mathbf{Q} = \mathbf{Q}_\ell$ is the matrix containing all the vectors $\mathbf{q}_i$ as columns. This implies that the matrix $\mathbf{X}$ containing the data vectors as rows can be decomposed as

$$\mathbf{X}' = \mathbf{Q}\mathbf{R},$$

where $\mathbf{R}$ is an upper triangular matrix with ith column

$$\mathbf{r}_i = \begin{pmatrix} \mathbf{Q}'_{i-1}\phi\left(\mathbf{x}_i\right) \\ \nu_i \\ \mathbf{0}_{\ell-i} \end{pmatrix}.$$

We can also view $\mathbf{r}_i$ as the respresentation of $\mathbf{x}_i$ in the basis

$$\{\mathbf{q}_1, \ldots, \mathbf{q}_\ell\}.$$

QR-decomposition This is the well-known *QR-decomposition* of the matrix $\mathbf{X}'$ into the product of an orthonormal matrix $\mathbf{Q}$ and upper triangular matrix $\mathbf{R}$ with positive diagonal entries.

We now consider the application of this technique in a kernel-defined feature space. Consider the matrix $\mathbf{X}$ whose rows are the projections of a dataset

$$S = \{\mathbf{x}_1, \ldots, \mathbf{x}_\ell\}$$

into a feature space defined by a kernel κ with corresponding feature mapping ϕ. Applying the Gram–Schmidt method in the feature space would lead to the decomposition

$$\mathbf{X}' = \mathbf{Q}\mathbf{R},$$

defined above. This gives the following decomposition of the kernel matrix

$$\mathbf{K} = \mathbf{XX'} = \mathbf{R'Q'QR} = \mathbf{R'R}.$$

Definition 5.10 This is the *Cholesky decomposition* of a positive semi-definite matrix into the product of a lower triangular and upper triangular matrix that are transposes of each other.

Since the Cholesky decomposition is unique, performing a Cholesky decomposition of the kernel matrix is equivalent to performing Gram–Schmidt orthonormalisation in the feature space and hence we can view Cholesky decomposition as the dual implementation of the Gram–Schmidt orthonormalisation. ∎

Cholesky implementation The computation of the (j, i)th entry in the matrix $\mathbf{R}$ corresponds to evaluating the inner product between the ith vector $\phi(\mathbf{x}_i)$ with the jth basis vector $\mathbf{q}_j$, for $i > j$. Since we can decompose $\phi(\mathbf{x}_i)$ into a component lying in the subspace spanned by the basis vectors up to the jth for which we have already computed the inner products and the perpendicular complement, this inner product is given by

$$\nu_j \langle \mathbf{q}_j, \phi(\mathbf{x}_i) \rangle = \langle \phi(\mathbf{x}_j), \phi(\mathbf{x}_i) \rangle - \sum_{t=1}^{j-1} \langle \mathbf{q}_t, \phi(\mathbf{x}_j) \rangle \langle \mathbf{q}_t, \phi(\mathbf{x}_i) \rangle,$$

which corresponds to the Cholesky computation performed for $j = 1, \ldots, \ell$

$$\mathbf{R}_{ji} = \nu_j^{-1} \left(\mathbf{K}_{ji} - \sum_{t=1}^{j-1} \mathbf{R}_{tj} \mathbf{R}_{ti} \right), \ i = j+1, \ldots, \ell,$$

where ν_j is obtained by keeping track of the residual norm squared d_i of the vectors in the orthogonal complement. This is done by initialising with the diagonal of the kernel matrix

$$d_i = \mathbf{K}_{ii}$$

and updating with

$$d_i \leftarrow d_i - \mathbf{R}_{ji}^2$$

as the ith entry is computed. The value of ν_j is then the residual norm of the next vector; that is

$$\nu_j = \sqrt{d_j}.$$

Note that the new representation of the data as the columns of the matrix $\mathbf{R}$ gives rise to exactly the same kernel matrix. Hence, we have found a new projection function

$$\hat{\phi} : \mathbf{x}_i \longmapsto \mathbf{r}_i$$

which gives rise to the same kernel matrix on the set S; that is

$$\kappa(\mathbf{x}_i, \mathbf{x}_j) = \hat{\kappa}(\mathbf{x}_i, \mathbf{x}_j) = \left\langle \hat{\phi}(\mathbf{x}_i), \hat{\phi}(\mathbf{x}_j) \right\rangle, \text{ for all } i, j = 1, \ldots, \ell.$$

This new projection maps data into the coordinate system determined by the orthonormal basis $\mathbf{q}_1, \ldots, \mathbf{q}_\ell$. Hence, to compute $\hat{\phi}$ and thus $\hat{\kappa}$ for new examples, we must evaluate the projections onto these basis vectors in the feature space. This can be done by effectively computing an additional column denoted by $\mathbf{r}$ of an extension of the matrix $\mathbf{R}$ from an additional column of $\mathbf{K}$ denoted by $\mathbf{k}$

$$\mathbf{r}_j = \nu_j^{-1}\left(\mathbf{k}_j - \sum_{t=1}^{j-1} R_{tj}\mathbf{r}_t \right), \ j = 1, \ldots, \ell.$$

We started this section by asking how we might find a basis for the data when it lies in a subspace, or close to a subspace, of the feature space. If the data are not linearly independent the corresponding residual norm d_j will be equal to 0 when we come to process an example that lies in the subspace spanned by the earlier examples. This will occur if and only if the data lies in a subspace of dimension $j-1$, which is equivalent to saying that the rank of the matrix $\mathbf{X}$ is $j-1$. But this is equivalent to deriving

$$\mathbf{K} = \mathbf{R}'\mathbf{R}$$

with $\mathbf{R}$ a $(j-1) \times \ell$ matrix, or in other words to $\mathbf{K}$ having rank $j-1$. We have shown the following result.

Proposition 5.11 *The rank of the dataset S is equal to that of the kernel matrix $\mathbf{K}$ and by symmetry that of the matrix $\mathbf{X}'\mathbf{X}$.*

We can therefore compute the rank of the data in the feature space by computing the rank of the kernel matrix that only involves the inner products between the training points. Of course in high-dimensional feature spaces we may expect the rank to be equal to the number of data points. If we use the Gaussian kernel this will always be the case if the points are distinct.

Clearly the size of d_j indicates how independent the next example is from the examples processed so far. If we wish to capture the most important dimensions of the data points it is therefore natural to vary the order that the examples are processed in the Cholesky decomposition by always choosing the point with largest residual norm, while those with small residuals are eventually ignored altogether. This leads to a reordering of the order in which the examples are processed. The reordering is computed by the statement

$$[\texttt{a}, \texttt{I}(\texttt{j}+1)] \;=\; \texttt{max}(\texttt{d});$$

in the Matlab code below with the array I storing the permutation.

This approach corresponds to pivoting in Cholesky decomposition, while failing to include all the examples is referred to as an *incomplete Cholesky decomposition*. The corresponding approach in the feature space is known as *partial Gram–Schmidt orthonormalisation*.

Algorithm 5.12 [Cholesky decomposition or dual Gram–Schmidt] Matlab code for the incomplete Cholesky decomposition, equivalent to the dual partial Gram–Schmidt orthonormalisation is given in Code Fragment 5.4. ∎

Notice that the index array I stores the indices of the vectors in the order in which they are chosen, while the parameter η allows for the possibility that the data is only approximately contained in a subspace. The residual norms will all be smaller than this value, while the dimension of the feature space obtained is given by T. If η is set small enough then T will be equal to the rank of the data in the feature space. Hence, we can determine the rank of the data in the feature space using Code Fragment 5.4.

The partial Gram–Schmidt procedure can be viewed as a method of reducing the size of the residuals by a greedy strategy of picking the largest at each iteration. This naturally raises the question of whether smaller residuals could result if the subspace was chosen globally to minimise the residuals. The solution to this problem will be given by choosing the eigensubspace that will be shown to minimise the sum-squared residuals. The next section begins to examine this approach to assessing the spread of the data in the feature space, though final answers to these questions will be given in Chapter 6.

5.3 Measuring the spread of the data

The mean estimates where the data is centred, while the variance measures the extent to which the data is spread. We can compare two zero-mean uni-

```
% original kernel matrix stored in variable K
% of size ell x ell.
% new features stored in matrix R of size T x ell
% eta gives threshold residual cutoff
j = 0;
R = zeros(ell,ell);
d = diag(K);
[a,I(j+1)] = max(d);
while a > eta
    j = j + 1;
    nu(j) = sqrt(a);
    for i = 1:ell
        R(j,i) = (K(I(j),i) - R(:,i)'*R(:,I(j)))/nu(j);
        d(i) = d(i) - R(j,i)^2;
    end
    [a,I(j+1)] = max(d);
end
T = j;
R = R(1:T,:);
% for new example with vector of inner products
% k of size ell x 1 to compute new features r
r = zeros(T, 1);
for j=1:T
    r(j) = (k(I(j)) - r'*R(:,I(j)))/nu(j);
end
```

Code Fragment 5.4. Matlab code for performing incomplete Cholesky decomposition or dual partial Gram–Schmidt orthogonalisation.

variate random variables using a measure known as the *covariance* defined to be the expectation of their product

$$\mathrm{cov}\,(x,y) = \mathbb{E}_{xy}[xy].$$

Frequently, raw feature components from different sensors are difficult to compare because the units of measurement are different. It is possible to compensate for this by standardising the features into unitless quantities. The standardisation $\hat{x}$ of a feature x is

$$\hat{x} = \frac{x - \mu_x}{\sigma_x},$$

where μ_x and σ_x are the mean and standard deviation of the random variable x. The measure $\hat{x}$ is known as the standard score. The covariance

$$\mathbb{E}_{\hat{x}\hat{y}}[\hat{x}\hat{y}]$$

of two such scores gives a measure of *correlation*

$$\rho_{xy} = \text{corr}(x, y) = \mathbb{E}_{xy}\left[\frac{(x - \mu_x)(y - \mu_y)}{\sigma_x \sigma_y}\right]$$

between two random variables. A standardised score $\hat{x}$ has the property that $\mu_{\hat{x}} = 0$, $\sigma_{\hat{x}} = 1$. Hence, the correlation can be seen as the cosine of the angle between the standardised scores. The value ρ_{xy} is also known as the Pearson correlation coefficient. Note that for two random vectors x and y the following three conditions are equivalent:

$$\rho_{xy} = 1;$$
$$\hat{x} = \hat{y};$$
$$y = b + wx \text{ for some } b \text{ and for some } w > 0.$$

Similarly $\rho_{xy} = -1$ if and only if $\hat{x} = -\hat{y}$ and the same holds with a negative w. This means that by comparing their standardised scores we can measure for linear correlations between two (univariate) random variables. In general we have

$$\rho_{xy} = \begin{cases} 0; & \text{if the two variables are linearly uncorrelated,} \\ \pm 1; & \text{if there is an exact linear relation between them.} \end{cases}$$

More generally

$$|\rho_{xy}| \approx 1 \text{ if and only if } y \approx b + wx,$$

and we talk about positive and negative linear correlations depending on the sign of ρ_{xy}. Hence, we can view $|\rho_{xy}|$ as an indicator for the presence of a pattern function of the form $g(x, y) = y - b - wx$.

The above observations suggest the following preprocessing might be helpful if we are seeking linear models.

Algorithm 5.13 [Standardising data] When building a linear model it is natural to standardise the features in order to make linear relations more apparent. Code Fragment 5.5 gives Matlab code to standardise input features by estimating the mean and standard deviation over a training set.

∎

Variance of projections The above standardisation treats each coordinate independently. We will now consider measures that can take into account the interaction between different features. As discussed above if we are working with a kernel-induced feature space, we cannot access the coordinates of the points $\phi(S)$. Despite this we can learn about the spread in the

```
% original data stored in ell x N matrix X
% output uses the same variable X
% M is a row vector storing the column averages
% SD stores the column standard deviations
ell = size(X,1);
M = sum(X) / ell;
M2 = sum(X.^2)/ell;
SD = sqrt(M2 - M.^2);
X = (X - ones(ell,1)*M)./(ones(ell,1)*SD);
```

Code Fragment 5.5. Matlab code for standardising data.

feature space. Consider the $\ell \times N$ matrix $\mathbf{X}$ whose rows are the projections of the training points into the N-dimensional feature space

$$\mathbf{X} = \left[\begin{array}{cccc} \phi(\mathbf{x}_1) & \phi(\mathbf{x}_2) & \cdots & \phi(\mathbf{x}_\ell) \end{array}\right]'.$$

Note that the feature vectors themselves are column vectors. If we assume that the data has zero mean or has already been centred then the covariance matrix $\mathbf{C}$ has entries

$$\mathbf{C}_{st} = \frac{1}{\ell}\sum_{i=1}^{\ell} \phi(\mathbf{x}_i)_s \phi(\mathbf{x}_i)_t, \ s,t = 1,\ldots,N.$$

Observe that

$$\ell \mathbf{C}_{st} = \sum_{i=1}^{\ell} \phi(\mathbf{x}_i)_s \phi(\mathbf{x}_i)_t = \left(\sum_{i=1}^{\ell} \phi(\mathbf{x}_i)\phi(\mathbf{x}_i)'\right)_{st} = (\mathbf{X}'\mathbf{X})_{st}.$$

If we consider a unit vector $\mathbf{v} \in \mathbb{R}^N$ then the expected value of the norm of the projection $\|P_{\mathbf{v}}(\phi(\mathbf{x}))\| = \mathbf{v}'\phi(\mathbf{x})/(\mathbf{v}'\mathbf{v}) = \mathbf{v}'\phi(\mathbf{x})$ of the training points onto the space spanned by $\mathbf{v}$ is

$$\mu_{\mathbf{v}} = \hat{\mathbb{E}}\left[\|P_{\mathbf{v}}(\phi(\mathbf{x}))\|\right] = \hat{\mathbb{E}}\left[\mathbf{v}'\phi(\mathbf{x})\right] = \mathbf{v}'\hat{\mathbb{E}}\left[\phi(\mathbf{x})\right] = 0,$$

where we have again used the fact that the data is centred. Hence, if we wish to compute the variance of the norms of the projections onto $\mathbf{v}$ we have

$$\sigma_{\mathbf{v}}^2 = \hat{\mathbb{E}}\left[(\|P_{\mathbf{v}}(\phi(\mathbf{x}))\| - \mu_{\mathbf{v}})^2\right] = \hat{\mathbb{E}}\left[\|P_{\mathbf{v}}(\phi(\mathbf{x}))\|^2\right] = \frac{1}{\ell}\sum_{i=1}^{\ell}\|P_{\mathbf{v}}(\phi(\mathbf{x}_i))\|^2$$

but we have

$$\frac{1}{\ell}\sum_{i=1}^{\ell}\|P_{\mathbf{v}}(\phi(\mathbf{x}))\|^2 = \frac{1}{\ell}\sum_{i=1}^{\ell}\mathbf{v}'\phi(\mathbf{x}_i)\phi(\mathbf{x}_i)'\mathbf{v} = \hat{\mathbb{E}}\left[\mathbf{v}'\phi(\mathbf{x}_i)\phi(\mathbf{x}_i)'\mathbf{v}\right] \quad (5.9)$$

$$= \frac{1}{\ell}\mathbf{v}'\mathbf{X}'\mathbf{X}\mathbf{v}.$$

So the covariance matrix contains the information needed to compute the variance of the data along any projection direction. If the data has not been centred we must subtract the square of the mean projection since the variance is given by

$$
\sigma_{\mathbf{v}}^2 = \hat{\mathbb{E}}\left[\left(\|P_{\mathbf{v}}\left(\phi(\mathbf{x})\right)\| - \mu_{\mathbf{v}}\right)^2\right] = \hat{\mathbb{E}}\left[\|P_{\mathbf{v}}\left(\phi(\mathbf{x})\right)\|^2\right] - \mu_{\mathbf{v}}^2
$$
$$
= \frac{1}{\ell}\mathbf{v}'\mathbf{X}'\mathbf{X}\mathbf{v} - \left(\frac{1}{\ell}\mathbf{v}'\mathbf{X}'\mathbf{j}\right)^2,
$$

where $\mathbf{j}$ is the all 1s vector.

Variance of projections in a feature space It is natural to ask if we can compute the variance of the projections onto a fixed direction $\mathbf{v}$ in the feature space using only inner product information. Clearly, we must choose the direction $\mathbf{v}$ so that we can express it as a linear combination of the projections of the training points

$$
\mathbf{v} = \sum_{i=1}^{\ell} \alpha_i \phi(\mathbf{x}_i) = \mathbf{X}'\boldsymbol{\alpha}.
$$

For this $\mathbf{v}$ we can now compute the variance as

$$
\sigma_{\mathbf{v}}^2 = \frac{1}{\ell}\mathbf{v}'\mathbf{X}'\mathbf{X}\mathbf{v} - \left(\frac{1}{\ell}\mathbf{v}'\mathbf{X}'\mathbf{j}\right)^2 = \frac{1}{\ell}\boldsymbol{\alpha}'\mathbf{X}\mathbf{X}'\mathbf{X}\mathbf{X}'\boldsymbol{\alpha} - \left(\frac{1}{\ell}\boldsymbol{\alpha}'\mathbf{X}\mathbf{X}'\mathbf{j}\right)^2
$$
$$
= \frac{1}{\ell}\boldsymbol{\alpha}'\left(\mathbf{X}\mathbf{X}'\right)^2\boldsymbol{\alpha} - \frac{1}{\ell^2}\left(\boldsymbol{\alpha}'\mathbf{X}\mathbf{X}'\mathbf{j}\right)^2
$$
$$
= \frac{1}{\ell}\boldsymbol{\alpha}'\mathbf{K}^2\boldsymbol{\alpha} - \frac{1}{\ell^2}\left(\boldsymbol{\alpha}'\mathbf{K}\mathbf{j}\right)^2,
$$

again computable from the kernel matrix.

Being able to compute the variance of projections in the feature space suggests implementing a classical method for choosing a linear classifier known as the Fisher discriminant. Using the techniques we have developed we will be able to implement this algorithm in the space defined by the kernel.

5.4 Fisher discriminant analysis I

The Fisher discriminant is a classification function

$$
f(x) = \text{sgn}\left(\langle \mathbf{w}, \phi(x) \rangle + b\right),
$$

where the weight vector $\mathbf{w}$ is chosen to maximise the quotient

$$J(\mathbf{w}) = \frac{\left(\mu_{\mathbf{w}}^+ - \mu_{\mathbf{w}}^-\right)^2}{\left(\sigma_{\mathbf{w}}^+\right)^2 + \left(\sigma_{\mathbf{w}}^-\right)^2}, \qquad (5.10)$$

where $\mu_{\mathbf{w}}^+$ is the mean of the projection of the positive examples onto the direction $\mathbf{w}$, $\mu_{\mathbf{w}}^-$ the mean for the negative examples, and $\sigma_{\mathbf{w}}^+$, $\sigma_{\mathbf{w}}^-$ the corresponding standard deviations. Figure 5.2 illustrates the projection onto a particular direction $\mathbf{w}$ that gives good separation of the means with small variances of the positive and negative examples. The Fisher discriminant maximises the ratio between these quantities. The motivation for this choice

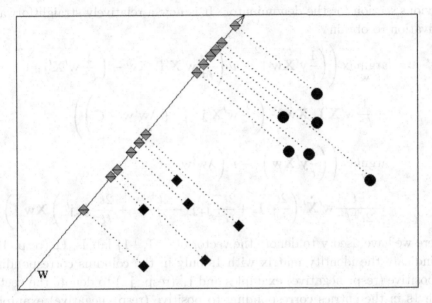

Fig. 5.2. The projection of points on to a direction $\mathbf{w}$ with positive and negative examples grouped separately.

is that the direction chosen maximises the separation of the means scaled according to the variances in that direction. Since we are dealing with kernel-defined feature spaces, it makes sense to introduce a regularisation on the norm of the weight vector $\mathbf{w}$ as motivated by Theorem 4.12. Hence, we consider the following optimisation.

Computation 5.14 [Regularised Fisher discriminant] The regularised Fisher discriminant chooses $\mathbf{w}$ to solve the following optimisation problem

$$\max_{\mathbf{w}} J(\mathbf{w}) = \frac{\left(\mu_{\mathbf{w}}^+ - \mu_{\mathbf{w}}^-\right)^2}{\left(\sigma_{\mathbf{w}}^+\right)^2 + \left(\sigma_{\mathbf{w}}^-\right)^2 + \lambda \|\mathbf{w}\|^2} \qquad (5.11)$$

■

First observe that the quotient is invariant under rescalings of the vector $\mathbf{w}$ so that we can constrain the denominator to have a fixed value C. Using a Lagrange multiplier ν we obtain the solution vector as

$$\mathbf{w}^\star = \operatorname*{argmax}_{\mathbf{w}} \left(\left(\hat{\mathbb{E}}\left[y\mathbf{w}'\phi(\mathbf{x}) \right] \right)^2 - \nu \left(\frac{1}{\ell^+}\mathbf{w}'\mathbf{X}'\mathbf{I}_+\mathbf{I}_+\mathbf{X}\mathbf{w} - \left(\frac{1}{\ell^+}\mathbf{w}'\mathbf{X}'\mathbf{j}_+ \right)^2 \right. \right.$$
$$\left. \left. + \frac{1}{\ell^-}\mathbf{w}'\mathbf{X}'\mathbf{I}_-\mathbf{I}_-\mathbf{X}\mathbf{w} - \left(\frac{1}{\ell^-}\mathbf{w}'\mathbf{X}'\mathbf{j}_- \right)^2 + \lambda\mathbf{w}'\mathbf{w} - C \right) \right),$$

where we have used a simplification of the numerator and the results of the previous section for the denominator. It is now a relatively straightforward derivation to obtain

$$\mathbf{w}^\star = \operatorname*{argmax}_{\mathbf{w}} \left(\left(\frac{1}{\ell}\mathbf{y}'\mathbf{X}\mathbf{w} \right)^2 - \nu \left(\frac{1}{\ell^+}\mathbf{w}'\mathbf{X}'\mathbf{I}_+\mathbf{X}\mathbf{w} - \left(\frac{1}{\ell^+}\mathbf{w}'\mathbf{X}'\mathbf{j}_+ \right)^2 \right. \right.$$
$$\left. \left. + \frac{1}{\ell^-}\mathbf{w}'\mathbf{X}'\mathbf{I}_-\mathbf{X}\mathbf{w} - \left(\frac{1}{\ell^-}\mathbf{w}'\mathbf{X}'\mathbf{j}_- \right)^2 + \lambda\mathbf{w}'\mathbf{w} - C \right) \right)$$
$$= \operatorname*{argmax}_{\mathbf{w}} \left(\left(\frac{1}{\ell}\mathbf{y}'\mathbf{X}\mathbf{w} \right)^2 - \nu \left(\lambda\mathbf{w}'\mathbf{w} - C \right. \right.$$
$$\left. \left. + \frac{\ell}{2\ell^+\ell^-}\mathbf{w}'\mathbf{X}' \left(\frac{2\ell^-}{\ell}\mathbf{I}_+ + \frac{2\ell^-}{\ell\ell^+}\mathbf{j}_+\mathbf{j}_+' - \frac{2\ell^+}{\ell}\mathbf{I}_- + \frac{2\ell^+}{\ell\ell^-}\mathbf{j}_-\mathbf{j}_-' \right) \mathbf{X}\mathbf{w} \right) \right),$$

where we have used $\mathbf{y}$ to denote the vector of $\{-1, +1\}$ labels, $\mathbf{I}_+$ (resp. $\mathbf{I}_-$) to indicate the identity matrix with 1s only in the columns corresponding to positive (resp. negative) examples and $\mathbf{j}_+$ (resp. $\mathbf{j}_-$) to denote the vector with 1s in the entries corresponding to positive (resp. negative) examples and otherwise 0s. Letting

$$\mathbf{B} = \mathbf{D} - \mathbf{C}^+ - \mathbf{C}^- \tag{5.12}$$

where $\mathbf{D}$ is a diagonal matrix with entries

$$\mathbf{D}_{ii} = \begin{cases} 2\ell^-/\ell & \text{if } y_i = +1 \\ 2\ell^+/\ell & \text{if } y_i = -1, \end{cases} \tag{5.13}$$

and $\mathbf{C}^+$ and $\mathbf{C}^-$ are given by

$$\mathbf{C}_{ij}^+ = \begin{cases} 2\ell^-/(\ell\ell^+) & \text{if } y_i = +1 = y_j \\ 0 & \text{otherwise} \end{cases} \tag{5.14}$$

and

$$\mathbf{C}_{ij}^- = \begin{cases} 2\ell^+/(\ell\ell^-) & \text{if } y_i = -1 = y_j \\ 0 & \text{otherwise,} \end{cases} \tag{5.15}$$

we can write

$$\mathbf{w}^\star = \operatorname*{argmax}_{\mathbf{w}} \left(\left(\frac{1}{\ell} \mathbf{y}'\mathbf{X}\mathbf{w} \right)^2 - \nu \left(\lambda \mathbf{w}'\mathbf{w} - C + \frac{\ell}{2\ell + \ell^-} \mathbf{w}'\mathbf{X}'\mathbf{B}\mathbf{X}\mathbf{w} \right) \right).$$

(5.16)

Varying C will only cause the solution to be rescaled since any rescaling of the weight vector will not affect the ratio of the numerator to the quantity constrained. If we now consider the optimisation

$$\mathbf{w}^\star = \operatorname*{argmax}_{\mathbf{w}} \left(\mathbf{y}'\mathbf{X}\mathbf{w} - \nu' \left(\lambda \mathbf{w}'\mathbf{w} - C + \frac{\ell}{2\ell + \ell^-} \mathbf{w}'\mathbf{X}'\mathbf{B}\mathbf{X}\mathbf{w} \right) \right), \quad (5.17)$$

it is clear that the solutions of problems (5.16) and (5.17) will be identical up to reversing the direction of $\mathbf{w}^\star$, since once the denominator is constrained to have value C the weight vector $\mathbf{w}$ that maximises (5.17) will maximise (5.16). This holds since the maxima of $\mathbf{y}'\mathbf{X}\mathbf{w}$ and $(\mathbf{y}'\mathbf{X}\mathbf{w})^2$ coincide with a possible change of sign of $\mathbf{w}$. Hence, with an appropriate re-definition of ν, λ and C

$$\mathbf{w}^\star = \operatorname*{argmax}_{\mathbf{w}} \left(\mathbf{y}'\mathbf{X}\mathbf{w} - \frac{\nu}{2} \mathbf{w}'\mathbf{X}'\mathbf{B}\mathbf{X}\mathbf{w} + C - \frac{\lambda\nu}{2} \mathbf{w}'\mathbf{w} \right).$$

Taking derivatives with respect to $\mathbf{w}$ we obtain

$$0 = \mathbf{X}'\mathbf{y} - \nu \mathbf{X}'\mathbf{B}\mathbf{X}\mathbf{w} - \lambda\nu\mathbf{w},$$

so that $\lambda\nu\mathbf{w} = \mathbf{X}'(\mathbf{y} - \nu\mathbf{B}\mathbf{X}\mathbf{w}),$

Dual expression This implies that we can express $\mathbf{w}$ in the dual form as a linear combination of the training examples $\mathbf{w} = \mathbf{X}'\boldsymbol{\alpha}$, where $\boldsymbol{\alpha}$ is given by

$$\boldsymbol{\alpha} = \frac{1}{\lambda\nu} (\mathbf{y} - \nu\mathbf{B}\mathbf{X}\mathbf{w}). \quad (5.18)$$

Substituting for $\mathbf{w}$ in equation (5.18) we obtain

$$\lambda\nu\boldsymbol{\alpha} = \mathbf{y} - \nu\mathbf{B}\mathbf{X}\mathbf{X}'\boldsymbol{\alpha} = \mathbf{y} - \nu\mathbf{B}\mathbf{K}\boldsymbol{\alpha}.$$

giving

$$(\nu\mathbf{B}\mathbf{K} + \lambda\nu\mathbf{I})\boldsymbol{\alpha} = \mathbf{y}.$$

Since the classification function is invariant to rescalings of the weight vector, we can rescale $\boldsymbol{\alpha}$ by ν to obtain

$$(\mathbf{B}\mathbf{K} + \lambda\mathbf{I})\boldsymbol{\alpha} = \mathbf{y}.$$

Notice the similarity with the ridge regression solution considered in Chapter 2, but here the real-valued outputs are replaced by the binary labels and the additional matrix $\mathbf{B}$ is included, though for balanced datasets this will be close to $\mathbf{I}$. In general the solution is given by

$$\boldsymbol{\alpha} = (\mathbf{BK} + \lambda \mathbf{I})^{-1} \mathbf{y},$$

so that the corresponding classification function is

$$h(\mathbf{x}) = \operatorname{sgn}\left(\sum_{i=1}^{\ell} \alpha_i \kappa(\mathbf{x}, \mathbf{x}_i) - b\right) = \operatorname{sgn}\left(\mathbf{k}'(\mathbf{BK} + \lambda \mathbf{I})^{-1} \mathbf{y} - b\right), \quad (5.19)$$

where $\mathbf{k}$ is the vector with entries $\kappa(\mathbf{x}, \mathbf{x}_i)$, $i = 1, \dots, \ell$ and b is an appropriate offset. The value of b is chosen so that $\mathbf{w}' \boldsymbol{\mu}^+ - b = b - \mathbf{w}' \boldsymbol{\mu}^-$, that is so that the decision boundary bisects the line joining the two centres of mass. Taking the weight vector $\mathbf{w} = \mathbf{X}' \boldsymbol{\alpha}$, we have

$$b = 0.5 \boldsymbol{\alpha}' \mathbf{X} \left(\frac{1}{\ell^+} \mathbf{X}' \mathbf{j}_+ + \frac{1}{\ell^-} \mathbf{X}' \mathbf{j}_-\right) = 0.5 \boldsymbol{\alpha}' \mathbf{XX}' \mathbf{t} = 0.5 \boldsymbol{\alpha}' \mathbf{Kt}, \quad (5.20)$$

where $\mathbf{t}$ is the vector with entries

$$t_i = \begin{cases} 1/\ell^+ & \text{if } y_i = +1 \\ 1/\ell^- & \text{if } y_i = -1. \end{cases} \quad (5.21)$$

We summarise in the following computation.

Computation 5.15 [Regularised kernel Fisher discriminant] The regularised kernel Fisher discriminant chooses the dual variables $\boldsymbol{\alpha}$ as follows

$$\boldsymbol{\alpha} = (\mathbf{BK} + \lambda \mathbf{I})^{-1} \mathbf{y},$$

where $\mathbf{K}$ is the kernel matrix, $\mathbf{B}$ is given by (5.12)-(5.15), and the resulting classification function is given by (5.19) and the threshold b by (5.20) and (5.21). ∎

Finally, we give a more explicit description of the dual algorithm.

Algorithm 5.16 [Dual Fisher discriminant] Matlab code for the dual Fisher discriminant algorithm is given in Code Fragment 5.6. ∎

Proposition 5.17 *Consider the classification training set*

$$S = \{(\mathbf{x}_1, y_1), \dots, (\mathbf{x}_\ell, y_\ell)\},$$

with a feature space implicitly defined by the kernel $\kappa(\mathbf{x}, \mathbf{z})$. *Let*

$$f(\mathbf{x}) = \mathbf{y}'(\mathbf{BK} + \lambda \mathbf{I})^{-1} \mathbf{k} - b,$$

```
% K is the kernel matrix of ell training points
% lambda the regularisation parameter
% y the labels
% The inner products between the training and t test points
% are stored in the matrix Ktest of dimension ell x t
% the true test labels are stored in ytruetest
ell = size(K,1);
ellplus = (sum(y) + ell)/2;
yplus = 0.5*(y + 1);
ellminus = ell - ellplus;
yminus = yplus - y;
t = size(Ktest,2);
rescale = ones(ell,1)+y*((ellminus-ellplus)/ell);
plusfactor = 2*ellminus/(ell*ellplus);
minusfactor = 2*ellplus/(ell*ellminus);
B = diag(rescale) - (plusfactor * yplus) * yplus'
     - (minusfactor * yminus) * yminus';
alpha = (B*K + lambda*eye(ell,ell))\y;
b = 0.25*(alpha'*K*rescale)/(ellplus*ellminus);
ytest = sign(Ktest'*alpha - b);
error = sum(abs(ytruetest - ytest))/(2*t)
```

Code Fragment 5.6. Kernel Fisher discriminant algorithm

where $\mathbf{K}$ is the $\ell \times \ell$ matrix with entries $\mathbf{K}_{ij} = \kappa(\mathbf{x}_i, \mathbf{x}_j)$, $\mathbf{k}$ is the vector with entries $\mathbf{k}_i = \kappa(\mathbf{x}_i, \mathbf{x})$, $\mathbf{B}$ is defined by equations (5.12)–(5.15) and b is defined by equations (5.20)–(5.21). Then the function $f(\mathbf{x})$ is equivalent to the hyperplane in the feature space implicitly defined by the kernel $\kappa(\mathbf{x}, \mathbf{z})$ that solves the Fisher discriminant problem (5.10) regularised by the parameter λ.

Remark 5.18 [Statistical properties] In this example of the kernel Fisher discriminant we did not obtain an explicit performance guarantee. If we observe that the function obtained has a non-zero margin γ we could apply Theorem 4.17 but this in itself does not motivate the particular choice of optimisation criterion. Theorem 4.12 as indicated above can motivate the regularisation of the norm of the weight vector, but a direct optimisation of the bound will lead to the more advanced algorithms considered in Chapter 7. ∎

5.5 Summary

- Many properties of the data in the embedding space can be calculated using only information obtained through kernel evaluations. These include distances between points, distances of points from the centre of mass, dimensionality of the subspace spanned by the data, and so on.

- Many transformations of the data in the embedding space can be realised through operations on the kernel matrix. For example, translating a dataset so that its centre of mass coincides with the origin corresponds to a set of operations on the kernel matrix; normalisation of the data produces a mapping to vectors of norm 1, and so on.

- Certain transformations of the kernel matrix correspond to performing projections in the kernel-defined feature space. Deflation corresponds to one such projection onto the orthogonal complement of a 1-dimensional subspace. Using these insights it is shown that incomplete Cholesky decomposition of the kernel matrix is a dual implementation of partial Gram–Schmidt orthonormalisation in the feature space.

- Three simple pattern analysis algorithms, one for novelty-detection and the other two for classification, have been described using the basic geometric relations derived in this chapter.

- The Fisher discriminant can be viewed as optimising a measure of the separation of the projections of the data onto a 1-dimensional subspace.

5.6 Further reading and advanced topics

In this chapter we have shown how to evaluate a number of properties of a set of points in a kernel defined feature space, typically the image of a generic dataset through the embedding map ϕ. This discussion is important both as a demonstration of techniques and methods that will be used in the following three chapters, and because the properties discussed can be directly used to analyse data, albeit in simple ways. In this sense, they are some of the first pattern analysis algorithms we have presented.

It is perhaps surprising how much information about a dataset can be obtained simply from its kernel matrix. The idea of using Mercer kernels as inner products in an embedding space in order to implement a learning algorithm dates back to Aizermann, Braverman and Rozonoer [1], who considered a dual implementation of the perceptron algorithm. However, its introduction to mainstream machine learning literature had to wait until 1992 with the first paper on support vector machines [16]. For some time after that paper, kernels were only used in combination with the maximal margin algorithm, while the idea that other types of algorithms could be implemented in this way began to emerge. The possibility of using kernels in any algorithm that can be formulated in terms of inner products was first mentioned in the context of kernel PCA (discussed in Chapter 6) [121], [20].

The centre of mass, the distance, the expected squared distance from the centre are all straight-forward applications of the kernel concept, and appear to have been introduced independently by several authors since the early days of research in this field. The connection between Parzen windows and the centres of mass of the two classes was pointed out by Schölkopf and is discussed in the book [120]. Also the normalisation procedure is well-known, while the centering procedure was first published in the paper [121]. Kernel Gram–Schmidt was introduced in [31] and can also be seen as an approximation of kernel PCA. The equivalent method of incomplete Cholesky decomposition was presented by [7]. See [49] for a discussion of QR decomposition.

Note that in Chapter 6 many of these ideas will be re-examined, including the kernel Fisher discriminant and kernel PCA, so more references can be found in Section 6.9.

For constantly updated pointers to online literature and free software see the book's companion website: www.kernel-methods.net.

6

Pattern analysis using eigen-decompositions

The previous chapter saw the development of some basic tools for working in a kernel-defined feature space resulting in some useful algorithms and techniques. The current chapter will extend the methods in order to understand the spread of the data in the feature space. This will be followed by examining the problem of identifying correlations between input vectors and target values. Finally, we discuss the task of identifying covariances between two different representations of the same object.

All of these important problems in kernel-based pattern analysis can be reduced to performing an eigen- or generalised eigen-analysis, that is the problem of finding solutions of the equation $\mathbf{Aw} = \lambda \mathbf{Bw}$ given symmetric matrices $\mathbf{A}$ and $\mathbf{B}$. These problems range from finding a set of k directions in the embedding space containing the maximum amount of variance in the data (principal components analysis (PCA)), through finding correlations between input and output representations (partial least squares (PLS)), to finding correlations between two different representations of the same data (canonical correlation analysis (CCA)). Also the Fisher discriminant analysis from Chapter 5 can be cast as a generalised eigenvalue problem.

The importance of this class of algorithms is that the generalised eigenvectors problem provides an efficient way of optimising an important family of cost functions; it can be studied with simple linear algebra and can be solved or approximated efficiently using a number of well-known techniques from computational algebra. Furthermore, we show that the problems can be solved in a kernel-defined feature space using a dual representation, that is, they only require information about inner products between datapoints.

6.1 Singular value decomposition

We have seen how we can sometimes learn something about the covariance matrix $\mathbf{C}$ by using the kernel matrix $\mathbf{K} = \mathbf{XX}'$. For example in the previous chapter the variances were seen to be given by the covariance matrix, but could equally be evaluated using the kernel matrix. The close connection between these two matrices will become more apparent if we consider the eigen-decomposition of both matrices

$$\ell\mathbf{C} = \mathbf{X}'\mathbf{X} = \mathbf{U}\tilde{\mathbf{\Lambda}}_N\mathbf{U}' \text{ and } \mathbf{K} = \mathbf{XX}' = \mathbf{V}\mathbf{\Lambda}_\ell\mathbf{V}',$$

where the columns $\mathbf{u}_i$ of the orthonormal matrix $\mathbf{U}$ are the eigenvectors of $\ell\mathbf{C}$, and the columns $\mathbf{v}_i$ of the orthonormal matrix $\mathbf{V}$ are the eigenvectors of $\mathbf{K}$. Now consider an eigenvector–eigenvalue pair $\mathbf{v}$, λ of $\mathbf{K}$. We have

$$\ell\mathbf{C}(\mathbf{X}'\mathbf{v}) = \mathbf{X}'\mathbf{XX}'\mathbf{v} = \mathbf{X}'\mathbf{Kv} = \lambda\mathbf{X}'\mathbf{v},$$

implying that $\mathbf{X}'\mathbf{v}$, λ is an eigenvector–eigenvalue pair for $\ell\mathbf{C}$. Furthermore, the norm of $\mathbf{X}'\mathbf{v}$ is given by

$$\|\mathbf{X}'\mathbf{v}\|^2 = \mathbf{v}'\mathbf{XX}'\mathbf{v} = \lambda,$$

so that the corresponding normalised eigenvector of $\ell\mathbf{C}$ is $\mathbf{u} = \lambda^{-1/2}\mathbf{X}'\mathbf{v}$. There is a symmetry here since we also have that

$$\lambda^{-1/2}\mathbf{Xu} = \lambda^{-1}\mathbf{XX}'\mathbf{v} = \mathbf{v}.$$

We can summarise these relations as follows

$$\mathbf{u} = \lambda^{-1/2}\mathbf{X}'\mathbf{v} \text{ and } \mathbf{v} = \lambda^{-1/2}\mathbf{Xu}.$$

We can deflate both $\ell\mathbf{C}$ and $\mathbf{K}$ of the corresponding eigenvalues by making the following deflation of $\mathbf{X}$:

$$\mathbf{X} \longmapsto \tilde{\mathbf{X}} = \mathbf{X} - \mathbf{vv}'\mathbf{X} = \mathbf{X} - \lambda^{1/2}\mathbf{vu}' = \mathbf{X} - \mathbf{Xuu}'. \tag{6.1}$$

This follows from the equalities

$$\tilde{\mathbf{X}}\tilde{\mathbf{X}}' = (\mathbf{X} - \mathbf{vv}'\mathbf{X})(\mathbf{X} - \mathbf{vv}'\mathbf{X})' = \mathbf{XX}' - \lambda\mathbf{vv}',$$

and

$$\tilde{\mathbf{X}}'\tilde{\mathbf{X}} = (\mathbf{X} - \mathbf{vv}'\mathbf{X})'(\mathbf{X} - \mathbf{vv}'\mathbf{X}) = \mathbf{X}'\mathbf{X} - \mathbf{X}'\mathbf{vv}'\mathbf{X} = \mathbf{X}'\mathbf{X} - \lambda\mathbf{uu}'.$$

Hence, the first $t = \operatorname{rank}(\mathbf{XX}') \leq \min(N, \ell)$ columns $\mathbf{U}_t$ of $\mathbf{U}$ can be chosen as

$$\mathbf{U}_t = \mathbf{X}'\mathbf{V}_t\mathbf{\Lambda}_t^{-1/2}, \tag{6.2}$$

where we assume the t non-zero eigenvalues of $\mathbf{K}$ and $\ell\mathbf{C}$ appear in descending order. But by the symmetry of $\ell\mathbf{C}$ and $\mathbf{K}$ these are the only non-zero eigenvalues of $\ell\mathbf{C}$, since we can transform any eigenvector–eigenvalue pair $\mathbf{u}$, λ of $\ell\mathbf{C}$ to an eigenvector–eigenvalue pair $\mathbf{Xu}$, λ of $\mathbf{K}$. It follows, as we have already seen, that

$$t = \text{rank}(\mathbf{XX'}) = \text{rank}(\mathbf{X'X}).$$

By extending $\mathbf{U}_t$ to $\mathbf{U}$ and $\mathbf{\Lambda}_t^{1/2}$ to an $N \times \ell$ matrix whose additional entries are all zero, we obtain the *singular value decomposition (SVD)* of the matrix $\mathbf{X'}$ defined as a decomposition

$$\mathbf{X'} = \mathbf{U\Sigma V'},$$

where $\mathbf{\Sigma}$ is an $N \times \ell$ matrix with all entries 0 except the leading diagonal which has entries $\sigma_i = \sqrt{\lambda_i}$ satisfying $\sigma_1 \geq \sigma_2 \geq \cdots \geq \sigma_t > 0$ for $t = \text{rank}(\mathbf{X}) \leq \min(N, \ell)$ with $\mathbf{U}$ and $\mathbf{V}$ square matrices satisfying

$$\mathbf{V'V} = \mathbf{I} \quad \text{so that} \quad \mathbf{V'} = \mathbf{V}^{-1} \text{ and similarly } \mathbf{U'} = \mathbf{U}^{-1},$$

also known as *orthogonal* matrices.

Consequences of singular value decomposition There are a number of interesting consequences. Notice how equation (6.2) implies a dual representation for the jth eigenvector $\mathbf{u}_j$ of $\ell\mathbf{C}$ with the coefficients given by the corresponding eigenvector $\mathbf{v}_j$ of $\mathbf{K}$ scaled by $\lambda_j^{-1/2}$, that is

$$\mathbf{u}_j = \lambda_j^{-1/2} \sum_{i=1}^{\ell} (\mathbf{v}_j)_i \, \phi(\mathbf{x}_i) = \sum_{i=1}^{\ell} \alpha_i^j \phi(\mathbf{x}_i), \; j = 1, \ldots, t,$$

where the dual variables $\boldsymbol{\alpha}^j$ for the jth vector $\mathbf{u}_j$ are given by

$$\boldsymbol{\alpha}^j = \lambda_j^{-1/2} \mathbf{v}_j. \tag{6.3}$$

and $\mathbf{v}_j$, λ_j are the jth eigenvector–eigenvalue pair of the kernel matrix.

It is important to remark that if we wish to compute the projection of a new data point $\phi(\mathbf{x})$ onto the direction $\mathbf{u}_j$ in the feature space, this is given by

$$P_{\mathbf{u}_j}(\phi(\mathbf{x})) \;=\; \mathbf{u}_j' \phi(\mathbf{x}) = \left\langle \sum_{i=1}^{\ell} \alpha_i^j \phi(\mathbf{x}_i), \phi(\mathbf{x}) \right\rangle = \sum_{i=1}^{\ell} \alpha_i^j \langle \phi(\mathbf{x}_i), \phi(\mathbf{x}) \rangle$$

$$= \sum_{i=1}^{\ell} \alpha_i^j \kappa(\mathbf{x}_i, \mathbf{x}), \tag{6.4}$$

Hence we will be able to project new data onto the eigenvectors in the feature space by performing an eigen-decomposition of the kernel matrix. We will present the details of this algorithm in Section 6.2.1 after introducing primal principal components analysis in the next section.

Remark 6.1 [Centering not needed] Although the definition of the covariance matrix assumes the data to be centred, none of the derivations given in this section make use of this fact. Hence, we need not assume that the covariance matrix is computed for centred data to obtain dual representations of the projections. ∎

Remark 6.2 [Notation conventions] We have used the notation $\mathbf{u}_j$ for the primal eigenvectors in contrast to our usual $\mathbf{w}_j$. This is to maintain consistency with the standard notation for the singular value decomposition of a matrix. Note that we have used the standard notation for the dual variables. ∎

6.2 Principal components analysis

In the previous chapter we saw how the variance in any fixed direction in the feature space could be measured using only the kernel matrix. This made it possible to find the Fisher discriminant function in a kernel-defined feature space by appropriate manipulation of the kernel matrix. We now consider finding a direction that maximises the variance in the feature space.

Maximising variance If we assume that the data has been centred in the feature space using for example Code Fragment 5.2, then we can compute the variance of the projection onto a normalised direction $\mathbf{w}$ as

$$\frac{1}{\ell} \sum_{i=1}^{\ell} \left(P_{\mathbf{w}} \left(\phi(\mathbf{x}_i) \right) \right)^2 = \hat{\mathbb{E}} \left[\mathbf{w}' \phi(\mathbf{x}) \phi(\mathbf{x})' \mathbf{w} \right] = \mathbf{w}' \hat{\mathbb{E}} \left[\phi(\mathbf{x}) \phi(\mathbf{x})' \right] \mathbf{w}$$

$$= \frac{1}{\ell} \mathbf{w}' \mathbf{X}' \mathbf{X} \mathbf{w} = \mathbf{w}' \mathbf{C} \mathbf{w},$$

where we again use $\hat{\mathbb{E}} \left[f(\mathbf{x}) \right]$ to denote the empirical mean of $f(\mathbf{x})$

$$\hat{\mathbb{E}} \left[f(\mathbf{x}) \right] = \frac{1}{\ell} \sum_{i=1}^{\ell} f(\mathbf{x}_i),$$

and $\mathbf{C} = \frac{1}{\ell} \mathbf{X}' \mathbf{X}$ is the covariance matrix of the data sample. Hence, finding the directions of maximal variance reduces to the following computation.

Computation 6.3 [Maximising variance] The direction that maximises the variance can be found by solving the following problem

$$\max_{\mathbf{w}} \quad \mathbf{w}'\mathbf{C}\mathbf{w}, \\ \text{subject to} \quad \|\mathbf{w}\|_2 = 1. \tag{6.5}$$

∎

Eigenvectors for maximising variance Consider the quotient

$$\rho(\mathbf{w}) = \frac{\mathbf{w}'C\mathbf{w}}{\mathbf{w}'\mathbf{w}}.$$

Since rescaling $\mathbf{w}$ has a quadratic effect on $\rho(\mathbf{w})$, the solution of (6.5) is the direction that maximises $\rho(\mathbf{w})$. Observe that this is the optimisation of the Raleigh quotient given in (3.2), where it was observed that the solution is given by the eigenvector corresponding to the largest eigenvalue with the value of $\rho(\mathbf{w})$ given by the eigenvalue. We can search for the direction of second largest variance in the orthogonal subspace, by looking for the largest eigenvector in the matrix obtained by deflating the matrix $\mathbf{C}$ with respect to $\mathbf{w}$. This gives the eigenvector of $\mathbf{C}$ corresponding to the second-largest eigenvalue. Repeating this step shows that the mutually orthogonal directions of maximum variance in order of decreasing size are given by the eigenvectors of $\mathbf{C}$.

Remark 6.4 [Explaining variance] We have seen that the size of the eigenvalue is equal to the variance in the chosen direction. Hence, if we project into a number of orthogonal directions the total variance is equal to the sum of the corresponding eigenvalues, making it possible to say what percentage of the overall variance has been captured, where the overall variance is given by the sum of all the eigenvalues, which equals the trace of the kernel matrix or the sum of the squared norms of the data.   ∎

Since rescaling a matrix does not alter the eigenvectors, but simply rescales the corresponding eigenvalues, we can equally search for the directions of maximum variance by analysing the matrix $\ell\mathbf{C} = \mathbf{X}'\mathbf{X}$. Hence, the first eigenvalue of the matrix $\ell\mathbf{C}$ equals the sum of the squares of the projections of the data into the first eigenvector in the feature space. A similar conclusion can be reached using the Courant–Fisher Theorem 3.6 applied to the first eigenvalue λ_1. By the above observations and equation (5.9) we have

$$\lambda_1(\ell\mathbf{C}) = \lambda_1(\mathbf{X}'\mathbf{X}) = \max_{\dim(T)=1} \min_{0\neq\mathbf{u}\in T} \frac{\mathbf{u}'\mathbf{X}'\mathbf{X}\mathbf{u}}{\mathbf{u}'\mathbf{u}}$$

$$= \max_{0 \neq \mathbf{u}} \frac{\mathbf{u}'\mathbf{X}'\mathbf{X}\mathbf{u}}{\mathbf{u}'\mathbf{u}} = \max_{0 \neq \mathbf{u}} \frac{\|\mathbf{X}\mathbf{u}\|^2}{\|\mathbf{u}\|^2} = \max_{0 \neq \mathbf{u}} \sum_{i=1}^{\ell} P_{\mathbf{u}} \left(\phi(\mathbf{x}_i) \right)^2$$

$$= \sum_{i=1}^{\ell} \|\phi(\mathbf{x}_i)\|^2 - \min_{0 \neq \mathbf{u}} \sum_{i=1}^{\ell} \left\| P_{\mathbf{u}}^{\perp} \left(\phi(\mathbf{x}_i) \right) \right\|^2,$$

where $P_{\mathbf{u}}^{\perp}(\phi(\mathbf{x}))$ is the projection of $\phi(\mathbf{x})$ into the space orthogonal to $\mathbf{u}$. The last equality follows from Pythagoras's theorem since the vectors are the sum of two orthogonal projections. Furthermore, the unit vector that realises the max and min is the first column $\mathbf{u}_1$ of the matrix $\mathbf{U}$ of the eigen-decomposition

$$\mathbf{X}'\mathbf{X} = \mathbf{U}\mathbf{\Lambda}\mathbf{U}'$$

of $\mathbf{X}'\mathbf{X}$.

A similar application of the Courant–Fisher Theorem 3.6 to the ith eigenvalue of the matrix $\ell\mathbf{C}$ gives

$$\lambda_i(\ell\mathbf{C}) = \lambda_i(\mathbf{X}'\mathbf{X}) = \max_{\dim(T)=i} \min_{0 \neq \mathbf{u} \in T} \frac{\mathbf{u}'\mathbf{X}'\mathbf{X}\mathbf{u}}{\mathbf{u}'\mathbf{u}}$$

$$= \max_{\dim(T)=i} \min_{0 \neq \mathbf{u} \in T} \sum_{j=1}^{\ell} P_{\mathbf{u}} \left(\phi(\mathbf{x}_j) \right)^2 = \sum_{j=1}^{\ell} P_{\mathbf{u}_i} \left(\phi(\mathbf{x}_j) \right)^2,$$

that is, the sum of the squares of the projections of the data in the direction of the ith eigenvector $\mathbf{u}_i$ in the feature space. If we consider projecting into the space U_k spanned by the first k eigenvectors, we have

$$\sum_{i=1}^{k} \lambda_i = \sum_{i=1}^{k} \sum_{j=1}^{\ell} P_{\mathbf{u}_i} \left(\phi(\mathbf{x}_j) \right)^2 = \sum_{j=1}^{\ell} \sum_{i=1}^{k} P_{\mathbf{u}_i} \left(\phi(\mathbf{x}_j) \right)^2 = \sum_{j=1}^{\ell} \| P_{U_k} \left(\phi(\mathbf{x}_j) \right) \|^2,$$

where we have used $P_{U_k}(\phi(\mathbf{x}))$ to denote the orthogonal projection of $\phi(\mathbf{x})$ into the subspace U_k. Furthermore, notice that if we consider $k = N$ the projection becomes the identity and we have

$$\sum_{i=1}^{N} \lambda_i = \sum_{j=1}^{\ell} \| P_{U_N} \left(\phi(\mathbf{x}_j) \right) \|^2 = \sum_{j=1}^{\ell} \| \phi(\mathbf{x}_j) \|^2, \tag{6.6}$$

something that also follows from the fact that the expressions are the traces of two similar matrices $\ell\mathbf{C}$ and $\mathbf{\Lambda}$.

Definition 6.5 [Principal components analysis] Principal components analysis (PCA) takes an initial subset of the principal axes of the training data and projects the data (both training and test) into the space spanned by this set of eigenvectors. We effectively preprocess a set of data by projecting it into the subspace spanned by the first k eigenvectors of the covariance matrix of the training set for some $k < \ell$. The new coordinates are known as the *principal coordinates* with the eigenvectors referred to as the *principal axes*.　■

Algorithm 6.6 [Primal principal components analysis] The primal principal components analysis algorithm performs the following computation:

input	Data $S = \{\mathbf{x}_1, \ldots, \mathbf{x}_\ell\} \subset \mathbb{R}^n$, dimension k.
process	$\boldsymbol{\mu} = \frac{1}{\ell} \sum_{i=1}^{\ell} \mathbf{x}_i$
	$\mathbf{C} = \frac{1}{\ell} \sum_{i=1}^{\ell} (\mathbf{x}_i - \boldsymbol{\mu})(\mathbf{x}_i - \boldsymbol{\mu})'$
	$[\mathbf{U}, \boldsymbol{\Lambda}] = \text{eig}(\ell \mathbf{C})$
	$\tilde{\mathbf{x}}_i = \mathbf{U}_k'\mathbf{x}_i,\; i = 1, \ldots, \ell.$
output	Transformed data $\tilde{S} = \{\tilde{\mathbf{x}}_1, \ldots, \tilde{\mathbf{x}}_\ell\}$.

　■

Remark 6.7 [Data lying in a subspace] Suppose that we have a data matrix in which one column is exactly constant for all examples. Clearly, this feature carries no information and will be set to zero by the centering operation. Hence, we can remove it by projecting onto the other dimensions without losing any information about the data. Data may in fact lie in a lower-dimensional subspace even if no individual feature is constant. This corresponds to the subspace not being aligned with any of the axes. The principal components analysis is nonetheless able to detect such a subspace. For example if the data has rank r then only the first r eigenvalues are non-zero and so the corresponding eigenvectors span the subspace containing the data. Therefore, projection into the first r principal axes exactly captures the training data.　■

Remark 6.8 [Denoising] More generally if the eigenvalues beyond the kth are small we can think of the data as being approximately k-dimensional, the features beyond the kth being approximately constant the data has little variance in these directions. In such cases it can make sense to project the data into the space spanned by the first k eigenvectors. It is possible that the variance in the dimensions we have removed is actually the result of noise, so that their removal can in some cases improve the representation of the data. Hence, performing principal components analysis can be regarded as an example of *denoising*.　■

Remark 6.9 [Applications to document analysis] We will also see in Chapter 10 how principal components analysis has a semantic focussing effect when applied in document analysis, with the eigenvectors representing concepts or themes inferred from the statistics of the data. The representation of an input in the principal coordinates can then be seen as an indication of how much it is related to these different themes. ∎

Remark 6.10 [PCA for visualisation] In Chapter 8 we will also see how a low-dimensional PCA projection can be used as a visualisation tool. In the case of non-numeric datasets this is particularly powerful since the data itself does not have a natural geometric structure, but only a high-dimensional implicit representation implied by the choice of kernel. Hence, in this case kernel PCA can be seen as a way of inferring a low-dimensional explicit geometric feature space that best captures the structure of the data. ∎

PCA explaining variance The eigenvectors of the covariance matrix ordered by decreasing eigenvalue correspond to directions of decreasing variance in the data, with the eigenvalue giving the amount of variance captured by its eigenvector. The larger the dimension k of the subspace U_k the greater percentage of the variance that is captured. These approximation properties are explored further in the alternative characterisation given below. We can view identification of a low-dimensional subspace capturing a high proportion of the variance as a pattern identified in the training data. This of course raises the question of whether the pattern is stable, that is, if the subspace we have identified will also capture the variance of new data arising from the same distribution. We will examine this statistical question once we have introduced a dual version of the algorithm.

Remark 6.11 [Centering not needed] The above derivation does not make use of the fact that the data is centred. It therefore follows that if we define

$$\mathbf{C} = \frac{1}{\ell}\mathbf{X}'\mathbf{X}$$

with $\mathbf{X}$ not centred, the same derivation holds as does the proposition given below. Centering the data has the advantage of reducing the overall sum of the eigenvalues, hence removing irrelevant variance arising from a shift of the centre of mass, but we can use principal components analysis on uncentred data. ∎

Alternative characterisations An alternative characterisation of the principal components (or principal axes) of a dataset will be important for the analysis of kernel PCA in later sections. We first introduce some additional notation. We have used $P_U(\phi(\mathbf{x}))$ to denote the orthogonal projection of an embedded point $\phi(\mathbf{x})$ into the subspace U. We have seen above that we are also interested in the error resulting from using the projection rather than the actual vector $\phi(\mathbf{x})$. This difference

$$P_U^\perp(\phi(\mathbf{x})) = \phi(\mathbf{x}) - P_U(\phi(\mathbf{x}))$$

is the projection into the orthogonal subspace and will be referred to as the *residual*. We can compute its norm from the norms of $\phi(\mathbf{x})$ and $P_U(\phi(\mathbf{x}))$ using Pythagoras's theorem. We will typically assess the quality of a projection by the average of the squared norms of the residuals of the training data

$$\frac{1}{\ell}\sum_{i=1}^{\ell}\left\|P_U^\perp(\phi(\mathbf{x}_i))\right\|^2 = \frac{1}{\ell}\|\boldsymbol{\xi}\|^2, \text{ where } \xi_i = \left\|P_U^\perp(\phi(\mathbf{x}_i))\right\|.$$

The next proposition shows that using the space spanned by the first k principal components of the covariance matrix minimises this quantity.

Proposition 6.12 *Given a training set S with covariance matrix $\mathbf{C}$, the orthogonal projection $P_{U_k}(\phi(\mathbf{x}))$ into the subspace U_k spanned by the first k eigenvectors of $\mathbf{C}$ is the k-dimensional orthogonal projection minimising the average squared distance between each training point and its image, in other words U_k solves the optimisation problem*

$$\begin{aligned}\min_U \quad & J^\perp(U) = \sum_{i=1}^{\ell}\left\|P_U^\perp(\phi(\mathbf{x}_i))\right\|_2^2 \\ \text{subject to} \quad & \dim U = k.\end{aligned} \tag{6.7}$$

Furthermore, the value of $J^\perp(U)$ at the optimum is given by

$$J^\perp(U) = \sum_{i=k+1}^{N}\lambda_i, \tag{6.8}$$

where $\lambda_1, \ldots, \lambda_N$ are the eigenvalues of the matrix $\ell\mathbf{C}$ in decreasing order.

Proof A demonstration of this fact will also illuminate various features of the principal coordinates. Since, $P_U(\phi(\mathbf{x}_i))$ is an orthogonal projection it follows from Pythagoras's theorem that

$$J^\perp(U) = \sum_{i=1}^{\ell}\left\|P_U^\perp(\phi(\mathbf{x}_i))\right\|_2^2 = \sum_{i=1}^{\ell}\|\phi(\mathbf{x}_i) - P_U(\phi(\mathbf{x}_i))\|_2^2$$

$$= \sum_{i=1}^{\ell} \|\phi(\mathbf{x}_i)\|^2 - \sum_{i=1}^{\ell} \|P_U(\phi(\mathbf{x}_i))\|_2^2. \tag{6.9}$$

Hence, the optimisation (6.7) has the same solution as the optimisation problem

$$\begin{array}{ll} \max_U & J(U) = \sum_{i=1}^{\ell} \|P_U(\phi(\mathbf{x}_i))\|_2^2 \\ \text{subject to} & \dim U = k. \end{array} \tag{6.10}$$

Let $\mathbf{w}^1, \ldots, \mathbf{w}^k$ be a basis for a general space U expressed in the principal axes. We can then evaluate $J(U)$ as follows

$$\begin{aligned} J(U) &= \sum_{i=1}^{\ell} \|P_U(\phi(\mathbf{x}_i))\|_2^2 = \sum_{i=1}^{\ell} \sum_{j=1}^{k} P_{\mathbf{w}^j}(\phi(\mathbf{x}_i))^2 \\ &= \sum_{j=1}^{k} \sum_{i=1}^{\ell} P_{\mathbf{w}^j}(\phi(\mathbf{x}_i))^2 = \sum_{j=1}^{k} \sum_{s=1}^{\ell} \left(\mathbf{w}_s^j\right)^2 \sum_{i=1}^{\ell} P_{\mathbf{u}_s}(\phi(\mathbf{x}_i))^2 \\ &= \sum_{j=1}^{k} \sum_{s=1}^{\ell} \left(\mathbf{w}_s^j\right)^2 \lambda_s = \sum_{s=1}^{\ell} \lambda_s \sum_{j=1}^{k} \left(\mathbf{w}_s^j\right)^2. \end{aligned}$$

Since, the $\mathbf{w}^j$ are orthogonal we must have

$$a_s = \sum_{j=1}^{k} \left(\mathbf{w}_s^j\right)^2 \leq 1,$$

for all s (consider extending to an orthonormal basis

$$\mathbf{W} = \left[\mathbf{w}^1 \cdots \mathbf{w}^k \mathbf{w}^{k+1} \cdots \mathbf{w}^\ell\right]$$

and observing that

$$\left(\mathbf{W}\mathbf{W}'\right)_{ss} = \sum_{j=1}^{\ell} \left(\mathbf{w}_s^j\right)^2 = 1$$

for all s), while

$$\sum_{s=1}^{\ell} a_s = \sum_{s=1}^{\ell} \sum_{j=1}^{k} \left(\mathbf{w}_s^j\right)^2 = \sum_{j=1}^{k} \sum_{s=1}^{\ell} \left(\mathbf{w}_s^j\right)^2 = k.$$

Therefore we have

$$J(U) = \sum_{s=1}^{\ell} \lambda_s a_s \leq \sum_{s=1}^{k} \lambda_s = J(U_k), \tag{6.11}$$

showing that U_k does indeed optimise both (6.7) and (6.10). The value of the optimum follows from (6.9), (6.11) and (6.6). $\qquad\square$

Principal axes capturing variance If we take $k = \ell$ nothing is lost in the projection and so summing all the eigenvalues gives us the sum of the norms of the feature vectors

$$\sum_{i=1}^{\ell} \|\phi(\mathbf{x}_i)\|^2 = \sum_{i=1}^{\ell} \lambda_i,$$

a fact that also follows from the invariance of the trace to the orthogonal transformation

$$\ell \mathbf{C} \longmapsto \ell \mathbf{U}'\mathbf{C}\mathbf{U} = \mathbf{\Lambda}_\ell.$$

The individual eigenvalues say how much of the sum of the norms squared lies in the space spanned by the ith eigenvector. By the above discussion the eigenvectors of the matrix $\mathbf{X}'\mathbf{X}$ give the directions of maximal variance of the data in descending order with the corresponding eigenvalues giving the size of the variance in that direction multiplied by ℓ. It is the fact that projection into the space U_k minimises the resulting average squared residual that motivates the use of these eigenvectors as a coordinate system.

We now consider how this analysis can be undertaken using only inner product information and hence exploiting a dual representation and kernels.

6.2.1 Kernel principal components analysis

Kernel PCA is the application of PCA in a kernel-defined feature space making use of the dual representation. Section 6.1 has demonstrated how projections onto the feature space eigenvectors can be computed through a dual representation computed from the eigenvectors and eigenvalues of the kernel matrix.

We now present the details of the kernel PCA algorithm before providing a stability analysis assessing when the resulting projection captures a stable pattern of the data. We continue to use U_k to denote the subspace spanned by the first k eigenvectors in the feature space. Using equation (6.4) we can compute the k-dimensional vector projection of new data into this subspace as

$$P_{U_k}\left(\phi(\mathbf{x})\right) = \left(\mathbf{u}_j'\phi(\mathbf{x})\right)_{j=1}^{k} = \left(\sum_{i=1}^{\ell} \alpha_i^j \kappa(\mathbf{x}_i, \mathbf{x})\right)_{j=1}^{k}, \qquad (6.12)$$

where

$$\boldsymbol{\alpha}^j = \lambda_j^{-1/2} \mathbf{v}_j$$

is given in terms of the corresponding eigenvector and eigenvalue of the kernel matrix. Equation (6.12) forms the basis of kernel PCA.

Algorithm 6.13 [Kernel PCA] The kernel PCA algorithm performs the following computation:

input	Data $S = \{\mathbf{x}_1, \ldots, \mathbf{x}_\ell\}$, dimension k.
process	$\mathbf{K}_{ij} = \kappa(\mathbf{x}_i, \mathbf{x}_j), \; i, j = 1, \ldots, \ell$
	$\mathbf{K} = \mathbf{K} - \frac{1}{\ell} \mathbf{j} \mathbf{j}' \mathbf{K} - \frac{1}{\ell} \mathbf{K} \mathbf{j} \mathbf{j}' + \frac{1}{\ell^2} (\mathbf{j}' \mathbf{K} \mathbf{j}) \mathbf{j} \mathbf{j}',$
	$[\mathbf{V}, \boldsymbol{\Lambda}] = \text{eig}(\mathbf{K})$
	$\boldsymbol{\alpha}^j = \frac{1}{\sqrt{\lambda_j}} \mathbf{v}_j, \; j = 1, \ldots, k.$
	$\tilde{\mathbf{x}}_i = \left(\sum_{i=1}^\ell \alpha_i^j \kappa(\mathbf{x}_i, \mathbf{x}) \right)_{j=1}^k$
output	Transformed data $\tilde{S} = \{\tilde{\mathbf{x}}_1, \ldots, \tilde{\mathbf{x}}_\ell\}$.

The Matlab code for this computation is given in Code Fragment 6.1. ∎

Figure 6.1 shows the first principal direction as a shading level for the sample data shown using primal PCA. Figure 6.2 shows the same data analysed using kernel PCA with a nonlinear kernel.

6.2.2 Stability of principal components analysis

The critical question for assessing the performance of kernel PCA is the extent to which the projection captures new data drawn according to the same distribution as the training data. The last line of the Matlab code in Code Fragment 6.1 computes the average residual of the test data. We would like to ensure that this is not much larger than the average residual of the training data given by the expression in the comment eight lines earlier. Hence, we assess the stability of kernel PCA through the pattern function

$$\begin{aligned} f(\mathbf{x}) &= \left\| P_{U_k}^\perp(\boldsymbol{\phi}(\mathbf{x})) \right\|^2 = \| \boldsymbol{\phi}(\mathbf{x}) - P_{U_k}(\boldsymbol{\phi}(\mathbf{x})) \|^2 \\ &= \| \boldsymbol{\phi}(\mathbf{x}) \|^2 - \| P_{U_k}(\boldsymbol{\phi}(\mathbf{x})) \|^2, \end{aligned}$$

that is, the squared norm of the orthogonal (residual) projection for the subspace U_k spanned by the first k eigenvectors. As always we wish the expected value of the pattern function to be small

$$\mathbb{E}_{\mathbf{x}}[f(\mathbf{x})] = \mathbb{E}_{\mathbf{x}}\left[\left\| P_{U_k}^\perp(\boldsymbol{\phi}(\mathbf{x})) \right\|^2 \right] \approx 0.$$

```
% K is the kernel matrix of the training points
% inner products between ell training and t test points
%    are stored in matrix Ktest of dimension (ell + 1) x t
%    last entry in each column is inner product with self
% k gives dimension of projection space
% V is ell x k matrix storing the first k eigenvectors
 % L is k x k diagonal matrix with eigenvalues
ell = size(K,1);
D = sum(K) / ell;
E = sum(D) / ell;
J = ones(ell,1) * D;
K = K - J - J' + E * ones(ell, ell);
[V, L] = eigs(K, k, 'LM');
 invL = diag(1./diag(L));          % inverse of L
 sqrtL = diag(sqrt(diag(L)));      % sqrt of eigenvalues
 invsqrtL = diag(1./diag(sqrtL)); % inverse of sqrtL
 TestFeat = invsqrtL * V' * Ktest(1:ell - 1,:);
 TrainFeat = sqrtL * V'; % = invsqrtL * V' * K;
% Note that norm(TrainFeat, 'fro') = sum-squares of
%    norms of projections = sum(diag(L)).
% Hence, average squared norm not captured (residual) =
%    (sum(diag(K)) - sum(diag(L)))/ell
% If we need the new inner product information:
Knew = V * L * V'; % = TrainFeat' * TrainFeat;
% between training and test
Ktestnew = V * V' * Ktest(1:ell - 1,:);
% and between test and test
Ktestvstest = Ktest(1:ell - 1,:)'*V*invL*V'*Ktest(1:ell - 1,:);
% The average sum-squared residual of the test points is
(sum(Ktest(ell + 1,:)  - diag(Ktestvstest)')/t
```

Code Fragment 6.1. Matlab code for kernel PCA algorithm.

Our aim is to relate the empirical value of the residual given by the pattern function $f(\mathbf{x})$ to its expected value. Since the eigenvalues of $\ell\mathbf{C}$ and the kernel matrix $\mathbf{K}$ are the same, it follows from equation (6.8) that ℓ times the empirical average of the pattern function is just the sum of those eigenvalues from $k + 1$ to ℓ. We introduce the notation $\lambda^{>t}(S) = \sum_{i=t+1}^{\ell} \lambda_i$ for these sums. Hence, the critical question is how much larger than the empirical expectation

$$\hat{\mathbb{E}}\left[\|P_{U_k}^{\perp}(\phi(\mathbf{x}))\|^2\right] = \frac{1}{\ell}\lambda^{>t}(S)$$

is the true expectation

$$\mathbb{E}\left[\left\|P_{U_t}^{\perp}(\phi(\mathbf{x}))\right\|^2\right].$$

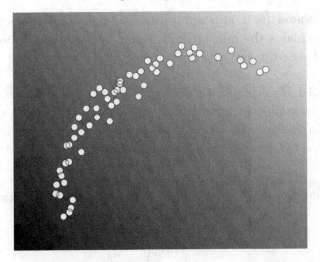

Fig. 6.1. The shading shows the value of the projection on to the first principal direction for linear PCA.

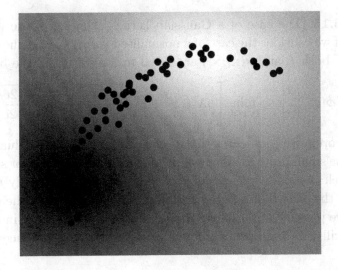

Fig. 6.2. The shading shows the the value of the projection on to the first principal direction for nonlinear PCA.

It is worth noting that if we can bound the difference between these for some value of t, for $k > t$ we have

$$\mathbb{E}\left[\left\|P_{U_k}^{\perp}(\boldsymbol{\phi}(\mathbf{x}))\right\|^2\right] \leq \mathbb{E}\left[\left\|P_{U_t}^{\perp}(\boldsymbol{\phi}(\mathbf{x}))\right\|^2\right],$$

so that the bound for t also applies to k-dimensional projections. This observation explains the min in the theorem below giving a bound on the difference between the two expectations.

Theorem 6.14 *If we perform PCA in the feature space defined by a kernel κ then with probability greater than $1 - \delta$, for any $1 \leq k \leq \ell$, if we project new data onto the space U_k spanned by the first k eigenvectors in the feature space, the expected squared residual is bounded by*

$$\mathbb{E}\left[\left\|P_{\hat{U}_k}^{\perp}(\phi(\mathbf{x}))\right\|^2\right] \leq \min_{1 \leq t \leq k}\left[\frac{1}{\ell}\lambda^{>t}(S) + \frac{8}{\ell}\sqrt{(t+1)\sum_{i=1}^{\ell}\kappa(\mathbf{x}_i,\mathbf{x}_i)^2}\right]$$
$$+ 3R^2\sqrt{\frac{\ln(2\ell/\delta)}{2\ell}},$$

where the support of the distribution is in a ball of radius R in the feature space.

Remark 6.15 [The case of a Gaussian kernel] Reading of the theorem is simplified if we consider the case of a normalised kernel such as the Gaussian. In this case both R and $\kappa(\mathbf{x}_i, \mathbf{x}_i)$ are equal to 1 resulting in the bound

$$\mathbb{E}\left[\left\|P_{\hat{U}_k}^{\perp}(\phi(\mathbf{x}))\right\|^2\right] \leq \min_{1 \leq t \leq k}\left[\frac{1}{\ell}\lambda^{>t}(S) + 8\sqrt{\frac{(t+1)}{\ell}}\right] + 3\sqrt{\frac{\ln(2\ell/\delta)}{2\ell}}.$$

Hence, Theorem 6.14 indicates that the expected squared residual of a test point will be small provided the residual eigenvalues are small for some value $t \leq k$, which is modest compared to ℓ. Hence, we should only use kernel PCA when the eigenvalues become small at an early stage in the spectrum. Provided we project into a space whose dimension exceeds the index of this stage, we will with high probability capture most of the variance of unseen data. ∎

The overall message is that capturing a high proportion of the variance of the data in a number of dimensions significantly smaller than the samples size indicates that a reliable pattern has been detected and that the same subspace will, with high probability, capture most of the variance of the test data. We can therefore view the theorem as stating that the percentage of variance captured by low-dimensional eigenspaces is concentrated and hence reliably estimated from the training sample.

A proof of this theorem appears in Appendix A.2. The basis for the statistical analysis are the Rademacher complexity results of Chapter 4. The difficulty in applying the method is that the function class does not appear to be linear, but interestingly it can be viewed as linear in the feature space defined by the quadratic kernel

$$\hat{\kappa}(\mathbf{x}, \mathbf{z}) = \kappa(\mathbf{x}, \mathbf{z})^2.$$

Hence, the use of kernels not only defines a feature space and provides the algorithmic tool to compute in that space, but also resurfaces as a proof technique for analysing the stability of principal components analysis. Though this provides an interesting and distinctive use of kernels we have preferred not to distract the reader from the main development of this chapter and have moved the proof details to an appendix.

Whitening PCA computed the directions of maximal variance and used them as the basis for dimensionality reduction. The resulting covariance matrix of the projected data retains the same eigenvalues corresponding to the eigenvectors used to define the projection space, but has a diagonal structure. This follows from the observation that given a centred data matrix $\mathbf{X}$, the projected data $\mathbf{X}\mathbf{U}_k$ has covariance matrix

$$\frac{1}{\ell}\mathbf{U}'_k\mathbf{X}'\mathbf{X}\mathbf{U}_k = \frac{1}{\ell}\mathbf{U}'_k\mathbf{U}\boldsymbol{\Lambda}\mathbf{U}'\mathbf{U}_k = \frac{1}{\ell}\boldsymbol{\Lambda}_k.$$

Whitening is a technique that transforms the projected data to make the resulting covariance matrix equal to the identity by rescaling the projection directions by $\boldsymbol{\Lambda}_k^{-1/2}$ to obtain $\mathbf{X}\mathbf{U}_k\boldsymbol{\Lambda}_k^{-1/2}$, so that the covariance becomes

$$\frac{1}{\ell}\boldsymbol{\Lambda}_k^{-1/2}\mathbf{U}'_k\mathbf{X}'\mathbf{X}\mathbf{U}_k\boldsymbol{\Lambda}_k^{-1/2} = \frac{1}{\ell}\boldsymbol{\Lambda}_k^{-1/2}\mathbf{U}'_k\mathbf{U}\boldsymbol{\Lambda}\mathbf{U}'\mathbf{U}_k\boldsymbol{\Lambda}_k^{-1/2} = \frac{1}{\ell}\boldsymbol{\Lambda}_k^{-1/2}\boldsymbol{\Lambda}_k\boldsymbol{\Lambda}_k^{-1/2}$$

$$= \frac{1}{\ell}\mathbf{I}.$$

This is motivated by the desire to make the different directions have equal weight, though we will see a further motivation for this in Chapter 12. The transformation can be implemented as a variant of kernel PCA.

Algorithm 6.16 [Whitening] The whitening algorithm is given in Code Fragment 6.2. Note that $\mathbf{j}$ denotes the all 1s vector. ∎

6.3 Directions of maximum covariance

Principal components analysis measures the variance in the data by identifying the so-called principal axes that give the directions of maximal variance in decreasing importance. PCA sets a threshold and discards the principal directions for which the variance is below that threshold.

input	Data $S = \{\mathbf{x}_1, \ldots, \mathbf{x}_\ell\}$, dimension k.
process	$\mathbf{K}_{ij} = \kappa\left(\mathbf{x}_i, \mathbf{x}_j\right),\ i, j = 1, \ldots, \ell$
	$\mathbf{K} = \mathbf{K} - \frac{1}{\ell}\mathbf{jj}'\mathbf{K} - \frac{1}{\ell}\mathbf{Kjj}' + \frac{1}{\ell^2}\left(\mathbf{j}'\mathbf{Kj}\right)\mathbf{jj}',$
	$[\mathbf{V}, \mathbf{\Lambda}] = \text{eig}\left(\mathbf{K}\right)$
	$\boldsymbol{\alpha}^j = \frac{1}{\lambda_j}\mathbf{v}_j,\ j = 1, \ldots, k.$
	$\tilde{\mathbf{x}}_i = \left(\sum_{i=1}^{\ell} \alpha_i^j \kappa(\mathbf{x}_i, \mathbf{x})\right)_{j=1}^{k}$
output	Transformed data $\tilde{S} = \{\tilde{\mathbf{x}}_1, \ldots, \tilde{\mathbf{x}}_\ell\}.$

Code Fragment 6.2. Pseudocode for the whitening algorithm.

Consider for a moment that we are tackling a regression problem. Performing PCA as a precursor to finding a linear regressor is referred to as *principal components regression (PCR)* and is motivated mainly through its potential for denoising and hence reducing the variance of the resulting regression error. There is, however, a danger inherent in this approach in that what is important for the regression estimation is not the size of the variance of the data, but how well it can be used to predict the output. It might be that the high variance directions identified by PCA are uncorrelated with the target, while a direction with relatively low variance nonetheless has high predictive potential.

In this section we will begin to examine methods for measuring when directions carry information useful for prediction. This will allow us again to isolate directions that optimise the derived criterion. The key is to look for relationships between two random variables.

In Section 5.3 we defined the covariance of two zero-mean univariate random variables x and y as $\mathbb{E}[xy]$. This is in contrast to the correlation coefficient which normalises with respect to the variances of the two variables. We now consider extending our consideration to multidimensional random vectors.

Consider two multivariate random vectors giving rise to a dataset S containing pairs $(\mathbf{x}, \mathbf{y})$ from two different spaces X and Y. We call such a dataset *paired* in the sense that the process generating the data generates items in pairs, one from X and one from Y.

Example 6.17 For example, if we have a set of labelled examples for a supervised learning task, we can view it as a paired dataset by letting the input space be X and the output space be Y. If the labels are binary this makes examples from Y a Bernoulli sequence, but more generally for regression $Y = \mathbb{R}$, and of course we can consider the case where $Y = \mathbb{R}^n$ or indeed has a more complex structure.   ∎

We are interested in studying the covariance between the two parts of a paired dataset even though those two parts live in different spaces. We achieve this by using an approach similar to that adopted to study the variance of random vectors. There we projected the data onto a direction vector $\mathbf{w}$ to create a univariate random variable, whose mean and standard deviation could subsequently be computed. Here we project the two parts onto two separate directions specified by unit vectors $\mathbf{w}_x$ and $\mathbf{w}_y$, to obtain two random variables $\mathbf{w}_x'\mathbf{x}$ and $\mathbf{w}_y'\mathbf{y}$ that are again univariate and hence whose covariance can be computed. In this way we can assess the relation between $\mathbf{x}$ and $\mathbf{y}$. Note that for the purposes of this exposition we are assuming that the input space is the feature space. When we come to apply this analysis in Section 6.7.1, we will introduce a kernel-defined feature space for the first component only. We give a definition of a paired dataset in which the two components correspond to distinct kernel mappings in Section 6.5.

Again following the analogy with the unsupervised case, given two directions $\mathbf{w}_x$ and $\mathbf{w}_y$, we can measure the covariance of the corresponding random variables as

$$\hat{\mathbb{E}}\left[\mathbf{w}_x'\mathbf{x}\mathbf{w}_y'\mathbf{y}\right] = \hat{\mathbb{E}}\left[\mathbf{w}_x'\mathbf{x}\mathbf{y}'\mathbf{w}_y\right] = \mathbf{w}_x'\hat{\mathbb{E}}\left[\mathbf{x}\mathbf{y}'\right]\mathbf{w}_y = \mathbf{w}_x'\mathbf{C}_{xy}\mathbf{w}_y,$$

where we have used $\mathbf{C}_{xy}$ to denote the sample covariance matrix $\hat{\mathbb{E}}\left[\mathbf{x}\mathbf{y}'\right]$ between X and Y. If we consider two matrices $\mathbf{X}$ and $\mathbf{Y}$ whose ith rows are the feature vectors of corresponding examples $\mathbf{x}_i$ and $\mathbf{y}_i$, we can write

$$\mathbf{C}_{xy} = \hat{\mathbb{E}}\left[\mathbf{x}\mathbf{y}'\right] = \frac{1}{\ell}\sum_{i=1}^{\ell}\mathbf{x}_i\mathbf{y}_i' = \frac{1}{\ell}\mathbf{X}'\mathbf{Y}.$$

Now that we are able to measure the covariance for a particular choice of directions, it is natural to ask if we can choose the directions to maximise this quantity. Hence, we would like to solve the following optimisation.

Computation 6.18 [Maximising Covariance] The directions $\mathbf{w}_x$, $\mathbf{w}_y$ of maximal covariance can be found as follows

$$\begin{aligned} \max_{\mathbf{w}_x,\mathbf{w}_y} \quad & C(\mathbf{w}_x,\mathbf{w}_y) = \mathbf{w}_x'\mathbf{C}_{xy}\mathbf{w}_y = \tfrac{1}{\ell}\mathbf{w}_x'\mathbf{X}'\mathbf{Y}\mathbf{w}_y, \\ \text{subject to} \quad & \|\mathbf{w}_x\|_2 = \|\mathbf{w}_y\|_2 = 1. \end{aligned} \tag{6.13}$$

We can again convert this to maximising a quotient by introducing an invariance to scaling

$$\max_{\mathbf{w}_x, \mathbf{w}_y} \frac{C(\mathbf{w}_x, \mathbf{w}_y)}{\|\mathbf{w}_x\| \, \|\mathbf{w}_y\|} = \max_{\mathbf{w}_x, \mathbf{w}_y} \frac{\mathbf{w}_x' \mathbf{C}_{xy} \mathbf{w}_y}{\|\mathbf{w}_x\| \, \|\mathbf{w}_y\|}. \tag{6.14}$$

∎

Remark 6.19 [Relation to Rayleigh quotient] Note the similarity to the Rayleigh quotient considered above, but in this case $\mathbf{C}_{xy}$ is not a square matrix since its row dimension is equal to the dimension of X, while its column dimension is given by the dimension of Y. Furthermore, even if these dimensions were equal, $\mathbf{C}_{xy}$ would not be symmetric and here we are optimising over two vectors. ∎

Proposition 6.20 *The directions that solve the maximal covariance optimisation (6.13) are the first singular vectors $\mathbf{w}_x = \mathbf{u}_1$ and $\mathbf{w}_y = \mathbf{v}_1$ of the singular value decomposition of $\mathbf{C}_{xy}$*

$$\mathbf{C}_{xy} = \mathbf{U} \boldsymbol{\Sigma} \mathbf{V}';$$

the value of the covariance is given by the corresponding singular value σ_1.

Proof Using the singular value decomposition of $\mathbf{C}_{xy}$ and taking into account that $\mathbf{U}$ and $\mathbf{V}$ are orthornormal matrices so that, for example, $\|\mathbf{V}\mathbf{w}\| = \|\mathbf{w}\|$ and any $\mathbf{w}_x$ can be expressed as $\mathbf{U}\mathbf{u}_x$ for some $\mathbf{u}_x$, the solution to problem (6.13) becomes

$$
\begin{aligned}
\max_{\mathbf{w}_x, \mathbf{w}_y : \|\mathbf{w}_x\|_2 = \|\mathbf{w}_y\|_2 = 1} C(\mathbf{w}_x, \mathbf{w}_y) &= \max_{\mathbf{u}_x, \mathbf{v}_y : \|\mathbf{U}\mathbf{u}_x\|_2 = \|\mathbf{V}\mathbf{v}_y\|_2 = 1} (\mathbf{U}\mathbf{u}_x)' \mathbf{C}_{xy} \mathbf{V}\mathbf{v}_y \\
&= \max_{\mathbf{u}_x, \mathbf{v}_y : \|\mathbf{u}_x\|_2 = \|\mathbf{v}_y\|_2 = 1} \mathbf{u}_x' \mathbf{U}' \mathbf{U} \boldsymbol{\Sigma} \mathbf{V}' \mathbf{V} \mathbf{v}_y \\
&= \max_{\mathbf{u}_x, \mathbf{v}_y : \|\mathbf{u}_x\|_2 = \|\mathbf{v}_y\|_2 = 1} \mathbf{u}_x' \boldsymbol{\Sigma} \mathbf{v}_y.
\end{aligned}
$$

The last line clearly has a maximum of the largest singular value σ_1, when we take $\mathbf{u}_x = \mathbf{e}_1$ and $\mathbf{v}_y = \mathbf{e}_1$ the first unit vector (albeit of different dimensions). Hence, the original problem is solved by taking $\mathbf{w}_x = \mathbf{u}_1 = \mathbf{U}\mathbf{e}_1$ and $\mathbf{w}_y = \mathbf{v}_1 = \mathbf{V}\mathbf{e}_1$, the first columns of $\mathbf{U}$ and $\mathbf{V}$ respectively. □

Proposition 6.20 shows how to compute the directions that maximise the covariance. If we wish to identify more than one direction, as we did for example with the principal components, we must apply the same strategy of projecting the data onto the orthogonal complement by deflation. From equation (5.8), this corresponds to the operations

$$\mathbf{X} \longleftarrow \mathbf{X} \left(\mathbf{I} - \mathbf{u}_1 \mathbf{u}_1' \right) \text{ and } \mathbf{Y} \longleftarrow \mathbf{Y} \left(\mathbf{I} - \mathbf{v}_1 \mathbf{v}_1' \right).$$

The resulting covariance matrix is therefore

$$
\begin{aligned}
\frac{1}{\ell}\left(\mathbf{I}-\mathbf{u}_1\mathbf{u}_1'\right)\mathbf{X}'\mathbf{Y}\left(\mathbf{I}-\mathbf{v}_1\mathbf{v}_1'\right) &= \left(\mathbf{I}-\mathbf{u}_1\mathbf{u}_1'\right)\mathbf{U}\boldsymbol{\Sigma}\mathbf{V}'\left(\mathbf{I}-\mathbf{v}_1\mathbf{v}_1'\right)\\
&= \mathbf{U}\boldsymbol{\Sigma}\mathbf{V}'-\sigma_1\mathbf{u}_1\mathbf{v}_1'\\
&= \mathbf{C}_{xy}-\sigma_1\mathbf{u}_1\mathbf{v}_1',
\end{aligned}
$$

implying that this corresponds to the deflation procedure for singular value decomposition given in equation (6.1). The next two directions of maximal covariance will now be given by the second singular vectors $\mathbf{u}_2$ and $\mathbf{v}_2$ with the value of the covariance given by σ_2. Proceeding in similar fashion we see that the singular vectors give the orthogonal directions of maximal covariance in descending order. This provides a series of directions in X and in Y that have the property of being maximally covariant resulting in the singular value decomposition of $\mathbf{C}_{xy}$

$$
\mathbf{C}_{xy} = \sum_{i=1}^{\ell}\sigma_i\mathbf{u}_i\mathbf{v}_i'.
$$

Computation and dual form If we wish to avoid performing a singular value decomposition of $\mathbf{C}_{xy}$, for example when working in a kernel-defined feature space, we can find the singular vectors through an eigenanalysis of the matrix $\mathbf{C}_{xy}\mathbf{C}_{xy}'$, to obtain $\mathbf{U}$, and of $\mathbf{C}_{xy}'\mathbf{C}_{xy}$, to obtain $\mathbf{V}$. Incidentally, this also reminds us that the singular directions are orthogonal, since they are the eigenvectors of a symmetric matrix. Now observe that

$$
\mathbf{C}_{xy}'\mathbf{C}_{xy} = \frac{1}{\ell^2}\mathbf{Y}'\mathbf{X}\mathbf{X}'\mathbf{Y} = \frac{1}{\ell^2}\mathbf{Y}'\mathbf{K}_x\mathbf{Y},
$$

where $\mathbf{K}_x$ is the kernel matrix associated with the space X. The dimension of this system will be N_y, the same as that of the Y space. It follows from a direct comparison with PCA that

$$
\mathbf{u}_j = \frac{1}{\sigma_j}\mathbf{C}_{xy}\mathbf{v}_j.
$$

Hence, the projection of a new point $\phi(\mathbf{x})$ onto $\mathbf{u}_j$ is given by

$$
\mathbf{u}_j'\phi(\mathbf{x}) = \frac{1}{\ell\sigma_j}\mathbf{v}_j'\mathbf{Y}'\mathbf{X}\phi(\mathbf{x}) = \sum_{i=1}^{\ell}\alpha_i^j\kappa(\mathbf{x}_i,\mathbf{x}),
$$

where

$$
\alpha^j = \frac{1}{\ell\sigma_j}\mathbf{Y}\mathbf{v}_j.
$$

Remark 6.21 [On stability analysis] We do not provide a stability analysis for the features selected by maximising the covariance, though it is clear that we can view them as eigenvectors of a corresponding eigen-decomposition based on a sample estimation of covariances. Hence, similar techniques to those used in Appendix A.2 could be used to show that provided the number of features extracted is small compared to the size of the sample, we can expect the test example performance to mimic closely that of the training sample. ∎

Alternative characterisation There is another characterisation of the largest singular vectors that motivates their use in choosing a prediction function from X to Y in the case of a supervised learning problem with $Y = \mathbb{R}^n$. We will discuss multi-variate regression in more detail at the end of the chapter, but present the characterisation here to complement the covariance approach presented above. The approach focuses on the choice of the orthogonal matrices of the singular value decomposition.

Suppose that we seek orthogonal matrices $\hat{\mathbf{U}}$ and $\hat{\mathbf{V}}$ such that the columns of $\mathbf{S} = \mathbf{X}\hat{\mathbf{U}}$ and $\mathbf{T} = \mathbf{Y}\hat{\mathbf{V}}$ are as similar as possible. By this we mean that we seek to minimise a simple discrepancy D between $\mathbf{S}$ and $\mathbf{T}$ defined as

$$D(\hat{\mathbf{U}}, \hat{\mathbf{V}}) = \sum_{i=1}^{m} |\mathbf{s}_i - \mathbf{t}_i|^2 + \sum_{i=m+1}^{n} |\mathbf{s}_i|^2, \qquad (6.15)$$

where we have assumed that $\mathbf{S}$ has more columns than $\mathbf{T}$. If we let $\bar{\mathbf{T}} = [\mathbf{T}, \mathbf{0}]$, or in other words $\mathbf{T}$ is padded with 0s to the size of $\mathbf{S}$, we have

$$
\begin{aligned}
D(\hat{\mathbf{U}}, \hat{\mathbf{V}}) &= \left\| \mathbf{S} - \bar{\mathbf{T}} \right\|_F^2 = \left\langle \mathbf{S} - \bar{\mathbf{T}}, \mathbf{S} - \bar{\mathbf{T}} \right\rangle_F \\
&= \left\langle \mathbf{S}, \mathbf{S} \right\rangle_F - 2 \left\langle \mathbf{S}, \bar{\mathbf{T}} \right\rangle_F + \left\langle \bar{\mathbf{T}}, \bar{\mathbf{T}} \right\rangle_F \\
&= \operatorname{tr} \mathbf{S}'\mathbf{S} - 2 \operatorname{tr} \mathbf{S}'\mathbf{T} + \operatorname{tr} \mathbf{T}'\mathbf{T} \\
&= \operatorname{tr} \hat{\mathbf{U}}'\mathbf{X}'\mathbf{X}\hat{\mathbf{U}} - 2 \operatorname{tr} \hat{\mathbf{U}}'\mathbf{X}'\mathbf{Y}\hat{\mathbf{V}} + \operatorname{tr} \hat{\mathbf{V}}'\mathbf{Y}'\mathbf{Y}\hat{\mathbf{V}} \\
&= \operatorname{tr} \mathbf{X}'\mathbf{X} + \operatorname{tr} \mathbf{Y}'\mathbf{Y} - 2 \operatorname{tr} \hat{\mathbf{U}}'\mathbf{X}'\mathbf{Y}\hat{\mathbf{V}}.
\end{aligned}
$$

Hence, the maximum of D is obtained when $\operatorname{tr} \hat{\mathbf{U}}'\mathbf{X}'\mathbf{Y}\hat{\mathbf{V}}$ is minimised. But we have

$$\operatorname{tr} \hat{\mathbf{U}}'\mathbf{X}'\mathbf{Y}\hat{\mathbf{V}} = \ell \operatorname{tr} \hat{\mathbf{U}}'\mathbf{U}\boldsymbol{\Sigma}\mathbf{V}'\hat{\mathbf{V}} = \ell \operatorname{tr} \tilde{\mathbf{V}}\tilde{\mathbf{U}}'\boldsymbol{\Sigma},$$

for appropriately sized orthogonal matrices $\tilde{\mathbf{V}}$ and $\tilde{\mathbf{U}}$. Since multiplying by an orthogonal matrix from the left will not change the two-norm of the columns, the value of the expression is clearly maximised when $\tilde{\mathbf{V}}\tilde{\mathbf{U}}' = \mathbf{I}$, the identity matrix. Hence, the choice of $\hat{\mathbf{U}}$ and $\hat{\mathbf{V}}$ that minimises $D(\hat{\mathbf{U}}, \hat{\mathbf{V}})$ is the orthogonal matrices of the singular value decomposition.

Before we continue our exploration of patterns that can be identified using eigen-decompositions, we must consider a more expanded class of techniques that solve the so-called generalised eigenvector problem.

6.4 The generalised eigenvector problem

A number of problems in kernel-based pattern analysis can be reduced to solving a generalised eigenvalue problem, a standard problem in multivariate statistics

$$\mathbf{Aw} = \lambda \mathbf{Bw}$$

with $\mathbf{A}$, $\mathbf{B}$ symmetric matrices, $\mathbf{B}$ positive definite. Hence, the normal eigenvalue problem is a special case obtained by taking $\mathbf{B} = \mathbf{I}$, the identity matrix. The problem arises as the solution of the maximisation of a generalised Rayleigh quotient

$$\rho(\mathbf{w}) = \frac{\mathbf{w}'\mathbf{Aw}}{\mathbf{w}'\mathbf{Bw}},$$

which has a positive quadratic form rather than a simple norm squared in the denominator. Since the ratio is invariant to rescaling of the vector $\mathbf{w}$, we can maximise the ratio by constraining the denominator to have value 1. Hence, the maximum quotient problem can be cast as the optimization problem

$$\begin{aligned} \max \quad & \mathbf{w}'\mathbf{Aw} \\ \text{subject to} \quad & \mathbf{w}'\mathbf{Bw} = 1. \end{aligned} \qquad (6.16)$$

Applying the Lagrange multiplier technique and differentiating with respect to $\mathbf{w}$ we arrive at the generalised eigenvalue problem

$$\mathbf{Aw} - \lambda \mathbf{Bw} = \mathbf{0}. \qquad (6.17)$$

Since by assumption $\mathbf{B}$ is positive definite we can convert to a standard eigenvalue problem by premultiplying by $\mathbf{B}^{-1}$ to obtain

$$\mathbf{B}^{-1}\mathbf{Aw} = \lambda \mathbf{w}.$$

But note that although both $\mathbf{A}$ and $\mathbf{B}$ are assumed to be symmetric, $\mathbf{B}^{-1}\mathbf{A}$ need not be. Hence we cannot make use of the main results of Section 3.1. In particular the eigenvectors will not in general be orthogonal. There is, however, a related symmetric eigenvalue problem that reveals something about the structure of the eigenvectors of (6.16). Since $\mathbf{B}$ is positive definite it possesses a symmetric square root $\mathbf{B}^{1/2}$ with the property that

$$\mathbf{B}^{1/2}\mathbf{B}^{1/2} = \mathbf{B}.$$

Consider premultiplying (6.17) by $\mathbf{B}^{1/2}$ and reparametrise the solution vector $\mathbf{w}$ as $\mathbf{B}^{-1/2}\mathbf{v}$. We obtain the standard eigenvalue problem

$$\mathbf{B}^{-1/2}\mathbf{A}\mathbf{B}^{-1/2}\mathbf{v} = \lambda\mathbf{v}, \tag{6.18}$$

where now the matrix $\mathbf{B}^{-1/2}\mathbf{A}\mathbf{B}^{-1/2} = (\mathbf{B}^{-1/2}\mathbf{A}\mathbf{B}^{-1/2})'$ is symmetric. Applying the results of Chapter 3, we can find a set of orthonormal eigenvector solutions of (6.18) λ_i, $\mathbf{v}_i$. Hence, the solutions of (6.17) have the form

$$\mathbf{w}_i = \mathbf{B}^{-1/2}\mathbf{v}_i,$$

where $\mathbf{v}_1, \ldots, \mathbf{v}_\ell$ are the orthonormal eigenvectors of (6.18) with the associated eigenvalues being the same. Since $\mathbf{B}^{1/2}$ is a bijection of the space $\mathbb{R}^\ell$ we can write

$$\rho = \frac{\mathbf{w}'\mathbf{A}\mathbf{w}}{\mathbf{w}'\mathbf{B}\mathbf{w}} = \frac{\left(\mathbf{B}^{1/2}\mathbf{w}\right)'\mathbf{B}^{-1/2}\mathbf{A}\mathbf{B}^{-1/2}\left(\mathbf{B}^{1/2}\mathbf{w}\right)}{\left\|\mathbf{B}^{1/2}\mathbf{w}\right\|^2}$$

the generalised Rayleigh quotient is given by the associated Rayleigh quotient for the standard eigenvalue problem (6.18) after the bijection $\mathbf{B}^{1/2}$ has been applied. We can therefore see the generalised eigenvalue problem as an eigenvalue problem in a transformed space. The following propositions are simple consequences of these observations.

Proposition 6.22 *Any vector $\mathbf{v}$ can be written as a linear combination of the eigenvectors $\mathbf{w}_i$, $i = 1, \ldots, \ell$. The generalised eigenvectors of the problem $\mathbf{A}\mathbf{w} = \lambda\mathbf{B}\mathbf{w}$ have the following generalised orthogonality properties: if the eigenvalues are distinct, then in the metrics defined by $\mathbf{A}$ and $\mathbf{B}$, the eigenvectors are orthonormal*

$$\mathbf{w}_i'\mathbf{B}\mathbf{w}_j = \delta_{ij}$$
$$\mathbf{w}_i'\mathbf{A}\mathbf{w}_j = \delta_{ij}\lambda_i.$$

Proof For $i \neq j$ we have (assuming without loss of generality that $\lambda_j \neq 0$)

$$0 = \mathbf{v}_i'\mathbf{v}_j = \mathbf{w}_i'\mathbf{B}^{1/2}\mathbf{B}^{1/2}\mathbf{w}_j = \mathbf{w}_i'\mathbf{B}\mathbf{w}_j = \frac{1}{\lambda_j}\mathbf{w}_i'\mathbf{A}\mathbf{w}_j,$$

which gives the result for $i \neq j$. Now consider

$$\lambda_i = \lambda_i\mathbf{v}_i'\mathbf{v}_i = \lambda_i\mathbf{w}_i'\mathbf{B}^{1/2}\mathbf{B}^{1/2}\mathbf{w}_i = \lambda_i\mathbf{w}_i'\mathbf{B}\mathbf{w}_i = \mathbf{w}_i'\mathbf{A}\mathbf{w}_i,$$

which covers the case of $i = j$. $\square$

Definition 6.23 [Conjugate vectors] The first property

$$\mathbf{w}_i' \mathbf{B} \mathbf{w}_j = \delta_{ij}, \text{ for } i, j = 1, \dots, \ell,$$

is also referred to as *conjugacy with respect to* $\mathbf{B}$, or equivalently that the vectors $\mathbf{w}_i$ are *conjugate*. $\blacksquare$

Proposition 6.24 *There is a global maximum and minimum of the generalised Rayleigh quotient. The quotient is bounded by the smallest and the largest eigenvalue*

$$\rho_\ell \le \rho \le \rho_1,$$

so that the global maximum ρ_1 is attained by the associated eigenvector.

Remark 6.25 [Second derivatives] We can also study the stationary points, by examining the second derivative or Hessian at the eigenvectors

$$\mathbf{H} = \frac{\partial^2 \rho}{\partial \mathbf{w}^2}|_{\mathbf{w}=\mathbf{w}_i} = \frac{2}{\mathbf{w}_i' \mathbf{B} \mathbf{w}_i} (\mathbf{A} - \rho_i \mathbf{B}).$$

For all $1 < i < \ell$, $\mathbf{H}$ has positive and negative eigenvalues, since

$$\left(\mathbf{B}^{-1/2} \mathbf{v}_1 \right)' (\mathbf{A} - \rho_i \mathbf{B}) \, \mathbf{B}^{-1/2} \mathbf{v}_1 = \mathbf{w}_1' \mathbf{A} \mathbf{w}_1 - \rho_i = \rho_1 - \rho_i > 0,$$

while

$$\left(\mathbf{B}^{-1/2} \mathbf{v}_\ell \right)' (\mathbf{A} - \rho_i \mathbf{B}) \, \mathbf{B}_{\mathbf{v}_\ell}^{-1/2} = \mathbf{w}_\ell' \mathbf{A} \mathbf{w}_\ell - \rho_i = \rho_\ell - \rho_i < 0.$$

It follows that all the eigensolutions besides the largest and smallest are saddle points. $\blacksquare$

Proposition 6.26 *If λ_i, $\mathbf{w}_i$ are the eigenvalues and eigenvectors of the generalised eigenvalue problem*

$$\mathbf{A} \mathbf{w} = \lambda \mathbf{B} \mathbf{w},$$

then the matrix $\mathbf{A}$ can be decomposed as

$$\mathbf{A} = \sum_{i=1}^{\ell} \lambda_i \mathbf{B} \mathbf{w}_i \, (\mathbf{B} \mathbf{w}_i)'.$$

Proof We can decompose

$$\mathbf{B}^{-1/2}\mathbf{A}\mathbf{B}^{-1/2} = \sum_{i=1}^{\ell} \lambda_i \mathbf{v}_i \mathbf{v}_i',$$

implying that

$$\mathbf{A} = \sum_{i=1}^{\ell} \lambda_i \mathbf{B}^{1/2}\mathbf{v}_i \left(\mathbf{B}^{1/2}\mathbf{v}_i\right)' = \sum_{i=1}^{\ell} \lambda_i \mathbf{B}\mathbf{w}_i \left(\mathbf{B}\mathbf{w}_i\right)',$$

as required. ☐

Definition 6.27 [Generalised deflation] The final proposition suggests how we can deflate the matrix $\mathbf{A}$ in an iterative direct solution of the generalised eigenvalue problem

$$\mathbf{A}\mathbf{w} = \lambda \mathbf{B}\mathbf{w}.$$

After finding a non-zero eigenvalue–eigenvector pair λ, $\mathbf{w}$ we deflate $\mathbf{A}$ by

$$\mathbf{A} \longleftarrow \mathbf{A} - \lambda \mathbf{B}\mathbf{w}\left(\mathbf{B}\mathbf{w}\right)' = \mathbf{A} - \lambda \mathbf{B}\mathbf{w}\mathbf{w}'\mathbf{B}',$$

leaving $\mathbf{B}$ unchanged. ∎

6.5 Canonical correlation analysis

We have looked at two ways of detecting stable patterns through the use of eigen-decompositions firstly to optimise variance of the training data in kernel PCA and secondly to maximise the covariance between two views of the data typically input and output vectors. We now again consider the case in which we have two views of the data which are paired in the sense that each example as a pair of representations. This situation is sometimes referred to as a paired dataset. We will show how to find correlations between the two views.

An extreme case would be where the second view is simply the labels of the examples. In general we are interested here in cases where we have a more complex 'output' that amounts to a different representation of the same object.

Example 6.28 A set of documents containing each document in two different languages is a paired dataset. The two versions give different views of the same underlying object, in this case the semantic content of the document. Such a dataset is known as a parallel corpus. By seeking correlations between the two views, we might hope to extract features that bring out the underlying semantic content. The fact that a pattern has been found in both views suggests that it is not related to the irrelevant representation specific aspects of one or other view, but rather to the common underlying semantic content. This example will be explored further in Chapter 10. ∎

This section will develop the methodology for finding these common patterns in different views through seeking correlations between projection values from the two views. Using an appropriate regularisation technique, the methods are extended to kernel-defined feature spaces.

Recall that in Section 5.3 we defined the correlation between two zero-mean univariate random variables x and y to be

$$\rho = \operatorname{corr}(x, y) = \frac{\mathbb{E}[xy]}{\sqrt{\mathbb{E}[xx]\,\mathbb{E}[yy]}} = \frac{\operatorname{cov}(x, y)}{\sqrt{\operatorname{var}(x)}\sqrt{\operatorname{var}(y)}}.$$

Definition 6.29 [Paired dataset] A paired dataset is created when each object $\mathbf{x} \in X$ can be viewed through two distinct projections into two feature spaces

$$\phi_a : \mathbf{x} \longrightarrow F_a \text{ and } \phi_b : \mathbf{x} \longrightarrow F_b,$$

where F_a is the feature space associated with one representation and F_b the feature space for the other. Figure 6.3 illustrates this configuration. The corresponding kernel functions are denoted κ_a and κ_b. Hence, we have a multivariate random vector $(\phi_a(\mathbf{x}), \phi_b(\mathbf{x}))$. Assume we are given a training set

$$S = \{(\phi_a(\mathbf{x}_1), \phi_b(\mathbf{x}_1)), \ldots, (\phi_a(\mathbf{x}_\ell), \phi_b(\mathbf{x}_\ell))\}$$

drawn independently at random according to the underlying distribution. We will refer to such a set as a *paired* or *aligned dataset* in the feature space defined by the kernels κ_a and κ_b. ∎

We now seek to maximise the empirical correlation between $x_a = \mathbf{w}'_a \phi_a(\mathbf{x})$ and $x_b = \mathbf{w}'_b \phi_b(\mathbf{x})$ over the projection directions $\mathbf{w}_a$ and $\mathbf{w}_b$

$$\max \rho = \frac{\hat{\mathbb{E}}[x_a x_b]}{\sqrt{\hat{\mathbb{E}}[x_a x_a]\,\hat{\mathbb{E}}[x_b x_b]}}$$

$$= \frac{\hat{\mathbb{E}}\left[\mathbf{w}'_a \phi_a(\mathbf{x})\, \phi_b(\mathbf{x})'\, \mathbf{w}_b\right]}{\sqrt{\hat{\mathbb{E}}\left[\mathbf{w}'_a \phi_a(\mathbf{x})\, \phi_a(\mathbf{x})'\, \mathbf{w}_a\right]\,\hat{\mathbb{E}}\left[\mathbf{w}'_b \phi_b(\mathbf{x})\, \phi_b(\mathbf{x})'\, \mathbf{w}_b\right]}}$$

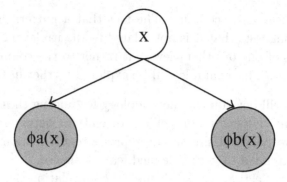

Fig. 6.3. The two embeddings of a paired dataset.

$$= \frac{\mathbf{w}_a' \mathbf{C}_{ab} \mathbf{w}_b}{\sqrt{\mathbf{w}_a' \mathbf{C}_{aa} \mathbf{w}_a \mathbf{w}_b' \mathbf{C}_{bb} \mathbf{w}_b}}, \tag{6.19}$$

where we have decomposed the empirical covariance matrix as follows

$$
\begin{aligned}
\mathbf{C} &= \frac{1}{\ell} \sum_{i=1}^{\ell} \left(\phi_a\left(\mathbf{x}\right), \phi_b\left(\mathbf{x}\right) \right) \left(\phi_a\left(\mathbf{x}\right), \phi_b\left(\mathbf{x}\right) \right)' \\
&= \begin{pmatrix} \frac{1}{\ell}\sum_{i=1}^{\ell} \phi_a\left(\mathbf{x}\right) \phi_a\left(\mathbf{x}\right)' & \frac{1}{\ell}\sum_{i=1}^{\ell} \phi_b\left(\mathbf{x}\right) \phi_a\left(\mathbf{x}\right)' \\ \frac{1}{\ell}\sum_{i=1}^{\ell} \phi_a\left(\mathbf{x}\right) \phi_b\left(\mathbf{x}\right)' & \frac{1}{\ell}\sum_{i=1}^{\ell} \phi_b\left(\mathbf{x}\right) \phi_b\left(\mathbf{x}\right)' \end{pmatrix} \\
&= \begin{pmatrix} \mathbf{C}_{aa} & \mathbf{C}_{ba} \\ \mathbf{C}_{ab} & \mathbf{C}_{bb} \end{pmatrix}.
\end{aligned}
$$

This optimisation is very similar to that given in (6.14). The only difference is that here the denominator of the quotient measures the norm of the projection vectors differently from the covariance case. In the current optimisation the vectors $\mathbf{w}_a$ and $\mathbf{w}_b$ are again only determined up to direction since rescaling $\mathbf{w}_a$ by λ_a and $\mathbf{w}_b$ by λ_b results in the quotient

$$
\frac{\lambda_a \lambda_b \mathbf{w}_a' \mathbf{C}_{ab} \mathbf{w}_b}{\sqrt{\lambda_a^2 \mathbf{w}_a' \mathbf{C}_{aa} \mathbf{w}_a \lambda_b^2 \mathbf{w}_b' \mathbf{C}_{bb} \mathbf{w}_b}} = \frac{\lambda_a \lambda_b \mathbf{w}_a' \mathbf{C}_{ab} \mathbf{w}_b}{\lambda_a \lambda_b \sqrt{\mathbf{w}_a' \mathbf{C}_{aa} \mathbf{w}_a \mathbf{w}_b' \mathbf{C}_{bb} \mathbf{w}_b}}
$$

$$
= \frac{\mathbf{w}_a' \mathbf{C}_{ab} \mathbf{w}_b}{\sqrt{\mathbf{w}_a' \mathbf{C}_{aa} \mathbf{w}_a \mathbf{w}_b' \mathbf{C}_{bb} \mathbf{w}_b}}.
$$

This implies that we can constrain the two terms in the denominator to individually have value 1. Hence, the problem is solved by the following optimisation problem.

Computation 6.30 [CCA] Given a paired dataset with covariance matrix

$\mathbf{C}_{ab}$, canonical correlation analysis finds the directions $\mathbf{w}_a, \mathbf{w}_b$ that maximise the correlation of corresponding projections by solving

$$\max_{\mathbf{w}_a, \mathbf{w}_b} \quad \mathbf{w}_a' \mathbf{C}_{ab} \mathbf{w}_b$$
$$\text{subject to} \quad \mathbf{w}_a' \mathbf{C}_{aa} \mathbf{w}_a = 1 \text{ and } \mathbf{w}_b' \mathbf{C}_{bb} \mathbf{w}_b = 1. \qquad (6.20)$$

∎

Solving CCA Applying the Lagrange multiplier technique to the optimisation (6.20) gives

$$\max \quad \mathbf{w}_a' \mathbf{C}_{ab} \mathbf{w}_b - \frac{\lambda_a}{2} \left(\mathbf{w}_a' \mathbf{C}_{aa} \mathbf{w}_a - 1 \right) - \frac{\lambda_b}{2} \left(\mathbf{w}_b' \mathbf{C}_{bb} \mathbf{w}_b - 1 \right).$$

Taking derivatives with respect to $\mathbf{w}_a$ and $\mathbf{w}_b$ we obtain the equations

$$\mathbf{C}_{ab} \mathbf{w}_b - \lambda_a \mathbf{C}_{aa} \mathbf{w}_a = \mathbf{0} \quad \text{and} \quad \mathbf{C}_{ba} \mathbf{w}_a - \lambda_b \mathbf{C}_{bb} \mathbf{w}_b = \mathbf{0}. \qquad (6.21)$$

Subtracting $\mathbf{w}_a'$ times the first from $\mathbf{w}_b'$ times the second we have

$$\lambda_a \mathbf{w}_a' \mathbf{C}_{aa} \mathbf{w}_a - \lambda_b \mathbf{w}_b' \mathbf{C}_{bb} \mathbf{w}_b = 0,$$

which, taking into account the two constraints, implies $\lambda_a = \lambda_b$. Using λ to denote this value we obtain the following algorithm for computing the correlations.

Algorithm 6.31 [Primal CCA] The following method finds the directions of maximal correlation:

Input	covariance matrices $\mathbf{C}_{aa}$, $\mathbf{C}_{bb}$, $\mathbf{C}_{ba}$ and $\mathbf{C}_{ab}$
Process	solve the generalised eigenvalue problem:
	$\begin{pmatrix} \mathbf{0} & \mathbf{C}_{ab} \\ \mathbf{C}_{ba} & \mathbf{0} \end{pmatrix} \begin{pmatrix} \mathbf{w}_a \\ \mathbf{w}_b \end{pmatrix} = \lambda \begin{pmatrix} \mathbf{C}_{aa} & \mathbf{0} \\ \mathbf{0} & \mathbf{C}_{bb} \end{pmatrix} \begin{pmatrix} \mathbf{w}_a \\ \mathbf{w}_b \end{pmatrix}$
Output	eigenvectors and eigenvalues $\mathbf{w}_a^j$, $\mathbf{w}_b^j$ and $\lambda_j > 0$, $j = 1, \ldots, \ell$.

$$(6.22)$$

∎

This is an example of a generalised eigenvalue problem described in the last section. Note that the value of the eigenvalue for a particular eigenvector gives the size of the correlation since $\mathbf{w}_a'$ times the top portion of (6.22) gives

$$\rho = \mathbf{w}_a' \mathbf{C}_{ab} \mathbf{w}_b = \lambda_a \mathbf{w}_a' \mathbf{C}_{aa} \mathbf{w}_a = \lambda.$$

Hence, we have all eigenvalues lying in the interval $[-1, +1]$, with each λ_i and eigenvector

$$\begin{pmatrix} \mathbf{w}_a \\ \mathbf{w}_b \end{pmatrix}$$

paired with an eigenvalue $-\lambda_i$ with eigenvector

$$\begin{pmatrix} \mathbf{w}_a \\ -\mathbf{w}_b \end{pmatrix}.$$

We are therefore only interested in half the spectrum which we can take to be the positive eigenvalues. The eigenvectors corresponding to the largest eigenvalues are those that identify the strongest correlations. Note that in this case by Proposition 6.22 the eigenvectors will be conjugate with respect to the matrix

$$\begin{pmatrix} \mathbf{C}_{aa} & \mathbf{0} \\ \mathbf{0} & \mathbf{C}_{bb} \end{pmatrix},$$

so that for $i \neq j$ we have

$$0 = \begin{pmatrix} \mathbf{w}_a^j \\ \mathbf{w}_b^j \end{pmatrix}' \begin{pmatrix} \mathbf{C}_{aa} & \mathbf{0} \\ \mathbf{0} & \mathbf{C}_{bb} \end{pmatrix} \begin{pmatrix} \mathbf{w}_a^i \\ \mathbf{w}_b^i \end{pmatrix} = \left(\mathbf{w}_a^j\right)' \mathbf{C}_{aa} \mathbf{w}_a^i + \left(\mathbf{w}_b^j\right)' \mathbf{C}_{bb} \mathbf{w}_b^i$$

and

$$0 = \begin{pmatrix} \mathbf{w}_a^j \\ \mathbf{w}_b^j \end{pmatrix}' \begin{pmatrix} \mathbf{C}_{aa} & \mathbf{0} \\ \mathbf{0} & \mathbf{C}_{bb} \end{pmatrix} \begin{pmatrix} \mathbf{w}_a^i \\ -\mathbf{w}_b^i \end{pmatrix} = \left(\mathbf{w}_a^j\right)' \mathbf{C}_{aa} \mathbf{w}_a^i - \left(\mathbf{w}_b^j\right)' \mathbf{C}_{bb} \mathbf{w}_b^i$$

yielding

$$\left(\mathbf{w}_a^j\right)' \mathbf{C}_{aa} \mathbf{w}_a^i = 0 = \left(\mathbf{w}_b^j\right)' \mathbf{C}_{bb} \mathbf{w}_b^i.$$

This implies that, as with PCA, we obtain a diagonal covariance matrix if we project the data into the coordinate system defined by the eigenvectors, whether we project each view independently or simply the sum of the projections of the two views in the common space. The directions themselves will not, however, be orthogonal in the standard inner product of the feature space.

Dual form of CCA Naturally we wish to solve the problem in the dual formulation. Hence, we consider expressing $\mathbf{w}_a$ and $\mathbf{w}_b$ in terms of their respective parts of the training sample by creating a matrix $\mathbf{X}_a$ whose rows are the vectors $\phi_a(\mathbf{x}_i)$, $i = 1, \ldots, \ell$ and the matrix $\mathbf{X}_b$ with rows $\phi_b(\mathbf{x}_i)$

$$\mathbf{w}_a = \mathbf{X}_a' \boldsymbol{\alpha}_a \text{ and } \mathbf{w}_b = \mathbf{X}_b' \boldsymbol{\alpha}_b.$$

Substituting into (6.20) gives

$$\begin{aligned} \max & \quad \boldsymbol{\alpha}_a' \mathbf{X}_a \mathbf{X}_a' \mathbf{X}_b \mathbf{X}_b' \boldsymbol{\alpha}_b \\ \text{subject to} & \quad \boldsymbol{\alpha}_a' \mathbf{X}_a \mathbf{X}_a' \mathbf{X}_a \mathbf{X}_a' \boldsymbol{\alpha}_a = 1 \text{ and } \boldsymbol{\alpha}_b' \mathbf{X}_b \mathbf{X}_b' \mathbf{X}_b \mathbf{X}_b' \boldsymbol{\alpha}_b = 1, \end{aligned}$$

or equivalently the following optimisation problem.

Computation 6.32 [Kernel CCA] Given a paised dataset with respect to kernels κ_a and κ_b, kernel canonical correlation analysis finds the directions of maximal correlation by solving

$$\max_{\alpha_a,\alpha_b} \quad \alpha_a' \mathbf{K}_a \mathbf{K}_b \alpha_b$$
$$\text{subject to} \quad \alpha_a' \mathbf{K}_a^2 \alpha_a = 1 \text{ and } \alpha_b' \mathbf{K}_b^2 \alpha_b = 1,$$

where $\mathbf{K}_a$ and $\mathbf{K}_b$ are the kernel matrices for the two representations. ∎

Figure 6.4 shows the two feature spaces with the projections of 7 points. The shading corresponds to the value of the projection on the first correlation direction using a Gaussian kernel in each feature space.

Overfitting in CCA Again applying the Lagrangian techniques this leads to the equations

$$\mathbf{K}_a \mathbf{K}_b \alpha_b - \lambda \mathbf{K}_a^2 \alpha_a = 0 \text{ and } \mathbf{K}_b \mathbf{K}_a \alpha_a - \lambda \mathbf{K}_b^2 \alpha_b = 0.$$

These equations highlight the potential problem of overfitting that arises in high-dimensional feature spaces. If the dimension N_a of the feature space F_a satisfies $N_a \gg \ell$, it is likely that the data will be linearly independent in the feature space. For example this is always true for a Gaussian kernel. But if the data are linearly independent in F_a the matrix $\mathbf{K}_a$ will be full rank and hence invertible. This gives

$$\alpha_a = \frac{1}{\lambda} \mathbf{K}_a^{-1} \mathbf{K}_b \alpha_b \tag{6.23}$$

and so

$$\mathbf{K}_b^2 \alpha_b - \lambda^2 \mathbf{K}_b^2 \alpha_b = 0.$$

This equation will hold for all vectors α_b with $\lambda = 1$. Hence, we are able to find perfect correlations between arbitrary projections in F_b and an appropriate choice of the projection in F_a. Clearly these correlations are failing to distinguish spurious features from those capturing the underlying semantics. This is perhaps most clearly demonstrated if we consider a random permutation σ of the examples for the second projections to create the vectors

$$\left(\phi_a\left(\mathbf{x}_i \right), \phi_b\left(\mathbf{x}_{\sigma(i)} \right) \right), i = 1, \ldots, \ell.$$

The kernel matrix $\mathbf{K}_a$ will be unchanged and hence still invertible. We are therefore still able to find perfect correlations even though the underlying semantics are no longer correlated in the two representations.

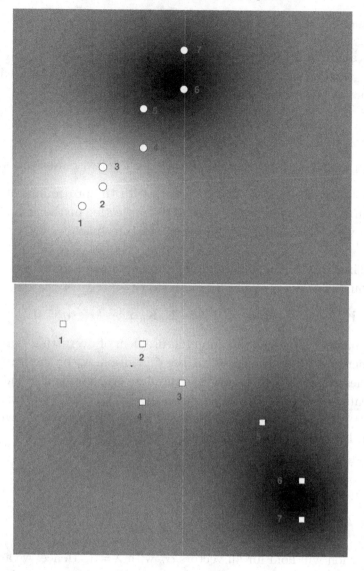

Fig. 6.4. Two feature spaces for a paired dataset with shading indicating the value of the projection onto the first correlation direction.

These observations show that the class of pattern functions we have selected are too flexible. We must introduce some regularisation to control the flexibility. We must, therefore, investigate the statistical stability of CCA, if we are to ensure that meaningful patterns are found.

Stability analysis of CCA Maximising correlation corresponds to minimising the empirical expectation of the pattern function

$$g_{\mathbf{w}_a, \mathbf{w}_b}(\mathbf{x}) = \left\| \mathbf{w}'_a \phi_a(\mathbf{x}) - \mathbf{w}'_b \phi_b(\mathbf{x}) \right\|^2,$$

subject to the same conditions, since

$$
\begin{aligned}
\hat{\mathbb{E}} \left[\left\| \mathbf{w}'_a \phi_a(\mathbf{x}) - \mathbf{w}'_b \phi_b(\mathbf{x}) \right\|^2 \right] &= \hat{\mathbb{E}} \left[\left\| \mathbf{w}'_a \phi_a(\mathbf{x}) \right\|^2 \right] + \hat{\mathbb{E}} \left[\left\| \mathbf{w}'_b \phi_b(\mathbf{x}) \right\|^2 \right] - \\
&\quad 2 \hat{\mathbb{E}} \left[\left\langle \mathbf{w}'_a \phi_a(\mathbf{x}), \mathbf{w}'_b \phi_b(\mathbf{x}) \right\rangle \right] \\
&= 2 \left(1 - \mathbf{w}'_a C_{ab} \mathbf{w}_b \right).
\end{aligned}
$$

The function $g_{\mathbf{w}_a, \mathbf{w}_b}(\mathbf{x}) \approx 0$ captures the property of the pattern that we are seeking. It assures us that the feature $\mathbf{w}'_a \phi_a(\mathbf{x})$ that can be obtained from one view of the data is almost identical to $\mathbf{w}'_b \phi_b(\mathbf{x})$ computable from the second view. Such pairs of features are therefore able to capture underlying properties of the data that are present in both views. If our assumption is correct, that what is essential is common to both views, then these features must be capturing some important properties. We can obtain a stability analysis of the function by simply viewing $g_{\mathbf{w}_a, \mathbf{w}_b}(\mathbf{x})$ as a regression function, albeit with special structure, attempting to learn the constant 0 function. Applying the standard Rademacher bound, observe that the empirical expected value of $g_{\mathbf{w}_a, \mathbf{w}_b}(\mathbf{x})$ is simply $2 \left(1 - \mathbf{w}'_a C_{ab} \mathbf{w}_b \right)$. Furthermore, we can use the same technique as that described in Theorem A.3 of Appendix A.2 to represent the function as a linear function in the feature space determined by the quadratic kernel

$$\hat{\kappa}(\mathbf{x}, \mathbf{z}) = \left(\kappa_a(\mathbf{x}, \mathbf{z}) + \kappa_b(\mathbf{x}, \mathbf{z}) \right)^2,$$

with norm-squared

$$2 \left\| \mathbf{w}_a \mathbf{w}'_b \right\|_F^2 = 2 \operatorname{tr} \left(\mathbf{w}_b \mathbf{w}'_a \mathbf{w}_a \mathbf{w}'_b \right) = \left\| \mathbf{w}_a \right\|^2 \left\| \mathbf{w}_b \right\|^2.$$

This gives the following theorem.

Theorem 6.33 *Fix A and B in $\mathbb{R}^+$. If we obtain a feature given by the pattern function $g_{\mathbf{w}_a, \mathbf{w}_b}(\mathbf{x})$ with $\left\| \mathbf{w}_a \right\| \le A$ and $\left\| \mathbf{w}_b \right\| \le B$, on a paired training set S of size ℓ in the feature space defined by the kernels κ_a and κ_b drawn i.i.d. according to a distribution $\mathcal{D}$, then with probability greater than $1 - \delta$ over the generation of S, the expected value of $g_{\mathbf{w}_a, \mathbf{w}_b}(\mathbf{x})$ on new data is bounded by*

$$\mathbb{E}_{\mathcal{D}} \left[g_{\mathbf{w}_a, \mathbf{w}_b}(\mathbf{x}) \right] \le 2 \left(1 - \mathbf{w}'_a C_{ab} \mathbf{w}_b \right)$$

$$\frac{4(A^2 + B^2)}{\ell} \sqrt{\sum_{i=1}^{\ell} (\kappa_a(\mathbf{x}_i, \mathbf{x}_i) + \kappa_b(\mathbf{x}_i, \mathbf{x}_i))^2}$$

$$+ 3R(A^2 + B^2) \sqrt{\frac{\ln(2/\delta)}{2\ell}},$$

where

$$R = \max_{\mathbf{x} \in \text{supp}(\mathcal{D})} (\kappa_a(\mathbf{x}, \mathbf{x}) + \kappa_b(\mathbf{x}, \mathbf{x})).$$

The theorem indicates that the empirical value of the pattern function will be close to its expectation, provided that the norms of the two direction vectors are controlled. Hence, we must trade-off between finding good correlations while not allowing the norms to become too large.

Regularisation of CCA Theorem 6.33 shows that the quality of the generalisation of the associated pattern function is controlled by the product of the norms of the weight vectors $\mathbf{w}_a$ and $\mathbf{w}_b$. We therefore introduce a penalty on the norms of these weight vectors. This gives rise to the primal optimisation problem.

Computation 6.34 [Regularised CCA] The regularised version of CCA is solved by the optimisation:

$$\max_{\mathbf{w}_a, \mathbf{w}_b} \rho(\mathbf{w}_a, \mathbf{w}_b) \tag{6.24}$$

$$= \frac{\mathbf{w}_a' \mathbf{C}_{ab} \mathbf{w}_b}{\sqrt{\left((1 - \tau_a) \mathbf{w}_a' \mathbf{C}_{aa} \mathbf{w}_a + \tau_a \|\mathbf{w}_a\|^2\right) \left((1 - \tau_b) \mathbf{w}_b' \mathbf{C}_{bb} \mathbf{w}_b + \tau_b \|\mathbf{w}_b\|^2\right)}},$$

where the two regularisation parameters τ_a and τ_b control the flexibility in the two feature spaces.   ∎

Notice that τ_a, τ_b interpolate smoothly between the maximisation of the correlation and the maximisation of the covariance described in Section 6.3. Dualising we arrive at the following optimisation problem.

Computation 6.35 [Kernel regularised CCA] The dual regularised CCA is solved by the optimisation

$$\max_{\boldsymbol{\alpha}_a, \boldsymbol{\alpha}_b} \quad \boldsymbol{\alpha}_a' \mathbf{K}_a \mathbf{K}_b \boldsymbol{\alpha}_b$$
$$\text{subject to} \quad (1 - \tau_a) \boldsymbol{\alpha}_a' \mathbf{K}_a^2 \boldsymbol{\alpha}_a + \tau_a \boldsymbol{\alpha}_a' \mathbf{K}_a \boldsymbol{\alpha}_a = 1$$
$$\text{and } (1 - \tau_b) \boldsymbol{\alpha}_b' \mathbf{K}_b^2 \boldsymbol{\alpha}_b + \tau_b \boldsymbol{\alpha}_b' \mathbf{K}_b \boldsymbol{\alpha}_b = 1.$$

∎

Note that as with ridge regression we regularised by penalising the norms of the weight vectors. Nonetheless, the resulting form of the equations obtained does not in this case correspond to a simple addition to the diagonal of the kernel matrix, the so-called ridge of ridge regression.

Solving dual regularised CCA Using the Lagrangian technique, we can now obtain the equations

$$\mathbf{K}_a \mathbf{K}_b \boldsymbol{\alpha}_b - \lambda \left(1 - \tau_a\right) \mathbf{K}_a^2 \boldsymbol{\alpha}_a - \lambda \tau_a \mathbf{K}_a \boldsymbol{\alpha}_a = 0$$
$$\text{and } \mathbf{K}_b \mathbf{K}_a \boldsymbol{\alpha}_a - \lambda \left(1 - \tau_b\right) \mathbf{K}_b^2 \boldsymbol{\alpha}_b - \lambda \tau_b \mathbf{K}_b \boldsymbol{\alpha}_b = 0,$$

hence forming the generalised eigenvalue problem

$$\begin{pmatrix} 0 & \mathbf{K}_a \mathbf{K}_b \\ \mathbf{K}_b \mathbf{K}_a & 0 \end{pmatrix} \begin{pmatrix} \boldsymbol{\alpha}_a \\ \boldsymbol{\alpha}_b \end{pmatrix}$$
$$= \lambda \begin{pmatrix} \left(1 - \tau_a\right) \mathbf{K}_a^2 + \tau_a \mathbf{K}_a & 0 \\ 0 & \left(1 - \tau_b\right) \mathbf{K}_b^2 + \tau_b \mathbf{K}_b \end{pmatrix} \begin{pmatrix} \boldsymbol{\alpha}_a \\ \boldsymbol{\alpha}_b \end{pmatrix}.$$

One difficulty with this approach can be the size of the resulting generalised eigenvalue problem, since it will be twice the size of the training set. A method of tackling this is to use the partial Gram–Schmidt orthonormalisation of the data in the feature space to form a lower-dimensional approximation to the feature representation of the data. As described in Section 5.2 this is equivalent to performing an incomplete Cholesky decomposition of the kernel matrices

$$\mathbf{K}_a = \mathbf{R}_a' \mathbf{R}_a \text{ and } \mathbf{K}_b = \mathbf{R}_b' \mathbf{R}_b,$$

with the columns of $\mathbf{R}_a$ and $\mathbf{R}_b$ being the new feature vectors of the training points in the orthonormal basis created by the Gram–Schmidt process. Performing an incomplete Cholesky decomposition ensures that $\mathbf{R}_a \in \mathbb{R}^{n_a \times \ell}$ has linearly independent rows so that $\mathbf{R}_a \mathbf{R}_a'$ is invertible. The same holds for $\mathbf{R}_b \mathbf{R}_b'$ with $\mathbf{R}_b \in \mathbb{R}^{n_b \times \ell}$.

We can now view our problem as a primal canonical correlation analysis with the feature vectors given by the columns of $\mathbf{R}_a$ and $\mathbf{R}_b$. This leads to the equations

$$\mathbf{R}_a \mathbf{R}_b' \mathbf{w}_b - \lambda \left(1 - \tau_a\right) \mathbf{R}_a \mathbf{R}_a' \mathbf{w}_a - \lambda \tau_a \mathbf{w}_a = 0 \qquad (6.25)$$
$$\text{and } \mathbf{R}_b \mathbf{R}_a' \mathbf{w}_a - \lambda \left(1 - \tau_b\right) \mathbf{R}_b \mathbf{R}_b' \mathbf{w}_b - \lambda \tau_b \mathbf{w}_b = 0.$$

From the first equation, we can now express $\mathbf{w}_a$ as

$$\mathbf{w}_a = \frac{1}{\lambda} \left(\left(1 - \tau_a\right) \mathbf{R}_a \mathbf{R}_a' + \tau_a \mathbf{I}\right)^{-1} \mathbf{R}_a \mathbf{R}_b' \mathbf{w}_b,$$

which on substitution in the second gives the normal (albeit non-symmetric) eigenvalue problem

$$\left((1-\tau_b)\,\mathbf{R}_b\mathbf{R}_b' + \tau_b\mathbf{I}\right)^{-1}\mathbf{R}_b\mathbf{R}_a'\left((1-\tau_a)\,\mathbf{R}_a\mathbf{R}_a' + \tau_a\mathbf{I}\right)^{-1}\mathbf{R}_a\mathbf{R}_b'\mathbf{w}_b = \lambda^2\mathbf{w}_b$$

of dimension $n_b \times n_b$. After performing a full Cholesky decomposition

$$\mathbf{R}'\mathbf{R} = \left((1-\tau_b)\,\mathbf{R}_b\mathbf{R}_b' + \tau_b\mathbf{I}\right)$$

of the non-singular matrix on the right hand side, we then take

$$\mathbf{u}_b = \mathbf{R}\mathbf{w}_b,$$

which using the fact that the transpose and inversion operations commute leads to the equivalent symmetric eigenvalue problem

$$\left(\mathbf{R}'\right)^{-1}\mathbf{R}_b\mathbf{R}_a'\left((1-\tau_a)\,\mathbf{R}_a\mathbf{R}_a' + \tau_a\mathbf{I}\right)^{-1}\mathbf{R}_a\mathbf{R}_b'\mathbf{R}^{-1}\mathbf{u}_b = \lambda^2\mathbf{u}_b.$$

By symmetry we could have created an eigenvalue problem of dimension $n_a \times n_a$. Hence, the size of the eigenvalue problem can be reduced to the smaller of the two partial Gram–Schmidt dimensions.

We can of course recover the full unapproximated kernel canonical correlation analysis if we simply choose $n_a = \text{rank}\,(\mathbf{K}_a)$ and $n_b = \text{rank}\,(\mathbf{K}_b)$. Even in this case we have avoided the need to solve a generalised eigenvalue problem, while at the same time reducing the dimension of the problem by at least a factor of two since $\min(n_a, n_b) \le \ell$. The overall algorithm is as follows.

Algorithm 6.36 [Kernel CCA] Kernel canonical correlation analysis can be solved as shown in Code Fragment 6.3. ∎

This means that we can have two views of an object that together create a paired dataset S through two different representations or kernels. We use this procedure to compute correlations between the two sets that are stable in the sense that they capture properties of the underlying distribution rather than of the particular training set or view.

Remark 6.37 [Bilingual corpora] Example 6.28 has already mentioned as examples of paired datasets so-called parallel corpora in which each document appears with its translation to a second language. We can apply the kernel canonical correlation analysis to such a corpus using kernels for text that will be discussed in Chapter 10. This will provide a means of projecting documents from either language into a common semantic space. ∎

Input	kernel matrices $\mathbf{K}_a$ and $\mathbf{K}_b$ with parameters τ_a and τ_b
Process	Perform (incomplete) Cholesky decompositions: $\mathbf{K}_a = \mathbf{R}_a'\mathbf{R}_a$ and $\mathbf{K}_b = \mathbf{R}_b'\mathbf{R}_b$ of dimensions n_a and n_b; perform a complete Cholesky decomposition: $(1 - \tau_b)\,\mathbf{R}_b\mathbf{R}_b' + \tau_b\mathbf{I} = \mathbf{R}'\mathbf{R}$ solve the eigenvalue problem: $(\mathbf{R}')^{-1}\mathbf{R}_b\mathbf{R}_a'\left((1-\tau_a)\,\mathbf{R}_a\mathbf{R}_a' + \tau_a\mathbf{I}\right)^{-1}\mathbf{R}_a\mathbf{R}_b'\mathbf{R}^{-1}\mathbf{u}_b = \lambda^2\mathbf{u}_b$ to give each λ_j, $\mathbf{u}_b^j$ compute $\mathbf{w}_b^j = \mathbf{R}^{-1}\mathbf{u}_b$, $\mathbf{w}_b^j = \mathbf{w}_b^j/\|\mathbf{w}_b^j\|$ $\mathbf{w}_a^j = \left((1-\tau_a)\,\mathbf{R}_a\mathbf{R}_a' + \tau_a\mathbf{I}\right)^{-1}\mathbf{R}_a\mathbf{R}_b'\mathbf{w}_b^j$ $\mathbf{w}_a^j = \mathbf{w}_a^j/\|\mathbf{w}_a^j\|$
Output	eigenvectors and values $\mathbf{w}_a^j$, $\mathbf{w}_b^j$ and $\lambda_j > 0,$. $j = 1,\ldots,\min(n_a, n_b)$

Code Fragment 6.3. Pseudocode for the kernel CCA algorithm.

Remark 6.38 [More than 2 representations] Notice that a simple manipulation of equation (6.22) gives the alternative formulation

$$\begin{pmatrix} C_{aa} & C_{ab} \\ C_{ba} & C_{bb} \end{pmatrix} \begin{pmatrix} \mathbf{w}_a \\ \mathbf{w}_b \end{pmatrix} = (1+\lambda) \begin{pmatrix} C_{aa} & 0 \\ 0 & C_{bb} \end{pmatrix} \begin{pmatrix} \mathbf{w}_a \\ \mathbf{w}_b \end{pmatrix}$$

which suggests a natural generalisation, namely seeking correlations between three or more views. Given k multivariate random variables, it reduces to the generalised eigenvalue problem

$$\begin{pmatrix} \mathbf{C}_{11} & \mathbf{C}_{12} & \cdots & \mathbf{C}_{1k} \\ \mathbf{C}_{21} & \mathbf{C}_{22} & \cdots & \vdots \\ \vdots & \vdots & \ddots & \vdots \\ \mathbf{C}_{k1} & \cdots & \cdots & \mathbf{C}_{kk} \end{pmatrix} \begin{pmatrix} \mathbf{w}_1 \\ \vdots \\ \vdots \\ \mathbf{w}_k \end{pmatrix}$$

$$= \rho \begin{pmatrix} \mathbf{C}_{11} & 0 & \cdots & 0 \\ 0 & \mathbf{C}_{22} & \cdots & 0 \\ \vdots & \vdots & \ddots & \vdots \\ 0 & 0 & \cdots & \mathbf{C}_{kk} \end{pmatrix} \begin{pmatrix} \mathbf{w}_1 \\ \vdots \\ \vdots \\ \mathbf{w}_k \end{pmatrix},$$

where we use C_{ij} to denote the covariance matrix between the ith and jth views. Note that for $k > 2$ there is no obvious way of reducing such a generalised eigenvalue problem to a lower-dimensional eigenvalue problem as was possible using the Cholesky decomposition in the case $k = 2$. ∎

6.6 Fisher discriminant analysis II

We considered the Fisher discriminant in Section 5.4, arriving at a dual formulation that could be solved by solving a set of linear equations. We revisit it here to highlight the fact that it can also be viewed as the solution of a generalised eigenvalue problem and so is closely related to the correlation and covariance analysis we have been studying in this chapter. Recall that Computation 5.14 characterised the regularised Fisher discriminant as choosing its discriminant vector to maximise the quotient

$$\frac{(\mu_{\mathbf{w}}^+ - \mu_{\mathbf{w}}^-)^2}{(\sigma_{\mathbf{w}}^+)^2 + (\sigma_{\mathbf{w}}^-)^2 + \lambda \|\mathbf{w}\|^2}.$$

This can be expressed using the notation of Section 5.4 as

$$\max_{\mathbf{w}} \frac{\mathbf{w}'\mathbf{X}'\mathbf{y}\mathbf{y}'\mathbf{X}\mathbf{w}}{\lambda\mathbf{w}'\mathbf{w} + \frac{\ell}{2\ell+\ell-}\mathbf{w}'\mathbf{X}'\mathbf{B}\mathbf{X}\mathbf{w}} = \max_{\mathbf{w}} \frac{\mathbf{w}'\mathbf{E}\mathbf{w}}{\mathbf{w}'\mathbf{F}\mathbf{w}},$$

where

$$\mathbf{E} = \mathbf{X}'\mathbf{y}\mathbf{y}'\mathbf{X} \text{ and } \mathbf{F} = \lambda\mathbf{I} + \frac{\ell}{2\ell+\ell-}\mathbf{X}'\mathbf{B}\mathbf{X}.$$

Hence, the solution is the eigenvector corresponding to the largest eigenvalue of the generalised eigenvalue problem

$$\mathbf{E}\mathbf{w} = \mu\mathbf{F}\mathbf{w},$$

as outlined in Section 6.4. Note that the matrix $\mathbf{E}$ has rank 1 since it can be decomposed as

$$\mathbf{E} = (\mathbf{X}'\mathbf{y})(\mathbf{y}'\mathbf{X}),$$

where $\mathbf{X}'\mathbf{y}$ has just one column. This implies that only the first eigenvector contains useful information and that it can be found by the matrix inversion procedure described in Section 5.4.

6.7 Methods for linear regression

The previous section showed how the Fisher discriminant is equivalent to choosing a feature by solving a generalised eigenvalue problem and then defining a threshold in that one-dimensional space. This section will return to the problem of regression and consider how the feature spaces derived from solving eigenvalue problems might be used to enhance regression accuracy.

We first met regression in Chapter 2 when we considered simple linear regression subsequently augmented with a regularisation of the regression vector **w** to create so-called ridge regression defined in Computation 7.21. In this section we consider performing linear regression using a new set of coordinates that has been extracted from the data with the methods presented above. This will lead to an easier understanding of some popular regression algorithms.

First recall the optimisation of least squares regression. We seek a vector **w** that solves

$$\min_{\mathbf{w}} \|\mathbf{Xw} - \mathbf{y}\|_2^2,$$

where as usual the rows of **X** contain the feature vectors of the examples and the desired outputs are stored in the vector **y**. If we wish to consider a more general multivariate regression both **w** and **y** become matrices **W** and **Y** and the norm is taken as the Frobenius matrix norm

$$\min_{\mathbf{W}} \|\mathbf{XW} - \mathbf{Y}\|_F^2,$$

since this is equivalent to summing the squared norms of the individual errors.

Principal components regression Perhaps the simplest method to consider is the use of the features returned by PCA. If we were to use the first k eigenvectors of $\mathbf{X'X}$ as our features and leave **Y** unchanged, this would correspond to performing PCA and regressing in the feature space given by the first k principal axes, so the data matrix now becomes $\mathbf{XU}_k$, where $\mathbf{U}_k$ contains the first k columns of the matrix **U** from the singular value decomposition $\mathbf{X'} = \mathbf{U\Sigma V'}$. Using the fact that premultiplying by an orthogonal matrix does not affect the norm, we obtain

$$\min_{\mathbf{B}} \|\mathbf{XU}_k\mathbf{B} - \mathbf{Y}\|_F^2 = \min_{\mathbf{B}} \|\mathbf{V'V\Sigma'U'U}_k\mathbf{B} - \mathbf{V'Y}\|_F^2$$
$$= \min_{\mathbf{B}} \|\mathbf{\Sigma}_k'\mathbf{B} - \mathbf{V'Y}\|_F^2,$$

where $\mathbf{\Sigma}_k$ is the matrix obtained by taking the first k rows of $\mathbf{\Sigma}$. Letting $\mathbf{\Sigma}_k^{-1}$ denote the matrix obtained from $\mathbf{\Sigma}_k$ by inverting its diagonal elements, we have $\mathbf{\Sigma}_k^{-1}\mathbf{\Sigma}_k' = \mathbf{I}_k$, so the solution **B** with minimal norm is given by

$$\mathbf{B} = \mathbf{\Sigma}_k^{-1}\mathbf{V'Y} = \bar{\mathbf{\Sigma}}_k^{-1}\mathbf{V}_k'\mathbf{Y},$$

where $\mathbf{V}_k$ contains the first k columns of **V** and $\bar{\mathbf{\Sigma}}_k^{-1}$ is the square matrix containing the first k columns of $\mathbf{\Sigma}_k^{-1}$. It follows from the singular value decomposition that

$$\mathbf{V}_k' = \bar{\mathbf{\Sigma}}_k^{-1}\mathbf{U}_k'\mathbf{X'}, \tag{6.26}$$

so we can also write

$$\mathbf{B} = \bar{\Sigma}_k^{-2} \mathbf{U}_k' \mathbf{X}' \mathbf{Y}.$$

This gives the primal form emphasising that the components are computed by an inner product between the corresponding feature vectors $\mathbf{u}_j$ that form the columns of $\mathbf{U}$ and the data matrix $\mathbf{X}'\mathbf{Y}$ weighted by the inverse of the corresponding eigenvalue.

If we recall that $\mathbf{V}$ contains the eigenvectors $\mathbf{v}_j$ of the kernel matrix and that kernel PCA identifies the dual variables of the directions $\mathbf{u}_j$ as

$$\frac{1}{\sigma_j}\mathbf{v}_j,$$

it follows from equation (6.26) that the regression coefficient for the jth principal component is given by the inner product between its dual representation and the target outputs again with an appropriate weighting of the inverse of the corresponding singular value. We can therefore write the resulting regression function for the univariate case in the dual form as

$$f(\mathbf{x}) = \sum_{j=1}^{k} \frac{1}{\sigma_j} \sum_{s=1}^{\ell} v_{js} y_s \sum_{i=1}^{\ell} \frac{1}{\sigma_j} v_{ji} \kappa(\mathbf{x}_i, \mathbf{x}),$$

where v_{js} denotes the sth component of the jth eigenvector $\mathbf{v}_j$. Hence

$$f(\mathbf{x}) = \sum_{i=1}^{\ell} \alpha_i \kappa(\mathbf{x}_i, \mathbf{x})$$

where

$$\boldsymbol{\alpha} = \sum_{j=1}^{k} \frac{1}{\lambda_j} \left(\mathbf{v}_j' \mathbf{y} \right) \mathbf{v}_j.$$

The form of the solution has an intuitive feel in that we work out the covariances with the target values of the different eigenvectors and weight their contribution to $\boldsymbol{\alpha}$ proportionately. This also implies that we can continue to add additional dimensions without recomputing the previous coefficients in the primal space but by simply adding in a vector to $\boldsymbol{\alpha}$ in the dual respresentation. This is summarised in Algorithm 6.39.

Algorithm 6.39 [Principal components regression] The dual principal components regression (PCR) algorithm is given in Code Fragment 6.4. ∎

input	Data $S = \{\mathbf{x}_1, \ldots, \mathbf{x}_\ell\}$, dimension k and target output vectors $\mathbf{y}^s$, $s = 1, \ldots, m$.
process	$\mathbf{K}_{ij} = \kappa\left(\mathbf{x}_i, \mathbf{x}_j\right)$, $i, j = 1, \ldots, \ell$ $\mathbf{K} = \mathbf{K} - \frac{1}{\ell}\mathbf{j}\mathbf{j}'\mathbf{K} - \frac{1}{\ell}\mathbf{K}\mathbf{j}\mathbf{j}' + \frac{1}{\ell^2}\left(\mathbf{j}'\mathbf{K}\mathbf{j}\right)\mathbf{j}\mathbf{j}'$, $[\mathbf{V}, \mathbf{\Lambda}] = \text{eig}\,(\mathbf{K})$ $\boldsymbol{\alpha}^s = \sum_{j=1}^{k} \frac{1}{\lambda_j}\left(\mathbf{v}_j'\mathbf{y}^s\right)\mathbf{v}_j$, $s = 1, \ldots, m$.
output	Regression functions $f_s\left(\mathbf{x}\right) = \sum_{i=1}^{\ell} \alpha_i^s \kappa\left(\mathbf{x}_i, \mathbf{x}\right)$, $s = 1, \ldots, m$.

Code Fragment 6.4. Pseudocode for dual principal components regression.

Regression features from maximal covariance We can see from the previous example that the critical measure for the different coordinates is their covariance with the matrix $\mathbf{X}'\mathbf{Y}$, since the regression coefficient is proportional to this quantity. This suggests that rather than using PCA to choose the features, we should select directions that maximise the covariance. Proposition 6.20 showed that the directions that maximise the covariance are given by the singular vectors of the matrix $\mathbf{X}'\mathbf{Y}$. Furthermore, the characterisation of the minimisers of equation (6.15) as the orthogonal matrices of the singular value decomposition of $\mathbf{X}'\mathbf{Y}$ suggests that they may provide a useful set of features when solving a regression problem from an input space $X = \mathbb{R}^n$ to an output space $Y = \mathbb{R}^m$. There is an implicit restriction as there are only m non-zero singular values of the matrix $\mathbf{X}'\mathbf{Y}$. We must therefore consider performing regression of the variables $\mathbf{Y}$ in terms of $\mathbf{X}\mathbf{U}_k$, where $\mathbf{U}_k$ is the matrix formed of the first $k \leq m$ columns of $\mathbf{U}$. We seek a $k \times m$ matrix of coefficients $\mathbf{B}$ that solves the optimisation

$$
\begin{aligned}
\min_{\mathbf{B}} \|\mathbf{X}\mathbf{U}_k\mathbf{B} - \mathbf{Y}\|_F^2 &= \min_{\mathbf{B}} \langle \mathbf{X}\mathbf{U}_k\mathbf{B} - \mathbf{Y}, \mathbf{X}\mathbf{U}_k\mathbf{B} - \mathbf{Y}\rangle_F \\
&= \min_{\mathbf{B}} \left(\text{tr}(\mathbf{B}'\mathbf{U}_k'\mathbf{X}'\mathbf{X}\mathbf{U}_k\mathbf{B}) - 2\,\text{tr}(\mathbf{B}'\mathbf{U}_k'\mathbf{X}'\mathbf{Y}) \right. \\
&\qquad\left. +\,\text{tr}(\mathbf{Y}'\mathbf{Y})\right) \\
&= \min_{\mathbf{B}} \left(\text{tr}(\mathbf{B}'\mathbf{U}_k'\mathbf{X}'\mathbf{X}\mathbf{U}_k\mathbf{B}) - 2\,\text{tr}(\mathbf{B}'\mathbf{U}_k'\mathbf{X}'\mathbf{Y})\right).
\end{aligned}
$$

The final regression coefficients are given by $\mathbf{U}_k\mathbf{B}$. We seek the minimum by computing the gradient with respect to $\mathbf{B}$ and setting to zero. This results in the equation

$$
\mathbf{U}_k'\mathbf{X}'\mathbf{X}\mathbf{U}_k\mathbf{B} = \mathbf{U}_k'\mathbf{X}'\mathbf{Y} = \mathbf{U}_k'\mathbf{U}\boldsymbol{\Sigma}\mathbf{V}' = \boldsymbol{\Sigma}_k\mathbf{V}_k'.
$$

The solution for $\mathbf{B}$ can be computed using, for example, a Cholesky decomposition of $\mathbf{U}_k'\mathbf{X}'\mathbf{X}\mathbf{U}_k$, though for the case where $k = 1$, it is given by

$$\mathbf{B} = \frac{\sigma_1}{\mathbf{u}_1'\mathbf{X}'\mathbf{X}\mathbf{u}_1}\mathbf{v}_1'.$$

If we wish to compute the dual representation of this regression coefficient, we must express

$$\mathbf{u}_1\mathbf{B} = \frac{\sigma_1}{\mathbf{u}_1'\mathbf{X}'\mathbf{X}\mathbf{u}_1}\mathbf{u}_1\mathbf{v}_1' = \mathbf{X}'\boldsymbol{\alpha},$$

for some $\boldsymbol{\alpha}$. By observing that $\mathbf{u}_1 = \frac{1}{\sigma_1}\mathbf{X}'\mathbf{Y}\mathbf{v}_1$ we obtain

$$\boldsymbol{\alpha} = \frac{1}{\mathbf{u}_1'\mathbf{X}'\mathbf{X}\mathbf{u}_1}\mathbf{Y}\mathbf{v}_1\mathbf{v}_1'.$$

Note that the $\frac{1}{\sigma_1}\mathbf{Y}\mathbf{v}_1$ are the dual variables of $\mathbf{u}_1$, so that we again see the dual variables of the feature playing a role in determining the dual representation of the regression coefficients. For $k > 1$, there is no avoiding solving a system of linear equations.

When we compare PCR and the use of maximal covariance features, PCR has two advantages. Firstly, the coefficients can be obtained by simple inner products rather than solving linear equations, and secondly, the restriction to take $k \leq m$ does not apply. The disadvantage of PCR is that the choice of features does not take into account the output vectors $\mathbf{Y}$ so that the features are unable to align with the maximal covariance directions. As discussed above the features that carry the regression information may be of relatively low variance and so could potentially be removed by the PCA phase of the algorithm.

The next section will describe an algorithm known as *partial least squares* that combines the advantages of both methods while further improving the covariance obtained and providing a simple method for iteratively computing the feature directions.

6.7.1 Partial least squares

When developing a regression algorithm, it appears that it may not be the variance of the inputs, but their covariance with the target that is more important. The partial least squares approach uses the covariance to guide the selection of features before performing least-squares regression in the derived feature space. It is very popular in the field of chemometrics, where high-dimensional and correlated representations are commonplace. This situation will also arise if we use kernels to project the data into spaces where the new coordinates are far from uncorrelated and where the dimension of the space is much higher than the sample size. The combination of PLS with kernels produces a powerful algorithm that we will describe in the next subsection after first deriving the primal version here.

Our first goal is to find the directions of maximum covariance. Since we have already described in Section 6.3 that these are computed by the singular value decomposition of $\mathbf{X'Y}$ and have further discussed the difficulties of using the resulting features at the end of the previous section, it seems a contradiction that we should be able to further improve the covariance. This is certainly true of the first direction and indeed the first direction that is chosen by the partial least squares algorithm is that given by the singular vector corresponding to the largest singular value. Consider now performing regression using only this first direction. The regression coefficient is the one for the case $k = 1$ given in the previous subsection as $b\mathbf{v}_1'$, where

$$b = \frac{\sigma_1}{\mathbf{u}_1'\mathbf{X'Xu}_1},$$

while the approximation of $\mathbf{Y}$ will be given by

$$b\mathbf{Xu}_1\mathbf{v}_1'.$$

Hence, the values across the training set of the hidden feature that has been used are given in the vector $\mathbf{Xu}_1$. This suggests that rather than deflate $\mathbf{X'Y}$ by $\sigma_1\mathbf{u}_1\mathbf{v}_1'$ as required for the singular value decomposition, we deflate $\mathbf{X}$ by projecting its columns into the space orthogonal to $\mathbf{Xu}_1$. Using equation (5.8) which gives the projection matrix for a normalised vector $\mathbf{w}$ as

$$\left(\mathbf{I} - \mathbf{ww'}\right),$$

we obtain the deflation of $\mathbf{X} = \mathbf{X}_1$ as

$$\mathbf{X}_2 = \left(\mathbf{I} - \frac{\mathbf{X}_1\mathbf{u}_1\mathbf{u}_1'\mathbf{X}_1'}{\mathbf{u}_1'\mathbf{X}_1'\mathbf{X}_1\mathbf{u}_1}\right)\mathbf{X}_1 = \mathbf{X}_1 - \frac{\mathbf{X}_1\mathbf{u}_1\mathbf{u}_1'\mathbf{X}_1'\mathbf{X}_1}{\mathbf{u}_1'\mathbf{X}_1'\mathbf{X}_1\mathbf{u}_1} = \mathbf{X}_1\left(\mathbf{I} - \frac{\mathbf{u}_1\mathbf{u}_1'\mathbf{X}_1'\mathbf{X}_1}{\mathbf{u}_1'\mathbf{X}_1'\mathbf{X}_1\mathbf{u}_1}\right).$$
$$(6.27)$$

If we now recursively choose a new direction, the result will be that the vector of values of the next hidden feature will necessarily be orthogonal to $\mathbf{Xu}_1$ since it will be a linear combination of the columns of the deflated matrix all of which are othogonal to that vector.

Remark 6.40 [Conjugacy] It is important to distinguish between the orthogonality between the values of a feature across the training examples, and the orthogonality of the feature vectors. Vectors that satisfy the orthogonality considered here are referred to as *conjugate*. Furthermore, this will imply that the coefficients can be computed iteratively at each stage since there can be no interaction between a set of conjugate features. ∎

Remark 6.41 [Conjugacy of eigenvectors] It may seem surprising that deflating using $\mathbf{X}\mathbf{u}_1$ leads to orthogonal features when, for an eigenvalue decomposition, we deflate by the equivalent of $\mathbf{u}_1$; that is, the first eigenvector. The reason that the eigenvalue deflation leads to conjugate features is that for the eigenvalue case $\mathbf{X}\mathbf{u}_1 = \sigma_1 \mathbf{v}_1$ is the first eigenvector of the kernel matrix. Hence, using the eigenvectors results in features that are automatically conjugate. ∎

Since we have removed precisely the direction that contributed to the maximal covariance, namely $\mathbf{X}\mathbf{u}_1$, the maximal covariance of the deflated matrix must be at least as large as σ_2, the second singular value of the original matrix. In general, the covariance of the deflated matrix will be larger than σ_2. Furthermore, this also means that the restriction to $k \leq m$ no longer applies since we do not need to deflate $\mathbf{Y}$ at all. We summarise the PLS feature extraction in Algorithm 6.42.

Algorithm 6.42 [PLS feature extraction] The PLS feature extraction algorithm is given in Code Fragment 6.5. ∎

input	Data matrix $\mathbf{X} \in \mathbb{R}^{\ell \times N}$, dimension k, target vectors $\mathbf{Y} \in \mathbb{R}^{\ell \times m}$.

process	$\mathbf{X}_1 = \mathbf{X}$
	 for $j = 1, \ldots, k$
	    let $\mathbf{u}_j, \mathbf{v}_j, \sigma_j$ be the first singular vector/value of $\mathbf{X}_j'\mathbf{Y}$,
	    $\mathbf{X}_{j+1} = \left(\mathbf{I} - \frac{\mathbf{X}_j \mathbf{u}_j \mathbf{u}_j' \mathbf{X}_j'}{\mathbf{u}_j' \mathbf{X}_j' \mathbf{X}_j \mathbf{u}_j} \right) \mathbf{X}_j$
	 end

output	Feature directions $\mathbf{u}_j$, $j = 1, \ldots, k$.

Code Fragment 6.5. Pseudocode for PLS feature extraction.

Remark 6.43 [Deflating $\mathbf{Y}$] We can if we wish use a similar deflation strategy for $\mathbf{Y}$ giving, for example

$$\mathbf{Y}_2 = \left(\mathbf{I} - \frac{\mathbf{X}_1 \mathbf{u}_1 \mathbf{u}_1' \mathbf{X}_1'}{\mathbf{u}_1' \mathbf{X}_1' \mathbf{X}_1 \mathbf{u}_1} \right) \mathbf{Y}.$$

Surprisingly even if we do, the fact that we are only removing the explained covariance means it will have no effect on the extraction of subsequent features. An alternative way of seeing this is that we are projecting into the space spanned by the columns of $\mathbf{X}_2$ and so are only removing components parallel to $\mathbf{X}_1\mathbf{u}_1$. This also ensures that we can continue to extract hidden features as long as there continues to be explainable variance in $\mathbf{Y}$, typically for values of $k > m$. Deflating $\mathbf{Y}$ will, however, be needed for dual partial least squares. ∎

Remark 6.44 [Relation to Gram–Schmidt orthonormalisation] For one-dimensional outputs the PLS feature extraction can be viewed as a Gram–Schmidt orthonormalisation of the so-called Krylov space of vectors

$$\mathbf{X}'\mathbf{y}, (\mathbf{X}'\mathbf{X})^1\mathbf{X}'\mathbf{y}, \ldots, (\mathbf{X}'\mathbf{X})^{k-1}\mathbf{X}'\mathbf{y}$$

with respect to the inner product

$$\langle \mathbf{a}, \mathbf{b} \rangle = \mathbf{a}'(\mathbf{X}'\mathbf{X})\,\mathbf{b}.$$

It is also closely related to the conjugate gradient method as applied to minimising the expression

$$\frac{1}{2}\mathbf{u}'(\mathbf{X}'\mathbf{X})\,\mathbf{u} - \mathbf{y}\mathbf{X}'\mathbf{u}.$$

∎

Orthogonality and conjugacy of PLS features There are some nice properties of the intermediate quantities computed in the algorithm. For example the vectors $\mathbf{u}_i$ are not only conjugate but also orthogonal as vectors, as the following derivation demonstrates. Suppose $i < j$, then we can write

$$\mathbf{X}_j = \mathbf{Z}\left(\mathbf{X}_i - \frac{\mathbf{X}_i\mathbf{u}_i\mathbf{u}_i'\mathbf{X}_i'\mathbf{X}_i}{\mathbf{u}_i'\mathbf{X}_i'\mathbf{X}_i\mathbf{u}_i}\right),$$

for some matrix $\mathbf{Z}$. Hence

$$\mathbf{X}_j\mathbf{u}_i = \mathbf{Z}\left(\mathbf{X}_i - \frac{\mathbf{X}_i\mathbf{u}_i\mathbf{u}_i'\mathbf{X}_i'\mathbf{X}_i}{\mathbf{u}_i'\mathbf{X}_i'\mathbf{X}_i\mathbf{u}_i}\right)\mathbf{u}_i = 0. \tag{6.28}$$

Note that $\mathbf{u}_j$ is in the span of the rows of $\mathbf{X}_j$, that is $\mathbf{u}_j = \mathbf{X}_j'\boldsymbol{\alpha}$, for some $\boldsymbol{\alpha}$. It follows that

$$\mathbf{u}_j'\mathbf{u}_i = \boldsymbol{\alpha}'\mathbf{X}_j\mathbf{u}_i = 0.$$

Furthermore, if we let

$$\mathbf{p}_j = \frac{\mathbf{X}_j'\mathbf{X}_j\mathbf{u}_j}{\mathbf{u}_j'\mathbf{X}_j'\mathbf{X}_j\mathbf{u}_j},$$

we have $\mathbf{u}_i'\mathbf{p}_j = 0$ for $i < j$. This follows from

$$\mathbf{u}_i'\mathbf{p}_j = \frac{\mathbf{u}_i'\mathbf{X}_j'\mathbf{X}_j\mathbf{u}_j}{\mathbf{u}_j'\mathbf{X}_j'\mathbf{X}_j\mathbf{u}_j} = 0, \tag{6.29}$$

again from equation (6.28). Furthermore, we clearly have $\mathbf{u}_j'\mathbf{p}_j = 1$. The projection of $\mathbf{X}_j$ can also now be expressed as

$$\mathbf{X}_{j+1} = \mathbf{X}_j \left(\mathbf{I} - \frac{\mathbf{u}_j\mathbf{u}_j'\mathbf{X}_j'\mathbf{X}_j}{\mathbf{u}_j'\mathbf{X}_j'\mathbf{X}_j\mathbf{u}_j} \right) = \mathbf{X}_j \left(\mathbf{I} - \mathbf{u}_j\mathbf{p}_j' \right). \tag{6.30}$$

Computing the regression coefficients If we consider a test point with feature vector $\phi(\mathbf{x})$ the transformations that we perform at each step should also be applied to $\phi_1(\mathbf{x}) = \phi(\mathbf{x})$ to create a series of feature vectors

$$\phi_{j+1}(\mathbf{x})' = \phi_j(\mathbf{x})' \left(\mathbf{I} - \mathbf{u}_j\mathbf{p}_j' \right).$$

This is the same operation that is performed on the rows of $\mathbf{X}_j$ in equation (6.30). We can now write

$$\phi(\mathbf{x})' = \phi_{k+1}(\mathbf{x})' + \sum_{j=1}^{k} \phi_j(\mathbf{x})' \mathbf{u}_j\mathbf{p}_j'.$$

The feature vector that we need for the regression $\hat{\phi}(\mathbf{x})$ has components

$$\hat{\phi}(\mathbf{x}) = \left(\phi_j(\mathbf{x})' \mathbf{u}_j \right)_{j=1}^{k},$$

since these are the projections of the residual vector at stage j onto the next feature vector $\mathbf{u}_j$. Rather than compute $\phi_j(\mathbf{x})'$ iteratively, consider using the inner products between the original $\phi(\mathbf{x})'$ and the feature vectors $\mathbf{u}_j$ stored as the columns of the matrix $\mathbf{U}$

$$\begin{aligned} \phi(\mathbf{x})'\mathbf{U} &= \phi_{k+1}(\mathbf{x})'\mathbf{U} + \sum_{j=1}^{k} \phi_j(\mathbf{x})' \mathbf{u}_j\mathbf{p}_j'\mathbf{U} \\ &= \phi_{k+1}(\mathbf{x})'\mathbf{U} + \hat{\phi}(\mathbf{x})' \mathbf{P}'\mathbf{U}, \end{aligned}$$

where $\mathbf{P}$ is the matrix whose columns are $\mathbf{p}_j$, $j = 1, \ldots, k$. Finally, since for $s > j$, $(\mathbf{I} - \mathbf{u}_s\mathbf{p}_s')\mathbf{u}_j = \mathbf{u}_j$, we can write

$$\phi_{k+1}(\mathbf{x})' \mathbf{u}_j = \phi_k(\mathbf{x})' \left(\mathbf{I} - \mathbf{u}_k\mathbf{p}_k' \right) \mathbf{u}_j = 0, \text{ for } j = 1, \ldots, k.$$

It follows that the new feature vector can be expressed as

$$\hat{\phi}(\mathbf{x})' = \phi(\mathbf{x})' \mathbf{U} \left(\mathbf{P}'\mathbf{U} \right)^{-1}.$$

As observed above the regression coefficients for the jth dimension of the new feature vector is

$$\frac{\sigma_j}{\mathbf{u}_j' \mathbf{X}_j' \mathbf{X}_j \mathbf{u}_j} \mathbf{v}_j',$$

where $\mathbf{v}_j$ is the complementary singular vector associated with $\mathbf{u}_j$ so that

$$\sigma_j \mathbf{v}_i = \mathbf{Y}' \mathbf{X}_i \mathbf{u}_i$$

It follows that the overall regression coefficients can be computed as

$$\mathbf{W} = \mathbf{U} \left(\mathbf{P}' \mathbf{U} \right)^{-1} \mathbf{C}', \tag{6.31}$$

where $\mathbf{C}$ is the matrix with columns

$$\mathbf{c}_j = \frac{\mathbf{Y}' \mathbf{X}_j \mathbf{u}_j}{\mathbf{u}_j' \mathbf{X}_j' \mathbf{X}_j \mathbf{u}_j}.$$

This appears to need a matrix inversion, but equation (6.29) implies that the matrix $\mathbf{P}' \mathbf{U}$ is upper triangular with constant diagonal 1 so that the computation of

$$\left(\mathbf{P}' \mathbf{U} \right)^{-1} \mathbf{C}'$$

only involves the solution of m sets of k linear equations in k unknowns with an upper triangular matrix.

Iterative computation of singular vectors The final promised ingredient of the new algorithm is an iterative method for computing the maximal singular value and associated singular vectors. The technique is known as the iterative power method and can also be used to find the largest eigenvalue of a matrix. It simply involves repeatedly multiplying a random initial vector by the matrix and then renormalising. Supposing that $\mathbf{Z} \mathbf{\Lambda} \mathbf{Z}'$ is the eigen-decomposition of a matrix $\mathbf{A}$, then the computation

$$\mathbf{A}^s \mathbf{x} = \left(\mathbf{Z} \mathbf{\Lambda} \mathbf{Z}' \right)^s \mathbf{x} = \mathbf{Z} \mathbf{\Lambda}^s \mathbf{Z}' \mathbf{x} \approx \mathbf{z}_1 \lambda_1^s \mathbf{z}_1' \mathbf{x}$$

shows that the vector converges to the largest eigenvector and the renormalisation coefficient to the largest eigenvalue provided $\mathbf{z}_1' \mathbf{x} \neq 0$.

In general this is not very efficient, but in the case of low-rank matrices such as $\mathbf{C}_{xy}$ when the output dimension m is small, it proves very effective. Indeed for the case when $m = 1$ a single iteration is sufficient to find the exact solution. Hence, for solving a standard regression problem this is more efficient than performing an SVD of $\mathbf{X}' \mathbf{Y}$.

Algorithm 6.45 [Primal PLS] The primal PLS algorithm is given in Code Fragment 6.6. The repeat loop computes the first singular value by the

input	Data matrix $\mathbf{X} \in \mathbb{R}^{\ell \times N}$, dimension k, target outputs $\mathbf{Y} \in \mathbb{R}^{\ell \times m}$.
process	$\boldsymbol{\mu} = \frac{1}{\ell}\mathbf{X}'\mathbf{j}$ computes the means of components
	$\mathbf{X}_1 = \mathbf{X} - \mathbf{j}\boldsymbol{\mu}'$ centering the data
	$\hat{\mathbf{Y}} = \mathbf{0}$
	for $j = 1, \ldots, k$
	$\quad \mathbf{u}_j$=first column of $\mathbf{X}_j'\mathbf{Y}$
	$\quad \mathbf{u_j} = \mathbf{u_j}/\|\mathbf{u_j}\|$
	$\quad$ repeat
	$\quad\quad \mathbf{u}_j = \mathbf{X}_j'\mathbf{Y}\mathbf{Y}'\mathbf{X}_j\mathbf{u}_j$
	$\quad\quad \mathbf{u_j} = \mathbf{u_j}/\|\mathbf{u_j}\|$
	$\quad$ until convergence
	$\quad \mathbf{p}_j = \frac{\mathbf{X}_j'\mathbf{X}_j\mathbf{u}_j}{\mathbf{u}_j'\mathbf{X}_j'\mathbf{X}_j\mathbf{u}_j}$
	$\quad \mathbf{c}_j = \frac{\mathbf{Y}'\mathbf{X}_j\mathbf{u}_j}{\mathbf{u}_j'\mathbf{X}_j'\mathbf{X}_j\mathbf{u}_j}$
	$\quad \hat{\mathbf{Y}} = \hat{\mathbf{Y}} + \mathbf{X}_j\mathbf{u}_j\mathbf{c}_j'$
	$\quad \mathbf{X}_{j+1} = \mathbf{X}_j\left(\mathbf{I} - \mathbf{u}_j\mathbf{p}_j'\right)$
	end
	$\mathbf{W} = \mathbf{U}\left(\mathbf{P}'\mathbf{U}\right)^{-1}\mathbf{C}'$
output	Mean vector $\boldsymbol{\mu}$, training outputs $\hat{\mathbf{Y}}$, regression coefficients $\mathbf{W}$

Code Fragment 6.6. Pseudocode for the primal PLS algorithm.

iterative method. This results in $\mathbf{u}_j$ converging to the first right singular vector $\mathbf{Y}'\mathbf{X}_j$. Following the loop we compute $\mathbf{p}_j$ and $\mathbf{c}_j$, followed by the deflation of $\mathbf{X}_j$ given by

$$\mathbf{X} \rightarrow \mathbf{X} - \mathbf{X}\mathbf{u}_j\mathbf{p}_j'.$$

as required. We can deflate $\mathbf{Y}$ to its residual but it does not affect the correlations discovered since the deflation removes components in the space spanned by $\mathbf{X}_j\mathbf{u}_j$, to which $\mathbf{X}_{j+1}$ has now become orthogonal. From our observations above it is clear that the vectors $\mathbf{X}_j\mathbf{u_j}$ generated at each stage are orthogonal to each other.

We must now allow the algorithm to classify new data. The regression coefficients $\mathbf{W}$ are given in equation (6.31).

Code Fragment 6.7 gives Matlab code for the complete PLS algorithm in primal form. Note that it begins by centering the data since covariances are computed on centred data.   ■

We would now like to show how this selection can be mimicked in the dual space.

```
% X is an ell x n matrix whose rows are the training inputs
% Y is ell x m containing the corresponding output vectors
% T gives the number of iterations to be performed
mux = mean(X); muy = mean(Y); jj = ones(size(X,1),1);
X = X - jj*mux; Y = Y - jj*muy;
for i=1:T
  YX = Y'*X;
  u(:,i) = YX(1,:)'/norm(YX(1,:));
  if size(Y,2) > 1, % only loop if dimension greater than 1
     uold = u(:,i) + 1;
     while norm(u(:,i) - uold) > 0.001,
        uold = u(:,i);
        tu = YX'*YX*u(:,i);
        u(:,i) = tu/norm(tu);
     end
  end
  t = X*u(:,i);
  c(:,i) = Y'*t/(t'*t);
  p(:,i) = X'*t/(t'*t);
  trainY = trainY + t*c(:,i)';
  trainerror = norm(Y - trainY,'fro')/sqrt(ell)
  X = X - t*p(:,i)';
  % compute residual Y = Y - t*c(:,i)';
end
% Regression coefficients for new data
W = u * ((p'*u)\c'));
% Xtest gives new data inputs as rows, Ytest true outputs
elltest = size(Xtest,1); jj = ones(elltest,1);
testY = (Xtest - jj*mux) * W + jj*muy;
testerror = norm(Ytest - testY,'fro')/sqrt(elltest)
```

Code Fragment 6.7. Matlab code for the primal PLS algorithm.

6.7.2 Kernel partial least squares

The projection direction in the feature space at each stage is given by the vector $\mathbf{u}_j$. This vector is in the primal space while we must work in the dual space. We therefore express a multiple of $\mathbf{u}_j$ as

$$a_j \mathbf{u}_j = \mathbf{X}'_j \boldsymbol{\beta}_j,$$

which is clearly consistent with the derivation of $\mathbf{u}_j$ in the primal PLS algorithm. For the dual PLS algorithm we must implement the deflation of $\mathbf{Y}$. This redundant step for the primal will be needed to get the required dual representations. We use the notation $\mathbf{Y}_j$ to denote the jth deflation. This leads to the following recursion for $\boldsymbol{\beta}$

$$\boldsymbol{\beta} = \mathbf{Y}_j \mathbf{Y}'_j \mathbf{X}_j \mathbf{X}'_j \boldsymbol{\beta} = \mathbf{Y}_j \mathbf{Y}'_j \mathbf{K}_j \boldsymbol{\beta}$$

with the normalisation $\quad \boldsymbol{\beta} \;=\; \dfrac{\boldsymbol{\beta}}{\|\boldsymbol{\beta}\|}.$

This converges to a dual representation $\boldsymbol{\beta}_j$ of a scaled version $a_j \mathbf{u}_j$ of $\mathbf{u}_j$, where note that we have moved to a kernel matrix $\mathbf{K}_j$. Now we need to compute a rescaled $\boldsymbol{\tau}_j = a_j \mathbf{X}_j \mathbf{u}_j$ and $\mathbf{c}_j$ from $\boldsymbol{\beta}_j$. We have

$$\boldsymbol{\tau}_j = a_j \mathbf{X}_j \mathbf{u}_j = \mathbf{X}_j \mathbf{X}_j' \boldsymbol{\beta}_j = \mathbf{K}_j \boldsymbol{\beta}_j,$$

while we work with a rescaled version $\hat{\mathbf{c}}_j$ of $\mathbf{c}_j$

$$\hat{\mathbf{c}}_j = \frac{\mathbf{Y}_j' \boldsymbol{\tau}_j}{\boldsymbol{\tau}_j' \boldsymbol{\tau}_j} = \frac{\mathbf{Y}_j' \mathbf{X}_j \mathbf{u}_j}{a_j \mathbf{u}_j' \mathbf{X}_j' \mathbf{X}_j \mathbf{u}_j} = \frac{1}{a_j} \mathbf{c}_j,$$

so that we can consider $\boldsymbol{\tau}_j$ as a rescaled dual representation of the output vector $\mathbf{c}_j$. However, when we compute the contribution to the training output values

$$\boldsymbol{\tau}_j \hat{\mathbf{c}}_j' = \mathbf{X}_j \mathbf{u}_j \left(\frac{\mathbf{Y}_j' \mathbf{X}_j \mathbf{u}_j}{\mathbf{u}_j' \mathbf{X}_j' \mathbf{X}_j \mathbf{u}_j} \right)',$$

the rescalings cancel to give the correct result. Again with an automatic correction for the rescaling, Algorithm 6.42 gives the deflation of $\mathbf{X}_j$ as

$$\mathbf{X}_{j+1} = \left(\mathbf{I} - \frac{\boldsymbol{\tau}_j \boldsymbol{\tau}_j'}{\boldsymbol{\tau}_j' \boldsymbol{\tau}_j} \right) \mathbf{X}_j,$$

with an equivalent deflation of the kernel matrix given by

$$
\begin{aligned}
\mathbf{K}_{j+1} &= \mathbf{X}_{j+1} \mathbf{X}_{j+1}' \\[2mm]
&= \left(\mathbf{I} - \frac{\boldsymbol{\tau}_j \boldsymbol{\tau}_j'}{\boldsymbol{\tau}_j' \boldsymbol{\tau}_j} \right) \mathbf{X}_j \mathbf{X}_j' \left(\mathbf{I} - \frac{\boldsymbol{\tau}_j \boldsymbol{\tau}_j'}{\boldsymbol{\tau}_j' \boldsymbol{\tau}_j} \right) \\[2mm]
&= \left(\mathbf{I} - \frac{\boldsymbol{\tau}_j \boldsymbol{\tau}_j'}{\boldsymbol{\tau}_j' \boldsymbol{\tau}_j} \right) \mathbf{K}_j \left(\mathbf{I} - \frac{\boldsymbol{\tau}_j \boldsymbol{\tau}_j'}{\boldsymbol{\tau}_j' \boldsymbol{\tau}_j} \right),
\end{aligned}
$$

all computable without explicit feature vectors. We also need to consider the vectors $\mathbf{p}_j$

$$\mathbf{p}_j = \frac{\mathbf{X}_j' \mathbf{X}_j \mathbf{u}_j}{\mathbf{u}_j' \mathbf{X}_j' \mathbf{X}_j \mathbf{u}_j} = a_j \frac{\mathbf{X}_j' \boldsymbol{\tau}_j}{\boldsymbol{\tau}_j' \boldsymbol{\tau}_j}.$$

Properties of the dual computations We now consider the properties of these new quantities. First observe that the τ_j are orthogonal since for $j > i$

$$\tau_j' \tau_i = a_j a_i \mathbf{u}_j' \mathbf{X}_j' \mathbf{X}_i \mathbf{u}_i = 0,$$

as the columns of $\mathbf{X}_j$ are all orthogonal to $\mathbf{X}_i \mathbf{u}_i$. This furthermore means that for $i < j$

$$\left(\mathbf{I} - \frac{\tau_i \tau_i'}{\tau_i' \tau_i} \right) \tau_j = \tau_j,$$

implying

$$\mathbf{X}_j' \tau_j = \mathbf{X}' \tau_j,$$

so that

$$\mathbf{p}_j = a_j \frac{\mathbf{X}' \tau_j}{\tau_j' \tau_j}.$$

Note $\boldsymbol{\beta}_j$ can be written as $\mathbf{Y}_j \mathbf{x}_j$ for $\mathbf{x}_j = b_j \mathbf{Y}_j' \mathbf{K}_j \boldsymbol{\beta}_j$, for some scaling b_j. This implies that provided we deflate $\mathbf{Y}$ using

$$\mathbf{Y}_{j+1} = \left(\mathbf{I} - \frac{\tau_j \tau_j'}{\tau_j' \tau_j} \right) \mathbf{Y}_j,$$

so the columns of $\mathbf{Y}_j$ are also orthogonal to $\mathbf{X}_i \mathbf{u}_i$ for $i < j$, it follows that

$$\boldsymbol{\beta}_j' \tau_i = \mathbf{x}_j' \mathbf{Y}_j' \mathbf{X}_i \mathbf{u}_i = 0.$$

From this we have

$$\left(\mathbf{I} - \frac{\tau_i \tau_i'}{\tau_i' \tau_i} \right) \boldsymbol{\beta}_j = \boldsymbol{\beta}_j,$$

for $i < j$, so that

$$\mathbf{X}_j' \boldsymbol{\beta}_j = \mathbf{X}' \boldsymbol{\beta}_j$$

Computing the regression coefficients All that remains to be computed are the regression coefficients. These again must be computed in dual form, that is we require

$$\mathbf{W} = \mathbf{X}' \boldsymbol{\alpha},$$

so that a new input $\phi(\mathbf{x})$ can be processed using

$$\phi(\mathbf{x})' \mathbf{W} = \phi(\mathbf{x})' \mathbf{X}' \boldsymbol{\alpha} = \mathbf{k}' \boldsymbol{\alpha},$$

where $\mathbf{k}$ is the vector of inner products between the test point and the training inputs. From the analysis of the primal PLS in equation (6.31) we have

$$\mathbf{W} = \mathbf{U}\left(\mathbf{P}'\mathbf{U}\right)^{-1}\mathbf{C}'.$$

Using $\mathbf{B}$ to denote the matrix with columns $\boldsymbol{\beta}_j$ and diag $(\mathbf{a})$ for the diagonal matrix with entries diag $(\mathbf{a})_{ii} = a_i$, we can write

$$\mathbf{U} = \mathbf{X}'\mathbf{B}\operatorname{diag}\left(\mathbf{a}\right)^{-1}.$$

Similarly using $\mathbf{T}$ to denote the matrix with columns $\boldsymbol{\tau}_j$

$$\begin{aligned}
\mathbf{P}'\mathbf{U} &= \operatorname{diag}\left(\mathbf{a}\right)\operatorname{diag}\left(\boldsymbol{\tau}_i'\boldsymbol{\tau}_i\right)^{-1}\mathbf{T}'\mathbf{X}\mathbf{X}'\mathbf{B}\operatorname{diag}\left(\mathbf{a}\right)^{-1} \\
&= \operatorname{diag}\left(\mathbf{a}\right)\operatorname{diag}\left(\boldsymbol{\tau}_i'\boldsymbol{\tau}_i\right)^{-1}\mathbf{T}'\mathbf{K}\mathbf{B}\operatorname{diag}\left(\mathbf{a}\right)^{-1}.
\end{aligned}$$

Here diag $(\boldsymbol{\tau}_i'\boldsymbol{\tau}_i)$ is the diagonal matrix with entries diag $(\boldsymbol{\tau}_i'\boldsymbol{\tau}_i)_{ii} = \boldsymbol{\tau}_i'\boldsymbol{\tau}_i$. Finally, again using the orthogonality of $\mathbf{X}_j\mathbf{u}_j$ to $\boldsymbol{\tau}_i$, for $i < j$, we obtain

$$\mathbf{c}_j = \frac{\mathbf{Y}_j'\mathbf{X}_j\mathbf{u}_j}{\mathbf{u}_j'\mathbf{X}_j'\mathbf{X}_j\mathbf{u}_j} = \frac{\mathbf{Y}'\mathbf{X}_j\mathbf{u}_j}{\mathbf{u}_j'\mathbf{X}_j'\mathbf{X}_j\mathbf{u}_j} = a_j\frac{\mathbf{Y}'\boldsymbol{\tau}_j}{\boldsymbol{\tau}_j'\boldsymbol{\tau}_j},$$

making

$$\mathbf{C} = \mathbf{Y}'\mathbf{T}\operatorname{diag}\left(\boldsymbol{\tau}_i'\boldsymbol{\tau}_i\right)^{-1}\operatorname{diag}\left(\mathbf{a}\right).$$

Putting the pieces together we can compute the dual regression variables as

$$\boldsymbol{\alpha} = \mathbf{B}\left(\mathbf{T}'\mathbf{K}\mathbf{B}\right)^{-1}\mathbf{T}'\mathbf{Y}.$$

Finally, the dual solution is given component-wise by

$$f_j(\mathbf{x}) = \sum_{i=1}^{\ell}\alpha_i^j\kappa\left(\mathbf{x}_i,\mathbf{x}\right),\quad j = 1,\ldots,m.$$

Remark 6.46 [Rescaling matrices] Observe that

$$\mathbf{T}'\mathbf{K}\mathbf{B} = \operatorname{diag}\left(\boldsymbol{\tau}_i'\boldsymbol{\tau}_i\right)\operatorname{diag}\left(\mathbf{a}\right)^{-1}\mathbf{P}'\mathbf{U}\operatorname{diag}\left(\mathbf{a}\right)$$

and so is also upper triangular, but with rows and columns rescaled. The rescaling caused by diag $(\boldsymbol{\tau}_i'\boldsymbol{\tau}_i)$ could be removed since we can easily compute this matrix. This might be advantageous to increase the numerical stability, since $\mathbf{P}'\mathbf{U}$ was optimally stable with diagonal entries 1, so the smaller the rescalings the better. The matrix diag $(\mathbf{a})$ on the other hand is not readily accessible. ∎

Remark 6.47 [Notation] The following table summarises the notation used in the above derivations:

$\mathbf{u}_j$	primal projection directions	$\boldsymbol{\beta}_j$	dual projection directions
$\mathbf{U}$	matrix with columns $\mathbf{u}_j$	$\mathbf{B}$	matrix with columns $\boldsymbol{\beta}_j$
$\mathbf{c}_j$	primal output vector	$\boldsymbol{\tau}_j$	dual of scaled output vector
$\mathbf{C}$	matrix with columns $\mathbf{c}_j$	$\mathbf{T}$	matrix with columns $\boldsymbol{\tau}_j$
$\mathbf{W}$	primal regression coefficients	$\boldsymbol{\alpha}$	dual regression coefficients
$\mathbf{P}$	matrix with columns $\mathbf{p}_j$	$\mathbf{K}$	kernel matrix

∎

Algorithm 6.48 [Kernel PLS] The kernel PLS algorithm is given in Code Fragment 6.8. Code Fragment 6.9 gives Matlab code for the complete PLS

input	Data $S = \{\mathbf{x}_1, \ldots, \mathbf{x}_\ell\}$, dimension k, target outputs $\mathbf{Y} \in \mathbb{R}^{\ell \times m}$.
process	$\mathbf{K}_{ij} = \kappa(\mathbf{x}_i, \mathbf{x}_j),\ i, j = 1, \ldots, \ell$ $\mathbf{K}_1 = \mathbf{K}$ $\hat{\mathbf{Y}} = \mathbf{Y}$ for $j = 1, \ldots, k$ $\quad \boldsymbol{\beta}_j =$ first column of $\hat{\mathbf{Y}}$ $\quad \boldsymbol{\beta}_j = \boldsymbol{\beta}_j / \|\boldsymbol{\beta}_j\|$ $\quad$ repeat $\qquad \boldsymbol{\beta}_j = \hat{\mathbf{Y}}\hat{\mathbf{Y}}'\mathbf{K}_j\boldsymbol{\beta}_j$ $\qquad \boldsymbol{\beta}_j = \boldsymbol{\beta}_j / \|\boldsymbol{\beta}_j\|$ $\quad$ until convergence $\quad \boldsymbol{\tau}_j = \mathbf{K}_j\boldsymbol{\beta}_j$ $\quad \mathbf{c}_j = \hat{\mathbf{Y}}'\boldsymbol{\tau}_j / \|\boldsymbol{\tau}_j\|^2$ $\quad \hat{\mathbf{Y}} = \hat{\mathbf{Y}} - \boldsymbol{\tau}_j\mathbf{c}_j'$ $\quad \mathbf{K}_{j+1} = \left(\mathbf{I} - \boldsymbol{\tau}_j\boldsymbol{\tau}_j'/\|\boldsymbol{\tau}_j\|^2\right)\mathbf{K}_j\left(\mathbf{I} - \boldsymbol{\tau}_j\boldsymbol{\tau}_j'/\|\boldsymbol{\tau}_j\|^2\right)$ end $\mathbf{B} = [\boldsymbol{\beta}_1, \ldots, \boldsymbol{\beta}_k]\ \mathbf{T} = [\boldsymbol{\tau}_1, \ldots, \boldsymbol{\tau}_k]$ $\boldsymbol{\alpha} = \mathbf{B}\left(\mathbf{T}'\mathbf{K}\mathbf{B}\right)^{-1}\mathbf{T}'\mathbf{Y}$
output	Training outputs $\mathbf{Y} - \hat{\mathbf{Y}}$ and dual regression coefficients $\boldsymbol{\alpha}$

Code Fragment 6.8. Pseudocode for the kernel PLS algorithm.

algorithm in dual form. Note that it should also begin by centering the data but we have for brevity omitted this step (see Code Fragment 5.2 for Matlab code for centering). ∎

```
% K is an ell x ell kernel matrix
% Y is ell x m containing the corresponding output vectors
% T gives the number of iterations to be performed
KK = K; YY = Y;
for i=1:T
 YYK = YY*YY'*KK;
 beta(:,i) = YY(:,1)/norm(YY(:,1));
 if size(YY,2) > 1, % only loop if dimension greater than 1
   bold = beta(:,i) + 1;
   while norm(beta(:,i) - bold) > 0.001,
     bold = beta(:,i);
     tbeta = YYK*beta(:,i);
     beta(:,i) = tbeta/norm(tbeta);
   end
 end
 tau(:,i) = KK*beta(:,i);
 val = tau(:,i)'*t(:,i);
 c(:,i) = YY'*tau(:,i)/val;
 trainY = trainY + tau(:,i)*c(:,i)';
 trainerror = norm(Y - trainY,'fro')/sqrt(ell)
 w = KK*tau(:,i)/val;
 KK = KK - tau(:,i)*w' - w*tau(:,i)'
       + tau(:,i)*tau(:,i)'*(tau(:,i)'*w)/val;
 YY = YY - tau(:,i)*c(:,i)';
end
% Regression coefficients for new data
alpha = beta * ((tau'*K*beta)\tau')*Y;
% Ktest gives new data inner products as rows, Ytest true outputs
elltest = size(Xtest,1);
testY = Ktest * alpha;
testerror = norm(Ytest - testY,'fro')/sqrt(elltest)
```

Code Fragment 6.9. Matlab code for the dual PLS algorithm.

6.8 Summary

- Eigenanalysis can be used to detect patterns within sets of vectors.
- Principal components analysis finds directions based on the variance of the data.
- The singular value decomposition of a covariance matrix finds directions of maximal covariance.
- Canonical correlation analysis finds directions of maximum correlation.
- Fisher discriminant analysis can also be derived as the solution of a generalised eigenvalue problem.
- The methods can be implemented in kernel-defined feature spaces.
- The patterns detected can also be used as feature selection methods for subsequent analysis, as for example principal components regression.

- The iterative use of directions of maximal covariance in regression gives the state-of-the-art partial least squares regression procedure, again implementable in kernel-defined feature spaces.

6.9 Further reading and advanced topics

The use of eigenproblems to solve statistical problems dates back to the 1930s. In 1936 Sir Ronald Fisher, the English statistician who pioneered modern data analysis, published 'The use of multiple measurements in taxonomic problems', where his linear discriminant algorithm is described [44]. The basic ideas behind principal components analysis (PCA) date back to Karl Pearson in 1901, but the general procedure as described in this book was developed by Harold Hotelling, whose pioneering paper 'Analysis of a Complex of Statistical Variables with Principal Component' appeared in 1933 [61]. A few years later in 1936, Hotelling [62] further introduced canonical correlation analysis (CCA), with the article 'Relations between two sets of variables'.

So in very few years much of multivariate statistics had been introduced, although it was not until the advent of modern computers that it could show its full power. All of these algorithms were linear and were not regularised. Classically they were justified under the assumption that the data was generated according to a Gaussian distribution, but the main computational steps are the same as the ones described and generalised in this chapter. For an introduction to classical multivariate statistics see [159]. The statistical analysis of PCA is based on the papers [127] and [126]. Many of these methods suffer from overfitting when directly applied to high-dimensional data. The need for regularisation was, for example, recognised by Vinod in [151]. A nice unified survey of eigenproblems in pattern recognition can be found in [15].

The development of the related algorithm of partial least squares has in contrast been rather different. It was introduced by Wold [162] in 1966 and developed in [164], [163], see also Höskuldsson [60] and Wold [165] for a full account. It has mostly been developed and applied in the field of chemometrics, where it is common to have very high-dimensional data. Based on ideas motivated by conjugate gradient methods in least squares problems (see for example conjugate gradient in [49]), it has been used in applications for many years. Background material on SVD and generalised eigenproblems can be found in many linear algebra books, for example [98].

The enhancement of these classical methods with the use of kernels has been a recurring theme over the last few years in the development of kernel methods. Schölkopf *et al.* introduced it with kernel PCA [121]. Later several groups produced versions of kernel CCA [7], [83], [2], and of kernel FDA [100], [11]. Kernel PLS was introduced by Rosipal and Trejo [112].

Applications of kernel CCA in cross-lingual information retrieval are described in [151] while applications in bioinformatics are covered in [168], [149]. A more thorough description of kernel CCA is contained in [52], with applications to image retrieval and classification given in [152, 51]. Kernel CCA is also described in the book [131].

For constantly updated pointers to online literature and free software see the book's companion website: www.kernel-methods.net

7

Pattern analysis using convex optimisation

This chapter presents a number of algorithms for particular pattern analysis tasks such as novelty-detection, classification and regression. We consider criteria for choosing particular pattern functions, in many cases derived from stability analysis of the corresponding tasks they aim to solve. The optimisation of the derived criteria can be cast in the framework of convex optimization, either as linear or convex quadratic programs. This ensures that as with the algorithms of the last chapter the methods developed here do not suffer from the problem of local minima. They include such celebrated methods as support vector machines for both classification and regression.

We start, however, by describing how to find the smallest hypersphere containing the training data in the embedding space, together with the use and analysis of this algorithm for detecting anomalous or novel data. The techniques introduced for this problem are easily adapted to the task of finding the maximal margin hyperplane or support vector solution that separates two sets of points again possibly allowing some fraction of points to be exceptions. This in turn leads to algorithms for the case of regression.

An important feature of many of these systems is that, while enforcing the learning biases suggested by the stability analysis, they also produce 'sparse' dual representations of the hypothesis, resulting in efficient algorithms for both training and test point evaluation. This is a result of the Karush–Kuhn–Tucker conditions, which play a crucial role in the practical implementation and analysis of these algorithms.

7.1 The smallest enclosing hypersphere

In Chapter 1 novelty-detection was cited as one of the pattern analysis algorithms that we aimed to develop in the course of this book. A novelty-detection algorithm uses a training set to learn the support of the distribution of the 'normal' examples. Future test examples are then filtered by the resulting pattern function to identify any abnormal examples that appear not to have been generated from the same training distribution.

In Chapter 5 we developed a simple novelty-detection algorithm in a general kernel-defined feature space by estimating when new data is outside the hypersphere around the centre of mass of the distribution with radius large enough to contain all the training data. In this section we will further investigate the use of feature space hyperspheres as novelty detectors, where it is understood that new examples that lie outside the hypersphere are treated as 'abnormal' or 'novel'.

Clearly the smaller the hypersphere the more finely tuned the novelty-detection that it realises. Hence, our aim will be to define smaller hyperspheres for which we can still guarantee that with high probability they contain most of the support of the training distribution. There are two respects in which the novelty-detection hypersphere considered in Chapter 5 may be larger than is necessary. Firstly, the centre of the hypersphere was fixed at the centre of mass, or an estimate thereof, based on the training data. By allowing its centre to move it may be possible to find a smaller hypersphere that still contains all the training data. The second concern is that just one unlucky training example may force a much larger radius than should really be needed, implying that the solution is not robust. Ideally we would therefore like to find the smallest hypersphere that contains all but some small proportion of extreme training data.

Given a set of data embedded in a space, the problem of finding the smallest hypersphere containing a specified non-trivial fraction of the data is unfortunately NP-hard. Hence, there are no known algorithms to solve this problem exactly. It can, however, be solved exactly for the case when the hypersphere is required to include all of the data. We will therefore first tackle this problem. The solution is of interest in its own right, but the techniques developed will also indicate a route towards an approximate solution for the other case. Furthermore, the approach adopted for novelty-detection points the way towards a solution of the classification problem that we tackle in Section 7.2.

7.1.1 The smallest hypersphere containing a set of points

Let us assume that we are given a training set $S = \{\mathbf{x}_1, \ldots, \mathbf{x}_\ell\}$ with an associated embedding ϕ into a Euclidean feature space F with associated kernel κ satisfying

$$\kappa(\mathbf{x}, \mathbf{z}) = \langle \phi(\mathbf{x}), \phi(\mathbf{z}) \rangle.$$

The centre of the smallest hypersphere containing S is the point $\mathbf{c}$ that minimises the distance r from the furthest datapoint, or more precisely

$$\mathbf{c}^* = \operatorname*{argmin}_{\mathbf{c}} \max_{1 \le i \le \ell} \|\phi(\mathbf{x}_i) - \mathbf{c}\|,$$

with R the value of the expression at the optimum. We have derived the following computation.

Computation 7.1 [Smallest enclosing hypersphere] Given a set of points

$$S = \{\mathbf{x}_1, \ldots, \mathbf{x}_\ell\}$$

the hypersphere $(\mathbf{c}, r)$ that solves the optimisation problem

$$\begin{aligned}
&\min_{\mathbf{c}, r} && r^2 \\
&\text{subject to} && \|\phi(\mathbf{x}_i) - \mathbf{c}\|^2 = (\phi(\mathbf{x}_i) - \mathbf{c})'(\phi(\mathbf{x}_i) - \mathbf{c}) \le r^2 \\
& && i = 1, \ldots, \ell,
\end{aligned} \tag{7.1}$$

is the hypersphere containing S with smallest radius r. ∎

We can solve constrained optimisation problems of this type by defining a Lagrangian involving one Lagrange multiplier $\alpha_i \ge 0$ for each constraint

$$L(\mathbf{c}, r, \boldsymbol{\alpha}) = r^2 + \sum_{i=1}^{\ell} \alpha_i \left[\|\phi(\mathbf{x}_i) - \mathbf{c}\|^2 - r^2 \right].$$

We then solve by setting the derivatives with respect to $\mathbf{c}$ and r equal to zero

$$\frac{\partial L(\mathbf{c}, r, \boldsymbol{\alpha})}{\partial \mathbf{c}} = 2 \sum_{i=1}^{\ell} \alpha_i (\phi(\mathbf{x}_i) - \mathbf{c}) = \mathbf{0}, \text{ and}$$

$$\frac{\partial L(\mathbf{c}, r, \boldsymbol{\alpha})}{\partial r} = 2r \left(1 - \sum_{i=1}^{\ell} \alpha_i \right) = 0,$$

giving the following equations

$$\sum_{i=1}^{\ell} \alpha_i = 1 \text{ and as a consequence } \mathbf{c} = \sum_{i=1}^{\ell} \alpha_i \phi(\mathbf{x}_i).$$

The second equality implies that the centre of the smallest hypersphere containing the datapoints always lies in their span. This shows that the centre can be expressed in the dual representation. Furthermore, the first equality implies that the centre lies in the convex hull of the training set. Inserting these relations into the Lagrangian we obtain

$$
L(\mathbf{c}, r, \boldsymbol{\alpha}) = r^2 + \sum_{i=1}^{\ell} \alpha_i \left[\|\boldsymbol{\phi}(\mathbf{x}_i) - \mathbf{c}\|^2 - r^2 \right]
$$

$$
= \sum_{i=1}^{\ell} \alpha_i \langle \boldsymbol{\phi}(\mathbf{x}_i) - \mathbf{c}, \boldsymbol{\phi}(\mathbf{x}_i) - \mathbf{c} \rangle
$$

$$
= \sum_{i=1}^{\ell} \alpha_i \left(\kappa(\mathbf{x}_i, \mathbf{x}_i) + \sum_{k,j=1}^{\ell} \alpha_j \alpha_k \kappa(\mathbf{x}_j, \mathbf{x}_k) - 2 \sum_{j=1}^{\ell} \alpha_j \kappa(\mathbf{x}_i, \mathbf{x}_j) \right)
$$

$$
= \sum_{i=1}^{\ell} \alpha_i \kappa(\mathbf{x}_i, \mathbf{x}_i) + \sum_{k,j=1}^{\ell} \alpha_k \alpha_j \kappa(\mathbf{x}_j, \mathbf{x}_k) - 2 \sum_{i,j=1}^{\ell} \alpha_i \alpha_j \kappa(\mathbf{x}_i, \mathbf{x}_j)
$$

$$
= \sum_{i=1}^{\ell} \alpha_i \kappa(\mathbf{x}_i, \mathbf{x}_i) - \sum_{i,j=1}^{\ell} \alpha_i \alpha_j \kappa(\mathbf{x}_i, \mathbf{x}_k),
$$

where we have used the relation $\sum_{i=1}^{\ell} \alpha_i = 1$ to obtain line 2 and to take the middle expression out of the brackets after line 3. The Lagrangian has now been expressed wholly in terms of the Lagrange parameters, something referred to as the *dual Lagrangian*. The solution is obtained by maximising the resulting expression. We have therefore shown the following algorithm, where we use $\mathcal{H}$ to denote the Heaviside function $\mathcal{H}(x) = 1$, if $x \geq 0$ and 0 otherwise.

Algorithm 7.2 [Smallest hypersphere enclosing data] The smallest hypersphere in a feature space defined by a kernel κ enclosing a dataset S is computed given in Code Fragment 7.1. ∎

We have certainly achieved our goal of decreasing the size of the hypersphere since now we have located the hypersphere of minimal volume that contains the training data.

Remark 7.3 [On sparseness] The solution obtained here has an additional important property that results from a theorem of optimization known as the Kuhn-Tucker Theorem. This theorem states that the Lagrange parameters can be non-zero only if the corresponding inequality constraint is an

Input	training set $S = \{\mathbf{x}_1, \ldots, \mathbf{x}_\ell\}$
Process maximise subject to	find $\boldsymbol{\alpha}^*$ as solution of the optimisation problem: $W(\boldsymbol{\alpha}) = \sum_{i=1}^{\ell} \alpha_i \kappa(\mathbf{x}_i, \mathbf{x}_i) - \sum_{i,j=1}^{\ell} \alpha_i \alpha_j \kappa(\mathbf{x}_i, \mathbf{x}_j)$ $\sum_{i=1}^{\ell} \alpha_i = 1$ and $\alpha_i \geq 0$, $i = 1, \ldots, \ell$.
4 5 6 7	$r^* = \sqrt{W(\boldsymbol{\alpha}^*)}$ $D = \sum_{i,j=1}^{\ell} \alpha_i^* \alpha_j^* \kappa(\mathbf{x}_i, \mathbf{x}_j) - r^{*2}$ $f(\mathbf{x}) = \mathcal{H}\left[\kappa(\mathbf{x}, \mathbf{x}) - 2\sum_{i=1}^{\ell} \alpha_i^* \kappa(\mathbf{x}_i, \mathbf{x}) + D \right]$ $\mathbf{c}^* = \sum_{i=1}^{\ell} \alpha_i^* \boldsymbol{\phi}(\mathbf{x}_i)$
Output	centre of sphere $\mathbf{c}^*$ and/or function f testing for inclusion

Code Fragment 7.1. Pseudocode for computing the minimal hypersphere.

equality at the solution. These so-called Karush–Kuhn–Tucker (KKT) complementarity conditions are satisfied by the optimal solutions $\boldsymbol{\alpha}^*$, $(\mathbf{c}^*, r^*)$

$$\alpha_i^* \left[\|\boldsymbol{\phi}(\mathbf{x}_i) - \mathbf{c}^*\|^2 - r^{*2} \right] = 0, \quad i = 1, \ldots, \ell.$$

This implies that only the training examples $\mathbf{x}_i$ that lie on the surface of the optimal hypersphere have their corresponding α_i^* non-zero. For the remaining examples, the corresponding parameter satisfies $\alpha_i^* = 0$. Hence, in the expression for the centre only the points on the surface are involved. It is for this reason that they are sometimes referred to as *support vectors*.

We will denote the set of indices of the support vectors with sv. Using this notation the pattern function becomes

$$f(\mathbf{x}) = \mathcal{H}\left[\kappa(\mathbf{x}, \mathbf{x}) - 2\sum_{i \in \mathrm{sv}} \alpha_i^* \kappa(\mathbf{x}, \mathbf{x}_i) + D \right],$$

hence involving the evaluation of only $\#\mathrm{sv}$ inner products rather than ℓ as was required for the hypersphere of Chapter 5.   ∎

Remark 7.4 [On convexity] In Chapter 3 we showed that for a kernel function the matrix with entries $(\kappa(\mathbf{x}_i, \mathbf{x}_j))_{i,j=1}^{\ell}$ is positive semi-definite for all training sets, the so-called finitely positive semi-definite property. This in turn means that the optimisation problem of Algorithm 7.2 is always convex. Hence, the property required for a kernel function to define a feature space also ensures that the minimal hypersphere optimisation problem has a unique solution that can be found efficiently. This rules out the problem of encountering local minima.   ∎

Note that the function f output by Algorithm 7.2 outputs 1, if the new point lies outside the chosen sphere and so is considered novel, and 0 otherwise. The next section considers bounds on the probability that the novelty detector identifies a point as novel that has been generated by the original distribution, a situation that constitutes an erroneous output. Such examples will be false positives in the sense that they will be normal data identified by the algorithm as novel.

Data arising from novel conditions will be generated by a different distribution and hence we have no way of guaranteeing what output f will give. In this sense we have no way of bounding the negative positive rate. The intuition behind the approach is that the smaller the sphere used to define f, the more likely that novel data will fall outside and hence be detected as novel. Hence, in the subsequent development we will examine ways of shrinking the sphere, while still retaining control of the false positive rate.

7.1.2 Stability of novelty-detection

In the previous section we developed an algorithm for computing the smallest hypersphere enclosing a training sample and for testing whether a new point was contained in that hypersphere. It was suggested that the method could be used as a novelty-detection algorithm where points lying outside the hypersphere would be considered abnormal. But is there any guarantee that points from the same distribution will lie in the hypersphere? Even in the hypersphere based on the centre of gravity of the distribution we had to effectively leave some slack in its radius to allow for the inaccuracy in our estimation of their centre. But if we are to allow some slack in the radius of the minimal hypersphere, how much should it be?

In this section we will derive a stability analysis based on the techniques developed in Chapter 4 that will answer this question and give a novelty-detection algorithm with associated stability guarantees on its performance.

Theorem 7.5 *Fix $\gamma > 0$ and $\delta \in (0,1)$. Let $(\mathbf{c}, r)$ be the centre and radius of a hypersphere in a feature space determined by a kernel κ from a training sample $S = \{\mathbf{x}_1, \ldots, \mathbf{x}_\ell\}$ drawn randomly according to a probability distribution $\mathcal{D}$. Let $g(\mathbf{x})$ be the function defined by*

$$g(\mathbf{x}) = \begin{cases} 0, & \text{if } \|\mathbf{c} - \phi(\mathbf{x})\| \leq r; \\ \left(\|\mathbf{c} - \phi(\mathbf{x})\|^2 - r^2\right)/\gamma, & \text{if } r^2 \leq \|\mathbf{c} - \phi(\mathbf{x})\|^2 \leq r^2 + \gamma; \\ 1, & \text{otherwise.} \end{cases}$$

Then with probability at least $1 - \delta$ *over samples of size* ℓ *we have*

$$\mathbb{E}_D \left[g(\mathbf{x}) \right] \leq \frac{1}{\ell} \sum_{i=1}^{\ell} g(\mathbf{x}_i) + \frac{6R^2}{\gamma \sqrt{\ell}} + 3\sqrt{\frac{\ln(2/\delta)}{2\ell}},$$

where R *is the radius of a ball in feature space centred at the origin containing the support of the distribution.*

Proof Consider the loss function $\mathcal{A} : \mathbb{R} \to [0, 1]$, given by

$$\mathcal{A}(a) = \begin{cases} 0, & \text{if } R^2 a < r^2 - \|\mathbf{c}\|^2; \\ \left(R^2 a + \|\mathbf{c}\|^2 - r^2 \right)/\gamma, & \text{if } r^2 - \|\mathbf{c}\|^2 \leq R^2 a \leq r^2 - \|\mathbf{c}\|^2 + \gamma; \\ 1, & \text{otherwise.} \end{cases}$$

Hence, we can write $g(\mathbf{x}) = \mathcal{A}(f(\mathbf{x}))$, where

$$f(\mathbf{x}) = \|\mathbf{c} - \phi(\mathbf{x})\|^2 / R^2 - \|\mathbf{c}\|^2 / R^2 = \|\phi(\mathbf{x})\|^2 / R^2 - 2\langle \mathbf{c}, \phi(\mathbf{x}) \rangle / R^2.$$

Hence, by Theorem 4.9 we have that

$$\mathbb{E}_D \left[g(\mathbf{x}) \right] \leq \hat{\mathbb{E}} \left[g(\mathbf{x}) \right] + \hat{R}_\ell \left(\mathcal{A} \circ \left(\mathcal{F} + \|\phi(\mathbf{x})\|^2 / R^2 \right) \right) + 3\sqrt{\frac{\ln(2/\delta)}{2\ell}}, \quad (7.2)$$

where $\mathcal{F}$ is the class of linear functions with norm bounded by 1 with respect to the kernel

$$\hat{\kappa}(\mathbf{x}_i, \mathbf{x}_j) = 4\kappa(\mathbf{x}_i, \mathbf{x}_j) / R^2 = \langle 2\phi(\mathbf{x}_i)/R, 2\phi(\mathbf{x}_j)/R \rangle.$$

Since $\mathcal{A}(0) = 0$, we can apply part 4 of Theorem 4.15 with $L = R^2/\gamma$ to give

$$\hat{R}_\ell \left(\mathcal{A} \circ \left(\mathcal{F} + \|\phi(\mathbf{x})\|^2 / R^2 \right) \right) \leq 2R^2 \hat{R}_\ell \left(\mathcal{F} + \|\phi(\mathbf{x})\|^2 / R^2 \right)/\gamma.$$

By part 5 of Theorem 4.15, we have

$$\hat{R}_\ell (\mathcal{F} + \|\phi(\mathbf{x})\|^2 / R^2) \leq \hat{R}_\ell(\mathcal{F}) + 2\sqrt{\hat{\mathbb{E}} \left[\|\phi(\mathbf{x})\|^4 / R^4 \right] / \ell}$$

$$\leq \hat{R}_\ell(\mathcal{F}) + \frac{2}{\sqrt{\ell}},$$

while by Theorem 4.12 we have

$$\hat{R}_\ell(\mathcal{F}) = \frac{2}{\ell} \sqrt{\sum_{i=1}^{\ell} \hat{\kappa}(\mathbf{x}_i, \mathbf{x}_i)} = \frac{4}{R\ell} \sqrt{\sum_{i=1}^{\ell} \kappa(\mathbf{x}_i, \mathbf{x}_i)} = \frac{4}{\sqrt{\ell}}.$$

Putting the pieces into (7.2) gives the result. $\qquad \square$

Consider applying Theorem 7.5 to the minimal hypersphere $(\mathbf{c}^*, r^*)$ containing the training data. The first term vanishes since

$$\frac{1}{\ell} \sum_{i=1}^{\ell} g(\mathbf{x}_i) = 0.$$

If a test point $\mathbf{x}$ lies outside the hypersphere of radius $r = \sqrt{r^{*2} + \gamma}$ with centre $\mathbf{c}^*$ it will satisfy $g(\mathbf{x}_i) = 1$. Hence with probability greater than $1 - \delta$ we can bound the probability p of such points by

$$\frac{6R^2}{\gamma\sqrt{\ell}} + 3\sqrt{\frac{\ln(2/\delta)}{2\ell}},$$

since their contribution to $\mathbb{E}_{\mathcal{D}}[g(\mathbf{x})]$ is p, implying that $p \leq \mathbb{E}_{\mathcal{D}}[g(\mathbf{x})]$. Since $\left(r^* + \sqrt{\gamma}\right)^2 = r^{*2} + 2r^*\sqrt{\gamma} + \gamma \geq r^{*2} + \gamma$ we also have that, with probability greater than $1 - \delta$, points from the training distribution will lie outside a hypersphere of radius $r^* + \sqrt{\gamma}$ centred at $\mathbf{c}^*$ with probability less than

$$\frac{6R^2}{\gamma\sqrt{\ell}} + 3\sqrt{\frac{\ln(2/\delta)}{2\ell}}.$$

Hence, by choosing a radius slightly larger than r^* we can ensure that test data lying outside the hypersphere can be considered 'novel'.

Remark 7.6 [Size of the hypersphere] The results of this section formalise the intuition that small radius implies high sensitivity to novelties. If for a given kernel the radius is small we can hope for good novelty-detection. The next section will consider ways in which the radius of the ball can be reduced still further, while still retaining control of the sensitivity of the detector. ∎

7.1.3 Hyperspheres containing most of the points

We have seen in the last section how enlarging the radius of the smallest hypersphere containing the data ensures that we can guarantee with high probability that it contains the support of most of the distribution. This still leaves unresolved the sensitivity of the solution to the position of just one point, something that undermines the reliability of the parameters, resulting in a pattern analysis system that is not robust.

Theorem 7.5 also suggests a solution to this problem. Since the bound also applies to hyperspheres that fail to contain some of the training data, we can consider smaller hyperspheres provided we control the size of the term

$$\frac{1}{\ell} \sum_{i=1}^{\ell} g\left(\mathbf{x}_i\right) \leq \frac{1}{\gamma\ell} \sum_{i=1}^{\ell} \left(\|\mathbf{c} - \phi(\mathbf{x}_i)\|^2 - r^2\right)_+ . \tag{7.3}$$

In this way we can consider hyperspheres that balance the loss incurred by missing a small number of points with the reduction in radius that results. These can potentially give rise to more sensitive novelty detectors.

In order to implement this strategy we introduce a notion of *slack variable* $\xi_i = \xi_i(\mathbf{c}, r, \mathbf{x}_i)$ defined as

$$\xi_i = \left(\|\mathbf{c} - \phi(\mathbf{x}_i)\|^2 - r^2\right)_+ ,$$

which is zero for points inside the hypersphere and measures the degree to which the distance squared from the centre exceeds r^2 for points outside. Let $\boldsymbol{\xi}$ denote the vector with entries ξ_i, $i = 1, \ldots, \ell$. Using the upper bound of inequality (7.3), we now translate the bound of Theorem 7.5 into the objective of the optimisation problem (7.1) with a parameter C to control the trade-off between minimising the radius and controlling the slack variables.

Computation 7.7 [Soft minimal hypersphere] The sphere that optimises a trade off between equation (7.3) and the radius of the sphere is given as the solution of

$$\begin{aligned} \min_{\mathbf{c}, r, \boldsymbol{\xi}} \quad & r^2 + C \|\boldsymbol{\xi}\|_1 \\ \text{subject to} \quad & \|\phi(\mathbf{x}_i) - \mathbf{c}\|^2 = (\phi(\mathbf{x}_i) - \mathbf{c})'(\phi(\mathbf{x}_i) - \mathbf{c}) \leq r^2 + \xi_i \\ & \xi_i \geq 0, \quad i = 1, \ldots, \ell. \end{aligned} \tag{7.4}$$

We will refer to this approach as the *soft minimal hypersphere.* ∎

An example of such a sphere obtained using a linear kernel is shown in Figure 7.1. Note how the centre of the sphere marked by a × obtained by the algorithm is now very close to the centre of the Gaussian distribution generating the data marked by a diamond.

Again introducing Lagrange multipliers we arrive at the Lagrangian

$$L(\mathbf{c}, r, \boldsymbol{\alpha}, \boldsymbol{\xi}) = r^2 + C \sum_{i=1}^{\ell} \xi_i + \sum_{i=1}^{\ell} \alpha_i \left[\|\phi(\mathbf{x}_i) - \mathbf{c}\|^2 - r^2 - \xi_i\right] - \sum_{i=1}^{\ell} \beta_i \xi_i.$$

Differentiating with respect to the primal variables gives

$$\frac{\partial L(\mathbf{c}, r, \boldsymbol{\alpha}, \boldsymbol{\xi})}{\partial \mathbf{c}} = 2 \sum_{i=1}^{\ell} \alpha_i (\phi(\mathbf{x}_i) - \mathbf{c}) = 0;$$

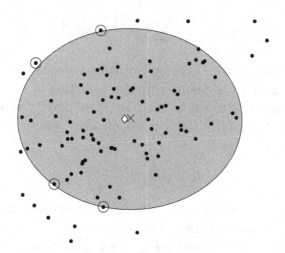

Fig. 7.1. The 'sphere' found by Computation 7.7 using a linear kernel.

$$\frac{\partial L(\mathbf{c}, r, \boldsymbol{\alpha}, \boldsymbol{\xi})}{\partial r} = 2r\left(1 - \sum_{i=1}^{\ell} \alpha_i\right) = 0;$$

$$\frac{\partial L(\mathbf{c}, r, \boldsymbol{\alpha}, \boldsymbol{\xi})}{\partial \xi_i} = C - \alpha_i - \beta_i = 0.$$

The final equation implies that $\alpha_i \leq C$ since $\beta_i = C - \alpha_i \geq 0$. Substituting, we obtain

$$\begin{aligned}
L(\mathbf{c}, r, \boldsymbol{\alpha}, \boldsymbol{\xi}) &= r^2 + C\sum_{i=1}^{\ell} \xi_i + \sum_{i=1}^{\ell} \alpha_i \left[\|\boldsymbol{\phi}(\mathbf{x}_i) - \mathbf{c}\|^2 - r^2 - \xi_i\right] - \sum_{i=1}^{\ell} \beta_i \xi_i \\
&= \sum_{i=1}^{\ell} \alpha_i \left\langle \boldsymbol{\phi}(\mathbf{x}_i) - \mathbf{c}, \boldsymbol{\phi}(\mathbf{x}_i) - \mathbf{c}\right\rangle \\
&= \sum_{i=1}^{\ell} \alpha_i \kappa\left(\mathbf{x}_i, \mathbf{x}_i\right) - \sum_{i,j=1}^{\ell} \alpha_i \alpha_j \kappa\left(\mathbf{x}_i, \mathbf{x}_j\right),
\end{aligned}$$

which is the dual Lagrangian.

Hence, we obtain the following algorithm.

Algorithm 7.8 [Soft hypersphere minimisation] The hypersphere that optimises the soft bound of Computation 7.7 is computed in Code Fragment 7.2.

∎

Input	training set $S = \{\mathbf{x}_1, \ldots, \mathbf{x}_\ell\}$, $\delta > 0$, $\gamma > 0$, $C > 0$
Process maximise subject to	find $\boldsymbol{\alpha}^*$ as solution of the optimisation problem: $W(\boldsymbol{\alpha}) = \sum_{i=1}^{\ell} \alpha_i \kappa(\mathbf{x}_i, \mathbf{x}_i) - \sum_{i,j=1}^{\ell} \alpha_i \alpha_j \kappa(\mathbf{x}_i, \mathbf{x}_j)$ $\sum_{i=1}^{\ell} \alpha_i = 1$ and $0 \le \alpha_i \le C$, $i = 1, \ldots, \ell$.
4	choose i such that $0 < \alpha_i^* < C$
5	$r^* = \sqrt{\kappa(\mathbf{x}_i, \mathbf{x}_i) - 2\sum_{j=1}^{\ell} \alpha_j^* \kappa(\mathbf{x}_j, \mathbf{x}_i) + \sum_{i,j=1}^{\ell} \alpha_i^* \alpha_j^* \kappa(\mathbf{x}_i, \mathbf{x}_j)}$
6	$D = \sum_{i,j=1}^{\ell} \alpha_i^* \alpha_j^* \kappa(\mathbf{x}_i, \mathbf{x}_j) - (r^*)^2 - \gamma$
7	$f(\cdot) = \mathcal{H}\left[\kappa(\cdot, \cdot) - 2\sum_{i=1}^{\ell} \alpha_i^* \kappa(\mathbf{x}_i, \cdot) + D\right]$
8	$\|\boldsymbol{\xi}^*\|_1 = \left(W(\boldsymbol{\alpha}^*) - (r^*)^2\right)/C$
9	$\mathbf{c}^* = \sum_{i=1}^{\ell} \alpha_i^* \boldsymbol{\phi}(\mathbf{x}_i)$
Output	centre of sphere $\mathbf{c}^*$ and/or function f testing for containment sum of slacks $\|\boldsymbol{\xi}^*\|_1$, the radius r^*

Code Fragment 7.2. Pseudocode for soft hypersphere minimisation.

The function f again outputs 1 to indicate as novel new data falling outside the sphere. The size of the sphere has been reduced, hence increasing the chances that data generated by a different distribution will be identified as novel. The next theorem shows that this increase in sensitivity has not compromised the false positive rate, that is the probability of data generated according to the same distribution being incorrectly labelled as novel.

Theorem 7.9 *Fix $\delta > 0$ and $\gamma > 0$. Consider a training sample $S = \{\mathbf{x}_1, \ldots, \mathbf{x}_\ell\}$ drawn according to a distribution $\mathcal{D}$ and let $\mathbf{c}^*$, f and $\|\boldsymbol{\xi}^*\|_1$ be the output of Algorithm 7.8. Then the vector $\mathbf{c}^*$ is the centre of the soft minimal hypersphere that minimises the objective $r^2 + C\|\boldsymbol{\xi}\|_1$ for the image $\phi(S)$ of the set S in the feature space F defined by the kernel $\kappa(\mathbf{x}_i, \mathbf{x}_j) = \langle \phi(\mathbf{x}_i), \phi(\mathbf{x}_j) \rangle$. Furthermore, r^* is the radius of the hypersphere, while the sum of the slack variables is $\|\boldsymbol{\xi}^*\|_1$. The function f outputs 1 on test points $\mathbf{x} \in X$ drawn according to the distribution $\mathcal{D}$ with probability at most*

$$\frac{1}{\gamma\ell}\|\boldsymbol{\xi}^*\|_1 + \frac{6R^2}{\gamma\sqrt{\ell}} + 3\sqrt{\frac{\ln(2/\delta)}{2\ell}}, \tag{7.5}$$

where R is the radius of a ball in feature space centred at the origin containing the support of the distribution.

Proof The first part of the theorem follows from the previous derivations.

The expression for the radius r^* follows from two applications of the Karush–Kuhn–Tucker conditions using the fact that $0 < \alpha_i^* < C$. Firstly, since $\beta_i^* = C - \alpha_i^* \neq 0$, we have that $\xi_i^* = 0$, while $\alpha_i^* \neq 0$ implies

$$0 = \|\mathbf{x}_i - \mathbf{c}^*\|^2 - (r^*)^2 - \xi_i^* = \|\mathbf{x}_i - \mathbf{c}^*\|^2 - (r^*)^2.$$

The expression for $\|\boldsymbol{\xi}^*\|_1$ follows from the fact that

$$W(\boldsymbol{\alpha}^*) = (r^*)^2 + C\,\|\boldsymbol{\xi}^*\|_1,$$

while (7.5) follows from Theorem 7.5 and the fact that

$$\frac{1}{\ell}\sum_{i=1}^{\ell} g\,(\mathbf{x}_i) \leq \frac{1}{\gamma\ell}\,\|\boldsymbol{\xi}^*\|_1,$$

while

$$P_{\mathcal{D}}\,(f\,(\mathbf{x}) = 1) \leq \mathbb{E}_{\mathcal{D}}\,[g(\mathbf{x})],$$

where $g(\mathbf{x})$ is the function from Theorem 7.5 with $\mathbf{c} = \mathbf{c}^*$ and $r = r^*$. $\qquad\square$

The algorithm is designed to optimise the bound on the probability of new points lying outside the hypersphere. Despite this there may be any number of training points excluded. We are also not guaranteed to obtain the smallest hypersphere that excludes the given number of points.

ν-**formulation** There is an alternative way of parametrising the problem that allows us to exert some control over the fraction of points that are excluded from the hypersphere. Note that in Theorem 7.9 the parameter C must be chose larger than $1/\ell$, since otherwise the constraint

$$\sum_{i=1}^{\ell} \alpha_i = 1$$

cannot be satisfied.

Computation 7.10 [ν-soft minimal hypersphere] If we consider setting the parameter $C = 1/(\nu\ell)$, as C varies between $1/\ell$ and ∞ in Theorem 7.9, the same solutions are obtained as the parameter ν varies between 0 and 1 in the optimisation problem

$$\begin{aligned}
&\min_{\mathbf{c},r,\boldsymbol{\xi}} && \tfrac{1}{\ell}\,\|\boldsymbol{\xi}\|_1 + \nu r^2 \\
&\text{subject to} && \|\phi\,(\mathbf{x}_i) - \mathbf{c}\|^2 = (\phi(\mathbf{x}_i) - \mathbf{c})'(\phi(\mathbf{x}_i) - \mathbf{c}) \leq r^2 + \xi_i && (7.6) \\
&&& \xi_i \geq 0, \quad i = 1,\dots,\ell.
\end{aligned}$$

The solutions clearly correspond since this is just a rescaling of the objective. This approach will be referred to as the ν-*soft minimal hypersphere*. $\qquad\blacksquare$

An example of novelty-detection using a radial basis function kernel is given in Figure 7.2. Note how the area of the region has again reduced though since the distribution is a circular Gaussian the performance has probably not improved.

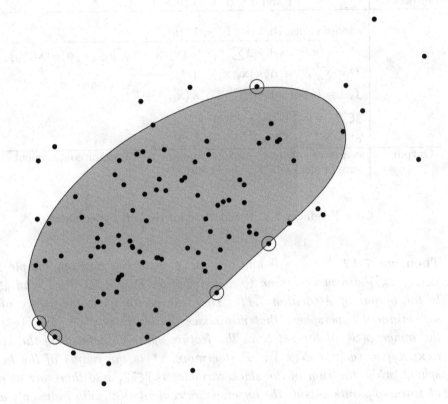

Fig. 7.2. Novelty detection in a kernel defined feature space.

The analysis for the soft hypersphere is identical to the ν-soft minimal hypersphere with an appropriate redefinition of the parameters. Using this fact we obtain the following algorithm.

Algorithm 7.11 [ν-soft minimal hypersphere] The hypersphere that optimises the ν-soft bound is computed in Code Fragment 7.3. ∎

As with the previous novelty-detection algorithms, the function f indicates as novel points for which its output is 1. The next theorem is again concerned with bounding the false positive rate, but also indicates the role of the parameter ν.

Input	training set $S = \{\mathbf{x}_1, \ldots, \mathbf{x}_\ell\}$, $\delta > 0$, $\gamma > 0$, $0 < \nu < 1$
Process maximise subject to	find $\boldsymbol{\alpha}^*$ as solution of the optimisation problem: $W(\boldsymbol{\alpha}) = \sum_{i=1}^{\ell} \alpha_i \kappa(\mathbf{x}_i, \mathbf{x}_i) - \sum_{i,j=1}^{\ell} \alpha_i \alpha_j \kappa(\mathbf{x}_i, \mathbf{x}_j)$ $\sum_{i=1}^{\ell} \alpha_i = 1$ and $0 \le \alpha_i \le 1/(\nu\ell)$, $i = 1, \ldots, \ell$.
4	choose i such that $0 < \alpha_i^* < 1/(\nu\ell)$
5	$r^* = \sqrt{\kappa(\mathbf{x}_i, \mathbf{x}_i) - 2\sum_{j=1}^{\ell} \alpha_j^* \kappa(\mathbf{x}_j, \mathbf{x}_i) + \sum_{i,j=1}^{\ell} \alpha_i^* \alpha_j^* \kappa(\mathbf{x}_i, \mathbf{x}_j)}$
6	$D = \sum_{i,j=1}^{\ell} \alpha_i^* \alpha_j^* \kappa(\mathbf{x}_i, \mathbf{x}_j) - (r^*)^2 - \gamma$
7	$f(\cdot) = \mathcal{H}\left[\kappa(\cdot, \cdot) - 2\sum_{i=1}^{\ell} \alpha_i^* \kappa(\mathbf{x}_i, \cdot) + D\right]$
8	$\|\boldsymbol{\xi}^*\|_1 = \nu\ell\left(W(\boldsymbol{\alpha}^*) - (r^*)^2\right)$
9	$\mathbf{c}^* = \sum_{i=1}^{\ell} \alpha_i^* \boldsymbol{\phi}(\mathbf{x}_i)$
Output	centre of sphere $\mathbf{c}^*$ and/or function f testing for containment sum of slacks $\|\boldsymbol{\xi}^*\|_1$, the radius r^*

Code Fragment 7.3. Pseudocode for the soft hypersphere.

Theorem 7.12 *Fix $\delta > 0$ and $\gamma > 0$. Consider a training sample $S = \{\mathbf{x}_1, \ldots, \mathbf{x}_\ell\}$ drawn according to a distribution $\mathcal{D}$ and let $\mathbf{c}^*$, f and $\|\boldsymbol{\xi}^*\|_1$ be the output of Algorithm 7.11. Then the vector $\mathbf{c}^*$ is the centre of the soft minimal hypersphere that minimises the objective $r^2 + \|\boldsymbol{\xi}\|_1 / (\nu\ell)$ for the image $\phi(S)$ of the set S in the feature space F defined by the kernel $\kappa(\mathbf{x}_i, \mathbf{x}_j) = \langle \phi(\mathbf{x}_i), \phi(\mathbf{x}_j) \rangle$. Furthermore, r^* is the radius of the hypersphere, while the sum of the slack variables is $\|\boldsymbol{\xi}^*\|_1$ and there are at most $\nu\ell$ training points outside the hypersphere centred at $\mathbf{c}^*$ with radius r^*, while at least $\nu\ell$ of the training points do not lie in the interior of the hypersphere. The function f outputs 1 on test points $\mathbf{x} \in X$ drawn according to the distribution $\mathcal{D}$ with probability at most*

$$\frac{1}{\gamma\ell} \|\boldsymbol{\xi}^*\|_1 + \frac{6R^2}{\gamma\sqrt{\ell}} + 3\sqrt{\frac{\ln(2/\delta)}{2\ell}},$$

where R is the radius of a ball in feature space centred at the origin containing the support of the distribution.

Proof Apart from the observations about the number of training points lying inside and outside the hypersphere the result follows directly from an application of Theorem 7.9 using the fact that the objective can be scaled by ν to give $\nu r^{*2} + \ell^{-1} \|\boldsymbol{\xi}^*\|_1$. For a point $\mathbf{x}_i$ lying outside the hypersphere we have $\xi_i^* > 0$ implying that $\beta_i^* = 0$, so that $\alpha_i^* = 1/(\nu\ell)$. Since

$$\sum_{i=1}^{\ell} \alpha_i^* = 1,$$

there can be at most $\nu\ell$ such points. Furthermore this equation together with the upper bound on α_i^* implies that at least $\nu\ell$ training points do not lie in the interior of the hypersphere, since for points inside the hypersphere $\alpha_i^* = 0$.   □

Remark 7.13 [Varying γ] Theorem 7.12 applies for a fixed value of γ. In practice we would like to choose γ based on the performance of the algorithm. This can be achieved by applying the theorem for a set of k values of γ with the value of δ set to δ/k. This ensures that with probability $1 - \delta$ the bound holds for all k choices of γ. Hence, we can apply the most useful value for the given situation at the cost of a slight weakening of the bound. The penalty is an additional $\frac{\ln(k)}{\ell}$ under the square root in the probability bound. We omit this derivation as it is rather technical without giving any additional insight. We will, however, assume that we can choose γ in response to the training data in the corollary below.   ∎

Theorem 7.12 shows how ν places a lower bound on the fraction of points that fail to be in the interior of the hypersphere and an equal upper bound on those lying strictly outside the hypersphere. Hence, modulo the points lying on the surface of the hypersphere, ν determines the fraction of points not enclosed in the hypersphere. This gives a more intuitive parametrisation of the problem than that given by the parameter C in Theorem 7.9. This is further demonstrated by the following appealing corollary relating the choice of ν to the false positive error rate.

Corollary 7.14 *If we wish to fix the probability bound of Theorem 7.12 to be*

$$p + 3\sqrt{\frac{\ln(2/\delta)}{2\ell}} = \frac{1}{\gamma\ell}\|\boldsymbol{\xi}^*\|_1 + \frac{6R^2}{\gamma\sqrt{\ell}} + 3\sqrt{\frac{\ln(2/\delta)}{2\ell}} \qquad (7.7)$$

for some $0 < p < 1$, and can choose γ accordingly, we will minimise the volume of the corresponding test hypersphere obtained by choosing $\nu = p$.

Proof Using the freedom to choose γ, it follows from equation (7.7) that

$$\gamma = \frac{1}{p}\left(\frac{1}{\ell}\|\boldsymbol{\xi}^*\|_1 + \frac{6R^2}{\sqrt{\ell}}\right)$$

so that the radius squared of the test hypersphere is

$$r^{*2} + \gamma = r^{*2} + \frac{1}{p}\left(\frac{1}{\ell}\,\|\boldsymbol{\xi}^*\|_1 + \frac{6R^2}{\sqrt{\ell}}\right)$$

$$= r^{*2} + \frac{1}{p\ell}\,\|\boldsymbol{\xi}^*\|_1 + \frac{6R^2}{p\sqrt{\ell}},$$

implying that p times the volume is

$$pr^{*2} + \frac{1}{\ell}\,\|\boldsymbol{\xi}^*\|_1 + \frac{6R^2}{\sqrt{\ell}},$$

which is equivalent to the objective of Computation 7.10 if $\nu = p$. $\qquad\square$

Remark 7.15 [Combining with PCA] During this section we have restricted our consideration to hyperspheres. If the data lies in a subspace of the feature space the hypersphere will significantly overestimate the support of the distribution in directions that are perpendicular to the subspace. In such cases we could further reduce the volume of the estimation by performing kernel PCA and applying Theorem 6.14 with δ set to $\delta/2$ to rule out points outside a thin slab around the k-dimensional subspace determined by the first k principal axes. Combining this with Theorem 7.12 also with δ set to $\delta/2$ results in a region estimated by the intersection of the hypersphere with the slab. $\qquad\blacksquare$

Remark 7.16 [Alternative approach] If the data is normalised it can be viewed as lying on the surface of a hypersphere in the feature space. In this case there is a correspondence between hyperspheres in the feature space and hyperplanes, since the decision boundary determined by the intersection of the two hyperspheres can equally well be described by the intersection of a hyperplane with the unit hypersphere. The weight vector of the hyperplane is that of the centre of the hypersphere containing the data. This follows immediately from the form of the test function if we assume that $\kappa(\mathbf{x}, \mathbf{x}) = 1$, since

$$f(\mathbf{x}) = \mathcal{H}\left[\kappa(\mathbf{x}, \mathbf{x}) - 2\sum_{i=1}^{\ell} \alpha_i^* \kappa(\mathbf{x}_i, \mathbf{x}) + D\right]$$

$$= \mathcal{H}\left[-2\sum_{i=1}^{\ell} \alpha_i^* \kappa(\mathbf{x}_i, \mathbf{x}) + D + 1\right].$$

This suggests that an alternative strategy could be to search for a hyperplane that maximally separates the data from the origin with an appropriately adjusted threshold. For normalised data this will result in exactly the same solution, but for data that is not normalised it will result in the slightly different optimisation problem. The approach taken for classification in the next section parallels this idea. ∎

7.2 Support vector machines for classification

In this section we turn our attention to the problem of classification. For novelty-detection we have seen how the stability analysis of Theorem 7.5 guides Computation 7.7 for the soft minimal hypersphere. Such an approach gives a principled way of choosing a pattern function for a particular pattern analysis task. We have already obtained a stability bound for classification in Theorem 4.17 of Chapter 4. This gives a bound on the test misclassification error or generalisation error of a linear function $g(\mathbf{x})$ with norm 1 in a kernel-defined feature space of

$$P_D\left(y \neq g(\mathbf{x})\right) \leq \frac{1}{\ell\gamma} \sum_{i=1}^{\ell} \xi_i + \frac{4}{\ell\gamma}\sqrt{\mathrm{tr}(\mathbf{K})} + 3\sqrt{\frac{\ln(2/\delta)}{2\ell}}, \qquad (7.8)$$

where $\mathbf{K}$ is the kernel matrix for the training set and $\xi_i = \xi\left((\mathbf{x}_i, y_i), \gamma, g\right) = (\gamma - y_i g(\mathbf{x}_i))_+$. We now use this bound to guide the choice of linear function returned by the learning algorithm. As with the (soft) minimal hyperspheres this leads to a quadratic optimisation problem though with some slight additional complications. Despite these we will follow a similar route to that outlined above starting with separating hyperplanes and moving to soft solutions and eventually to ν-soft solutions.

Remark 7.17 [Choosing γ and the threshold] Again as with the bound for the stability of novelty-detection, strictly speaking the bound of (7.8) only applies if we have chosen γ a priori, while in practice we will choose γ after running the learning algorithm. A similar strategy to that described above involving the application of Theorem 4.17 for a range of values of γ ensures that we can use the bound for approximately the observed value at the cost of a small penalty under the square root. We will again omit these technical details for the sake of readability and treat (7.8) as if it held for all choices of γ. Similarly, the bound was proven for $g(\mathbf{x})$ a simple linear function, while below we will consider the additional freedom of choosing a threshold without adapting the bound to take this into account. ∎

7.2.1 The maximal margin classifier

Let us assume initially that for a given training set

$$S = \{(\mathbf{x}_1, y_1), \ldots, (\mathbf{x}_\ell, y_\ell)\},$$

there exists a norm 1 linear function

$$g(\mathbf{x}) = \langle \mathbf{w}, \phi(\mathbf{x}_i) \rangle + b$$

determined by a weight vector $\mathbf{w}$ and threshold b and that there exists $\gamma > 0$, such that $\xi_i = (\gamma - y_i g(\mathbf{x}_i))_+ = 0$ for $1 \leq i \leq \ell$. This implies that the first term on the right-hand side of (7.8) vanishes. In the terminology of Chapter 4 it implies that the margin $m(S, g)$ of the training set S satisfies

$$m(S, g) = \min_{1 \leq i \leq \ell} y_i g(\mathbf{x}_i) \geq \gamma.$$

Informally, this implies that the two classes of data can be separated by a hyperplane with a margin of γ as shown in Figure 7.3. We will call such

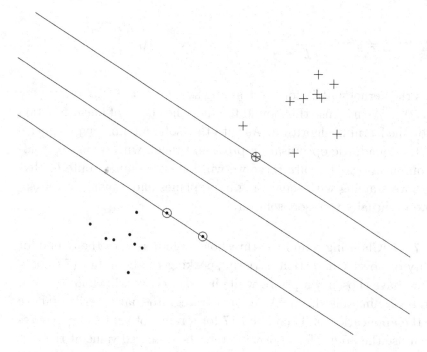

Fig. 7.3. Example of large margin hyperplane with support vectors circled.

a training set *separable* or more precisely *linearly separable* with margin γ. More generally a classifier is called *consistent* if it correctly classifies all of the training set.

Since the function $\mathbf{w}$ has norm 1 the expression $\langle \mathbf{w}, \phi(\mathbf{x}_i) \rangle$ measures the length of the perpendicular projection of the point $\phi(\mathbf{x}_i)$ onto the ray determined by $\mathbf{w}$ and so

$$y_i g(\mathbf{x}_i) = y_i \left(\langle \mathbf{w}, \phi(\mathbf{x}_i) \rangle + b \right)$$

measures how far the point $\phi(\mathbf{x}_i)$ is from the boundary hyperplane, given by

$$\{\mathbf{x} : g(\mathbf{x}) = 0\},$$

measuring positively in the direction of correct classification. For this reason we refer to the functional margin of a linear function with norm 1 as the *geometric margin* of the associated classifier. Hence $m(S, g) \geq \gamma$ implies that S is correctly classified by g with a geometric margin of at least γ.

For such cases we consider optimising the bound of (7.8) over all functions g for which such a γ exists. Clearly, the larger the value of γ the smaller the bound. Hence, we optimise the bound by maximising the margin $m(S, g)$.

Remark 7.18 [Robustness of the maximal margin] Although the stability of the resulting hyperplane is guaranteed provided $m(S, g) = \gamma$ is large, the solution is not robust in the sense that a single additional *training* point can reduce the value of γ very significantly potentially even rendering the training set non-separable. ∎

In view of the above criterion our task is to find the linear function that maximises the geometric margin. This function is often referred to as the *maximal margin hyperplane* or the *hard margin support vector machine*.

Computation 7.19 [Hard margin SVM] Hence, the choice of hyperplane should be made to solve the following optimisation problem

$$
\begin{aligned}
&\max_{\mathbf{w}, b, \gamma} \quad \gamma \\
&\text{subject to} \quad y_i \left(\langle \mathbf{w}, \phi(\mathbf{x}_i) \rangle + b \right) \geq \gamma,\ i = 1, \ldots, \ell, \\
&\qquad\qquad \text{and } \|\mathbf{w}\|^2 = 1.
\end{aligned}
\tag{7.9}
$$

∎

Remark 7.20 [Canonical hyperplanes] The traditional way of formulating the optimisation problem makes use of the observation that rescaling the weight vector and threshold does not change the classification function. Hence we can fix the functional margin to be 1 and minimise the norm of the weight vector. We have chosen to use the more direct method here as it follows more readily from the novelty detector of the previous section and leads more directly to the ν-support vector machine discussed later. ■

For the purposes of conversion to the dual it is better to treat the optimisation as minimising $-\gamma$. As with the novelty-detection optimisation we derive a Lagrangian in order to arrive at the dual optimisation problem. Introducing Lagrange multipliers we obtain

$$L(\mathbf{w}, b, \gamma, \boldsymbol{\alpha}, \lambda) = -\gamma - \sum_{i=1}^{\ell} \alpha_i \left[y_i \left(\langle \mathbf{w}, \phi(\mathbf{x}_i) \rangle + b \right) - \gamma \right] + \lambda \left(\|\mathbf{w}\|^2 - 1 \right).$$

Differentiating with respect to the primal variables gives

$$\frac{\partial L(\mathbf{w}, b, \gamma, \boldsymbol{\alpha}, \lambda)}{\partial \mathbf{w}} = -\sum_{i=1}^{\ell} \alpha_i y_i \phi(\mathbf{x}_i) + 2\lambda \mathbf{w} = \mathbf{0},$$

$$\frac{\partial L(\mathbf{w}, b, \gamma, \boldsymbol{\alpha}, \lambda)}{\partial \gamma} = -1 + \sum_{i=1}^{\ell} \alpha_i = 0, \text{ and}$$

$$\frac{\partial L(\mathbf{w}, b, \gamma, \boldsymbol{\alpha}, \lambda)}{\partial b} = -\sum_{i=1}^{\ell} \alpha_i y_i = 0. \tag{7.10}$$

Substituting we obtain

$$\begin{aligned}
L(\mathbf{w}, b, \gamma, \boldsymbol{\alpha}, \lambda) &= -\sum_{i=1}^{\ell} \alpha_i y_i \langle \mathbf{w}, \phi(\mathbf{x}_i) \rangle + \lambda \|\mathbf{w}\|^2 - \lambda \\
&= \left(-\frac{1}{2\lambda} + \frac{1}{4\lambda} \right) \sum_{i,j=1}^{\ell} \alpha_i y_i \alpha_j y_j \langle \phi(\mathbf{x}_i), \phi(\mathbf{x}_j) \rangle - \lambda \\
&= -\frac{1}{4\lambda} \sum_{i,j=1}^{\ell} \alpha_i \alpha_j y_i y_j \kappa(\mathbf{x}_i, \mathbf{x}_j) - \lambda.
\end{aligned}$$

Finally, optimising the choice of λ gives

$$\lambda = \frac{1}{2} \left(\sum_{i,j=1}^{\ell} \alpha_i \alpha_j y_i y_j \kappa(\mathbf{x}_i, \mathbf{x}_j) \right)^{1/2},$$

resulting in

$$L(\boldsymbol{\alpha}) = -\left(\sum_{i,j=1}^{\ell} \alpha_i \alpha_j y_i y_j \kappa(\mathbf{x}_i, \mathbf{x}_j) \right)^{1/2}. \tag{7.11}$$

which we call the dual Lagrangian. We have therefore derived the following algorithm.

Algorithm 7.21 [Hard margin SVM] The hard margin support vector machine is implemented in Code Fragment 7.4. ∎

Input	training set $S = \{(\mathbf{x}_1, y_1), \ldots, (\mathbf{x}_\ell, y_\ell)\}$, $\delta > 0$
Process maximise subject to	find $\boldsymbol{\alpha}^*$ as solution of the optimisation problem: $W(\boldsymbol{\alpha}) = -\sum_{i,j=1}^{\ell} \alpha_i \alpha_j y_i y_j \kappa(\mathbf{x}_i, \mathbf{x}_j)$ $\sum_{i=1}^{\ell} y_i \alpha_i = 0$, $\sum_{i=1}^{\ell} \alpha_i = 1$ and $0 \leq \alpha_i$, $i = 1, \ldots, \ell$.
4 5 6 7 8	$\gamma^* = \sqrt{-W(\boldsymbol{\alpha}^*)}$ choose i such that $0 < \alpha_i^*$ $b = y_i (\gamma^*)^2 - \sum_{j=1}^{\ell} \alpha_j^* y_j \kappa(\mathbf{x}_j, \mathbf{x}_i)$ $f(\cdot) = \mathrm{sgn}\left(\sum_{j=1}^{\ell} \alpha_j^* y_j \kappa(\mathbf{x}_j, \cdot) + b\right)$; $\mathbf{w} = \sum_{j=1}^{\ell} y_j \alpha_j^* \phi(\mathbf{x}_j)$
Output	weight vector $\mathbf{w}$, dual solution $\boldsymbol{\alpha}^*$, margin γ^* and function f implementing the decision rule represented by the hyperplane

Code Fragment 7.4. Pseudocode for the hard margin SVM.

The following theorem characterises the output and analyses the statistical stability of Algorithm 7.21.

Theorem 7.22 *Fix $\delta > 0$. Suppose that a training sample*

$$S = \{(\mathbf{x}_1, y_1), \ldots, (\mathbf{x}_\ell, y_\ell)\},$$

is drawn according to a distribution $\mathcal{D}$ is linearly separable in the feature space implicitly defined by the kernel κ and suppose Algorithm 7.21 outputs $\mathbf{w}, \boldsymbol{\alpha}^*, \gamma^*$ and the function f. Then the function f realises the hard margin support vector machine in the feature space defined by κ with geometric margin γ^*. Furthermore, with probability $1 - \delta$, the generalisation error of the resulting classifier is bounded by

$$\frac{4}{\ell \gamma^*} \sqrt{\mathrm{tr}(\mathbf{K})} + 3\sqrt{\frac{\ln(2/\delta)}{2\ell}},$$

where $\mathbf{K}$ is the corresponding kernel matrix.

Proof The solution of the optimisation problem in Algorithm 7.21 clearly optimises (7.11) subject to the constraints of (7.10). Hence, the optimisation of $W(\boldsymbol{\alpha})$ will result in the same solution vector $\boldsymbol{\alpha}^*$. It follows that

$$\gamma^* = -L(\mathbf{w}^*, b^*, \gamma^*, \boldsymbol{\alpha}^*, \lambda^*) = \sqrt{-W(\boldsymbol{\alpha}^*)}.$$

The result follows from these observations and the fact that $\mathbf{w}$ is a simple rescaling of the solution vector $\mathbf{w}^*$ by twice the Lagrange multiplier λ^*. Furthermore

$$2\lambda^* = \frac{2}{2}\left(\sum_{i,j=1}^{\ell}\alpha_i^*\alpha_j^*y_iy_j\kappa\left(\mathbf{x}_i,\mathbf{x}_j\right)\right)^{1/2} = \sqrt{-W(\boldsymbol{\alpha}^*)}.$$

If $\mathbf{w}$ is the solution given by Algorithm 7.21, it is a rescaled version of the optimal solution $\mathbf{w}^*$. Since the weight vector $\mathbf{w}$ has norm and geometric margin equal to $\sqrt{-W(\boldsymbol{\alpha}^*)}$, its functional margin is $-W(\boldsymbol{\alpha}^*) = \gamma^*$, while the vectors with non-zero α_i^* have margin equal to the functional margin – see Remark 7.23 – this gives the formula for b. $\qquad\square$

Remark 7.23 [On sparseness] The Karush–Kuhn–Tucker complementarity conditions provide useful information about the structure of the solution. The conditions state that the optimal solutions $\boldsymbol{\alpha}^*$, $(\mathbf{w}^*, b^*)$ must satisfy

$$\alpha_i^*\left[y_i\left(\langle\mathbf{w}^*, \boldsymbol{\phi}\left(\mathbf{x}_i\right)\rangle + b^*\right) - \gamma^*\right] = 0, \qquad i = 1,\ldots,\ell.$$

This implies that only for inputs $\mathbf{x}_i$ for which the geometric margin is γ^*, and that therefore lie closest to the hyperplane, are the corresponding α_i^* non-zero. All the other parameters α_i^* are zero. This is a similar situation to that encountered in the novelty-detection algorithm of Section 7.1. For the same reason the inputs with non-zero α_i^* are called *support vectors* (see Figure 7.3) and again we will denote the set of indices of the support vectors with sv. $\qquad\blacksquare$

Remark 7.24 [On convexity] Note that the requirement that κ is a kernel means that the optimisation problem of Algorithm 7.21 is convex since the matrix $\mathbf{G} = (y_iy_j\kappa(\mathbf{x}_i,\mathbf{x}_j))_{i,j=1}^{\ell}$ is also positive semi-definite, as the following computation shows

$$\boldsymbol{\beta}'\mathbf{G}\boldsymbol{\beta} = \sum_{i,j=1}^{\ell}\beta_i\beta_jy_iy_j\kappa(\mathbf{x}_i,\mathbf{x}_j) = \left\langle\sum_{i=1}^{\ell}\beta_iy_i\boldsymbol{\phi}(\mathbf{x}_i), \sum_{j=1}^{\ell}\beta_jy_j\boldsymbol{\phi}(\mathbf{x}_j)\right\rangle$$

$$= \left\|\sum_{i=1}^{\ell}\beta_iy_i\boldsymbol{\phi}(\mathbf{x}_i)\right\|^2 \geq 0.$$

Hence, the property required of a kernel function to define a feature space also ensures that the maximal margin optimisation problem has a unique solution that can be found efficiently. This rules out the problem of local minima often encountered in for example training neural networks. ∎

Remark 7.25 [Duality gap] An important result from optimisation theory states that throughout the feasible regions of the primal and dual problems the primal objective is always bigger than the dual objective, when the primal is a minimisation. This is also indicated by the fact that we are minimising the primal and maximising the dual. Since the problems we are considering satisfy the conditions of strong duality, there is no duality gap at the optimal solution. We can therefore use any difference between the primal and dual objectives as an indicator of convergence. We will call this difference the duality gap. Let $\hat{\alpha}$ be the current value of the dual variables. The possibly still negative margin can be calculated as

$$\hat{\gamma} = \frac{\min_{y_i=1}\left(\langle \hat{\mathbf{w}}, \phi\left(\mathbf{x}_i\right)\rangle\right) - \max_{y_i=-1}\left(\langle \hat{\mathbf{w}}, \phi\left(\mathbf{x}_i\right)\rangle\right)}{2},$$

where the current value of the weight vector is $\hat{\mathbf{w}}$. Hence, the duality gap can be computed as

$$-\sqrt{-W(\hat{\alpha})} + \hat{\gamma}.$$

∎

Alternative formulation There is an alternative way of defining the maximal margin optimisation by constraining the functional margin to be 1 and minimising the norm of the weight vector that achieves this. Since the resulting classification is invariant to rescalings this delivers the same classifier. We can arrive at this formulation directly from the dual optimisation problem (7.10) if we use a Lagrange multiplier to incorporate the constraint

$$\sum_{i=1}^{\ell} \alpha_i = 1$$

into the optimisation. Again using the invariance to rescaling we can elect to fix the corresponding Lagrange variable to a value of 2. This gives the following algorithm.

Algorithm 7.26 [Alternative hard margin SVM] The alternative hard margin support vector machine is implemented in Code Fragment 7.5. ∎

Input	training set $S = \{(\mathbf{x}_1, y_1), \ldots, (\mathbf{x}_\ell, y_\ell)\}$, $\delta > 0$
Process maximise subject to	find $\boldsymbol{\alpha}^*$ as solution of the optimisation problem: $W(\boldsymbol{\alpha}) = \sum_{i=1}^{\ell} \alpha_i - \frac{1}{2} \sum_{i,j=1}^{\ell} \alpha_i \alpha_j y_i y_j \kappa(\mathbf{x}_i, \mathbf{x}_j)$ $\sum_{i=1}^{\ell} y_i \alpha_i = 0$ and $0 \le \alpha_i$, $i = 1, \ldots, \ell$.
4 5 6 7 8	$\gamma^* = \left(\sum_{i \in \mathrm{sv}} \alpha_i^*\right)^{-1/2}$ choose i such that $0 < \alpha_i^*$ $b = y_i - \sum_{j \in \mathrm{sv}} \alpha_j^* y_j \kappa(\mathbf{x}_j, \mathbf{x}_i)$ $f(\cdot) = \mathrm{sgn}\left(\sum_{j \in \mathrm{sv}} \alpha_j^* y_j \kappa(\mathbf{x}_j, \cdot) + b\right);$ $\mathbf{w} = \sum_{j \in \mathrm{sv}} y_j \alpha_j^* \phi(\mathbf{x}_j)$
Output	weight vector $\mathbf{w}$, dual solution $\boldsymbol{\alpha}^*$, margin γ^* and function f implementing the decision rule represented by the hyperplane

Code Fragment 7.5. Pseudocode for the alternative version of the hard SVM.

The following theorem characterises the output and analyses the stability of Algorithm 7.26.

Theorem 7.27 *Fix $\delta > 0$. Suppose that a training sample*

$$S = \{(\mathbf{x}_1, y_1), \ldots, (\mathbf{x}_\ell, y_\ell)\},$$

is drawn according to a distribution $\mathcal{D}$, is linearly separable in the feature space implicitly defined by the kernel $\kappa(\mathbf{x}_i, \mathbf{x}_j)$, and suppose Algorithm 7.26 outputs $\mathbf{w}$, $\boldsymbol{\alpha}^*$, γ^* and the function f. Then the function f realises the hard margin support vector machine in the feature space defined by κ with geometric margin γ^*. Furthermore, with probability $1 - \delta$, the generalisation error is bounded by

$$\frac{4}{\ell\gamma^*}\sqrt{\mathrm{tr}(\mathbf{K})} + 3\sqrt{\frac{\ln(2/\delta)}{2\ell}},$$

where $\mathbf{K}$ is the corresponding kernel matrix.

Proof The generalisation follows from the equivalence of the two classifiers. It therefore only remains to show that the expression for γ^* correctly computes the geometric margin. Since we know that the solution is just a scaling of the solution of problem (7.10) we can seek the solution by optimising μ, where

$$\boldsymbol{\alpha} = \mu \boldsymbol{\alpha}^\dagger$$

and $\boldsymbol{\alpha}^\dagger$ is the solution to problem (7.10). Hence, μ is chosen to maximise

$$\mu \sum_{i=1}^{\ell} \alpha_i^\dagger - \frac{\mu^2}{2} \sum_{i,j=1}^{\ell} y_i y_j \alpha_i^\dagger \alpha_j^\dagger \kappa(\mathbf{x}_i, \mathbf{x}_j) = \mu - \frac{\mu^2}{2} \sum_{i,j=1}^{\ell} y_i y_j \alpha_i^\dagger \alpha_j^\dagger \kappa(\mathbf{x}_i, \mathbf{x}_j)$$

giving

$$\mu^* = \left(\sum_{i,j=1}^{\ell} y_i y_j \alpha_i^\dagger \alpha_j^\dagger \kappa(\mathbf{x}_i, \mathbf{x}_j) \right)^{-1} = -W(\boldsymbol{\alpha}^\dagger)^{-1} = (\gamma^*)^{-2},$$

implying

$$\gamma^* = (\mu^*)^{-1/2} = \left(\mu^* \sum_{i=1}^{\ell} \alpha_i^\dagger \right)^{-1/2} = \left(\sum_{i=1}^{\ell} \alpha_i^* \right)^{-1/2},$$

as required. □

An example using the Gaussian kernel is shown in Figure 7.4.

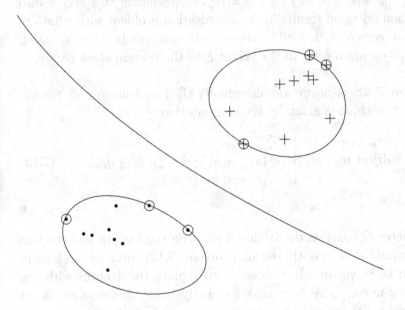

Fig. 7.4. Decision boundary and support vectors when using a gaussian kernel.

7.2.2 Soft margin classifiers

The maximal margin classifier is an important concept, but it can only be used if the data are separable. For this reason it is not applicable in many real-world problems where the data are frequently noisy. If we are to ensure linear separation in the feature space in such cases, we will need very complex kernels that may result in overfitting. Since the hard margin support vector machine always produces a consistent hypothesis, it is extremely sensitive to noise in the training data. The dependence on a quantity like the margin opens the system up to the danger of being very sensitive to a few points. For real data this will result in a non-robust estimator.

This problem motivates the development of more robust versions that can tolerate some noise and outliers in the training set without drastically altering the resulting solution. The motivation of the maximal margin hyperplane was the bound given in (7.8) together with the assumption that the first term vanishes. It is the second assumption that led to the requirement that the data be linearly separable. Hence, if we relax this assumption and just attempt to optimise the complete bound we will be able to tolerate some misclassification of the training data. Exactly as with the novelty detector we must optimise a combination of the margin and 1-norm of the vector $\boldsymbol{\xi}$, where $\xi_i = \xi\left((y_i, \mathbf{x}_i), \gamma, g\right) = (\gamma - y_i g(\mathbf{x}_i))_+$. Introducing this vector into the optimisation criterion results in an optimisation problem with what are known as *slack variables* that allow the margin constraints to be violated. For this reason we often refer to the vector $\boldsymbol{\xi}$ as the *margin slack vector*.

Computation 7.28 [1-norm soft margin SVM] The 1-norm soft margin support vector machine is given by the computation

$$
\begin{aligned}
&\min_{\mathbf{w},b,\gamma,\boldsymbol{\xi}} && -\gamma + C\sum_{i=1}^{\ell} \xi_i \\
&\text{subject to} && y_i\left(\langle \mathbf{w}, \phi\left(\mathbf{x}_i\right)\rangle + b\right) \geq \gamma - \xi_i, \ \xi_i \geq 0, \\
&&& i = 1, \ldots, \ell, \text{ and } \|\mathbf{w}\|^2 = 1.
\end{aligned}
\tag{7.12}
$$

■

The parameter C controls the trade-off between the margin and the size of the slack variables. The optimisation problem (7.12) controls the 1-norm of the margin slack vector. It is possible to replace the 1-norm with the square of the 2-norm. The generalisation analysis for this case is almost identical except for the use of the alternative squared loss function

$$
\mathcal{A}(a) = \begin{cases} 1, & \text{if } a < 0; \\ (1 - a/\gamma)^2, & \text{if } 0 \leq a \leq \gamma; \\ 0, & \text{otherwise.} \end{cases}
$$

The resulting difference when compared to Theorem 4.17 is that the empirical loss involves $1/\gamma^2$ rather than $1/\gamma$ and the Lipschitz constant is $2/\gamma$ in place of $1/\gamma$. Hence, the bound becomes

$$P_D\left(y \neq g(\mathbf{x})\right) \leq \frac{1}{\ell\gamma^2} \sum_{i=1}^{\ell} \xi_i^2 + \frac{8}{\ell\gamma}\sqrt{\mathrm{tr}(\mathbf{K})} + 3\sqrt{\frac{\ln(2/\delta)}{2\ell}}. \qquad (7.13)$$

In the next section we look at optimising the 1-norm bound and, following that, turn our attention to the case of the 2-norm of the slack variables.

1-Norm soft margin – the box constraint The corresponding Lagrangian for the 1-norm soft margin optimisation problem is

$$
\begin{aligned}
L(\mathbf{w}, b, \gamma, \boldsymbol{\xi}, \boldsymbol{\alpha}, \boldsymbol{\beta}, \lambda) &= -\gamma + C\sum_{i=1}^{\ell} \xi_i - \sum_{i=1}^{\ell} \alpha_i\left[y_i(\langle\phi\left(\mathbf{x}_i\right), \mathbf{w}\rangle + b) - \gamma + \xi_i\right] \\
&\quad - \sum_{i=1}^{\ell} \beta_i\xi_i + \lambda\left(\|\mathbf{w}\|^2 - 1\right)
\end{aligned}
$$

with $\alpha_i \geq 0$ and $\beta_i \geq 0$. The corresponding dual is found by differentiating with respect to $\mathbf{w}$, $\boldsymbol{\xi}$, γ and b, and imposing stationarity

$$
\begin{aligned}
\frac{\partial L(\mathbf{w}, b, \gamma, \boldsymbol{\xi}, \boldsymbol{\alpha}, \boldsymbol{\beta}, \lambda)}{\partial\mathbf{w}} &= 2\lambda\mathbf{w} - \sum_{i=1}^{\ell} y_i\alpha_i\phi\left(\mathbf{x}_i\right) = \mathbf{0}, \\
\frac{\partial L(\mathbf{w}, b, \gamma, \boldsymbol{\xi}, \boldsymbol{\alpha}, \boldsymbol{\beta}, \lambda)}{\partial\xi_i} &= C - \alpha_i - \beta_i = 0, \\
\frac{\partial L(\mathbf{w}, b, \gamma, \boldsymbol{\xi}, \boldsymbol{\alpha}, \boldsymbol{\beta}, \lambda)}{\partial b} &= \sum_{i=1}^{\ell} y_i\alpha_i = 0, \\
\frac{\partial L(\mathbf{w}, b, \gamma, \boldsymbol{\xi}, \boldsymbol{\alpha}, \boldsymbol{\beta}, \lambda)}{\partial\gamma} &= 1 - \sum_{i=1}^{\ell} \alpha_i = 0.
\end{aligned}
$$

Resubstituting the relations obtained into the primal, we obtain the following adaptation of the dual objective function

$$L(\boldsymbol{\alpha}, \lambda) = -\frac{1}{4\lambda} \sum_{i,j=1}^{\ell} y_iy_j\alpha_i\alpha_j\kappa\left(\mathbf{x}_i, \mathbf{x}_j\right) - \lambda,$$

which, again optimising with respect to λ, gives

$$\lambda^* = \frac{1}{2}\left(\sum_{i,j=1}^{\ell} y_iy_j\alpha_i\alpha_j\kappa\left(\mathbf{x}_i, \mathbf{x}_j\right)\right)^{1/2} \qquad (7.14)$$

resulting in

$$L(\boldsymbol{\alpha}) = -\left(\sum_{i,j=1}^{\ell} \alpha_i \alpha_j y_i y_j \kappa\left(\mathbf{x}_i, \mathbf{x}_j\right)\right)^{1/2}.$$

This is identical to that for the maximal margin, the only difference being that the constraint $C - \alpha_i - \beta_i = 0$, together with $\beta_i \geq 0$ enforces $\alpha_i \leq C$. The KKT complementarity conditions are therefore

$$\alpha_i \left[y_i(\langle \boldsymbol{\phi}\left(\mathbf{x}_i\right), \mathbf{w}\rangle + b) - \gamma + \xi_i\right] = 0, \quad i = 1, \dots, \ell,$$
$$\xi_i\left(\alpha_i - C\right) = 0, \quad\quad\quad\quad\quad\quad\quad i = 1, \dots, \ell.$$

Notice that the KKT conditions imply that non-zero slack variables can only occur when $\alpha_i = C$. The computation of b^* and γ^* from the optimal solution $\boldsymbol{\alpha}^*$ can be made from two points $\mathbf{x}_i$ and $\mathbf{x}_j$ satisfying $y_i = -1$, $y_j = +1$ and $C > \alpha_i^*, \alpha_j^* > 0$. It follows from the KKT conditions that

$$y_i(\langle \boldsymbol{\phi}\left(\mathbf{x}_i\right), \mathbf{w}^*\rangle + b^*) - \gamma^* = 0 = y_j(\langle \boldsymbol{\phi}\left(\mathbf{x}_j\right), \mathbf{w}^*\rangle + b^*) - \gamma^*$$

implying that

$$-\langle \boldsymbol{\phi}\left(\mathbf{x}_i\right), \mathbf{w}^*\rangle - b^* - \gamma^* \;=\; \langle \boldsymbol{\phi}\left(\mathbf{x}_j\right), \mathbf{w}^*\rangle + b^* - \gamma^*$$
$$\text{or } b^* \;=\; -0.5\left(\langle \boldsymbol{\phi}\left(\mathbf{x}_i\right), \mathbf{w}^*\rangle + \langle \boldsymbol{\phi}\left(\mathbf{x}_j\right), \mathbf{w}^*\rangle\right) \quad (7.15)$$
$$\text{while } \gamma^* \;=\; \langle \boldsymbol{\phi}\left(\mathbf{x}_j\right), \mathbf{w}^*\rangle + b^*. \quad\quad\quad\quad (7.16)$$

We therefore have the following algorithm.

Algorithm 7.29 [1-norm soft margin support vector machine] The 1-norm soft margin support vector machine is implemented in Code Fragment 7.6.

∎

The following theorem characterises the output and statistical stability of Algorithm 7.29.

Theorem 7.30 *Fix $\delta > 0$ and $C \in [1/\ell, \infty)$. Suppose that a training sample*

$$S = \{(\mathbf{x}_1, y_1), \dots, (\mathbf{x}_\ell, y_\ell)\}$$

is drawn according to a distribution $\mathcal{D}$ and suppose Algorithm 7.29 outputs $\mathbf{w}$, $\boldsymbol{\alpha}^*$, γ^* and the function f. Then the function f realises the 1-norm soft margin support vector machine in the feature space defined by κ. Furthermore, with probability $1 - \delta$, the generalisation error is bounded by

$$\frac{1}{C\ell} - \frac{\sqrt{-W(\boldsymbol{\alpha}^*)}}{C\ell\gamma^*} + \frac{4}{\ell\gamma^*}\sqrt{\mathrm{tr}(\mathbf{K})} + 3\sqrt{\frac{\ln(2/\delta)}{2\ell}},$$

Input	training set $S = \{(\mathbf{x}_1, y_1), \ldots, (\mathbf{x}_\ell, y_\ell)\}$, $\delta > 0$, $C \in [1/\ell, \infty)$
Process maximise subject to	find $\boldsymbol{\alpha}^*$ as solution of the optimisation problem: $W(\boldsymbol{\alpha}) = -\sum_{i,j=1}^{\ell} \alpha_i \alpha_j y_i y_j \kappa(\mathbf{x}_i, \mathbf{x}_j)$ $\sum_{i=1}^{\ell} y_i \alpha_i = 0$, $\sum_{i=1}^{\ell} \alpha_i = 1$ and $0 \le \alpha_i \le C$, $i = 1, \ldots, \ell$.
4	$\lambda^* = \frac{1}{2} \left(\sum_{i,j=1}^{\ell} y_i y_j \alpha_i^* \alpha_j^* \kappa(\mathbf{x}_i, \mathbf{x}_j) \right)^{1/2}$
5	choose i, j such that $-C < \alpha_i^* y_i < 0 < \alpha_j^* y_j < C$
6	$b^* = -0.5(\sum_{k=1}^{\ell} \alpha_k^* y_k \kappa(\mathbf{x}_k, \mathbf{x}_i) + \sum_{k=1}^{\ell} \alpha_k^* y_k \kappa(\mathbf{x}_k, \mathbf{x}_j))$
7	$\gamma^* = (2\lambda^*)^{-1}(\sum_{k=1}^{\ell} \alpha_k^* y_k \kappa(\mathbf{x}_k, \mathbf{x}_j) + b^*)$
8	$f(\cdot) = \mathrm{sgn}\left(\sum_{j=1}^{\ell} \alpha_j^* y_j \kappa(\mathbf{x}_j, \cdot) + b^* \right)$;
9	$\mathbf{w} = \sum_{j=1}^{\ell} y_j \alpha_j^* \phi(\mathbf{x}_j)$
Output	weight vector $\mathbf{w}$, dual solution $\boldsymbol{\alpha}^*$, margin γ^* and function f implementing the decision rule represented by the hyperplane

Code Fragment 7.6. Pseudocode for 1-norm soft margin SVM.

where $\mathbf{K}$ is the corresponding kernel matrix.

Proof Note that the rescaling of γ^* is required since the function $f(\mathbf{x})$ corresponds to the weight vector

$$\mathbf{w} = 2\lambda^* \mathbf{w}^* = \sum_{i=1}^{\ell} y_i \alpha_i^* \phi(\mathbf{x}_i).$$

All that remains to show is that the error bound can be derived from the general formula

$$P_D(y \ne g(\mathbf{x})) \le \frac{1}{\ell\gamma} \sum_{i=1}^{\ell} \xi_i + \frac{4}{\ell\gamma} \sqrt{\mathrm{tr}(\mathbf{K})} + 3\sqrt{\frac{\ln(2/\delta)}{2\ell}}.$$

We need to compute the sum of the slack variables. Note that at the optimum we have

$$L(\mathbf{w}^*, b^*, \gamma^*, \boldsymbol{\xi}^*, \boldsymbol{\alpha}^*, \boldsymbol{\beta}^*, \lambda^*) = -\sqrt{-W(\boldsymbol{\alpha}^*)} = -\gamma^* + C \sum_{i=1}^{\ell} \xi_i^*$$

and so

$$\sum_{i=1}^{\ell} \xi_i^* = \frac{\gamma^* - \sqrt{-W(\boldsymbol{\alpha}^*)}}{C}.$$

Substituting into the bound gives the result.   □

An example of the soft margin support vector solution using a Gaussian kernel is shown in Figure 7.5. The support vectors with zero slack variables are circled, though there are other support vectors that fall outside the positive and negative region corresponding to their having non-zero slack variables.

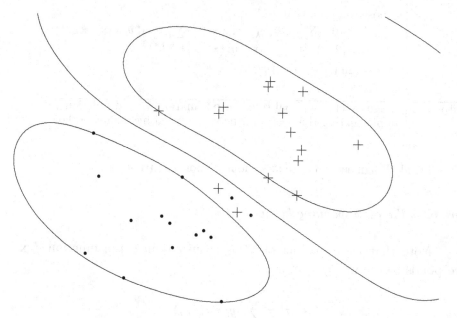

Fig. 7.5. Decision boundary for a soft margin support vector machine using a gauss-ian kernel.

Surprisingly the algorithm is equivalent to the maximal margin hyper-plane, with the additional constraint that all the α_i are upper bounded by C. This gives rise to the name *box constraint* that is frequently used to refer to this formulation, since the vector $\boldsymbol{\alpha}$ is constrained to lie inside the box with side length C in the positive orthant. The trade-off parameter between accuracy and regularisation directly controls the size of the α_i. This makes sense intuitively as the box constraints limit the influence of outliers, which would otherwise have large Lagrange multipliers. The constraint also en-sures that the feasible region is bounded and hence that the primal always has a non-empty feasible region.

Remark 7.31 [Tuning the parameter C] In practice the parameter C is varied through a wide range of values and the optimal performance assessed using a separate validation set or a technique known as cross-validation for verifying performance using only the training set. As the parameter C runs through a range of values, the margin γ^* varies smoothly through a corresponding range. Hence, for a given problem, choosing a particular value for C corresponds to choosing a value for γ^*, and then minimising $\|\boldsymbol{\xi}\|_1$ for that size of margin. ∎

As with novelty-detection, the parameter C has no intuitive meaning. However, the same restrictions on the value of C, namely that $C \geq 1/\ell$, that applied for the novelty-detection optimisation apply here. Again this suggests using

$$C = 1/\left(\nu\ell\right),$$

with $\nu \in (0, 1]$ as this leads to a similar control on the number of outliers in a way made explicit in the following theorem. This form of the support vector machine is known as the ν-support vector machine or new support vector machine.

Algorithm 7.32 [ν-support vector machine] The ν-support vector machine is implemented in Code Fragment 7.7. ∎

Input	training set $S = \{(\mathbf{x}_1, y_1), \ldots, (\mathbf{x}_\ell, y_\ell)\}$, $\delta > 0$, $\nu \in (0, 1]$
Process maximise subject to	find $\boldsymbol{\alpha}^*$ as solution of the optimisation problem: $W(\boldsymbol{\alpha}) = -\sum_{i,j=1}^{\ell} \alpha_i \alpha_j y_i y_j \kappa\left(\mathbf{x}_i, \mathbf{x}_j\right)$ $\sum_{i=1}^{\ell} y_i \alpha_i = 0$, $\sum_{i=1}^{\ell} \alpha_i = 1$ and $0 \leq \alpha_i \leq 1/\left(\nu\ell\right)$, $i = 1, \ldots, \ell$.
4 5 6 7 8 9	$\lambda^* = \frac{1}{2}\left(\sum_{i,j=1}^{\ell} y_i y_j \alpha_i^* \alpha_j^* \kappa\left(\mathbf{x}_i, \mathbf{x}_j\right)\right)^{1/2}$ choose i, j such that $-1/\left(\nu\ell\right) < \alpha_i^* y_i < 0 < \alpha_j^* y_j < 1/\left(\nu\ell\right)$ $b^* = -0.5(\sum_{k=1}^{\ell} \alpha_k^* y_k \kappa\left(\mathbf{x}_k, \mathbf{x}_i\right) + \sum_{k=1}^{\ell} \alpha_k^* y_k \kappa\left(\mathbf{x}_k, \mathbf{x}_j\right))$ $\gamma^* = (2\lambda^*)^{-1}(\sum_{k=1}^{\ell} \alpha_k^* y_k \kappa\left(\mathbf{x}_k, \mathbf{x}_j\right) + b^*)$ $f(\cdot) = \mathrm{sgn}\left(\sum_{j=1}^{\ell} \alpha_j^* y_j \kappa\left(\mathbf{x}_j, \cdot\right) + b^*\right)$; $\mathbf{w} = \sum_{j=1}^{\ell} y_j \alpha_j^* \phi(\mathbf{x}_j)$
Output	weight vector $\mathbf{w}$, dual solution $\boldsymbol{\alpha}^*$, margin γ^* and function f implementing the decision rule represented by the hyperplane

Code Fragment 7.7. Pseudocode for the soft margin SVM.

The following theorem characterises the output and analyses the statistical stability of Algorithm 7.32, while at the same time elucidating the role of the parameter ν.

Theorem 7.33 *Fix $\delta > 0$ and $\nu \in (0, 1]$. Suppose that a training sample*

$$S = \{(\mathbf{x}_1, y_1), \dots, (\mathbf{x}_\ell, y_\ell)\}$$

is drawn according to a distribution $\mathcal{D}$ and suppose Algorithm 7.32 outputs $\mathbf{w}$, $\boldsymbol{\alpha}^*$, γ^* and the function f. Then the function f realises the ν-support vector machine in the feature space defined by κ. Furthermore, with probability $1 - \delta$, the generalisation error of the resulting classifier is bounded by

$$\nu - \frac{\nu\sqrt{-W(\boldsymbol{\alpha}^*)}}{\gamma^*} + \frac{4}{\ell\gamma^*}\sqrt{\mathrm{tr}(\mathbf{K})} + 3\sqrt{\frac{\ln(2/\delta)}{2\ell}}, \qquad (7.17)$$

where $\mathbf{K}$ is the corresponding kernel matrix. Furthermore, there are at most $\nu\ell$ training points that fail to achieve a margin γ^*, while at least $\nu\ell$ of the training points have margin at most γ^*.

Proof This is a direct restatement of Proposition 7.30 with $C = 1/(\nu\ell)$. It remains only to show the bounds on the number of training points failing to achieve the margin γ^* and having margin at most γ^*. The first bound follows from the fact that points failing to achieve margin γ^* have a non-zero slack variable and hence $\alpha_i = 1/(\nu\ell)$. Since

$$\sum_{i=1}^{\ell} \alpha_i = 1,$$

it follows there can be at most $\nu\ell$ such points. Since $\alpha_i \leq 1/(\nu\ell)$ it similarly follows that at least $\nu\ell$ points have non-zero α_i implying that they have margin at most γ^*. ∎

Remark 7.34 [Tuning ν] The form of the generalisation error bound in Proposition 7.33 gives a good intuition about the role of the parameter ν. It corresponds to the noise level inherent in the data, a value that imposes a lower bound on the generalisation error achievable by any learning algorithm.

We can of course use the bound of (7.17) to guide the best choice of the parameter ν, though strictly speaking we should apply the bound for a range of values of ν, in order to work with the bound with non-fixed ν. This would lead to an additional $\log(\ell)/\ell$ factor under the final square root, but for simplicity we again omit these details. ∎

Remark 7.35 [Duality gap] In the case of the 1-norm support vector machine the feasibility gap can again be computed since the ξ_i, γ, and b are not specified when moving to the dual and so can be chosen to ensure that the primary problem is feasible. If we choose them to minimise the primal we can compute the difference between primal and dual objective functions. This can be used to detect convergence to the optimal solution. ∎

2-Norm soft margin – weighting the diagonal In order to minimise the bound (7.13) we can again formulate an optimisation problem, this time involving γ and the 2-norm of the margin slack vector

$$\begin{aligned} \min_{\mathbf{w},b,\gamma,\boldsymbol{\xi}} \quad & -\gamma + C\sum_{i=1}^{\ell}\xi_i^2 \\ \text{subject to} \quad & y_i\left(\langle\mathbf{w},\boldsymbol{\phi}\left(\mathbf{x}_i\right)\rangle + b\right) \geq \gamma - \xi_i,\ \xi_i \geq 0, \\ & i=1,\ldots,\ell,\ \text{and}\ \|\mathbf{w}\|^2 = 1. \end{aligned} \tag{7.18}$$

Notice that if $\xi_i < 0$, then the first constraint will still hold if we set $\xi_i = 0$, while this change will reduce the value of the objective function. Hence, the optimal solution for the problem obtained by removing the positivity constraint on ξ_i will coincide with the optimal solution of (7.18). Hence we obtain the solution to (7.18) by solving the following computation.

Computation 7.36 [2-norm soft margin SVM] The 2-norm soft margin support vector machine is given by the optimisation:

$$\begin{aligned} \min_{\mathbf{w},b,\gamma,\boldsymbol{\xi}} \quad & -\gamma + C\sum_{i=1}^{\ell}\xi_i^2 \\ \text{subject to} \quad & y_i\left(\langle\mathbf{w},\boldsymbol{\phi}\left(\mathbf{x}_i\right)\rangle + b\right) \geq \gamma - \xi_i, \\ & i=1,\ldots,\ell,\ \text{and}\ \|\mathbf{w}\|^2 = 1. \end{aligned} \tag{7.19}$$

∎

The Lagrangian for problem (7.19) of Computation 7.36 is

$$L(\mathbf{w},b,\gamma,\boldsymbol{\xi},\boldsymbol{\alpha},\lambda) = -\gamma + C\sum_{i=1}^{\ell}\xi_i^2 - \sum_{i=1}^{\ell}\alpha_i\left[y_i(\langle\boldsymbol{\phi}\left(\mathbf{x}_i\right),\mathbf{w}\rangle + b) - \gamma + \xi_i\right]$$
$$+ \lambda\left(\|\mathbf{w}\|^2 - 1\right)$$

with $\alpha_i \geq 0$. The corresponding dual is found by differentiating with respect to $\mathbf{w}$, $\boldsymbol{\xi}$, γ and b, imposing stationarity

$$\frac{\partial L(\mathbf{w}, b, \gamma, \boldsymbol{\xi}, \boldsymbol{\alpha}, \lambda)}{\partial \mathbf{w}} = 2\lambda \mathbf{w} - \sum_{i=1}^{\ell} y_i \alpha_i \phi(\mathbf{x}_i) = \mathbf{0},$$

$$\frac{\partial L(\mathbf{w}, b, \gamma, \boldsymbol{\xi}, \boldsymbol{\alpha}, \lambda)}{\partial \xi_i} = 2C\xi_i - \alpha_i = 0,$$

$$\frac{\partial L(\mathbf{w}, b, \gamma, \boldsymbol{\xi}, \boldsymbol{\alpha}, \lambda)}{\partial b} = \sum_{i=1}^{\ell} y_i \alpha_i = 0,$$

$$\frac{\partial L(\mathbf{w}, b, \gamma, \boldsymbol{\xi}, \boldsymbol{\alpha}, \lambda)}{\partial \gamma} = 1 - \sum_{i=1}^{\ell} \alpha_i = 0.$$

Resubstituting the relations obtained into the primal, we obtain the following adaptation of the dual objective function

$$L(\mathbf{w}, b, \gamma, \boldsymbol{\xi}, \boldsymbol{\alpha}, \lambda) = -\frac{1}{4C} \sum_{i=1}^{\ell} \alpha_i^2 - \frac{1}{4\lambda} \sum_{i,j=1}^{\ell} y_i y_j \alpha_i \alpha_j \kappa(\mathbf{x}_i, \mathbf{x}_j) - \lambda,$$

which, again optimising with respect to λ, gives

$$\lambda^* = \frac{1}{2} \left(\sum_{i,j=1}^{\ell} y_i y_j \alpha_i \alpha_j \kappa(\mathbf{x}_i, \mathbf{x}_j) \right)^{1/2} \tag{7.20}$$

resulting in

$$L(\boldsymbol{\alpha}, \lambda) = -\frac{1}{4C} \sum_{i=1}^{\ell} \alpha_i^2 - \left(\sum_{i,j=1}^{\ell} \alpha_i \alpha_j y_i y_j \kappa(\mathbf{x}_i, \mathbf{x}_j) \right)^{1/2}.$$

We can see that adding the 2-norm regularisation of the slack variables in the primal corresponds to regularising the dual with the 2-norm of the Lagrange multipliers. As C is varied, the size of this 2-norm squared will vary from a minimum of $1/\ell$ corresponding to a uniform allocation of

$$\alpha_i = \frac{1}{\ell},$$

to a maximum of 0.5 when exactly one positive and one negative example each get weight 0.5. Maximising the above objective over $\boldsymbol{\alpha}$ for a particular value C is equivalent to maximising

$$W(\boldsymbol{\alpha}) = -\mu \sum_{i=1}^{\ell} \alpha_i^2 - \sum_{i,j=1}^{\ell} \alpha_i \alpha_j y_i y_j \kappa(\mathbf{x}_i, \mathbf{x}_j)$$

$$= -\sum_{i,j=1}^{\ell} y_i y_j \alpha_i \alpha_j \left(\kappa\left(\mathbf{x}_i, \mathbf{x}_j\right) + \mu \delta_{ij} \right),$$

for some value of $\mu = \mu\left(C\right)$, where δ_{ij} is the Kronecker δ defined to be 1 if $i = j$ and 0 otherwise. But this is just the objective of Algorithm 7.21 with the kernel $\kappa\left(\mathbf{x}_i, \mathbf{x}_j\right)$ replaced by $\left(\kappa\left(\mathbf{x}_i, \mathbf{x}_j\right) + \mu \delta_{ij}\right)$.

Hence, we have the following algorithm.

Algorithm 7.37 [2-norm soft margin SVM] The 2-norm soft margin support vector machine is implemented in Code Fragment 7.8. ∎

Input	training set $S = \{(\mathbf{x}_1, y_1), \ldots, (\mathbf{x}_\ell, y_\ell)\}$, $\delta > 0$
Process maximise subject to	find $\boldsymbol{\alpha}^*$ as solution of the optimisation problem: $W(\boldsymbol{\alpha}) = -\sum_{i,j=1}^{\ell} \alpha_i \alpha_j y_i y_j \left(\kappa\left(\mathbf{x}_i, \mathbf{x}_j\right) + \mu \delta_{ij}\right)$ $\sum_{i=1}^{\ell} y_i \alpha_i = 0, \sum_{i=1}^{\ell} \alpha_i = 1$ and $0 \le \alpha_i,\ i = 1, \ldots, \ell$.
4 5 6 7 8	$\gamma^* = \sqrt{-W(\boldsymbol{\alpha}^*)}$ choose i such that $0 < \alpha_i^*$ $b = y_i \left(\gamma^*\right)^2 - \sum_{j=1}^{\ell} \alpha_j^* y_j \left(\kappa\left(\mathbf{x}_i, \mathbf{x}_j\right) + \mu \delta_{ij}\right)$ $f(\mathbf{x}) = \operatorname{sgn}\left(\sum_{j=1}^{\ell} \alpha_j^* y_j \kappa\left(\mathbf{x}_j, \mathbf{x}\right) + b\right);$ $\mathbf{w} = \sum_{j=1}^{\ell} y_j \alpha_j^* \phi(\mathbf{x}_j)$
Output	weight vector $\mathbf{w}$, dual solution $\boldsymbol{\alpha}^*$, margin γ^* and function f implementing the decision rule represented by the hyperplane

Code Fragment 7.8. Pseudocode for the 2-norm SVM.

The following theorem characterises the output and analyses the statistical stability of Algorithm 7.37.

Theorem 7.38 *Fix $\delta > 0$. Suppose that a training sample*

$$S = \{(\mathbf{x}_1, y_1), \ldots, (\mathbf{x}_\ell, y_\ell)\}$$

drawn according to a distribution $\mathcal{D}$ in the feature space implicitly defined by the kernel κ and suppose Algorithm 7.37 outputs $\mathbf{w}$, $\boldsymbol{\alpha}^*$, γ^* and the function f. Then the function f realises the hard margin support vector machine in the feature space defined by $\left(\kappa\left(\mathbf{x}_i, \mathbf{x}_j\right) + \mu \delta_{ij}\right)$ with geometric margin γ^*. This is equivalent to minimising the expression $-\gamma + C \sum_{i=1}^{\ell} \xi_i^2$ involving the 2-norm of the slack variables for some value of C, hence realising the

2-norm support vector machine. Furthermore, with probability $1 - \delta$, the generalisation error of the resulting classifier is bounded by

$$\min\left(\frac{\mu\,\|\boldsymbol{\alpha}^*\|^2}{\ell\gamma^{*4}} + \frac{8\sqrt{\mathrm{tr}(\mathbf{K})}}{\ell\gamma^*} + 3\sqrt{\frac{\ln(4/\delta)}{2\ell}},\; \frac{4\sqrt{\mathrm{tr}(\mathbf{K}) + \ell\mu}}{\ell\gamma^*} + 3\sqrt{\frac{\ln(4/\delta)}{2\ell}}\right),$$

where $\mathbf{K}$ is the corresponding kernel matrix.

Proof The value of the slack variable ξ_i^* can be computed by observing that the contribution to the functional output of the $\mu\delta_{ij}$ term is $\mu\alpha_i^*$ for the unnormalised weight vector $\mathbf{w}$ whose norm is given by

$$\|\mathbf{w}\|^2 = -W(\boldsymbol{\alpha}^*) = \gamma^{*2}.$$

Hence, for the normalised weight vector its value is $\mu\alpha_i^*/\gamma^*$. Plugging this into the bound (7.13) for the 2-norm case shows that the first term of the minimum holds with probability $1 - (\delta/2)$. The second term of the minimum holds with probability $1 - (\delta/2)$ through an application of the hard margin bound in the feature space defined by the kernel

$$(\kappa(\mathbf{x}_i, \mathbf{x}_j) + \mu\delta_{ij}).$$

$\square$

The 2-norm soft margin algorithm reduces to the hard margin case with an extra constant added to the diagonal. In this sense it is reminiscent of the ridge regression algorithm. Unlike ridge regression the 2-norm soft margin algorithm does not lose the sparsity property that is so important for practical applications. We now return to give a more detailed consideration of ridge regression including a strategy for introducing sparsity.

7.3 Support vector machines for regression

We have already discussed the problem of learning a real-valued function in both Chapters 2 and 6. The partial least squares algorithm described in Section 6.7.1 can be used for learning functions whose output is in any Euclidean space, so that the 1-dimensional output of a real-valued function can be seen as a special case. The term regression is generally used to refer to such real-valued learning. Chapter 2 used the ridge regression algorithm to introduce the dual representation of a linear function. We were not, however, in a position to discuss the stability of regression or extensions to the basic algorithm at that stage. We therefore begin this section by redressing this shortcoming of our earlier presentation. Following that we will give a fuller description of ridge regression and other support vector regression methods.

7.3.1 Stability of regression

In order to assess the stability of ridge regression we must choose a pattern function similar to that used for classification functions, namely a measure of discrepancy between the generated output and the desired output. The most common choice is to take the squared loss function between prediction and true output

$$f(\mathbf{z}) = f(\mathbf{x}, y) = \mathcal{L}(y, g(\mathbf{x})) = (y - g(\mathbf{x}))^2.$$

The function g is here the output of the ridge regression algorithm with the form

$$g(\mathbf{x}) = \sum_{i=1}^{\ell} \alpha_i \kappa(\mathbf{x}_i, \mathbf{x}),$$

where $\boldsymbol{\alpha}$ is given by

$$\boldsymbol{\alpha} = (\mathbf{K} + \lambda \mathbf{I}_\ell)^{-1} \mathbf{y}.$$

We can now apply Theorem 4.9 to this function to obtain the following result.

Theorem 7.39 *Fix $B > 0$ and $\delta \in (0, 1)$. Let $\mathcal{F}_B$ be the class of linear functions with norm at most B, mapping from a feature space defined by the kernel κ over a space X. Let*

$$S = \{(\mathbf{x}_1, y_1), \ldots, (\mathbf{x}_\ell, y_\ell)\}$$

be drawn independently according to a probability distribution $\mathcal{D}$ on $X \times \mathbb{R}$, the image of whose support in the feature space is contained in a ball of radius R about the origin, while the support of the output value y lies in the interval $[-BR, BR]$. Then with probability at least $1 - \delta$ over the random draw of S, we have, for all $g \in \mathcal{F}_B$

$$\mathbb{E}_{\mathcal{D}} \left[(y - g(\mathbf{x}))^2 \right] \leq \frac{1}{\ell} \sum_{i=1}^{\ell} (y_i - g(\mathbf{x}_i))^2 + \frac{16RB}{\ell} \left(B\sqrt{\mathrm{tr}(\mathbf{K})} + \|\mathbf{y}\|_2 \right)$$

$$+ 12(RB)^2 \sqrt{\frac{\ln(2/\delta)}{2\ell}},$$

where $\mathbf{K}$ is the kernel matrix of the training set S.

Proof We define the loss function class $\mathcal{L}_{\mathcal{F}, h, 2}$ to be

$$\mathcal{L}_{\mathcal{F}, h, 2} = \left\{ (g - h)^2 \Big| g \in \mathcal{F} \right\}.$$

We will apply Theorem 4.9 to the function $(y - g(\mathbf{x}))^2 / (2RB)^2 \in \mathcal{L}_{\mathcal{F},h,2}$ with $\mathcal{F} = \mathcal{F}_{B/(2RB)} = \mathcal{F}_{1/(2R)}$ and $h(\mathbf{x}, y) = y/(2RB)$. Since this ensures that in the support of the distribution the class is bounded in the interval $[0, 1]$, we have

$$\mathbb{E}_{\mathcal{D}}\left[(y - g(\mathbf{x}))^2 / (2RB)^2\right] \leq \hat{\mathbb{E}}\left[(y - g(\mathbf{x}))^2 / (2RB)^2\right]$$

$$+ \hat{R}_\ell(\mathcal{L}_{\mathcal{F},h,2}) + 3\sqrt{\frac{\ln(2/\delta)}{2\ell}}.$$

Multiplying through by $(2RB)^2$ gives

$$\mathbb{E}_{\mathcal{D}}\left[(y - g(\mathbf{x}))^2\right] \leq \hat{\mathbb{E}}\left[(y - g(\mathbf{x}))^2\right] + (2RB)^2\,\hat{R}_\ell(\mathcal{L}_{\mathcal{F},h,2})$$

$$+ 12\,(RB)^2\,\sqrt{\frac{\ln(2/\delta)}{2\ell}}.$$

The first term on the right-hand side is simply the empirical squared loss. By part (vi) of Proposition 4.15 we have

$$\hat{R}_\ell(\mathcal{L}_{\mathcal{F},h,2}) \leq 4\left(\hat{R}_\ell(\mathcal{F}_{1/(2R)}) + 2\sqrt{\hat{\mathbb{E}}\left[y^2/(2RB)^2\right]/\ell}\right).$$

This together with Theorem 4.12 gives the result. $\qquad\square$

7.3.2 Ridge regression

Theorem 7.39 shows that the expected value of the squared loss can be bounded by its empirical value together with a term that involves the trace of the kernel matrix and the 2-norm of the output values, but involving a bound on the norm of the weight vector of the linear functions. It therefore suggests that we can optimise the off-training set performance by solving the computation:

Computation 7.40 [Ridge regression optimisation] The ridge regression optimisation is achieved by solving

$$\begin{aligned}
\min_{\mathbf{w}} \quad & \textstyle\sum_{i=1}^{\ell} \xi_i^2 \\
\text{subject to} \quad & y_i - \langle \mathbf{w}, \phi(\mathbf{x}_i) \rangle = \xi_i, \\
& i = 1, \dots, \ell, \text{ and } \|\mathbf{w}\| \leq B.
\end{aligned} \qquad (7.21)$$

Applying the Lagrange multiplier technique we obtain the Lagrangian

$$L(\mathbf{w}, \boldsymbol{\xi}, \boldsymbol{\beta}, \lambda) = \sum_{i=1}^{\ell} \xi_i^2 + \sum_{i=1}^{\ell} \beta_i \left[y_i - \langle \phi(\mathbf{x}_i), \mathbf{w} \rangle - \xi_i \right] + \lambda \left(\|\mathbf{w}\|^2 - B^2 \right).$$

Again taking derivatives with respect to the primal variables gives

$$2\lambda \mathbf{w} = \sum_{i=1}^{\ell} \beta_i \phi(\mathbf{x}_i) \text{ and } 2\xi_i = \beta_i, \ i = 1, \dots, \ell.$$

Resubstituting into L we have

$$L(\boldsymbol{\beta}, \lambda) = -\frac{1}{4} \sum_{i=1}^{\ell} \beta_i^2 + \sum_{i=1}^{\ell} \beta_i y_i - \frac{1}{4\lambda} \sum_{i,j=1}^{\ell} \beta_i \beta_j \kappa(\mathbf{x}_i, \mathbf{x}_j) - \lambda B^2.$$

Letting $\alpha_i = \beta_i / (2\lambda)$ be the dual coefficients of the solution weight vector results in the optimisation

$$\min_{\boldsymbol{\alpha}} -\lambda \sum_{i=1}^{\ell} \alpha_i^2 + 2 \sum_{i=1}^{\ell} \alpha_i y_i - \sum_{i,j=1}^{\ell} \alpha_i \alpha_j \kappa(\mathbf{x}_i, \mathbf{x}_j).$$

Differentiating with respect to the parameters and setting the derivative equal to zero leads to the following algorithm.

Algorithm 7.41 [Kernel ridge regression] The ridge regression algorithm is implemented as follows:

Input	training set $S = \{(\mathbf{x}_1, y_1), \dots, (\mathbf{x}_\ell, y_\ell)\}$, $\lambda > 0$
Process	$\boldsymbol{\alpha}^* = (\mathbf{K} + \lambda \mathbf{I}_\ell)^{-1} \mathbf{y}$
2	$f(\mathbf{x}) = \sum_{j=1}^{\ell} \alpha_j^* \kappa(\mathbf{x}_j, \mathbf{x})$
3	$\mathbf{w} = \sum_{j=1}^{\ell} \alpha_j^* \phi(\mathbf{x}_j)$
Output	weight vector $\mathbf{w}$, dual $\boldsymbol{\alpha}^*$ and/or function f implementing ridge regression

The algorithm was already introduced in Chapter 2 (see (2.6)). Strictly speaking we should have optimised over λ, but clearly different values of λ correspond to different choices of B, hence varying λ is equivalent to varying B.

The example of ridge regression shows how once again the form of the bound on the stability of the pattern function leads to the optimisation problem that defines the solution of the learning task. Despite this well-founded motivation, dual ridge regression like dual partial least squares suffers from the disadvantage that the solution vector $\boldsymbol{\alpha}^*$ is not sparse. Hence, to evaluate the learned function on a novel example we must evaluate the kernel with each of the training examples. For large training sets this will make the response time very slow.

The sparsity that arose in the case of novelty-detection and classification had its roots in the inequalities used to define the optimisation criterion. This follows because at the optimum those points for which the function output places them in a region where the loss function has zero derivative must have their Lagrange multipliers equal to zero. Clearly for the 2-norm loss this is never the case.

We therefore now examine how the square loss function of ridge regression can be altered with a view to introducing sparsity into the solutions obtained. This will then lead to the use of the optimisation techniques applied above for novelty-detection and classification but now used to solve regression problems, hence developing the support vector regression (SVR) algorithms.

7.3.3 ε-insensitive regression

In order to encourage sparseness, we need to define a loss function that involves inequalities in its evelation. This can be achieved by ignoring errors that are smaller than a certain threshold $\varepsilon > 0$. For this reason the band around the true output is sometimes referred to as a *tube*. This type of loss function is referred to as an ε-insensitive loss function. Using ε-insensitive loss functions leads to the support vector regression algorithms.

Figure 7.6 shows an example of a one-dimensional regression function with an ε-insensitive band. The variables ξ measure the cost of the errors on the training points. These are zero for all points inside the band. Notice that when $\varepsilon = 0$ we recover standard loss functions such as the squared loss used in the previous section as the following definition makes clear.

Definition 7.42 The *(linear) ε-insensitive loss function* $\mathcal{L}^\varepsilon(\mathbf{x}, y, g)$ is defined by

$$\mathcal{L}^\varepsilon(\mathbf{x}, y, g) = |y - g(\mathbf{x})|_\varepsilon = \max\left(0, |y - g(\mathbf{x})| - \varepsilon\right),$$

where g is a real-valued function on a domain X, $\mathbf{x} \in X$ and $y \in \mathbb{R}$. Similarly the *quadratic ε-insensitive loss* is given by

$$\mathcal{L}_2^\varepsilon(\mathbf{x}, y, g) = |y - g(\mathbf{x})|_\varepsilon^2.$$

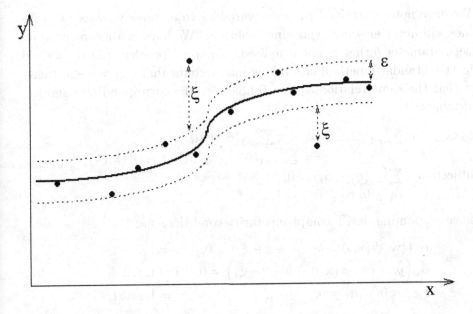

Fig. 7.6. Regression using ε-insensitive loss.

Continuing the development that we began with ridge regression it is most natural to consider taking the square of the ε-insensitive loss to give the so-called quadratic ε-insensitive loss.

Quadratic ε-insensitive loss We can optimise the sum of the quadratic ε-insensitive losses again subject to the constraint that the norm is bounded. This can be cast as an optimisation problem by introducing separate slack variables for the case where the output is too small and the output is too large. Rather than have a separate constraint for the norm of the weight vector we introduce the norm into the objective function together with a parameter C to measure the trade-off between the norm and losses. This leads to the following computation.

Computation 7.43 [Quadratic ε-insensitive SVR] The weight vector $\mathbf{w}$ and threshold b for the quadratic ε-insensitive support vector regression are chosen to optimise the following problem

$$
\left.
\begin{array}{ll}
\min_{\mathbf{w},b,\boldsymbol{\xi},\hat{\boldsymbol{\xi}}} & \|\mathbf{w}\|^2 + C\sum_{i=1}^{\ell}(\xi_i^2 + \hat{\xi}_i^2), \\
\text{subject to} & (\langle \mathbf{w}, \boldsymbol{\phi}(\mathbf{x}_i)\rangle + b) - y_i \leq \varepsilon + \xi_i,\ i = 1,\ldots,\ell, \\
& y_i - (\langle \mathbf{w}, \boldsymbol{\phi}(\mathbf{x}_i)\rangle + b) \leq \varepsilon + \hat{\xi}_i,\ i = 1,\ldots,\ell.
\end{array}
\right\}
\tag{7.22}
$$

∎

We have not constrained the slack variables to be positive since negative values will never arise at the optimal solution. We have further included an offset parameter b that is not penalised. The dual problem can be derived using the standard method and taking into account that $\xi_i \hat{\xi}_i = 0$ and therefore that the same relation $\alpha_i \hat{\alpha}_i = 0$ holds for the corresponding Lagrange multipliers

$$\max_{\hat{\alpha}, \alpha} \quad \sum_{i=1}^{\ell} y_i (\hat{\alpha}_i - \alpha_i) - \varepsilon \sum_{i=1}^{\ell} (\hat{\alpha}_i + \alpha_i)$$
$$- \frac{1}{2} \sum_{i,j=1}^{\ell} (\hat{\alpha}_i - \alpha_i)(\hat{\alpha}_j - \alpha_j) \left(\kappa(\mathbf{x}_i, \mathbf{x}_j) + \frac{1}{C} \delta_{ij} \right),$$

subject to $\quad \sum_{i=1}^{\ell} (\hat{\alpha}_i - \alpha_i) = 0,$
$$\hat{\alpha}_i \geq 0, \ \alpha_i \geq 0, \ i = 1, \ldots, \ell.$$

The corresponding KKT complementarity conditions are

$$\alpha_i \left(\langle \mathbf{w}, \phi(\mathbf{x}_i) \rangle + b - y_i - \varepsilon - \xi_i \right) = 0, \quad i = 1, \ldots, \ell,$$
$$\hat{\alpha}_i \left(y_i - \langle \mathbf{w}, \phi(\mathbf{x}_i) \rangle - b - \varepsilon - \hat{\xi}_i \right) = 0, \quad i = 1, \ldots, \ell,$$
$$\xi_i \hat{\xi}_i = 0, \ \alpha_i \hat{\alpha}_i = 0, \quad\quad\quad\quad\quad\quad i = 1, \ldots, \ell,$$

Remark 7.44 [Alternative formulation] Note that by substituting $\beta = \hat{\alpha} - \alpha$ and using the relation $\alpha_i \hat{\alpha}_i = 0$, it is possible to rewrite the dual problem in a way that more closely resembles the classification case

$$\max_{\beta} \quad \sum_{i=1}^{\ell} y_i \beta_i - \varepsilon \sum_{i=1}^{\ell} |\beta_i| - \frac{1}{2} \sum_{i,j=1}^{\ell} \beta_i \beta_j \left(\kappa(\mathbf{x}_i, \mathbf{x}_j) + \frac{1}{C} \delta_{ij} \right),$$
subject to $\quad \sum_{i=1}^{\ell} \beta_i = 0.$

Notice that if we set $\varepsilon = 0$ we recover ridge regression, but with an unpenalised offset that gives rise to the constraint

$$\sum_{i=1}^{\ell} \beta_i = 0.$$

We will in fact use $\boldsymbol{\alpha}$ in place of $\boldsymbol{\beta}$ when we use this form later. ∎

Hence, we have the following result for a regression technique that will typically result in a sparse solution vector $\boldsymbol{\alpha}^*$.

Algorithm 7.45 [2-norm support vector regression] The 2-norm support vector regression algorithm is implemented in Code Fragment 7.9. ∎

Though the move to the use of the ε-insensitive loss was motivated by the desire to introduce sparsity into the solution, remarkably it can also improve the generalisation error as measured by the expected value of the squared error as is bourne out in practical experiments.

Input	training set $S = \{(\mathbf{x}_1, y_1), \ldots, (\mathbf{x}_\ell, y_\ell)\}$, $C > 0$
Process	find $\boldsymbol{\alpha}^*$ as solution of the optimisation problem:
$\max_{\boldsymbol{\alpha}}$	$W(\boldsymbol{\alpha}) = \sum_{i=1}^{\ell} y_i \alpha_i - \varepsilon \sum_{i=1}^{\ell} |\alpha_i| - \frac{1}{2} \sum_{i,j=1}^{\ell} \alpha_i \alpha_j \left(\kappa(\mathbf{x}_i, \mathbf{x}_j) + \frac{1}{C} \delta_{ij} \right)$
subject to	$\sum_{i=1}^{\ell} \alpha_i = 0$.

4	$\mathbf{w} = \sum_{j=1}^{\ell} \alpha_j^* \phi(\mathbf{x}_j)$
5	$b^* = -\varepsilon - (\alpha_i^*/C) + y_i - \sum_{j=1}^{\ell} \alpha_j^* \kappa(\mathbf{x}_j, \mathbf{x}_i)$ for i with $\alpha_i^* > 0$.
6	$f(\mathbf{x}) = \sum_{j=1}^{\ell} \alpha_j^* \kappa(\mathbf{x}_j, \mathbf{x}) + b^*$,
Output	weight vector $\mathbf{w}$, dual $\boldsymbol{\alpha}^*$, b^* and/or function f implementing 2-norm support vector regression

Code Fragment 7.9. Pseudocode for 2-norm support vector regression.

The quadratic ε-insensitive loss follows naturally from the loss function used in ridge regression. There is, however, an alternative that parallels the use of the 1-norm of the slack variables in the support vector machine. This makes use of the linear ε-insensitive loss.

Linear ε-insensitive loss A straightforward rewriting of the optimisation problem (7.22) that minimises the linear loss is as follows:

Computation 7.46 [Linear ε-insensitive SVR] The weight vector $\mathbf{w}$ and threshold b for the linear ε-insensitive support vector regression are chosen to optimise the following problem

$$\left. \begin{array}{ll} \min_{\mathbf{w}, b, \boldsymbol{\xi}, \hat{\boldsymbol{\xi}}} & \frac{1}{2} \|\mathbf{w}\|^2 + C \sum_{i=1}^{\ell} (\xi_i + \hat{\xi}_i), \\ \text{subject to} & (\langle \mathbf{w}, \phi(\mathbf{x}_i) \rangle + b) - y_i \leq \varepsilon + \xi_i, \ i = 1, \ldots, \ell, \\ & y_i - (\langle \mathbf{w}, \phi(\mathbf{x}_i) \rangle + b) \leq \varepsilon + \hat{\xi}_i, \ i = 1, \ldots, \ell, \\ & \xi_i, \hat{\xi}_i \geq 0, \ i = 1, \ldots, \ell. \end{array} \right\} \quad (7.23)$$

■

The corresponding dual problem can be derived using the now standard techniques

$$\begin{array}{ll} \max & \sum_{i=1}^{\ell} (\hat{\alpha}_i - \alpha_i) y_i - \varepsilon \sum_{i=1}^{\ell} (\hat{\alpha}_i + \alpha_i) \\ & \qquad - \frac{1}{2} \sum_{i,j=1}^{\ell} (\hat{\alpha}_i - \alpha_i)(\hat{\alpha}_j - \alpha_j) \kappa(\mathbf{x}_i, \mathbf{x}_j), \\ \text{subject to} & 0 \leq \alpha_i, \hat{\alpha}_i \leq C, \ i = 1, \ldots, \ell, \\ & \sum_{i=1}^{\ell} (\hat{\alpha}_i - \alpha_i) = 0, \ i = 1, \ldots, \ell. \end{array}$$

The KKT complementarity conditions are

$$\alpha_i \left(\langle \mathbf{w}, \phi\left(\mathbf{x}_i\right) \rangle + b - y_i - \varepsilon - \xi_i \right) = 0, \quad i = 1, \ldots, \ell,$$
$$\hat{\alpha}_i \left(y_i - \langle \mathbf{w}, \phi\left(\mathbf{x}_i\right) \rangle - b - \varepsilon - \hat{\xi}_i \right) = 0, \quad i = 1, \ldots, \ell,$$
$$\xi_i \hat{\xi}_i = 0, \ \alpha_i \hat{\alpha}_i = 0, \quad i = 1, \ldots, \ell,$$
$$(\alpha_i - C)\, \xi_i = 0, \ (\hat{\alpha}_i - C)\, \hat{\xi}_i = 0, \quad i = 1, \ldots, \ell.$$

Again as mentioned in Remark 7.44 substituting α_i for $\hat{\alpha}_i - \alpha_i$, and taking into account that $\alpha_i \hat{\alpha}_i = 0$, we obtain the following algorithm.

Algorithm 7.47 [1-norm support vector regression] The 1-norm support vector regression algorithm is implemented in Code Fragment 7.10. ∎

Input	training set $S = \{(\mathbf{x}_1, y_1), \ldots, (\mathbf{x}_\ell, y_\ell)\}$, $C > 0$
Process $\max_{\boldsymbol{\alpha}}$ subject to	find $\boldsymbol{\alpha}^*$ as solution of the optimisation problem: $W(\boldsymbol{\alpha}) = \sum_{i=1}^{\ell} y_i \alpha_i - \varepsilon \sum_{i=1}^{\ell} |\alpha_i| - \frac{1}{2} \sum_{i,j=1}^{\ell} \alpha_i \alpha_j \kappa(\mathbf{x}_i, \mathbf{x}_j)$ $\sum_{i=1}^{\ell} \alpha_i = 0, \ -C \leq \alpha_i \leq C, \ i = 1, \ldots, \ell.$
4 5 6	$\mathbf{w} = \sum_{j=1}^{\ell} \alpha_j^* \phi(\mathbf{x}_j)$ $b^* = -\varepsilon + y_i - \sum_{j=1}^{\ell} \alpha_j^* \kappa(\mathbf{x}_j, \mathbf{x}_i)$ for i with $0 < \alpha_i^* < C$. $f(\mathbf{x}) = \sum_{j=1}^{\ell} \alpha_j^* \kappa(\mathbf{x}_j, \mathbf{x}) + b^*,$
Output	weight vector $\mathbf{w}$, dual $\boldsymbol{\alpha}^*$, b^* and/or function f implementing 1-norm support vector regression

Code Fragment 7.10. Pseudocode for 1-norm support vector regression.

Remark 7.48 [Support vectors] If we consider the band of $\pm\varepsilon$ around the function output by the learning algorithm, the points that are not strictly inside the tube are support vectors. Those not touching the tube will have the absolute value of the corresponding α_i equal to C. ∎

Stability analysis of ε-insensitive regression The linear ε-insensitive loss for support vector regression raises the question of what stability analysis is appropriate. When the output values are real there are a large range of possibilities for loss functions all of which reduce to the discrete loss in the case of classification. An example of such a loss function is the loss that counts an error if the function output deviates from the true output by more than an error bound γ

$$\mathcal{H}^\gamma(\mathbf{x}, y, g) = \begin{cases} 0, & \text{if } |y - g(\mathbf{x})| \leq \gamma; \\ 1, & \text{otherwise.} \end{cases}$$

We can now apply a similar generalisation analysis to that developed for classification by introducing a loss function

$$\mathcal{A}(a) = \begin{cases} 0, & \text{if } a < \varepsilon, \\ (a - \varepsilon) / (\gamma - \varepsilon), & \text{if } \varepsilon \leq a \leq \gamma, \\ 1, & \text{otherwise.} \end{cases}$$

Observe that $\mathcal{H}^\gamma(\mathbf{x}, y, g) \leq \mathcal{A}(|y - g(\mathbf{x})|) \leq |y - g(\mathbf{x})|_\varepsilon$, so that we can apply Theorem 4.9 to $\mathcal{A}(|y - g(\mathbf{x})|)$ to give an upper bound on $\mathbb{E}_D[\mathcal{H}^\gamma(\mathbf{x}, y, g)]$ while the empirical error can be upper bounded by

$$\sum_{i=1}^\ell |y_i - g(\mathbf{x}_i)|_\varepsilon = \sum_{i=1}^\ell (\xi_i + \hat{\xi}_i).$$

Putting the pieces together gives the following result.

Theorem 7.49 *Fix $B > 0$ and $\delta \in (0, 1)$. Let $\mathcal{F}_B$ be the class of linear functions with norm at most B, mapping from a feature space defined by the kernel κ over a space X. Let*

$$S = \{(\mathbf{x}_1, y_1), \ldots, (\mathbf{x}_\ell, y_\ell)\}$$

be drawn independently according to a probability distribution D on $X \times \mathbb{R}$. Then with probability at least $1 - \delta$ over the random draw of S, we have for all $g \in \mathcal{F}_B$

$$P_D(|y - g(\mathbf{x})| > \gamma) = \mathbb{E}_D[\mathcal{H}^\gamma(\mathbf{x}, y, g)]$$

$$\leq \frac{\|\boldsymbol{\xi} + \hat{\boldsymbol{\xi}}\|_1}{\ell(\gamma - \varepsilon)} + \frac{4B\sqrt{\mathrm{tr}(\mathbf{K})}}{\ell(\gamma - \varepsilon)} + 3\sqrt{\frac{\ln(2/\delta)}{2\ell}},$$

where $\mathbf{K}$ is the kernel matrix of the training set S.

The result shows that bounding a trade-off between the sum of the linear slack variables and the norm of the weight vector will indeed lead to an improved bound on the probability that the output error exceeds γ.

ν-**support vector regression** One of the attractive features of the 1-norm support vector machine was the ability to reformulate the problem so that the regularisation parameter specifies the fraction of support vectors in the so-called ν-support vector machine. The same approach can be adopted here in what is known as ν-support vector regression. The reformulation involves the automatic adaptation of the size ε of the tube.

Computation 7.50 [ν-support vector regression] The weight vector $\mathbf{w}$ and threshold b for the ν-support vector regression are chosen to optimise the following problem:

$$
\left.
\begin{array}{ll}
\min_{\mathbf{w},b,\varepsilon,\boldsymbol{\xi},\hat{\boldsymbol{\xi}}} & \frac{1}{2}\|\mathbf{w}\|^2 + C\left(\nu\varepsilon + \frac{1}{\ell}\sum_{i=1}^{\ell}(\xi_i + \hat{\xi}_i)\right), \\
\text{subject to} & (\langle\mathbf{w},\phi(\mathbf{x}_i)\rangle + b) - y_i \leq \varepsilon + \xi_i, \\
& y_i - (\langle\mathbf{w},\phi(\mathbf{x}_i)\rangle + b) \leq \varepsilon + \hat{\xi}_i, \\
& \xi_i, \hat{\xi}_i \geq 0, \ i = 1,\ldots,\ell,
\end{array}
\right\}
\tag{7.24}
$$

■

Applying the now usual analysis leads to the following algorithm.

Algorithm 7.51 [ν-support vector regression] The ν-support vector regression algorithm is implemented in Code Fragment 7.11.   ■

Input	training set $S = \{(\mathbf{x}_1, y_1), \ldots, (\mathbf{x}_\ell, y_\ell)\}$, $C > 0$, $0 < \nu < 1$.
Process $\max_{\boldsymbol{\alpha}}$ subject to	find $\boldsymbol{\alpha}^*$ as solution of the optimisation problem: $W(\boldsymbol{\alpha}) = \sum_{i=1}^{\ell} y_i\alpha_i - \varepsilon\sum_{i=1}^{\ell}|\alpha_i| - \frac{1}{2}\sum_{i,j=1}^{\ell}\alpha_i\alpha_j\kappa(\mathbf{x}_i,\mathbf{x}_j)$ $\sum_{i=1}^{\ell}\alpha_i = 0, \ \sum_{i=1}^{\ell}|\alpha_i| \leq C\nu, \ -C/\ell \leq \alpha_i \leq C/\ell, \ i = 1,\ldots,\ell.$
4 5 6	$\mathbf{w} = \sum_{j=1}^{\ell}\alpha_j^*\phi(\mathbf{x}_j)$ $b^* = -\varepsilon + y_i - \sum_{j=1}^{\ell}\alpha_j^*\kappa(\mathbf{x}_j,\mathbf{x}_i)$ for i with $0 < \alpha_i^* < C/\ell$. $f(\mathbf{x}) = \sum_{j=1}^{\ell}\alpha_j^*\kappa(\mathbf{x}_j,\mathbf{x}) + b^*,$
Output	weight vector $\mathbf{w}$, dual $\boldsymbol{\alpha}^*$, b^* and/or function f implementing ν-support vector regression

Code Fragment 7.11. Pseudocode for new SVR.

As with the ν-support vector machine the parameter ν controls the fraction of errors in the sense that there are at most $\nu\ell$ training points that fall outside the tube, while at least $\nu\ell$ of the training points are support vectors and so lie either outside the tube or on its surface.

7.4 On-line classification and regression

The algorithms we have described in this section have all taken a training set S as input and processed all of the training examples at once. Such an algorithm is known as a *batch* algorithm.

In many practical tasks training data must be processed one at a time as it is received, so that learning is started as soon as the first example is received. The learning follows the following protocol. As each example is received the learner makes a prediction of the correct output. The true output is then made available and the degree of mismatch or loss made in the prediction is recorded. Finally, the learner can update his current pattern function in response to the feedback received on the current example. If updates are only made when non-zero loss is experience, the algorithm is said to be *conservative*.

Learning that follows this protocol is known as *on-line learning*. The aim of the learner is to adapt his pattern function as rapidly as possible. This is reflected in the measures of performance adopted to analyse on-line learning. Algorithms are judged according to their ability to control the accumulated loss that they will suffer in processing a sequence of examples. This measure takes into account the rate at which learning takes place.

We first consider a simple on-line algorithm for learning linear functions in an on-line fashion.

The perceptron algorithm The algorithm learns a thresholded linear function

$$h\left(\mathbf{x}\right) = \text{sgn}\left\langle \mathbf{w}, \phi\left(\mathbf{x}\right)\right\rangle$$

in a kernel-defined feature space in an on-line fashion making an update whenever a misclassified example is processed. If the weight vector after t updates is denoted by $\mathbf{w}_t$ then the update rule for the $(t+1)$st update when an example $(\mathbf{x}_i, y_i)$ is misclassified is given by

$$\mathbf{w}_{t+1} = \mathbf{w}_t + y_i \phi\left(\mathbf{x}_i\right).$$

Hence, the corresponding dual update rule is simply

$$\alpha_i = \alpha_i + 1,$$

if we assume that the weight vector is expressed as

$$\mathbf{w}_t = \sum_{i=1}^{\ell} \alpha_i y_i \phi\left(\mathbf{x}_i\right).$$

This is summarised in the following algorithm.

Algorithm 7.52 [Kernel perceptron] The dual perceptron algorithm is implemented in Code Fragment 7.12.   ■

Input	training sequence $(\mathbf{x}_1, y_1), \ldots, (\mathbf{x}_\ell, y_\ell), \ldots$
Process	$\boldsymbol{\alpha} = 0$, $i = 0$, loss $= 0$
2	repeat
3	$\quad i = i + 1$
4	$\quad$ if sgn $\left(\sum_{j=1}^{\ell} \alpha_j y_j \kappa(\mathbf{x}_j, \mathbf{x}_i) \right) \neq y_i$
5	$\quad\quad \alpha_i = \alpha_i + 1$
6	$\quad\quad$ loss $=$ loss $+1$
7	$\quad$ until finished
8	$f(\mathbf{x}) = \sum_{j=1}^{\ell} \alpha_j y_j \kappa(\mathbf{x}_j, \mathbf{x})$
Output	dual variables $\boldsymbol{\alpha}$, loss and function f

Code Fragment 7.12. Pseudocode for the kernel perceptron algorithm.

We can apply the perceptron algorithm as a batch algorithm to a full training set by running through the set repeating the updates until all of the examples are correctly classified.

Assessing the performance of the perceptron algorithm The algorithm does not appear to be aiming for few updates, but for the batch case the well-known perceptron convergence theorem provides a bound on their number in terms of the margin of the corresponding hard margin support vector machine as stated in the theorem due to Novikoff.

Theorem 7.53 (Novikoff) *If the training points*

$$S = \{(\mathbf{x}_1, y_1), \ldots, (\mathbf{x}_\ell, y_\ell)\}$$

are contained in a ball of radius R about the origin, the hard margin support vector machine weight vector $\mathbf{w}^*$ with no bias has geometric margin γ and we begin with the weight vector

$$\mathbf{w}_0 = \mathbf{0} = \sum_{i=1}^{\ell} 0 \phi(\mathbf{x}_i) ;$$

then the number of updates of the perceptron algorithm is bounded by

$$\frac{R^2}{\gamma^2}.$$

Proof The result follows from two sequences of inequalities. The first shows that as the updates are made the norm of the resulting weight vector cannot grow too fast, since if i is the index of the example used for the tth update, we have

$$\|\mathbf{w}_{t+1}\|^2 = \langle \mathbf{w}_t + y_i\boldsymbol{\phi}(\mathbf{x}_i), \mathbf{w}_t + y_i\boldsymbol{\phi}(\mathbf{x}_i)\rangle$$
$$= \|\mathbf{w}_t\|^2 + 2y_i\langle \mathbf{w}_t, \boldsymbol{\phi}(\mathbf{x}_i)\rangle + \|\boldsymbol{\phi}(\mathbf{x}_i)\|^2$$
$$\leq \|\mathbf{w}_t\|^2 + R^2 \leq (t+1)R^2,$$

since the fact we made the update implies the middle term cannot be positive. The other sequence of inequalities shows that the inner product between the sequence of weight vectors and the vector $\mathbf{w}^*$ (assumed without loss of generality to have norm 1) increases by a fixed amount each update

$$\langle \mathbf{w}^*, \mathbf{w}_{t+1}\rangle = \langle \mathbf{w}^*, \mathbf{w}_t\rangle + y_i\langle \mathbf{w}^*, \boldsymbol{\phi}(\mathbf{x}_i)\rangle \geq \langle \mathbf{w}^*, \mathbf{w}_t\rangle + \gamma \geq (t+1)\gamma.$$

The two inequalities eventually become incompatible as they imply that

$$t^2\gamma^2 \leq \langle \mathbf{w}^*, \mathbf{w}_t\rangle^2 \leq \|\mathbf{w}_t\|^2 \leq tR^2.$$

Clearly, we must have

$$t \leq \frac{R^2}{\gamma^2},$$

as required. $\qquad\square$

The bound on the number of updates indicates that each time we make a mistake we are effectively offsetting the cost of that mistake with some progress towards learning a function that correctly classifies the training set. It is curious that the bound on the number of updates is reminiscent of the bound on the generalisation of the hard margin support vector machine.

Despite the number of updates not being a bound on the generalisation performance of the resulting classifier, we now show that it does imply such a bound. Indeed the type of analysis we now present will also imply a bound on the generalisation of the hard margin support vector machine in terms of the number of support vectors.

Recall that for the various support vector machines for classification and the ε-insensitive support vector machine for regression only a subset of the Lagrange multipliers is non-zero. This property of the solutions is referred to as *sparseness*. Furthermore, the support vectors contain all the information necessary to reconstruct the hyperplane or regression function. Hence, for classification even if all of the other points were removed the same maximal separating hyperplane would be found from the remaining subset of the support vectors. This shows that the maximal margin hyperplane is a compression scheme in the sense that from the subset of support vectors we can reconstruct the maximal margin hyperplane that correctly classifies the whole training set.

For the perceptron algorithm the bound is in terms of the number of updates made to the hypothesis during learning, that is the number bounded by Novikoff's theorem. This is because the same hypothesis would be generated by performing the same sequence of updates while ignoring the examples on which updates were not made. These examples can then be considered as test examples since they were not involved in the generation of the hypothesis. There are ℓ^k ways in which a sequence of k updates can be created from a training set of size ℓ, so we have a bound on the number of hypotheses considered. Putting this together using a union bound on probability gives the following proposition.

Theorem 7.54 *Fix $\delta > 0$. If the perceptron algorithm makes $1 \leq k \leq \ell/2$ updates before converging to a hypothesis $f(\mathbf{x})$ that correctly ranks a training set*

$$S = \{(\mathbf{x}_1, y_1), \ldots, (\mathbf{x}_\ell, y_\ell)\}$$

drawn independently at random according to a distribution $\mathcal{D}$, then with probability at least $1 - \delta$ over the draw of the set S, the generalisation error of $f(x)$ is bounded by

$$P_\mathcal{D}(f(\mathbf{x}) \neq y) \leq \frac{1}{\ell - k}\left(k \ln \ell + \ln \frac{\ell}{2\delta}\right). \tag{7.25}$$

Proof We first fix $1 \leq k \leq \ell/2$ and consider the possible hypotheses that can be generated by sequences of k examples. The proof works by bounding the probability that we choose a hypothesis for which the generalisation error is worse than the bound. We use bold $\mathbf{i}$ to denote the sequence of indices on which the updates are made and $\mathbf{i}_0$ to denote some a priori fixed sequence of indices. With $f_\mathbf{i}$ we denote the function obtained by updating on the sequence $\mathbf{i}$

$$P\left\{S : \exists \mathbf{i} \text{ s.t. } P_\mathcal{D}(f_\mathbf{i}(\mathbf{x}) \neq y) > \frac{1}{\ell - k}\left(k \ln \ell + \ln \frac{\ell}{2\delta}\right)\right\}$$

$$\leq \ell^k P\left\{S : P_\mathcal{D}(f_{\mathbf{i}_0}(\mathbf{x}) \neq y) > \frac{1}{\ell - k}\left(k \ln \ell + \ln \frac{\ell}{2\delta}\right)\right\}$$

$$\leq \ell^k \left(1 - \frac{1}{\ell - k}\left(k \ln \ell + \ln \frac{\ell}{2\delta}\right)\right)^{\ell - k}$$

$$\leq \ell^k \exp\left(-\frac{\ell - k}{\ell - k}\left(k\ln\ell + \ln\frac{\ell}{2\delta}\right)\right)$$

$$\leq \frac{2\delta}{\ell}.$$

Hence, the total probability of the bound failing over the different choices of k is at most δ as required. $\qquad\square$

Combining this with the bound on the number of updates provided by Novikoff's theorem gives the following corollary.

Corollary 7.55 *Fix $\delta > 0$. Suppose the hard margin support vector machine has margin γ on the training set*

$$S = \{(\mathbf{x}_1, y_1), \ldots, (\mathbf{x}_\ell, y_\ell)\}$$

drawn independently at random according to a distribution $\mathcal{D}$ and contained in a ball of radius R about the origin. Then with probability at least $1 - \delta$ over the draw of the set S, the generalisation error of the function $f(\mathbf{x})$ obtained by running the perceptron algorithm on S in batch mode is bounded by

$$P_{\mathcal{D}}(f(\mathbf{x}) \neq y) \leq \frac{2}{\ell}\left(\frac{R^2}{\gamma^2}\ln\ell + \ln\frac{\ell}{2\delta}\right),$$

provided

$$\frac{R^2}{\gamma^2} \leq \frac{\ell}{2}.$$

There is a similar bound on the generalisation of the hard margin support vector machine in terms of the number of support vectors. The proof technique mimics that of Theorem 7.54, the only difference being that the order of the support vectors does not affect the function obtained. This gives the following bound on the generalisation quoted without proof.

Theorem 7.56 *Fix $\delta > 0$. Suppose the hard margin support vector machine has margin γ on the training set*

$$S = \{(\mathbf{x}_1, y_1), \ldots, (\mathbf{x}_\ell, y_\ell)\}$$

drawn independently at random according to a distribution $\mathcal{D}$. Then with probability at least $1 - \delta$ over the draw of the set S, its generalisation error is bounded by

$$\frac{1}{\ell - d}\left(d\log\frac{e\ell}{d} + \log\frac{\ell}{\delta}\right),$$

where $d = \#\,\mathrm{sv}$ is the number of support vectors.

The theorem shows that the smaller the number of support vectors the better the generalisation that can be expected. If we were to use the bound to guide the learning algorithm a very different approach would result. Indeed we can view the perceptron algorithm as a greedy approach to optimising this bound, in the sense that it only makes updates and hence creates non-zero α_i when this is forced by a misclassification.

Curiously the generalisation bound for the perceptron algorithm is at least as good as the margin bound obtained for the hard margin support vector machine! In practice the support vector machine typically gives better generalisation, indicating that the apparent contradiction arises as a result of the tighter proof technique that can be used in this case.

Remark 7.57 [Expected generalisation error] A slightly tighter bound on the *expected* generalisation error of the support vector machine in terms of the same quantities can be obtained by a leave-one-out argument. Since, when a non-support vector is omitted, it is correctly classified by the remaining subset of the training data the leave-one-out estimate of the generalisation error is

$$\frac{\#\,\mathrm{sv}}{\ell}.$$

A cyclic permutation of the training set shows that the expected error of a test point is bounded by this quantity. The use of an expected generalisation bound gives no guarantee about its variance and hence its reliability. Indeed leave-one-out bounds are known to suffer from this problem. Theorem 7.56 can be seen as showing that in the case of maximal margin classifiers a slightly weaker bound does hold with high probability and hence that in this case the variance cannot be too high.   ∎

Remark 7.58 [Effects of the margin] Note that in SVMs the margin has two effects. Its maximisation ensures a better bound on the generalisation, but at the same time it is the margin that is the origin of the sparseness of the solution vector, as the inequality constraints generate the KKT complementarity conditions. As indicated above the maximal margin classifier does not attempt to control the number of support vectors and yet in practice there are frequently few non-zero α_i. This sparseness of the solution can be exploited by implementation techniques for dealing with large datasets.   ∎

Kernel adatron There is an on-line update rule that models the hard margin support vector machine with fixed threshold 0. It is a simple adaptation of the perceptron algorithm.

Algorithm 7.59 [Kernel adatron] The kernel adatron algorithm is implemented in Code Fragment 7.13. ∎

Input	training set $S = \{(\mathbf{x}_1, y_1), \ldots, (\mathbf{x}_\ell, y_\ell)\}$
Process	$\boldsymbol{\alpha} = 0$, $i = 0$, loss $= 0$
2	repeat
3	for $i = 1 : \ell$
4	$\alpha_i \leftarrow \alpha_i + \left(1 - y_i \sum_{j=1}^{\ell} \alpha_j y_j \kappa\left(\mathbf{x}_j, \mathbf{x}_i\right)\right) \Big/ \kappa\left(\mathbf{x}_i, \mathbf{x}_i\right)$
5	if $\alpha_i < 0$ then $\alpha_i \leftarrow 0$.
6	end
7	until $\boldsymbol{\alpha}$ unchanged
8	$f(\mathbf{x}) = \text{sgn}\left(\sum_{j=1}^{\ell} \alpha_j y_j \kappa(\mathbf{x}_j, \mathbf{x})\right)$
Output	dual variables $\boldsymbol{\alpha}$, loss and function f

Code Fragment 7.13. Pseudocode for the kernel adatron algorithm.

For each α_i this can be for one of two reasons. If the first update did not change α_i then

$$1 - y_i \sum_{j=1}^{\ell} \alpha_j y_j \kappa\left(\mathbf{x}_j, \mathbf{x}_i\right) = 0$$

and so $(\mathbf{x}_i, y_i)$ has functional margin 1. If, on the other hand, the value of α_i remains 0 as a result of the second update, we have

$$1 - y_i \sum_{j=1}^{\ell} \alpha_j y_j \kappa\left(\mathbf{x}_j, \mathbf{x}_i\right) < 0$$

implying $(\mathbf{x}_i, y_i)$ has functional margin greater than 1. It follows that at convergence the solution satisfies the KKT complementarity conditions for the alternative hard margin support vector machine of Algorithm 7.26 once the condition

$$\sum_{i=1}^{\ell} \alpha_i y_i = 0$$

arising from a variable threshold has been removed. The algorithm can be adapted to handle a version of the 1-norm soft margin support vector machine by introducing an upper bound on the value of α_i, while a version of the 2-norm support vector machine can be implemented by adding a constant to the diagonal of the kernel matrix.

Remark 7.60 [SMO algorithm] If we want to allow a variable threshold the updates must be made on a pair of examples, an approach that results in the SMO algorithm. The rate of convergence of both of these algorithms is strongly affected by the order in which the examples are chosen for updating. Heuristic measures such as the degree of violation of the KKT conditions can be used to ensure very effective convergence rates in practice. ∎

On-line regression On-line learning algorithms are not restricted to classification problems. Indeed in the next chapter we will describe such an algorithm for ranking that will be useful in the context of collaborative filtering. The update rule for the kernel adatron algorithm also suggests a general methodology for creating on-line versions of the optimisations we have described. The objective function for the alternative hard margin SVM is

$$W(\boldsymbol{\alpha}) = \sum_{i=1}^{\ell} \alpha_i - \frac{1}{2} \sum_{i,j=1}^{\ell} \alpha_i \alpha_j y_i y_j \kappa(\mathbf{x}_i, \mathbf{x}_j).$$

If we consider the gradient of this quantity with respect to an individual α_i we obtain

$$\frac{\partial W(\boldsymbol{\alpha})}{\partial \alpha_i} = 1 - y_i \sum_{j=1}^{\ell} \alpha_j y_j \kappa(\mathbf{x}_j, \mathbf{x}_i)$$

making the first update of the kernel adatron algorithm equivalent to

$$\alpha_i \leftarrow \alpha_i + \frac{\partial W(\boldsymbol{\alpha})}{\partial \alpha_i}$$

making it a simple gradient ascent algorithm augmented with corrections to ensure that the additional constraints are satisfied. If, for example, we apply this same approach to the linear ε-insensitive loss version of the support vector regression algorithm with fixed offset 0, we obtain the algorithm.

Algorithm 7.61 [On-line support vector regression] On-line support vector regression is implemented in Code Fragment 7.14. ∎

Input	training set $S = \{(\mathbf{x}_1, y_1), \ldots, (\mathbf{x}_\ell, y_\ell)\}$
Process	$\boldsymbol{\alpha} = 0$, $i = 0$, loss $= 0$
2	repeat
3	for $i = 1 : \ell$
4	$\hat{\alpha}_i \leftarrow \alpha_i$;
5	$\alpha_i \leftarrow \alpha_i + y_i - \varepsilon \operatorname{sgn}(\alpha_i) - \sum_{j=1}^{\ell} \alpha_j \kappa(\mathbf{x}_j, \mathbf{x}_i)$;
6	if $\hat{\alpha}_i \alpha_i < 0$ then $\alpha_i \leftarrow 0$;
7	end
8	until $\boldsymbol{\alpha}$ unchanged
9	$f(\mathbf{x}) = \sum_{j=1}^{\ell} \alpha_j \kappa(\mathbf{x}_j, \mathbf{x})$
Output	dual variables $\boldsymbol{\alpha}$, loss and function f

where for $\alpha_i = 0$, $\operatorname{sgn}(\alpha_i)$ is interpreted to be the number in $[-1, +1]$ that gives the update in line 5 the smallest absolute value.

Code Fragment 7.14. Pseudocode for the on-line support vector regression.

7.5 Summary

- The smallest hypersphere enclosing all points in the embedding space can be found by solving a convex quadratic program. This suggests a simple novelty-detection algorithm.

- The stability analysis suggests a better novelty detector may result from a smaller hypersphere containing a fixed fraction of points that minimises the sum of the distances to the external points. This can again be computed by a convex quadratic program. Its characteristic function can be written in terms of a kernel expansion, where only certain points have non-zero coefficients. They are called support vectors and because of the many zero coefficients the expansion is called 'sparse'.

- If there is a maximal margin hyperplane separating two sets of points in the embedding space, it can be found by solving a convex quadratic program. This gives the hard margin support vector machine classification algorithm.

- The stability analysis again suggests improved generalisation will frequently result from allowing a certain (prefixed) fraction of points to be 'margin' errors while minimising the sizes of those errors. This can again be found by solving a convex quadratic program and gives the well-known soft margin support vector machines. Also in this case, the kernel expansion of the classification function can be sparse, as a result of the Karush–Kuhn–Tucker conditions. The pre-image of this hyperplane in the input space can be very complex, depending on the choice of kernel. Hence, these algorithms are able to optimise over highly nonlinear function classes through an application of the kernel trick.

- A nonlinear regression function that realises a trade-off between loss and smoothness can be found by solving a convex quadratic program. This corresponds to a regularised linear function in the embedding space. Fixing the regularization term to be the 2-norm of the linear function in the embedding space, different choices of loss can be made. The quadratic loss yields the nonlinear version of ridge regression introduced in Chapter 2. Both linear and quadratic ε-insensitive losses yield support vector machines for regression. Unlike ridge regression these again result in sparse kernel expansions of the solutions.

- The absence of local minima from the above algorithms marks a major departure from traditional systems such as neural networks, and jointly with sparseness properties makes it possible to create very efficient implementations.

7.6 Further reading and advanced topics

The systematic use of optimisation in pattern recognition dates back at least to Mangasarian's pioneering efforts [95] and possibly earlier. Many different authors have independently proposed algorithms for data classification or other tasks based on the theory of Lagrange multipliers, and this approach is now part of the standard toolbox in pattern analysis.

The problem of calculating the smallest sphere containing a set of data was first posed in the hard-margin case by [117], [20] for the purpose of calculating generalisation bounds that depend on the radius of the enclosing sphere. It was subsequently addressed by Tax and Duin [136] in a soft margin setting for the purpose of modeling the input distribution and hence detecting novelties. This approach to novelty detection was cast in a ν-SVM setting by Schölkopf *et al.* [119].

The problem of separating two sets of data with a maximal margin hyperplane has been independently addressed by a number of authors over a long period of time. Large margin hyperplanes in the input space were, for example, discussed by Duda and Hart [39], Cover [28], Smith [129], Vapnik *et al.* [146], [143], and several statistical mechanics papers (for example [3]). It is, however, the combination of this optimisation problem with kernels that produced support vector machines, as we discuss briefly below. See Chapter 6 of [32] for a more detailed reconstruction of the history of SVMs.

The key features of SVMs are the use of kernels, the absence of local minima, the sparseness of the solution and the capacity control obtained by optimising the margin. Although many of these components were already used in different ways within machine learning, it is their combination that was first realised in the paper [16]. The use of slack variables for noise tolerance, tracing back to [13] and further to [129], was introduced to the SVM algorithm in 1995 in the paper of Cortes and Vapnik [27]. The ν-support vector algorithm for classification and regression is described in [122].

Extensive work has been done over more than a decade by a fast growing community of theoreticians and practitioners, and it would be difficult to document all the variations on this theme. In a way, this entire book is an attempt to systematise this body of literature.

Among many connections, it is worth emphasising the connection between SVM regression, ridge regression and regularisation networks. The concept of regularisation was introduced by Tikhonov [138], and was introduced into machine learning in the form of regularisation networks by Girosi *et al.* [48]. The relation between regularisation networks and support vector machines has been explored by a number of authors [47], [157], [131], [43].

Finally for a background on convex optimisation and Kuhn–Tucker theory see for example [94], and for a brief introduction see Chapter 5 of [32].

For constantly updated pointers to online literature and free software see the book's companion website: www.kernel-methods.net.

8

Ranking, clustering and data visualisation

In this chapter we conclude our presentation of kernel-based pattern analysis algorithms by discussing three further common tasks in data analysis: ranking, clustering and data visualisation.

Ranking is the problem of learning a ranking function from a training set of ranked data. The number of ranks need not be specified though typically the training data comes with a relative ordering specified by assignment to one of an ordered sequence of labels.

Clustering is perhaps the most important and widely used method of unsupervised learning: it is the problem of identifying groupings of similar points that are relatively 'isolated' from each other, or in other words to partition the data into dissimilar groups of similar items. The number of such clusters may not be specified a priori. As exact solutions are often computationally hard to find, effective approximations via relaxation procedures need to be sought.

Data visualisation is often overlooked in pattern analysis and machine learning textbooks, despite being very popular in the data mining literature. It is a crucial step in the process of data analysis, enabling an understanding of the relations that exist within the data by displaying them in such a way that the discovered patterns are emphasised. These methods will allow us to visualise the data in the kernel-defined feature space, something very valuable for the kernel selection process. Technically it reduces to finding low-dimensional embeddings of the data that approximately retain the relevant information.

8.1 Discovering rank relations

Ranking a set of objects is an important task in pattern analysis, where the relation sought between the datapoints is their relative rank. An example of an application would be the ranking of documents returned to the user in an information retrieval task, where it is hard to define a precise absolute relevance measure, but it is possible to sort by the user's preferences. Based on the query, and possibly some partial feedback from the user, the set of documents must be ordered according to their suitability as answers to the query.

Another example of ranking that uses different information is the task known as collaborative filtering. Collaborative filtering aims to rank items for a new user based only on rankings previously obtained from other users. The system must make recommendations to the new user based on information gleaned from earlier users. This problem can be cast in the framework of learning from examples if we treat each new user as a new learning task. We view each item as an example and the previous users' preferences as its features.

Example 8.1 If we take the example of a movie recommender system, a film is an example whose features are the gradings given by previous users. For users who have not rated a particular film the corresponding feature value can be set to zero, while positive ratings are indicated by a positive feature value and negative ratings by a negative value. Each new user corresponds to a new learning task. Based on a small set of supplied ratings we must learn to predict the ranking the user would give to films he or she has not yet seen. ■

In general we consider the following ranking task. Given a set of ranked examples, that is objects $\mathbf{x} \in X$ assigned to a label from an ordered set Y, we are required to predict the rank of new instances. Ranking could be tackled as a regression or classification problem by treating the ranks as real-values or the assignment to a particular rank value as a classification. The price of making these reductions is not to make full use of the available information in the reduction to classification or the flexibility inherent in the ordering requirement in the reduction to regression. It is therefore preferable to treat it as a problem in its own right and design specific algorithms able to take advantage of the specific nature of that problem.

Definition 8.2 [Ranking] A *ranking problem* is specified by a set

$$S = \{(\mathbf{x}_1, y_1), \ldots, (\mathbf{x}_\ell, y_\ell)\}$$

of instance/rank pairs. We assume an implicit kernel-defined feature space with corresponding feature mapping ϕ so that $\phi(\mathbf{x}_i)$ is in $\mathbb{R}^n$ for some n, $1 \leq n \leq \infty$. Furthermore, we assume its rank y_i is an element of a finite set Y with a total order relation. We say that $\mathbf{x}_i$ is preferred over $\mathbf{x}_j$ (or vice versa) if $y_i \succ y_j$ (or $y_i \prec y_j$). The objects $\mathbf{x}_i$ and $\mathbf{x}_j$ are not comparable if $y_i = y_j$. The induced relation on X is a partial ordering that partitions the input space into equivalence classes. A ranking rule is a mapping from instances to ranks $r : X \rightarrow Y$. ∎

Remark 8.3 [An alternative reduction] One could also transform it into the problem of predicting the relative ordering of all possible pairs of examples, hence obtaining a 2-class classification problem. The problem in this approach would be the extra computational cost since the sample size for the algorithm would grow quadratically with the number of examples. If on the other hand the training data is given in the form of all relative orderings, we can generate a set of ranks as the equivalence classes of the equality relation with the induced ordering. ∎

Definition 8.4 [Linear ranking rules] A *linear ranking rule* first embeds the input data into the real axis $\mathbb{R}$ by means of a linear function in the kernel-defined feature space $f(\mathbf{x}) = \langle \mathbf{w}, \phi(\mathbf{x}) \rangle$. The real-value is subsequently converted to a rank by means of $|Y|$ thresholds b_y, $y \in Y$ that respect the ordering of Y, meaning that $y \prec y'$ implies $b_y \leq b_{y'}$. We will denote by $\mathbf{b}$ the k-dimensional vector of thresholds. The ranking of an instance $\mathbf{x}$ is then given by

$$r_{\mathbf{w},\mathbf{b}}(\mathbf{x}) = \min \{ y \in Y : f(\mathbf{x}) = \langle \mathbf{w}, \phi(\mathbf{x}) \rangle < b_y \},$$

where we assume that the largest label has been assigned a sufficiently large value to ensure the minimum always exists. If $\mathbf{w}$ is given in a dual representation

$$\mathbf{w} = \sum_{i=1}^{\ell} \alpha_i \phi(\mathbf{x}_i),$$

the ranking function is

$$r_{\mathbf{w},\mathbf{b}}(\mathbf{x}) = \min \left\{ y \in Y : f(\mathbf{x}) = \sum_{i=1}^{\ell} \alpha_i \kappa(\mathbf{x}_i, \mathbf{x}) < b_y \right\}.$$

∎

A linear ranking rule partitions the input space into $|Y| + 1$ equivalence classes corresponding to parallel bands defined by the direction **w** and the thresholds b_i as shown in the two upper diagrams of Figure 8.1. The lower diagrams give examples of nonlinear rankings arising from the use of appropriate kernel functions.

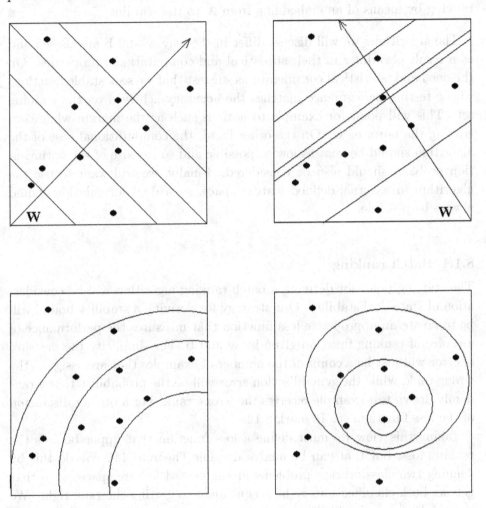

Fig. 8.1. Examples of the partitioning resulting from linear and nonlinear ranking functions.

Remark 8.5 [Degrees of freedom] The example of Figure 8.1 shows an important freedom available to ranking algorithms namely that the classes need not be equally spaced, we just need the ordering right. This is the key difference between the ranking functions we are considering and using regression on, for example, integer-ranking values. ∎

Remark 8.6 [Ordering within ranks] The ranking functions described above have an additional feature in that the elements within each equivalence class can also be ordered by the value of the function $g(\mathbf{x})$, though we will ignore this information. This is a consequence of the fact that we represent the ranking by means of an embedding from X to the real line. ∎

The algorithms we will discuss differ in the way $\mathbf{w}$ and $\mathbf{b}$ are chosen and as a result also differ in their statistical and computational properties. On the one hand, statistical considerations suggest that we seek stable functions whose testing performance matches the accuracy achieved on the training set. This will point for example to notions such as the margin while controlling the norm of $\mathbf{w}$. On the other hand, the computational cost of the algorithm should be kept as low as possible and so the size of the optimization problem should also be considered. Finally, we will want to use the algorithm in a kernel-defined feature space, so a dual formulation should always be possible.

8.1.1 Batch ranking

The starting point for deriving a batch-ranking algorithm will be consideration of statistical stability. Our strategy for deriving a stability bound will be to create an appropriate loss function that measures the performance of a choice of ranking function given by $\mathbf{w}$ and $\mathbf{b}$. For simplicity the measure of error will just be a count of the number of examples that are assigned the wrong rank, while the generalisation error will be the probability that a randomly drawn test example receives the wrong rank. For a further discussion of the loss function, see Remark 8.12.

Taking this view we must define a loss function that upper bounds the ranking loss, but that can be analysed using Theorem 4.9. We do this by defining two classification problems in augmented feature spaces such that getting both classifications right is equivalent to getting the rank right. We can think of one classification guaranteeing the rank is big enough, and the other that it is not too big.

Recoding the problem The key idea is to add one extra feature to the input vectors for each rank, setting their values to zero for all but the rank corresponding to the correct rank. The feature corresponding to the correct rank if available is set to 1. We use ϕ to denote this augmented vector

$$\phi\left(\mathbf{x}, y\right) = \left[\phi\left(\mathbf{x}\right), 0, \ldots, 0, 1, 0, \ldots, 0\right] = \left[\phi\left(\mathbf{x}\right), \mathbf{e}_y\right],$$

where we use $\mathbf{e}_y$ to denote the unit vector with yth coordinate equal to 1. We now augment the weight vector by a coordinate of $-b_y$ in the position of the feature corresponding to rank $y \in Y$

$$\hat{\mathbf{w}}_{\mathbf{b}} = \left[\mathbf{w}, -b_0, -b_1, -b_2, \ldots, -b_{|Y|}\right],$$

where for simplicity of notation we have assumed that $Y = \{1, \ldots, |Y|\}$ and have chosen b_0 to be some value smaller than $\langle \mathbf{w}, \phi(\mathbf{x}) \rangle$ for all $\mathbf{w}$ and $\mathbf{x}$. Using this augmented representation we how have

$$\langle \hat{\mathbf{w}}_{\mathbf{b}}, \phi(\mathbf{x}, y) \rangle = \langle \mathbf{w}, \phi(\mathbf{x}) \rangle - b_y,$$

where y is the rank of $\mathbf{x}$. Now if $(\mathbf{w}, \mathbf{b})$ correctly ranks an example $(\mathbf{x}, y)$ then

$$
\begin{aligned}
y &= r_{\mathbf{w}, \mathbf{b}}(\mathbf{x}) = \min\{y' \in Y : \langle \mathbf{w}, \phi(\mathbf{x}) \rangle < b_{y'}\} \\
&= \min\{y' \in Y : \langle \hat{\mathbf{w}}_{\mathbf{b}}, \phi(\mathbf{x}, y) \rangle < b_{y'} - b_y\},
\end{aligned}
$$

implying that

$$\langle \hat{\mathbf{w}}_{\mathbf{b}}, \phi(\mathbf{x}, y) \rangle < 0. \tag{8.1}$$

Furthermore, we have

$$\langle \hat{\mathbf{w}}_{\mathbf{b}}, \phi(\mathbf{x}, y-1) \rangle = \langle \mathbf{w}, \phi(\mathbf{x}) \rangle - b_{y-1},$$

and so if $(\mathbf{w}, \mathbf{b})$ correctly ranks $(\mathbf{x}, y)$ then

$$
\begin{aligned}
y &= r_{\mathbf{w}, \mathbf{b}}(\mathbf{x}) = \min\{y' \in Y : \langle \mathbf{w}, \phi(\mathbf{x}) \rangle < b_{y'}\} \\
&= \min\{y' \in Y : \langle \hat{\mathbf{w}}_{\mathbf{b}}, \phi(\mathbf{x}, y-1) \rangle < b_{y'} - b_{y-1}\},
\end{aligned}
$$

implying that

$$\langle \hat{\mathbf{w}}_{\mathbf{b}}, \phi(\mathbf{x}, y-1) \rangle \geq 0. \tag{8.2}$$

Suppose that inequalities (8.1) and (8.2) hold for $(\mathbf{w}, \mathbf{b})$ on an example $(\mathbf{x}, y)$. Then since $\langle \hat{\mathbf{w}}_{\mathbf{b}}, \phi(\mathbf{x}, y) \rangle < 0$, it follows that $\langle \mathbf{w}, \phi(\mathbf{x}) \rangle < b_y$ and so

$$y \in \{y' \in Y : \langle \mathbf{w}, \phi(\mathbf{x}) \rangle < b_{y'}\},$$

while $\langle \hat{\mathbf{w}}_{\mathbf{b}}, \phi(\mathbf{x}, y-1) \rangle \geq 0$ implies $\langle \mathbf{w}, \phi(\mathbf{x}) \rangle \geq b_{y-1}$ hence

$$y - 1 \notin \{y' \in Y : \langle \mathbf{w}, \phi(\mathbf{x}) \rangle < b_{y'}\},$$

giving

$$r_{\mathbf{w}, \mathbf{b}}(\mathbf{x}) = \min\{y' \in Y : \langle \mathbf{w}, \phi(\mathbf{x}) \rangle < b_{y'}\} = y,$$

the correct rank. Hence we have shown the following proposition

Proposition 8.7 *The ranker* $r_{\mathbf{w},\mathbf{b}}(\cdot)$ *correctly ranks* $(\mathbf{x}, y)$ *if and only if* $\langle \hat{\mathbf{w}}_{\mathbf{b}}, \boldsymbol{\phi}(\mathbf{x}, y) \rangle < 0$ *and* $\langle \hat{\mathbf{w}}_{\mathbf{b}}, \boldsymbol{\phi}(\mathbf{x}, y-1) \rangle \geq 0$.

Hence the error rate of $r_{\mathbf{w},\mathbf{b}}(\mathbf{x})$ is bounded by the classifier rate on the extended set. The proposition therefore reduces the analysis of the ranker $r_{\mathbf{w},\mathbf{b}}(\mathbf{x})$ to that of a classifier in an augmented space.

Stability of ranking In order to analyse the statistical stability of ranking, we need to extend the data distribution $\mathcal{D}$ on $X \times Y$ to the augmented space. We simply divide the probability of example $(\mathbf{x}, y)$ equally between the two examples $(\boldsymbol{\phi}(\mathbf{x}, y), -1)$ and $(\boldsymbol{\phi}(\mathbf{x}, y-1), 1)$. We then apply Theorem 4.17 to upper bound the classifier error rate with probability $1 - \delta$ by

$$\frac{1}{\ell\gamma} \sum_{i=1}^{\ell} \left(\xi_i^l + \xi_i^u \right) + \frac{4}{\ell\gamma} \sqrt{\mathrm{tr}(\mathbf{K})} + 3\sqrt{\frac{\ln(2/\delta)}{2\ell}},$$

where ξ_i^u, ξ_i^l are the slack variables measuring the amount by which the example $(\mathbf{x}_i, y_i)$ fails to meet the margin γ for the lower and upper thresholds. Hence, we can bound the error of the ranker by

$$P_{\mathcal{D}}\left(r_{\mathbf{w},\mathbf{b}}(\mathbf{x}) \neq y\right) \leq \frac{2}{\ell\gamma} \sum_{i=1}^{\ell} \left(\xi_i^l + \xi_i^u \right) + \frac{8}{\ell\gamma} \sqrt{\mathrm{tr}(\mathbf{K})} + 6\sqrt{\frac{\ln(2/\delta)}{2\ell}}, \quad (8.3)$$

where the factor 2 arises from the fact that either derived example being misclassified will result in a ranking error.

Ranking algorithms If we ignore the effects of the vector $\mathbf{b}$ on the norm of $\hat{\mathbf{w}}_{\mathbf{b}}$ we can optimise the bound by performing the following computation.

Computation 8.8 [Soft ranking] The soft ranking bound is optimised as follows

$$\begin{aligned}
\min_{\mathbf{w},\mathbf{b},\gamma,\boldsymbol{\xi}^u,\boldsymbol{\xi}^l} \quad & -\gamma + C \sum_{i=1}^{\ell} \left(\xi_i^u + \xi_i^l \right) \\
\text{subject to} \quad & \langle \mathbf{w}, \boldsymbol{\phi}(\mathbf{x}_i) \rangle \leq b_{y_i} - \gamma + \xi_i^l, \ y_i \neq |Y|, \ \xi_i^l \geq 0, \\
& \langle \mathbf{w}, \boldsymbol{\phi}(\mathbf{x}_i) \rangle \geq b_{y_i-1} + \gamma - \xi_i^u, \ y_i \neq 1, \ \xi_i^u \geq 0, \\
& i = 1, \ldots, \ell, \text{ and } \|\mathbf{w}\|^2 = 1.
\end{aligned} \quad (8.4)$$

$\blacksquare$

Applying the usual technique of creating the Lagrangian and setting derivatives equal to zero gives the relationships

$$1 = \sum_{i=1}^{\ell} \left(\alpha_i^u + \alpha_i^l \right),$$

$$\mathbf{w} = \frac{1}{2\lambda} \sum_{i=1}^{\ell} \left(\alpha_i^u - \alpha_i^l \right) \phi\left(\mathbf{x}_i\right),$$

$$\sum_{i:y_i=y} \alpha_i^l = \sum_{i:y_i=y-1} \alpha_i^u, \ y = 2, \ldots, |Y|,$$

$$0 \ \leq \ \alpha_i^u, \alpha_i^l \leq C.$$

Resubstituting into the Lagrangian results in the dual Lagrangian

$$L(\boldsymbol{\alpha}^u, \boldsymbol{\alpha}^l, \lambda) = -\frac{1}{4\lambda} \sum_{i,j=1}^{\ell} \left(\alpha_i^u - \alpha_i^l \right) \left(\alpha_j^u - \alpha_j^l \right) \kappa\left(\mathbf{x}_i, \mathbf{x}_j\right) - \lambda.$$

As in previous cases optimising for λ gives an objective that is the square root of the objective of the equivalent dual optimisation problem contained in the following algorithm.

Algorithm 8.9 [ν-ranking] The ν-ranking algorithm is implemented in Code Fragment 8.1. ∎

Input	$S = \{(\mathbf{x}_1, y_1), \ldots, (\mathbf{x}_\ell, y_\ell)\}, \ \nu \in (0, 1]$
$\max_{\boldsymbol{\alpha}^u, \boldsymbol{\alpha}^l}$ subject to	$W(\boldsymbol{\alpha}^u, \boldsymbol{\alpha}^l) = -\sum_{i,j=1}^{\ell} \left(\alpha_i^u - \alpha_i^l\right) \left(\alpha_j^u - \alpha_j^l\right) \kappa(\mathbf{x}_i, \mathbf{x}_j),$ $\sum_{i:y_i=y} \alpha_i^l = \sum_{i:y_i=y-1} \alpha_i^u, \ y = 2, \ldots, |Y|,$ $0 \leq \alpha_i^u, \alpha_i^l \leq 1/(\nu\ell), \ i = 1, \ldots, \ell, \ \sum_{i=1}^{\ell} \left(\alpha_i^u + \alpha_i^l\right) = 1$
compute	$\alpha_i = \alpha_i^{u*} - \alpha_i^{l*}$ $f(\mathbf{x}) = \sum_{i=1}^{\ell} \alpha_i \kappa(\mathbf{x}_i, \mathbf{x})$ $\mathbf{b} = (b_1, \ldots, b_{|Y|-1}, \infty)$
where	$b_y = 0.5\left(f\left(\mathbf{x}_i\right) + f\left(\mathbf{x}_j\right)\right)$ $\gamma = 0.5\left(f\left(\mathbf{x}_j\right) - f\left(\mathbf{x}_i\right)\right)$
where	$(\mathbf{x}_i, y), (\mathbf{x}_j, y+1)$ satisfy $0 < \alpha_i^{l*} < 1/(\nu\ell)$ and $0 < \alpha_j^{u*} < 1/(\nu\ell),$
output	$r_{\boldsymbol{\alpha}, \mathbf{b}}(\mathbf{x}), \gamma$

Code Fragment 8.1. Pseudocode for the soft ranking algorithm.

The next theorem characterises the output of Algorithm 8.9.

Theorem 8.10 *Fix $\nu \in (0, 1]$. Suppose that a training sample*

$$S = \{(\mathbf{x}_1, y_1), \ldots, (\mathbf{x}_\ell, y_\ell)\}$$

drawn according to a distribution $\mathcal{D}$ over $X \times Y$, where $Y = \{1, \ldots, |Y|\}$ is a finite set of ranks and suppose $r_{\boldsymbol{\alpha}, \mathbf{b}}(\mathbf{x}), \gamma$ is the output of Algorithm

8.9, then $r_{\alpha, b}(\mathbf{x})$ *optimises the bound of (8.3). Furthermore, there are at most* $\nu \ell$ *training points that fail to achieve a margin* γ *from both adjacent thresholds and hence have non-zero slack variables, while at least* $\nu \ell$ *of the training points have margin at least* γ.

Proof By the derivation given above setting $C = 1/(\nu \ell)$, the solution vector is a rescaled version of the solution of the optimisation problem (8.4). The setting of the values b_y follows from the Karush–Kuhn–Tucker conditions that ensure $\xi_i^{l*} = 0$ and the appropriate rescaling of $f(\mathbf{x}_i)$ is γ^* from the upper boundary if $0 < \alpha_i^{l*} < C$, with the corresponding result when $0 < \alpha_j^{u*} < C$. The bounds on the number of training points achieving the margin follow from the bounds on α_i^u and α_i^l. $\qquad\square$

Remark 8.11 [Measuring stability] We have omitted an explicit generalisation bound from the proposition to avoid the message getting lost in technical details. The bound could be computed by ignoring $b_{|Y|}$ and b_0 and removing one of the derived examples for points with rank 1 or $|Y|$ and hence computing the margin and slack variables for the normalised weight vector. These could then be plugged into (8.3). $\qquad\blacksquare$

Remark 8.12 [On the loss function] We have measured loss by counting the number of wrong ranks, but the actual slack variables get larger the further the distance to the correct rank. Intuitively, it does seem reasonable to count a bigger loss if the rank is out by a greater amount. Defining a loss that takes the degree of mismatch into account and deriving a corresponding convex relaxation is beyond the scope of this book. $\qquad\blacksquare$

This example again shows the power and flexibility of the overall approach we are advocating. The loss function that characterises the performance of the task under consideration is upper bounded by a loss function to which the Rademacher techniques can be applied. This in turn leads to a uniform bound on the performance of the possible functions on randomly generated test data. By designing an algorithm to optimise the bound we therefore directly control the stability of the resulting pattern function. A careful choice of the loss function ensures that the optimisation problem is convex and hence has a unique optimum that can be found efficiently using standard optimisation algorithms.

8.1.2 On-line ranking

With the exception of Section 7.4 all of the algorithms that we have so far considered for classification, regression, novelty-detection and, in the current subsection, for ranking all assume that we are given a set of training examples that can be used to drive the learning algorithm towards a good solution. Unfortunately, training sets are not always available before we start to learn.

Example 8.13 A case in point is Example 8.1 given above describing the use of collaborative filtering to recommend a film. Here we start with no information about the new user. As we obtain his or her views of a few films we must already begin to learn and hence direct our recommendations towards films that are likely to be of interest. ∎

The learning paradigm that considers examples being presented one at a time with the system being allowed to update the inferred pattern function after each presentation is known as *on-line learning*.

Perhaps the best known on-line learning algorithm is the *perceptron algorithm* given in Algorithm 7.52. We now describe an on-line ranking algorithm that follows the spirit of the perceptron algorithm. Hence, it considers one example at a time ranking it using its current estimate of the weight vector $\mathbf{w}$ and ranking thresholds $\mathbf{b}$. We again assume that the weight vector is expressed in the dual representation

$$\mathbf{w} = \sum_{i=1}^{\ell} \alpha_i \phi(\mathbf{x}_i),$$

where now the value of α_i can be positive or negative. The α_i are initialised to 0. The vector $\mathbf{b}$ must be initialised to an ordered set of integer values, which can, for example, be taken to be all 0, except for $b_{|Y|}$, which is set to ∞ and remains fixed throughout.

If an example is correctly ranked then no change is made to the current ranking function $r_{\boldsymbol{\alpha},\mathbf{b}}(\mathbf{x})$. If on the other hand the estimated rank is wrong for an example $(\mathbf{x}_i, y_i)$, an update is made to the dual variable α_i as well as to one or more of the rank thresholds in the vector $\mathbf{b}$.

Suppose that the estimated rank $y < y_i$. In this case we decrement thresholds $b_{y'}$ for $y' = y, \ldots, y_i - 1$ by 1 and increment α_i by $y_i - y$. When $y > y_i$ we do the reverse by incrementing the thresholds $b_{y'}$ for $y' = y_i, \ldots, y - 1$ by 1 and decrementing α_i by $y - y_i$. This is given in the following algorithm.

Algorithm 8.14 [On-line ranking] The on-line ranking algorithm is implemented in Code Fragment 8.2. ■

Input	training sequence $(\mathbf{x}_1, y_1), \ldots, (\mathbf{x}_\ell, y_\ell), \ldots$
Process	$\boldsymbol{\alpha} = \mathbf{0}, \mathbf{b} = \mathbf{0}, b_{|Y|} = \infty, i = 0$
2	repeat
3	$i = i + 1$
4	$y = r_{\boldsymbol{\alpha}, \mathbf{b}}(\mathbf{x}_i)$
3	if $y < y_i$
4	$\alpha_i = \alpha_i + y_i - y$
5	$y' = y' - 1$ for $y' = y, \ldots, y_i - 1$
6	else if $y > y_i$
7	$\alpha_i = \alpha_i + y_i - y$
8	$y' = y' + 1$ for $y' = y_i, \ldots, y - 1$
9	end
10	until finished
Output	$r_{\boldsymbol{\alpha}, \mathbf{b}}(\mathbf{x})$

Code Fragment 8.2. Pseudocode for on-line ranking.

In order to verify the correctness of Algorithm 8.14 we must check that the update rule preserves a valid ranking function or in other words that the vector of thresholds remains correctly ordered

$$y < y' \implies b_y \leq b_{y'}.$$

In view of the initialisation of $\mathbf{b}$ to integer values and the integral updates, the property could only become violated in one of two cases. The first is if $b_y = b_{y+1}$ and we increment b_y by 1, while leaving b_{y+1} fixed. It is clear from the update rule above that this could only occur if the estimated rank was $y+1$, a rank that cannot be returned when $b_y = b_{y+1}$. A similar contradiction shows that the other possible violation of decrementing b_{y+1} when $b_y = b_{y+1}$ is also ruled out. Hence, the update rule does indeed preserve the ordering of the vector of thresholds.

Stability analysis of on-line ranking We will give an analysis of the stability of Algorithm 8.14 based on the bound given in Theorem 7.54 for the perceptron algorithm. Here, the bound is in terms of the number of updates made to the hypothesis. Since the proof is identical to that of Theorem 7.54, we do not repeat it here.

Theorem 8.15 *Fix $\delta > 0$. If the ranking perceptron algorithm makes $1 \leq k \leq \ell/2$ updates before converging to a hypothesis $r_{\boldsymbol{\alpha}, \mathbf{b}}(\mathbf{x})$ that correctly* *ranks a training set*

$$S = \{(\mathbf{x}_1, y_1), \ldots, (\mathbf{x}_\ell, y_\ell)\}$$

drawn independently at random according to a distribution $\mathcal{D}$, then with probability at least $1 - \delta$ over the draw of the set S, the generalisation error of $r_{\alpha,\mathbf{b}}(\mathbf{x})$ is bounded by

$$P_{\mathcal{D}}(r_{\alpha,\mathbf{b}}(\mathbf{x}) \neq y) \leq \frac{1}{\ell - k}\left(k \ln \ell + \ln \frac{\ell}{2\delta}\right). \tag{8.5}$$

Thus, a bound on the number of updates of the perceptron-ranking algorithm can be translated into a generalisation bound of the resulting classifier if it has been run until correct ranking of the (batch) training set has been achieved. For practical purposes this gives a good indication of how well the resulting ranker will perform since we can observe the number of updates made and plug the number into the bound (7.25). From a theoretical point of view one would like to have some understanding of when the number of updates can be expected to be small for the chosen algorithm.

We now give an a priori bound on the number of updates of the perceptron-ranking algorithm by showing that it can be viewed as the application of the perceptron algorithm for a derived classification problem and then applying Novikoff's Theorem 7.53. The weight vector $\mathbf{w}^*$ will be the vector solving the maximal margin problem for the derived training set

$$\hat{S} = \{(\boldsymbol{\phi}(\mathbf{x}, y), -1), (\boldsymbol{\phi}(\mathbf{x}, y - 1), 1) : (\mathbf{x}, y) \in S\}$$

for a ranking training set S. The updates of the perceptron-ranking algorithm correspond to slightly more complex examples

$$\boldsymbol{\phi}(\mathbf{x}, y : y') = \sum_{u=y}^{y'-1} \boldsymbol{\phi}(\mathbf{x}, u).$$

When the estimated rank $y < y_i$ the example $(\boldsymbol{\phi}(\mathbf{x}, y : y_i), 1)$ is misclassified and updating on this example is equivalent to the perceptron-ranking algorithm update. Similarly, when the estimated rank $y > y_i$ the example $(\boldsymbol{\phi}(\mathbf{x}, y_i : y), -1)$ is misclassified and the updates again correspond. Hence, since

$$\|\boldsymbol{\phi}(\mathbf{x}, y : y')\|^2 \leq (|Y| - 1)\left(\|\boldsymbol{\phi}(\mathbf{x})\|^2 + 1\right),$$

we can apply Theorem 7.53 to bound the number of updates by

$$\frac{(|Y| - 1)(R^2 + 1)}{\gamma^2},$$

where R is a bound on the norm of the feature vectors $\phi(\mathbf{x})$ and γ is the margin obtained by the corresponding hard margin batch algorithm. This gives the following corollary.

Corollary 8.16 *Fix $\delta > 0$. Suppose the batch ranking algorithm with $\nu = 1/\ell$ has margin γ on the training set*

$$S = \{(\mathbf{x}_1, y_1), \dots, (\mathbf{x}_\ell, y_\ell)\}$$

drawn independently at random according to a distribution $\mathcal{D}$ and contained in a ball of radius R about the origin. Then with probability at least $1 - \delta$ over the draw of the set S, the generalisation error of the ranking function $r_{\alpha, \mathbf{b}}(\mathbf{x})$ obtained by running the on-line ranking algorithm on S in batch mode is bounded by

$$P_{\mathcal{D}}\left(r_{\alpha, \mathbf{b}}(\mathbf{x}) \neq y\right) \leq \frac{2}{\ell}\left(\frac{(|Y| - 1)(R^2 + 1)}{\gamma^2}\ln \ell + \ln \frac{\ell}{2\delta}\right),$$

provided

$$\frac{(|Y| - 1)(R^2 + 1)}{\gamma^2} \leq \frac{\ell}{2}.$$

8.2 Discovering cluster structure in a feature space

Cluster analysis aims to discover the internal organisation of a dataset by finding structure within the data in the form of 'clusters'. This generic word indicates separated groups of similar data items. Intuitively, the division into clusters should be characterised by within-cluster similarity and between-cluster (external) dissimilarity. Hence, the data is broken down into a number of groups composed of similar objects with different groups containing distinctive elements. This methodology is widely used both in multivariate statistical analysis and in machine learning.

Clustering data is useful for a number of different reasons. Firstly, it can aid our understanding of the data by breaking it into subsets that are significantly more uniform than the overall dataset. This could assist for example in understanding consumers by identifying different 'types' of behaviour that can be regarded as prototypes, perhaps forming the basis for targeted marketing exercises. It might also form the initial phase of a more complex data analysis. For example, rather than apply a classification algorithm to the full dataset, we could use a separate application for each cluster with the intention of rendering the local problem within a single cluster easier to solve accurately. In general we can view the clustering as making the data simpler to describe, since a new data item can be specified by indicating its cluster and then its relation to the cluster centre.

Each application might suggest its own criterion for assessing the quality of the clustering obtained. Typically we would expect the quality to involve some measure of fit between a data item and the cluster to which it is assigned. This can be viewed as the pattern function of the cluster analysis. Hence, a stable clustering algorithm will give assurances about the expected value of this fit for a new randomly drawn example. As with other pattern analysis algorithms this will imply that the pattern of clusters identified in the training set is not a chance occurrence, but characterises some underlying property of the distribution generating the data.

Perhaps the most common choice for the measure assumes that each cluster has a centre and assesses the fit of a point by its squared distance from the centre of the cluster to which it is assigned. Clearly, this will be minimised if new points are assigned to the cluster whose centre is nearest. Such a division of the space creates what is known as a *Voronoi diagram* of regions each containing one of the cluster centres. The boundaries between the regions are composed of intersecting hyperplanes each defined as the set of points equidistant from some pair of cluster centres.

Throughout this section we will adopt the squared distance criterion for assessing the quality of clustering, initially based on distances in the input space, but subsequently generalised to distances in a kernel-defined feature space. In many ways the use of kernel methods for clustering is very natural, since the kernel-defines pairwise similarities between data items, hence providing all the information needed to assess the quality of a clustering. Furthermore, using kernels ensures that the algorithms can be developed in full generality without specifying the particular similarity measure being used.

Ideally, all possible arrangements of the data into clusters should be tested and the best one selected. This procedure is computationally infeasible in all but very simple examples since the number of all possible partitions of a dataset grows exponentially with the number of data items. Hence, efficient algorithms need to be sought. We will present a series of algorithms that make use of the distance in a kernel-defined space as a measure of dissimilarity and use simple criteria of performance that can be used to drive practical, efficient algorithms that approximate the optimal solution.

We will start with a series of general definitions that are common to all approaches, before specifying the problem as a (non-convex) optimisation problem. We will then present a greedy algorithm to find sub-optimal solutions (local minima) and a spectral algorithm that can be solved globally at the expense of relaxing the optimisation criterion.

8.2.1 Measuring cluster quality

Given an unlabelled set of data

$$S = \{\mathbf{x}_1, \ldots, \mathbf{x}_\ell\},$$

we wish to find an assignment of each point to one of a finite – but not necessarily prespecified – number N of classes. In other words, we seek a map

$$f : S \rightarrow \{1, 2, \ldots, N\}.$$

This partition of the data should be chosen among all possible assignments in such a way as to solve the measure of clustering quality given in the following computation.

Computation 8.17 [Cluster quality] The clustering function should be chosen to optimise

$$f = \underset{f:S\rightarrow\{1,2,\ldots,N\}}{\operatorname{argmin}} \sum_{i,j:f_i=f(\mathbf{x}_i)=f(\mathbf{x}_j)=f_j} \|\phi(\mathbf{x}_i) - \phi(\mathbf{x}_j)\|^2, \qquad (8.6)$$

where we have as usual assumed a projection function ϕ into a feature space F, in which the kernel κ computes the inner product

$$\kappa(\mathbf{x}_i, \mathbf{x}_j) = \langle \phi(\mathbf{x}_i), \phi(\mathbf{x}_j) \rangle.$$

∎

We will use the short notation $f_i = f(\mathbf{x}_i)$ throughout this section and assume N is fixed. Figure 8.2 shows an example of a clustering of a set of data into two clusters with an indication of the contributions to (8.6). As indicated above this is not the most general clustering criterion that could be considered, but we begin by showing that it does have a number of useful properties and does subsume some apparently more general criteria. A first criticism of the criterion is that it does not seem to take into account the between-cluster separation, but only the within-cluster similarity. We might want to consider a criterion that balanced both of these two factors

$$\min_f \left\{ \sum_{i,j:f_i=f_j} \|\phi(\mathbf{x}_i) - \phi(\mathbf{x}_j)\|^2 - \lambda \sum_{i,j:f_i\neq f_j} \|\phi(\mathbf{x}_i) - \phi(\mathbf{x}_j)\|^2 \right\}. \qquad (8.7)$$

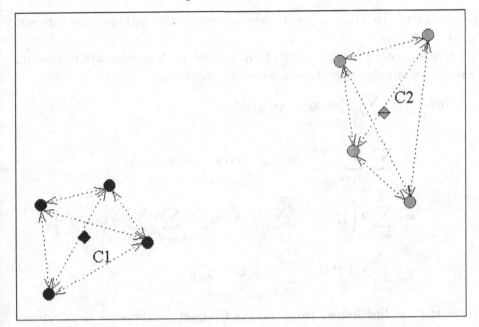

Fig. 8.2. An example of a clustering of a set of data.

However, observe that we can write

$$\sum_{i,j:f_i \neq f_j} \|\phi(\mathbf{x}_i) - \phi(\mathbf{x}_j)\|^2 = \sum_{i,j=1}^{\ell} \|\phi(\mathbf{x}_i) - \phi(\mathbf{x}_j)\|^2$$

$$- \sum_{i,j:f_i = f_j} \|\phi(\mathbf{x}_i) - \phi(\mathbf{x}_j)\|^2$$

$$= A - \sum_{i,j:f_i = f_j} \|\phi(\mathbf{x}_i) - \phi(\mathbf{x}_j)\|^2,$$

where A is constant for a given dataset. Hence, equation (8.7) can be expressed as

$$\min_f \left\{ \sum_{i,j:f_i = f_j} \|\phi(\mathbf{x}_i) - \phi(\mathbf{x}_j)\|^2 - \lambda \sum_{i,j:f_i \neq f_j} \|\phi(\mathbf{x}_i) - \phi(\mathbf{x}_j)\|^2 \right\}$$

$$= \min_f \left\{ (1 + \lambda) \sum_{i,j:f_i = f_j} \|\phi(\mathbf{x}_i) - \phi(\mathbf{x}_j)\|^2 - \lambda A \right\},$$

showing that the same clustering function f solves the two optimisations (8.6) and (8.7). These derivations show that minimising the within-cluster distances for a fixed number of clusters automatically maximises the between-cluster distances.

There is another nice property of the solution of the optimisation criterion (8.6). If we simply expand the expression, we obtain

$$
\begin{aligned}
\text{opt} \;&=\; \sum_{i,j:f_i=f_j} \|\phi\left(\mathbf{x}_i\right) - \phi\left(\mathbf{x}_j\right)\|^2 \\[2mm]
&=\; \sum_{k=1}^{N} \sum_{i:f_i=k} \sum_{j:f_j=k} \langle \phi\left(\mathbf{x}_i\right) - \phi\left(\mathbf{x}_j\right), \phi\left(\mathbf{x}_i\right) - \phi\left(\mathbf{x}_j\right) \rangle \\[2mm]
&=\; \sum_{k=1}^{N} 2 \left(\left|f^{-1}\left(k\right)\right| \sum_{i:f_i=k} \kappa\left(\mathbf{x}_i, \mathbf{x}_i\right) - \sum_{i:f_i=k} \sum_{j:f_j=k} \kappa\left(\mathbf{x}_i, \mathbf{x}_j\right) \right) \\[2mm]
&=\; \sum_{k=1}^{N} 2 \left|f^{-1}\left(k\right)\right| \sum_{i:f_i=k} \|\phi(\mathbf{x}_i) - \mu_k\|^2 ,
\end{aligned}
$$

where the last line follows from (5.4) of Chapter 5 expressing the average-squared distance of a set of points from their centre of mass, and

$$
\mu_k = \frac{1}{\left|f^{-1}\left(k\right)\right|} \sum_{i \in f^{-1}(k)} \phi\left(\mathbf{x}_i\right) \tag{8.8}
$$

is the centre of mass of those examples assigned to cluster k, a point often referred to as the *centroid* of the cluster. This implies that if we enforce equal sized clusters the optimisation criterion (8.6) is also equivalent to the criterion

$$
f = \operatorname*{argmin}_{f} \sum_{k=1}^{N} \left(\sum_{i:f_i=k} \|\phi(\mathbf{x}_i) - \mu_k\|^2 \right) = \operatorname*{argmin}_{f} \sum_{i=1}^{\ell} \left\| \phi(\mathbf{x}_i) - \mu_{f(\mathbf{x}_i)} \right\|^2 ,
$$

$$\tag{8.9}$$

that seeks a clustering of points minimising the sum-squared distances to the centres of mass of the clusters. One might be tempted to assume that this implies the points are assigned to the cluster whose centroid is nearest. The following theorem shows that indeed this is the case.

Theorem 8.18 *The solution of the clustering optimisation criterion*

$$
f = \operatorname*{argmin}_{f} \sum_{i,j:f_i=f_j} \|\phi\left(\mathbf{x}_i\right) - \phi\left(\mathbf{x}_j\right)\|^2
$$

under the constraint of equal sized clusters satisfies

$$
f\left(\mathbf{x}_i\right) = \operatorname*{argmin}_{1 \leq k \leq N} \|\phi\left(\mathbf{x}_i\right) - \mu_k\| ,
$$

where μ_j is the centroid of the points assigned to cluster j.

Proof Let μ_k be as in equation (8.8). If we consider a clustering function g defined on S that assigns points to the nearest centroid

$$g\left(\mathbf{x}_i\right) = \operatorname*{argmin}_{1 \leq k \leq N} \left\| \phi\left(\mathbf{x}_i\right) - \mu_k \right\|,$$

we have, by the definition of g

$$\sum_{i=1}^{\ell} \left\| \phi(\mathbf{x}_i) - \mu_{g(\mathbf{x}_i)} \right\|^2 \leq \sum_{i=1}^{\ell} \left\| \phi(\mathbf{x}_i) - \mu_{f(\mathbf{x}_i)} \right\|^2. \tag{8.10}$$

Furthermore, if we let

$$\hat{\mu}_k = \frac{1}{\left| g^{-1}(k) \right|} \sum_{i \in g^{-1}(k)} \phi\left(\mathbf{x}_i\right)$$

it follows that

$$\sum_{i=1}^{\ell} \left\| \phi(\mathbf{x}_i) - \hat{\mu}_{g(\mathbf{x}_i)} \right\|^2 \leq \sum_{i=1}^{\ell} \left\| \phi(\mathbf{x}_i) - \mu_{g(\mathbf{x}_i)} \right\|^2 \tag{8.11}$$

by Proposition 5.2. But the left-hand side is the value of the optimisation criterion (8.9) for the function g. Since f was assumed to be optimal we must have

$$\sum_{i=1}^{\ell} \left\| \phi(\mathbf{x}_i) - \hat{\mu}_{g(\mathbf{x}_i)} \right\|^2 \geq \sum_{i=1}^{\ell} \left\| \phi(\mathbf{x}_i) - \mu_{f(\mathbf{x}_i)} \right\|^2,$$

implying with (8.10) and (8.11) that the two are in fact equal. The result follows. $\qquad\square$

The characterisation given in Proposition 8.18 also indicates how new data should be assigned to the clusters. We simply use the natural generalisation of the assignment as

$$f\left(\mathbf{x}\right) = \operatorname*{argmin}_{1 \leq k \leq N} \left\| \phi\left(\mathbf{x}\right) - \mu_k \right\|.$$

Once we have chosen the cost function of Computation 8.17 and observed that its test performance is bound solely in terms of the number of centres and the value of equation (8.6) on the training examples, it is clear that any clustering algorithm must attempt to minimise the cost function. Typically we might expect to do this for different numbers of centres, finally selecting the number for which the bound on $\mathbb{E}_{\mathcal{D}} \min_{1 \leq k \leq N} \left\| \phi\left(\mathbf{x}\right) - \mu_k \right\|^2$ is acceptable.

Hence, the core task is given a fixed number of centres N find the partition into clusters which minimises equation (8.6). In view of Proposition 8.18, we therefore arrive at the following clustering optimisation strategy.

Computation 8.19 [Clustering optimisation strategy] The clustering optimisation strategy is given by

input	$S = \{\mathbf{x}_1, \ldots, \mathbf{x}_\ell\}$, integer N
process	$\boldsymbol{\mu} = \mathrm{argmin}_{\boldsymbol{\mu}} \sum_{i=1}^{\ell} \min_{1 \leq k \leq N} \|\boldsymbol{\phi}(\mathbf{x}_i) - \mu_k\|^2$
output	$f(\cdot) = \mathrm{argmin}_{1 \leq k \leq N} \|\boldsymbol{\phi}(\cdot) - \mu_k\|$

∎

Figure 8.3 illustrates this strategy by showing the distances (dotted arrows) involved in computed the sum-squared criterion. The minimisation of this sum automatically maximises the indicated distance (dot-dashed arrow) between the cluster centres provided the clusters have equal sizes.

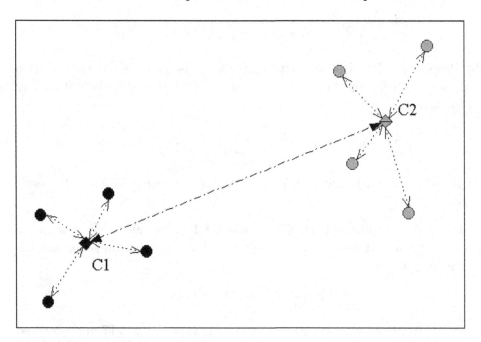

Fig. 8.3. The clustering criterion reduces to finding cluster centres to minimise sum-squared distances.

Remark 8.20 [Stability analysis] Furthermore we can see that this strategy suggests an appropriate pattern function for our stability analysis to estimate

$$\mathbb{E}_{\mathcal{D}} \min_{1 \le k \le N} \|\phi(\mathbf{x}) - \mu_k\|^2 \, ;$$

the smaller the bound obtained the better the quality of the clustering achieved. ∎

Unfortunately, unlike the optimisation problems that we have described previously, this problem is not convex. Indeed the task of checking if there exists a solution with value better than some threshold turns out to be NP-complete. This class of problems is generally believed not to be solvable in polynomial time, and we are therefore forced to consider heuristic or approximate algorithms that seek solutions that are close to optimal.

We will describe two such approaches in the next section. The first will use a greedy iterative method to seek a local optimum of the cost function, hence failing to be optimal precisely because of its non-convexity. The second method will consider a relaxation of the cost function to give an approximation that can be globally optimised. This is reminiscent of the approach taken to minimise the number of misclassification when applying a support vector machine to non-separable data. By introducing slack variables and using their 1-norm to upper bound the number of misclassifications we can approximately minimise this number through solving a convex optimisation problem.

The greedy method will lead to the well-known k-means algorithm, while the relaxation method gives spectral clustering algorithms. In both cases the approaches can be applied in kernel-defined feature spaces.

Remark 8.21 [Kernel matrices for well-clustered data] We have seen how we can compute distances in a kernel-defined feature space. This will provide the technology required to apply the methods in these spaces. It is often more natural to consider spaces in which unrelated objects have zero inner product. For example using a Gaussian kernel ensures that all distances between points are less than $\sqrt{2}$ with the distances becoming larger as the inputs become more orthogonal. Hence, a good clustering is achieved when the data in the same cluster are concentrated close to the prototype and the prototypes are nearly orthogonal. This means that the kernel matrix for clustered data – assuming without loss of generality that the data are sorted by cluster – will be a perturbation of a block-diagonal matrix with one block for each cluster

$$\begin{pmatrix} B_1 & 0 & 0 & 0 \\ 0 & B_2 & 0 & 0 \\ 0 & 0 & B_3 & 0 \\ 0 & 0 & 0 & B_4 \end{pmatrix}$$

Note that this would not be the case for other distance functions where, for example, negative inner products were possible.   ∎

On between cluster distances There is one further property of this minimisation that relates to the means of the clusters. If we consider the covariance matrix of the data, we can perform the following derivation

$$\ell \mathbf{C} = \sum_{i=1}^{\ell} \left(\phi(\mathbf{x}_i) - \phi_S \right) \left(\phi(\mathbf{x}_i) - \phi_S \right)'$$

$$= \sum_{i=1}^{\ell} \left(\phi(\mathbf{x}_i) - \mu_{f_i} + \mu_{f_i} - \phi_S \right) \left(\phi(\mathbf{x}_i) - \mu_{f_i} + \mu_{f_i} - \phi_S \right)'$$

$$= \sum_{i=1}^{\ell} \left(\phi(\mathbf{x}_i) - \mu_{f_i} \right) \left(\phi(\mathbf{x}_i) - \mu_{f_i} \right)'$$

$$+ \sum_{k=1}^{N} \left(\sum_{i:f_i=k} \left(\phi(\mathbf{x}_i) - \mu_k \right) \right) \left(\mu_k - \phi_S \right)'$$

$$+ \sum_{k=1}^{N} \left(\mu_k - \phi_S \right) \sum_{i:f_i=k} \left(\phi(\mathbf{x}_i) - \mu_k \right)'$$

$$+ \sum_{i=1}^{\ell} \left(\mu_{f_i} - \phi_S \right) \left(\mu_{f_i} - \phi_S \right)'$$

$$= \sum_{i=1}^{\ell} \left(\phi(\mathbf{x}_i) - \mu_{f_i} \right) \left(\phi(\mathbf{x}_i) - \mu_{f_i} \right)'$$

$$+ \sum_{k=1}^{N} \left| f^{-1}(k) \right| \left(\mu_k - \phi_S \right) \left(\mu_k - \phi_S \right)'.$$

Taking traces of both sides of the equation we obtain

$$\mathrm{tr}\left(\ell \mathbf{C} \right) = \sum_{i=1}^{\ell} \left\| \phi(\mathbf{x}_i) - \mu_{f_i} \right\|^2 + \sum_{k=1}^{N} \left| f^{-1}(k) \right| \left\| \mu_k - \phi_S \right\|^2.$$

The first term on the right-hand side is just the value of the Computation 8.19 that is minimised by the clustering function, while the value of the left-hand side is independent of the clustering. Hence, the clustering criterion automatically maximises the trace of the second term on the right-hand side. This corresponds to maximising

$$\sum_{k=1}^{N} |f^{-1}(k)| \, \|\mu_k - \phi_S\|^2 \, ;$$

in other words the sum of the squares of the distances from the overall mean of the cluster means weighted by their size. We again see that optimising the tightness of the clusters automatically forces their centres to be far apart.

8.2.2 Greedy solution: k-means

Proposition 8.18 confirms that we can solve Computation 8.17 by identifying centres of mass of the members of each cluster. The first algorithm we will describe attempts to do just this and is therefore referred to as the k-means algorithm. It keeps a set of cluster centroids $C_1, C_2, \ldots, C_N$ that are initialised randomly and then seeks to minimise the expression

$$\sum_{i=1}^{\ell} \left\| \phi(\mathbf{x}_i) - C_{f(\mathbf{x}_i)} \right\|^2, \tag{8.12}$$

by adapting both f as well as the centres. It will converge to a solution in which C_k is the centre of mass of the points assigned to cluster k and hence will satisfy the criterion of Proposition 8.18.

The algorithm alternates between updating f to adjust the assignment of points to clusters and updating the C_k giving the positions of the centres in a two-stage iterative procedure. The first stage simply assigns points to the cluster whose cluster centre is closest. Clearly this will reduce the value of the expression in (8.12). The second stage repositions the centre of each cluster at the centre of mass of the points assigned to that cluster. We have already analysed this second stage in Proposition 5.2 showing that moving the cluster centre to the centre of mass of the points does indeed reduce the criterion of (8.12).

Hence, each stage can only reduce the expression (8.12). Since the number of possible clusterings is finite, it follows that after a finite number of iterations the algorithm will converge to a stable clustering assignment provided ties are broken in a deterministic way. If we are to implement in a dual form we must represent the clusters by an indicator matrix $\mathbf{A}$ of dimension $\ell \times N$

containing a 1 to indicate the containment of an example in a cluster

$$\mathbf{A}_{ik} = \begin{cases} 1 & \text{if } \mathbf{x}_i \text{ is in cluster } k; \\ 0 & \text{otherwise.} \end{cases}$$

We will say that the *clustering is given* by matrix $\mathbf{A}$. Note that each row of $\mathbf{A}$ contains exactly one 1, while the column sums give the number of points assigned to the different clusters. Matrices that have this form will be known as *cluster matrices*. We can therefore compute the coordinates of the centroids C_k as the N columns of the matrix

$$\mathbf{X}'\mathbf{AD},$$

where $\mathbf{X}$ contains the training example feature vectors as rows and $\mathbf{D}$ is a diagonal $N \times N$ matrix with diagonal entries the inverse of the column sums of $\mathbf{A}$, indicating the number of points ascribed to that cluster. The distances of a new test vector $\phi(\mathbf{x})$ from the centroids is now given by

$$\begin{aligned} \|\phi(\mathbf{x}) - C_k\|^2 &= \|\phi(\mathbf{x})\|^2 - 2\langle\phi(\mathbf{x}), C_k\rangle + \|C_k\|^2 \\ &= \kappa(\mathbf{x}, \mathbf{x}) - 2\left(\mathbf{k}'\mathbf{AD}\right)_k + \left(\mathbf{DA}'\mathbf{XX}'\mathbf{AD}\right)_{kk}, \end{aligned}$$

where $\mathbf{k}$ is the vector of inner products between $\phi(\mathbf{x})$ and the training examples. Hence, the cluster to which $\phi(\mathbf{x})$ should be assigned is given by

$$\underset{1 \le k \le N}{\text{argmin}} \|\phi(\mathbf{x}) - C_k\|^2 = \underset{1 \le k \le N}{\text{argmin}} \left(\mathbf{DA}'\mathbf{KAD}\right)_{kk} - 2\left(\mathbf{k}'\mathbf{AD}\right)_k,$$

where $\mathbf{K}$ is the kernel matrix of the training set. This provides the rule for classifying new data. The update rule consists in reassigning the entries in the matrix $\mathbf{A}$ according to the same rule in order to redefine the clusters.

Algorithm 8.22 [Kernel k-means] Matlab code for the kernel k-means algorithm is given in Code Fragment 8.3. ∎

Despite its popularity, this algorithm is prone to local minima since the optimisation is not convex. Considerable effort has been devoted to finding good initial guesses or inserting additional constraints in order to limit the effect of this fact on the quality of the solution obtained. In the next section we see two relaxations of the original problem for which we can find the global solution.

8.2.3 Relaxed solution: spectral methods

In this subsection, rather than relying on gradient descent methods to tackle a non-convex problem, we make a convex relaxation of the problem in order

```
% original kernel matrix stored in variable K
% clustering given by a ell x N binary matrix A
% and cluster allocation function f
% d gives the distances to cluster centroids
A = zeros(ell,N);
f = ceil(rand(ell,1)* N);
for i=1,ell
  A(i,f(i)) = 1;
end
change = 1;
while change = 1
  change = 0;
  E = A * diag(1./sum(A));
  Z = ones(ell,1)* diag(E'*K*E)'- 2*K*E;
  [d, ff] = min(Z, [], 2);
  for i=1,ell
    if f(i) ~= ff(i)
      A(i,ff(i)) = 1;
      A(i, f(i)) = 0;
      change = 1;
    end
  end
  f = ff;
end
```

Code Fragment 8.3. Matlab code to perform k-means clustering.

to obtain a closed form approximation. We can then study the approximation and statistical properties of its solutions.

Clustering into two classes We first consider the simpler case when there are just two clusters. In this relaxation we represent the cluster assignment by a vector $\mathbf{y} \in \{-1, +1\}^\ell$, that associates to each point a $\{-1, +1\}$ label. For the two classes case the clustering quality criterion described above is minimised by maximising

$$\sum_{y_i \neq y_j} \|\phi(\mathbf{x}_i) - \phi(\mathbf{x}_j)\|^2.$$

Assuming that the data is normalised and the sizes of the clusters are equal this will correspond to minimising the so-called cut cost

$$2 \sum_{y_i \neq y_j} \kappa(\mathbf{x}_i, \mathbf{x}_j) = \sum_{i,j=1}^{\ell} \kappa(\mathbf{x}_i, \mathbf{x}_j) - \sum_{i,j=1}^{\ell} y_i y_j \kappa(\mathbf{x}_i, \mathbf{x}_j),$$

$$\text{subject to } \mathbf{y} \in \{-1, +1\}^\ell, \sum_{i=1}^{\ell} y_i = 0$$

since it measures the kernel 'weight' between vertices in different clusters. Hence, we must solve

$$\max \qquad \mathbf{y}'\mathbf{K}\mathbf{y}$$

$$\text{subject to} \quad \mathbf{y} \in \{-1, +1\}^\ell, \sum_{i=1}^{\ell} y_i = 0$$

We can relax this optimisation by removing the restriction that $\mathbf{y}$ be a binary vector while controlling its norm. This is achieved by maximising the Raleigh quotient (3.2)

$$\max \frac{\mathbf{y}'\mathbf{K}\mathbf{y}}{\mathbf{y}'\mathbf{y}}.$$

As observed in Chapter 3 this is solved by the eigenvector of the matrix $\mathbf{K}$ corresponding to the largest eigenvalue with the value of the quotient equal to the eigenvalue λ_1. Hence, we obtain a lower bound on the cut cost of

$$0.5 \left(\sum_{i,j=1}^{\ell} \kappa\left(\mathbf{x}_i, \mathbf{x}_j\right) - \lambda_1 \right),$$

giving a corresponding lower bound on the value of the sum-squared criterion. Though such a lower bound is useful, the question remains as to whether the approach can suggest useful clusterings of the data. A very natural way to do so in this two-cluster case is simply to threshold the vector $\mathbf{y}$ hence converting it to a binary clustering vector. This naive approach can deliver surprisingly good results though there is no a priori guarantee attached to the quality of the solution.

Remark 8.23 [Alternative criterion] It is also possible to consider minimising a ratio between the cut size and a measure of the size of the clusters. This leads through similar relaxations to different eigenvalue problems. For example if we let $\mathbf{D}$ be the diagonal matrix with entries

$$\mathbf{D}_{ii} = \sum_{j=1}^{\ell} \mathbf{K}_{ij},$$

then useful partitions can be derived from the eigenvectors of

$$\mathbf{D}^{-1}\mathbf{K}, \quad \mathbf{D}^{-1/2}\mathbf{K}\mathbf{D}^{-1/2} \quad \text{and} \quad \mathbf{K} - \mathbf{D}$$

with varying justifications. In all cases thresholding the resulting vectors delivers the corresponding partitions. Generally the approach is motivated using the Gaussian kernel with its useful properties discussed above. ∎

Multiclass clustering We now consider the more general problem of multiclass clustering. We start with an equivalent formulation of the sum-of-squares minimization problem as a trace maximization under special constraints. By successively relaxing these constraints we are led to an approximate algorithm with nice global properties.

Consider the derivation and notation introduced to obtain the program for k-means clustering. We can compute the coordinates of the centroids C_k as the N columns of the matrix

$$\mathbf{X'AD},$$

where $\mathbf{X}$ is the data matrix, $\mathbf{A}$ a matrix assigning points to clusters and $\mathbf{D}$ a diagonal matrix with inverses of the cluster sizes on the diagonal. Consider now the matrix

$$\mathbf{X'ADA'}.$$

It has ℓ columns with the ith column a copy of the cluster centroid corresponding to the ith example. Hence, we can compute the sum-squares of the distances from the examples to their corresponding cluster centroid as

$$
\begin{aligned}
\left\| \mathbf{X'ADA'} - \mathbf{X'} \right\|_F^2 &= \left\| \left(\mathbf{I}_\ell - \mathbf{ADA'}\right) \mathbf{X} \right\|_F^2 \\
&= \mathrm{tr}\left(\mathbf{X'} \left(\mathbf{I}_\ell - \mathbf{ADA'}\right) \mathbf{X} \right) \\
&= \mathrm{tr}\left(\mathbf{XX'} \right) - \mathrm{tr}\left(\sqrt{\mathbf{D}}\mathbf{A'XX'A}\sqrt{\mathbf{D}} \right),
\end{aligned}
$$

since

$$\left(\mathbf{I}_\ell - \mathbf{ADA'}\right)^2 = \left(\mathbf{I}_\ell - \mathbf{ADA'}\right)$$

as $\mathbf{A'AD} = \sqrt{\mathbf{D}}\mathbf{A'A}\sqrt{\mathbf{D}} = \mathbf{I}_N$, indicating that $\left(\mathbf{I}_\ell - \mathbf{ADA'}\right)$ is a projection matrix. We have therefore shown the following proposition.

Proposition 8.24 *The sum-squares cost function* ss$(\mathbf{A})$ *of a clustering, given by matrix* $\mathbf{A}$ *can be expressed as*

$$\mathrm{ss}(\mathbf{A}) = \mathrm{tr}\left(\mathbf{K}\right) - \mathrm{tr}\left(\sqrt{\mathbf{D}}\mathbf{A'KA}\sqrt{\mathbf{D}} \right),$$

where $\mathbf{K}$ *is the kernel matrix and* $\mathbf{D} = \mathbf{D}\left(\mathbf{A}\right)$ *is the diagonal matrix with the inverses of the column sums of* $\mathbf{A}$.

Since the first term is not affected by the choice of clustering, the proposition leads to the Computation.

Computation 8.25 [Multiclass clustering] We can minimise the cost $\mathrm{ss}(\mathbf{A})$ by solving

$$\max_{\mathbf{A}} \quad \mathrm{tr}\left(\sqrt{\mathbf{D}}\mathbf{A}'\mathbf{K}\mathbf{A}\sqrt{\mathbf{D}}\right)$$
$$\text{subject to} \quad \mathbf{A} \text{ is a cluster matrix and } \mathbf{D} = \mathbf{D}\left(\mathbf{A}\right).$$

∎

Remark 8.26 [Distances of the cluster centres from the origin] We can see that $\mathrm{tr}\left(\sqrt{\mathbf{D}}\mathbf{A}'\mathbf{K}\mathbf{A}\sqrt{\mathbf{D}}\right)$ is the sum of the squares of the cluster centroids, relating back to our previous observations about the sum-square criterion corresponding to maximising the sum-squared distances of the centroids from the overall centre of mass of the data. This shows that this holds for the origin as well and since an optimal clustering is invariant to translations of the coordinate axes, this will be true of the sum-squared distances to any fixed point.

∎

We have now arrived at a constrained optimisation problem whose solution solves to the min-squared clustering criterion. Our aim now is to relax the constraints to obtain a problem that can be optimised exactly, but whose solution will not correspond precisely to a clustering. Note that the matrices $\mathbf{A}$ and $\mathbf{D} = \mathbf{D}\left(\mathbf{A}\right)$ satisfy

$$\sqrt{\mathbf{D}}\mathbf{A}'\mathbf{A}\sqrt{\mathbf{D}} = \mathbf{I}_N = \mathbf{H}'\mathbf{H}, \tag{8.13}$$

where $\mathbf{H} = \mathbf{A}\sqrt{\mathbf{D}}$. Hence, only requiring that this $\ell \times N$ matrix satisfies equation (8.13), we obtain the relaxed maximization problem given in the computation.

Computation 8.27 [Relaxed multiclass clustering] The relaxed maximisation for multiclass clustering is obtained by solving

$$\max \quad \mathrm{tr}\left(\mathbf{H}'\mathbf{K}\mathbf{H}\right)$$
$$\text{subject to} \quad \mathbf{H}'\mathbf{H} = \mathbf{I}_N,$$

∎

The solutions of Computation 8.27 will not correspond to clusterings, but may lead to good clusterings. The important property of the relaxation is that it can be solved in closed-form.

Proposition 8.28 *The maximum of the trace* $\mathrm{tr}\left(\mathbf{H}'\mathbf{K}\mathbf{H}\right)$ *over all* $\ell \times N$ *matrices satisfying* $\mathbf{H}'\mathbf{H} = \mathbf{I}_N$ *is equal to the sum of the first N eigenvalues* *of* $\mathbf{K}$

$$\max_{\mathbf{H'H}=\mathbf{I}_N} \text{tr}\left(\mathbf{H'KH}\right) = \sum_{k=1}^{N} \lambda_k$$

while the $\mathbf{H}^*$ *realising the optimum is given by*

$$\mathbf{V}_N\mathbf{Q},$$

where $\mathbf{Q}$ *is an arbitrary* $N \times N$ *orthonormal matrix and* $\mathbf{V}_N$ *is the* $\ell \times N$ *matrix composed of the first* N *eigenvectors of* $\mathbf{K}$*. Furthermore, we can lower bound the sum-squared error of the best clustering by*

$$\min_{\substack{\mathbf{A} \text{ clustering matrix}}} \text{ss}(\mathbf{A}) = \text{tr}\left(\mathbf{K}\right) - \max_{\substack{\mathbf{A} \text{ clustering matrix}}} \text{tr}\left(\sqrt{\mathbf{D}}\mathbf{A'KA}\sqrt{\mathbf{D}}\right)$$

$$\geq \text{tr}\left(\mathbf{K}\right) - \max_{\mathbf{H'H}=\mathbf{I}_N} \text{tr}\left(\mathbf{H'KH}\right) = \sum_{k=N+1}^{\ell} \lambda_k.$$

Proof Since $\mathbf{H'H} = \mathbf{I}_N$ the operator $\mathbf{P} = \mathbf{HH'}$ is a rank N projection. This follows from the fact that $(\mathbf{HH'})^2 = \mathbf{HH'HH'} = \mathbf{HI}_N\mathbf{H'} = \mathbf{HH'}$ and $\text{rank}\,\mathbf{H} = \text{rank}\,\mathbf{H'H} = \text{rank}\,\mathbf{I}_N = N$. Therefore

$$\mathbf{I}_N\mathbf{H'KHI}_N = \mathbf{H'HH'XX'HH'H} = \left\|\mathbf{H'PX}\right\|_F^2 = \left\|\mathbf{PX}\right\|_F^2.$$

Hence, we seek the N-dimensional projection of the columns of $\mathbf{X}$ that maximises the resulting sum of the squared norms. Treating these columns as the training vectors and viewing maximising the projection as minimising the residual we can apply Proposition 6.12. It follows that the maximum will be realised by the eigensubspace spanned by the N eigenvectors corresponding to the largest eigenvalues for the matrix $\mathbf{XX'} = \mathbf{K}$. Clearly, the projection is only specified up to an arbitrary $N \times N$ orthonormal transformation $\mathbf{Q}$.
$\square$

At first sight we have not gained a great deal by moving to the relaxed version of the problem. It is true that we have obtained a strict lower bound on the quality of clustering that can be achieved, but the matrix $\mathbf{H}$ that realises that lower bound does not in itself immediately suggest a method of performing a clustering that comes close to the bound. Furthermore, in the case of multi-class clustering we do not have an obvious simple thresholding algorithm for converting the result of the eigenvector analysis into a clustering as we found in the two cluster examples. We mention three possible approaches.

Re-clustering One approach is to apply a different clustering algorithm in the reduced N-dimensional representation of the data, when we map each example to the corresponding row of the matrix $\mathbf{V}_N$, possibly after performing a renormalisation.

Eigenvector approach We will describe a different method that is related to the proof of Proposition 8.28. Consider the choice $\mathbf{H}^* = \mathbf{V}_N$ that realises the optimum bound of the proposition. Let $\mathbf{W} = \mathbf{V}_N\sqrt{\mathbf{\Lambda}_N}$ be obtained from $\mathbf{V}_N$ by multiplying column i by $\sqrt{\lambda_i}$, $i = 1, \ldots, N$. We now form the cluster matrix $\mathbf{A}$ by setting the largest entry in each row of $\mathbf{W}$ to 1 and the remaining entries to 0.

QR approach An alternative approach is inspired by a desire to construct an approximate cluster matrix which is related to $\mathbf{V}_N$ by an orthonormal transformation

$$\mathbf{A} \approx \mathbf{V}_N\mathbf{Q},$$

implying that

$$\mathbf{V}'_N \approx \mathbf{Q}\mathbf{A}'.$$

If we perform a QR decomposition of $\mathbf{V}'_N$ we obtain

$$\mathbf{V}'_N = \hat{\mathbf{Q}}\mathbf{R}$$

with $\hat{\mathbf{Q}}$ an $N \times N$ orthogonal matrix and $\mathbf{R}$ an $N \times \ell$ upper triangular. By assigning vector i to the cluster index by the row with largest entry in the column i of matrix $\mathbf{R}$, we obtain a cluster matrix $\mathbf{A}' \approx \mathbf{R}$, hence giving a value of $\mathrm{ss}(\mathbf{A})$ close to that given by the bound.

8.3 Data visualisation

Visualisation refers to techniques that can present a dataset

$$S = \{\mathbf{x}_1, \ldots, \mathbf{x}_\ell\}$$

in a manner that reveals some underlying structure of the data in a way that is easily understood or appreciated by a user. A clustering is one type of structure that can be visualised. If for example there is a natural clustering of the data into say four clusters, each one grouped tightly around a separate centroid, our understanding of the data is greatly enhanced by displaying the four centroids and indicating the tightness of the clustering around them. The centroids can be thought of as prototypical data items.

Hence, for example in a market analysis, customers might be clustered into a set of typical types with individual customers assigned to the type to which they are most similar.

In this section we will consider a different type of visualisation. Our aim is to provide a two- or three-dimensional 'mapping' of the data, hence displaying the data points as dots on a page or as points in a three-dimensional image. This type of visualisation is of great importance in many data mining tasks, but it assumes a special role in kernel methods, where we typically embed the data into a high-dimensional vector space. We have already considered measures for assessing the quality of an embedding such as the classifier margin, correlation with output values and so on. We will also in later chapters be looking into procedures for transforming prior models into embeddings. However once we arrive at the particular embedding, it is also important to have ways of visually displaying the data in the chosen feature space. Looking at the data helps us get a 'feel' for the structure of the data, hence suggesting why certain points are outliers, or what type of relations can be found. This can in turn help us pick the best algorithm out of the toolbox of methods we have been assembling since Chapter 5. In other words being able to 'see' the relative positions of the data in the feature space plays an important role in guiding the intuition of the data analyst.

Using the first few principal components, as computed by the PCA algorithm of Chapter 6, is a well-known method of visualisation forming the core of the classical multidimensional scaling algorithm. As already demonstrated in Proposition 6.12 PCA minimises the sum-squared norms of the residuals between the subspace representation and the actual data.

Naturally if one wants to look at the data from an angle that emphasises a certain property, such as a given dichotomy, other projections can be better suited, for example using the first two partial least squares features. In this section we will assume that the feature space has already been adapted to best capture the view of the data we are concerned with but typically using a high-dimensional kernel representation. Our main concern will therefore be to develop algorithms that can find low-dimensional representations of high-dimensional data.

Multidimensional scaling This problem has received considerable attention in multivariate statistics under the heading of multidimensional scaling (MDS). This is a series of techniques directly aimed at finding optimal low-dimensional embeddings of data mostly for visualisation purposes. The starting point for MDS is traditionally a matrix of distances or similarities rather than a Gram matrix of inner products or even a Euclidean embedding. Indeed the first stages of the MDS process aim to convert the matrix of similarities into a matrix of inner products. For metric MDS it is assumed that the distances correspond to embeddings in a Euclidean space, while for non-metric MDS these similarities can be measured in any way. Once an approximate inner product matrix has been formed, classical MDS then uses the first two or three eigenvectors of the eigen-decomposition of the resulting Gram matrix to define two- or three-dimensional projections of the points for visualisation. Hence, if we make use of a kernel-defined feature space the first stages are no longer required and MDS reduces to computing the first two or three kernel PCA projections.

Algorithm 8.29 [MDS for kernel-embedded data] The MDS algorithm for data in a kernel-defined feature space is as follows:

input	Data $S = \{\mathbf{x}_1, \ldots, \mathbf{x}_\ell\}$, dimension $k = 2, 3$.
process	$\mathbf{K}_{ij} = \kappa(\mathbf{x}_i, \mathbf{x}_j), \ i, j = 1, \ldots, \ell$
	$\mathbf{K} - \frac{1}{\ell}\mathbf{jj}'\mathbf{K} - \frac{1}{\ell}\mathbf{Kjj}' + \frac{1}{\ell^2}(\mathbf{j}'\mathbf{Kj})\mathbf{jj}',$
	$[\mathbf{V}, \mathbf{\Lambda}] = \mathrm{eig}(\mathbf{K})$
	$\boldsymbol{\alpha}^j = \frac{1}{\sqrt{\lambda_j}}\mathbf{v}_j, \ j = 1, \ldots, k.$
	$\tilde{\mathbf{x}}_i = \left(\sum_{i=1}^{\ell} \alpha_i^j \kappa(\mathbf{x}_i, \mathbf{x})\right)_{j=1}^{k}$
output	Display transformed data $\tilde{S} = \{\tilde{\mathbf{x}}_1, \ldots, \tilde{\mathbf{x}}_\ell\}$.

■

Visualisation quality We will consider a further method of visualisation strongly related to MDS, but which is motivated by different criteria for assessing the quality of the representation of the data.

We can define the problem of visualisation as follows. Given a set of points

$$S = \{\phi(\mathbf{x}_1), \ldots, \phi(\mathbf{x}_\ell)\}$$

in a kernel-defined feature space F with

$$\phi : X \longrightarrow F,$$

find a projection $\boldsymbol{\tau}$ from X into $\mathbb{R}^k$, for small k such that

$$\|\boldsymbol{\tau}(\mathbf{x}_i) - \boldsymbol{\tau}(\mathbf{x}_j)\| \approx \|\phi(\mathbf{x}_i) - \phi(\mathbf{x}_j)\|, \text{ for } i, j = 1, \ldots, \ell.$$

We will use $\boldsymbol{\tau}_s$ to denote the projection onto the sth component of $\boldsymbol{\tau}$ and with a slight abuse of notation, as a vector of these projection values indexed by the training examples. As mentioned above it follows from Proposition 6.12

that the embedding determined by kernel PCA minimises the sum-squared residuals

$$\sum_{i=1}^{\ell} \|\boldsymbol{\tau}(\mathbf{x}_i) - \boldsymbol{\phi}(\mathbf{x}_i)\|^2,$$

where we make $\boldsymbol{\tau}$ an embedding into a k-dimensional subspace of the feature space F. Our next method aims to control more directly the relationship between the original and projection distances by solving the following computation.

Computation 8.30 [Visualisation quality] The quality of a visualisation can be optimsed as follows

$$
\begin{aligned}
\min_{\boldsymbol{\tau}} E(\boldsymbol{\tau}) &= \sum_{i,j=1}^{\ell} \langle \boldsymbol{\phi}(\mathbf{x}_i), \boldsymbol{\phi}(\mathbf{x}_j) \rangle \|\boldsymbol{\tau}(\mathbf{x}_i) - \boldsymbol{\tau}(\mathbf{x}_j)\|^2 \\
&= \sum_{i,j=1}^{\ell} \kappa(\mathbf{x}_i, \mathbf{x}_j) \|\boldsymbol{\tau}(\mathbf{x}_i) - \boldsymbol{\tau}(\mathbf{x}_j)\|^2,
\end{aligned}
$$
$$
\begin{aligned}
\text{subject to } \|\boldsymbol{\tau}_s\| &= 1, \quad \boldsymbol{\tau}_s \perp \mathbf{j}, \quad s = 1, \ldots, k, \\
\text{and } \boldsymbol{\tau}_s &\perp \boldsymbol{\tau}_t, \quad s, t = 1, \ldots, k.
\end{aligned}
\tag{8.14}
$$

∎

Observe that it follows from the constraints that

$$
\begin{aligned}
\sum_{i,j=1}^{\ell} \|\boldsymbol{\tau}(\mathbf{x}_i) - \boldsymbol{\tau}(\mathbf{x}_j)\|^2 &= \sum_{i,j=1}^{\ell} \sum_{s=1}^{k} (\boldsymbol{\tau}_s(\mathbf{x}_i) - \boldsymbol{\tau}_s(\mathbf{x}_j))^2 \\
&= \sum_{s=1}^{k} \sum_{i,j=1}^{\ell} (\boldsymbol{\tau}_s(\mathbf{x}_i) - \boldsymbol{\tau}_s(\mathbf{x}_j))^2 \\
&= 2 \sum_{s=1}^{k} \left(\ell \sum_{i=1}^{\ell} \boldsymbol{\tau}_s(\mathbf{x}_i)^2 - \sum_{i,j=1}^{\ell} \boldsymbol{\tau}_s(\mathbf{x}_i) \boldsymbol{\tau}_s(\mathbf{x}_j) \right) \\
&= 2\ell k - 2 \sum_{s=1}^{k} \sum_{i=1}^{\ell} \boldsymbol{\tau}_s(\mathbf{x}_i) \sum_{j=1}^{\ell} \boldsymbol{\tau}_s(\mathbf{x}_j) = 2\ell k.
\end{aligned}
$$

It therefore follows that, if the data is normalised, solving Computation 8.30 corresponds to minimising

$$E(\boldsymbol{\tau}) = \sum_{i,j=1}^{\ell} \left(1 - 0.5 \|\boldsymbol{\phi}(\mathbf{x}_i) - \boldsymbol{\phi}(\mathbf{x}_j)\|^2 \right) \|\boldsymbol{\tau}(\mathbf{x}_i) - \boldsymbol{\tau}(\mathbf{x}_j)\|^2$$

$$= 2\ell k - \sum_{i,j=1}^{\ell} 0.5 \left\| \phi\left(\mathbf{x}_i\right) - \phi\left(\mathbf{x}_j\right)\right\|^2 \left\| \boldsymbol{\tau}(\mathbf{x}_i) - \boldsymbol{\tau}(\mathbf{x}_j)\right\|^2,$$

hence optimising the correlation between the original and projected squared distances. More generally we can see minimisation as aiming to put large distances between points with small inner products and small distances between points having large inner products. The constraints ensure equal scaling in all dimensions centred around the origin, while the different dimensions are required to be mutually orthogonal to ensure no structure is unnecessarily reproduced.

Our next theorem will characterise the solution of the above optimisation using the eigenvectors of the so-called Laplacian matrix. This matrix can also be used in clustering as it frequently possesses more balanced properties than the kernel matrix. It is defined as follows.

Definition 8.31 [Laplacian matrix] The *Laplacian matrix* $\mathbf{L}\left(\mathbf{K}\right)$ of a kernel matrix $\mathbf{K}$ is defined by

$$\mathbf{L}\left(\mathbf{K}\right) = \mathbf{D} - \mathbf{K},$$

where $\mathbf{D}$ is the diagonal matrix with entries

$$\mathbf{D}_{ii} = \sum_{j=1}^{\ell} \mathbf{K}_{ij}.$$

∎

Observe the following simple property of the Laplacian matrix. Given any real vector $\mathbf{v} = (v_1, \ldots, v_\ell) \in \mathbb{R}^\ell$

$$\sum_{i,j=1}^{\ell} \mathbf{K}_{ij} \left(v_i - v_j\right)^2 = 2 \sum_{i,j=1}^{\ell} \mathbf{K}_{ij} v_i^2 - 2 \sum_{i,j=1}^{\ell} \mathbf{K}_{ij} v_i v_j$$

$$= 2\mathbf{v}'\mathbf{D}\mathbf{v} - 2\mathbf{v}'\mathbf{K}\mathbf{v} = 2\mathbf{v}'\mathbf{L}\left(\mathbf{K}\right)\mathbf{v}.$$

It follows that the all 1s vector $\mathbf{j}$ is an eigenvector of $\mathbf{L}\left(\mathbf{K}\right)$ with eigenvalue 0 since the sum is zero if $v_i = v_j = 1$. It also implies that if the kernel matrix has positive entries then $\mathbf{L}\left(\mathbf{K}\right)$ is positive semi-definite. In the statement of the following theorem we separate out λ_1 as the eigenvalue 0, while ordering the remaining eigenvalues in ascending order.

Theorem 8.32 *Let*

$$S = \{\mathbf{x}_1, \ldots, \mathbf{x}_\ell\}$$

be a set of points with kernel matrix $\mathbf{K}$. The visualisation problem given in Computation 8.30 is solved by computing the eigenvectors $\mathbf{v}^1, \mathbf{v}^2, \ldots, \mathbf{v}^\ell$ with corresponding eigenvalues $0 = \lambda_1, \lambda_2 \leq \ldots \leq \lambda_\ell$ of the Laplacian matrix $\mathbf{L}(\mathbf{K})$. An optimal embedding $\boldsymbol{\tau}$ is given by $\boldsymbol{\tau}_i = \mathbf{v}^{i+1}$, $i = 1, \ldots, k$ and the minimal value of $E(\boldsymbol{\tau})$ is

$$2 \sum_{\ell=2}^{k+1} \lambda_\ell.$$

If $\lambda_{k+1} < \lambda_{k+2}$ then the optimal embedding is unique up to orthonormal transformations in $\mathbb{R}^k$.

Proof The criterion to be minimised is

$$\sum_{i,j=1}^{\ell} \kappa(\mathbf{x}_i, \mathbf{x}_j) \|\boldsymbol{\tau}(\mathbf{x}_i) - \boldsymbol{\tau}(\mathbf{x}_j)\|^2 = \sum_{s=1}^{k} \sum_{i,j=1}^{\ell} \kappa(\mathbf{x}_i, \mathbf{x}_j) (\boldsymbol{\tau}_s(\mathbf{x}_i) - \boldsymbol{\tau}_s(\mathbf{x}_j))^2$$

$$= 2 \sum_{s=1}^{k} \boldsymbol{\tau}_s' \mathbf{L}(\mathbf{K}) \boldsymbol{\tau}_s.$$

Taking into account the normalisation and orthogonality constraints gives the solution as the eigenvectors of $\mathbf{L}(\mathbf{K})$ by the usual characterisation of the Raleigh quotients. The uniqueness again follows from the invariance under orthonormal transformations together with the need to restrict to the subspace spanned by the first k eigenvectors. $\square$

The implementation of this visualisation technique is very straightforward.

Algorithm 8.33 [Data visualisation] Matlab code for the data visualisation algorithm is given in Code Fragment 8.4. ∎

```
% original kernel matrix stored in variable K
% tau gives the embedding in k dimensions
D = diag(sum(K));
L = D - K;
[V,Lambda] = eig(L);
Lambda = diag(Lambda);
I = find(abs(Lambda) > 0.00001)
objective = 2*sum(Lambda(I(1:k)))
Tau = V(:,I(1:k));
plot(Tau(:,1), Tau(:,2), 'x')
```

Code Fragment 8.4. Matlab code to implementing low-dimensional visualisation.

8.4 Summary

- The problem of learning a ranking function can be solved using kernel methods.
- Stability analysis motivates the development of an optimisation criterion that can be efficiently solved using convex quadratic programming.
- Practical considerations suggest an on-line version of the method. A stability analysis is derived for the application of a perceptron-style algorithm suitable for collaborative filtering.
- The quality of a clustering of points can be measured by the expected within cluster distances.
- Analysis of this measure shows that it has many attractive properties. Unfortunately, minimising the criterion on the training sample is NP-hard.
- Two kernel approaches to approximating the solution are presented. The first is the dual version of the k-means algorithm. The second relies on solving exactly a relaxed version of the problem in what is known as spectral clustering.
- Data in the feature space can be visualised by finding low-dimensional embeddings satisfying certain natural criteria.

8.5 Further reading and advanced topics

The problem of identifying clusters in a set of data has been a classic topic of statistics and machine learning for many years. The book [40] gives a general introduction to many of the main ideas, particularly to the various cost functions that can be optimised, as well as presenting the many convenient properties of the cost function described in this book, the expected square distance from cluster-centre. The classical k-means algorithm greedily attempts to optimise this cost function.

On the other hand, the clustering approach based on spectral analysis is relatively new, and still the object of current research. In the NIPS conference 2001, for example, the following independent works appeared: [34], [169], [103], [12]. Note also the article [74]. The statistical stability of spectral clustering has been investigated in [126], [103].

The kernelisation of k-means is a folk algorithm within the kernel machines community, being used as an example of kernel-based algorithms for some time. The combination of spectral clustering with kernels is more recent.

Also the problem of learning to rank data has been addressed by several authors in different research communities. For recent examples, see Herbrich *et al.* [56] and Crammer and Singer [30]. Our discussion in this chapter mostly follows Crammer and Singer.

Visualising data has for a long time been a vital component of data mining, as well as of graph theory, where visualising is also known as graph drawing. Similar ideas were developed in multivariate statistics, with the problem of multidimensional scaling [159]. The method presented in this chapter was developed in the chemical literature, but it has natural equivalents in graph drawing [105].

For constantly updated pointers to online literature and free software see the book's companion website: www.kernel-methods.net

Part III

Constructing kernels

9

Basic kernels and kernel types

There are two key properties that are required of a kernel function for an application. Firstly, it should capture the measure of similarity appropriate to the particular task and domain, and secondly, its evaluation should require significantly less computation than would be needed in an explicit evaluation of the corresponding feature mapping ϕ. Both of these issues will be addressed in the next four chapters but the current chapter begins the consideration of the efficiency question.

A number of computational methods can be deployed in order to short-cut the computation: some involve using closed-form analytic expressions, others exploit recursive relations, and others are based on sampling. This chapter aims to show several different methods in action, with the aim of illustrating how to design new kernels for specific applications. It will also pave the way for the final three chapters that carry these techniques into the design of advanced kernels.

We will also return to an important theme already broached in Chapter 3, namely that kernel functions are not restricted to vectorial inputs: kernels can be designed for objects and structures as diverse as strings, graphs, text documents, sets and graph-nodes. Given the different evaluation methods and the diversity of the types of data on which kernels can be defined, together with the methods for composing and manipulating kernels outlined in Chapter 3, it should be clear how versatile this approach to data modelling can be, allowing as it does for refined customisations of the embedding map ϕ to the problem at hand.

9.1 Kernels in closed form

We have already seen polynomial and Gaussian kernels in Chapters 2 and 3. We start by revisiting these important examples, presenting them in a different light in order to illustrate a series of important design principles that will lead us to more sophisticated kernels. The polynomial kernels in particular will serve as a thread linking this section with those that follow.

Polynomial kernels In Chapter 3, Proposition 3.24 showed that the space of valid kernels is closed under the application of polynomials with positive coefficients. We now give a formal definition of the polynomial kernel.

Definition 9.1 [Polynomial kernel] The *derived polynomial kernel* for a kernel κ_1 is defined as

$$\kappa(\mathbf{x}, \mathbf{z}) = p(\kappa_1(\mathbf{x}, \mathbf{z})),$$

where $p(\cdot)$ is any polynomial with positive coefficients. Frequently, it also refers to the special case

$$\kappa_d(\mathbf{x}, \mathbf{z}) = (\langle \mathbf{x}, \mathbf{z} \rangle + R)^d,$$

defined over a vector space X of dimension n, where R and d are parameters.

∎

Expanding the polynomial kernel κ_d using the binomial theorem we have

$$\kappa_d(\mathbf{x}, \mathbf{z}) = \sum_{s=0}^{d} \binom{d}{s} R^{d-s} \langle \mathbf{x}, \mathbf{z} \rangle^s. \tag{9.1}$$

Our discussion in Chapter 3 showed that the features for each component in the sum together form the features of the whole kernel. Hence, we have a reweighting of the features of the polynomial kernels

$$\hat{\kappa}_s(\mathbf{x}, \mathbf{z}) = \langle \mathbf{x}, \mathbf{z} \rangle^s, \text{ for } s = 0, \dots, d.$$

Recall from Chapter 3 that the feature space corresponding to the kernel $\hat{\kappa}_s(\mathbf{x}, \mathbf{z})$ has dimensions indexed by all monomials of degree s, for which we use the notation

$$\phi_{\mathbf{i}}(\mathbf{x}) = \mathbf{x}^{\mathbf{i}} = x_1^{i_1} x_2^{i_2} \dots x_n^{i_n},$$

where $\mathbf{i} = (i_1, \dots, i_n) \in \mathbb{N}^n$ satisfies

$$\sum_{j=1}^{n} i_j = s.$$

The features corresponding to the kernel $\kappa_d(\mathbf{x}, \mathbf{z})$ are therefore all functions of the form $\phi_{\mathbf{i}}(\mathbf{x})$ for $\mathbf{i}$ satisfying

$$\sum_{j=1}^{n} i_j \leq d.$$

Proposition 9.2 *The dimension of the feature space for the polynomial kernel* $\kappa_d(\mathbf{x}, \mathbf{z}) = (\langle \mathbf{x}, \mathbf{z} \rangle + R)^d$ *is*

$$\binom{n+d}{d}.$$

Proof We will prove the result by induction over n. For $n = 1$, the number is correctly computed as $d + 1$. Now consider the general case and divide the monomials into those that contain at least one factor x_1 and those that have $i_1 = 0$. Using the induction hypothesis there are $\binom{n+d-1}{d-1}$ of the first type of monomial, since there is a 1-1 correspondence between monomials of degree at most d with one factor x_1 and monomials of degree at most $d - 1$ involving all base features. The number of monomials of degree at most d satisfying $i_1 = 0$ is on the other hand equal to $\binom{n-1+d}{d}$ since this corresponds to a restriction to one fewer input feature. Hence, the total number of all monomials of degree at most d is equal to

$$\binom{n+d-1}{d-1} + \binom{n-1+d}{d} = \binom{n+d}{d},$$

as required. $\qquad\qquad\qquad\qquad\qquad\qquad\qquad\qquad\qquad\qquad\qquad\qquad\qquad\square$

Remark 9.3 [Relative weightings] Note that the parameter R allows some control of the relative weightings of the different degree monomials, since by equation (9.1), we can write

$$\kappa_d(\mathbf{x}, \mathbf{z}) = \sum_{s=0}^{d} a_s \hat{\kappa}_s(\mathbf{x}, \mathbf{z}),$$

where

$$a_s = \binom{d}{s} R^{d-s}.$$

Hence, increasing R decreases the relative weighting of the higher order polynomials. $\qquad\qquad\qquad\qquad\qquad\qquad\qquad\qquad\qquad\qquad\qquad\qquad\quad\blacksquare$

Remark 9.4 [On computational complexity] One of the reasons why it is possible to reduce the evaluation of polynomial kernels to a very simple computation is that we are using *all* of the monomials. This has the effect of reducing the freedom to control the weightings of individual monomials. Paradoxically, it can be much more expensive to use only a subset of them, since, if no pattern exists that can be exploited to speed the overall computation, we are reduced to enumerating each monomial feature in turn. For some special cases, however, recursive procedures can be used as a shortcut as we now illustrate. ∎

All-subsets kernel As an example of a different combination of features consider a space with a feature ϕ_A for each subset $A \subseteq \{1, 2, \ldots, n\}$ of the input features, including the empty subset. Equivalently we can represent them as we did for the polynomial kernel as features

$$\phi_{\mathbf{i}}(\mathbf{x}) = x_1^{i_1} x_2^{i_2} \ldots x_n^{i_n},$$

with the restriction that $\mathbf{i} = (i_1, \ldots, i_n) \in \{0, 1\}^n$. The feature ϕ_A is given by multiplying together the input features for all the elements of the subset

$$\phi_A(\mathbf{x}) = \prod_{i \in A} x_i.$$

This generates all monomial features for all combinations of up to n different indices but here, unlike in the polynomial case, each factor in the monomial has degree 1.

Definition 9.5 [All-subsets embedding] The *all-subsets kernel* is defined by the embedding

$$\phi : \mathbf{x} \longmapsto (\phi_A(\mathbf{x}))_{A \subseteq \{1,\ldots,n\}},$$

with the corresponding kernel $\kappa_\subseteq(\mathbf{x}, \mathbf{z})$ given by

$$\kappa_\subseteq(\mathbf{x}, \mathbf{z}) = \langle \phi(\mathbf{x}), \phi(\mathbf{z}) \rangle.$$

∎

There is a simple computation that evaluates the all-subsets kernel as the following derivation shows

$$\kappa_\subseteq(\mathbf{x}, \mathbf{z}) = \langle \phi(\mathbf{x}), \phi(\mathbf{z}) \rangle = \sum_{A \subseteq \{1,\ldots,n\}} \phi_A(\mathbf{x}) \phi_A(\mathbf{z}) = \sum_{A \subseteq \{1,\ldots,n\}} \prod_{i \in A} x_i z_i$$

$$= \prod_{i=1}^{n} (1 + x_i z_i),$$

where the last step follows from an application of the distributive law. We summarise this in the following computation.

Computation 9.6 [All-subsets kernel] The all-subsets kernel is computed by

$$\kappa_\subseteq (\mathbf{x}, \mathbf{z}) = \prod_{i=1}^{n} (1 + x_i z_i)$$

for n-dimensional input vectors. ∎

Note that each subset in this feature space is assigned equal weight unlike the variable weightings characteristic of the polynomial kernel. We will see below that the same kernel can be formulated in a recursive way, giving rise to a class known as the ANOVA kernels. They build on a theme already apparent in the above where we see the kernel expressed as a sum of products, but computed as a product of sums.

Remark 9.7 [Recursive computation] We can clearly compute the polynomial kernel of degree d recursively in terms of lower degree kernels using the recursion

$$\kappa_d (\mathbf{x}, \mathbf{z}) = \kappa_{d-1} (\mathbf{x}, \mathbf{z}) (\langle \mathbf{x}, \mathbf{z} \rangle + R).$$

Interestingly it is also possible to derive a recursion in terms of the input dimensionality n. This recursion follows the spirit of the inductive proof for the dimension of the feature space given for polynomial kernels. We use the notation

$$\kappa_s^m (\mathbf{x}, \mathbf{z}) = (\langle \mathbf{x}_{1:m}, \mathbf{z}_{1:m} \rangle + R)^s,$$

where $\mathbf{x}_{1:m}$ denotes the restriction of $\mathbf{x}$ to its first m features. Clearly we can compute

$$\kappa_s^0 (\mathbf{x}, \mathbf{z}) = R^s \text{ and } \kappa_0^m (\mathbf{x}, \mathbf{z}) = 1.$$

For general m and s, we divide the products in the expansion of

$$(\langle \mathbf{x}_{1:m}, \mathbf{z}_{1:m} \rangle + R)^s$$

into those that contain at least one factor $x_m z_m$ and those that contain no such factor. The sum of the first group is equal to $s\kappa_{s-1}^m (\mathbf{x}, \mathbf{z}) x_m z_m$ since there is a choice of s factors in which the $x_m z_m$ arises, while the remaining factors are drawn in any way from the other $s - 1$ components in the overall product. The sum over the second group equals $\kappa_s^{m-1}(\mathbf{x}, \mathbf{z})$, resulting in the recursion

$$\kappa_s^m(\mathbf{x}, \mathbf{z}) = s\kappa_{s-1}^m(\mathbf{x}, \mathbf{z})\, x_m z_m + \kappa_s^{m-1}(\mathbf{x}, \mathbf{z}).$$

Clearly, this is much less efficient than the direct computation of the definition, since we must compute $O(nd)$ intermediate values giving a complexity of $O(nd)$, even if we save all the intermediate values, as compared to $O(n+d)$ for the direct method. The approach does, however, motivate the use of recursion introduced below for the computation of kernels for which a direct route does not exist. ∎

Gaussian kernels Gaussian kernels are the most widely used kernels and have been extensively studied in neighbouring fields. Proposition 3.24 of Chapter 3 verified that the following kernel is indeed valid.

Definition 9.8 [Gaussian kernel] For $\sigma > 0$, the *Gaussian kernel* is defined by

$$\kappa(\mathbf{x}, \mathbf{z}) = \exp\left(-\frac{\|\mathbf{x} - \mathbf{z}\|^2}{2\sigma^2}\right).$$

∎

For the Gaussian kernel the images of all points have norm 1 in the resulting feature space as $\kappa(\mathbf{x}, \mathbf{x}) = \exp(0) = 1$. The feature space can be chosen so that the images all lie in a single orthant, since all inner products between mapped points are positive.

Note that we are not restricted to using the Euclidean distance in the input space. If for example $\kappa_1(\mathbf{x}, \mathbf{z})$ is a kernel corresponding to a feature mapping ϕ_1 into a feature space F_1, we can create a Gaussian kernel in F_1 by observing that

$$\|\phi_1(\mathbf{x}) - \phi_1(\mathbf{z})\|^2 = \kappa_1(\mathbf{x}, \mathbf{x}) - 2\kappa_1(\mathbf{x}, \mathbf{z}) + \kappa_1(\mathbf{z}, \mathbf{z}),$$

giving the derived Gaussian kernel as

$$\kappa(\mathbf{x}, \mathbf{z}) = \exp\left(-\frac{\kappa_1(\mathbf{x}, \mathbf{x}) - 2\kappa_1(\mathbf{x}, \mathbf{z}) + \kappa_1(\mathbf{z}, \mathbf{z})}{2\sigma^2}\right).$$

The parameter σ controls the flexibility of the kernel in a similar way to the degree d in the polynomial kernel. Small values of σ correspond to large values of d since, for example, they allow classifiers to fit any labels, hence risking overfitting. In such cases the kernel matrix becomes close to the identity matrix. On the other hand, large values of σ gradually reduce the kernel to a constant function, making it impossible to learn any non-trivial classifier. The feature space has infinite-dimension for every value of σ but for large values the weight decays very fast on the higher-order features. In other words although the rank of the kernel matrix will be full, for all practical purposes the points lie in a low-dimensional subspace of the feature space.

Remark 9.9 [Visualising the Gaussian feature space] It can be hard to form a picture of the feature space corresponding to the Gaussian kernel. As described in Chapter 3 another way to represent the elements of the feature space is as functions in a Hilbert space

$$\mathbf{x} \longmapsto \phi(\mathbf{x}) = \kappa(\mathbf{x}, \cdot) = \exp\left(-\frac{\|\mathbf{x} - \cdot\|^2}{2\sigma^2}\right),$$

with the inner product between functions given by

$$\left\langle \sum_{i=1}^{\ell} \alpha_i \kappa(\mathbf{x}_i, \cdot), \sum_{j=1}^{\ell} \beta_j \kappa(\mathbf{x}_j, \cdot) \right\rangle = \sum_{i=1}^{\ell} \sum_{j=1}^{\ell} \alpha_i \beta_j \kappa(\mathbf{x}_i, \mathbf{x}_j).$$

To a first approximation we can think of each point as representing a new potentially orthogonal direction, but with the overlap to other directions being bigger the closer the two points are in the input space. ∎

9.2 ANOVA kernels

The polynomial kernel and the all-subsets kernel have limited control of what features they use and how they weight them. The polynomial kernel can only use all monomials of degree d or of degree up to d with a weighting scheme depending on just one parameter R. As its name suggests, the all-subsets kernel is restricted to using all the monomials corresponding to possible subsets of the n input space features. We now present a method that allows more freedom in specifying the set of monomials.

The ANOVA kernel κ_d of degree d is like the all-subsets kernel except that it is restricted to subsets of the given cardinality d. We can use the above notation $\mathbf{x^i}$ to denote the expression $x_1^{i_1} x_2^{i_2} \ldots x_n^{i_n}$, where $\mathbf{i} = (i_1, \ldots, i_n) \in \{0, 1\}^n$ with the further restriction that

$$\sum_{j=1}^{n} i_j = d.$$

For the case $d = 0$ there is one feature with constant value 1 corresponding to the empty set. The difference between the ANOVA and polynomial kernel $\kappa_d(\mathbf{x}, \mathbf{z})$ is the exclusion of repeated coordinates.

ANOVA stands for ANalysis Of VAriance, the first application of Hoeffding's decompositions of functions that led to this kernel (for more about the history of the method see Section 9.10). We now give the formal definition.

Definition 9.10 [ANOVA embedding] The embedding of the ANOVA kernel of degree d is given by

$$\phi_d : \mathbf{x} \longmapsto (\phi_A(\mathbf{x}))_{|A|=d},$$

where for each subset A the feature is given by

$$\phi_A(\mathbf{x}) = \prod_{i \in A} x_i = \mathbf{x}^{\mathbf{i}_A},$$

where $\mathbf{i}_A$ is the indicator function of the set A. ∎

The dimension of the resulting embedding is clearly $\binom{n}{d}$, since this is the number of such subsets, while the resulting inner product is given by

$$
\begin{aligned}
\kappa_d(\mathbf{x}, \mathbf{z}) &= \langle \phi_d(\mathbf{x}), \phi_d(\mathbf{z}) \rangle = \sum_{|A|=d} \phi_A(\mathbf{x}) \phi_A(\mathbf{z}) \\
&= \sum_{1 \le i_1 < i_2 < \cdots < i_d \le n} (x_{i_1} z_{i_1})(x_{i_2} z_{i_2}) \ldots (x_{i_d} z_{i_d}) \\
&= \sum_{1 \le i_1 < i_2 < \cdots < i_d \le n} \prod_{j=1}^{d} x_{i_j} z_{i_j}.
\end{aligned}
$$

Note again the sums of products in the definition of the kernel.

Remark 9.11 [Feature space] Notice that this is a proper subspace of the embedding space generated by a polynomial kernel of degree d, since instead of imposing $1 \le i_1 < i_2 < \cdots < i_d \le n$, the polynomial kernel only requires the weaker restriction $1 \le i_1 \le i_2 \le \cdots \le i_d \le n$. The weighting of the subspace of features considered for the ANOVA kernel is also uniform in the polynomial kernel, but the weightings of the features with repeated indices is higher. ∎

We have been keen to stress that it should be possible to evaluate a kernel faster than by an explicit computation of the feature vectors. Here, for an explicit computation, the number of operations grows as $d\binom{n}{d}$ since there are $\binom{n}{d}$ features each of which requires $O(d)$ operations to evaluate. We now consider a recursive method of computation following the spirit of the recursive evaluation of the polynomial kernel given in Remark 9.7.

Naive recursion We again introduce a series of intermediate kernels. Again using the notation $\mathbf{x}_{1:m} = (x_1, \ldots, x_m)$ we introduce, for $m \geq 1$ and $s \geq 0$

$$\kappa_s^m(\mathbf{x}, \mathbf{z}) = \kappa_s(\mathbf{x}_{1:m}, \mathbf{z}_{1:m}),$$

which is the ANOVA kernel of degree s applied to the inputs restricted to the first m coordinates. In order to evaluate $\kappa_s^m(\mathbf{x}, \mathbf{z})$ we now argue inductively that its features can be divided into two groups: those that contain x_m and the remainder. There is a 1-1 correspondence between the first group and subsets of size $d - 1$ restricted to $\mathbf{x}_{1:m-1}$, while the second group are subsets of size d restricted to $\mathbf{x}_{1:m-1}$. It follows that

$$\kappa_s^m(\mathbf{x}, \mathbf{z}) = (x_m z_m) \kappa_{s-1}^{m-1}(\mathbf{x}, \mathbf{z}) + \kappa_s^{m-1}(\mathbf{x}, \mathbf{z}). \tag{9.2}$$

The base of the recursion occurs when $m < s$ or $s = 0$. Clearly, we have

$$\kappa_s^m(\mathbf{x}, \mathbf{z}) = 0, \text{ if } m < s, \tag{9.3}$$

since no subset of size s can be found, while

$$\kappa_0^m(\mathbf{x}, \mathbf{z}) = 1, \tag{9.4}$$

as the empty set has a feature value of 1. We summarise this in the following computation.

Computation 9.12 [ANOVA recursion] The ANOVA kernel is given by the following recursion

$$
\begin{aligned}
\kappa_0^m(\mathbf{x}, \mathbf{z}) &= 1, \text{ if } m \geq 0, \\
\kappa_s^m(\mathbf{x}, \mathbf{z}) &= 0, \text{ if } m < s, \\
\kappa_s^m(\mathbf{x}, \mathbf{z}) &= (x_m z_m) \kappa_{s-1}^{m-1}(\mathbf{x}, \mathbf{z}) + \kappa_s^{m-1}(\mathbf{x}, \mathbf{z})
\end{aligned}
$$

■

The computational framework presented here forms the basis for several further generalisations that will be discussed in this and subsequent chapters leading to the introduction of string kernels in Chapter 11.

Remark 9.13 [Cost of naive recursion] As we observed above, a direct computation of the kernel by explicit evaluation of the features would involve $O\left(d\binom{n}{d}\right)$ operations. If we were to implement the recursion given in equations (9.2) to (9.4), this would also remain very costly. If we denote with a function $T(m, s)$ the cost of performing the recursive calculation of

$\kappa_s^m(\mathbf{x}, \mathbf{z})$, we can use the recurrence relation to deduce the following estimate for the number of operations

$$\begin{aligned} T(m, s) &= T(m-1, s) + T(m-1, s-1) + 3 \\ &> T(m-1, s) + T(m-1, s-1), \end{aligned}$$

with $T(m, s) = 1$ for $m < s$ and $T(m, 0) = 1$. For these base values we have the inequality

$$T(m, s) \geq \binom{m}{s},$$

while using an inductive assumption gives

$$\begin{aligned} T(m, s) &> T(m-1, s) + T(m-1, s-1) \\ &\geq \binom{m-1}{s} + \binom{m-1}{s-1} = \binom{m}{s}. \end{aligned}$$

Hence the cost of computing the kernel $\kappa_d(\mathbf{x}, \mathbf{z})$ is at least $\binom{n}{d}$ which is still exponential in the degree d. ∎

Dynamic programming evaluation The naive recursion is inefficient because it repeats many of the same computations again and again. The key to a drastic reduction in the overall computational complexity is to save the values of $\kappa_s^m(\mathbf{x}, \mathbf{z})$ in a dynamic programming table indexed by s and m as they are computed:

DP	$m = 1$	2	$\cdots$	n	
$s = 0$	1	1	$\cdots$	1	
1	$x_1 z_1$	$x_1 z_1 + x_2 z_2$	$\cdots$	$\sum_{i=1}^{n} x_i z_i$	
2	0	$\kappa_2^2(\mathbf{x}, \mathbf{z})$	$\cdots$	$\kappa_2^n(\mathbf{x}, \mathbf{z})$	(9.5)
$\vdots$	$\vdots$	$\vdots$	$\ddots$	$\vdots$	
d	0	0	$\cdots$	$\kappa_d^n(\mathbf{x}, \mathbf{z})$	

If we begin computation with the first row from left to right and continue down the table taking each row in turn, the evaluation of a particular entry depends on the entry diagonally above to its left and the entry immediately to its left. Hence, both values will already be available in the table. The required kernel evaluation is the bottom rightmost entry in the table. We summarise in the following algorithm.

Algorithm 9.14 [ANOVA kernel] The ANOVA kernel κ_d is computed in Code Fragment 9.1. ∎

Input	vectors $\mathbf{x}$ and $\mathbf{z}$ of length n, degree d
Process	for $j = 0 : n$
2	$\quad$ DP $(0, j) = 1$;
3	end
6	for $k = 1 : d$
7	$\quad$ DP $(k, k - 1) = 0$;
9	$\quad$ for $j = k : n$
10	$\quad\quad$ DP $(k, j) = $ DP $(k, j - 1) + x\,(j)\,z\,(j)\,$DP $(k - 1, j - 1)$;
11	$\quad$ end
12	end
Output	kernel evaluation $\kappa_d\,(\mathbf{x}, \mathbf{z}) = $ DP (d, n)

Code Fragment 9.1. Pseudocode for ANOVA kernel.

Cost of the computation The computation involves

$$3\left(nd - \frac{d(d-1)}{2}\right)$$

numerical operations. If we take into account that entries $\kappa_s^m\,(\mathbf{x}, \mathbf{z})$ with $m > n - d + s$ cannot affect the result, this can be reduced still further.

Remark 9.15 [Dynamic programming notation] Such a staged recursive implementation is often referred to as a *dynamic programming*, though dynamic programs can involve more complex evaluations at each stage and can be run over more general structures such as graphs rather than simple tables. We will use a uniform notation for showing dynamic programming tables following the example of (9.5), with DP in the upper left corner indicating this type of table. See Appendix B for details of the different table types. ■

Remark 9.16 [On using different degrees] Observe that the final column in the table contains the ANOVA kernel evaluations for all degrees up to and including d. It is therefore possible, at very little extra cost, to evaluate the kernel

$$\kappa_{\le d}\,(\mathbf{x}, \mathbf{z}) = \sum_{s=0}^{d} \kappa_s\,(\mathbf{x}, \mathbf{z}),$$

or indeed any appropriate reweighting of the component kernels. If we take this to the extreme value of $d = n$, we recover the all-subsets kernel

$$\kappa_\subseteq(\mathbf{x}, \mathbf{z}) = \kappa_{\leq n}(\mathbf{x}, \mathbf{z}) = \sum_{s=0}^{n} \kappa_s(\mathbf{x}, \mathbf{z}),$$

though the method of computation described here is a lot less efficient than that given in Remark 9.1

$$\kappa_\subseteq(\mathbf{x}, \mathbf{z}) = \prod_{i=1}^{n}(1 + x_i z_i),$$

which provides a simpler recursion of complexity only $O(3n)$. Viewed recursively we can see

$$\kappa_\subseteq(\mathbf{x}_m, \mathbf{z}_m) = \kappa_\subseteq(\mathbf{x}_{m-1}, \mathbf{z}_{m-1})(1 + x_m z_m),$$

corresponding to dividing all subsets into those that contain m and those that do not. ∎

Remark 9.17 [Uneven term weighting] In both the ANOVA kernel and the all-subsets kernel, we have the freedom to downplay some features and emphasise others by simply introducing a weighting factor $a_i \geq 0$ whenever we evaluate

$$a_i x_i z_i,$$

so that, for example, the all-subsets kernel becomes

$$\kappa_\subseteq(\mathbf{x}, \mathbf{z}) = \prod_{i=1}^{n}(1 + a_i x_i z_i).$$

In the case of the ANOVA evaluation it is also possible to vary weightings of the features depending on the structure of the monomial. For example, monomials with non-consecutive indices can have their weights reduced. This will form a key ingredient in the string kernels. ∎

Computation 9.18 [Alternative recursion for the ANOVA kernel] Other recursive computations are possible for the ANOVA kernel. When originally introduced, the recursion given was as follows

$$\kappa_0(\mathbf{x}, \mathbf{z}) \;=\; 1$$

$$\kappa_d(\mathbf{x}, \mathbf{z}) \;=\; \frac{1}{d}\sum_{s=1}^{d}(-1)^{s+1}\kappa_{d-s}(\mathbf{x}, \mathbf{z})\,\bar{\kappa}_s(\mathbf{x}, \mathbf{z})$$

where $\bar{\kappa}_s(\mathbf{x}, \mathbf{z}) = \sum_{i=1}^{n} (x_i z_i)^s$. ∎

Remark 9.19 [Correctness of alternative recursion] The correctness of this alternative can be verified formally. Intuitively, since $\bar{\kappa}_s(\mathbf{x}, \mathbf{z}) = \langle \mathbf{x}, \mathbf{z} \rangle$, the first term in the sum is

$$\frac{1}{d} \kappa_{d-1}(\mathbf{x}, \mathbf{z}) \langle \mathbf{x}, \mathbf{z} \rangle,$$

which includes the d subsets as features with weighting 1, but also includes features $\phi_i(\mathbf{x})$ for which some components have repeated entries. The second term removes these but introduces others which are in turn removed by the following term and so on. The complexity of this method using tables is $O(nd + d^2)$, which is comparable to Algorithm 9.14. However the version discussed above is more useful for extensions to the case of strings and is numerically more stable. ∎

Remark 9.20 [Extensions to general kernels on structures] We can view the individual components $x_i z_i$ in the ANOVA kernel as a base kernel

$$\kappa_i(\mathbf{x}, \mathbf{z}) = x_i z_i.$$

Indeed the reweighting scheme discussed in Remark 9.17 can be seen as changing this base kernel to

$$\kappa_i(\mathbf{x}, \mathbf{z}) = a_i x_i z_i.$$

Taking this view suggests that we could compare data types more general than real numbers in each coordinate, be they discrete objects such as characters, or multi-coordinate vectors. More generally we can simply replace the n coordinates by n general base kernels that provide different methods of comparing the two objects. We do not require that the ith kernel depends only on the ith coordinate. It might depend on a set of coordinates that could overlap with the coordinates affecting other features. In general all of the base kernels could depend on all of the input coordinates. Given a sequence $\kappa_1(\mathbf{x}, \mathbf{z}), \ldots, \kappa_n(\mathbf{x}, \mathbf{z})$ of base kernels, this more general version of the ANOVA kernel therefore has the following form

$$\kappa_d^A(\mathbf{x}, \mathbf{z}) = \sum_{1 \le i_1 < i_2 < \cdots < i_d \le n} \prod_{j=1}^{d} \kappa_{i_j}(\mathbf{x}, \mathbf{z}).$$

There are many different applications where this might prove useful. For example it allows us to consider the case when the inputs are discrete structures with d components, with $\kappa_i(\mathbf{x}, \mathbf{z})$ providing a comparison of the ith subcomponent. Both recursions can still be used. For example the original recursion becomes

$$\kappa_s^m \left(\mathbf{x}, \mathbf{z} \right) = \kappa_m \left(\mathbf{x}, \mathbf{z} \right) \kappa_{s-1}^{m-1} \left(\mathbf{x}, \mathbf{z} \right) + \kappa_s^{m-1} \left(\mathbf{x}, \mathbf{z} \right),$$

while for the second recursion we must replace the evaluation of $\bar{\kappa}_s \left(\mathbf{x}, \mathbf{z} \right)$ by

$$\bar{\kappa}_s \left(\mathbf{x}, \mathbf{z} \right) = \sum_{i=1}^{n} \kappa_i \left(\mathbf{x}, \mathbf{z} \right)^s.$$

∎

9.3 Kernels from graphs

The ANOVA kernel is a method that allows us to be slightly more selective about which monomials are included. Clearly it is, however, very far from general. Ideally we would like to extend the range of selective options available while still retaining the efficient computation it affords. We will achieve this by first showing how the all-subsets kernel computation can be represented using a graph. This will suggest a more general family of methods that subsumes all three examples considered so far.

As a first example consider the all-subsets kernel. We can illustrate the computation

$$\kappa_\subseteq \left(\mathbf{x}, \mathbf{z} \right) = \prod_{i=1}^{n} \left(1 + x_i z_i \right)$$

with the graph shown in Figure 9.1. Here the computation flows from left

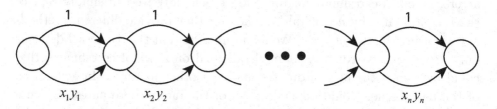

Fig. 9.1. Kernel graph for the all-subsets kernel.

to right with the value at a node given by summing over the edges reaching that node, the value at the previous node times the value on the edge. The double edges enable us to code the fact that the previous value is multiplied by the factor

$$\left(1 + x_i z_i \right).$$

We can view the graph as an illustration of the computational strategy, but it also encodes the features of the kernel as the set of directed paths from the leftmost to the rightmost vertex. Each such path must go through each vertex using either the upper or lower edge. Using the lower edge corresponds to including the feature while using the upper edge means that it is left out. It follows that there are 2^n paths in 1-1 correspondence with the subsets of $\{1, \ldots, n\}$, that is with the coordinates of the kernel feature mapping.

The perspective afforded by illustrating the kernel computation as a graph suggests defining a more general set of kernels in terms of a general graph structure.

Consider a directed (edges have an associated direction) graph $G = (V, E)$ where V is a set of vertices with two labelled vertices: s the source vertex and t the sink vertex. The set E of directed edges without loops is labelled with the base kernels. For the all-subsets kernel these were either a constant or $x_i z_i$ for some i, but in general we could consider the base kernels $\kappa_i(\mathbf{x}, \mathbf{z})$ in the spirit of Remark 9.20. If we treat a constant function as a kernel we can simply view the edges $e \in E$ as indexing a kernel $\kappa_e(\mathbf{x}, \mathbf{z})$. Note that we will denote path p by the sequence of vertices it contains, for example

$$p = (u_0 u_1 \ldots u_d),$$

where it is understood that $(u_i \to u_{i+1}) \in E$ for $i = 1, \ldots, d-1$. If $(u_d \to v) \in E$ then pv denotes the path

$$(u_0 u_1 \ldots u_d v).$$

We summarise in the following definition.

Definition 9.21 A *kernel graph* is a directed graph $G = (V, E)$ with a source vertex s of in-degree 0 and sink vertex t of out-degree 0. Furthermore, each edge e is labelled with a kernel κ_e. Let P_{st} be the set of directed paths from vertex s to vertex t and for a path $p = (u_0 u_1 \cdots u_d)$ let

$$\kappa_p(\mathbf{x}, \mathbf{z}) = \prod_{i=1}^{d} \kappa_{(u_{i-1} \to u_i)}(\mathbf{x}, \mathbf{z}),$$

that is, the product of the kernels associated with the edges of p. We now introduce the *graph kernel* specified by the graph G by

$$\kappa_G(\mathbf{x}, \mathbf{z}) = \sum_{p \in P_{st}} \kappa_p(\mathbf{x}, \mathbf{z}) = \sum_{p \in P_{st}} \prod_{i=1}^{d} \kappa_{(u_{i-1} \to u_i)}(\mathbf{x}, \mathbf{z}).$$

For simplicity we assume that no vertex has a directed edge to itself. If the graph has no directed loops we call the graph *simple*, while in general we allow directed loops involving more than one edge. ∎

A graph kernel can be seen to be a kernel since sums and products of kernels are kernels though for graphs with loops there will be an issue of convergence of the infinite sums involved. Notice that if the base kernels are the simple products $x_i z_i$ or the constant 1, then we have each path corresponding to a monomial feature formed as the product of the factors on that path.

Remark 9.22 [Vertex labelled versus edge labelled graphs] We have introduced kernel graphs by labelling the edges with base kernels. It is also possible to label the vertices of the graph and again define the kernel as the sum over all paths with the features for a path being the product of the features associated with nodes on the path. We omit these details as they do not add any additional insights. ∎

Remark 9.23 [Flexibility of graph kernels] Clearly the range of options available using different graphs G is very large. By adjusting the structure of the graph we can control which monomial features are included. We have even allowed the possibility of graphs with loops that would give rise to infinite feature spaces including monomials of arbitrary length. We have been able to significantly broaden the definition of the kernels, but can we retain the efficient computational methods characteristic of the all-subsets kernel? In particular if the graph is directed does the computation dictated by the directed graph really compute the kernel? ∎

Computation of graph kernels Given a kernel graph $G = (V, E)$, consider introducing a kernel for each vertex $u \in V$ defined by

$$\kappa_u(\mathbf{x}, \mathbf{z}) = \sum_{p \in P_{su}} \kappa_p(\mathbf{x}, \mathbf{z}).$$

Hence, we have $\kappa_G(\mathbf{x}, \mathbf{z}) = \kappa_t(\mathbf{x}, \mathbf{z})$ and we take $\kappa_s(\mathbf{x}, \mathbf{z}) = 1$. Consider a vertex u. All paths arriving at u from s must reach u by a directed edge into u. Similarly, any path p from s to a vertex v that has a directed edge e to u can be extended to a path pu from s to u. We can therefore decompose the sum

$$\kappa_u(\mathbf{x}, \mathbf{z}) = \sum_{p \in P_{su}} \kappa_p(\mathbf{x}, \mathbf{z}) = \sum_{v: v \to u} \sum_{p \in P_{sv}} \kappa_{pu}(\mathbf{x}, \mathbf{z})$$

$$= \sum_{v:v \to u} \kappa_{(v \to u)}(\mathbf{x}, \mathbf{z}) \sum_{p \in P_{sv}} \kappa_p(\mathbf{x}, \mathbf{z})$$

$$= \sum_{v:v \to u} \kappa_{(v \to u)}(\mathbf{x}, \mathbf{z}) \kappa_v(\mathbf{x}, \mathbf{z}). \tag{9.6}$$

This is a set of linear equations for the vector of unknown values

$$\boldsymbol{\kappa} = (\kappa_u(\mathbf{x}, \mathbf{z}))_{u \in V \backslash s}.$$

If we define the square matrix $\mathbf{A}$ indexed by $V \backslash s$ to have entries

$$\mathbf{A}_{uv} = \begin{cases} \kappa_{(v \to u)}(\mathbf{x}, \mathbf{z}) & \text{if } (v \to u) \in E \\ -1 & \text{if } u = v, \\ 0 & \text{otherwise,} \end{cases} \tag{9.7}$$

and the vector $\mathbf{b}$ to have entries

$$b_u = \begin{cases} -\kappa_{(s \to u)}(\mathbf{x}, \mathbf{z}) & \text{if } (s \to u) \in E \\ 0 & \text{otherwise,} \end{cases} \tag{9.8}$$

then we can rewrite equation (9.6) to give the computation:

Computation 9.24 [General graph kernels] Using $\mathbf{A}$ given by (9.7) and $\mathbf{b}$ by (9.8), the evaluation of the general graph kernel is obtained by solving

$$\mathbf{A}\boldsymbol{\kappa} = \mathbf{b},$$

and returning

$$\kappa(\mathbf{x}, \mathbf{z}) = \kappa_t(\mathbf{x}, \mathbf{z}).$$

∎

Hence, provided the matrix $\mathbf{A}$ is invertible, we can in general solve the system in $O\left(|V|^3\right)$ steps to evaluate the kernel. The question of invertibility is related to the fact that once the graph has loops we cannot guarantee in general that the kernel evaluation will be bounded. Hence, care must be taken in defining graphs with loops. There are several types of graph structures other than the simple graph kernels with no loops for which more efficient computations exist.

If the graph is simple we can order the computation so that the values needed to compute $\kappa_u(\mathbf{x}, \mathbf{z})$ have already been evaluated. We must perform a so-called topological sort of the vertices to obtain an order that is compatible with the partial order determined by the directed edges. This results in the computation described by the graph structure, multiplying the values stored at the previous nodes with the factor on the edge and summing, giving a complexity of $O(|E|)$.

Algorithm 9.25 [Simple graph kernels] Computation of simple graph kernels is given in Code Fragment 9.2. ∎

Input	vectors $\mathbf{x}$ and $\mathbf{z}$ of length n, simple graph kernel $G = (V, E)$
Process	Find an ordering u_i of the vertices of G
2	such that $u_i \to u_j$ implies $i < j$.
	DP $(1) = 1$;
6	for $i = 2 : |V|$
7	DP $(i) = 0$;
9	for $j : u_j \to u_i$
10	DP $(i) = $ DP $(i) + \kappa_{(u_j \to u_i)} (\mathbf{x}, \mathbf{z})$ DP (j);
11	end
12	end
Output	kernel evaluation $\kappa_G (\mathbf{x}, \mathbf{z}) = $ DP $(|V|)$

Code Fragment 9.2. Pseudocode for simple graph kernels.

Remark 9.26 [Message passing] The evaluation of the array entry DP (i) at the vertex u_i can be viewed as the result of a set of messages received from vertices u_j, for which there is an edge $u_j \to u_i$. The message passed by the vertex u_j is its computed value DP (j). Algorithms of this type are referred to as *message passing algorithms* and play an important role in Bayesian belief networks. ∎

Example 9.27 [Polynomial kernel] We can also represent the polynomial kernel as a simple graph kernel. The graph corresponding to its computation is shown in Figure 9.2. Clearly, paths from the leftmost to rightmost vertex

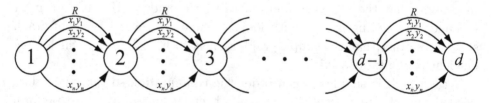

Fig. 9.2. Kernel graph for the polynomial kernel.

again correspond to its features, but notice how many different paths give rise to the same feature. It is this that gives rise to the different weightings that the various monomials receive. ∎

Example 9.28 [ANOVA kernel] Recall the recursive computation of the ANOVA kernel illustrated in Table (9.5). Now consider creating a graph whose vertices are the entries in the table with directed edges to a vertex from the entries used to compute the value stored at that vertex. The edges are labelled with the factor that is applied to the value in the computation. Hence, for example, the vertex $(1,2)$ corresponding to the entry for $s = 1$ and $m = 2$ has a directed edge labelled $x_2 y_2$ from vertex $(0,1)$ and an edge from $(1,1)$ labelled 1. This corresponds to the recursive computation

$$\kappa_1^2(\mathbf{x}, \mathbf{z}) = (x_2 z_2)\, \kappa_{1-1}^{2-1}(\mathbf{x}, \mathbf{z}) + \kappa_1^{2-1}(\mathbf{x}, \mathbf{z}).$$

We have included one extra vertex $(0,0)$ corresponding to $s = 0$ and $m = 0$ with edges labelled 1 from vertex $(0,i)$ to $(0,i+1)$ for $i = 0,\ldots,n-1$. Finally, vertices (s, m) with $s > m$ together with associated edges have been deleted since they correspond to entries that are always 0. The graph is shown in Figure 9.3. We can view the graph as an illustration of the computational strategy, but it also encodes the features of the kernel as the set of directed paths from the vertex $(0,0)$ to the vertex (d, n). Each such path corresponds to the monomial formed by the product of all the factors on the path. Hence, for example, the path $(0,0)(1,1)\cdots(d,d)(d,d+1)\cdots(d,n)$ corresponds to the feature $x_1 x_2 \cdots x_d$. Clearly, to reach the vertex (d,n) we must move down d rows; each time we do so the feature indexing that column is included. Hence, each path corresponds to one set of d features with different paths selecting a different subset. ∎

Remark 9.29 [Regular language kernels] There is a well-known equivalence between languages specified by regular expressions, also known as *regular languages*, and languages recognised by non-deterministic or deterministic finite state automata (FSA). We can use directed labelled graphs to specify non-deterministic FSAs. The nodes of the graph correspond to the states of the FSA, with the source being the initial state, and the sink the accepting state. The directed edges are labelled with symbols from the alphabet of the language or a symbol ε for so-called ε-transitions that do not generate a symbol. Hence, we can view a kernel graph as a non-deterministic FSA over the alphabet of base kernels, where ε-transitions correspond to edges labelled by 1. The languages of the non-deterministic FSA is the set of finite strings that are accepted by the FSA. This is exactly the set of monomial features specified by the kernel graph with the only difference that for the kernel graph a reordering of the base kernels specifies the same feature, while for the FSA, permuting the symbols in a string creates a distinct word in the language. Modulo this difference, we can use regular expressions as a

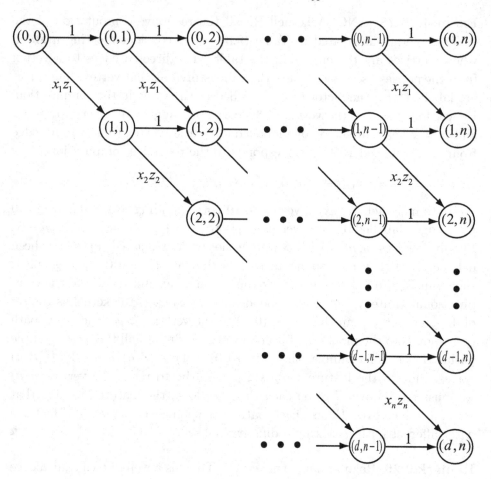

Fig. 9.3. Kernel graph for the ANOVA kernel.

shorthand for specifying the monomial features that we wish to include in our feature space, with the guarantee that the evaluation of the resulting kernel will be polynomial in the number of states of an equivalent non-deterministic FSA.   ∎

9.4 Diffusion kernels on graph nodes

One of the appeals of using kernel methods for pattern analysis is that they can be defined on non-vectorial data, making it possible to extend the application of the techniques to many different types of objects. In later chapters we will define specialist kernels for strings and trees to further illustrate this point, but here we introduce a method that can take any basic comparison rule and convert it into a valid kernel. All that is required is some measure of similarity that captures at the simplest level association between two objects, perhaps only non-zero for objects that are closely related. The construction will use this to construct a refined similarity that relates all objects and is guaranteed to be a kernel.

The method again uses paths in graphs to create more complex relations between objects. In the kernel graphs described in the previous section the labelling of the graph was adjusted for each kernel evaluation $\kappa_G(\mathbf{x}, \mathbf{z})$. In this section we describe how similar ideas can be used to define a new kernel over a set of data, where each data item is associated with a vertex of the graph.

Definition 9.30 [Base similarity graph] A *base similarity graph* for a dataset S is a graph $G = (S, E)$, whose vertices are the data items in S, while the (undirected) links between them are labelled with some base similarity measure $\tau(\mathbf{x}, \mathbf{z})$. The *(base) similarity matrix* $\mathbf{B} = \mathbf{B}_1$ of G is indexed by the elements of S with entries

$$\mathbf{B}_{\mathbf{xz}} = \tau(\mathbf{x}, \mathbf{z}) = \tau_1(\mathbf{x}, \mathbf{z}).$$

∎

In general, the base similarity could be a simple method of comparing the objects with the only restriction that it must be symmetric. Furthermore, no assumption is made that it corresponds to a kernel, though if it is a kernel the method will deliver derived kernels. This would therefore allow us to create more complex kernels in a principled way.

Remark 9.31 [Finite domains] In general a base similarity over a finite domain could be specified by the similarity matrix $\mathbf{B}$. This is the most general way to specify it. Both the kernels defined in this section are introduced for finite domains and deal directly with the similarity matrix. However, for large (or infinite) domains we require a compact function that exploits some features of the data, to create a similarity between objects. We will see that the kernels introduced here can be extended in this way when we treat a specific application area in Chapter 10. We want to emphasise here that the kernels can be defined between elements of non-metric spaces as long as some base comparisons are available. ∎

Consider now the similarity $\tau_2(\mathbf{x}, \mathbf{z})$ obtained by summing the products of the weights on all paths of length 2 between two vertices $\mathbf{x}$ and $\mathbf{z}$

$$\tau_2\left(\mathbf{x}, \mathbf{z}\right) = \sum_{(\mathbf{x}_0 \mathbf{x}_1 \mathbf{x}_2) \in P_{\mathbf{xz}}^2} \prod_{i=1}^{2} \tau_1\left(\mathbf{x}_{i-1}, \mathbf{x}_i\right),$$

where we use $P_{\mathbf{xz}}^k$ to denote the set of paths of length k starting at $\mathbf{x}$ and finishing at $\mathbf{z}$.

Remark 9.32 [Paths as features] Notice that in this case we cannot view the paths as features, since the set of paths used in the sum depends on the arguments of the kernel function. This is in contrast to the fixed set of paths used for the graph kernels. We cannot therefore conclude that this is a kernel simply by considering sums and products of kernels.   ∎

Now consider how to compute the corresponding similarity matrix $\mathbf{B}_2$

$$\begin{aligned}
\tau_2\left(\mathbf{x}, \mathbf{z}\right) &= \left(\mathbf{B}_2\right)_{\mathbf{xz}} = \sum_{(\mathbf{x}_0 \mathbf{x}_1 \mathbf{x}_2) \in P_{\mathbf{xz}}^2} \prod_{i=1}^{2} \tau_1\left(\mathbf{x}_{i-1}, \mathbf{x}_i\right) \\
&= \sum_{(\mathbf{x}, \mathbf{x}_1) \in E} \tau_1\left(\mathbf{x}, \mathbf{x}_1\right) \tau_1\left(\mathbf{x}_1, \mathbf{z}\right) \\
&= \mathbf{B}_{\mathbf{xz}}^2.
\end{aligned}$$

Hence, the new similarity matrix is simply the square of the base similarity matrix. It now is immediately apparent that the resulting function τ_2 is indeed a kernel, since the square of a symmetric matrix is always positive semi-definite, as its eigenvectors remain unchanged but the corresponding eigenvalues are each squared.

If we want to determine the features of this kernel we rewrite the sum as

$$\begin{aligned}
\left(\mathbf{B}_2\right)_{\mathbf{xz}} &= \sum_{(\mathbf{x}, \mathbf{x}_1) \in E} \tau_1\left(\mathbf{x}, \mathbf{x}_1\right) \tau_1\left(\mathbf{x}_1, \mathbf{z}\right) = \sum_{i=1}^{\ell} \tau_1\left(\mathbf{x}, \mathbf{x}_i\right) \tau_1\left(\mathbf{x}_i, \mathbf{z}\right) \\
&= \left\langle \left(\tau_1\left(\mathbf{x}, \mathbf{x}_i\right)\right)_{i=1}^{\ell}, \left(\tau_1\left(\mathbf{z}, \mathbf{x}_i\right)\right)_{i=1}^{\ell} \right\rangle,
\end{aligned}$$

where we have assumed that the datapoints are given as

$$S = \{\mathbf{x}_1, \mathbf{x}_2, \ldots, \mathbf{x}_\ell\}.$$

Hence, the kernel corresponds to the projection into the space with features given by the evaluation of the base similarity with each of the examples

$$\phi : \mathbf{x} \longmapsto \left(\tau_1\left(\mathbf{x}, \mathbf{x}_i\right)\right)_{i=1}^{\ell}.$$

The intuition behind this construction is that we can enhance the base similarity by linking objects that share a number of 'common friends'. Hence we might consider taking a combination of the two matrices

$$\mathbf{B}_1 + \mathbf{B}_2.$$

We can similarly extend the consideration to paths of length k

$$\tau_k(\mathbf{x}, \mathbf{z}) = \sum_{(\mathbf{x}_0 \mathbf{x}_1 ... \mathbf{x}_k) \in P_{\mathbf{xz}}^k} \prod_{i=1}^k \tau_1(\mathbf{x}_{i-1}, \mathbf{x}_i).$$

A simple inductive argument shows that the corresponding similarity matrix $\mathbf{B}_k$ satisfies

$$\mathbf{B}_k = \mathbf{B}^k.$$

We would expect the relevance of longer paths to decay since linking objects through long paths might create erroneous measures of similarity. We can control the contribution of longer paths by introducing a decay factor λ into a general sum. For example if we choose

$$\mathbf{K} = \sum_{k=0}^{\infty} \frac{1}{k!} \lambda^k \mathbf{B}^k,$$

we can write

$$\mathbf{K} = \exp(\lambda \mathbf{B}),$$

leading to the following definition.

Definition 9.33 [Exponential diffusion kernel] We will refer to

$$\mathbf{K} = \exp(\lambda \mathbf{B})$$

as the *exponential diffusion kernel* of the base similarity measure $\mathbf{B}$. ∎

Definition 9.34 [von Neumann diffusion kernel] An alternative combination gives rise to the so-called *von Neumann diffusion kernel*

$$\mathbf{K} = \sum_{k=0}^{\infty} \lambda^k \mathbf{B}^k = (\mathbf{I} - \lambda \mathbf{B})^{-1},$$

which will only exist provided

$$\lambda < \|\mathbf{B}\|_2^{-1},$$

where $\|\mathbf{B}\|_2$ is the spectral radius of $\mathbf{B}$. ∎

Note that the justification that the diffusion kernels are indeed valid kernels is contained in Remark 9.36 below.

Computation 9.35 [Evaluating diffusion kernels] We can evaluate these kernels by performing an eigen-decomposition of $\mathbf{B}$, apply the corresponding function to the eigenvalues and remultiply the components back together. This follows from the fact that for any polynomial $p(x)$

$$p\left(\mathbf{V}'\boldsymbol{\Lambda}\mathbf{V}\right) = \mathbf{V}'p\left(\boldsymbol{\Lambda}\right)\mathbf{V},$$

for any orthonormal matrix $\mathbf{V}$ and diagonal matrix $\boldsymbol{\Lambda}$. This strategy works since $\mathbf{B}$ is symmetric and so can be expressed in the form

$$\mathbf{B} = \mathbf{V}'\boldsymbol{\Lambda}\mathbf{V},$$

where $\boldsymbol{\Lambda}$ contains its real eigenvalues.   ∎

Remark 9.36 [Eigenvalues and relation to kernel PCA] The computation also re-emphasises the point that all of the kernels have the same eigenvectors as $\mathbf{B}$: they simply apply a reweighting to the eigenvalues. Note that using the diffusion construction when the base similarity measure is a kernel can therefore be viewed as a soft version of kernel PCA. PCA applies a threshold function to the eigenvalues, setting those smaller than λ_k to zero. In contrast the diffusion kernels apply a function to each eigenvalue: $(1 - \mu\lambda)^{-1}$ for the von Neumann kernel and $\exp(\mu\lambda)$ for the exponential kernel, that increases the relative weight of the larger eigenvalues when compared to the smaller ones. The fact that the functions $(1 - \mu\lambda)^{-1}$ and $\exp(\mu\lambda)$ have positive values for λ in the indicated range ensures that the kernel matrices are indeed positive semi-definite.   ∎

We will further explore these kernels in applications to textual data in Chapter 10.

9.5 Kernels on sets

As another example of a non-vectorial space consider the set of subsets $\mathcal{P}(D)$ of a fixed domain D, a set sometimes referred to as the *power set* of D. The elements of the input space are therefore sets. They could include all the subsets of D or some subselection of the whole power set

$$X \subseteq \mathcal{P}(D).$$

Consider now two elements A_1 and A_2 of X, that is two subsets of the domain D. In Chapter 2 we gave one example of a kernel $\kappa(A_1, A_2)$ on such subsets of D defined as

$$\kappa\left(A_1, A_2\right) = 2^{|A_1 \cap A_2|}.$$

In this section we will extend the range of available kernels.

Suppose that D is equipped with a measure or probability density function μ. If D is finite this is simply a mapping from D to the positive reals. For infinite D there are technical details involving a σ-algebra of subsets known as the measurable sets. We must assume that the sets included in X are all measurable. In either case μ defines an integration over the set D

$$\mu\left(f\right) = \int_D f\left(a\right) d\mu\left(a\right),$$

for so-called measurable functions. In particular the indicator function I_A of a measurable set A defines the measure (or probability) of the set by

$$\mu\left(A\right) = \mu\left(I_A\right) \in \mathbb{R}^+.$$

Definition 9.37 [Intersection kernel] We now define the *intersection kernel* over the subsets of D by

$$\kappa_\cap\left(A_1, A_2\right) = \mu\left(A_1 \cap A_2\right),$$

that is, the measure of the intersection between the two sets. ∎

This can be seen to be a valid kernel by considering the feature space of all measurable functions with the inner product defined by

$$\langle f_1, f_2 \rangle = \int_D f_1\left(a\right) f_2\left(a\right) d\mu\left(a\right).$$

The feature mapping is now given by

$$\phi : A \longmapsto I_A,$$

implying that

$$\begin{aligned}
\kappa_\cap\left(A_1, A_2\right) &= \mu\left(A_1 \cap A_2\right) = \int_D I_{A_1 \cap A_2}\left(a\right) d\mu\left(a\right) \\
&= \int_D I_{A_1}\left(a\right) I_{A_2}\left(a\right) d\mu\left(a\right) = \langle I_{A_1}, I_{A_2} \rangle \\
&= \langle \phi\left(A_1\right), \phi\left(A_2\right) \rangle,
\end{aligned}$$

as required. This construction also makes clear that we could have mapped to the indicator function of the complementary set provided the measure of this set is finite.

Definition 9.38 [Union complement kernel] Assuming that $\mu(D) = 1$, we have the *union complement kernel*

$$\tilde{\kappa}(A_1, A_2) = \mu((D \setminus A_1) \cap (D \setminus A_2)) = 1 - \mu(A_1 \cup A_2).$$

∎

There are many cases in which we may want to represent data items as sets. There is also the potential for an interesting duality, since we represent an object by the items it contains, while the items themselves can also be described by the set of objects they are contained in. This duality will be exploited in the case of kernels for text briefly discussed here but covered in detail in Chapter 10.

Example 9.39 Consider a document as a set of words from a dictionary D. The similarity between two documents d_1 and d_2 will then be the measure of the intersection between those two sets. The importance of a word can also be encoded in a distribution over D weighting the calculation of the measure of the intersection. As mentioned above we can also compare words by defining a function over documents indicating in which documents they appear. This induces a duality between term-based and document-based representations that can be exploited in many ways. This duality corresponds to the duality implied by kernel-based representations, and hence when using this kind of data there is an interesting interpretation of dual features that will be explored further in Chapter 10. ∎

Remark 9.40 [Agreement kernel] We can sum the two kernels $\kappa_\cap$ and $\tilde{\kappa}$ described above to obtain the kernel

$$\begin{aligned}
\kappa(A_1, A_2) &= \tilde{\kappa}(A_1, A_2) + \kappa_\cap(A_1, A_2) \\
&= 1 - \mu(A_1 \cup A_2) + \mu(A_1 \cap A_2) \\
&= 1 - \mu(A_1 \setminus A_2) - \mu(A_2 \setminus A_1),
\end{aligned}$$

that is, the measure of the points on which the two indicator functions agree. If we used indicator functions I_A^- which mapped elements not in the set to -1, then, after introducing a factor of $1/2$, this would give rise to the kernel

$$\begin{aligned}
\hat{\kappa}(A_1, A_2) &= \frac{1}{2}\left\langle I_{A_1}^-, I_{A_2}^- \right\rangle \\
&= \frac{1}{2}(\kappa(A_1, A_2) - \mu(A_1 \setminus A_2) - \mu(A_2 \setminus A_1)) \\
&= \frac{1}{2} - \mu(A_1 \setminus A_2) - \mu(A_2 \setminus A_1).
\end{aligned}$$

The second kernel is simply the first minus $1/2$. This will be a better starting point since it leaves more options open – we can always add $1/2$ as this is equivalent to adding an extra feature with constant value $\sqrt{1/2}$, but in general we cannot subtract a constant from the kernel matrix. ∎

Derived subsets kernel Our final example of defining kernels over sets considers the case where we already have a kernel κ_0 defined on the elements of a universal set U.

Definition 9.41 [Derived subsets kernel] Given a base kernel κ_0 on a set U, we define the *subset kernel* derived from κ_0 between finite subsets A and B of U by

$$\kappa(A, B) = \sum_{a \in A} \sum_{b \in B} \kappa_0(a, b).$$

∎

The following proposition verifies that a derived subsets kernel is indeed a kernel.

Proposition 9.42 *Given a kernel κ_0 on a set U the derived subsets kernel κ is an inner product in an appropriately defined feature space and hence is a kernel.*

Proof Let ϕ_0 be an embedding function into a feature space F_0 for the kernel κ_0 so that

$$\kappa_0(a, b) = \langle \phi_0(a), \phi_0(b) \rangle.$$

Consider the embedding function for a finite subset $A \subseteq U$ defined by

$$\phi(A) = \sum_{a \in A} \phi_0(a) \in F_0.$$

We have

$$\kappa(a, b) = \sum_{a \in A} \sum_{b \in B} \kappa_0(a, b) = \sum_{a \in A} \sum_{b \in B} \langle \phi_0(a), \phi_0(b) \rangle$$

$$= \left\langle \sum_{a \in A} \phi_0(a), \sum_{b \in B} \phi_0(b) \right\rangle = \langle \phi(A), \phi(B) \rangle,$$

as required. □

Example 9.43 Another application of the derived subsets kernel idea is in allowing deformed matches in normal kernels. This can be useful when we want to introduce specific invariances into the kernel design. Suppose we are computing the kernel between the images $\mathbf{x}, \mathbf{z} \in X$ of two handwritten characters. We know that the two arguments should be considered equivalent if slight transformations of the images are applied, such as small rotations, translations, thickenings and even the addition of some noise. Suppose we devise a function

$$\phi : X \to \mathcal{P}(X)$$

that expands the argument to a set of arguments that are all equivalent to it, hence introducing a 'jittering' effect. The similarity of two images $\mathbf{x}$ and $\mathbf{z}$ can now be measured in $\mathcal{P}(X)$ between the sets of images $\phi(\mathbf{x})$ and $\phi(\mathbf{z})$ using the derived subsets kernel for a base kernel for comparing images. ∎

9.6 Kernels on real numbers

There is an interesting application of the intersection kernel that defines further kernels for real numbers. This can in turn be combined with the ANOVA kernel construction to obtain new kernels between vectors. Let us first consider real numbers $x, z \in \mathbb{R}$. The simplest and most obvious kernel is of course

$$\kappa(x, z) = xz,$$

though we can equally use the polynomial or Gaussian kernel construction in one-dimension to obtain for example

$$\kappa(x, z) = \exp\left(-\frac{(x - z)^2}{2\sigma^2}\right).$$

Now consider representing $x \in \mathbb{R}^+$ by the interval $[0, x]$, that is the set $\{y : 0 \le y \le x\}$. Applying an intersection kernel with the standard integration measure we obtain

$$\kappa(x, z) = \min(x, z). \tag{9.9}$$

Hence, normalising we obtain that

$$\kappa(x, z) = \frac{\min(x, z)}{\sqrt{\min(x, x)\min(z, z)}} = \frac{\min(x, z)}{\sqrt{xz}}$$

is a kernel. Similarly representing $x \in \mathbb{R}^+$ by the interval $[0, x^{-p}]$ for some $p > 0$ and applying the intersection construction, we obtain that

$$\kappa(x, z) = \frac{1}{\max(x, z)^p}$$

is a kernel, which when normalised gives the kernel

$$\kappa(x, z) = \frac{(xz)^{p/2}}{\max(x, z)^p}.$$

For $p = 1$ we have

$$\kappa(x, z) = \frac{\sqrt{xz}}{\max(x, z)}, \tag{9.10}$$

while for $p = 2$ we get an interesting variant of the standard inner product

$$\kappa(x, z) = \frac{xz}{\max(x, z)^2}.$$

If there is an upper bound C on the value of x we can map to the interval $[x, C]$ to obtain the kernel

$$\kappa(x, z) = C - \max(x, z).$$

Furthermore we are not restricted to using 1-dimensional sets. For example mapping $x \in \mathbb{R}^+$ to the rectangle

$$[0, x] \times [0, x^{-1}],$$

results in an intersection kernel

$$\kappa(x, z) = \frac{\min(x, z)}{\max(x, z)}.$$

Of course the 2-dimensional construction is more natural for two-dimensional vectors and gives kernels such as

$$\kappa((x_1, x_2), (z_1, z_2)) = \min(x_1, z_1) \min(x_2, z_2)$$

and

$$\kappa((x_1, x_2), (z_1, z_2)) = \frac{\sqrt{x_1 x_2 z_1 z_2}}{\max(x_1, z_1) \max(x_2, z_2)}.$$

Actually these last two kernels could have been obtained by applying the generalised ANOVA construction of degree 2 (see Remark 9.20) using the base kernels given in equations (9.9) and (9.10) respectively.

Finally consider mapping $z \in \mathbb{R}$ to the function $g(|\cdot - z|) \in L_2(\mu)$ for some fixed g and defining the inner product via the integration

$$\kappa(z_1, z_2) = \int g(|x - z_1|) g(|x - z_2|) d\mu(x).$$

This is clearly a kernel since the image of z is a point in the corresponding Hilbert space. Taking μ to be the standard measure, the choice of the function g could be a Gaussian to give a soft comparison of two numbers or for example a threshold function

$$g(x) = \begin{cases} 1 & \text{if } x \leq C; \\ 0 & \text{otherwise.} \end{cases}$$

This results in the kernel

$$\kappa(z_1, z_2) = \max(0, 2C - |z_1 - z_2|). \tag{9.11}$$

Remark 9.44 [Distance induced by min kernel] The distance induced by the 'min' kernel of equation (9.9) is

$$\begin{aligned} \|\phi(x) - \phi(z)\|^2 &= x + z - 2\min(x, z) \\ &= \max(x, z) - \min(x, z) = |x - z|, \end{aligned}$$

as opposed to the normal Euclidean distance induced by the standard kernel xz. ∎

Remark 9.45 [Spline kernels] Notice that we can put together the ideas of the generalised ANOVA construction of Remark 9.20 with the the 'min' kernel

$$\kappa(x, z) = \min(x, z)$$

to obtain the so-called spline kernels for multi-dimensional data. ∎

9.7 Randomised kernels

There are cases of kernels where the feature space is explicitly constructed by a vector

$$\phi(\mathbf{x}) = (\phi_i(\mathbf{x}))_{i \in I},$$

and each of the individual $\phi_i(\mathbf{x})$ are simple to compute, but the size of the set I makes complete evaluation of the feature vector prohibitively expensive. If the feature space inner product is given by

$$\kappa(\mathbf{x}, \mathbf{z}) = \langle (\phi_i(\mathbf{x}))_{i \in I}, (\phi_i(\mathbf{z}))_{i \in I} \rangle = \sum_{i \in I} \mu_i \phi_i(\mathbf{x}) \phi_i(\mathbf{z}),$$

with $\sum_i \mu_i = 1$ then we can estimate the value of the inner product by sampling indices according to μ and forming an empirical estimate of the inner product through an average of N randomly drawn features

$$\hat{\kappa}(\mathbf{x}, \mathbf{z}) = \frac{1}{N} \sum_{i \sim \mu} \phi_i(\mathbf{x}) \phi_i(\mathbf{z}).$$

We can bound the maximal deviation that can be caused by changing a single feature by $2c/N$ where $[-c, c]$ is a bound on the range of the functions ϕ_i. Applying McDiarmid's Theorem 4.5 we obtain

$$P\{\hat{\kappa}(\mathbf{x}, \mathbf{z}) - \mathbb{E}\hat{\kappa}(\mathbf{x}, \mathbf{z}) \geq \epsilon\} \leq \exp\left(\frac{-2\epsilon^2}{\sum_{i=1}^N 4c^2/N^2}\right) = \exp\left(\frac{-N\epsilon^2}{2c^2}\right).$$

Observing that $\mathbb{E}\hat{\kappa}(\mathbf{x}, \mathbf{z}) = \kappa(\mathbf{x}, \mathbf{z})$ and that the same argument can be applied to $-\hat{\kappa}(\mathbf{x}, \mathbf{z})$ gives

$$P\{|\hat{\kappa}(\mathbf{x}, \mathbf{z}) - \kappa(\mathbf{x}, \mathbf{z})| \geq \epsilon\} \leq 2\exp\left(\frac{-N\epsilon^2}{2c^2}\right).$$

Hence, with high probability we obtain a good estimate of the true kernel evaluation even using only a modest number of features. If for example we require that with probability at least $1 - \delta$ all of the entries in an $\ell \times \ell$ kernel matrix are within ϵ of their true values, we should choose N so that

$$2\exp\left(\frac{-N\epsilon^2}{2c^2}\right) \leq \frac{2\delta}{\ell(\ell+1)},$$

implying that

$$N \geq \frac{2c^2}{\epsilon^2} \ln \frac{\ell(\ell+1)}{\delta}.$$

This leads to the following computation.

Computation 9.46 [Evaluating randomised kernels] With probability at least $1 - \delta$ we can estimate all the entries of the kernel matrix of a randomised kernel to accuracy ϵ by sampling

$$N \geq \frac{2c^2}{\epsilon^2} \ln \frac{\ell(\ell+1)}{\delta}$$

features ϕ_k and setting

$$\hat{\kappa}(\mathbf{x}_i, \mathbf{x}_j) = \frac{1}{N} \sum_{k=1}^N \phi_k(\mathbf{x}_i) \phi_k(\mathbf{x}_j),$$

for $i, j = 1, \ldots, \ell$, where the range of the features is bounded in $[-c, c]$. ∎

Remark 9.47 [Sampling intersection kernels] One example where this could arise is in kernels defined in terms of intersection of sets

$$\kappa_\cap(A_1, A_2) = \mu(A_1 \cap A_2).$$

The features here are the elements of the domain D. If the structure of the sets makes it difficult to integrate the measure over their intersection, we may be able to use the randomisation approach. This is equivalent to estimating the integral

$$\mu\left(A_1 \cap A_2\right) = \int_D I_{A_1 \cap A_2}\left(a\right) d\mu\left(a\right)$$

via a Monte Carlo random sampling. Hence, if we can efficiently generate random examples according to μ, we can apply the randomisation approach. An example where this might be relevant is for a kernel between boolean functions. Estimating when a boolean function has any satisfying assignment becomes NP-hard even if, for example, we restrict the structure of the function to a disjunctive normal form with 3 literals per clause. Hence, an exact evaluation of the integral would be computationally infeasible. We can, however, sample binary vectors and check if they satisfy both functions. Note that such a kernel would be needed in an application where the examples were boolean functions and we were looking for patterns among them.

■

9.8 Other kernel types

This section concludes this chapter's overview of methods for designing kernels by outlining the three kernel types to be presented in the last three chapters of the book. Although they will be discussed in detail later, it is worth placing them in the context of the current survey to furnish a fuller picture of the diversity of data and techniques available.

9.8.1 Kernels from successive embeddings

We saw in Chapter 3 that the class of kernel functions satisfies a series of closure properties. Furthermore, we saw that as long as we can show the existence of an embedding function ϕ such that

$$\kappa\left(\mathbf{x}, \mathbf{z}\right) = \langle \phi\left(\mathbf{x}\right), \phi\left(\mathbf{z}\right)\rangle$$

then we know that κ is a kernel, even if we are not able either computationally or explicitly to construct ϕ. These two facts open up the possibility of defining kernels by successive adjustments, either performing successive embeddings or manipulating the given kernel function (or matrix). In this way we can sculpt the feature space for the particular application.

We must exploit knowledge of the domain by designing a series of simple embeddings each of which could for example introduce some invariance into the embedding by ensuring that all transformations of an example under a particular invariance are mapped to the same image. Any classifier using the resulting kernel will be invariant to that transformation. Note also that further embeddings cannot undo this invariance. Hence, the final kernel will exhibit invariance to all of the transformations considered.

The overall kernel resulting from a sequence of such embeddings is by definition a valid kernel, although we might not be able to explicitly construct its features. The proof of validity follows the stages of its construction by composing the sequence of successive embeddings to create the embedding corresponding to the overall kernel

$$\phi(\mathbf{x}) = \psi_1(\mathbf{x}) \circ \psi_2(\mathbf{x}) \circ \cdots \circ \psi_n(\mathbf{x}).$$

Figure 9.4 illustrates this point with a sequence of two embeddings progressively increasing the separation of the datapoints associated with the two classes of a classification problem.

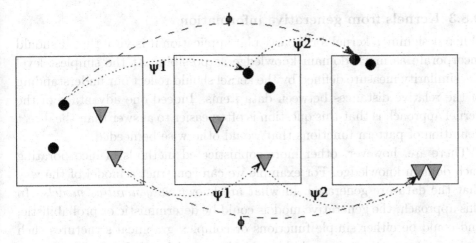

Fig. 9.4. A sequence of two embeddings can be composed to create an overall embedding with desirable properties.

Example 9.48 In Chapter 10 we will see this approach applied in the case of text documents, where we can successively embed a document to gradually take care of synonymy, semantics, stop words, removal of document length information, and so on. Each of these properties is realised by composing with an additional embedding function and can be seen as implementing an invariance. A similar approach may well be applicable in other domains such as, for example, machine vision. ∎

9.8.2 Kernels over general structures

In Remark 9.20 we saw how the ANOVA construction could be used to define a kernel in a recursive fashion, provided a set of base kernels was available. This situation is not uncommon in recursively-defined data structures, such as strings and trees. For example, comparing two symbols in the sequence provides a base kernel for the case of strings. We will show how this can be used to recursively build a kernel between sequences of symbols, hence enabling pattern analysis of documents, DNA sequences, etc.

This approach makes it possible to build general kernels defined over structured data objects, provided we have a way to compare the elementary components of such structures. Typically the method of combination corresponds to a recursive computation. The approach is not restricted to strings or mathematical structures such as trees or graphs, but can be applied to complex objects that arise in particular application domains such as web pages, chemometrics, and so on.

9.8.3 Kernels from generative information

When designing a kernel for a particular application it is vital that it should incorporate as much domain knowledge as possible. At the simplest level the similarity measure defined by the kernel should reflect our understanding of the relative distances between data items. Indeed one advantage of the kernel approach is that this question is often easier to answer than the direct definition of pattern functions that would otherwise be needed.

There are, however, other more sophisticated methods of incorporating such domain knowledge. For example we can construct a model of the way that the data are generated, in what are known as *generative models*. In this approach, the generative models could be deterministic or probabilistic, and could be either simple functions or complex graphical structures such as finite state automata or hidden Markov models (HMMs). In Chapter 12 we will explore methods for converting these models of the data into kernel functions, hence developing several frameworks for incorporating prior knowledge in a principled way including the well-known Fisher kernels.

9.9 Summary

- Many kernels can be computed in closed form including the polynomial and Gaussian kernels.
- Many kernels can be defined using recursive relations including the polynomial kernel, the all-subsets kernel and the ANOVA kernel.

- Graph kernels generalise the family of recursively-defined kernels allowing more detailed sculpting of which features are to be included.

- Kernels over graph nodes can be defined in terms of diffusion processes starting from a general base similarity measure.

- Simple kernels can be defined based on fundamental set operations.

- Sampling can enable accurate estimation of kernels whose feature set prohibits efficient exact evaluation.

9.10 Further reading and advanced topics

In the early years of research on kernel methods only functions in closed form were considered. The introduction of ANOVA kernels gave the first example of kernels defined by means of a recursive relation, which could be efficiently evaluated using dynamic programming. That in turn triggered the observation that other kernels could be defined in terms of recursive relations, or even in terms of very general computational procedures. At the same time, the idea that kernels need to be defined on vectorial inputs was been recognised as unnecessarily restrictive. From 1999 the first kernels between strings defined by means of recursions started to appear [158], [157], [54]. After those first contributions, a flood of different approaches have been proposed, the main ones are summarised in this chapter with more detailed presentations of many of them deferred to Chapter 11. More recently it has been recognised that one does not even need to have a kernel function at all, just a kernel matrix for the available data. This has led to optimisation procedures for directly inferring the kernel matrix, which are not discussed here.

Gaussian and polynomial kernels were already discussed in the first paper on support vector machines [16]. Gaussian kernels in particular have been investigated for a long time within the literature on reproducing kernel Hilbert spaces [156]. ANOVA kernels were first suggested by Burges and Vapnik (under the name of Gabor kernels) in 1995 [21] in the form described in Computation 9.18. The recursion described in Algorithm 9.14 was proposed by Chris Watkins in 1999 [157]. The paper of Takimoto and Warmuth [132] introduces the 'all subsets kernel' as well as the idea of kernels based on paths in a graph.

These regular language kernels are related to the rational kernels proposed in [26].

Diffusion kernels were proposed by Imre Kondor in [82], while von Neumann kernels were introduced in [71]. The bag-of-words kernels were proposed by Thorsten Joachims [67] and can be considered as an example of kernels between sets.

The discussion of kernels over sets or between numbers is largely a collection of folk results, but strongly influenced by discussions with Chris Watkins.

Kernels over general structures were simultaneouly elaborated by Watkins and by Haussler [158], [157], [54] and will be discussed in further detail in Chapter 11.

Kernels based on data compression ideas from information theory have been proposed [36] and form yet another approach for defining similarity measures satisfying the finitely positive semi-definite property. Kernels defined on sets of points have also been recently explored in [65], while an interesting approach for graph kernels has been proposed by [75].

For constantly updated pointers to online literature and free software see the book's companion website: www.kernel-methods.net.

10

Kernels for text

The last decade has seen an explosion of readily available digital text that has rendered attempts to analyse and classify by hand infeasible. As a result automatic processing of natural language text documents has become a main research interest of Artificial Intelligence (AI) and computer science in general. It is probably fair to say that after multivariate data, natural language text is the most important data format for applications. Its particular characteristics therefore deserve specific attention.

We will see how well-known techniques from Information Retrieval (IR), such as the rich class of vector space models, can be naturally reinterpreted as kernel methods. This new perspective enriches our understanding of the approach, as well as leading naturally to further extensions and improvements. The approach that this perspective suggests is based on detecting and exploiting statistical patterns of words in the documents. An important property of the vector space representation is that the primal–dual dialectic we have developed through this book has an interesting counterpart in the interplay between term-based and document-based representations.

The goal of this chapter is to introduce the Vector Space family of kernel methods highlighting their construction and the primal–dual dichotomy that they illustrate. Other kernel constructions can be applied to text, for example using probabilistic generative models and string matching, but since these kernels are not specific to natural language text, they will be discussed separately in Chapters 11 and 12.

10.1 From bag of words to semantic space

Although the task of automatically analysing the meaning of a document falls under the heading of natural language processing, it was the IR community that developed the relatively simple representation that is today most commonly used to assess the topic of a document. This representation is known as the vector space model (VSM) or the 'bag-of-words' approach. It is this technique that forms the basis of the kernels developed in this chapter. As mentioned above, other representations of text are certainly possible including those relying on a string level analysis or on probabilistic models. These approaches will be mentioned as special cases in later chapters that are mainly concerned with other data formats.

One of the aims of this chapter is to show that by using the VSM to create kernels, it is possible to extend its applicability beyond IR to the full range of tasks that can be solved using the kernel approach, including correlation analysis, novelty-detection, classification, ranking, clustering and so on. Some of these tasks reappear with different names in the context of document analysis. For example document classification is often referred to as *categorisation*, on-line classification as *filtering*, while novelty detection is known as *new topic detection*.

10.1.1 Representing text

The simplest possible version of the VSM is the representation of a document as a *bag-of-words*. A bag is a set in which repeated elements are allowed, so that not only the presence of a word but also its frequency is taken into account. Hence, a document is represented by the words it contains, with the ordering of the words and punctuation being ignored. This implies that some grammatical information is lost, since there is no representation of the word ordering. This furthermore implies that phrases are also broken into their constituent words and hence the meaning of a phrase such as 'bread winner' is lost. We begin with some definitions.

Definition 10.1 [Vector space model] *Words* are any sequence of letters from the basic alphabet separated by punctuation or spaces. We use *term* synonymously with word. A dictionary can be defined by some permanent predefined set of terms, but in practice we only need to consider those words actually appearing in the documents being processed. We refer to this full set of documents as the *corpus* and the set of terms occurring in the corpus as the *dictionary*. Hence, we can view a document as a bag of terms or *bag-of-words*. We can represent a bag as a vector in a space in which each dimension is associated with one term from the dictionary

$$\phi : d \longmapsto \phi(d) = (\text{tf}(t_1, d), \text{tf}(t_2, d), \ldots, \text{tf}(t_N, d)) \in \mathbb{R}^N,$$

where $\text{tf}(t_i, d)$ is the frequency of the term t_i in the document d. Hence, a document is mapped into a space of dimensionality N being the size of the dictionary, typically a very large number. ∎

Despite the high-dimensionality of the dictionary, the vector associated with a given document is sparse, i.e. has most of its entries equal to 0, since it will contain only very few of the vast number of possible words.

Definition 10.2 [Document–term matrix] The document–term matrix of a corpus is the matrix whose rows are indexed by the documents of the corpus and whose columns are indexed by the terms. The (i, j)th entry gives the frequency of term t_j in document d_i

$$\mathbf{D} = \begin{pmatrix} \text{tf}(t_1, d_1) & \cdots & \text{tf}(t_N, d_1) \\ \vdots & \ddots & \vdots \\ \text{tf}(t_1, d_\ell) & \cdots & \text{tf}(t_N, d_\ell) \end{pmatrix}.$$

The term–document matrix is the transpose $\mathbf{D}'$ of the document–term matrix. The term-by-term matrix is given by $\mathbf{D}'\mathbf{D}$ while the document-by-document matrix is $\mathbf{D}\mathbf{D}'$. ∎

Note that the document–term matrix is simply the data matrix $\mathbf{X}$ we have used consistently throughout this book. Hence, the term-by-term matrix is ℓ times the covariance matrix, while the document-by-document matrix is the corresponding kernel matrix.

Remark 10.3 [Interpreting duality] An interesting feature of the VSM will be an additional interpretation of the duality between representations of kernel algorithms. Here the dual representation corresponds to a document view of the problem, while the primal description provides a term view. In the same way that a document can be seen as the counts of the terms that appear in it, a term can be regarded as the counts of the documents in which it appears. These two views are represented by the rows of a document–term matrix with the rows of its transpose giving the representation of terms. ∎

Since it is often the case that the corpus size is less than the number of terms or dictionary size, it is sometimes useful to compute in a document-based or dual representation, whereas for intuitive and interpretational purposes it is usually better to work in the term-based or primal representation.

We can exploit the power of duality in kernel methods by stating the problem in the intuitive term representation, and then dualising it to provide a document-based implementation.

10.1.2 Semantic issues

The representation of documents provided by the VSM ignores any semantic relation between words. One important issue is to improve the vector space representation to ensure that documents containing semantically equivalent words are mapped to similar feature vectors.

For example synonymous words give two ways of saying the same thing, but are assigned distinct components. Hence, the VSM despite retaining enough information to take account of this similarity, is unable to do so without extra processing. We will present a range of methods that aim to address this and related problems.

On the other hand, the case of homonymy when a single word has two distinct meanings is an example that the VSM will be less able to handle since it has thrown away the contextual information that could disambiguate the meaning. Despite this, some context can be derived from the statistics of the words in the document. We begin, however, by mentioning two simpler operations that can improve the quality of the embedding.

The first is to apply different weights w_i to each coordinate or equivalently to give varying weights to the terms. Perhaps the simplest example of this is the removal of uninformative terms such as 'and', 'of', 'the', and so on. This is equivalent to assigning a weight of 0 to these coordinates. This technique was pioneered in the IR literature, where such words are referred to as *stop words*, with the complete set known as the *stop list*. We consider more general weighting schemes in the next section.

The second effect that can cause problems is the influence of the length of a document. Clearly, the longer a document the more words it contains and hence, the greater the norm of its associated vector. If the length of the document is not relevant for the tasks we are trying to solve, for example categorisation by topic, it makes sense to remove this effect by normalising the embedding vectors. Using the technique developed in Chapter 5 and given in (5.1), we define a kernel that discards this information as follows

$$\hat{\kappa}(\mathbf{x}, \mathbf{y}) = \left\langle \frac{\phi(\mathbf{x})}{\|\phi(\mathbf{x})\|}, \frac{\phi(\mathbf{y})}{\|\phi(\mathbf{y})\|} \right\rangle = \frac{\kappa(\mathbf{x}, \mathbf{y})}{\sqrt{\kappa(\mathbf{x}, \mathbf{x})\kappa(\mathbf{y}, \mathbf{y})}}.$$

Typically the normalisation is implemented as either the first transformation or as the final embedding. We will not consider the normalisation for each of the different semantic embeddings but assume that when required it is included as a final stage.

Remark 10.4 [On successive embeddings] The operations can be performed in sequence, creating a series of successive embeddings, each of which adds some additional refinement to the semantics of the representation, for example term weighting followed by normalisation. This chapter will describe a number of operations designed to refine the semantic quality of the representation. Any of these refinements can be included in a sequence. As described in the last chapter, if we compose these successive embeddings we create a single map that incorporates different aspects of domain knowledge into the representation. ∎

10.2 Vector space kernels

Given a document, we have seen how it can be represented by a row vector

$$\phi(d) = (\text{tf}(t_1, d), \text{tf}(t_2, d), \dots, \text{tf}(t_N, d)) \in \mathbb{R}^N,$$

in which each entry records how many times a particular term is used in the document. Typically $\phi(d)$ can have tens of thousands of entries, often more than the number of training examples. Nonetheless, for a particular document the representation is extremely sparse, having only relatively few non-zero entries. This preliminary embedding can then be refined by successive operations that we will examine later in the chapter.

As indicated in Definition 10.2 we can create a document–term matrix $\mathbf{D}$ whose rows are the vectors associated with the documents of the corpus. It is common in IR to work with the transpose or term–document matrix $\mathbf{D}'$, but we have chosen to maintain consistency with our use in earlier chapters of the matrix $\mathbf{X}$, whose rows are the feature vectors of the training examples. Hence, there is a direct correspondence between $\mathbf{X}$ and $\mathbf{D}$ where features become terms and examples become documents.

Definition 10.5 [Vector space kernel] Within the VSM we can create a kernel matrix as

$$\mathbf{K} = \mathbf{DD}'$$

corresponding to the *vector space kernel*

$$\kappa(d_1, d_2) = \langle \phi(d_1), \phi(d_2) \rangle = \sum_{j=1}^{N} \text{tf}(t_j, d_1) \, \text{tf}(t_j, d_2).$$

∎

Cost of the computation In order to compute the kernel κ we must first convert the document into a list of the terms that they contain. This process is known as *tokenisation*. It has been a fundamental processing technique of computer science since the design of the first compilers. Each term encountered in the corpus is assigned its own unique number. This ensures that the list of terms in a document can be reordered into ascending term order together with an associated frequency count. In this way the document is converted into a list $L(d)$ rather than the impractically long explicit vector $\phi(d)$. It is now a relatively simple and efficient task to compute

$$\kappa(d_1, d_2) = A(L(d_1), L(d_2)),$$

using the lists $L(d_1)$ and $L(d_2)$ as inputs, where the algorithm $A(\cdot, \cdot)$ traverses the lists, computing products of frequencies whenever the term numbers match. In summary, the computation of the kernel does not involve explicit evaluation of the feature vectors $\phi(d)$, but uses an intermediate representation of a list $L(d)$ of terms. Hence, although we are working in a space that is typically of very high dimension, the computation of the projections and subsequent inner product evaluation can be implemented in a time proportional to the sum of the lengths of the two documents

$$O(|d_1| + |d_2|).$$

We should contrast this approach with systems that require explicit weights to be maintained for each component.

Remark 10.6 [Nonlinear embeddings] Throughout this chapter we will restrict ourselves to considering linear transformations of the basic VSM, always laying emphasis on the power of capturing important domain knowledge. However, it is of course possible to consider nonlinear embeddings using standard kernel constructions. For example a polynomial kernel over the normalised bag-of-words representation

$$\bar{\kappa}(d_1, d_2) = (\kappa(d_1, d_2) + 1)^d = (\langle \phi(d_1), \phi(d_2) \rangle + 1)^d,$$

uses all n-tuples of words for $0 \leq n \leq d$ as features. The same approach can be used for any of the vector space kernels using polynomial kernels or other kernel constructions such as the Gaussian kernel. ∎

10.2.1 Designing semantic kernels

As indicated above the bag-of-words representation has many shortcomings, partly the neglecting of the word order but also of the semantic content of the words themselves. In order to address this second omission, we will consider transformations of the document vectors $\phi(d)$. The VSM considers only the simplest case of linear transformations of the type $\tilde{\phi}(d) = \phi(d)\,\mathbf{S}$, where $\mathbf{S}$ is a matrix that could be diagonal, square or, in general, any $N \times k$ matrix. Using this transformation the corresponding kernel takes the form

$$\tilde{\kappa}(d_1, d_2) = \phi(d_1)\,\mathbf{SS}'\phi(d_2)' = \tilde{\phi}(d_1)\,\tilde{\phi}(d_2)'.$$

That this is a kernel follows directly from the explicit construction of a feature vector. We refer to $\mathbf{S}$ as the *semantic matrix*. Different choices of the matrix $\mathbf{S}$ lead to different variants of the VSMs. As indicated in Remark 10.4 we will often create $\mathbf{S}$ as a composition of several stages. We will examine some of these in the coming subsections. Hence, we might define

$$\mathbf{S} = \mathbf{RP},$$

where $\mathbf{R}$ is a diagonal matrix giving the term weightings or relevances, while $\mathbf{P}$ is a *proximity* matrix defining the semantic spreading between the different terms of the corpus.

Term weighting As mentioned in the previous section not all words have the same importance in establishing the topic of a document. Indeed, in IR the so-called stop words are removed before the analysis starts. The entropy or the frequency of a word across the documents in a corpus can be used to quantify the amount of information carried by a word. This is an 'absolute' measure in the sense that it takes no account of particular topics or tasks. For categorisation one could also define a relative measure of the importance of a word with respect to the given topic, such as the mutual information. Here we consider an absolute measure known as *idf* that weights terms as a function of their *inverse document frequency*. Suppose that there are ℓ documents in the corpus and let df (t) be the number of documents containing the term t. The usual measure of inverse document frequency for a term t is then given by

$$w(t) = \ln\left(\frac{\ell}{\mathrm{df}(t)}\right).$$

Implicit in this weighting is the possibility of stop words, since if a term is contained in every document then df $(t) = \ell$ and $w(t) = 0$, effectively excluding the term from the dictionary and hence reducing the dimensionality of the feature space. For efficiency reasons it is still preferable to create an explicit stop list of terms that should a priori be excluded from the features.

The use of the logarithmic function ensures that none of the weights can become too large relative to the weight of a term that occurs in roughly half of the documents. This is occasionally further controlled by removing words that occur in fewer than one or two documents, since they are viewed as too exceptional to be of use in analysing future documents.

Given a term weighting $w(t)$ whether defined by the *idf* rule or some alternative scheme, we can now define a new VSM by choosing the matrix $\mathbf{R}$ to be diagonal with entries

$$\mathbf{R}_{tt} = w(t).$$

The associated kernel simply computes the inner product

$$\tilde{\kappa}(d_1, d_2) = \phi(d_1)\,\mathbf{R}\mathbf{R}'\phi(d_2)' = \sum_t w(t)^2\,\mathrm{tf}(t, d_1)\,\mathrm{tf}(t, d_2),$$

again clearly implementable by a weighted version A_w of the algorithm A:

$$\tilde{\kappa}(d_1, d_2) = A_w(L(d_1), L(d_2)).$$

The evaluation of this kernel involves both term frequencies and inverse document frequencies. It is therefore often referred to as the *tf–idf* representation. Since these measures do not use label information, they could also be estimated from an external, larger unlabelled corpus that provides background knowledge for the system.

Term proximity matrix The *tf–idf* representation implements a down-weighting of irrelevant terms as well as highlighting potentially discriminative ones, but nonetheless is still not capable of recognising when two terms are semantically related. It is therefore not able to establish a connection between two documents that share no terms, even when they address the same topic through the use of synonyms. The only way that this can be achieved is through the introduction of semantic similarity between terms. Within the VSM this requires that a proximity matrix $\mathbf{P}$ has non-zero off-diagonal entries $\mathbf{P}_{ij} > 0$ when the term i is semantically related to the term j. Given such a matrix, the vector space kernel

$$\tilde{\kappa}(d_1, d_2) = \phi(d_1)\,\mathbf{P}\mathbf{P}'\phi(d_2)' \tag{10.1}$$

corresponds to representing a document by a less sparse vector $\phi(d)\,\mathbf{P}$ that has non-zero entries for all terms that are semantically similar to those present in the document $\dot{d}$. This is closely related to a technique from IR known as 'query expansion', where a query is expanded to include not only the actual query terms but any terms that are semantically related. Alternatively, we can view the matrix $\mathbf{PP}'$ as encoding a semantic strength between terms. This is perhaps most clearly apparent if we let $\mathbf{Q} = \mathbf{PP}'$ and expand the equation (10.1)

$$\tilde{\kappa}(d_1, d_2) = \sum_{i,j} \phi(d_1)_i \, \mathbf{Q}_{ij} \phi(d_2)_j,$$

so that we can view $\mathbf{Q}_{ij}$ as encoding the amount of semantic relation between terms i and j. Note that defining the similarity by inferring $\mathbf{Q}$ requires the additional constraint that $\mathbf{Q}$ be positive semi-definite, suggesting that defining $\mathbf{P}$ will in general be more straightforward.

Remark 10.7 [Stemming] One method of detecting some semantic similarities is known as *stemming*. This technique, implemented as part of the tokeniser, automatically removes inflexions from words, hence ensuring that different forms of the same word are treated as equivalent terms. For example 'structural', 'structure' and 'structured' would all be mapped to the common stem 'structure' and so be treated as the same term. This effectively performs a dimension reduction, while linking the different forms of the word as semantically identical. We can implement this within the VSM by setting $\mathbf{P}_{ij} = s^{-1/2}$, for all terms i, j that are reduced to the same stem, where s is the number of distinct terms involved. Of course this is just of theoretical interest as in practice the terms are all mapped to a single stemmed term in the list $L(d)$. ∎

10.2.2 Designing the proximity matrix

Remark 10.7 suggests a way of defining the proximity matrix $\mathbf{P}$ by putting non-zero entries between those terms whose semantic relation is apparent from their common stem. The question remains of how we can obtain more general semantic matrices that link synonymous or related terms that do not share a common core. We now give a series of methods for obtaining semantic relationships or learning them directly from a corpus be it the training corpus or a separate set of documents. Though we present the algorithms in a term-based representation, we will in many cases show how to implement them in dual form, hence avoiding the explicit computation of the matrix $\mathbf{P}$.

Explicit construction of the proximity matrix Perhaps the most natural method of incorporating semantic information is by inferring the relatedness of terms from an external source of domain knowledge. In this section we briefly describe one such approach. In the next section we will see how we can use co-occurrence information to infer semantic relations between terms, hence avoiding the need to make use of such external information.

A semantic network such as Wordnet provides a way to obtain term-similarity information. A semantic network encodes relationships between words of a dictionary in a hierarchical fashion, where the more general terms occur higher in the tree structure, so that for example 'spouse' occurs above 'husband' and 'wife', since it is their hypernym. We can use the distance between two terms in the hierarchical tree provided by Wordnet to give an estimate of their semantic proximity. This can then be used to modify the metric of the vector space of the bag-of-words feature space.

In order to introduce this information into the kernel, we can handcraft the matrix $\mathbf{P}$ by setting the entry $\mathbf{P}_{ij}$ to reflect the semantic proximity between the terms i and j. A simple but effective choice is to set this equal to the inverse of their distance in the tree, that is the length of the shortest path connecting them. The use of this semantic proximity gives rise to the vector space kernel

$$\tilde{\kappa}\left(d_{1}, d_{2}\right) = \phi\left(d_{1}\right) \mathbf{P} \mathbf{P}' \phi\left(d_{2}\right)'.$$

Generalised vector space model An early attempt to overcome the limitations of the VSMs by introducing semantic similarity between terms is known as the generalised VSM or GVSM. This method aims at capturing term–term correlations by looking at co-occurrence information. Two terms are considered semantically related if they frequently co-occur in the same documents. Indeed this simple observation forms the basis of most of the techniques we will develop in this chapter. This means that two documents can be seen as similar even if they do not share any terms, but the terms they contain co-occur in other documents. The GVSM method represents a document by a vector of its similarities with the different documents in the corpus, in other words a document is represented by the embedding

$$\phi\left(d\right) = \phi\left(d\right) \mathbf{D}',$$

where $\mathbf{D}$ is the document–term matrix, equivalent to taking $\mathbf{P} = \mathbf{D}'$. This definition does not make immediately clear that it implements a semantic similarity, but if we compute the corresponding kernel

$$\tilde{\kappa}\left(d_{1}, d_{2}\right) = \phi\left(d_{1}\right) \mathbf{D}'\mathbf{D}\phi\left(d_{2}\right)'.$$

Now we can observe that the matrix $\mathbf{D}'\mathbf{D}$ has a nonzero (i, j)th entry if and only if there is a document in the corpus in which the ith and jth terms co-occur, since

$$\left(\mathbf{D}'\mathbf{D}\right)_{ij} = \sum_{d} \text{tf}\left(i, d\right) \text{tf}\left(j, d\right).$$

So two terms co-occurring in a document are considered related with the strength of the relationship given by the frequency and number of their co-occurrences. If there are fewer documents than terms, this has the effect of dimensionality reduction by mapping from the vectors indexed by terms to a lower-dimensional space indexed by the documents of the corpus. Though appealing, the GVSM is too naive in its use of the co-occurrence information. The coming subsections examine more subtle uses of this information to create more refined semantics.

Latent semantic kernels The IR community developed a very effective vector space representation of documents that can capture semantic information through the use of co-occurrence information known as latent semantic indexing (LSI). Conceptually, LSI follows the same approach as GVSMs, only that the technique used to extract the semantic information from the co-occurrences is very different making use as it does of singular value decomposition (SVD). We will see that this amounts to a special choice of the matrix $\mathbf{P}$ with some useful properties.

Recall from Section 6.1 that the SVD of the matrix $\mathbf{D}'$ is

$$\mathbf{D}' = \mathbf{U}\mathbf{\Sigma}\mathbf{V}'$$

where $\mathbf{\Sigma}$ is a diagonal matrix of the same dimensions as $\mathbf{D}$, and $\mathbf{U}$ and $\mathbf{V}$ are unitary matrices whose columns are the eigenvectors of $\mathbf{D}'\mathbf{D}$ and $\mathbf{D}\mathbf{D}'$ respectively. LSI now projects the documents into the space spanned by the first k columns of $\mathbf{U}$, using these new k-dimensional vectors for subsequent processing

$$d \longmapsto \phi\left(d\right) \mathbf{U}_{k},$$

where $\mathbf{U}_{k}$ is the matrix containing the first k columns of $\mathbf{U}$. This choice can be motivated by recalling that the eigenvectors define the subspace that minimises the sum-squared differences between the points and their projections, that is it defines the subspace with minimal sum-squared residuals as spelled out in Proposition 6.12. Hence, the eigenvectors for a set of documents can be viewed as concepts described by linear combinations of terms chosen in such a way that the documents are described as accurately as possible using only k such concepts.

Note that terms that co-occur frequently will tend to align in the same eigenvectors, since SVD merges highly correlated dimensions in order to define a small number of dimensions able to reconstruct the whole feature vector. Hence, the SVD is using the co-occurrence information in a sophisticated algorithm that can maximise the amount of information extracted by a given number of dimensions.

The definition of LSI shows that it is identical to performing PCA in the feature space as described in (6.12). Hence, the new kernel becomes that of kernel PCA

$$\tilde{\kappa}\left(d_1, d_2\right) = \phi\left(d_1\right)\mathbf{U}_k\mathbf{U}_k'\phi\left(d_2\right)',$$

showing that the matrix $\mathbf{P}$ has in this case been chosen equal to $\mathbf{U}_k$. If we compare this with the GVSM we can write its projection as

$$\kappa_{\mathrm{GSVM}}\left(d_1, d_2\right) = \phi\left(d_1\right)\mathbf{D}'\mathbf{D}\phi\left(d_2\right)' = \phi\left(d_1\right)\mathbf{U}'\mathbf{\Sigma}\mathbf{U}\phi\left(d_2\right)'.$$

Hence, there are two adaptations that have taken place when compared to GVSM. Firstly, dimensionality reduction has been introduced through the restriction to k eigenvectors, and secondly the removal of the matrix $\mathbf{\Sigma}$ has ensured that the projections of the data are orthonormal.

The fact that LSI is equivalent to PCA also implies that we can implement the algorithm in the dual representation to obtain from (6.12) the evaluation of the projection as follows.

Computation 10.8 [Latent semantic kernels]Latent semantic kernels are implemented by projecting onto the features

$$\phi(d)\mathbf{U}_k = \left(\lambda_i^{-1/2}\sum_{j=1}^{\ell}\left(\mathbf{v}_i\right)_j\kappa(d_j, d)\right)_{i=1}^k,$$

where κ is the base kernel, and $\lambda_i, \mathbf{v}_i$ are the eigenvalue, eigenvector pairs of the kernel matrix.   ∎

The base kernel can now be chosen as the bag-of-words kernel or more generally a complex kernel involving term weightings or even the polynomial construction. For this reason we refer to this dual construction as *latent semantic kernels (LSK)*.

Again we see the sculpting of the feature space through a series of transformations each using additional domain knowledge to further refine the semantics of the embedding. If we wish to represent the LSKs with a proximity matrix we can do so by taking

$$\mathbf{P} = \mathbf{U}_k \mathbf{U}_k'$$

since this leads to an identical kernel, while the matrix $\mathbf{P}$ is now square and so defines connection strengths between the different terms. Notice how as k increases, the matrix tends to the identity, returning to the treatment of all terms as semantically distinct. Hence, the value of k controls the amount of semantic smoothing that is introduced into the representation.

Exploiting multilingual corpora Aligned corpora are formed of pairs of documents that are translations of each other in two languages. They are examples of the paired training sets introduced when we considered canonical correlation analysis in Section 6.5. We can treat the translation as a complex label for the first document, or consider the two versions as two views of the same object.

In this way we can use a bilingual corpus to learn a semantic mapping that is useful for tasks that have nothing to do with the second language. The translations can be seen as complex labels that enable us to elicit refined semantic mappings that project the documents onto key directions that are able to remove semantically irrelevant aspects of the representation.

LSKs can be used to derive a more refined language independent representation. This is achieved by concatenating the two versions of the document into a single bilingual text. LSI is then applied to create a set of k semantic dimensions. A new document or query in only one language is projected using the projections derived from the eigenvectors obtained from the concatenated documents.

The latent semantic approach looks for directions of maximum variance but is restricted by its concatenation of the feature spaces of the two languages. An alternative method for creating semantic features is to use kernel CCA. This method treats the two versions of the document as two views of the same semantic object. It therefore finds independent projections for the two languages that map to a common semantic space. This space can be used for further document analysis.

Remark 10.9 [Cross-lingual information retrieval] Cross-lingual information retrieval (CLIR) is concerned with the task of retrieving documents in one language with queries from a different language. The technique is intended for users who have a passive knowledge of a language enabling them to read documents, but not sufficient expertise to choose a suitable query for the information they require. The semantic space provides an ideal representation for performing CLIR.   ∎

Semantic diffusion kernels We would like to continue our exploitation of the dual perspective between document-based and term-based representations. If we regard documents as similar that share terms, we have seen how we can equally well regard as related terms that co-occur in many documents. This suggests we might extend the similarity implications even further by, for example, regarding documents that share terms that co-occur as similar – this is the effect of using the co-occurrence analysis in further processing. Extrapolating this interaction suggests the introduction of a recurrence relation. For this section we will denote the matrix $\mathbf{D'D}$ with $\mathbf{G}$ and as usual $\mathbf{DD'}$ is the base kernel matrix $\mathbf{K}$. Consider refined similarity matrices $\hat{\mathbf{K}}$ between documents and $\hat{\mathbf{G}}$ between terms defined recursively by

$$\hat{\mathbf{K}} = \mu\mathbf{D}\hat{\mathbf{G}}\mathbf{D}' + \mathbf{K} \quad \text{and} \quad \hat{\mathbf{G}} = \mu\mathbf{D}'\hat{\mathbf{K}}\mathbf{D} + \mathbf{G}. \quad (10.2)$$

We can interpret this as augmenting the similarity given by $\mathbf{K}$ through indirect similarities measured by $\mathbf{G}$ and vice versa. The factor $\mu < \|\mathbf{K}\|^{-1}$ ensures that the longer range effects decay exponentially (recall that $\|\mathbf{K}\| = \max_{\lambda \in \lambda(\mathbf{K})} |\lambda|$ denotes the spectral norm of $\mathbf{K}$).

Recall Definition 9.34 of the von Neumann diffusion kernel $\bar{\mathbf{K}}$ over a base kernel $\mathbf{K}_1$ in Section 9.4

$$\bar{\mathbf{K}} = (\mathbf{I} - \lambda\mathbf{K}_1)^{-1}$$

We can characterise the solution of the above recurrences in the following proposition.

Proposition 10.10 *Provided* $\mu < \|\mathbf{K}\|^{-1} = \|\mathbf{G}\|^{-1}$, *the kernel* $\hat{\mathbf{K}}$ *that solves the recurrences (10.2) is* $\mathbf{K}$ *times the von Neumann kernel over the base kernel* $\mathbf{K}$, *while the matrix* $\hat{\mathbf{G}}$ *satisfies*

$$\hat{\mathbf{G}} = \mathbf{G}(\mathbf{I} - \mu\mathbf{G})^{-1}.$$

The proof of the proposition is given in Appendix A.3.

Note that we can view $\hat{\mathbf{K}}(\mu)$ as a kernel based on the proximity matrix $\mathbf{P} = \sqrt{\mu\hat{\mathbf{G}} + \mathbf{I}}$ since

$$\mathbf{DPP'D'} = \mathbf{D}(\mu\hat{\mathbf{G}} + \mathbf{I})\mathbf{D}' = \mu\mathbf{D}\hat{\mathbf{G}}\mathbf{D}' + \mathbf{K} = \hat{\mathbf{K}}(\mu).$$

Hence, the solution $\hat{\mathbf{G}}$ defines a refined similarity between terms.

The kernel $\hat{\mathbf{K}}$ combines these indirect link kernels with an exponentially decaying weight. This and the diffusion kernels suggest an alternative weighting scheme that shows faster decay. Given a kernel $\mathbf{K}$, consider the exponential diffusion kernel of Definition 9.33

$$\bar{\mathbf{K}}(\mu) = \mathbf{K} \sum_{t=1}^{\infty} \frac{\mu^t \mathbf{K}^t}{t!} = \mathbf{K} \exp(\mu \mathbf{K}).$$

One advantage of this definition is that the series is convergent for all values of μ, so that no restrictions need to be placed on this parameter. The next proposition gives the semantic proximity matrix corresponding to $\bar{\mathbf{K}}(\mu)$.

Proposition 10.11 *Let* $\bar{\mathbf{K}}(\mu) = \mathbf{K} \exp(\mu \mathbf{K})$. *Then* $\bar{\mathbf{K}}(\mu)$ *corresponds to a semantic proximity matrix*

$$\exp\left(\frac{\mu}{2}\mathbf{G}\right).$$

Again the proof of the proposition can be found in Appendix A.3.

Remark 10.12 [Applying the diffusion kernels to unseen data] Note that for the case of text the application of the derived kernel is not restricted to the examples used in the kernel matrix. As with kernel PCA we can project new examples into the coordinate system determined by the principal axes and reweight them with the appropriate function of the corresponding eigenvalue. Hence, we can compute the diffusion construction on a modestly sized training set, but apply it to previously unseen data. ∎

10.3 Summary

- The VSM developed in the IR community provides a rich source of kernels for the analysis of text documents.
- The simplest example is the bag-of-words kernel that treats all terms in the corpus as independent features.
- Refinements of the VSM are characterised by the use of different semantic matrices $\mathbf{S}$.

Term weighting schemes lead to diagonal semantic matrices

Off-diagonal entries can be set using external sources such as semantic nets.

Alternatively we can learn semantic relations through co-occurrence analysis of the training corpus.

The GVSM gives the simplest approach, with latent semantic kernels and diffusion kernels making more refined use of the co-occurrence information.

Multilingual corpora can further refine the choice of semantic concepts as well as enabling cross-lingual information analysis.

10.4 Further reading and advanced topics

Kernel methods provide a natural framework for pattern analysis in text. This is not just through their interpretation of duality, but also because the function of a kernel in deciding if two documents, sentences or words have a similar meaning is much easier than actually analysing that meaning. This similarity measure can often be obtained by borrowing methods from different disciplines, as is evident from the diverse literature on which this chapter has been based.

The conventional VSM was introduced in 1975 by Salton *et al.* [114], and became the standard representation of documents in IR. Its use as a kernel, proposed by Joachims [68], is equivalent to setting the matrix $\mathbf{P} = \mathbf{I}$. A number of variations on that theme have been suggested, for example the GVSM [167], LSI [37] and many others, all of which have an obvious kernel counterpart.

Following this first embedding, a number of other, possibly nonlinear, mappings can be performed. Both Joachims, and Dumais *et al.* [41] used polynomial and Gaussian kernels to further refine the vector space representation, so further mapping the data into a richer space, for classification tasks using support vector machines.

The European project KerMIT has developed a number of new and sophisticated representations, kernels and algorithms, and their website contains a number of publications concerned with kernels for text, see www.euro-kermit.org. Also the book by Thorsten Joachims [69] is entirely devoted to text classification using kernel methods.

The survey paper [66] contains a framework using as a unifying concept the proximity matrix. The paper [128] discusses the semantic smoothing as performed by means of semantic networks and a particular choice of proximity matrix. The paper on latent semantic kernels [35, 31] discusses the use of those ideas within kernel methods, and the paper by [86] compares a number of choices of term weighting schemes, and hence indirectly of embedding maps.

The use of kCCA for cross language analysis is presented in [153] and the use of diffusion kernels in [71] (more background information about kernel

CCA can be found in Section 6.9 and diffusion kernels in Section 9.10). Other methods for cross-language analysis include adaptations of LSI described in [92]. Combinations of text and hyperlink information, in hypertext kernels, are described in [69].

Of course other kernels for text can be devised which do not use the VSM, as those based on string matching [93], and and probabilistic modeling, as in [59], but are better addressed within the context of Chapters 11 and 12. See Section 11.9 and Section 12.4 for more references.

For constantly updated pointers to online literature and free software see the book's companion website: www.kernel-methods.net

11

Kernels for structured data: strings, trees, etc.

Probably the most important data type after vectors and free text is that of symbol strings of varying lengths. This type of data is commonplace in bioinformatics applications, where it can be used to represent proteins as sequences of amino acids, genomic DNA as sequences of nucleotides, promoters and other structures. Partly for this reason a great deal of research has been devoted to it in the last few years. Many other application domains consider data in the form of sequences so that many of the techniques have a history of development within computer science, as for example in stringology, the study of string algorithms.

Kernels have been developed to compute the inner product between images of strings in high-dimensional feature spaces using dynamic programming techniques. Although sequences can be regarded as a special case of a more general class of structures for which kernels have been designed, we will discuss them separately for most of the chapter in order to emphasise their importance in applications and to aid understanding of the computational methods. In the last part of the chapter, we will show how these concepts and techniques can be extended to cover more general data structures, including trees, arrays, graphs and so on.

Certain kernels for strings based on probabilistic modelling of the data-generating source will not be discussed here, since Chapter 12 is entirely devoted to these kinds of methods. There is, however, some overlap between the structure kernels presented here and those arising from probabilistic modelling covered in Chapter 12. Where appropriate we will point out the connections.

The use of kernels on strings, and more generally on structured objects, makes it possible for kernel methods to operate in a domain that traditionally has belonged to syntactical pattern recognition, in this way providing a bridge between that field and statistical pattern analysis.

11.1 Comparing strings and sequences

In this chapter we consider the problem of embedding two sequences in a high-dimensional space in such a way that their relative distance in that space reflects their similarity and that the inner product between their images can be computed efficiently. The first decision to be made is what similarity notion should be reflected in the embedding, or in other words what features of the sequences are revealing for the task at hand. Are we trying to group sequences by length, composition, or some other properties? What type of patterns are we looking for? This chapter will describe a number of possible embeddings providing a toolkit of techniques that either individually or in combination can be used to meet the needs of many applications.

Example 11.1 The different approaches all reduce to various ways of counting substrings or subsequences that the two strings have in common. This is a meaningful similarity notion in biological applications, since evolutionary proximity is thought to result both in functional similarity and in sequence similarity, measured by the number of insertions, deletions and symbol replacements. Measuring sequence similarity should therefore give a good indication about the functional similarity that bioinformatics researchers would like to capture. ∎

We begin by defining what we mean by a string, substring and subsequence of symbols. Note that we will use the term substring to indicate that a string occurs contiguously within a string s, and subsequence to allow the possibility that gaps separate the different characters resulting in a non-contiguous occurrence within s.

Definition 11.2 [Strings and substrings] An *alphabet* is a finite set Σ of $|\Sigma|$ symbols. A *string*

$$s = s_1 \ldots s_{|s|},$$

is any finite sequence of symbols from Σ, including the empty sequence denoted ε, the only string of length 0. We denote by Σ^n the set of all finite strings of length n, and by Σ^* the set of all strings

$$\Sigma^* = \bigcup_{n=0}^{\infty} \Sigma^n.$$

We use $[s = t]$ to denote the function that returns 1 if the strings s and t are identical and 0 otherwise. More generally $[p(s, t)]$ where $p(s, t)$ is a boolean expression involving s and t, returns 1 if $p(s, t)$ is true and 0 otherwise. For strings s, t, we denote by $|s|$ the *length* of the string s and by st the string obtained by concatenating the strings s and t. The string t is a substring of s if there are (possibly empty) strings u and v such that

$$s = utv.$$

If $u = \varepsilon$, we say that t is a *prefix* of s, while if $v = \varepsilon$, t is known as a *suffix*. For $1 \leq i \leq j \leq |s|$, the string $s(i : j)$ is the substring $s_i \ldots s_j$ of s. The substrings of length k are also referred to as *k-grams* or *k-mers*. ∎

Definition 11.3 [Subsequence] We say that u is a *subsequence* of a string s, if there exist indices $\mathbf{i} = (i_1, \ldots, i_{|u|})$, with $1 \leq i_1 < \cdots < i_{|u|} \leq |s|$, such that $u_j = s_{i_j}$, for $j = 1, \ldots, |u|$. We will use the short-hand notation $u = s(\mathbf{i})$ if u is a subsequence of s in the positions given by $\mathbf{i}$. We denote by $|\mathbf{i}| = |u|$ the number of indices in the sequence, while the length $l(\mathbf{i})$ of the subsequence is $i_{|u|} - i_1 + 1$, that is, the number of characters of s covered by the subsequence. The empty tuple is understood to index the empty string ε. Throughout this chapter we will use the convention that bold indices $\mathbf{i}$ and $\mathbf{j}$ range over strictly ordered tuples of indices, that is, over the sets

$$I_k = \{(i_1, \ldots, i_k) : 1 \leq i_1 < \cdots < i_k\} \subset \mathbb{N}^k, \ k = 0, 1, 2, \ldots.$$

∎

Example 11.4 For example, the words in this sentence are all strings from the alphabet $\Sigma = \{a, b, ..., z\}$. Consider the string $s =$"kernels". We have $|s| = 7$, while $s(1 : 3) =$"ker" is a prefix of s, $s(4 : 7) =$"nels" is a suffix of s, and together with $s(2 : 5) =$"erne" all three are substrings of s. The string $s(1, 2, 4, 7) =$"kens" is a subsequence of length 4, whose length $l(1, 2, 4, 7)$ in s is 7. Another example of a subsequence is $s(2, 4, 6) =$"enl". ∎

Remark 11.5 [Binary representation] There is a 1–1 correspondence between the set I_k and the binary strings with exactly k 1s. The tuple $(i_1, \ldots, i_k)$ corresponds to the binary string with 1s in positions i_j, $j = 1, \ldots, k$. For some of the discussions below it can be easier to think in terms of binary strings or vectors, as in Example 11.18. ∎

Remark 11.6 [On strings and sequences] There is some ambiguity between the terms 'string' and 'sequence' across different traditions. They are sometimes used equivalently both in computer science and biology, but in most of the computer science literature the term 'string' requires contiguity, whereas 'sequence' implies only order. This makes a difference when moving to substrings and subsequences. What in the biological literature are called 'sequences' are usually called 'strings' in the computer science literature. In this chapter we will follow the computer science convention, though frequently including an indication as to whether the given substring is contiguous or not in order to minimise possible confusion. ∎

Embedding space All the kernels presented in this chapter can be defined by an explicit embedding map from the space of all finite sequences over an alphabet Σ to a vector space F. The coordinates of F are indexed by a subset I of strings over Σ, that is by a subset of the input space. In some cases I will be the set Σ^p of strings of length p giving a vector space of dimension $|\Sigma|^p$, while in others it will be the infinite-dimensional space indexed by Σ^*. As usual we use ϕ to denote the feature mapping

$$\phi: s \longmapsto (\phi_u(s))_{u \in I} \in F.$$

For each embedding space F, there will be many different maps ϕ to choose from. For example, one possibility is to set the value of the coordinate $\phi_u(s)$ indexed by the string u to be a count of how many times u occurs as a contiguous substring in the input string s, while another possible choice is to count how many times u occurs as a (non-contiguous) subsequence. In this second case the weight of the count can also be tuned to reflect how many gaps there are in the different occurrences. We can also count approximate matches appropriately weighting for the number of mismatches.

In the next section we use the example of a simple string kernel to introduce some of the techniques. This will set the scene for the subsequent sections where we develop string kernels more tuned to particular applications.

11.2 Spectrum kernels

Perhaps the most natural way to compare two strings in many applications is to count how many (contiguous) substrings of length p they have in common. We define the *spectrum of order p* (or *p-spectrum*) of a sequence s to be the histogram of frequencies of all its (contiguous) substrings of length p. Comparing the p-spectra of two strings can give important information about their similarity in applications where contiguity plays an important role. We can define a kernel as the inner product of their p-spectra.

Definition 11.7 [The p-spectrum kernel] The feature space F associated with the p-spectrum kernel is indexed by $I = \Sigma^p$, with the embedding given by

$$\phi_u^p (s) = |\{(v_1, v_2) : s = v_1 u v_2\}|, \ u \in \Sigma^p.$$

The associated kernel is defined as

$$\kappa_p (s, t) = \langle \phi^p (s), \phi^p (t) \rangle = \sum_{u \in \Sigma^p} \phi_u^p (s) \phi_u^p (t).$$

∎

Example 11.8 [2-spectrum kernel] Consider the strings `"bar"`, `"bat"`, `"car"` and `"cat"`. Their 2-spectra are given in the following table:

ϕ	ar	at	ba	ca
bar	1	0	1	0
bat	0	1	1	0
car	1	0	0	1
cat	0	1	0	1

with all the other dimensions indexed by other strings of length 2 having value 0, so that the resulting kernel matrix is:

K	bar	bat	car	cat
bar	2	1	1	0
bat	1	2	0	1
car	1	0	2	1
cat	0	1	1	2

∎

Example 11.9 [3-spectrum kernel] As a further example, consider the following two sequences

$$s = \texttt{"statistics"}$$
$$t = \texttt{"computation"}$$

The two strings contain the following substrings of length 3

`"sta"`, `"tat"`, `"ati"`, `"tis"`, `"ist"`, `"sti"`, `"tic"`, `"ics"`
`"com"`, `"omp"`, `"mpu"`, `"put"`, `"uta"`, `"tat"`, `"ati"`, `"tio"`, `"ion"`

and they have in common the substrings `"tat"` and `"ati"`, so their inner product would be $\kappa (s, t) = 2$.

∎

Many alternative recursions can be devised for the calculation of this kernel with different costs and levels of complexity. We will present a few of them spread through the rest of this chapter, since they illustrate different points about the design of string kernels.

In this section we present the first having a cost $O\left(p\left|s\right|\left|t\right|\right)$. Our aim in later sections will be to show how the cost can be reduced to $O\left(p\left(\left|s\right|+\left|t\right|\right)\right)=O\left(p\max\left(\left|s\right|,\left|t\right|\right)\right)$ making it linear in the length of the longer sequence.

The first method will nonetheless be useful because it will introduce some methods that are important when considering more sophisticated kernels, for example ones that can tolerate partial matches and insertions of irrelevant symbols. It will also illustrate an important consideration that makes it possible to use partial results of the evaluation of one entry in the kernel matrix to speed up the computation of other entries in the same row or column. In such cases the complexity of computing the complete kernel matrix can be less than $O\left(\ell^2\right)$ times the cost of evaluating a single entry.

Computation 11.10 [p-spectrum recursion] We can first define an 'auxiliary' kernel known as the k-suffix kernel to assist in the computation of the p-spectrum kernel. The k-suffix kernel $\kappa_k^S\left(s,t\right)$ is defined by

$$\kappa_k^S\left(s,t\right)=\begin{cases}1 & \text{if } s=s_1u,\ t=t_1u,\ \text{for } u\in\Sigma^k \\ 0 & \text{otherwise.}\end{cases}$$

Clearly the evaluation of $\kappa_k^S\left(s,t\right)$ requires $O\left(k\right)$ comparisons, so that the p-spectrum kernel can be evaluated using the equation

$$\kappa_p\left(s,t\right)=\sum_{i=1}^{|s|-p+1}\sum_{j=1}^{|t|-p+1}\kappa_p^S\left(s\left(i:i+p\right),t\left(j:j+p\right)\right)$$

in $O\left(p\left|s\right|\left|t\right|\right)$ operations. ∎

Example 11.11 The evaluation of the 3-spectrum kernel using the above recurrence is illustrated in the following Table 11.1 and 11.2, where each entry computes the kernel between the corresponding prefixes of the two strings. ∎

Remark 11.12 [Computational cost] The evaluation of one row of the table for the p-suffix kernel corresponds to performing a search in the string t for the p-suffix of a prefix of s. Fast string matching algorithms such as the Knuth–Morris–Pratt algorithm can identify the matches in time $O\left(\left|t\right|+p\right)=O\left(\left|t\right|\right)$, suggesting that the complexity could be improved to

DP : κ_3^S	ε	c	o	m	p	u	t	a	t	i	o	n
ε	0	0	0	0	0	0	0	0	0	0	0	0
s	0	0	0	0	0	0	0	0	0	0	0	0
t	0	0	0	0	0	0	0	0	0	0	0	0
a	0	0	0	0	0	0	0	0	0	0	0	0
t	0	0	0	0	0	0	0	0	1	0	0	0
i	0	0	0	0	0	0	0	0	0	1	0	0
s	0	0	0	0	0	0	0	0	0	0	0	0
t	0	0	0	0	0	0	0	0	0	0	0	0
i	0	0	0	0	0	0	0	0	0	0	0	0
c	0	0	0	0	0	0	0	0	0	0	0	0
s	0	0	0	0	0	0	0	0	0	0	0	0

Table 11.1. *3-spectrum kernel between two strings.*

DP : κ_3	ε	c	o	m	p	u	t	a	t	i	o	n
ε	0	0	0	0	0	0	0	0	0	0	0	0
s	0	0	0	0	0	0	0	0	0	0	0	0
t	0	0	0	0	0	0	0	0	0	0	0	0
a	0	0	0	0	0	0	0	0	0	0	0	0
t	0	0	0	0	0	0	0	0	1	1	1	1
i	0	0	0	0	0	0	0	0	1	2	2	2
s	0	0	0	0	0	0	0	0	1	2	2	2
t	0	0	0	0	0	0	0	0	1	2	2	2
i	0	0	0	0	0	0	0	0	1	2	2	2
c	0	0	0	0	0	0	0	0	1	2	2	2
s	0	0	0	0	0	0	0	0	1	2	2	2

Table 11.2. *3-spectrum kernel between strings.*

$O(|s| |t|)$ operations using this approach. We do not pursue this further since we will consider even faster implementations later in this chapter. ∎

Remark 11.13 [Blended spectrum kernel] We can also consider a 'blended' version of this kernel $\tilde{\kappa}_p$, where the spectra corresponding to all values $1 \leq d \leq p$ are simultaneously compared, and weighted according to λ^d. This requires the use of an auxiliary p-suffix kernel $\tilde{\kappa}_p^S$ that records the level of similarity of the suffices of the two strings. This kernel is defined recursively as follows

$$\tilde{\kappa}_0^S(sa, tb) = 0,$$

$$\tilde{\kappa}_p^S (sa, tb) = \begin{cases} \lambda^2 \left(1 + \tilde{\kappa}_{p-1}^S (s,t)\right), & \text{if } a = b; \\ 0, & \text{otherwise.} \end{cases}$$

The blended spectrum kernel can be defined using the same formula as the p-spectrum kernel as follows

$$\tilde{\kappa}_p (s,t) = \sum_{i=1}^{|s|-p+1} \sum_{j=1}^{|t|-p+1} \tilde{\kappa}_p^S (s(i:i+p), t(j:j+p)),$$

resulting in the same time complexity as the original p-spectrum kernel. ∎

As mentioned above later in this chapter we will give a more efficient method for computing the p-spectrum kernel. This will be based on a tree-like data structure known as a trie. We first turn to considering subsequences rather than substrings as features in our next example.

11.3 All-subsequences kernels

In this section we consider a feature mapping defined by all contiguous or non-contiguous subsequences of a string.

Definition 11.14 [All-subsequences kernel] The feature space associated with the embedding of the all-subsequences kernel is indexed by $I = \Sigma^*$, with the embedding given by

$$\phi_u (s) = |\{\mathbf{i} : u = s(\mathbf{i})\}|, \ u \in I,$$

that is, the count of the number of times the indexing string u occurs as a subsequence in the string s. The associated kernel is defined by

$$\kappa(s,t) = \langle \phi(s), \phi(t) \rangle = \sum_{u \in \Sigma^*} \phi_u(s) \phi_u(t).$$

∎

An explicit computation of this feature map will be computationally infeasible even if we represent $\phi_u(s)$ by a list of its non-zero components, since if $|s| = m$ we can expect of the order of

$$\min\left(\binom{m}{k}, |\Sigma|^k \right)$$

distinct subsequences of length k. Hence, for $m > 2|\Sigma|$ the number of non-zero entries considering only strings u of length $m/2$ is likely to be at least $|\Sigma|^{m/2}$, which is exponential in the length m of the string s.

Remark 11.15 [Set intersection] We could also consider this as a case of a kernel between multisets, as outlined in Chapter 9. The measure of the intersection is a valid kernel. Neither definition suggests how the computation of the kernel might be effected efficiently.   ∎

Example 11.16 All the (non-contiguous) subsequences in the words "bar", "baa", "car" and "cat" are given in the following two tables:

ϕ	ε	a	b	c	r	t	aa	ar	at	ba	br	bt
bar	1	1	1	0	1	0	0	1	0	1	1	0
baa	1	2	1	0	0	0	1	0	0	2	0	0
car	1	1	0	1	1	0	0	1	0	0	0	0
cat	1	1	0	1	0	1	0	0	1	0	0	0

ϕ	ca	cr	ct	bar	baa	car	cat
bar	0	0	0	1	0	0	0
baa	0	0	0	0	1	0	0
car	1	1	0	0	0	1	0
cat	1	0	1	0	0	0	1

and since all other (infinite) coordinates must have value zero, the kernel matrix is

K	bar	baa	car	cat
bar	8	6	4	2
baa	6	12	3	3
car	4	3	8	4
cat	2	3	4	8

Notice that in general, the diagonal elements of this kernel matrix can vary greatly with the length of a string and even as illustrated here between words of the same length, when they have different numbers of repeated subsequences. Of course this effect can be removed if we choose to normalise this kernel. Notice also that all the entries are always positive placing all the feature vectors in the positive orthant. This suggests that centering may be advisable in some situations (see Code Fragment 5.2).   ∎

Evaluating the kernel We now consider how the kernel κ can be evaluated more efficiently than via an explicit computation of the feature vectors. This will involve the definition of a recursive relation similar to that derived for ANOVA kernels in Chapter 9. Its computation will also follow similar dynamic programming techniques in order to complete a table of values with the resulting kernel evaluation given by the final entry in the table. In presenting this introductory kernel, we will introduce terminology, definitions and techniques that will be used throughout the rest of the chapter.

First consider restricting our attention to the feature indexed by a string u. The contribution of this feature to the overall inner product can be expressed as

$$\phi_u(s)\,\phi_u(t) = \sum_{\mathbf{i}:u=s(\mathbf{i})} 1 \sum_{\mathbf{j}:u=t(\mathbf{j})} 1 = \sum_{(\mathbf{i},\mathbf{j}):u=s(\mathbf{i})=t(\mathbf{j})} 1,$$

where it is understood that $\mathbf{i}$ and $\mathbf{j}$ range over strictly ordered tuples of indices. Hence, the overall inner product can be expressed as

$$\kappa(s,t) = \langle \phi(s), \phi(t) \rangle = \sum_{u \in I} \sum_{(\mathbf{i},\mathbf{j}):u=s(\mathbf{i})=t(\mathbf{j})} 1 = \sum_{(\mathbf{i},\mathbf{j}):s(\mathbf{i})=t(\mathbf{j})} 1. \tag{11.1}$$

The key to the recursion is to consider the addition of one extra symbol a to one of the strings s. In the final sum of equation (11.1) there are two possibilities for the tuple $\mathbf{i}$: either it is completely contained within s or its final index corresponds to the final a. In the first case the subsequence is a subsequence of s, while in the second its final symbol is a. Hence, we can split this sum into two parts

$$\sum_{(\mathbf{i},\mathbf{j}):sa(\mathbf{i})=t(\mathbf{j})} 1 = \sum_{(\mathbf{i},\mathbf{j}):s(\mathbf{i})=t(\mathbf{j})} 1 + \sum_{u:t=uav} \sum_{(\mathbf{i},\mathbf{j}):s(\mathbf{i})=u(\mathbf{j})} 1, \tag{11.2}$$

where for the second contribution we have used the fact that the last character of the subsequence is a which must therefore occur in some position within t.

Computation 11.17 [All-subsequences kernel] Equation (11.2) leads to the following recursive definition of the kernel

$$\begin{aligned}
\kappa(s,\varepsilon) &= 1, & (11.3)\\
\kappa(sa,t) &= \kappa(s,t) + \sum_{k:t_k=a} \kappa(s,t(1:k-1))
\end{aligned}$$

where we have used the fact that every string contains the empty string ε exactly once. By the symmetry of kernels, an analogous recurrence relation can be given for $\kappa(s,ta)$

$$\begin{aligned}
\kappa(\varepsilon,t) &= 1\\
\kappa(s,ta) &= \kappa(s,t) + \sum_{k:s_k=a} \kappa(s(1:k-1),t).
\end{aligned}$$

Similar symmetric definitions will exist for other recurrences given in this chapter, though in future we will avoid pointing out these alternatives. ∎

An intuitive reading of the recurrence states that common subsequences are either contained completely within s and hence included in the first term of the recurrence or must end in the symbol a, in which case their final symbol can be matched with occurrences of a in the second string.

Example 11.18 Consider computing the kernel between the strings $s =$ "gatt" and $t =$"cata", where we add the symbol $a =$"a" to the string "gatt" to obtain the string $sa =$ "gatta". The rows of the tables are indexed by the pairs $(\mathbf{i}, \mathbf{j})$ such that $sa(\mathbf{i}) = t(\mathbf{j})$ with those not involving the final character of sa listed in the first table, while those involving the final character are given in the second table. The binary vectors below each string show the positions of the entries in the vectors $\mathbf{i}$ and $\mathbf{j}$.

g	a	t	t	a	$sa(\mathbf{i}) = t(\mathbf{j})$	c	a	t	a
0	0	0	0	0	ε	0	0	0	0
0	1	1	0	0	at	0	1	1	0
0	1	0	1	0	at	0	1	1	0
0	1	0	0	0	a	0	1	0	0
0	0	1	0	0	t	0	0	1	0
0	0	0	1	0	t	0	0	1	0
0	1	0	0	0	a	0	0	0	1

g	a	t	t	a	$sa(\mathbf{i}) = t(\mathbf{j})$	c	a	t	a
0	0	0	0	1	a	0	1	0	0
0	0	0	0	1	a	0	0	0	1
0	1	0	0	1	aa	0	1	0	1
0	0	0	1	1	ta	0	0	1	1
0	0	1	0	1	ta	0	0	1	1
0	1	1	0	1	ata	0	1	1	1
0	1	0	1	1	ata	0	1	1	1

Hence, we see that the 14 rows implying $\kappa(sa, t) = 14$ are made up of the 7 rows of the first table giving $\kappa(s, t) = 7$ plus $\kappa($"gatt"$,$"c"$) = 1$ given by the first row of the second table and $\kappa($"gatt"$,$"cat"$) = 6$ corresponding to rows 2 to 7 of the second table. ∎

Cost of the computation As for the case of the ANOVA kernels discussed in Chapter 9 a recursive evaluation of this kernel would be very expensive.

Clearly, a similar strategy of computing the entries into a table based on dynamic programming methods will result in an efficient computation. The table has one row for each symbol of the string s and one column for each symbol of the string t; the entries $\kappa_{ij} = \kappa\left(s\left(1:i\right), t\left(1:j\right)\right)$ give the kernel evaluations on the various prefices of the two strings:

DP	ε	t_1	t_2	$\cdots$	t_m
ε	1	1	1	$\cdots$	1
s_1	1	κ_{11}	κ_{12}	$\cdots$	κ_{1m}
s_2	1	κ_{21}	κ_{22}	$\cdots$	κ_{2m}
$\vdots$	$\vdots$	$\vdots$	$\vdots$	$\ddots$	$\vdots$
s_n	1	κ_{n1}	κ_{n2}	$\cdots$	$\kappa_{nm} = \kappa\left(s,t\right)$

The first row and column are given by the base case of the recurrence. The general recurrence of (11.3) allows us to compute the (i,j)th entry as the sum of the $(i-1,j)$th entry together with all the entries $(i-1, k-1)$ with $1 \le k < j$ for which $t_k = s_i$. Clearly, filling the rows in sequential order ensures that at each stage the values required to compute the next entry have already been computed at an earlier stage.

The number of operations to evaluate the single (i,j)th entry is $O(j)$ since we must check through all the symbols in t up to jth. Hence, to fill the complete table will require $O\left(|s| |t|^2\right)$ operations using this still slightly naive approach.

Example 11.19 Example 11.18 leads to the following table:

DP	ε	g	a	t	t	a
ε	1	1	1	1	1	1
c	1	1	1	1	1	1
a	1	1	2	2	2	3
t	1	1	2	4	6	7
a	1	1	3	5	7	14

■

Speeding things up We can improve the complexity still further by observing that as we fill the ith row the sum

$$\sum_{k \le j : t_k = s_i} \kappa\left(s\left(1:i-1\right), t\left(1:k-1\right)\right)$$

required when we reach the jth position could have been precomputed into an array P by the following computation

```
last = 0;
P(0) = 0;
for k = 1 : m
  P(k) = P(last);
  if t_k = s_i then
    P(k) = P(last) + DP(i − 1, k − 1);
    last = k;
  end
end
```

Using the array p we can now compute the next row with the simple loop

```
for k = 1 : m
  DP(i, k) = DP(i − 1, k) + P(k);
end
```

We now summarise the algorithm.

Algorithm 11.20 [All-non-contiguous subsequences kernel] The all–non-contiguous subsequences kernel is computed in Code Fragment 11.1.   ∎

Input	strings s and t of lengths n and m
Process	for $j = 1 : m$
2	$\quad$ DP $(0, j) = 1$;
3	end
4	for $i = 1 : n$
5	$\quad$ last $= 0$; $P(0) = 0$;
6	$\quad$ for $k = 1 : m$
7	$\quad\quad$ $P(k) = P(\text{last})$;
8	$\quad\quad$ if $t_k = s_i$ then
9	$\quad\quad\quad$ $P(k) = P(\text{last}) + $ DP $(i − 1, k − 1)$
10	$\quad\quad\quad$ last $= k$;
11	$\quad\quad$ end
12	$\quad$ end
13	$\quad$ for $k = 1 : m$
14	$\quad\quad$ DP $(i, k) = $ DP $(i − 1, k) + P(k)$;
15	$\quad$ end
16	end
Output	kernel evaluation $\kappa(s, t) = $ DP (n, m)

Code Fragment 11.1. Pseudocode for the all-non-contiguous subsequences kernel.

Example 11.21 The array p for each row is interleaved with the evaluations of DP for the Example 11.18 in the following table:

DP	ε	g	a	t	t	a
ε	1	1	1	1	1	1
p	0	0	0	0	0	0
c	1	1	1	1	1	1
p	0	0	1	1	1	2
a	1	1	2	2	2	3
p	0	0	0	2	4	4
t	1	1	2	4	6	7
p	0	0	1	1	1	7
a	1	1	3	5	7	14

∎

Cost of the computation Since the complexity of both loops individually is $O(|t|)$ their complexity performed sequentially is also $O(|t|)$, making the overall complexity $O(|s|\,|t|)$.

Algorithm 11.20 is deceptively simple. Despite this simplicity it is giving the exponential improvement in complexity that we first observed in the ANOVA computation. We are evaluating an inner product in a space whose dimension is exponential in $|s|$ and in $|t|$ with just $O(|s|\,|t|)$ operations.

Remark 11.22 [Computational by-products] We compute the kernel $\kappa(s,t)$ by solving the *more general* problem of computing $\kappa(s(1:i),t(1:j))$ for all values of $i \leq |s|$ and $j \leq |t|$. This means that at the end of the computation we could also read off from the table the evaluation of the kernel between any prefix of s and any prefix of t. Hence, from the table of Example 11.19 we can see that $\kappa(\texttt{"gatt"},\texttt{"cat"}) = 6$ by reading off the value of DP $(4,3)$.

∎

11.4 Fixed length subsequences kernels

We can adapt the recursive relation presented above in a number of ways, until we are satisfied that the feature space implicitly defined by the kernel is tuned to the particular task at hand.

Our first adaptation reduces the dimensionality of the feature space by only considering non-contiguous substrings that have a given *fixed* length p.

Definition 11.23 [Fixed Length Subsequences Kernel] The feature space associated with the fixed length subsequences kernel of length p is indexed by Σ^p, with the embedding given by

$$\phi_u^p (s) = |\{\mathbf{i}: u = s\,(\mathbf{i})\}|,\ u \in \Sigma^p.$$

The associated kernel is defined as

$$\kappa_p (s,t) = \langle \phi^p (s), \phi^p (t) \rangle = \sum_{u \in \Sigma^p} \phi_u^p (s)\, \phi_u^p (t).$$

∎

Evaluating the kernel We can perform a similar derivation as for the all-subsequences kernel except that we must now restrict the index sequences to the set I_p of those with length p

$$\kappa (s,t) = \langle \phi (s), \phi (t) \rangle = \sum_{u \in \Sigma^p} \sum_{(\mathbf{i},\mathbf{j}):u=s(\mathbf{i})=t(\mathbf{j})} 1 = \sum_{(\mathbf{i},\mathbf{j}) \in I_p \times I_p : s(\mathbf{i})=t(\mathbf{j})} 1.$$

Following the derivations of the previous section we arrive at

$$\sum_{(\mathbf{i},\mathbf{j}) \in I_p \times I_p : sa(\mathbf{i})=t(\mathbf{j})} 1 = \sum_{(\mathbf{i},\mathbf{j}) \in I_p \times I_p : s(\mathbf{i})=t(\mathbf{j})} 1 + \sum_{u:t=uav} \sum_{(\mathbf{i},\mathbf{j}) \in I_{p-1} \times I_{p-1} : s(\mathbf{i})=u(\mathbf{j})} 1,$$

where, as before, the lengths of the sequences considered in the two components of the sum differ.

Computation 11.24 [Fixed length subsequence kernel] This leads to the following recursive definition of the fixed length subsequences kernel

$$
\begin{aligned}
\kappa_0 (s,t) &= 1, \\
\kappa_p (s,\varepsilon) &= 0,\ \text{for } p > 0, \\
\kappa_p (sa,t) &= \kappa_p (s,t) + \sum_{k:t_k=a} \kappa_{p-1} (s,t\,(1:k-1)).
\end{aligned}
\tag{11.4}
$$

∎

Note that now we not only have a recursion over the prefixes of the strings, but also over the lengths of the subsequences considered. The following algorithm includes this extra recursion to compute the kernel by storing the evaluation of the previous kernel in the table DPrec.

Algorithm 11.25 [Fixed length subsequences kernel] The fixed length subsequences kernel is computed in Code Fragment 11.2. ∎

Input	strings s and t of lengths n and m length p
Process	DP $(0:n, 0:m) = 1$;
2	for $l = 1:p$
3	DPrec = DP;
4	for $j = 1:m$
5	DP $(0, j) = 1$;
6	end
7	for $i = 1:n-p+l$
8	last $= 0$; $P(0) = 0$;
9	for $k = 1:m$
10	$P(k) = P(\text{last})$;
11	if $t_k = s_i$ then
12	$P(k) = P(\text{last}) + \text{DPrec}(i-1, k-1)$;
13	last $= k$;
14	end
15	end
16	for $k = 1:m$
17	DP $(i, k) = \text{DP}(i-1, k) + P(k)$;
18	end
19	end
20	end
Output	kernel evaluation $\kappa_p(s, t) = \text{DP}(n, m)$

Code Fragment 11.2. Pseudocode for the fixed length subsequences kernel.

Cost of the computation At the pth stage we must be able to access the row above both in the current table and in the table DPrec from the previous stage. Hence, we must create a series of tables by adding an extra loop to the overall algorithm making the overall complexity $O(p|s||t|)$. On the penultimate stage when $l = p - 1$ we need only compute up to row $n - 1$, since this is all that is required in the final loop with $l = p$. In the implementation given above we have made use of this fact at each stage, so that for the lth stage we have only computed up to row $n - p + l$, for $l = 1, \ldots, p$.

Example 11.26 Using the strings from Example 11.18 leads to the following computations for $p = 0, 1, 2, 3$ given in Table 11.3. Note that the sum of all four tables is identical to that for the all-subsequences kernel. This is because the two strings do not share any sequences longer than 3 so that summing over lengths $0, 1, 2, 3$ subsumes all the common subsequences. This also suggests that if we compute the p subsequences kernel we can, at almost no extra cost, compute the kernel κ_l for $l \leq p$. Hence, we have the flexibility

DP : κ_0	ε	g	a	t	t	a	DP : κ_1	ε	g	a	t	t	a
ε	1	1	1	1	1	1	ε	0	0	0	0	0	0
c	1	1	1	1	1	1	c	0	0	0	0	0	0
a	1	1	1	1	1	1	a	0	0	1	1	1	2
t	1	1	1	1	1	1	t	0	0	1	2	3	4
a	1	1	1	1	1	1	a	0	0	2	3	4	6
DP : κ_2	ε	g	a	t	t	a	DP : κ_3	ε	g	a	t	t	a
ε	0	0	0	0	0	0	ε	0	0	0	0	0	0
c	0	0	0	0	0	0	c	0	0	0	0	0	0
a	0	0	0	0	0	0	a	0	0	0	0	0	0
t	0	0	0	1	2	2	t	0	0	0	0	0	0
a	0	0	0	1	2	5	a	0	0	0	0	0	2

Table 11.3. *Computations for the fixed length subsequences kernel.*

to define a kernel that combines these different subsequences kernels with different weightings $a_l \geq 0$

$$\kappa(s,t) = \sum_{l=1}^{p} a_l \kappa_l(s,t).$$

The only change to the above algorithm would be that the upper bound of the loop for the variable i would need to become n rather than $n - p + l$ and we would need to accumulate the sum at the end of the l loop with the assignment

$$\text{Kern} = \text{Kern} + a(l)\, \text{DP}(n,m),$$

where the variable Kern is initialised to 0 at the very beginning of the algorithm.   ∎

11.5 Gap-weighted subsequences kernels

We now move to a more general type of kernel still based on subsequences, but one that weights the occurrences of subsequences according to how spread out they are. In other words the kernel considers the degree of presence of a subsequence to be a function of how many gaps are interspersed within it. The computation of this kernel will follow the approach developed in the previous section for the fixed length subsequences kernel. Indeed we also restrict consideration to fixed length subsequences in this section.

The kernel described here has often been referred to as the *string kernel* in the literature, though this name has also been used to refer to the p-spectrum kernel. We have chosen to use long-winded descriptive names for the kernels introduced here in order to avoid further proliferating the existing confusion around different names. We prefer to regard 'string kernel' as a generic term applicable to all of the kernels covered in this chapter.

The key idea behind the gap-weighted subsequences kernel is still to compare strings by means of the subsequences they contain – the more subsequences in common, the more similar they are – but rather than weighting all occurrences equally, the degree of contiguity of the subsequence in the input string s determines how much it will contribute to the comparison.

Example 11.27 For example: the string `"gon"` occurs as a subsequence of the strings `"gone"`, `"going"` and `"galleon"`, but we consider the first occurrence as more important since it is contiguous, while the final occurrence is the weakest of all three.   ∎

The feature space has the same coordinates as for the fixed subsequences kernel and hence the same dimension. In order to deal with non-contiguous substrings, it is necessary to introduce a decay factor $\lambda \in (0, 1)$ that can be used to weight the presence of a certain feature in a string. Recall that for an index sequence $\mathbf{i}$ identifying the occurrence of a subsequence $u = s(\mathbf{i})$ in a string s, we use $l(\mathbf{i})$ to denote the length of the string in s. In the gap-weighted kernel, we weight the occurrence of u with the exponentially decaying weight $\lambda^{l(\mathbf{i})}$.

Definition 11.28 [Gap-weighted subsequences kernel] The feature space associated with the gap-weighted subsequences kernel of length p is indexed by $I = \Sigma^p$, with the embedding given by

$$\phi_u^p(s) = \sum_{\mathbf{i}:u=s(\mathbf{i})} \lambda^{l(\mathbf{i})}, \ u \in \Sigma^p.$$

The associated kernel is defined as

$$\kappa_p(s, t) = \langle \phi^p(s), \phi^p(t) \rangle = \sum_{u \in \Sigma^p} \phi_u^p(s) \phi_u^p(t).$$

∎

Remark 11.29 [Two limits] Observe that we can recover the fixed length subsequences kernel by choosing $\lambda = 1$, since the weight of all occurrences will then be 1 so that

$$\phi_u^p(s) = \sum_{\mathbf{i}:u=s(\mathbf{i})} 1^{l(\mathbf{i})} = |\{\mathbf{i}: u = s(\mathbf{i})\}|, \; u \in \Sigma^p.$$

On the other hand, as $\lambda \to 0$, the kernel approximates the p-spectrum kernel since the relative weighting of strings longer than p tends to zero. Hence, we can view the gap-weighted kernel as interpolating between these two kernels. ∎

Example 11.30 Consider the simple strings "cat", "car", "bat", and "bar". Fixing $p = 2$, the words are mapped as follows:

ϕ	ca	ct	at	ba	bt	cr	ar	br
cat	λ^2	λ^3	λ^2	0	0	0	0	0
car	λ^2	0	0	0	0	λ^3	λ^2	0
bat	0	0	λ^2	λ^2	λ^3	0	0	0
bar	0	0	0	λ^2	0	0	λ^2	λ^3

So the unnormalised kernel between "cat" and "car" is $\kappa(\text{"cat"},\text{"car"}) = \lambda^4$, while the normalised version is obtained using

$$\kappa(\text{"cat"},\text{"cat"}) = \kappa(\text{"car"},\text{"car"}) = 2\lambda^4 + \lambda^6$$

as $\hat{\kappa}(\text{"cat"},\text{"car"}) = \lambda^4/(2\lambda^4 + \lambda^6) = (2 + \lambda^2)^{-1}$. ∎

11.5.1 Naive implementation

The computation of this kernel will involve both techniques developed for the fixed subsequences kernel and for the p-spectrum kernel. When computing the p-spectrum kernel we considered substrings that occurred as a suffix of a prefix of the string. This suggests considering subsequences whose final occurrence is the last character of the string. We introduce this as an auxiliary kernel.

Definition 11.31 [Gap-weighted suffix subsequences kernel] The feature space associated with the gap-weighted subsequences kernel of length p is indexed by $I = \Sigma^p$, with the embedding given by

$$\phi_u^{p,S}(s) = \sum_{\mathbf{i} \in I_p^{|s|}:u=s(\mathbf{i})} \lambda^{l(\mathbf{i})}, \; u \in \Sigma^p,$$

where we have used I_p^k to denote the set of p-tuples of indices $\mathbf{i}$ with $i_p = k$. The associated kernel is defined as

$$\kappa_p^S (s, t) = \left\langle \phi^{p,S} (s), \phi^{p,S} (t) \right\rangle = \sum_{u \in \Sigma^p} \phi_u^{p,S} (s) \, \phi_u^{p,S} (t).$$

∎

Example 11.32 Consider again the simple strings "cat", "car", "bat", and "bar". Fixing $p = 2$, the words are mapped for the suffix version as follows:

$\phi_u^{2,S} (s)$	ca	ct	at	ba	bt	cr	ar	br
cat	0	λ^3	λ^2	0	0	0	0	0
car	0	0	0	0	0	λ^3	λ^2	0
bat	0	0	λ^2	0	λ^3	0	0	0
bar	0	0	0	0	0	0	λ^2	λ^3

Hence, the suffix kernel between "cat" and "car" is $\kappa_2^S(\text{"cat"},\text{"car"}) = 0$, while suffix kernel between "cat" and "bat" is $\kappa_2^S(\text{"cat"},\text{"bat"}) = \lambda^4$. ∎

Figure 11.1 shows a visualisation of a set of strings derived from an embedding given by the gap-weighted subsequences kernel of length 4, with $\lambda = 0.8$. As in the case of the p-spectrum kernel, we can express the gap-

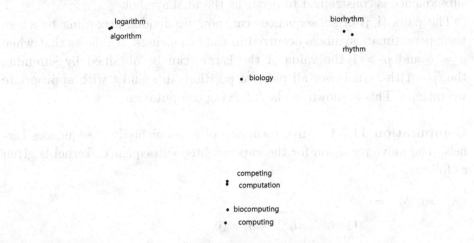

Fig. 11.1. Visualisation of the embedding created by the gap-weighted subsequences kernel.

weighted subsequences kernel in terms of its suffix version as

$$\kappa_p\left(s,t\right) = \sum_{i=1}^{|s|}\sum_{j=1}^{|t|}\kappa_p^S\left(s\left(1:i\right),t\left(1:j\right)\right),$$

since

$$
\begin{aligned}
\kappa_p\left(s,t\right) &= \sum_{u\in\Sigma^p}\sum_{\mathbf{i}\in I_p:u=s(\mathbf{i})}\lambda^{l(\mathbf{i})}\sum_{\mathbf{j}\in I_p:u=t(\mathbf{j})}\lambda^{l(\mathbf{j})} = \sum_{(\mathbf{i},\mathbf{j})\in I_p\times I_p:s(\mathbf{i})=t(\mathbf{j})}\lambda^{l(\mathbf{i})+l(\mathbf{j})} \\
&= \sum_{i=1}^{|s|}\sum_{j=1}^{|t|}\sum_{(\mathbf{i},\mathbf{j})\in I_p^i\times I_p^j:s(\mathbf{i})=t(\mathbf{j})}\lambda^{l(\mathbf{i})+l(\mathbf{j})} \\
&= \sum_{i=1}^{|s|}\sum_{j=1}^{|t|}\kappa_p^S\left(s\left(1:i\right),t\left(1:j\right)\right).
\end{aligned}
$$

Recall that $[u=v]$ denotes the function that returns 1 if the strings u and v are identical and 0 otherwise. We can therefore evaluate the suffix version for the case $p=1$ simply as

$$\kappa_1^S\left(s,t\right) = \left[s_{|s|}=t_{|t|}\right]\lambda^2.$$

We can now devise a recursion for the suffix version of the kernel by observing that, for extensions of s and t by single symbols a and b respectively, the suffix version is only non-zero if $a=b$, since the last character of the subsequence is constrained to occur as the final symbol.

The pairs $(\mathbf{i},\mathbf{j})$ of subsequences can now be divided according to where their penultimate symbols occurred in the two strings. It follows that when $a=b$ and $p>1$ the value of the kernel can be obtained by summing the $(p-1)$th kernel over all pairs of positions in s and t with appropriate weightings. This is shown in the following computation.

Computation 11.33 [Naive recursion of gap-weighted subsequences kernels] The naive recursion for the gap-weighted subsequences kernel is given as follows

$$
\begin{aligned}
\kappa_p^S\left(sa,tb\right) &= \sum_{(\mathbf{i},\mathbf{j})\in I_p^{|s|+1}\times I_p^{|t|+1}:sa(\mathbf{i})=tb(\mathbf{j})}\lambda^{l(\mathbf{i})+l(\mathbf{j})} \\
&= \left[a=b\right]\sum_{i=1}^{|s|}\sum_{j=1}^{|t|}\lambda^{2+|s|-i+|t|-j}\sum_{(\mathbf{i},\mathbf{j})\in I_{p-1}^i\times I_{p-1}^j:s(\mathbf{i})=t(\mathbf{j})}\lambda^{l(\mathbf{i})+l(\mathbf{j})}
\end{aligned}
$$

$$= [a = b] \sum_{i=1}^{|s|} \sum_{j=1}^{|t|} \lambda^{2+|s|-i+|t|-j} \kappa_{p-1}^S (s(1:i), t(1:j)). \quad (11.5)$$

∎

Example 11.34 Using the strings from Example 11.18 leads to the computations shown in Table 11.4 for the suffix version for $p = 1, 2, 3$. Hence

DP : κ_1^S	g	a	t	t	a
c	0	0	0	0	0
a	0	λ^2	0	0	λ^2
t	0	0	λ^2	λ^2	0
a	0	λ^2	0	0	λ^2

DP : κ_2^S	g	a	t	t	a
c	0	0	0	0	0
a	0	0	0	0	0
t	0	0	λ^4	λ^5	0
a	0	0	0	0	$\lambda^7 + \lambda^5 + \lambda^4$

DP : κ_3^S	g	a	t	t	a
c	0	0	0	0	0
a	0	0	0	0	0
t	0	0	0	0	0
a	0	0	0	0	$2\lambda^7$

Table 11.4. *Computations for the gap-weighted subsequences kernel.*

the gap-weighted subsequences kernels between $s =$"gatta" and $t =$"cata" for $p = 1, 2, 3$ are

$$\kappa_1 (\text{"gatta"}, \text{"cata"}) = 6\lambda^2,$$
$$\kappa_2 (\text{"gatta"}, \text{"cata"}) = \lambda^7 + 2\lambda^5 + 2\lambda^4$$
$$\text{and } \kappa_3 (\text{"gatta"}, \text{"cata"}) = 2\lambda^7.$$

∎

Cost of the computation If we were to implement a naive evaluation of the gap-weighted suffix subsequences kernel using the recursive definition of Computation 11.33, then for each value of p we must sum over all the entries in the previous table. This leads to a complexity of $O\left(|t|^2 |s|^2\right)$ to complete the table. Since there will be p tables required to evaluate κ_p this gives an overall complexity of $O\left(p|t|^2 |s|^2\right)$.

Remark 11.35 [Possible Computational Strategy] There are two different ways in which this complexity could be reduced. The first is to observe that the only non-zero entries in the tables for the suffix versions are the positions (i, j) for which $s_i = t_j$. Hence, we could keep a list $L(s, t)$ of these pairs

$$L(s, t) = \{(i, j) : s_i = t_j\},$$

and sum over the list $L(s, t)$ rather than over the complete arrays. The entries in the list could be inserted in lexicographic order of the index pairs. When summing over the list to compute an entry in position (k, l) we would need to consider all entries in the list before the (k, l)th entry, but only include those (i, j) with $i < k$ and $j < l$. This approach could also improve the memory requirements of the algorithm while the complexity would reduce to

$$O\left(p\,|L(s, t)|^2\right) \leq O\left(p\,|t|^2\,|s|^2\right).$$

The list version will be competitive when the list is short. This is likely to occur when the size of the alphabet is large, so that the chances of two symbols being equal becomes correspondingly small. ∎

We will not develop this approach further but consider a method that reduces the complexity to $O(p\,|t|\,|s|)$. For small alphabets this will typically be better than using the list approach.

11.5.2 Efficient implementation

Consider the recursive equation for the gap-weighted subsequences kernel given in equation (11.5). We now consider computing an intermediate dynamic programming table DP_p whose entries are

$$\mathrm{DP}_p(k, l) = \sum_{i=1}^{k} \sum_{j=1}^{l} \lambda^{k-i+l-j} \kappa_{p-1}^{S}(s(1:i), t(1:j)).$$

Given this table we can evaluate the kernel by observing that

$$\kappa_p^{S}(sa, tb) = \begin{cases} \lambda^2 \, \mathrm{DP}_p(|s|, |t|) & \text{if } a = b; \\ 0 & \text{otherwise.} \end{cases}$$

Computation 11.36 [Gap-weighted subsequences kernel] There is a natural recursion for evaluating $\mathrm{DP}_p(k, l)$ in terms of $\mathrm{DP}_p(k-1, l)$, $\mathrm{DP}_p(k, l-1)$

and $\mathrm{DP}_p\left(k-1,l-1\right)$

$$
\begin{aligned}
\mathrm{DP}_p\left(k,l\right) &= \sum_{i=1}^{k}\sum_{j=1}^{l}\lambda^{k-i+l-j}\kappa_{p-1}^{S}\left(s\left(1:i\right),t\left(1:j\right)\right) \\
&= \kappa_{p-1}^{S}\left(s\left(1:k\right),t\left(1:l\right)\right)+\lambda\,\mathrm{DP}_p\left(k,l-1\right) \qquad (11.6) \\
&\quad +\lambda\,\mathrm{DP}_p\left(k-1,l\right)-\lambda^2\,\mathrm{DP}_p\left(k-1,l-1\right).
\end{aligned}
$$

∎

Correctness of the recursion The correctness of this recursion can be seen by observing that the contributions to the sum can be divided into three groups: when $(i,j)=(k,l)$ we obtain the first term; those with $i=k$, $j<l$ are included in the second term with the correct weighting; those with $j=l$ and $i<k$ are included in the third term; while those with $i<k$, $j<l$, are included in the second, third and fourth terms with opposite weighting in the fourth, leading to their correct inclusion in the overall sum.

Example 11.37 Using the strings from Example 11.18 leads to the DP computations of Table 11.5 for $p=2,3$. Note that we do not need to compute the last row and column. The final evaluation of κ_3 ("gatta", "cata") is given by the sum of the entries in the κ_3^{S} table. ∎

The complexity of the computation required to compute the table DP_p for a single value of p is clearly $O\left(|t|\,|s|\right)$ as is the complexity of computing κ_p^{S} from DP_p making the overall complexity of computing the kernel $\kappa_p\left(s,t\right)$ equal to $O\left(p\,|t|\,|s|\right)$.

Algorithm 11.38 [Gap-weighted subsequences kernel] The gap-weighted subsequences kernel is computed in Code Fragment 11.3. ∎

Remark 11.39 [Improving the complexity] Algorithm 11.38 seems to fail to make use of the fact that in many cases most of the entries in the table DPS are zero. This fact forms the basis of the list algorithm with complexity $O\left(p\,|L\left(s,t\right)|^2\right)$. It would be very interesting if the two approaches could be combined to create an algorithm with complexity $O\left(p\,|L\left(s,t\right)|\right)$, though this seems to be a non-trivial task. ∎

11.5.3 Variations on the theme

The inspiration for the gap-weighted subsequences kernel is first and foremost from the consideration of DNA sequences where it is likely that inser-

DP : κ_1^S	g	a	t	t	a
c	0	0	0	0	0
a	0	λ^2	0	0	λ^2
t	0	0	λ^2	λ^2	0
a	0	λ^2	0	0	λ^2

DP$_2$	g	a	t	t
c	0	0	0	0
a	0	λ^2	λ^3	λ^4
t	0	λ^3	$\lambda^4+\lambda^2$	$\lambda^5+\lambda^3+\lambda^2$

DP : κ_2^S	g	a	t	t	a
c	0	0	0	0	0
a	0	0	0	0	0
t	0	0	λ^4	λ^5	0
a	0	0	0	0	$\lambda^7+\lambda^5+\lambda^4$

DP$_3$	g	a	t	t
c	0	0	0	0
a	0	0	0	0
t	0	0	λ^4	$2\lambda^5$

DP : κ_3^S	g	a	t	t	a
c	0	0	0	0	0
a	0	0	0	0	0
t	0	0	0	0	0
a	0	0	0	0	$2\lambda^7$

Table 11.5. *Computations for the dynamic programming tables of the gap-weighted subsequences kernel.*

tions and deletions of base pairs could occur as genes evolve. This suggests that we should be able to detect similarities between strings that have common subsequences with some gaps.

This consideration throws up a number of possible variations and generalisations of the gap-weighted kernel that could be useful for particular applications. We will discuss how to implement some of these variants in order to show the flexibility inherent in the algorithms we have developed.

Character-weightings string kernel Our first variant is to allow different weightings for different characters that are skipped over by a sub-

Input	strings s and t of lengths n and m, length p, parameter λ
Process	$\mathrm{DPS}\,(1:n,1:m) = 0;$
2	for $i = 1:n$
3	for $j = 1:m$
4	if $s_i = t_j$
5	$\mathrm{DPS}\,(i,j) = \lambda^2;$
6	end
7	end
8	end
9	$\mathrm{DP}\,(0,0:m) = 0;$
10	$\mathrm{DP}\,(1:n,0) = 0;$
11	for $l = 2:p$
12	$\mathrm{Kern}\,(l) = 0;$
13	for $i = 1:n-1$
14	for $j = 1:m-1$
15	$\mathrm{DP}\,(i,j) = \mathrm{DPS}\,(i,j) + \lambda\,\mathrm{DP}\,(i-1,j) +$
16	$\lambda\,\mathrm{DP}\,(i,j-1) - \lambda^2\,\mathrm{DP}\,(i-1,j-1);$
17	if $s_i = t_j$
18	$\mathrm{DPS}\,(i,j) = \lambda^2\,\mathrm{DP}\,(i-1,j-1);$
19	$\mathrm{Kern}\,(l) = \mathrm{Kern}\,(l) + \mathrm{DPS}\,(i,j);$
20	end
21	end
22	end
23	end
Output	kernel evaluation $\kappa_p\,(s,t) = \mathrm{Kern}\,(p)$

Code Fragment 11.3. Pseudocode for the gap-weighted subsequences kernel.

sequence. In the DNA example, this might perhaps be dictated by the expectation that certain base pairs are more likely to become inserted than others.

These gap-weightings will be denoted by λ_a for $a \in \Sigma$. Similarly, we will consider different weightings for characters that actually occur in a subsequence, perhaps attaching greater importance to certain symbols. These weightings will be denoted by μ_a for $a \in \Sigma$. With this generalisation the basic formula governing the recursion of the suffix kernel becomes

$$\kappa_p^S\,(sa, tb) = [a = b]\,\mu_a^2 \sum_{i=1}^{n}\sum_{j=1}^{m} \lambda\,(s\,(i+1:n))\,\lambda\,(t\,(j+1:m))$$

$$\kappa_{p-1}^S\,(s\,(1:i), t\,(1:j)),$$

where $n = |s|$, $m = |t|$ and we have used the notation $\lambda(u)$ for

$$\lambda(u) = \prod_{i=1}^{|u|} \lambda_{u_i}.$$

The corresponding recursion for $\mathrm{DP}_p(k, l)$ becomes

$$\begin{aligned}
\mathrm{DP}_p(k, l) = {} & \kappa_{p-1}^S(s(1:k), t(1:l)) + \lambda_{t_l}\,\mathrm{DP}_p(k, l-1) \\
& + \lambda_{s_k}\,\mathrm{DP}_p(k-1, l) - \lambda_{t_l}\lambda_{s_k}\,\mathrm{DP}_p(k-1, l-1),
\end{aligned}$$

with $\kappa_p^S(sa, tb)$ now given by

$$\kappa_p^S(sa, tb) = \begin{cases} \mu_a^2\,\mathrm{DP}_p(|s|, |t|) & \text{if } a = b; \\ 0 & \text{otherwise.} \end{cases}$$

Algorithm 11.40 [Character weightings string kernel] An implementation of this variant can easily be effected by corresponding changes to lines 5, 15 and 17 of Algorithm 11.38

5	$\mathrm{DPS}(i, j) = \mu(s_i)^2\,;$
15a	$\mathrm{DP}(i, j) = \mathrm{DPS}(i, j) + \lambda(s_i)\,\mathrm{DP}(i-1, j) +$
15b	$\qquad \lambda(t_j)\,(\mathrm{DP}(i, j-1) - \lambda(s_i)\,\mathrm{DP}(i-1, j-1))\,;$
17	$\mathrm{DPS}(i, j) = \mu(s_i)^2\,\mathrm{DP}(i-1, j-1)\,;$

∎

Soft matching So far, distinct symbols have been considered entirely unrelated. This may not be an accurate reflection of the application under consideration. For example, in DNA sequences it is more likely that certain base pairs will arise as a mutation of a given base pair, suggesting that some non-zero measure of similarity should be set between them.

We will assume that a similarity matrix $\mathbf{A}$ between symbols has been given. We may expect that many of the entries in $\mathbf{A}$ are zero, that the diagonal is equal to 1, but that some off-diagonal entries are non-zero. We must also assume that $\mathbf{A}$ is positive semi-definite in order to ensure that a valid kernel is defined, since $\mathbf{A}$ is the kernel matrix of the set of all single character strings when $p = 1$.

With this generalisation the basic formula governing the recursion of the suffix kernel becomes

$$\kappa_p^S(sa, tb) = \lambda^2 \mathbf{A}_{ab} \sum_{i=1}^{|s|} \sum_{j=1}^{|t|} \lambda^{|s|-i+|t|-j} \kappa_{p-1}^S(s(1:i), t(1:j)).$$

The corresponding recursion for $DP_p(k, l)$ remains unchanged as in (11.6), while $\kappa_p^S(sa, tb)$ is now given by

$$\kappa_p^S(sa, tb) = \lambda^2 \mathbf{A}_{ab} \underset{p}{DP}(|s|, |t|).$$

Algorithm 11.41 [Soft matching string kernel] An implementation of soft matching requires the alteration of lines 4, 5, 16 and 17 of Algorithm 11.38

4	if $A(s(i), t(j)) \neq 0$
5	$\quad DPS(i, j) = \lambda^2 A(s_i, t_j);$
16	$\quad$ if $A(s_i, t_j) \neq 0$
17	$\quad DPS(i, j) = \lambda^2 A(s_i, t_j) DP(i-1, j-1);$

∎

Weighting by number of gaps It may be that once an insertion occurs its length is not important. In other words we can expect bursts of inserted characters and wish only to penalise the similarity of two subsequences by the number and not the length of the bursts. For this variant the recursion becomes

$$\kappa_p^S(sa, tb) = [a = b] \sum_{i=1}^{|s|} \sum_{j=1}^{|t|} \lambda^{[i \neq |s|]} \lambda^{[j \neq |t|]} \kappa_{p-1}^S(s(1:i), t(1:j)),$$

since we only apply the penalty λ if the previous character of the subsequence occurs before position $|s|$ in s and before position $|t|$ in t.

In this case we must create the dynamic programming table DP_p whose entries are

$$DP_p(k, l) = \sum_{i=1}^{k} \sum_{j=1}^{l} \kappa_{p-1}^S(s(1:i), t(1:j)),$$

using the recursion

$$DP_p(k, l) = \kappa_{p-1}^S(s(1:k), t(1:l)) + DP_p(k, l-1) \\ + DP_p(k-1, l) - DP_p(k-1, l-1),$$

corresponding to $\lambda = 1$. Given this table we can evaluate the kernel by observing that if $a = b$ then

$$\kappa_p^S(sa, tb) = DP_p(|s|, |t|) + (\lambda - 1)(DP_p(|s|, |t| - 1) + DP_p(|s| - 1, |t|)) \\ + (\lambda^2 - 2\lambda + 1) DP_p(|s| - 1, |t| - 1),$$

since the first term ensures the correct weighting of $\kappa_{p-1}^{S}(s, t)$, while the second corrects the weighting of those entries involving a single λ factor and the third term adjusts the weighting of the remaining contributions.

Algorithm 11.42 [Gap number weighting string kernel] An implementation of weighting by number of gaps requires setting $\lambda = 1$ in lines 5 and 15 and altering line 17 to

17a $\qquad \mathrm{DPS}(i, j) = \mathrm{DP}(i - 1, j - 1) + (\lambda - 1)(\mathrm{DP}(i - 2, j - 1)$

17b $\qquad\qquad + \mathrm{DP}(i - 1, j - 2) + (\lambda - 1)\mathrm{DP}(i - 2, j - 2));$

∎

Remark 11.43 [General symbol strings] Though we have introduced the kernels in this chapter with character symbols in mind, they apply to any alphabet of symbols. For example if we consider the alphabet to be the set of reals we could compare numeric sequences. Clearly we will need to use the soft matching approach described above. The gap-weighted kernel is only appropriate if the matrix **A** comparing individual numbers has many entries equal to zero. An example of such a kernel is given in (9.11). ∎

11.6 Beyond dynamic programming: trie-based kernels

A very efficient, although less general, class of methods for implementing string kernels can be obtained by following a different computational approach. Instead of using dynamic programming as the core engine of the computation, one can exploit an efficient data structure known as a 'trie' in the string matching literature. The name trie is derived from 'retrieval tree'. Here we give the definition of a trie – see Definition 11.56 for a formal definition of trees.

Definition 11.44 [Trie] A *trie* over an alphabet Σ is a tree whose internal nodes have their children indexed by Σ. The edges connecting a parent to its child are labelled with the corresponding symbol from Σ. A *complete trie of depth p* is a trie containing the maximal number of nodes consistent with the depth of the tree being p. A *labelled trie* is a trie for which each node has an associated label. ∎

In a complete trie there is a 1–1 correspondence between the nodes at depth k and the strings of length k, the correspondence being between the node and the string on the path to that node from the root. The string associated with the root node is the empty string ε. Hence, we will refer to the nodes of a trie by their associated string. The key observation behind the trie-based approach is that one can therefore regard the *leaves* of the complete trie of depth p as the indices of the feature space indexed by the set Σ^p of strings of length p.

The algorithms extract relevant substrings from the source string being analysed and attach them to the root. The substrings are then repeatedly moved into the subtree or subtrees corresponding to their next symbol until the leaves corresponding to that substring are reached.

For a source string s there are $\frac{1}{2}|s|(|s|+1)$ non-trivial substrings $s(i:j)$ being determined by an initial index in $i \in \{1,\ldots,|s|\}$ and a final index $j \in \{i,\ldots,|s|\}$. Typically the algorithms will only consider a restricted subset of these possible substrings. Each substring can potentially end up at a number of leaves through being processed into more than one subtree. Once the substrings have been processed for each of the two source strings, their inner product can be computed by traversing the leaves, multiplying the corresponding weighted values at each leaf and summing.

Computation 11.45 [Trie-based String Kernels] Hence we can summarise the algorithm into its four main phases:

phase 1: Form all substrings $s(i:j)$ satisfying initial criteria;
phase 2: work the substrings of string s down from root to leaves;
phase 3: work the substrings of string t down from root to leaves;
phase 4: compute products at leaves and sum over the tree.

∎

This breakdown is just conceptual, but it does suggest an added advantage of the approach when we are computing a kernel matrix for a set

$$S = \left\{ s^1, \ldots, s^\ell \right\}$$

of strings. We need to perform phase 2 only once for each row of the kernel, subsequently repeating phases 3 and 4 as we cycle through the set S with the results of phase 2 for the string indexing the row retained at the leaves throughout.

Despite these advantages it is immediately clear that the approach does have its restrictions. Clearly, if all the leaves are populated then the complexity will be at least $|\Sigma|^p$, which for large values of p will become inefficient. Similarly, we must restrict the number of strings that can arrive at each leaf. If we were to consider the general gap-weighted kernel this could be of the order of the number of substrings of the source string s further adding to the complexity. For the examples we consider below we are able to place a bound on the number of populated leaves.

11.6.1 Trie computation of the p-spectrum kernels

As a simple first example let us consider this approach being used to compute the p-spectrum kernel. In this case the strings that are filtered down the trie are the substrings of length p of the source string s. The algorithm creates a list $L_s(\varepsilon)$ attached to the root node ε containing these $|s| - p + 1$ strings u, each with an associated index i initialised to 0. A similar list $L_t(\varepsilon)$ is created for the second string t. We now process the nodes recursively beginning with the call 'processnode(ε)' using the following strategy after initialising the global variable 'Kern' to 0. The complete algorithm is given here.

Algorithm 11.46 [Trie-based p-spectrum] The trie-based computation of the p-spectrum is given in Code Fragment 11.4. ∎

Input	strings s and t, parameter p
Process	Let $L_s(\varepsilon) = \{(s(i:i+p-1),0) : i = 1 : |s| - p + 1\}$
2	Let $L_t(\varepsilon) = \{(t(i:i+p-1),0) : i = 1 : |t| - p + 1\}$
3	Kern $= 0$;
4	processnode($\varepsilon, 0$);
where	processnode(v, depth)
6	let $L_s(v)$, $L_t(v)$ be the lists associated with v;
7	if depth $= p$
8	Kern $=$ Kern $+ |L_s(v)|\,|L_t(v)|$;
9	end
10	else if $L_s(v)$ and $L_t(v)$ both not empty
11	while there exists (u, i) in the list $L_s(v)$
12	add $(u, i+1)$ to the list $L_s(vu_{i+1})$;
13	end
14	while there exists (u, i) in the list $L_t(v)$
15	add $(u, i+1)$ to the list $L_t(vu_{i+1})$;
16	end
17	for $a \in \Sigma$
18	processnode(va, depth $+1$);
19	end
20	end
Output	$\kappa_p(s, t) =$ Kern

Code Fragment 11.4. Pseudocode for trie-based implementation of spectrum kernel.

Correctness of the algorithm The correctness of the algorithm follows from the observation that for all the pairs (u, i) in the list $L_s(v)$ we have $v = u(1:i)$, similarly for $L_t(v)$. This is certainly true at the start of the algorithm and continues to hold since $(u, i + 1)$ is added to the list at the vertex $vu_{i+1} = u(1:i+1)$. Hence, the substrings reaching a leaf vertex v are precisely those substrings equal to v. The length of the list $L_s(v)$ is therefore equal to

$$\phi_v^p(s) = |\{(v_1, v_2) : s = v_1 v v_2\}|,$$

implying the algorithm correctly computes the p-spectrum kernel.

Cost of the computation The complexity of the computation can be divided into the preprocessing which involves $O(|s| + |t|)$ steps, followed by the processing of the lists. Each of the $|s| - p + 1 + |t| - p + 1$ substrings processed gets passed down at most p times, so the complexity of the main processing is $O(p(|s| - p + 1 + |t| - p + 1))$ giving an overall complexity of

$$O(p(|s| + |t|)).$$

At first sight there appears to be a contradiction between this complexity and the size of the feature space $|\Sigma|^p$, which is exponential in p. The reason for the difference is that even for moderate p there are far fewer substrings than leaves in the complete trie of depth p. Hence, the recursive algorithm will rapidly find subtrees that are not populated, i.e. nodes u for which one of the lists $L_s(u)$ or $L_t(u)$ is empty. The algorithm effectively prunes the subtree below these nodes since the recursion halts at this stage. Hence, although the complete tree is exponential in size, the tree actually processed $O(p(|s| + |t|))$ nodes.

Remark 11.47 [Computing the kernel matrix] As already discussed above we can use the trie-based approach to complete a whole row of a kernel matrix more efficiently than if we were to evaluate each entry independently. We first process the string s indexing that row, hence populating the leaves of the trie with the lists arising from the string s. The cost of this processing is $O(p|s|)$. For each string t^i, $i = 1, \ldots, \ell$, we now process it into the trie and evaluate its kernel with s. For the ith string this takes time $O(p|t^i|)$. Hence, the overall complexity is

$$O\left(p\left(|s| + \sum_{i=1}^{\ell} |t^i|\right)\right),$$

rather than

$$O\left(p\left(\ell\,|s| + \sum_{i=1}^{\ell}|t^i|\right)\right),$$

that would be required if the information about s is not retained. This leads to the overall complexity for computing the kernel matrix

$$O\left(p\ell\sum_{i=1}^{\ell}|t^i|\right).$$

Despite the clear advantages in terms of computational complexity, there is one slight drawback of this method discussed in the next remark.   ∎

Remark 11.48 [Memory requirements] If we are not following the idea of evaluating a row of the kernel matrix, we can create and dismantle the tree as we process the strings. As we return from a recursive call all of the information in that subtree is no longer required and so it can be deleted. This means that at every stage of the computation there are at most $p\,|\Sigma|$ nodes held in memory with the substrings distributed among their lists. The factor of $|\Sigma|$ in the number of nodes arises from the fact that as we process a node we potentially create all of its $|\Sigma|$ children before continuing the recursion into one of them.   ∎

Remark 11.49 [By-product information] Notice that the trie also contains information about the spectra of order less than p so one could use it to calculate a blended spectrum kernel of the type

$$\kappa_{p,\mathbf{a}}(s,t) = \sum_{i=1}^{p} a_i\kappa_i(s,t),$$

by simply making the variable 'Kern' an array indexed by depth and updating the appropriate entry as each node is processed.   ∎

11.6.2 Trie-based mismatch kernels

We are now in a position to consider some extensions of the trie-based technique developed above for the p-spectrum kernel. In this example we will stick with substrings, but consider allowing some errors in the substring. For two strings u and v of the same length, we use $d(u,v)$ to denote the number of characters in which u and v differ.

Definition 11.50 [Mismatch kernel] The mismatch kernel $\kappa_{p,m}$ is defined by the feature mapping

$$\phi_u^{p,m}(s) = |\{(v_1, v_2) : s = v_1 v v_2 : |u| = |v| = p, d(u, v) \leq m\}|,$$

that is the feature associated with string u counts the number of substrings of s that differ from u by at most m symbols. The associated kernel is defined as

$$\kappa_{p,m}(s, t) = \langle \phi^{p,m}(s), \phi^{p,m}(t) \rangle = \sum_{u \in \Sigma^p} \phi_u^{p,m}(s) \phi_u^{p,m}(t).$$

∎

In order to apply the trie-based approach we initialise the lists at the root of the trie in exactly the same way as for the p-spectrum kernel, except that each substring u has two numbers attached (u, i, j), the current index i as before and the number j of mismatches allowed so far. The key difference in the processing is that when we process a substring it can be added to lists associated with more than one child node, though in all but one case the number of mismatches will be incremented. We give the complete algorithm before discussing its complexity.

Algorithm 11.51 [Trie-based mismatch kernel] The trie-based computation of the mismatch kernel is given in Code Fragment 11.5. ∎

Cost of the computation The complexity of the algorithm has been somewhat compounded by the mismatches. Each substring at a node potentially gives rise to $|\Sigma|$ substrings in the lists associated with its children. If we consider a single substring u at the root node it will reach all the leaves that are at a distance at most m from u. If we consider those at a distance k for some $0 \leq k \leq m$ there are

$$\binom{p}{k} |\Sigma|^k$$

such strings. So we can bound the number of times they are processed by

$$O\left(p^{k+1} |\Sigma|^k\right),$$

hence the complexity of the overall computation is bounded by

$$O\left(p^{m+1} |\Sigma|^m (|s| + |t|)\right),$$

taking into account the number of substrings at the root node. Clearly, we must restrict the number of mismatches if we wish to control the complexity of the algorithm.

Input	strings s and t, parameters p and m
Process	Let $L_s(\varepsilon) = \{(s(i:i+p-1),0,0) : i = 1 : |s| - p + 1\}$
2	Let $L_t(\varepsilon) = \{(t(i:i+p-1),0,0) : i = 1 : |t| - p + 1\}$
3	Kern $= 0$;
4	processnode$(\varepsilon, 0)$;
where	processnode(v, depth)
6	let $L_s(v)$, $L_t(v)$ be the lists associated with v;
7	if depth $= p$
8	Kern $=$ Kern $+ |L_s(v)|\,|L_t(v)|$;
9	end
10	else if $L_s(v)$ and $L_t(v)$ both not empty
11	while there exists (u,i,j) in the list $L_s(v)$
12	add $(u,i+1,j)$ to the list $L_s(vu_{i+1})$;
13	if $j < m$
14	for $a \in \Sigma$, $a \neq u_{i+1}$
15	add $(u,i+1,j+1)$ to the list $L_s(va)$;
16	end
17	while there exists (u,i,j) in the list $L_t(v)$
18	add $(u,i+1,j)$ to the list $L_t(vu_{i+1})$;
19	if $j < m$
20	for $a \in \Sigma$, $a \neq u_{i+1}$
21	add $(u,i+1,j+1)$ to the list $L_t(va)$;
22	end
23	for $a \in \Sigma$
24	processnode$(va, \text{depth} +1)$;
25	end
26	end
Output	$\kappa_{p,m}(s,t) =$ Kern

Code Fragment 11.5. Pseudocode for the trie-based implementation of the mismatch kernel.

Remark 11.52 [Weighting mismatches] As discussed in the previous section when we considered varying the substitution costs for different pairs of symbols, it is possible that some mismatches may be more costly than others. We can assume a matrix of mismatch costs $\mathbf{A}$ whose entries $\mathbf{A}_{ab}$ give the cost of symbol b substituting symbol a. We could now define a feature mapping for a substring u to count the number of substrings whose total mismatch cost is less than a threshold σ. We can evaluate this kernel with a few adaptations to Algorithm 11.51. Rather than using the third component of the triples (u,i,j) to store the number of mismatches, we store the total cost of mismatches included so far. We now replace lines 13–16 of the algorithm with

13	for $a \in \Sigma$, $a \neq u_{i+1}$
14	if $j + A(a, u_{i+1}) < \sigma$
15	add $(u, i + 1, j + C(a, u_{i+1}))$ to the list $L_s(va)$;
16	end

with similar changes made to lines 19–22.   ∎

11.6.3 Trie-based restricted gap-weighted kernels

Our second extension considers the gap-weighted features of the subsequences kernels. As indicated in our general discussion of the trie-based approach, it will be necessary to restrict the sets of subsequences in some way. Since they are typically weighted by an exponentially-decaying function of their length it is natural to restrict the subsequences by the lengths of their occurrences. This leads to the following definition.

Definition 11.53 [Restricted gap-weighted subsequences kernel] The feature space associated with the *m-restricted gap-weighted subsequences kernel* $\kappa_{p,m}$ *of length* p is indexed by $I = \Sigma^p$, with the embedding given by

$$\phi_u^{p,m}(s) = \sum_{i:u=s(i)} [l(\mathbf{i}) \leq m + p]\, \lambda^{l(\mathbf{i})-p}, \ u \in \Sigma^p.$$

The associated kernel is defined as

$$\kappa_{p,m}(s,t) = \langle \phi^{p,m}(s), \phi^{p,m}(t) \rangle = \sum_{u \in \Sigma^p} \phi_u^{p,m}(s)\, \phi_u^{p,m}(t).$$

∎

In order to apply the trie-based approach we again initialise the lists at the root of the trie in a similar way to the previous kernels, except that each substring should now have length $p + m$ since we must allow for as many as m gaps. Again each substring u has two numbers attached (u, i, j), the current index i as before and the number j of gaps allowed so far. We must restrict the first character of the subsequence to occur at the beginning of u as otherwise we would count subsequences with fewer than m gaps more than once. We avoid this danger by inserting the strings directly into the lists associated with the children of the root node.

At an internal node the substring can be added to the same list more than once with different numbers of gaps. When we process a substring (u, i, j) we consider adding every allowable number of extra gaps (the variable k in the next algorithm is used to store this number) while still ensuring that the overall number is not more than m. Hence, the substring can be inserted into as many as m of the lists associated with a node's children.

There is an additional complication that arises when we come to compute the contribution to the inner product at the leaf nodes, since not all of the substrings reaching a leaf should receive the same weighting. However, the number of gaps is recorded and so we can evaluate the correct weighting from this information. Summing for each list and multiplying the values obtained gives the overall contribution. For simplicity we will simply denote this computation by $\kappa\left(L_s\left(v\right), L_t\left(v\right)\right)$ in the algorithm given below.

Algorithm 11.54 [Trie-based restricted gap-weighted subsequences kernel] The trie-based computation of the restricted gap-weighted subsequences kernel is given in Code Fragment 11.6. ∎

Cost of the computation Again the complexity of the algorithm is considerably expanded since each of the original $|s| - p - m + 1$ substrings will give rise to

$$\binom{p + m - 1}{m - 1}$$

different entries at leaf nodes. Hence, the complexity of the overall algorithm can be bounded this number of substrings times the cost of computation on the path from root to leaf, which is at most $O\left(p + m\right)$ for each substring, giving an overall complexity of

$$O\left(\left(|s| + |t|\right)\left(p + m\right)^m\right).$$

In this case it is the number of gaps we allow that has a critical impact on the complexity. If this number is made too large then the dynamic programming algorithm will become more efficient. For small values of the decay parameter λ it is, however, likely that we can obtain a good approximation to the full gap-weighted subsequences kernel with modest values of m resulting in the trie-based approach being more efficient.

Remark 11.55 [Linear time evaluation] For all the trie-based kernels, it is worth noting that if we do not normalise the data it is possible to evaluate a linear function

$$f\left(s\right) = \sum_{i \in \mathrm{sv}} \alpha_i \kappa\left(s_i, s\right)$$

Input	strings s and t, parameters p and m
Process	for $i = 1 : |s| - m + 1$
2	add $(s\,(i : \min(i + p + m - 1, |s|)), 1, 0)$ to the list $L_s\,(s_i)$
3	end
4	for $i = 1 : |t| - m + 1$
5	add $(t\,(i : \min(i + p + m - 1, |t|)), 1, 0)$ to the list $L_t\,(t_i)$
6	end
7	Kern = 0;
8	for $a \in \Sigma$
9	processnode$(a, 1)$;
10	end

where	processnode(v, depth)
12	let $L_s\,(v)$, $L_t\,(v)$ be the lists associated with v;
13	if depth $= p$
14	Kern = Kern $+\kappa\,(L_s\,(v), L_t\,(v))$;
15	end
16	else if $L_s\,(v)$ and $L_t\,(v)$ both not empty
17	while there exists (u, i, j) in the list $L_s\,(v)$
18	for $k = 0 : m - j$
19	add $(u, i + k + 1, k + j)$ to the list $L_s\,(vu_{i+k+1})$;
20	end
21	while there exists (u, i, j) in the list $L_t\,(v)$
22	for $k = 0 : m - j$
23	add $(u, i + k + 1, k + j)$ to the list $L_t\,(vu_{i+k+1})$;
24	end
25	for $a \in \Sigma$
26	processnode$(va, \text{depth} + 1)$;
27	end
28	end
Output	$\kappa_p\,(s, t) = $ Kern

Code Fragment 11.6. Pseudocode for trie-based restricted gap-weighted subsequences kernel.

in linear time. This is achieved by creating a tree by processing all of the support vectors in sv weighting the substrings from s_i at the corresponding leaves by α_i. The test string s is now processed through the tree and the appropriately weighted contributions to the overall sum computed directedly at each leaf. ∎

11.7 Kernels for structured data

In this chapter we have shown an increasingly sophisticated series of kernels that perform efficient comparisons between strings of symbols of different lengths, using as features:

- all contiguous and non-contiguous subsequences of any size;
- all subsequences of a fixed size; all contiguous substrings of a fixed size or up to a fixed size, and finally;
- all non-contiguous substrings with a penalisation related to the size of the gaps.

The evaluation of the resulting kernels can in all cases be reduced to a dynamic programming calculation of low complexity in the length of the sequences and the length of the subsequences used for the matching. In some cases we have also shown how the evaluation can be sped up by the use of tries to achieve a complexity that is linear in the sum of the lengths of the two input strings.

Our aim in this section is to show that, at least for the case of dynamic programming, the approaches we have developed are not restricted to strings, but can be extended to a more general class we will refer to as 'structured data'.

By structured data we mean data that is formed by combining simpler components into more complex items frequently involving a recursive use of simpler objects of the same type. Typically it will be easier to compare the simpler components either with base kernels or using an inductive argument over the structure of the objects. Examples of structured data include the familiar examples of vectors, strings and sequences, but also subsume more complex objects such as trees, images and graphs.

From a practical viewpoint, it is difficult to overemphasise the importance of being able to deal in a principled way with data of this type as they almost invariably arise in more complex applications. Dealing with this type of data has been the objective of a field known as structural pattern recognition. The design of kernels for data of this type enables the same algorithms and analyses to be applied to entirely new application domains.

While in Part II of this book we presented algorithms for detecting and analysing several different types of patterns, the extension of kernels to structured data paves the way for analysing very diverse sets of data-types. Taken together, the two advances open up possibilities such as discovering clusters in a set of trees, learning classifications of graphs, and so on.

It is therefore by designing specific kernels for structured data that kernel methods can demonstrate their full flexibility. We have already discussed one kernel of this type when we pointed out that both the ANOVA and string kernels can be viewed as combining kernel evaluations over substructures of the objects being compared.

In this final section, we will provide a more general framework for designing kernels for this type of data, and we will discuss the connection between statistical and structural pattern analysis that this approach establishes. Before introducing this framework, we will discuss one more example with important practical implications that will not only enable us to illustrate many of the necessary concepts, but will also serve as a building block for a method to be discussed in Chapter 12.

11.7.1 Comparing trees

Data items in the form of trees can be obtained as the result of biological investigation, parsing of natural language text or computer programs, XML documents and in some representations of images in machine vision. Being able to detect patterns within sets of trees can therefore be of great practical importance, especially in web and biological applications. In this section we derive two kernel functions that can be used for this task, as well as provide a conceptual stepping stone towards certain kernels that will be defined in the next chapter.

We will design a kernel between trees that follows a similar approach to those we have considered between strings, in that it will also exploit their recursive structure via dynamic programming.

Recall that for strings the feature space was indexed by substrings. The features used to describe trees will be 'subtrees' of the given tree. We begin by defining what we mean by a tree and subtree. We use the convention that the edges of a tree are directed away from the root towards the leaves.

Definition 11.56 [Trees] A *tree* T is a directed connected acyclic graph in which each vertex (usually referred to as *nodes* for trees) except one has in-degree one. The node with in-degree 0 is known as the *root* $r(T)$ of the tree. Nodes v with out-degree $d^+(v) = 0$ are known as *leaf* nodes, while those with non-zero out-degree are *internal nodes*. The nodes to which an internal node v is connected are known as its *children*, while v is their parent. Two children of the same parent are said to be *siblings*. A *structured tree* is one in which the children of a node are given a fixed ordering, $\mathrm{ch}_1(v), \ldots, \mathrm{ch}_{d^+(v)}(v)$. Two trees are *identical* if there is a 1–1 correspondence between their nodes that respects the parent–child relation and the ordering of the children for each internal node. A *proper tree* is one that contains at least one edge. The size $|T|$ of a tree T is the number of its nodes.   ∎

Definition 11.57 [k-ary labelled trees] If the out-degrees of all the nodes are bounded by k we say the tree is k-*ary*; for example when $k = 2$, the tree is known as a *binary tree*. A *labelled* tree is one in which each node has an associated label. Two labelled trees are *identical* if they are identical as trees and corresponding nodes have the same labels. We use $\mathcal{T}$ to denote the set of all proper trees, with $\mathcal{T}_A$ denoting labelled proper trees with labels from the set A.   ∎

Definition 11.58 [Subtrees: general and co-rooted] A *complete subtree* $\tau(v)$ of a tree T at a node v is the tree obtained by taking the node v together with all vertices and edges reachable from v. A *co-rooted subtree* of a tree T is the tree resulting after removing a sequence of complete subtrees and replacing their roots. This is equivalent to deleting the complete subtrees of all the children of the selected nodes. Hence, if a node v is included in a co-rooted subtree then so are all of its siblings. The root of a tree T is included in every co-rooted subtree. A general subtree of a tree T is any co-rooted subtree of a complete subtree.   ∎

Remark 11.59 [Strings and trees] We can view strings as labelled trees in which the set of labels is the alphabet Σ and each node has at most one child. A complete subtree of a string tree corresponds to a suffix of the string, a rooted subtree to a prefix and a general subtree to a substring. ∎

For our purposes we will mostly be concerned with structured trees which are labelled with information that determines the number of children. We now consider the feature spaces that will be used to represent trees. Again following the analogy with strings the index set of the feature space will be the set of all trees, either labelled or unlabelled according to the context.

Embedding map All the kernels presented in this section can be defined by an explicit embedding map from the space of all finite trees possibly labelled with a set A to a vector space F, whose coordinates are indexed by a subset I of trees again either labelled or unlabelled. As usual we use ϕ to denote the feature mapping

$$\phi: T \longmapsto (\phi_S(T))_{S \in I} \in F$$

The aim is to devise feature mappings for which the corresponding kernel can be evaluated using a recursive calculation that proceeds bottom-up from the leaves to the root of the trees. The basic recursive relation connects the value of certain functions at a given node with the function values at its children. The base of the recursion will set the values at the leaves, ensuring that the computation is well-defined.

Remark 11.60 [Counting subtrees] As an example of a recursive computation over a tree consider evaluating the number $N(T)$ of proper co-rooted subtrees of a tree T. Clearly for a leaf node v there are no proper co-rooted subtrees of $\tau(v)$, so we have $N(\tau(v)) = 0$. Suppose that we know the value of $N(\tau(v_i))$ for each of the nodes $v_i = \text{ch}_i(r(T))$, $i = 1, \ldots, d^+(r(T))$ that are children of the root $r(T)$ of T. In order to create a proper co-rooted subtree of T we must include all of the nodes $r(T), v_1, \ldots, v_{d^+(r(T))}$, but we have the option of including any of the co-rooted subtrees of $\tau(v_i)$ or simply leaving the node v_i as a leaf. Hence, for node v_i we have $N(\tau(v_i)) + 1$ options. These observations lead to the following recursion for $N(T)$ for a proper tree T

$$N(T) = \prod_{i=1}^{d^+(r(T))} \left(N(\tau(\text{ch}_i(r(T)))) + 1 \right),$$

with $N(\tau(v)) = 0$, for a leaf node v. ∎

We are now in a position to consider two kernels over trees.

Co-rooted subtree kernel The feature space for this kernel will be indexed by all trees with the following feature mapping.

Definition 11.61 [Co-rooted subtree kernel] The feature space associated with the *co-rooted subtree kernel* is indexed by $I = \mathcal{T}$ the set of all proper trees with the embedding given by

$$\phi_S^r(T) = \begin{cases} 1 & \text{if } S \text{ is a co-rooted subtree of } T; \\ 0 & \text{otherwise.} \end{cases}$$

The associated kernel is defined as

$$\kappa_r(T_1, T_2) = \langle \phi^r(T_1), \phi^r(T_2) \rangle = \sum_{S \in \mathcal{T}} \phi_S^r(T_1) \phi_S^r(T_2).$$

∎

If either tree T_1 or T_2 is a single node then clearly

$$\kappa_r(T_1, T_2) = 0,$$

since for an improper tree T

$$\phi^r (T) = \mathbf{0}.$$

Furthermore if $d^+ (r (T_1)) \neq d^+ (r (T_1))$ then $\kappa_r (T_1, T_2) = 0$ since a co-rooted subtree of T_1 cannot be a co-rooted subtree of T_2. Assume therefore that

$$d^+ (r (T_1)) = d^+ (r (T_2)).$$

Now to introduce the recursive computation, assume we have evaluated the kernel between the complete subtrees on the corresponding children of $r (T_1)$ and $r (T_2)$; that is we have computed

$$\kappa_r (\tau (\mathrm{ch}_i (r (T_1))), \tau (\mathrm{ch}_i (r (T_2)))), \text{ for } i = 1, \dots, d^+ (r (T_1)).$$

We now have that

$$
\begin{aligned}
\kappa_r (T_1, T_2) &= \sum_{S \in \mathcal{T}} \phi^r_S (T_1) \phi^r_S (T_2) \\
&= \prod_{i=1}^{d^+ (r(T_1))} \sum_{S_i \in \mathcal{T}_0} \phi^r_{S_i} (\tau (\mathrm{ch}_i (r (T_1)))) \phi^r_{S_i} (\tau (\mathrm{ch}_i (r (T_2)))),
\end{aligned}
$$

where $\mathcal{T}_0$ denotes the set of all trees, both proper and improper, since the co-rooted proper subtrees of T are determined by any combination of co-rooted subtrees of $\tau (\mathrm{ch}_i (r (T)))$, $i = 1, \dots, d^+ (r (T_1))$.

Since there is only one improper co-rooted subtree we obtain the recursion

$$\kappa_r (T_1, T_2) = \prod_{i=1}^{d^+ (r(T_1))} (\kappa_r (\tau (\mathrm{ch}_i (r (T_1))), \tau (\mathrm{ch}_i (r (T_2)))) + 1).$$

We have the following algorithm.

Algorithm 11.62 [Co-rooted subtree kernel] The computation of the co-rooted subtree kernel is given in Code Fragment 11.7. ∎

Cost of the computation The complexity of the kernel computation is at most $O (\min (|T_1|, |T_2|))$ since the recursion can only process each node of the trees at most once. If the degrees of the nodes do not agree then the attached subtrees will not be visited and the computation will be correspondingly sped up.

Input	trees T_1 and T_2
Process	Kern $=$ processnode$(r(T_1), r(T_2))$;
where	processnode(v_1, v_2)
3	if $d^+(v_1) \neq d^+(v_2)$ or $d^+(v_1) = 0$
4	return 0;
5	end
6	else
7	Kern $= 1$;
8	for $i = 1 : d^+(v_1)$
9	Kern $=$ Kern $*$ (processnode $(\mathrm{ch}_i(v_1), \mathrm{ch}_i(v_2)) + 1)$;
10	end
11	return Kern;
12	end
Output	$\kappa_r(T_1, T_2) =$ Kern

Code Fragment 11.7. Pseudocode for the co-rooted subtree kernel.

Remark 11.63 [Labelled trees] If the tree is labelled we must include in line 3 of Algorithm 11.62 the test whether the labels of the nodes v_1 and v_2 match by replacing it by the line

3 | if $d^+(v_1) \neq d^+(v_2)$ or $d^+(v_1) = 0$ or label $(v_1) \neq$ label (v_2)

∎

All-subtree kernel We are now in a position to define a slightly more general tree kernel. The features will now be all subtrees rather than just the co-rooted ones. Again we are considering unlabelled trees. The definition is as follows.

Definition 11.64 [All-subtree kernel] The feature space associated with the *all-subtree kernel* is indexed by $I = \mathcal{T}$, the set of all proper trees with the embedding given by

$$\phi_S(T) = \begin{cases} 1 & \text{if } S \text{ is a subtree of } T; \\ 0 & \text{otherwise.} \end{cases}$$

The associated kernel is defined as

$$\kappa(T_1, T_2) = \langle \phi(T_1), \phi(T_2) \rangle = \sum_{S \in \mathcal{T}} \phi_S(T_1) \phi_S(T_2).$$

∎

The evaluation of this kernel can be reduced to the case of co-rooted subtrees by observing that

$$\kappa (T_1, T_2) = \sum_{v_1 \in T_1, v_2 \in T_2} \kappa_r (\tau (v_1), \tau (v_2)). \qquad (11.7)$$

In other words the all-subtree kernel can be computed by evaluating the co-rooted kernel for all pairs of nodes in the two trees. This follows from the fact that any subtree of a tree T is a co-rooted subtree of the complete subtree $\tau (v)$ for some node v of T.

Rather than use this computation we would like to find a direct recursion for $\kappa (T_1, T_2)$. Clearly if T_1 or T_2 is a leaf node we have

$$\kappa (T_1, T_2) = 0.$$

Furthermore, we can partition the sum (11.7) as follows

$$\begin{aligned}
\kappa (T_1, T_2) &= \sum_{v_1 \in T_1, v_2 \in T_2} \kappa_r (\tau (v_1), \tau (v_2)) \\
&= \kappa_r (T_1, T_2) + \sum_{i=1}^{d^+(r(T_1))} \kappa (\tau (\text{ch}_i (r (T_1))), T_2) \\
&\quad + \sum_{i=1}^{d^+(r(T_2))} \kappa (T_1, \tau (\text{ch}_i (r (T_2)))) \\
&\quad - \sum_{i=1}^{d^+(r(T_1))} \sum_{j=1}^{d^+(r(T_2))} \kappa (\tau (\text{ch}_i (r (T_1))), \tau (\text{ch}_j (r (T_2)))),
\end{aligned}$$

since the subtrees are either co-rooted in both T_1 and T_2 or are subtrees of a child of $r (T_1)$ or a child of $r (T_2)$. However, those that are not co-rooted with either T_1 or T_2 will be counted twice making it necessary to subtract the final sum. We therefore have Algorithm 11.65, again based on the construction of a table indexed by the nodes of the two trees using dynamic programming. We will assume that the n_j nodes $v_1^j, \ldots, v_{n_j}^j$ of the tree T_j have been ordered so that the parent of a node has a later index. Hence, the final node $v_{n_j}^j$ is the root of T_j. This ordering will be used to index the tables $\text{DP} (i_1, i_2)$ and $\text{DPr} (i_1, i_2)$. The algorithm first completes the table $\text{DPr} (i_1, i_2)$ with the value of the co-rooted tree kernel before it computes the all-subtree kernel in the array $\text{DP} (i_1, i_2)$. We will also assume for the purposes of the algorithm that $\text{child}_k^j (i)$ gives the index of the kth child of the node indexed by i in the tree T_j. Similarly, $d_j^+ (i)$ is the out-degree of the node indexed by i in the tree T_j.

Algorithm 11.65 [All-subtree kernel] The computation of the all-subtree kernel is given in Code Fragment 11.8. ∎

Input	unlabelled trees T_1 and T_2
Process	Assume $v_1^j, \ldots, v_{n_j}^j$ a compatible ordering of nodes of T_j, $j = 1, 2$
2	for $i_1 = 1 : n_1$
3	for $i_2 = 1 : n_2$
4	if $d_1^+(i_1) \neq d_2^+(i_2)$ or $d_1^+(i_1) = 0$
5	DPr $(i_1, i_2) = 0$;
6	else
7	DPr $(i_1, i_2) = 1$;
8	for $k = 1 : d_1^+(i_1)$
9	DPr $(i_1, i_2) =$ DPr $(i_1, i_2) * \left(\text{DPr}\left(\text{child}_k^1(i_1), \text{child}_k^2(i_2)\right) + 1\right)$;
10	end
11	end
12	end
13	for $i_1 = 1 : n_1$
14	for $i_2 = 1 : n_2$
15	if $d_1^+(i_1) = 0$ or $d_2^+(i_2) = 0$
16	DP $(i_1, i_2) = 0$;
17	else
18	DP $(i_1, i_2) =$ DPr (i_1, i_2);
19	for $j_1 = 1 : d_1^+(i_1)$
20	DP $(i_1, i_2) =$ DP $(i_1, i_2) +$ DP $\left(\text{child}_{j_1}^1(i_1), i_2\right)$;
21	for $j_2 = 1 : d_2^+(i_2)$
22	DP $(i_1, i_2) =$ DP $(i_1, i_2) +$ DP $\left(i_1, \text{child}_{j_2}^2(i_2)\right)$;
23	for $j_1 = 1 : d_1^+(i_1)$
24	DP $(i_1, i_2) =$ DP $(i_1, i_2) -$ DP $\left(\text{child}_{j_1}^1(i_1), \text{child}_{j_2}^2(i_2)\right)$;
25	end
26	end
27	end
28	end
Output	$\kappa(T_1, T_2) =$ DP (n_1, n_2)

Code Fragment 11.8. Pseudocode for the all-subtree kernel.

Cost of the computation The structure of the algorithm makes clear that the complexity of evaluating the kernel can be bounded by

$$O\left(|T_1|\,|T_2|\,d_{\max}^2\right),$$

where $d_{\max}$ is the maximal out-degree of the nodes in the two trees.

Remark 11.66 [On labelled trees] Algorithm 11.65 does not take into account possible labellings of the nodes of the tree. As we observed for the co-rooted tree kernel, the computation of the co-rooted table $\mathrm{DPr}\,(i_1, i_2)$ could be significantly sped up by replacing line 4 with

4 | if $d^+(v_1) \neq d^+(v_2)$ or $d^+(v_1) = 0$ or $\mathrm{label}\,(v_1) \neq \mathrm{label}\,(v_2)$.

However, no such direct simplification is possible for the computation of $\mathrm{DP}\,(i_1, i_2)$. If the labelling is such that very few nodes share the same label, it may be faster to create small separate DPr tables for each type and simply sum over all of these tables to compute

$$\kappa\,(T_1, T_2) = \mathrm{DP}\,(n_1, n_2),$$

avoiding the need to create the complete table for $\mathrm{DP}\,(i_1, i_2)$, $1 \leq i_1 < n_1$, $1 \leq i_2 < n_2$. ∎

Notice how the all-subtree kernel was defined in terms of the co-rooted subtrees. We first defined the simpler co-rooted kernel and then summed its evaluation over all possible choices of subtrees. This idea forms the basis of a large family of kernels, based on convolutions over substructures. We now turn to examine a more general framework for these kernels.

11.7.2 Structured data: a framework

The approach used in the previous sections for comparing strings, and subsequently trees, can be extended to handle more general types of data structures. The key idea in the examples we have seen has been first to define a way of comparing sub-components of the data such as substrings or subtrees and then to sum these sub-kernels over a set of decompositions of the data items.

We can think of this summing process as a kind of convolution in the sense that it averages over the different choices of sub-component. In general the operation can be thought of as a convolution if we consider the different ways of dividing the data into sub-components as analagous to dividing an interval into two subintervals. We will build this intuitive formulation into the notion of a *convolution kernel*. We begin by formalising what we mean by structured data.

As discussed at the beginning of Section 11.7, a data type is said to be 'structured' if it is possible to decompose it into smaller parts. In some cases there is a natural way in which this decomposition can occur. For example a vector is decomposed into its individual components. However, even here we can think of other possible decompositions by for example selecting a subset of the components as we did for the ANOVA kernel. A string is structured because it can be decomposed into smaller strings or symbols and a tree can be decomposed into subtrees.

The idea is to compute the product of sub-kernels comparing the parts before summing over the set of allowed decompositions. It is clear that when we create a decomposition we need to specify which kernels are applicable for which sub-parts.

Definition 11.67 [Decomposition Structure] A *decomposition structure* for a datatype $\mathcal{D}$ is specified by a multi-typed relation R between an element x of $\mathcal{D}$ and a finite set of tuples of sub-components each with an associated kernel

$$((x_1, \kappa_1), \ldots, (x_d, \kappa_d)),$$

for various values of d. Hence

$$\mathcal{R}(((x_1, \kappa_1), \ldots, (x_d, \kappa_d)), x)$$

indicates that x can be decomposed into components $x_1, \ldots, x_d$ each with an attached kernel. Note that the kernels may vary between different decompositions of the same x, so that just as x_1 depends on the particular decomposition, so does κ_1. The relation $\mathcal{R}$ is a subset of the disjoint sum of the appropriate cartesian product spaces. The set of all *admissible partitionings* of x is defined as

$$\mathcal{R}^{-1}(x) = \bigcup_{d=1}^{D} \{((x_1, \kappa_1), \ldots, (x_d, \kappa_d)) : \mathcal{R}(((x_1, \kappa_1), \ldots, (x_d, \kappa_d)), x)\},$$

while the *type* $\mathcal{T}(\mathbf{x})$ of the tuple $\mathbf{x} = ((x_1, \kappa_1), \ldots, (x_d, \kappa_d))$ is defined as

$$\mathcal{T}(\mathbf{x}) = (\kappa_1, \ldots, \kappa_d).$$

∎

Before we discuss how we can view many of the kernels we have met as exploiting decompositions of this type, we give a definition of the convolution or $\mathcal{R}$-kernel that arises from a decomposition structure $\mathcal{R}$.

Definition 11.68 [Convolution Kernels] Let $\mathcal{R}$ be a decomposition structure for a datatype $\mathcal{D}$. For x and z elements of $\mathcal{D}$ the associated convolution kernel is defined as

$$\kappa_{\mathcal{R}}(x, z) = \sum_{\mathbf{x} \in \mathcal{R}^{-1}(x)} \sum_{\mathbf{z} \in \mathcal{R}^{-1}(z)} [\mathcal{T}(\mathbf{x}) = \mathcal{T}(\mathbf{z})] \prod_{i=1}^{|\mathcal{T}(\mathbf{x})|} \kappa_i(x_i, z_i).$$

We also refer to this as the *$\mathcal{R}$-convolution kernel* or *$\mathcal{R}$-kernel* for short. Note that the product is only defined if the boolean expression is true, but if this is not the case the square bracket function is zero. ∎

Example 11.69 In the case of trees discussed above, we can define the decomposition structures $\mathcal{R}_1$ and $\mathcal{R}_2$ by:

$\mathcal{R}_1((S, \kappa_0), T)$ if and only if S is a co-rooted subtree of T;

$\mathcal{R}_2((S, \kappa_0), T)$ if and only if S is a subtree of T;

where $\kappa_0(S_1, S_2) = 1$ if $S_1 = S_2$ and 0 otherwise. The associated $\mathcal{R}$-kernels are clearly the co-rooted subtree kernel and the all-subtree kernel respectively. ∎

Example 11.70 For the case of the co-rooted tree kernel we could also create the recursive decomposition structure $\mathcal{R}$ by:

$\mathcal{R}_1(((T_1, \kappa_{\mathcal{R}} + 1), \ldots, (T_d, \kappa_{\mathcal{R}} + 1)), T)$

  if and only if $T_1, \ldots, T_d$ are the trees at the children of the root $r(T)$;

$\mathcal{R}_1((T, 0), T)$ if T is an improper tree.

By the definition of the associated $\mathcal{R}$-kernel we have

$$\kappa_{\mathcal{R}}(S, T) = \begin{cases} 0 & \text{if } d^+(r(S)) \neq d^+(r(T)) \text{ or } d^+(r(S)) = 0; \\ \prod_{i=1}^{d^+(r(T))} (\kappa_{\mathcal{R}}(\tau(\text{ch}_i(r(T))), \tau(\text{ch}_i(r(S)))) + 1) \\ \qquad \text{otherwise.} \end{cases}$$

This is precisely the recursive definition of the co-rooted subtree kernel. ∎

The two examples considered here give the spirit of the more flexible decomposition afforded by $\mathcal{R}$-decomposition structures. We now give examples that demonstrate how the definition subsumes many of the kernels we have considered in earlier chapters.

Example 11.71 Suppose X is a vector space of dimension n. Let κ_i be the kernel defined by

$$\kappa_i(\mathbf{x}, \mathbf{z}) = x_i z_i.$$

Consider the decomposition structure

$$\mathcal{R} = \{(((\mathbf{x}, \kappa_{i_1}), \ldots, (\mathbf{x}, \kappa_{i_d})), \mathbf{x}) : 1 \leq i_1 < i_2 < \cdots < i_d \leq n, \ \mathbf{x} \in \mathbb{R}^n\}.$$

Here the associated $\mathcal{R}$-kernel is defined as

$$\kappa_{\mathcal{R}}(\mathbf{x}, \mathbf{z}) = \sum_{1 \leq i_1 < \cdots < i_d \leq n} \prod_{j=1}^{d} \kappa_{i_j}(\mathbf{x}, \mathbf{z}) = \sum_{1 \leq i_1 < \cdots < i_d \leq n} \prod_{j=1}^{d} x_i z_i,$$

which we have already met in Chapter 9 as the ANOVA kernel. The generalisation of the ANOVA kernel to arbitrary subkernels described in Remark
9.20 seems even more natural in this presentation. Note how the kernel has
again the sum of products structure that we have seen recurring in many
different guises. ∎

Example 11.72 The more complex kernels defined over graphs can also
be recreated as $\mathcal{R}$-kernels if we index the subkernels κ_e by the edges $e \in E$
of the graph $G = (V, E)$. The $\mathcal{R}$-structure for a graph kernel defined by the
identified vertices a and b in G is now given by

$$\mathcal{R} =$$
$$\{(((\mathbf{x}, \kappa_{(u_0 \rightarrow u_1)}), \ldots, (\mathbf{x}, \kappa_{(u_{d-1} \rightarrow u_d)})), \mathbf{x}) : \mathbf{x} \in \mathbb{R}^n, (u_0, \ldots, u_d) \in P_{ab}\},$$

where P_{ab} is the set of paths from node a to node b, represented by the
sequence of edges. This follows straightforwardly from the definition of the
graph kernel as

$$\kappa_G(\mathbf{x}, \mathbf{z}) = \sum_{p \in P_{ab}} \prod_{i=1}^{d} \kappa_{(u_{i-1} \rightarrow u_i)}(\mathbf{x}, \mathbf{z}).$$

Notice that the type match in the definition of the $\mathcal{R}$-kernel ensures that
only matching paths enter into the sum. ∎

Example 11.73 A very similar structure to the ANOVA case can be used
to create the Gaussian kernel. Here we consider the base kernels to be

$$\kappa_i(\mathbf{x}, \mathbf{z}) = \exp\left(-\frac{(x_i - z_i)^2}{2\sigma^2}\right)$$

and the structure to be given by

$$\mathcal{R} = \{(((\mathbf{x}, \kappa_1), \ldots, (\mathbf{x}, \kappa_n)), \mathbf{x}) : \mathbf{x} \in \mathbb{R}^n\},$$

so that the associated $\mathcal{R}$-kernel is simply

$$
\begin{aligned}
\kappa_{\mathcal{R}}\left(\mathbf{x}, \mathbf{z}\right) &= \prod_{i=1}^{n} \kappa_i\left(\mathbf{x}, \mathbf{z}\right) = \prod_{i=1}^{d} \exp\left(-\frac{(x_i - z_i)^2}{2\sigma^2}\right) \\
&= \exp\left(-\frac{\sum_{i=1}^{d}(x_i - z_i)^2}{2\sigma^2}\right) = \exp\left(-\frac{\|\mathbf{x} - \mathbf{z}\|^2}{2\sigma^2}\right).
\end{aligned}
$$

∎

Example 11.74 It is very simple to construct decomposition structures for the various string kernels. For example the gap-weighted k-subsequences kernel is created using

$$
\mathcal{R} = \left\{\left(\left(u, \lambda^{l(\mathbf{i})}\kappa_0\right), s\right) : s \in \Sigma^*, \mathbf{i} \in I_k, u = s\left(\mathbf{i}\right)\right\},
$$

where κ_0 is the kernel returning 1 if the substrings are identical and 0 otherwise. ∎

$\mathcal{R}$-convolution kernels seem to provide a very natural generalisation of both ANOVA and graph kernels on the one hand and the tree and substring kernels on the other hand. There are clear distinctions between the structures in these two cases. In the ANOVA and graph kernels the components are chosen to be the whole structure and the variation is made between the kernels used to compare the objects, while in the tree and substring kernel the variation is mainly focussed on the substructure selection with the kernels usually being identical.

These observations suggest that there is much unexplored flexibility in the $\mathcal{R}$-kernels definition that has the potential to lead to many interesting new kernels. For example using a graph structure to determine how the kernels of different sub-components are combined might be a first step in this directions. The simplest example might be combining the ANOVA construction with the recursive definition of the co-rooted tree kernel given in Example 11.70.

Such combinations raise two questions. First, are the associated $\mathcal{R}$-kernels for decomposition structures always kernels? Second, when can we expect to be able to find efficient methods for computing the $\mathcal{R}$-kernel even when the sums involved are exponentially large? We will not attempt to investigate the second question any further, but provide a brief justification that $\mathcal{R}$-kernels are indeed kernels.

Proposition 11.75 *Let $\kappa_{\mathcal{R}}$ be the kernel defined by the decomposition structure $\mathcal{R}$. It follows that $\kappa_{\mathcal{R}}$ is an inner product in an appropriately defined feature space.*

Proof We will apply Proposition 9.42 by showing that the kernel $\kappa_{\mathcal{R}}$ is a subset kernel over an appropriately defined universal set. The set in question for a data item x is $\mathcal{R}^{-1}(x)$, which by the definition of a decomposition structure is finite as required. The elements of the set are compared using the product of valid kernels and hence the subset is defined with elements that are compared with a valid kernel. The result follows. In the case of a recursive definition, an additional inductive argument must be made using structural induction over the decomposition structure. $\square$

Remark 11.76 [Syntactical Pattern Recognition] The class of kernels we have developed in this section provides a link with the field of structural pattern recognition. Syntactic or structural pattern recognition deals with the problem of detecting common patterns in sets of structured data, typically representing them as rules. By using kernels that operate on structured data, we are 'interpolating' between statistical and syntactic pattern recognition, two branches of pattern analysis that rarely interact. ∎

11.8 Summary

- Strings of symbols can be compared by kernels that sum the number of common substrings or subsequences.
- Dynamic programming techniques allow us to compute such kernels efficiently.
- A whole range of variations on this theme allow one to tune a kernel to the particular application.
- Trie-based computation provides fast evaluation of some restrictions of these kernels.
- Kernels can also be defined over more complex structures such as trees.
- Convolution kernels define a framework that subsumes both structure and ANOVA style kernels.

11.9 Further reading and advanced topics

Although the first papers dealing with kernels for strings and trees appeared in 1999, there is already a considerable literature dealing with this problem. Watkins and Haussler [158], [157], [54] certainly are to be credited with starting this research direction, where ideas from classical string matching algorithms, based on dynamic programming, were used to construct recursive kernels. A good starting point for understanding the techniques used by them are the very readable books by Dan Gusfield [50] and Durbin *et al.* [42].

The first application of these theoretical ideas came in the field of text categorisation, with the paper of Lodhi *et al.* [93], followed by applications in bioinformatics. The computational cost of dynamic programming approaches to string kernels slowed down their uptake in larger-scale applications, until the publication of a series of papers demonstrating the use of different computational techniques for performing very similar computations at much cheaper cost, for example using tries [90], [89]. Spectrum kernels and the other methods have been applied to large real world problems in bioinformatics [87], [88]. Novel methods of computation using suffix trees are described in [154]. Our discussion of trie-based kernels was based on these papers, whereas the discussion on dynamic programming kernels goes back to Watkins.

Although motivated by string analysis, Haussler's framework is very general, and can motivate kernels for very diverse types of data. For example [23] presents the dynamic programming method for comparing two trees in the context of language parsing.

Ralf Herbrich's book presents some variations of the basic recursions for gappy string matching kernels [55]. An excellent introduction to string computations by means of dynamic programming is given in [50] and a discussion of the merits of bottom-up over top-down computations of recurrence relations can be found in [24].

Finally, recent work by Mohri, Cortes and Haffner [25] on Rational Kernels is closely related to what we have presented here, but is not discussed in this chapter for lack of space. For constantly updated pointers to online literature and free software see the book's companion website: www.kernel-methods.net

12

Kernels from generative models

It is often the case that we know something about the process generating the data. For example, DNA sequences have been generated through evolution in a series of modifications from ancestor sequences, text can be viewed as being generated by a source of words perhaps reflecting the topic of the document, a time series may have been generated by a dynamical system of a certain type, 2-dimensional images by projections of a 3-dimensional scene, and so on.

For all of these data sources we have some, albeit imperfect, knowledge about the source generating the data, and hence of the type of invariances, features and similarities (in a word, patterns) that we can expect it to contain. Even simple and approximate models of the data can be used to create kernels that take account of the insight thus afforded.

Models of data can be either deterministic or probabilistic and there are also several different ways of turning them into kernels. In fact some of the kernels we have already encountered can be regarded as derived from generative data models.

However in this chapter we put the emphasis on generative models of the data that are frequently pre-existing. We aim to show how these models can be exploited to provide features for an embedding function for which the corresponding kernel can be efficiently evaluated.

Although the emphasis will be mainly on two classes of kernels induced by probabilistic models, P-kernels and Fisher kernels, other methods exist to incorporate generative information into kernel design. Indeed in some sense every kernel can be regarded as embodying our generative assumptions about the data.

12.1 *P*-kernels

A very general type of kernel can be obtained by defining a joint probability distribution $P(x, z)$ on pairs of data items (x, z) from the product space $X \times X$ of a finite or countably infinite input space X. We assume the joint probability $P(x, z)$ does not depend on the order of the items so that P is symmetric, but to be a kernel

$$\kappa(x, z) = P(x, z),$$

it must also satisfy the finitely positive semi-definite property.

Definition 12.1 [*P*-kernel] A probability distribution $P(x, z)$ over a product space $X \times X$ that satisfies the finitely positive semi-definite property will be known as a *P*-kernel on the set X.   ∎

Given a kernel κ on a countably infinite space X, we can create a *P*-kernel that is essentially identical to κ provided

$$\sum_{x \in X} \sum_{z \in X} \kappa(x, z) = M < \infty,$$

since the distribution

$$P(x, z) = \frac{1}{M} \kappa(x, z)$$

satisfies the definition of a *P*-kernel.

On the other hand, not all distributions will be *P*-kernels, as the simple example of a two element set

$$X = \{x_1, x_2\},$$

with probabilities

$$
\begin{aligned}
P(x_1, x_1) &= P(x_2, x_2) = 0; \\
P(x_1, x_2) &= P(x_2, x_1) = 0.5
\end{aligned}
$$

shows, since the matrix

$$\begin{pmatrix} 0 & 0.5 \\ 0.5 & 0 \end{pmatrix}$$

indexed by x_1, x_2 has eigenvalues $\lambda = \pm 0.5$.

We have presented *P*-kernels for countably infinite input spaces since these are the types of data for which we take this approach. For uncountably infinite sets a *P*-kernel would be defined by a probability density function $p(x, z)$ again assumed symmetric and required to satisfy the finitely positive semi-definite property. A kernel κ would be equivalent to such a P-kernel through a renormalisation provided

$$\int_X \int_X \kappa(x, z)\, dx dz = M < \infty.$$

It follows for example that any bounded kernel over a compact domain can be regarded as a P-kernel.

Hence, a P-kernel is a very broad class of kernels that by itself does not provide interesting insights. Its real interest arises when we study how one might generate such joint probability distributions.

As a simple example consider a probability distribution $P(x)$ on the finite or countably infinite set X. We can define a 1-dimensional P-kernel using the following product

$$\kappa(x, z) = P(x)P(z).$$

This follows immediately from the observation that this kernel corresponds to the 1-dimensional embedding

$$\phi : x \longmapsto P(x).$$

This example suggests the following definition for a probabilistic model.

Definition 12.2 [Data model] A model m of a data generation process is an artificial distribution that assigns to each data item x a probability $P(x|m)$ of being generated. This can be seen as an estimate of the true distribution that generated the data. In practice we do not know precisely how the data was generated, but we may have a class of possible models M and a prior distribution P_M or belief as to which model was more likely to have generated the data. This is encoded in a distribution $P_M(m)$ over the set of models, where m is used to denote the individual model possibly described by a set of parameters. Hence, for example different settings of hidden variables are viewed as different models. ∎

Remark 12.3 [Modelling process] The definition of a data model only requires that it be a probability distribution. In practice we typically define the distribution in a way that reflects our understanding of the processes that actually generate the real data. It is for this reason that the term model is used since the distribution results from a model of the generation process. ∎

The first part of this chapter considers probability distributions arising from data models that give rise to more general and interesting classes of P-kernels.

12.1.1 Conditional-independence (CI) and marginalisation

Building on the example at the end of the previous section, we can create a joint distribution that is positive semi-definite by combining a number of different 1-dimensional distributions $P(x, z|m) = P(x|m)P(z|m)$. We choose m at random from a set M to combine the different distributions as follows

$$P(x, z) = \sum_{m \in M} P(x, z|m) P_M(m) = \sum_{m \in M} P(x|m)P(z|m)P_M(m),$$

where we have used $P_M(m)$ to denote the probability of drawing the distribution parametrised by m. We could again consider a probability density function in the case that M were an uncountably infinite set.

If we view the set M as a set of potential models of the data distribution each weighted according to our prior belief $P_M(m)$ in that particular model, the distribution corresponds to our prior estimation of the probability that x and z arise as a pair of independently generated examples. It is this view that also suggests the idea of marginalisation. If we view $P(x, z|m) P_M(m)$ as a probability distribution over triples (x, z, m), then the probability $P(x, z)$ is its marginal distribution, since it involves integrating over the unknown variable m. For this reason the kernels are sometimes referred to as marginal kernels.

In general, marginalising does not guarantee that the distribution satisfies the finitely positive semi-definite property. In our case it follows from the combination of marginalising over distributions each of which is finitely positive semi-definite because of the independence assumption in the generation of x and z. For this reason we say that x and z are conditionally independent given m. Hence, the assumption of conditional independence

$$P(x, z|m) = P(x|m)P(z|m)$$

is a sufficient (but not necessary) condition for positive semi-definiteness.

This class of kernels, obtained by marginalisation of conditionally independent functions, is extremely general, and can be efficiently computed for many classes of functions, using algorithmic tools developed in the theory of probabilistic graphical models. This often allows us to turn a generative model of the data into a kernel function. The dimensions of the embedding space are indexed by the elements of a set of probabilistic models $\phi_m(x) = P(x|m)$ as indicated in the following definition summarising the approach.

Definition 12.4 [Marginalisation kernels] Given a set of data models M and a prior distribution P_M on M, we can compute the probability that a pair of examples x and z is generated together

$$P_M(x, z) = \sum_{m \in M} P(x|m)P(z|m)P_M(m).$$

If we consider the projection function

$$\phi : x \longmapsto (P(x|m))_{m \in M} \in F,$$

in a feature space F indexed by M, $P_M(x, z)$ corresponds to the inner product

$$\langle f, g \rangle = \sum_{m \in M} f_m g_m P_M(m)$$

between $\phi(x)$ and $\phi(z)$. It follows that $P_M(x, z)$ is a P-kernel. We refer to $P_M(x, z)$ as the *marginalisation kernel* for the model class M. ∎

12.1.2 Representing multivariate distributions

Defining a data model requires us to create a class of multivariate probability distributions. The simplest form for such distributions is to assume independence between the different coordinates and hence use a collection of independent 1-dimensional distributions. Once we allow interactions between the different variables, the number of degrees of freedom increases substantially. For example to specify a multivariate Gaussian distribution we need $O(n^2)$ parameters to give the covariance matrix.

In view of these complications it is natural to search for models that lie somewhere between complete independence of the variables and full dependence. Graphical models are a representation that allows us to specify a dependence structure in the form of a directed acyclic graph whose nodes are the variables. The distribution of the variable A that labels a node becomes independent if we specify the values of the set $\mathcal{N}^-(A)$ of variables on vertices with edges $(B \to A)$ pointing at A. Hence, if the labelling $A_1, \ldots, A_n$ of the nodes is such that there are no edges from later to earlier vertices, then the distribution can be computed using

$$P(A_1, \ldots, A_n) = \prod_{i=1}^{n} P\left(A_i | \mathcal{N}^-(A_i)\right).$$

Specifying the individual conditional probabilities might involve a lookup table in the case of binary variables or some other distribution for more complex variables. Note that one can interpret an edge from node A to node B as implying that A is a partial cause for B.

Hence graphical models provide a compact representation of a joint probability distribution. For example the joint distribution

$$P(A, B, C, D) = P(A)P(B|A)P(C|A)P(D|C, B)$$

can be represented by the graphical model in Figure 12.1.

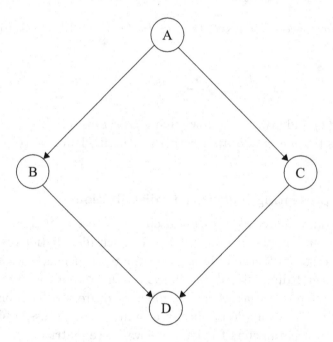

Fig. 12.1. A simple example of a graphical model.

So far we have considered graphical models in which the nodes are in one-to-one correspondence with the observed variables. In practice we may not be able to observe all of the relevant variables. In this case we distinguish between the observables and the so-called hidden variables, with the overall graphical model being defined over both sets of variables.

An example of a graphical model with hidden states is shown in Figure

12.3. It shows a sequence of hidden variables $(h_1, \ldots, h_n)$ linked so that the next variable is conditionally dependent on the previous hidden variable. Each hidden variable h_i conditions a corresponding distribution for the observable variable s_i. This is known as a 1-stage Markov model. We can also represent this by a sequence of nodes linked into a path, where the ith node has a state variable h_i that can take a number of possible values and the node emits a symbol depending on the value of h_i, while the value of h_i depends probabilistically on h_{i-1}. Hence, the symbol emission has been included into the function of the node.

We can make the diagram more explicit by creating a node for each state, that is each state variable–value pair. In this view the transitions take us from one state to another and we have a probabilistic finite state automata whose nodes emit symbols. We prefer to take this general framework as our definition of a hidden Markov model.

Definition 12.5 [Hidden Markov model] A hidden Markov model (HMM) M comprises a finite set of states A with an initial state a_I, a final state a_F, a probabilistic transition function $P_M(a|b)$ giving the probability of moving to state a given that the current state is b, and a probability distribution $P(\sigma|a)$ over symbols $\sigma \in \Sigma \cup \{\varepsilon\}$ for each state $a \in A$. ■

A hidden Markov model generates strings probabilistically by initialising the state to a_I and repeatedly performing random transitions each followed by a random generation of a symbol, until the state a_F is reached.

12.1.3 Fixed length strings generated by a hidden binomial model

The kernel presented in this subsection is a somewhat 'degenerate' example of an important class of models. Nonetheless its discussion sets the scene for two more complex generative models also for fixed length symbol sequences, each based on different assumptions about the hidden generating mechanism. These will be presented in the following two subsections followed by extensions to handle the case of strings of different lengths.

Consider comparing symbol strings that have the same length n with individual symbols drawn from a finite alphabet Σ. We assume that the symbols are generated by 'emission' from a sequence of hidden state variables represented by a string of the same length $h = (h_1 \ldots h_n)$, where the individual emission probabilities are independent that is

$$P(s|h) = \prod_{i=1}^{n} P(s_i|h_i),$$

and as posited in the general framework the probabilities of generating two strings s and t are also treated as independent. This generation model is illustrated in Figure 12.2. Note that to cast this in the framework of

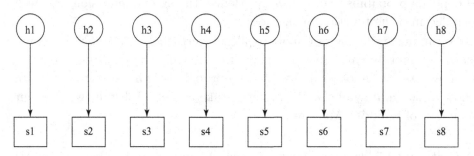

Fig. 12.2. A simple hidden model for generating fixed length strings.

Definition 12.5, we would need to expand each state variable into the set of states that it can assume and include transitions from the set of states for h_i to those for h_{i+1}, $i = 1, \ldots, n-1$, as well as including transitions from the initial state a_I and to the final state a_F. An example of this type of (formal) construction is given in the next subsection.

For the time being we leave the form of the distribution $P(s_i|h_i)$ unspecified, though there is a further assumption that the probabilities of the hidden states $P(h)$ can also be decomposed into a product over the individual symbols

$$P(h) = \prod_{i=1}^{n} P(h_i)$$

so that the kernel involves summing over all hidden strings and marginalising the probability to obtain the marginalisation kernel

$$\kappa(s,t) = \sum_{h \in \Sigma^n} P(s|h)P(t|h)P(h)$$

$$= \sum_{h \in \Sigma^n} \prod_{i=1}^{n} P(s_i|h_i)P(t_i|h_i)P(h_i).$$

We have already encountered sums of products within kernel calculations when we considered the kernels defined by summing over all paths in a graph. This form will also prove a recurring theme in this chapter. The sum is over a large number of hidden models, each of which can be used to compute a probability by means of a product. The key idea is that in certain important cases this can be computed as the product of sums by effectively exchanging the two operators, and hence achieving a significant computational saving. This will motivate a number of dynamic programming methods, but in the specific case considered here we will be able to obtain a closed form solution.

We can write

$$\kappa(s,t) = \sum_{h \in \Sigma^n} \prod_{i=1}^{n} P(s_i|h_i) P(t_i|h_i) P(h_i)$$

$$= \prod_{i=1}^{n} \sum_{\sigma \in \Sigma} P(s_i|\sigma) P(t_i|\sigma) P(\sigma), \tag{12.1}$$

where the expression on the right-hand side of the first line can be obtained by applying the distributive law to the product of sums given in the second line. The variable h_i tells us which term to take in the ith factor of the product with the overall expression given by the sum over all possible choices, that is over all strings h.

We have presented this example more as an illustration of the swapping step. In this case the result is rather trivial, since we could pre-compute a table of

$$P(a,b) = \sum_{\sigma \in \Sigma} P(a|\sigma) P(b|\sigma) P(\sigma), \text{ for } a, b \in \Sigma,$$

and then the kernel could be evaluated as

$$\kappa(s,t) = \prod_{i=1}^{n} P(s_i, t_i).$$

This is a simple product of base kernels

$$\kappa_i(s,t) = P(s_i, t_i)$$

and so could also be viewed as an ANOVA kernel of degree n.

It does, however, also illustrate a general property of P-kernels, namely that if we create P-kernels for each part X_i of a set of n disjoint components of data items from a set $X = X_1 \times \cdots \times X_n$, their product also becomes a P-kernel, since

$$\sum_{s \in X} \sum_{t \in X} P(s,t) = \sum_{s \in X} \sum_{t \in X} \prod_{i=1}^{n} P(s_i, t_i)$$

$$= \prod_{i=1}^{n} \sum_{s_i \in X_i} \sum_{t_i \in X_i} P(s_i, t_i)$$

$$= \prod_{i=1}^{n} 1 = 1.$$

Remark 12.6 [States and symbols] It is worth noting that although we discussed this example using the same set of symbols for the strings as for the states, these could be defined over different sets. In view of our final observations this will not have a very significant impact in this example, but we will see that in the next subsection this does afford us extra flexibility. ∎

12.1.4 Fixed length strings generated by a hidden markov model

The model above was not very realistic, but did demonstrate the type of computations that we are considering in this section, particularly the idea of marginalising over sums of products. For our next model we continue with the assumptions that the two strings s and t have fixed length n and are composed of symbols from an alphabet Σ. Furthermore we assume that they have been generated by a hidden model M, whose elements are represented by strings h of n states each from a set A, and that each symbol is generated independently, so that

$$P(s, t|h) = \prod_{i=1}^{n} P(s_i|h_i)P(t_i|h_i)$$

as before. Where we extend the previous model is in the structure of the distribution $P(h)$. Whereas before this distribution assumed independence of the individual states, we now introduce a 1-stage Markov structure into the hidden model for M, that is we let

$$P_M(h) = P_M(h_1)P_M(h_2|h_1)\dots P_M(h_n|h_{n-1}).$$

The hidden model is illustrated in Figure 12.3. Formally, if we wish to cast this in the framework of Definition 12.5, we must define the states of the model to be

$$\{a_I\} \cup A \times \{1, \dots, n\} \cup a_F,$$

with the transition probabilities given by

$$P_M((a, i)|a_I) = \begin{cases} P_M(a) & \text{if } i = 1; \\ 0 & \text{otherwise,} \end{cases}$$

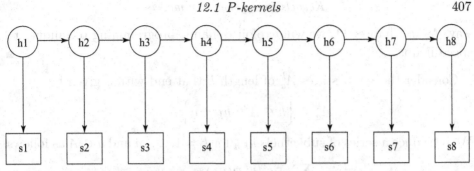

Fig. 12.3. The hidden Markov model for a fixed length string.

$$P_M\left((a,i)\,|\,(b,j)\right) = \begin{cases} P_M\left(a|b\right) & \text{if } i = j+1; \\ 0 & \text{otherwise,} \end{cases}$$

$$P_M\left(a_F|\,(b,j)\right) = \begin{cases} 1 & \text{if } i = n; \\ 0 & \text{otherwise.} \end{cases}$$

This means that in order to marginalise, we need to sum over a more complex probability distribution for the hidden states to obtain the corresponding marginalisation kernel

$$\kappa\left(s,t\right) = \sum_{h \in A^n} P(s|h)P(t|h)P_M(h)$$

$$= \sum_{h \in A^n} \prod_{i=1}^{n} P\left(s_i|h_i\right) P\left(t_i|h_i\right) P_M\left(h_i|h_{i-1}\right), \qquad (12.2)$$

where we have used the convention that $P_M(h_1|h_0) = P_M(h_1)$.

Remark 12.7 [Describing the models] We consider each hidden sequence h as a template for the sequences s, t in the sense that if we are in state h_i at position i, the probability that the observable sequence has a symbol s_i in that position is a function of h_i. In our generative model, sequences are generated independently from the hidden template with probabilities $P(s_i|h_i)$ that can be specified by a matrix of size $|\Sigma| \times |A|$. So given this matrix and a fixed h, we can compute $P(s|h)$ and $P(t|h)$. The problem is that there are $|A|^n$ different possible models for generating our sequences s, t, that is the feature space is spanned by a basis of $|A|^n$ dimensions. Furthermore, we consider a special generating process for h of Markov type: the probability of a state depends only on the preceeding state. The consequent marginalisation step will therefore be prohibitively expensive, if performed in a direct way. As in Chapter 11, we will exploit dynamic programming techniques to speed it up. ∎

Consider the set of states A_a^k of length k that end with a given by

$$A_a^k = \left\{ h \in A^k : h_k = a \right\}.$$

We introduce a series of subkernels $\kappa_{k,a}$ for $k = 1, \ldots, n$ and $a \in A$ as follows

$$
\begin{aligned}
\kappa_{k,a}(s,t) &= \sum_{h \in A_a^k} P(s|h) P(t|h) P_M(m) \\
&= \sum_{h \in A_a^k} \prod_{i=1}^k P(s_i|h_i) P(t_i|h_i) P_M(h_i|h_{i-1}),
\end{aligned}
$$

where we have implicitly extended the definitions of $P(s|h)$ and $P(h)$ to cover the case when h has fewer than n symbols by ignoring the rest of the string s.

Clearly, we can express the HMM kernel simply by

$$\kappa(s,t) = \sum_{a \in A} \kappa_{n,a}(s,t).$$

For $k = 1$ we have

$$\kappa_{1,a}(s,t) = P(s_1|a) P(t_1|a) P_M(a).$$

We now obtain recursive equations for computing $\kappa_{k+1,a}(s,t)$ in terms of $\kappa_{k,b}(s,t)$ for $b \in A$, as the following derivation shows

$$
\begin{aligned}
\kappa_{k+1,a}(s,t) &= \sum_{h \in A_a^{k+1}} \prod_{i=1}^{k+1} P(s_i|h_i) P(t_i|h_i) P_M(h_i|h_{i-1}) \\
&= \sum_{b \in A} P(s_{k+1}|a) P(t_{k+1}|a) P_M(a|b) \\
&\qquad \sum_{h \in A_b^k} \prod_{i=1}^k P(s_i|h_i) P(t_i|h_i) P_M(h_i|h_{i-1}) \\
&= \sum_{b \in A} P(s_{k+1}|a) P(t_{k+1}|a) P_M(a|b) \, \kappa_{k,b}(s,t).
\end{aligned}
$$

When computing these kernels we need to use the usual dynamic programming tables, one for each $\kappa_{k,b}(s,t)$, though of course we can overwrite those obtained for $k-1$ when computing $k+1$. The result is summarised in the following algorithm.

Algorithm 12.8 [Fixed length hidden Markov model kernel] The fixed length Hidden Markov Model kernel is computed in Code Fragment 12.1. ∎

Input	Symbol strings s and t, state transition probability matrix $P_M(a\mid b)$, initial state probabilities $P_M(a)$ and conditional probabilities $P(\sigma\mid a)$ of symbols given states.

Process
2
3
4
5
6
7
8
9
10
11
12
13
14
14
	Assume p states, $1, \ldots, p$.
	for $a = 1:p$
	   $\mathrm{DPr}(a) = P(s_1\mid a)\,P(t_1\mid a)\,P_M(a)$;
	end
	for $i = 1:n$
	  $\mathrm{Kern} = 0$;
	  for $a = 1:p$
	    $\mathrm{DP}(a) = 0$;
	    for $b = 1:p$
	      $\mathrm{DP}(a) = \mathrm{DP}(a) + P(s_i\mid a)\,P(t_i\mid a)\,P_M(a\mid b)\,\mathrm{DPr}(b)$;
	    end
	    $\mathrm{Kern} = \mathrm{Kern} + \mathrm{DP}(a)$;
	  end
	  $\mathrm{DPr} = \mathrm{DP}$;
	end

Output	$\kappa(s, t) = \mathrm{Kern}$

Code Fragment 12.1. Pseudocode for the fixed length HMM kernel.

The complexity of the kernel can be bounded from the structure of the algorithm by

$$O\left(n\,|A|^2\right).$$

Remark 12.9 [Reversing sums and products] It is possible to see the dynamic programming as partially reversing the sum and product of equation 12.2. At each stage we compute a product of the sums of the previous phase. This enable the algorithm to break down the very large sum of (12.2) into manageable stages. ∎

Example 12.10 The kernel presented here compares two strings of the same length under a hidden Markov model assumption. The strings are assumed to be 'aligned', that is the generic model h assumes that the ith symbol in each sequence was generated in a conditionally independent way, given the hidden state h_i, and that the sequence of hidden states has a

Markovian structure. This makes sense in those situations in which there is no possibility of insertions or deletions, but we can accurately model random substitutions or mutations of symbols. ∎

12.1.5 Pair hidden Markov model kernels

There are several possible ways to generalise the fixed length hidden Markov model kernel given above. In this and the next subsection we present two different extensions. The kernel presented above makes sense if we assume that two sequences have the same length and are generated by a 'template' sequence that has a Markov structure.

This subsection develops a kernel for strings of different lengths but again generated by an underlying Markov process, a case that has significant importance in computational biology. An alternative way to model the generative process of a fixed length sequence is to assume that all positions in the sequence are associated with the leaves of a tree, being generated simultaneously by an underlying evolution-like process. A generalisation to Markovian trees will be presented in the following section.

In this section we investigate the case when the two sequences have different lengths, generated by emission from hidden states that again satisfy the Markov property. This will make it possible to consider the insertion and deletion of symbols that could have created gaps in the pairwise alignment, hence creating alternative alignments between the sequences and possibly altering their lengths.

The change required to achieve this extra flexibility is at first sight very small. We simply augment the alphabet with the empty symbol ε. As a result a state can generate a symbol for one string while adding nothing to another. This means that the states will no longer correspond to the symbol positions. For this reason we must consider a general Markov model given by a set A of states with transition probabilities given by a matrix

$$M_{ab} = P_M(b|a)$$

giving the probability of moving to state b from state a. There is now no longer a linear ordering imposed on the states, which therefore can form a general probabilistic finite state automaton. We must, however, specify an initial state a_I with no associated emission and with no transitions to it. The model M comprises all possible trajectories h of states beginning at the initial state $h_0 = a_I$. It is also possible to require the trajectories to end a specified final state a_F, though to simplify the exposition we omit this restriction. It follows that the probability of a trajectory $h = (h_0, h_1, \ldots, h_N)$

is given by

$$P_M(h) = \prod_{i=1}^{N} P_M(h_i|h_{i-1}).$$

The emission probabilities for non-initial states are given by the probabilities

$$P(\sigma|a), \text{ for } a \in A \text{ and } \sigma \in \hat{\Sigma} = \Sigma \cup \{\varepsilon\},$$

with the probability that a trajectory h of length N generates a string s given by

$$P(s|h) = \sum_{\hat{s} \in \hat{\Sigma}^N} [\hat{s} = s] \prod_{i=1}^{N} P(s_i|h_i),$$

where we use $[\hat{s} = s]$ for the function outputting 1 when the two strings are equal after deletion of any empty symbols and 0 otherwise. As usual we consider the marginalisation kernel

$$\kappa(s, t) = \sum_{h \in M} P(s|h)P(t|h)P_M(h).$$

Remark 12.11 [Pair hidden Markov models] Our method of defining the generation is slightly unconventional. The more standard approach allows states to emit one symbol for each sequence, only one of which can be the empty character. Occasionally the symbol emission is also shifted from the states to the transitions. We have preferred to have emission from states to link with the previous and following subsections. Allowing states to emit pairs of characters complicates the verification of conditional independence, since we can no longer simply view the kernel as estimating the probability of the two strings arising from the modelling process, that is as a marginalisation kernel. The simplification achieved here results in some slight changes to the dynamic programme computations where we introduce pair hidden Markov models as a computational tool, but we feel that this is a price worth paying for the conceptual simplification. ∎

Example 12.12 We give an example to illustrate the computations of pair HMMs. Two proteins or genes are said to be homologous if they are both descendents from a common ancestor. The sequences may differ from the ancestor's as a result of deletions, insertions and mutations of symbols where these processes occurred independently for the two sequences after their first evolutionary divergence. The distance can be estimated by computing the alignments of the two sequences. For example the two sequences $s =$'AACGTACTGACTA' and $t =$'CGTAGAATA' may be aligned in the following way

AACGTACTGA-CTA

--CGTA--GAA-TA

among others. When assessing the probability that two sequences are homologous, a meaningful measure of similarity and hence potentially an interesting kernel, is given by computing the probabilities of the two sequences being generated from a common ancestor summed over all potential ancestors. The ancestors are modelled as a sequence of states encoding the changes that occurred at each point, deletion, insertion or mutation. The state sequence is assumed to be Markovian since the probabilities of specific changes depend only on the changes occurring at the previous step. This approach typically leads to different possible 'alignments' of the sequences, each with a given probability. For each possible hidden ancestor model h we can calculate the probability that each of the two sequences is its descendent $P(s|h)$ and $P(t|h)$, and we can sum this over all possible ancestors, marginalising in this way over all possible evolutionary ancestors: $P(s,t) = \sum_h P(s|h)P(t|h)P(h)$. ∎

The apparently small change we have introduced to handle gaps complicates the dynamic programming computations. We must now not only consider summing over all sequences ending in a certain stage, but also specify the positions we have reached in each of the strings in much the same way as we did for the string kernels in Chapter 11. Before we can do this we have an additional problem that states which emit ε can emit ε to both sequences complicating the recursion as in this case no new symbols are processed. This problem will be overcome by transforming our hidden Markov model into a so-called pair hidden Markov model generating the same distribution. We begin with a definition of pair hidden Markov models.

Definition 12.13 [Pair hidden Markov model] A data model whose states emit ordered pairs of data will be known as pair data model. Hence, a pair model M is specified by a set of distributions for $h \in M$ that assigns to each pair of data items (x_1, x_2) a probability $P_h(x_1, x_2) = P((x_1, x_2)|h)$. A pair hidden Markov model is a hidden Markov model whose states emit ordered pairs of data items. ∎

Note that in general a pair data model will not define a kernel if we take

$$\kappa(x_1, x_2) = \sum_{h \in M} P((x_1, x_2)|h), \qquad (12.3)$$

since the generation of the two examples is not necessarily independent. This will not, however, concern us since we use the pair hidden Markov model to generate a distribution that we know to be a valid kernel. Our use of the pair hidden Markov model is simply a stepping stone towards creating an efficient algorithm for evaluating that kernel.

The initial pair hidden Markov model is simply the hidden Markov model where each state uses its generating function to generate two symbols independently rather than the single symbol generated by the original model. The kernel defined by equation (12.3) is clearly the same as the marginalisation kernel by its definition.

The pair hidden Markov model is now adapted in two stages. The first creates a new model $\hat{M}$ from M by separating each state that can generate pairs $(\varepsilon, \varepsilon)$ as well as symbols from Σ into two states, one that generates only $(\varepsilon, \varepsilon)$ and one that only generates pairs with at least one symbol from Σ. The second stage involves the removal of the states that emit only $(\varepsilon, \varepsilon)$. In both cases we must verify that the distribution generated by the model remains unchanged.

For the first stage consider a state a that can emit $(\varepsilon, \varepsilon)$ as well as other combinations. We create a new state a^ε for each such state a. The state a^ε emits $(\varepsilon, \varepsilon)$ with probability 1, while the new emission probabilities $\hat{P}((\sigma_1, \sigma_2)|a)$ for a are given by

$$\hat{P}((\sigma_1, \sigma_2)|a) = \begin{cases} \frac{P(\sigma_1|a)P(\sigma_2|a)}{1 - P(\varepsilon|a)^2} & \text{if } \sigma_1 \neq \varepsilon \text{ or } \sigma_2 \neq \varepsilon; \\ 0 & \text{otherwise,} \end{cases}$$

so that a can no longer emit $(\varepsilon, \varepsilon)$. Furthermore the transition probabilities are adapted as follows

$$\begin{aligned} P_{\hat{M}}(a|b) &= P_M(a|b)\left(1 - P(\varepsilon|a)^2\right) \text{ for all } b \neq a, \\ P_{\hat{M}}(a|a) &= P_{\hat{M}}(a|a^\varepsilon) = P_M(a|a)\left(1 - P(\varepsilon|a)^2\right), \\ P_{\hat{M}}(a^\varepsilon|b) &= P_M(a|b)P(\varepsilon|a)^2 \text{ for all } b \neq a, \\ P_{\hat{M}}(a^\varepsilon|a) &= P_{\hat{M}}(a^\varepsilon|a^\varepsilon) = P_M(a|a)P(\varepsilon|a)^2. \end{aligned}$$

It is readily verified that the state a^ε in $\hat{M}$ corresponds to emitting the pair $(\varepsilon, \varepsilon)$ in state a in M, and so the pair hidden Markov model $\hat{M}$ generates an identical distribution over pairs to that generated by M.

The second state of the adaptation involves removing all the states that only emit the pair $(\varepsilon, \varepsilon)$. This is a standard operation on probabilistic finite state automata involving appropriately adjusting the transition probabilities between the remaining states. We omit the details as it is not central to our development.

We therefore now assume that we have a pair hidden Markov model none of whose states emit the pair $(\varepsilon, \varepsilon)$. Consider the sequences of states A_a that end with a given by

$$A_a = \left\{ h \in \hat{M} : h_{|h|} = a, h_0 = a_I \right\}.$$

We introduce a series of subkernels $\kappa_{i,j,a}$ for $a \in A$ as follows

$$\kappa_{i,j,a}(s,t) = \sum_{h \in A_a} \hat{P}(s(1:i), t(1:j) | h) P_{\hat{M}}(h).$$

Clearly, we can express the marginalisation kernel quite simply as

$$\kappa(s,t) = \sum_{a \in A} \kappa_{|s|,|t|,a}(s,t),$$

though if a finish state were specified we would only need the corresponding subkernel. The base of the dynamic programme recursion requires us to compute $\kappa_{0,0,a}(s,t)$ for all states $a \in A$. Clearly, for a_I we have $\kappa_{0,0,a_I}(s,t) = 1$, while for general $a \in A \setminus \{a_I\}$

$$\kappa_{0,0,a}(s,t) = 0.$$

We now obtain recursive equations for computing $\kappa_{i,j,a}(s,t)$ in terms of $\kappa_{i-1,j,b}(s,t)$, $\kappa_{i,j-1,b}(s,t)$ and $\kappa_{i-1,j-1,b}(s,t)$ for $b \in A$, as the following derivation shows

$$\begin{aligned}
\kappa_{i,j,a}(s,t) &= \sum_{h \in A_a} P((s,t) | h) P_{\hat{M}}(h) \\
&= \sum_{b \in A} P((s_i, \varepsilon) | a) P_{\hat{M}}(a|b) \kappa_{i-1,j,b}(s,t) \\
&\quad + \sum_{b \in A} P((\varepsilon, t_j) | a) P_{\hat{M}}(\hat{a}|b) \kappa_{i,j-1,b}(s,t) \\
&\quad + \sum_{b \in A} P((s_i, t_j) | a) P_{\hat{M}}(a|b) \kappa_{i-1,j-1,b}(s,t).
\end{aligned}$$

This is again a set of equations for $\kappa_{i,j,a}(s,t)$ assuming that we have previously computed $\kappa_{i-1,j,b}(s,t)$, $\kappa_{i,j-1,b}(s,t)$ and $\kappa_{i-1,j-1,b}(s,t)$ and results in the following algorithm.

Algorithm 12.14 [Pair hidden Markov models] The pair hidden Markov model kernel is computed in Code Fragment 12.2. ∎

Input	Symbol strings s and t, state transition probability matrix $P_M(a|b)$, initial state 0, final state p and conditional probabilities $P((\sigma_1, \sigma_2)|a)$ of pairs of symbols given states.
Process	Assume p states, $0, \ldots, p$. Lengths of s and t are n and m.
2	for $a = 0 : p$
3	$\quad$ Kern $(0, 0, a) = 0$;
4	$\quad$ for $i = 0 : n$ Kern $(i, -1, a) = 0$;
5	$\quad$ for $j = 0 : m$ Kern $(-1, j, a) = 0$;
8	end
9	Kern $(0, 0, 0) = 1$;
10	for $i = 1 : n$
11	$\quad$ for $a = 1 : p$
12	$\quad\quad$ Kern $(i, 0, a) = 0$;
13	$\quad\quad$ for $b = 0 : p$
14	$\quad\quad\quad$ Kern $(i, 0, a) =$ Kern $(i, 0, a)$ $\quad\quad\quad\quad\quad +P((s_i, \varepsilon)|a) P_M(a|b)$ Kern $(i - 1, 0, b)$;
15	$\quad\quad$ end
16	$\quad$ end
17	for $i = 0 : n$
18	$\quad$ for $j = 1 : m$
19	$\quad\quad$ for $a = 1 : p$
20	$\quad\quad\quad$ Kern $(i, j, a) = 0$;
21	$\quad\quad\quad$ for $b = 0 : p$
22	$\quad\quad\quad\quad$ Kern $(i, j, a) =$ Kern (i, j, a) $\quad\quad\quad\quad\quad +P((s_i, \varepsilon)|a) P_M(a|b)$ Kern $(i - 1, j, b)$
23	$\quad\quad\quad\quad\quad +P((\varepsilon, t_j)|a) P_M(a|b)$ Kern $(i, j - 1, b)$
24	$\quad\quad\quad\quad\quad +P((s_i, t_j)|a) P_M(a|b)$ Kern $(i - 1, j - 1, b)$;
25	$\quad\quad\quad$ end
26	$\quad\quad$ end
27	$\quad$ end
Output	$\kappa(s, t) =$ Kern (n, m, p)

Code Fragment 12.2. Pseudocode for the pair HMM kernel.

Remark 12.15 [Defining pair HMMs directly] We have introduced pair hidden Markov models as a stepping stone towards an efficient algorithm as they enable us to remove the possibility of no symbols at all being emitted by a state. Authors typically choose to define their models using pair hidden Markov models. This has the advantage of making the design more natural in some cases. The disadvantage is that extra conditions need to be applied to ensure that a valid kernel is generated, essentially ensuring that paths between states that emit two symbols are independent whether they emit symbols to one string or the other.   ∎

12.1.6 Hidden tree model kernels

The previous subsection considers unequal length sequences using a hidden Markov model. In this section we return to aligned equal length sequences, but consider a more complex generating model.

Another way to model the hidden structure generating two aligned strings of the same length n is to assume their symbols are associated to the n leaves of a tree, in which the state of each node depends probabilistically on the state of its parent node. The state of the leaves is assumed to represent the sequence. This is a probabilistic graphical model, and can be used as a generative model of the sequence and so to design a marginalisation kernel

$$P_M(s,t) = \sum_{h \in M} P(s|h)P(t|h)P_M(h).$$

The set M of models is therefore defined by a fixed tree of internal nodes $v_0, v_1, \ldots, v_N$ each labelled with $h(v_i)$ from a set A of states. We will assume that the state $a = h(n)$ of a node n is compatible with the number $\mathrm{child}(n) = \mathrm{child}(a)$ of its children and determines the distributions $P_{i,a}(b) = P_i(b|a)$ of probability that the ith child $\mathrm{ch}_i(v)$ is in state b given its parent is in state a. The state $h(l_k)$ of the leaf node determines the probability of $P(s_k|h(l_k))$ of the corresponding symbol s_i from Σ. Hence, after we specify a probability distribution $P_M(a)$ over the state $h(v_0)$ of the root node, this implies a distribution over the states of the n leaf nodes $l_1, \ldots, l_n$. This probabilistic graphical model describes a distribution of probability over all sequences from Σ^n given by

$$P(s) = \sum_{h \in M} \prod_{k=1}^{n} P(s_k|h(l_k)) \, P_M(h(v_0)) \prod_{i=0}^{N} \prod_{j=1}^{\mathrm{child}(h(v_i))} P_j(h(\mathrm{ch}_j(v_i))|h(v_i)).$$

Example 12.16 Consider the case of a fixed binary tree with binary states and symbols. Furthermore, we assume the conditional probabilities are the same for both children, so that we have only two degrees of freedom ϵ and δ for the internal nodes

$$P(0|1) = \epsilon \qquad P(1|0) = \delta$$
$$P(1|1) = 1 - \epsilon \qquad P(0|0) = 1 - \delta,$$

with another degree of freedom τ for the probability of the root-state

$$P(h(v_0) = 1) = \tau \text{ and } P(h(v_0) = 0) = 1 - \tau.$$

Hence, for this example we need only specify three parameters. ∎

Figure 12.4 shows an example of a hidden tree model. The tree model

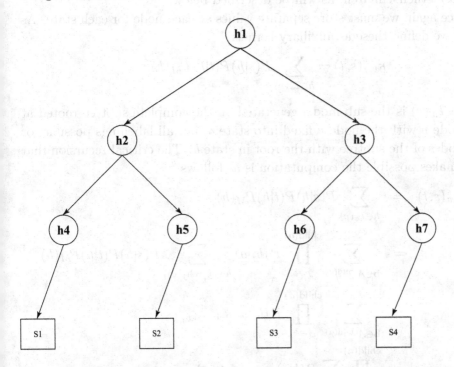

Fig. 12.4. A hidden tree model for generating a fixed length string.

is another example of a probabilistic graphical model. In general the number of different states of the tree make it impractical to perform a direct computation of the associated marginalisation kernel

$$\kappa(s,t) = \sum_{h \in M} P(s|h)P(t|h)P_M(h).$$

Since this probability is parametrised by the state of the internal nodes, there are exponentially many states h that can be used to measure the probability of a sequence corresponding to the exponentially many features $\phi_h(s) = P(s|h)$ for $h \in M$ that define the feature space. Once again we must devise a dynamic programme that can short-circuit the full computation by making use of the specific structure of the model.

This dynamic programme is an example of a message passing algorithm, that with a single depth-first traversal of the tree can compute the joint probability of the two input sequences summed over all compatible hidden states. This quantity is stored at the root node, after the traversal when the relative message passing is completed. At each node, a number of values or 'messages' are stored, and they are calculated based only on the values stored at their children, as will be described below.

Once again we must store separate values at each node for each state. As usual we define these as auxiliary kernels

$$\kappa_{v,a}(s,t) = \sum_{h \in T_a(v)} P(s|h)P(t|h)P_M(h),$$

where $T_a(v)$ is the sub-model generated on the complete subtree rooted at the node v with the node v fixed into state a, i.e. all labellings possible for the nodes of the subtree with the root in state a. The critical recursion that now makes possible the computation is as follows

$$\begin{aligned}
\kappa_{v,a}(s,t) &= \sum_{h \in T_a(v)} P(s|h)P(t|h)P_M(h) \\
&= \sum_{b \in A^{\text{child}(a)}} \prod_{j=1}^{\text{child}(a)} P(b_j|a) \sum_{h \in T_{b_j}(\text{ch}_j(v))} P(s|h)P(t|h)P_M(h) \\
&= \sum_{b \in A^{\text{child}(a)}} \prod_{j=1}^{\text{child}(a)} P(b_j|a) \, \kappa_{\text{ch}_j(v),b_j}(s,t) \\
&= \prod_{j=1}^{\text{child}(a)} \sum_{b \in A} P(b|a) \, \kappa_{\text{ch}_j(v),b}(s,t),
\end{aligned}$$

where the final line again follows from the use of the distributive law as in equation (12.1). If we consider the case of a binary tree with binary states, the computation at an internal node v involves two values

$$\kappa_{\text{ch}_j(v),0}(s,t) \text{ and } \kappa_{\text{ch}_j(v),1}(s,t)$$

being received from each of the two children $\text{ch}_1(v)$ and $\text{ch}_2(v)$. These four values are then combined with the probabilities $P(0|0)$, $P(0|1)$, $P(1|0)$ and $P(1|1)$ to compute the values

$$\kappa_{v,0}(s,t) \text{ and } \kappa_{v,1}(s,t)$$

subsequently passed on to its parent. In general there are $|A|$ messages from each child that must be received and appropriately processed.

The value of the kernel is given

$$\kappa(s,t) = \sum_{a \in A} P_M(a) \, \kappa_{v_o,a}(s,t),$$

that is the appropriately weighted sum of the kernels obtained by fixing the root node v_0 to each of the possible states. Similarly, the base of the recursion is given by

$$\kappa_{l_i,a}(s,t) = P(s_i|a)P(t_i|a),$$

since this corresponds to a deterministic state at the leaf l_i which either agrees with both of the corresponding symbols s_i and t_i or not. The result is summarised in the following algorithm that uses a recursive function returning an array of kernel values indexed by the states.

Algorithm 12.17 [Hidden tree model kernel] The hidden tree model kernel is computed in Code Fragment 12.3. ∎

The complexity of Algorithm 12.17 can be estimated by observing that each node v of the tree is visited once with a call to Treerecur (v) and that the computation involved for each call is bounded by $O\left(|A|^2 d^+\right)$, where d^+ is the maximum number of children of the tree nodes. Hence, the overall algorithm has complexity

$$O\left(N|A|^2 d^+\right),$$

since N is the number of nodes in the tree.

Remark 12.18 [Swapping sums and products] Note how the strategy succeeds in breaking down the overall sum of products into a staged sequence of manageable sums, one at each internal node. Hence, there has again been a partial swapping of the sums and products from the original definition, each swap leading to a corresponding reduction in the complexity. ∎

Example 12.19 Consider Example 12.16. Since this is a binary tree the recursion is somewhat simpler with all the indexing sets running from 0 to 1. For this case lines 17-26 of the algorithm can, for example, be replaced by

17	$\mathrm{Kern}\,(0) = ((1-\delta)\,\mathrm{Kerp}\,(0,0) + \epsilon\,\mathrm{Kerp}\,(0,1))$
18	$\qquad\qquad ((1-\delta)\,\mathrm{Kerp}\,(1,0) + \epsilon\,\mathrm{Kerp}\,(1,1))\,;$
19	$\mathrm{Kern}\,(1) = (\delta\,\mathrm{Kerp}\,(0,0) + (1-\epsilon)\,\mathrm{Kerp}\,(0,1))$
20	$\qquad\qquad (\delta\,\mathrm{Kerp}\,(1,0) + (1-\epsilon)\,\mathrm{Kerp}\,(1,1))\,;$

∎

Example 12.20 [Phylogenetic profiles] In its simplest form a phylogenetic profile of a gene or a protein is a string of bits each indicating the presence or absence of a homologue of the gene or protein in a different organism. It

Input	Symbol strings s and t, tree structure and conditional state probabilities $P_M(a\|b)$, initial state probabilities $P_M(a)$
Process	Assume p states, $1, \ldots, p$.
2	DP = Treerecur (v_0);
3	Kern = 0;
4	for $a = 1 : p$
5	Kern = Kern $+P_M(a)$ DP (a);
6	end
where	Treerecur (v)
8	if $v = l_i$
9	for $a = 1 : p$ DP$(a) = P(s_i\|a)P(t_i\|a)$;
10	return DP;
11	end
12	for $j = 1 : $ child (v)
13	DPp $(j, :)$ = Treerecur $(\text{ch}_j(v))$;
14	for $a = 1 : p$
15	DP $(a) = 1$;
16	for $j = 1 : $ child (a)
17	DPq $= 0$;
18	for $b = 1 : p$
19	DPq = DPq $+P_M(b\|a)$ DPp (j, b);
20	end
21	DP (a) = DP (a) DPq;
22	end
23	end
24	return DP;
Output	$\kappa(s, t) = $ Kern

Code Fragment 12.3. Pseudocode for the hidden tree model kernel.

is assumed that functionally related genes have similar phylogenetic profiles. In this context the question of defining similarity between such profiles is crucial. Instead of just counting the number of organisms in which the two genes are simultaneously present or absent, intuitively one could hope to obtain more information by comparing the entire evolutionary history of the two genes. Though the precise history is not available, it can be modeled by a phylogenetic tree and probabilities can be computed with it. A phylogenetic tree of a group of organisms is a rooted tree, where each leaf represents an organism currently existing, and each internal node represents an extinct species, with the edges of the tree indicating that the child species evolved from the parent. The transmission of genes during evolution can be modelled using the tree models considered in this section, that is a probabilistic graphical model that defines a joint probability distribution P for a set of random binary variables indexed by the nodes of the tree. The probabilities that a species has a gene when its parent does not is encoded in $P(0|1)$ and so on. Hence, assuming knowledge of the phylogenetic tree, the kernel we have defined can be used to measure the relatedness of two genes based on their phylogenetic profiles. ∎

Remark 12.21 [More general tree kernels] It is possible to extend the above kernel to consider all subtrees of the given tree structure, where the subtrees are obtained by pruning complete subtrees. Furthermore it is possible to consider the case in which we do not know the topology of the tree, and we want to marginalise over a large number of possible topologies. More information and pointers to the relevant literature can be found in Section 12.4. ∎

12.2 Fisher kernels

12.2.1 From probability to geometry

The main idea behind marginalisation kernels was to consider the probability of the data given one model $P(x|m)$ as a feature. Given a single model this is very little information that is potentially misleading since two very different data items could be given the same probability by the model without this indicating any similarity. The marginalisation kernels overcame this weakness by comparing the scores of data items under several different models, typically exponentially many models.

We now consider an alternative strategy known as the Fisher kernel that attempts to extract from a single generative model more information than simply their output probability. The aim is to analyse how the score depends on the model, which aspects of the model have been important in determining that score, and hence obtaining information about the internal representation of the data items within the model.

For such an approach to work we require the single model to be more flexible so that we can measure how it adapts to individual data items. We will therefore need the model to be smoothly parametrised so that derivatives of the model with respect to the parameters can be computed.

Remark 12.22 [Relation between generative model and Fisher kernels] These ideas are clearly related. In the case of marginalisation kernels we typically create a finite but very large set of models over which the scores are computed. We now consider a parametrised model with a particular parameter setting, but measure how the model changes in the neighbourhood of that setting. Hence, we can see the approach as considering a class of models obtained by deforming the current model. In this case, however, the information is summarised in a feature space whose dimension is equal to the number of parameters. Despite these connections the approaches are complementary in the sense that marginalisation kernels typically consider a set of models indexed by a discrete set, for example the paths of a hidden Markov model. Any smooth parameters are treated as constant. The Fisher kernel on the other hand is based only on the modelling of smooth parameters.   ∎

Remark 12.23 [Features from internal computations] Yet another approach would be to extract information from the 'internal computations' of the model in order to evaluate its probabilities. It is the generation process of a data point that should enable a fuller description in the feature space, so that the difference in the generation process and not just in the computed probability can be exploited for comparing two examples x and z.   ∎

Our starting point is a smooth parametric model $P_{\boldsymbol{\theta}^0}(x) = P\left(x|\boldsymbol{\theta}^0\right)$ of the data that computes the probability of a given input x being produced by the underlying generative process with the vector of parameters $\boldsymbol{\theta}$ set to $\boldsymbol{\theta}^0$.

We will construct features ϕ_i one for each model parameter θ_i by examining slight perturbations of that parameter around the given setting θ_i^0, in this way obtaining several models or perspectives by extracting information about how the different parameters affect the score of x.

More specifically, if one wanted to adapt the parameters of a model in order to accommodate a new data item by increasing its likelihood under the model, the parameters will have to be adapted in different ways. If we use a gradient approach to parameter tuning, the partial derivatives of the score $P_{\boldsymbol{\theta}^0}(x)$ with respect to the parameters contain the information about how much each parameter should be moved in order to accommodate the new point.

In this perspective, it seems natural to compare two data points through the directions in which they 'stretch' the parameters of the model, that is by viewing the score function at the two points as a function of the parameters and comparing the two gradients. If the gradient vectors are similar it means that the two data items would adapt the model in the same way, that is from the point of view of the given parametric model at the current parameter setting they are similar in the sense that they would require similar adaptations to the parameters.

Remark 12.24 [Features corresponding to constraints] There are other intuitive interpretations of the approach of describing the data items by the perturbations of the score caused by slight parameter movements. Consider a model that calculates the probability of a data item x being generated by checking if it satisfies certain constraints, with each constraint being assessed by one parameter. If some are violated, the data item is less representative of the model and so will receive a lower score, depending on the magnitude and number of the violations. The Fisher kernel compares two data points with respect to all relevant properties of the data model by comparing the pattern of behaviour of each with respect to the different constraints. One could also view these features as the Lagrange multipliers assessing the degree to which the input is attempting to violate the different constraints. ∎

What we have introduced in an intuitive way is a representation of the data that is based on a single parametrised probabilistic model. The purpose of Fisher kernels is to capture the internal representation of the data exploited by such models in order to compute its score.

Definition 12.25 [Smoothly parametrised model class] A *smoothly parametrised model class* is a set of probability distributions

$$M = \{P_{\boldsymbol{\theta}}(x) : \boldsymbol{\theta} \in \Theta\}$$

on an input space X, where $\Theta \subseteq \mathbb{R}^N$ for some finite N. We say that each parameter setting $\boldsymbol{\theta}$ determines a model $m(\boldsymbol{\theta})$ of the data. We define the *likelihood* of a data item x with respect to the model $m(\boldsymbol{\theta})$ for a given setting of the parameters $\boldsymbol{\theta}$ to be

$$\mathcal{L}_{\boldsymbol{\theta}}(x) = P(x|\boldsymbol{\theta}) = P_{\boldsymbol{\theta}}(x).$$

∎

Probabilistic models assess the degree of fit of a data point to a model by its likelihood. We can learn the model parameters θ by adapting them to maximise the likelihood of the training set, i.e. the probability

$$\prod_{i=1}^{\ell} \mathcal{L}_{\boldsymbol{\theta}}(x_i)$$

that all of the training points were generated independently in the model. The problem of learning a model in this way is something with which we are

not concerned in this book. We will assume throughout that the setting of
the parameters $\boldsymbol{\theta}^0$ has been determined. This can be done, for example, by
gradient ascent of the likelihood of the training set. From this perspective an
intuitive way to assess the relationship of a new point to the model is to see
what update would be necessary to the parameters in order to incorporate
it, that is what is the gradient of the likelihood at this point. If a point is
a prototypical example of the points accepted by the model, its likelihood
will already be close to maximal and little or no tuning of the parameters
will be necessary. If a point is very unusual with respect to some property,
the gradient in that direction will be large in order to incorporate the new
point.

As we have seen in the discussion so far the information we want to
exploit is contained in the gradient of the likelihood function of the given
data point taken with respect to the tunable parameters. In practice we
consider the log of the likelihood function since this means that products
of probabilities become sums, while at the same time the resulting gradient
vector is just rescaled. We can also use the second order derivatives to refine
the comparison.

Definition 12.26 [Fisher score and Fisher information matrix] The *log-
likelihood* of a data item x with respect to the model $m(\boldsymbol{\theta}^0)$ for a given
setting of the parameters $\boldsymbol{\theta}^0$ is defined to be

$$\log \mathcal{L}_{\boldsymbol{\theta}^0}(x).$$

Consider the vector gradient of the log-likelihood

$$\mathbf{g}\left(\boldsymbol{\theta}, x\right) = \left(\frac{\partial \log \mathcal{L}_{\boldsymbol{\theta}}(x)}{\partial \theta_i}\right)_{i=1}^{N}.$$

The *Fisher score* of a data item x with respect to the model $m(\boldsymbol{\theta}^0)$ for a
given setting of the parameters $\boldsymbol{\theta}^0$ is

$$\mathbf{g}\left(\boldsymbol{\theta}^0, x\right).$$

The *Fisher information matrix* with respect to the model $m(\boldsymbol{\theta}^0)$ for a given
setting of the parameters $\boldsymbol{\theta}^0$ is given by

$$\mathbf{I}_M = \mathbb{E}\left[\mathbf{g}\left(\boldsymbol{\theta}^0, x\right) \mathbf{g}\left(\boldsymbol{\theta}^0, x\right)'\right],$$

where the expectation is over the generation of the data point x according
to the data generating distribution.   ∎

The Fisher score gives us an embedding into the feature space $\mathbb{R}^N$ and hence immediately suggests a possible kernel. The matrix $\mathbf{I}_M$ can be used to define a non-standard inner product in that feature space.

Definition 12.27 [Fisher kernel] The invariant Fisher kernel with respect to the model $m(\boldsymbol{\theta}^0)$ for a given setting of the parameters $\boldsymbol{\theta}^0$ is defined as

$$\kappa(x, z) = \mathbf{g}\left(\boldsymbol{\theta}^0, x\right)' \mathbf{I}_M^{-1} \mathbf{g}\left(\boldsymbol{\theta}^0, z\right).$$

The practical Fisher kernel is defined as

$$\kappa(x, z) = \mathbf{g}\left(\boldsymbol{\theta}^0, x\right)' \mathbf{g}\left(\boldsymbol{\theta}^0, z\right).$$

∎

Remark 12.28 [Problem of small norms] Notice that this kernel may give a small norm to very typical points, while atypical points may have large derivatives and so a correspondingly larger norm. The derivative of the log implies division by $P(x|\boldsymbol{\theta})$, which will to some extent reinforce this effect. There is, therefore, a danger that the inner product between two typical points can become very small, despite their being similar in the model. This effect is can of course be overcome by normalising the kernel. ∎

Remark 12.29 [Using the Gaussian kernel] Another way to use the Fisher score that does not suffer from the problem described above is to use the Gaussian kernel based on distance in the Fisher score space

$$\kappa(x, z) = \exp\left(-\frac{\left\|\mathbf{g}\left(\boldsymbol{\theta}^0, x\right) - \mathbf{g}\left(\boldsymbol{\theta}^0, z\right)\right\|^2}{2\sigma^2}\right).$$

∎

We examine now some simple examples to illustrate the concepts introduced so far.

Example 12.30 [1-dim Gaussian Fisher kernel] Consider the model class M on $X = \mathbb{R}$ defined by the 1-dimensional Gaussian distributions

$$M = \left\{P(x|\boldsymbol{\theta}) = \frac{1}{\sqrt{2\pi}\sigma} \exp\left(-\frac{(x - \mu)^2}{2\sigma^2}\right) : \boldsymbol{\theta} = (\mu, \sigma) \in \mathbb{R}^2\right\}.$$

The log-likelihood of a point x as a function of the parameters $\boldsymbol{\theta} = (\mu, \sigma)$ is

$$\log \mathcal{L}_{(\mu,\sigma)}(x) = -\frac{(x - \mu)^2}{2\sigma^2} - \frac{1}{2}\log(2\pi\sigma).$$

Hence, the Fisher scores of a point x at parameter setting $\boldsymbol{\theta}^0 = (\mu_0, \sigma_0)$ is

$$\mathbf{g}\left(\boldsymbol{\theta}^0, x\right) = \left(\frac{(x - \mu_0)}{\sigma_0^2}, \frac{(x - \mu_0)^2}{\sigma_0^3} - \frac{1}{2\sigma_0}\right).$$

If we use the embedding

$$\phi(x) = \mathbf{g}\left(\boldsymbol{\theta}^0, x\right),$$

as in the practical Fisher kernel, then we obtain the following embedding for the case when $\mu_0 = 0$ and $\sigma_0 = 1$

$$\phi(x) = \left(x, x^2 - 0.5\right),$$

which is equivalent to the polynomial kernel of degree 2 with the real line being embedded onto the curve $y = x^2 - 0.5$ as shown in Figure 12.5. Using

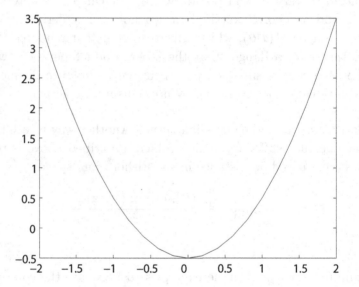

Fig. 12.5. Feature space embedding corresponding to the Fisher kernel of a one-dimensional Gaussians.

hyperplanes in this 2-dimensional space shows that the embedding will allow classifications that reflect exclusions of independent amounts of each tail of the Gaussian, something not possible with the standard (1-dimensional) inner product. Note that this will be true even if the true Gaussian is different from that given by the parameter setting $\boldsymbol{\theta}^0$, though the closer to the true distribution it is the easier it will be to achieve the separation. ∎

Example 12.31 [Two fixed width Gaussians] If we assume our data has been generated by two Gaussians with pre-fixed widths both equal to σ and means stored as the parameters $\boldsymbol{\theta} = (\mu^+, \mu^-)$, the gradient of the log-likelihood with respect to the two tunable parameters is

$$\mathbf{g}\left(\boldsymbol{\theta}^0, x\right) = \left(\frac{(x - \mu_0^+)}{\sigma^2}, \frac{(x - \mu_0^-)}{\sigma^2}\right).$$

This will not enrich the capacity of the function class since it maps to a line in the *two*-dimensional feature space. ∎

The two examples above illustrate how different assumptions on the source generating the data can change the embedding map, and a correct or even approximately correct guess of the model can improve the embedding.

We now show with examples how Fisher kernels can be used to deal with structured objects such as for example the strings of symbols in text or DNA. Frequently a generative model exists for such objects or can be inferred from easily available unlabelled data. We will gradually move from artificial to real cases, starting from fixed length strings of independently generated symbols, moving to Markov models and finally to HMMs. As before with exponential case, the same string can be embedded in different spaces depending on the generative model we decide to use.

Example 12.32 [Markov strings] We consider a generative model for strings of length n parametrised by probabilities $p_{u \to \sigma}$ that the next character following a string u of length k is σ. We therefore compute the likelihood of a string s as

$$\prod_{j=1}^{n-k} p_{s(j:j+k-1) \to s_{j+k}},$$

that is the product of the probabilities for each of the characters that have at least k predecessors in the string. If we assume that

$$\sum_{\sigma \in \Sigma} p_{u \to \sigma} = 1, \text{ for all } u \in \Sigma^k,$$

and that the first k symbols of the strings are fixed (if necessary these could be k special marker symbols added to the beginning of the string), the likelihoods corresponds to a distribution over the set of possible strings. This implies certain constraints on the parameters $p_{u \to \sigma}$ which would affect the calculation of the derivatives. We therefore choose to parametrise the model with arbitrary real-values $\boldsymbol{\theta} = (a_{u \to \sigma})_{u \in \Sigma^k, \sigma \in \Sigma}$ with

$$p_{u \to \sigma} = \frac{a_{u \to \sigma}}{\sum_{\sigma \in \Sigma} a_{u \to \sigma}}.$$

The Fisher score now becomes

$$
\begin{aligned}
\mathbf{g}\left(\boldsymbol{\theta}^0, s\right)_{u \to \sigma} &= \frac{\partial \log \mathcal{L}_{\boldsymbol{\theta}}(s)}{\partial a_{u \to \sigma}} \\
&= \sum_{j=1}^{n-k} \frac{\partial \log p_{s(j:j+k-1) \to s_{j+k}}}{\partial a_{u \to \sigma}} \\
&= \sum_{j=1}^{n-k} [s(j:j+k-1) = u] \left([s_{j+k} = \sigma] \frac{1}{a_{s(j:j+k-1) \to s_{j+k}}} \right. \\
&\qquad\qquad \left. - \frac{1}{\sum_{\sigma \in \Sigma} a_{s(j:j+k-1) \to \sigma}} \right).
\end{aligned}
$$

If we consider the parameter setting $\boldsymbol{\theta}^0$ for which all $a_{u \to \sigma} = p_{u \to \sigma} = |\Sigma|^{-1}$ the computation simplifies to

$$\mathbf{g}\left(\boldsymbol{\theta}^0, s\right)_{u \to \sigma} = |\{(v_1, v_2) : s = v_1 u \sigma v_2\}| \, |\Sigma| - |\{(v_1, v_2) : s = v_1 u v_2\}|.$$

Ignoring the second term this becomes the p-spectrum kernel of length $k+1$ scaled by $|\Sigma|$. The second term subtracts the first term for the given u averaged in s over the possible next characters σ, hence projecting the subset of features that include a k-string u to the hyperplane perpendicular to the all ones vector. ∎

Remark 12.33 [Arbitrary length strings] Example 12.32 can be extended to arbitrary length strings by introducing an end-of-string state to which we can transfer with certain probability at any time. More generally the approach suggests that we may improve the performance of the p-spectrum kernel by tuning the parameters $a_{u \to \sigma}$ for example using counts of the transitions in the whole corpus. This corresponds to learning the model from the training data.

Note how the states of the corresponding Markov model are labelled by subsequences $u\sigma$ of length $k + 1$, with the transitions defined by adding the next symbol to the suffix of length k. This suggests that we could generalise the approach by allowing states that correspond to different length subsequences perhaps chosen so that they are neither too frequent or too rare. The transition for a state u and symbol σ would be to the longest suffix of $u\sigma$ that corresponds to a state. Again the transition parameters could be inferred from the training data. ∎

The examples we have considered so far have all been for the practical Fisher kernel. The invariant Fisher kernel suffers from the drawback that it requires us to compute a random matrix

$$\mathbf{I}_M = \mathbb{E}\left[\mathbf{g}\left(\boldsymbol{\theta}^0, x\right)\mathbf{g}\left(\boldsymbol{\theta}^0, x\right)'\right]$$

where x is drawn according to the input distribution, something that we are not able to do in practice. Before considering this problem we will first indicate why the name 'invariant' is appropriate. If we reparametrise the model using an invertible differentiable transformation

$$\boldsymbol{\psi} = \boldsymbol{\psi}\left(\boldsymbol{\theta}\right),$$

we might expect that the resulting kernel would change. The embedding will certainly alter and so the practical Fisher kernel will change with it, but the invariant Fisher kernel is not affected by this reparametrisation since if $\tilde{\kappa}$ is the transformed kernel we have

$$\mathbf{g}\left(\boldsymbol{\theta}^0, x\right)' = \left(\frac{\partial \log \mathcal{L}_{\boldsymbol{\psi}}(x)}{\partial \psi_i}\right)_{i=1}^N \mathbf{J}\left(\boldsymbol{\psi}\right) = \mathbf{g}\left(\boldsymbol{\psi}^0, x\right)' \mathbf{J}\left(\boldsymbol{\psi}^0\right),$$

where $\mathbf{J}\left(\boldsymbol{\psi}^0\right)$ is the Jacobian of the transformation $\boldsymbol{\psi}$ evaluated at $\boldsymbol{\psi}^0$. It follows that

$$
\begin{aligned}
&\tilde{\kappa}(x_1, x_2) \\
&= \mathbf{g}\left(\boldsymbol{\psi}^0, x_1\right)' \tilde{\mathbf{I}}_M^{-1} \mathbf{g}\left(\boldsymbol{\psi}^0, x_2\right) \\
&= \mathbf{g}\left(\boldsymbol{\theta}^0, x_1\right)' \mathbf{J}\left(\boldsymbol{\psi}^0\right)^{-1} \\
&\quad \mathbb{E}\left[\mathbf{J}\left(\boldsymbol{\psi}^0\right)'^{-1} \mathbf{g}\left(\boldsymbol{\theta}^0, x\right) \mathbf{g}\left(\boldsymbol{\theta}^0, x\right)' \mathbf{J}\left(\boldsymbol{\psi}^0\right)^{-1}\right]^{-1} \mathbf{J}\left(\boldsymbol{\psi}^0\right)'^{-1} \mathbf{g}\left(\boldsymbol{\theta}^0, x_2\right) \\
&= \mathbf{g}\left(\boldsymbol{\theta}^0, x_1\right)' \mathbf{J}\left(\boldsymbol{\psi}^0\right)^{-1} \mathbf{J}\left(\boldsymbol{\psi}^0\right) \\
&\quad \mathbb{E}\left[\mathbf{g}\left(\boldsymbol{\theta}^0, x\right) \mathbf{g}\left(\boldsymbol{\theta}^0, x\right)'\right]^{-1} \mathbf{J}\left(\boldsymbol{\psi}^0\right)' \mathbf{J}\left(\boldsymbol{\psi}^0\right)'^{-1} \mathbf{g}\left(\boldsymbol{\theta}^0, x_2\right) \\
&= \mathbf{g}\left(\boldsymbol{\theta}^0, x_1\right)' \mathbb{E}\left[\mathbf{g}\left(\boldsymbol{\theta}^0, x\right) \mathbf{g}\left(\boldsymbol{\theta}^0, x\right)'\right]^{-1} \mathbf{g}\left(\boldsymbol{\theta}^0, x_2\right) = \kappa\left(x_1, x_2\right).
\end{aligned}
$$

The invariant Fisher kernel is indeed invariant to any smooth invertible reparametrisation of the model. This would appear to be a desirable property if we believe that the choice of parametrisation is somewhat arbitrary. We will see, however, that this view may be misleading.

Let us return to the question of computing the Fisher information matrix

$$\mathbf{I}_M = \mathbb{E}\left[\mathbf{g}\left(\boldsymbol{\theta}^0, x\right)\mathbf{g}\left(\boldsymbol{\theta}^0, x\right)'\right].$$

A natural approximation for the matrix is to take the empirical rather than the true expectation. In other words we estimate the matrix by averaging over the sample

$$\hat{\mathbf{I}}_M = \hat{\mathbb{E}}\left[\mathbf{g}\left(\boldsymbol{\theta}^0, x\right)\mathbf{g}\left(\boldsymbol{\theta}^0, x\right)'\right] = \frac{1}{\ell}\sum_{i=1}^{\ell}\mathbf{g}\left(\boldsymbol{\theta}^0, x_i\right)\mathbf{g}\left(\boldsymbol{\theta}^0, x_i\right)'.$$

In this case $\hat{\mathbf{I}}_M$ is simply the covariance matrix of the Fisher scores. Hence, the Fisher kernel becomes equivalent to whitening these scores (see Algorithm 6.16), with the associated dangers of amplifying noise if certain parameters are not relevant for the information contained in the training set. Hence, the invariance comes at the cost of possibly reducing the signal to noise ratio in the representation.

12.2.2 Fisher kernels for hidden Markov models

We now consider deriving Fisher kernels for the hidden Markov models that we developed to create generative kernels. Consider first the fixed length hidden Markov models described in Section 12.1.4. We now view the model as the sum over all of the state paths or individual models with the parameters the various transition and emission probabilities, so that for a particular parameter setting the probability of a sequence s is given by

$$P_M\left(s\right) = \sum_{m\in A^n} P(s|m)P_M(m) = \sum_{m\in A^n} P_M(s,m),$$

where

$$P_M(m) = P_M(m_1)P_M(m_2|m_1)\ldots P_M(m_n|m_{n-1}),$$

and

$$P(s|m) = \prod_{i=1}^{n} P\left(s_i|m_i\right)$$

so that

$$P_M(s,m) = \prod_{i=1}^{n} P\left(s_i|m_i\right)P\left(m_i|m_{i-1}\right).$$

The parameters of the model are the emission probabilities $P(s_i|m_i)$ and the transition probabilities $P_M(m_i|m_{i-1})$. For convenience we introduce parameters

$$\theta_{s_i|m_i} = P(s_i|m_i) \text{ and } \tau_{m_i|m_{i-1}} = P_M(m_i|m_{i-1}),$$

where we use the convention that $P_M(m_1) = P_M(m_1|m_0)$ with $m_0 = a_0$ for a special fixed state $a_0 \notin A$. We again have the difficulty experienced in Example 12.32 that these parameters are not independent. Using the same approach as was adopted in that example we introduce the unconstrained parameters

$$\theta_{\sigma,a} \text{ and } \tau_{a,b}$$

with

$$\theta_{\sigma|a} = \frac{\theta_{\sigma,a}}{\sum_{\sigma'\in\Sigma}\theta_{\sigma',a}} \text{ and } \tau_{a|b} = \frac{\tau_{a,b}}{\sum_{a'\in A}\tau_{a',b}}.$$

We assemble these values into a parameter vector $\boldsymbol{\theta}$. Furthermore we assume that the parameter setting at which the derivatives are computed satisfies

$$\sum_{\sigma\in\Sigma}\theta_{\sigma,a} = \sum_{a\in A}\tau_{a,b} = 1, \tag{12.4}$$

for all $a, b \in A$ in order to simplify the calculations.

We must compute the derivatives of the log-likelihood with respect to the parameters $\boldsymbol{\theta}$ and $\boldsymbol{\tau}$. The computations for both sets of parameters follow an identical pattern, so to simplify the presentation we first derive a template that subsumes both cases. Let

$$\bar{\psi}(b,a) = \frac{\psi(b,a)}{\sum_{b'\in B}\psi(b',a)}, \text{ for } a \in A \text{ and } b \in B.$$

Let

$$Q(\mathbf{a},\mathbf{b}) = \prod_{i=1}^{n}\bar{\psi}(b_i,a_i)\,c_i,$$

for some constants c_i. Consider the derivative of $Q(\mathbf{a},\mathbf{b})$ with respect to the parameter $\psi(b,a)$ at a point $(\mathbf{a}^0,\mathbf{b}^0)$ where

$$\sum_{b\in B}\psi(b,a_i^0) = 1 \text{ for all } i. \tag{12.5}$$

We have

$$\frac{\partial Q(\mathbf{a},\mathbf{b})}{\partial\psi(b,a)} =$$

$$= \sum_{k=1}^{n} c_k \prod_{i \neq k} \bar{\psi}\left(b_i^0, a_i^0\right) c_i \frac{\partial}{\partial \psi(b, a)} \frac{\psi(b_k, a_k)}{\sum_{b' \in B} \psi(b', a_k)}$$

$$= \sum_{k=1}^{n} \left(\frac{[b_k^0 = b][a_k^0 = a]}{\sum_{b' \in B} \psi(b', a_k^0)} - \frac{\psi(b_k^0, a_k^0)[a_k^0 = a]}{\left(\sum_{b' \in B} \psi(b', a_k^0)\right)^2} \right) c_k \prod_{i \neq k} \bar{\psi}\left(b_i^0, a_i^0\right) c_i$$

$$= \sum_{k=1}^{n} \left(\frac{[b_k^0 = b][a_k^0 = a]}{\bar{\psi}(b, a)} - [a_k^0 = a] \right) \prod_{i=k} \bar{\psi}\left(b_i^0, a_i^0\right) c_i$$

$$= \sum_{k=1}^{n} \left(\frac{[b_k^0 = b][a_k^0 = a]}{\bar{\psi}(b, a)} - [a_k^0 = a] \right) Q\left(\mathbf{a}^0, \mathbf{b}^0\right),$$

where we have made use (12.5) to obtain the third line from the second. We now return to considering the derivatives of the log-likelihood, first with respect to the parameter $\theta_{\sigma,a}$

$$\frac{\partial \log P_M(s|\boldsymbol{\theta})}{\partial \theta_{\sigma,a}} = \frac{1}{P_M(s|\boldsymbol{\theta})} \frac{\partial}{\partial \theta_{\sigma,a}} \sum_{m \in A^n} \prod_{i=1}^{n} P(s_i|m_i) P_M(m_i|m_{i-1})$$

$$= \frac{1}{P_M(s|\boldsymbol{\theta})} \sum_{m \in A^n} \frac{\partial}{\partial \theta_{\sigma,a}} \prod_{i=1}^{n} \frac{\theta_{s_i,m_i}}{\sum_{\sigma \in \Sigma} \theta_{\sigma,m_i}} \tau_{m_i|m_{i-1}}.$$

Letting $\mathbf{a}$ be the sequence of states m and $\mathbf{b}$ the string s, with $\psi(a, b) = \theta_{b,a}$ and $c_i = \tau_{m_i|m_{i-1}}$ we have

$$Q(\mathbf{a}, \mathbf{b}) = \prod_{i=1}^{n} \frac{\theta_{s_i,m_i}}{\sum_{\sigma \in \Sigma} \theta_{\sigma,m_i}} \tau_{m_i|m_{i-1}} = P_M(s, m|\boldsymbol{\theta}).$$

It follows from the derivative of Q that

$$\frac{\partial \log P_M(s|\boldsymbol{\theta})}{\partial \theta_{\sigma,a}} = \sum_{m \in A^n} \sum_{k=1}^{n} \left(\frac{[s_k = \sigma][m_k = a]}{\theta_{\sigma|a}} - [m_k = a] \right) \frac{P_M(s, m|\boldsymbol{\theta})}{P_M(s|\boldsymbol{\theta})}$$

$$= \sum_{k=1}^{n} \sum_{m \in A^n} \left(\frac{[s_k = \sigma][m_k = a]}{\theta_{\sigma|a}} - [m_k = a] \right) P_M(m|s, \boldsymbol{\theta})$$

$$= \sum_{k=1}^{n} \mathbb{E} \left[\frac{[s_k = \sigma][m_k = a]}{\theta_{\sigma|a}} - [m_k = a] \middle| s, \boldsymbol{\theta} \right]$$

$$= \frac{1}{\theta_{\sigma|a}} \sum_{k=1}^{n} \mathbb{E}\left[[s_k = \sigma][m_k = a]|s, \boldsymbol{\theta}\right] - \sum_{k=1}^{n} \mathbb{E}\left[[m_k = a]|s, \boldsymbol{\theta}\right],$$

where the expectations are over the hidden states that generate s. Now consider the derivatives with respect to the parameter $\tau_{a,b}$

$$\frac{\partial \log P_M(s|\boldsymbol{\theta})}{\partial \tau_{a,b}} = \frac{1}{P_M(s|\boldsymbol{\theta})} \frac{\partial}{\partial \tau_{a,b}} \sum_{m \in A^n} \prod_{i=1}^n P(s_i|m_i) P_M(m_i|m_{i-1})$$

$$= \frac{1}{P_M(s|\boldsymbol{\theta})} \sum_{m \in A^n} \frac{\partial}{\partial \tau_{a,b}} \prod_{i=1}^n \frac{\theta_{s_i,m_i}}{\sum_{\sigma \in \Sigma} \theta_{\sigma,m_i}} \tau_{m_i|m_{i-1}}.$$

Letting **a** and **b** be the sequence of states m and **b** be the same sequence of states shifted one position, with $\psi(a,b) = \tau_{a,b}$ and $c_i = \theta_{s_i|m_i}$, we have

$$Q(\mathbf{a}, \mathbf{b}) = \prod_{i=1}^n \theta_{s_i|m_i} \frac{\tau_{m_i, m_{i-1}}}{\sum_{a' \in A} \tau_{a', m_{i-1}}} \tau_{m_i|m_{i-1}} = P_M(s, m|\boldsymbol{\theta}).$$

It follows from the derivative of Q that

$$\frac{\partial \log P_M(s|\boldsymbol{\theta})}{\partial \tau_{a,b}}$$

$$= \sum_{k=1}^n \sum_{m \in A^n} \left(\frac{[m_{k-1} = b][m_k = a]}{\tau_{a|b}} - [m_k = a] \right) P_M(m|s, \boldsymbol{\theta})$$

$$= \frac{1}{\tau_{a|b}} \sum_{k=1}^n \mathbb{E}\left[[m_{k-1} = b][m_k = a]|s, \boldsymbol{\theta}\right] - \sum_{k=1}^n \mathbb{E}\left[[m_k = a]|s, \boldsymbol{\theta}\right],$$

It remains to compute the expectations in each of the sums. These are the expectations that the particular emissions and transitions occurred in the generation of the string s.

The computation of these quantities will rely on an algorithm known as the forwards–backwards algorithm. As the name suggests this is a two-stage algorithm that computes the quantities

$$f_a(i) = P(s_1 \ldots s_i, m_i = a),$$

in other words the probability that the ith hidden state is a with the prefix of the string s together with the probability $P(s)$ of the sequence. Following this the backwards algorithm computes

$$b_a(i) = P(s_{i+1} \ldots s_n|m_i = a).$$

Once these values have been computed it is possible to evaluate the expectation

$$\mathbb{E}\left[[s_k = \sigma][m_k = a]|s\right]$$
$$= P(s_k = \sigma, m_k = a|s)$$

$$= [s_k = \sigma] \frac{P(s_{k+1} \dots s_n | m_k = a) P(s_1 \dots s_k, m_k = a)}{P(s)}$$

$$= [s_k = \sigma] \frac{f_a(k) b_a(k)}{P(s)}.$$

Similarly

$$
\begin{aligned}
\mathbb{E}\left[[m_k = a] | s\right] &= P(m_k = a | s) \\
&= \frac{P(s_{k+1} \dots s_n | m_k = a) P(s_1 \dots s_k, m_k = a)}{P(s)} \\
&= \frac{f_a(k) b_a(k)}{P(s)}.
\end{aligned}
$$

Finally, for the second pair of expectations the only tricky evaluation is $\mathbb{E}\left[[m_{k-1} = b][m_k = a] | s\right]$, which equals

$$\frac{P(s_{k+1} \dots s_n | m_k = a) P(s_1 \dots s_{k-1}, m_{k-1} = b) P(a|b) P(s_k | m_k = a)}{P(s)}$$

$$= \frac{f_b(k-1) b_a(k) \tau_{a|b} \theta_{s_k|a}}{P(s)}.$$

Hence, the Fisher scores can be evaluated based on the results of the forwards–backwards algorithm. The forwards–backwards algorithm again uses a dynamic programming approach based on the recursion

$$f_b(i+1) = \theta_{s_{i+1}|b} \sum_{a \in A} f_a(i) \tau_{b|a},$$

with $f_{a_0}(0) = 1$ and $f_a(0) = 0$, for $a = a_0$. Once the forward recursion is complete we have

$$P(s) = \sum_{a \in A} f_a(n).$$

The initialisation for the backward algorithm is

$$b_a(n) = 1$$

with the recursion

$$b_b(i) = \sum_{a \in A} \tau_{a|b} \theta_{\sigma_{i+1}|a} b_a(i+1).$$

Putting all of these observations together we obtain the following algorithm, where we only evaluate the Fisher scores for the emission probabilities for brevity.

Algorithm 12.34 [Fixed length Markov model Fisher kernel] The Fisher scores for the fixed length Markov model Fisher kernel are computed in Code Fragment 12.4. ∎

Input	Symbol string s, state transition probability matrix $P_M(a|b)$, initial state probabilities $P_M(a) = P_M(a|a_0)$ and conditional probabilities $P(\sigma|a)$ of symbols given states.

Process	Assume p states, $0, 1, \ldots, p$.
2	score $(:, :) = 0$;
3	forw $(:, 0) = 0$;
4	back $(:, n) = 1$;
	$f(0, 0) = 1$; Prob $= 0$;
5	for $i = 1 : n$
7	for $a = 1 : p$
8	forw $(a, i) = 0$;
9	for $b = 1 : p$
10	forw $(a, i) = $ forw $(a, i) + P_M(a|b)$ forw $(b, i - 1)$;
11	end
12	forw $(a, i) = $ forw $(a, i) P(s_i|a)$;
13	end
14	end
15	for $a = 1 : p$
16	Prob $= $ Prob $+$ forw (a, n);
17	end
18	for $i = n - 1 : 1$
19	for $a = 1 : p$
20	back $(a, i) = 0$;
21	for $b = 1 : p$
22	back $(a, i) = $ back $(a, i) + P_M(b|a) P(s_{i+1}|b)$ back $(b, i + 1)$;
23	end
24	score $(a, s_i) = $ score $(a, s_i) + $ back (a, i) forw $(a, i) / (P(s_i|a)$ Prob$)$;
25	for $\sigma \in \Sigma$
26	score $(a, \sigma) = $ score $(a, \sigma) + $ back (a, i) forw $(a, i) /$ Prob;
27	end
28	end

Output	Fisher score $=$ score

Code Fragment 12.4. Pseudocode to compute the Fisher scores for the fixed length Markov model Fisher kernel.

12.3 Summary

- P-kernels arise from probability distributions over pairs of examples.
- marginalisation kernels compute the probability that two examples are generated over a class of models.
- marginalisation kernels can be computed efficiently for a number of com-

plex generative models including fixed length hidden Markov models, pair hidden Markov models and hidden tree models.

- Fisher kernels use the gradient of the log-likelihood as a feature vector.
- Fisher kernels can be efficiently evaluated for hidden Markov models.

12.4 Further reading and advanced topics

The notion of P-kernel was introduced by Haussler [54], while Watkins [158], [157] independently discussed conditional independence kernels, and the case of hidden Markov models. These ideas were later applied by Vert, defining first a family of kernels for strings based on simple probabilistic models [147] and then based on the hidden tree model [148] (our discussion of the hidden tree model is based on the work of Vert, while our discussion of the pair HMM kernel is derived from the work of Watkins, but more generally draws from the literature on context trees and on message-passing methods for marginalising probabilities in graphical models). The formal presentation of the pair-HMMs kernel is however based on the Durbin *et al.* 'forward' algorithm [42].

Pair HMMs have also been used as kernels by J.-P. Vert *et al.* [150]. Extensions of these ideas can be found in the papers of marginalised kernels of Koji Tsuda [139], [78], which also exploit stochastic context free grammars as generative models.

Another extension from trees to certain graphs is also possible using the techniques from [133], but overall the general problem is best attacked with the algorithms and concepts developed within the field of probabilistic graphical models, where the sum-product algorithm and its extension are used for marginalisation. A new book on this topic will be forthcoming shortly [70].

The notion of Fisher kernel was defined by Jaakkola and Haussler [63], [64] and later used by several authors, for example Hoffmann in [59]. For the treatment of string kernels as Fisher kernels, see [116].

Rational Kernels [25] are based on the definition of transducers. They can be related to pair HMMs but as with our presentation here have the advantage of automatically having the finitely positive semi-definite property. Furthermore, they define a very broad class of kernels. A more recent paper of Cuturi and Vert [36] also discusses string kernels based on probabilistic models and pair HMMs.

For constantly updated pointers to online literature and free software see the book's companion website: www.kernel-methods.net

Appendix A

Proofs omitted from the main text

A.1 Proof of McDiarmid's theorem

Theorem A.1 (McDiarmid [96]) *Let $X_1, \ldots, X_n$ be independent random variables taking values in a set A, and assume that $f : A^n \to \mathbb{R}$ satisfies*

$$\sup_{x_1, \ldots, x_n, \hat{x}_i \in A} |f(x_1, \ldots, x_n) - f(x_1, \ldots, \hat{x}_i, x_{i+1}, \ldots, x_n)| \leq c_i, \quad 1 \leq i \leq n.$$

Then for all $\epsilon > 0$,

$$P\{f(X_1, \ldots, X_n) - \mathbb{E}f(X_1, \ldots, X_n) \geq \epsilon\} \leq \exp\left(\frac{-2\epsilon^2}{\sum_{i=1}^n c_i^2}\right).$$

Proof Let $V_i = V_i(X_1, \ldots, X_i) = \mathbb{E}[f|X_1, \ldots, X_i] - \mathbb{E}[f|X_1, \ldots, X_{i-1}]$, where we have denoted $f(X_1, \ldots, X_n)$ with a simple f. Hence

$$f - \mathbb{E}[f] = \sum_{i=1}^n V_i.$$

We will denote the probability distribution of X_i by P_i, while with P we denote as above the overall distribution. So, for any $s > 0$, we have

$$
\begin{aligned}
P\{f - \mathbb{E}[f] \geq \varepsilon\} &= P\left\{\sum_{i=1}^n V_i \geq \varepsilon\right\} = P\left\{\exp\left(s\sum_{i=1}^n V_i\right)\exp(-s\varepsilon) \geq 1\right\} \\
&\leq \mathbb{E}\left[\exp\left(s\sum_{i=1}^n V_i\right)\right]\exp(-s\varepsilon) \\
&= \exp(-s\varepsilon)\,\mathbb{E}\left[\prod_{i=1}^n \exp(sV_i)\right]
\end{aligned}
$$

437

$$= \exp\left(-s\varepsilon\right)\mathbb{E}_{X_1\ldots X_{n-1}}\mathbb{E}_{X_n}\left[\prod_{i=1}^{n}\exp\left(sV_i\right)|X_1,\ldots,X_{n-1}\right]$$

$$= \exp\left(-s\varepsilon\right)\mathbb{E}_{X_1\ldots X_{n-1}}\left(\left[\prod_{i=1}^{n-1}\exp\left(sV_i\right)\right]\right. \tag{A.1}$$

$$\mathbb{E}_{X_n}\left[\exp\left(sV_n\right)|X_1,\ldots,X_{n-1}\right]\biggr),$$

where we have used the independence of the V_i from X_n, for $i=1,\ldots,n-1$ and the fact that the expectation of a product of independent variables equals the product of their expectations. The random variables V_i satisfy

$$\mathbb{E}[V_i|X_1,\ldots,X_{i-1}] = \mathbb{E}[\mathbb{E}[f|X_1,\ldots,X_i]|X_1,\ldots,X_{i-1}] - \mathbb{E}[f|X_1,\ldots,X_{i-1}]$$
$$= \mathbb{E}[f|X_1,\ldots,X_{i-1}] - \mathbb{E}[f|X_1,\ldots,X_{i-1}] = 0.$$

while their range can be bounded by

$$L_i = \inf_a V_i(X_1,\ldots,X_{i-1},a) \le V_i(X_1,\ldots,X_i) \le \sup_a V_i(X_1,\ldots,X_{i-1},a) = U_i.$$

If a_l and a_u are the values at which the inf and sup are attained, we have

$$|U_i - L_i|$$
$$= |\mathbb{E}[f|X_1,\ldots,X_{i-1},X_i=a_u] - \mathbb{E}[f|X_1,\ldots,X_{i-1},X_i=a_l]|$$
$$= \left|\int_{A^{n-i}} f\left(X_1,\ldots,X_{i-1},a_u,x_{i+1},\ldots x_n\right) dP_{i+1}(x_{i+1})\ldots dP_n(x_n)\right.$$
$$\left. - \int_{A^{n-i}} f\left(X_1,\ldots,X_{i-1},a_l,x_{i+1},\ldots,x_n\right) dP_{i+1}(x_{i+1})\ldots dP_n(x_n)\right|$$
$$\le \int_{A^{n-i}} dP_{i+1}(x_{i+1})\ldots dP_n(x_n)\,|f\left(X_1,\ldots,X_{i-1},a_u,x_{i+1},\ldots,x_n\right)$$
$$- f\left(X_1,\ldots,X_{i-1},a_l,x_{i+1},\ldots,x_n\right)|$$
$$\le |c_i|.$$

Letting $Z(X_i) = V_i(X_1,\ldots,X_{i-1},X_i)$ be the random variable depending only on X_i for given fixed values of $X_1,\ldots,X_{i-1}$, note that

$$\exp\left(sZ\right) \le \frac{Z-L_i}{U_i-L_i}\exp(sU_i) + \frac{U_i-Z}{U_i-L_i}\exp(sL_i),$$

by the convexity of the exponential function. Using the fact that

$$\mathbb{E}[Z] = \mathbb{E}[V_i|X_1,\ldots,X_{i-1}] = 0,$$

it follows that

$$\mathbb{E}\left[\exp\left(sV_i\right)|X_1,\ldots,X_{i-1}\right] = \mathbb{E}[\exp\left(sZ\right)]$$

$$\leq \frac{-L_i}{U_i - L_i} \exp(sU_i) + \frac{U_i}{U_i - L_i} \exp(sL_i)$$
$$= \exp(\psi(s)),$$

where $\psi(s) = \ln(\frac{-L_i}{U_i-L_i} \exp(sU_i) + \frac{U_i}{U_i-L_i} \exp(sL_i))$. It is not hard to check that $\psi(0) = \psi'(0) = 0$, while $\psi''(s) \leq 0.25(U_i - L_i)^2 \leq 0.25c_i^2$ for $s \geq 0$. Hence, taking three terms of the Taylor series with remainder, we have that

$$\mathbb{E}\left[\exp\left(sV_i\right)|X_1,\ldots,X_{i-1}\right] \leq \exp\left(\frac{s^2 c_i^2}{8}\right).$$

Plugging this into inequality (A.1) for $i = n$ gives

$$P\{f - \mathbb{E}[f] \geq \varepsilon\} \leq \exp\left(-s\varepsilon\right) \exp\left(\frac{s^2 c_n^2}{8}\right) \mathbb{E}_{X_1 \ldots X_{n-1}} \left[\prod_{i=1}^{n-1} \exp\left(sV_i\right)\right].$$

By iterating the same argument for $n-1, n-2, \ldots, 1$, we can show that

$$P\{f(X_1,\ldots,X_n) - \mathbb{E}f(X_1,\ldots,X_n) \geq \epsilon\}$$
$$\leq \exp\left(-s\varepsilon\right) \prod_{i=1}^{n} \exp\left(\frac{s^2 c_i^2}{8}\right)$$
$$= \exp\left(-s\varepsilon + \frac{s^2}{8} \sum_{i=1}^{n} c_i^2\right)$$
$$= \exp\left(-\frac{2\epsilon^2}{\sum_{i=1}^{n} c_i^2}\right),$$

where we have chosen $s = 4\epsilon \left(\sum_{i=1}^{n} c_i^2\right)^{-1}$ to minimise the expression. $\square$

A.2 Stability of principal components analysis

In this appendix we prove the following theorem from Chapter 6.

Theorem A.2 (Theorem 6.14) *If we perform PCA in the feature space defined by a kernel $\kappa(\mathbf{x}, \mathbf{z})$ then with probability greater than $1 - \delta$, for any $1 \leq k \leq \ell$, if we project new data onto the space U_k, the expected squared residual is bounded by*

$$\mathbb{E}\left[\left\|P_{U_k}^\perp(\phi(\mathbf{x}))\right\|^2\right] \leq \min_{1 \leq t \leq k} \left[\frac{1}{\ell}\lambda^{>t}(S) + \frac{8}{\ell}\sqrt{(t+1)\sum_{i=1}^{\ell} \kappa(\mathbf{x}_i, \mathbf{x}_i)^2}\right]$$
$$+ 3R^2\sqrt{\frac{\ln(2\ell/\delta)}{2\ell}},$$

where the support of the distribution is in a ball of radius R in the feature space.

The observation that makes the analysis possible is contained in the following theorem.

Theorem A.3 *The projection norm $\|P_{U_k}(\phi(\mathbf{x}))\|^2$ is a linear function $\hat{f}$ in a feature space $\hat{F}$ for which the kernel function is given by*

$$\hat{\kappa}(\mathbf{x}, \mathbf{z}) = \kappa(\mathbf{x}, \mathbf{z})^2.$$

Furthermore the 2-norm of the function $\hat{f}$ is $\sqrt{k}$.

Proof Let $\mathbf{X}' = \mathbf{U}\mathbf{\Sigma}\mathbf{V}'$ be the singular value decomposition of the matrix $\mathbf{X}'$ whose rows are the images of the training examples in the feature space. The projection norm is then given by

$$\hat{f}(\mathbf{x}) = \|P_{U_k}(\phi(\mathbf{x}))\|^2 = \phi(\mathbf{x})'\mathbf{U}_k\mathbf{U}_k'\phi(\mathbf{x}),$$

where $\mathbf{U}_k$ is the matrix containing the first k columns of $\mathbf{U}$. Hence we can write

$$\|P_{U_k}(\phi(\mathbf{x}))\|^2 = \sum_{i,j=1}^{N} \alpha_{ij}\phi(\mathbf{x})_i\phi(\mathbf{x})_j = \sum_{i,j=1}^{N} \alpha_{ij}\hat{\phi}(\mathbf{x})_{ij},$$

where $\hat{\phi}$ is the mapping into the feature space $\hat{F}$ composed of all pairs of F features and $\alpha_{ij} = (\mathbf{U}_k\mathbf{U}_k')_{ij}$. The standard polynomial construction gives the corresponding kernel $\hat{\kappa}$ as

$$
\begin{aligned}
\hat{\kappa}(\mathbf{x}, \mathbf{z}) &= \kappa(\mathbf{x}, \mathbf{z})^2 = \left(\sum_{i=1}^{N} \phi(\mathbf{x})_i\phi(\mathbf{z})_i \right)^2 \\
&= \sum_{i,j=1}^{N} \phi(\mathbf{x})_i\phi(\mathbf{z})_i\phi(\mathbf{x})_j\phi(\mathbf{z})_j = \sum_{i,j=1}^{N} (\phi(\mathbf{x})_i\phi(\mathbf{x})_j)(\phi(\mathbf{z})_i\phi(\mathbf{z})_j) \\
&= \langle \hat{\phi}(\mathbf{x}), \hat{\phi}(\mathbf{z}) \rangle.
\end{aligned}
$$

It remains to show that the norm of the linear function is $\sqrt{k}$. The norm satisfies (note that $\|\cdot\|_F$ denotes the Frobenius norm and $\mathbf{u}_i$, $i = 1, \ldots, N$, the orthonormal columns of $\mathbf{U}$)

$$\|\hat{f}\|^2 = \sum_{i,j=1}^{N} \alpha_{ij}^2 = \|\mathbf{U}_k\mathbf{U}_k'\|_F^2 = \left\langle \sum_{i=1}^{k} \mathbf{u}_i\mathbf{u}_i', \sum_{j=1}^{k} \mathbf{u}_j\mathbf{u}_j' \right\rangle_F = \sum_{i,j=1}^{k} (\mathbf{u}_i'\mathbf{u}_j)^2 = k,$$

as required.   □

Since the norm of the residual can be viewed as a linear function we can now apply the methods developed in Chapter 4.

Theorem A.4 *If we perform PCA on a training set S of size ℓ in the feature space defined by a kernel $\kappa(\mathbf{x}, \mathbf{z})$ and project new data onto the space U_k spanned by the first k eigenvectors, with probability greater than $1 - \delta$ over the generation of the sample S the expected squared residual is bounded by*

$$\mathbb{E}\left[\|P_{U_k}^{\perp}(\phi(\mathbf{x}))\|^2\right] \leq \frac{1}{\ell}\lambda^{>k}(S) + \frac{8}{\ell}\sqrt{(k+1)\sum_{i=1}^{\ell}\kappa(\mathbf{x}_i, \mathbf{x}_i)^2 + 3R^2\sqrt{\frac{\ln(2/\delta)}{2\ell}}},$$

where

$$R^2 = \max_{\mathbf{x} \in \operatorname{supp}(\mathcal{D})} \kappa(\mathbf{x}, \mathbf{x}).$$

Proof Prompted by Theorem A.3 we consider the linear function class

$$\hat{\mathcal{F}}_{\sqrt{k}} = \left\{\mathbf{x} \rightarrow \langle \mathbf{w}, \phi(\mathbf{x}) \rangle : \|\mathbf{w}\| \leq \sqrt{k}\right\}$$

with respect to the kernel

$$\hat{\kappa}(\mathbf{x}, \mathbf{z}) = \kappa(\mathbf{x}, \mathbf{z})^2 = \langle \hat{\phi}(\mathbf{x}), \hat{\phi}(\mathbf{z}) \rangle,$$

with corresponding feature mapping $\hat{\phi}$. However, we further augment the corresponding primal weight vectors with one further dimension while augmenting the corresponding feature vectors with a feature

$$\|\phi(\mathbf{x}))\|^2 = \kappa(\mathbf{x}, \mathbf{x}) = \sqrt{\hat{\kappa}(\mathbf{x}, \mathbf{x})} = \|\hat{\phi}(\mathbf{x}))\|$$

that is the norm squared in the original feature space. We now apply Theorem 4.9 to the loss class

$$\hat{F}_{\mathcal{L}} = \left\{f_{\mathcal{L}} : (\hat{\phi}(\mathbf{x}), \|\hat{\phi}(\mathbf{x}))\|) \mapsto A(\|\hat{\phi}(\mathbf{x}))\| - f(\hat{\phi}(\mathbf{x}))) \mid f \in \hat{\mathcal{F}}_{\sqrt{k}}\right\} \quad \text{(A.2)}$$
$$\subseteq A \circ \hat{\mathcal{F}}'_{\sqrt{k+1}},$$

where $\hat{\mathcal{F}}'_{\sqrt{k+1}}$ is the class of linear functions with norm bounded by $\sqrt{k+1}$ in the feature space defined by the kernel

$$\hat{\kappa}'(\mathbf{x}, \mathbf{z}) = \hat{\kappa}(\mathbf{x}, \mathbf{z}) + \kappa(\mathbf{x}, \mathbf{x})\kappa(\mathbf{z}, \mathbf{z}) = \kappa(\mathbf{x}, \mathbf{z})^2 + \kappa(\mathbf{x}, \mathbf{x})\kappa(\mathbf{z}, \mathbf{z})$$

and A is the function

$$A(x) = \begin{cases} 0 & \text{if } x \leq 0; \\ x/R^2 & \text{if } 0 \leq x \leq R^2; \\ 1 & \text{otherwise.} \end{cases}$$

The theorem is applied to the pattern function $\mathcal{A} \circ \hat{f}_{\mathcal{L}}$ where $\hat{f}$ is the projection function of Theorem A.3 and $\hat{f}_{\mathcal{L}}$ is defined in (A.2). We conclude that with probability $1 - \delta$

$$\mathbb{E}_{\mathcal{D}}\left[\mathcal{A} \circ \hat{f}_{\mathcal{L}}(\mathbf{x})\right] \leq \hat{\mathbb{E}}\left[\mathcal{A} \circ \hat{f}_{\mathcal{L}}(\mathbf{x})\right] + \hat{R}_{\ell}(\mathcal{A} \circ \hat{\mathcal{F}}'_{\sqrt{k+1}}) + 3\sqrt{\frac{\ln(2/\delta)}{2\ell}}. \quad (A.3)$$

First note that the left-hand side of the inequality is equal to

$$\frac{1}{R^2}\mathbb{E}\left[\|P_{U_k}^{\perp}(\phi(\mathbf{x}))\|^2\right],$$

since $\mathcal{A}$ acts as the identity in the range achieved by the function $\hat{f}_{\mathcal{L}}$. Hence, to obtain the result it remains to evaluate the first two expressions on the right-hand side of equation (A.3). Again observing that $\mathcal{A}$ acts as the identity in the range achieved, the first is a scaling of the squared residual of the training set when projecting into the space U_k, that is

$$\frac{1}{R^2}\hat{\mathbb{E}}\left[\|P_{U_k}^{\perp}(\phi(\mathbf{x}))\|^2\right] = \frac{1}{\ell R^2}\sum_{i=k+1}^{\ell}\lambda_i = \frac{1}{\ell R^2}\lambda^{>k}(S).$$

The second expression is $\hat{R}_{\ell}(\mathcal{A} \circ \hat{\mathcal{F}}'_{\sqrt{k+1}})$. Here we apply Theorem 4.12 and Theorem 4.15 part 4 to obtain

$$\hat{R}_{\ell}(\mathcal{A} \circ \hat{\mathcal{F}}'_{\sqrt{k+1}}) \leq \frac{4\sqrt{k+1}}{\ell R^2}\sqrt{\text{tr}\left(\hat{\mathbf{K}}'\right)} = \frac{4}{R^2}\sqrt{\frac{k+1}{\ell}}\sqrt{\frac{4}{\ell}\sum_{i=1}^{\ell}\kappa(\mathbf{x}_i, \mathbf{x}_i)^2}.$$

Assembling all the components and multiplying by R^2 gives the result. $\quad\square$

We now apply the bound ℓ times to obtain a proof of Theorem 6.14.

Proof [Proof of Theorem 6.14] We apply Theorem A.4 for $k = 1, \ldots, \ell$, in each case replacing δ by δ/ℓ. This ensures that with probability $1 - \delta$ the assertion holds for all ℓ applications. The result follows from the observation that for $k \geq t$

$$\mathbb{E}\left[\|P_{U_k}^{\perp}(\phi(\mathbf{x}))\|^2\right] \leq \mathbb{E}\left[\|P_{U_t}^{\perp}(\phi(\mathbf{x}))\|^2\right].$$

$\quad\square$

A.3 Proofs of diffusion kernels

Proposition A.5 *Provided* $\mu < \|\mathbf{K}\|^{-1} = \|\mathbf{G}\|^{-1}$, *the kernel* $\hat{\mathbf{K}}$ *that solves the recurrences (10.2) is* $\mathbf{K}$ *times the von Neumann kernel over the base* *kernel* $\mathbf{K}$, *while the matrix* $\hat{\mathbf{G}}$ *satisfies*

$$\hat{\mathbf{G}} = \mathbf{G}(\mathbf{I} - \mu\mathbf{G})^{-1}.$$

Proof First observe that

$$
\begin{aligned}
\mathbf{K}(\mathbf{I} - \mu\mathbf{K})^{-1} &= \mathbf{K}(\mathbf{I} - \mu\mathbf{K})^{-1} - \frac{1}{\mu}(\mathbf{I} - \mu\mathbf{K})^{-1} + \frac{1}{\mu}(\mathbf{I} - \mu\mathbf{K})^{-1} \\
&= -\frac{1}{\mu}(\mathbf{I} - \mu\mathbf{K})(\mathbf{I} - \mu\mathbf{K})^{-1} + \frac{1}{\mu}(\mathbf{I} - \mu\mathbf{K})^{-1} \\
&= \frac{1}{\mu}(\mathbf{I} - \mu\mathbf{K})^{-1} - \frac{1}{\mu}\mathbf{I}.
\end{aligned}
$$

Now if we substitute the second recurrence into the first we obtain

$$
\begin{aligned}
\hat{\mathbf{K}} &= \mu^2 \mathbf{DD}'\hat{\mathbf{K}}\mathbf{DD}' + \mu\mathbf{DD}'\mathbf{DD}' + \mathbf{K} \\
&= \mu^2 \mathbf{K}(\mathbf{K}(\mathbf{I} - \mu\mathbf{K})^{-1})\mathbf{K} + \mu\mathbf{K}^2 + \mathbf{K} \\
&= \mu^2 \mathbf{K}(\frac{1}{\mu}(\mathbf{I} - \mu\mathbf{K})^{-1} - \frac{1}{\mu}\mathbf{I})\mathbf{K} + \mu\mathbf{K}^2 + \mathbf{K} \\
&= \mu\mathbf{K}(\mathbf{I} - \mu\mathbf{K})^{-1}\mathbf{K} + \mathbf{K}(\mathbf{I} - \mu\mathbf{K})^{-1}(\mathbf{I} - \mu\mathbf{K}) \\
&= \mathbf{K}(\mathbf{I} - \mu\mathbf{K})^{-1},
\end{aligned}
$$

showing that the expression does indeed satisfy the recurrence. Clearly, by the symmetry of the definition the expression for $\hat{\mathbf{G}}$ also satisfies the recurrence. $\square$

Proposition A.6 *Let* $\bar{\mathbf{K}}(\mu) = \mathbf{K}\exp(\mu\mathbf{K})$. *Then* $\bar{\mathbf{K}}(\mu)$ *corresponds to a semantic proximity matrix*

$$\exp\left(\frac{\mu}{2}\mathbf{G}\right).$$

Proof Let $\mathbf{D}' = \mathbf{U}\boldsymbol{\Sigma}\mathbf{V}'$ be the singular value decomposition of $\mathbf{D}'$, so that $\mathbf{K} = \mathbf{V}\boldsymbol{\Lambda}\mathbf{V}'$ is the eigenvalue decomposition of $\mathbf{K}$, where $\boldsymbol{\Lambda} = \boldsymbol{\Sigma}'\boldsymbol{\Sigma}$. We can write $\bar{\mathbf{K}}$ as

$$
\begin{aligned}
\bar{\mathbf{K}} &= \mathbf{V}\boldsymbol{\Lambda}\exp(\mu\boldsymbol{\Lambda})\mathbf{V}' = \mathbf{DU}\boldsymbol{\Sigma}\exp(\mu\boldsymbol{\Lambda})\boldsymbol{\Sigma}^{-1}\mathbf{U}'\mathbf{D}' \\
&= \mathbf{DU}\exp(\mu\boldsymbol{\Lambda})\mathbf{U}'\mathbf{D}' = \mathbf{D}\exp(\mu\mathbf{G})\mathbf{D}',
\end{aligned}
$$

as required. $\square$

Appendix B

Notational conventions

B.1 List of symbols

N	dimension of feature space	L	primal Lagrangian
$y \in Y$	output and output space	W	dual Lagrangian
$\mathbf{x} \in X$	input and input space	$\|\cdot\|_p$	p-norm, default is 2-norm
$\|\mathbf{A}\|_F$	Frobenius norm of a matrix	$\|\mathbf{A}\|$	spectral/2-norm of a matrix
F	feature space	$\ln$	natural logarithm
$\mathcal{F}$	class of real-valued functions	e	base of the natural log
$\mathcal{L}$	class of linear functions	$\log$	log to the base 2
$\langle \mathbf{x}, \mathbf{z} \rangle$	inner product of $\mathbf{x}$ and $\mathbf{z}$	$\mathbf{x}', \mathbf{X}'$	transpose of vector, matrix
ϕ	mapping to feature space	$\mathbb{N}, \mathbb{R}$	natural, real numbers
$\kappa(\mathbf{x}, \mathbf{z})$	kernel $\langle \phi(\mathbf{x}), \phi(\mathbf{z}) \rangle$	S	training set
$f(\mathbf{x})$	real-valued function	ℓ	training set size
n	dimension of input space	$\phi(S)$	training set in feature space
R	radius containing the data	η	learning rate
$\mathcal{H}$	Heaviside function	ε	error probability
$\mathbf{w}$	weight vector	δ	confidence
b	bias	γ	margin
α	dual variables	ξ	slack variables
$\mathbf{C}$	covariance matrix	$\mathbf{I}$	identity matrix
$(x)_+$	equals x, if $x \geq 0$ else 0	$\mathbf{K}$	kernel matrix
$\text{sgn}(x)$	equals 1, if $x \geq 0$ else -1	$\#$	cardinality of a set
$\mathbf{j}$	all 1s vector		

B.2 Notation for Tables

Definition B.1 [Kernel matrix displays] We use a standard notation for displaying kernel matrices as

$\mathbf{K}$	1	2	$\cdots$	ℓ
1	$\kappa(\mathbf{x}_1, \mathbf{x}_1)$	$\kappa(\mathbf{x}_1, \mathbf{x}_2)$	$\cdots$	$\kappa(\mathbf{x}_1, \mathbf{x}_\ell)$
2	$\kappa(\mathbf{x}_2, \mathbf{x}_1)$	$\kappa(\mathbf{x}_2, \mathbf{x}_2)$	$\cdots$	$\kappa(\mathbf{x}_2, \mathbf{x}_\ell)$
$\vdots$	$\vdots$	$\vdots$	$\ddots$	$\vdots$
ℓ	$\kappa(\mathbf{x}_\ell, \mathbf{x}_1)$	$\kappa(\mathbf{x}_\ell, \mathbf{x}_2)$	$\cdots$	$\kappa(\mathbf{x}_\ell, \mathbf{x}_\ell)$

where the symbol $\mathbf{K}$ in the top right corner indicates that the table represents a kernel matrix. ∎

Definition B.2 [Dynamic programming tables] Dynamic programming tables are displayed in a table with first row and column used for indices and the top left cell marked with DP, as, for example, in the ANOVA dynamic programming table:

DP	1	2	$\cdots$	n
0	1	1	$\cdots$	1
1	$x_1 z_1$	$x_1 z_1 + x_2 z_2$	$\cdots$	$\sum_{i=1}^{n} x_i z_i$
2	0	$\kappa_2^2(\mathbf{x}, \mathbf{z})$	$\cdots$	$\kappa_2^n(\mathbf{x}, \mathbf{z})$
$\vdots$	$\vdots$	$\vdots$	$\ddots$	$\vdots$
d	0	0	$\cdots$	$\kappa_d^n(\mathbf{x}, \mathbf{z})$

∎

Appendix C

List of pattern analysis methods

C.1 Pattern analysis computations

C.2 Pattern analysis algorithms

Appendix D

List of kernels

D.1 Kernel definitions and computations

D.2 Kernel algorithms

References

[1] M. Aizerman, E. Braverman, and L. Rozonoer. Theoretical foundations of the potential function method in pattern recognition learning. *Automation and Remote Control*, **25** (1964): 821–837.

[2] S. Akaho. A kernel method for canonical correlation analysis. In *Proceedings of the International Meeting of the Psychometric Society (IMPS2001)*. Springer-Verlag, 2001.

[3] J.K. Anlauf and M. Biehl. The adatron: an adaptive perceptron algorithm. *Europhys. Letters*, **10** (1989): 687–692.

[4] M. Anthony and P. Bartlett. *Neural Network Learning: Theoretical Foundations*. Cambridge University Press, 1999.

[5] M. Anthony and N. Biggs. *Computational Learning Theory*, volume 30 of *Cambridge Tracts in Theoretical Computer Science*. Cambridge University Press, 1992.

[6] N. Aronszajn. Theory of reproducing kernels. *Transactions of the American Mathematical Society*, **68** (1950): 337–404.

[7] F.R. Bach and M.I. Jordan. Kernel independent component analysis. *Journal of Machine Learning Research*, **3** (2002): 1–48.

[8] P.L. Bartlett. The sample complexity of pattern classification with neural networks: the size of the weights is more important than the size of the network. *IEEE Transactions on Information Theory*, **44**(2) (1998): 525–536.

[9] P.L. Bartlett, S. Boucheron, and G. Lugosi. Model selection and error estimation. *Machine Learning*, **48** (2002): 85–113.

[10] P.L. Bartlett and S. Mendelson. Rademacher and Gaussian complexities: risk bounds and structural results. *Journal of Machine Learning Research*, **3** (2002): 463–482.

[11] G. Baudat and F. Anouar. Generalized discriminant analysis using a kernel approach. *Neural Computation*, **12**(10) (2000): 2385-2404.

[12] M. Belkin and P. Niyogi. Laplacian eigenmaps and spectral techniques for embedding and clustering. In T.G. Dietterich, S. Becker, and Z. Ghahramani, editors, *Advances in Neural Information Processing Systems 14*. MIT Press, 2002, pp. 585–591.

[13] K.P. Bennett and O.L. Mangasarian. Robust linear programming discrimination of two linearly inseparable sets. *Optimization Methods and Software*, **1** (1992): 23–34.

[14] C.M. Bishop. *Neural Networks for Pattern Recognition*. Clarendon Press, 1995.

[15] M. Borga, T. Landelius, and H. Knutsson. A Unified Approach to PCA, PLS, MLR and CCA. Report LiTH-ISY-R-1992, ISY, SE-581 83 Linköping, Sweden, November 1997.

[16] B.E. Boser, I.M. Guyon, and V.N. Vapnik. A training algorithm for optimal margin classifiers. In D. Haussler, editor, *Proceedings of the 5th Annual ACM Workshop on Computational Learning Theory (COLT)* ACM Press, July 1992, pp. 144–152.

[17] S. Boucheron, G. Lugosi, and P. Massart. A sharp concentration inequality with applications. *Random Structures and Algorithms*, **16** (2000):277–292, 2000.

[18] O. Bousquet and A. Elisseeff. Algorithmic stability and generalization performance. In T.K. Leen, T.G. Dietterich, and T., Volker editors, *Advances in Neural Information Processing Systems 13* MIT Press, 2001, pp. 196–202.

[19] L. Breiman, J. Friedman, R. Olshen, and C. Stone. *Classification and Regression Trees*. Wadsworth International, 1984.

[20] C.J.C. Burges. A tutorial on support vector machines for pattern recognition. *Data Mining and Knowledge Discovery*, **2**(2) (1998): 121–167.

[21] C.J.C. Burges and V. Vapnik. A new method for constructing artificial neural networks: Interim technical report, ONR contract N00014-94-C-0186. Technical report, AT&T Bell Laboratories, 1995.

[22] G. Chaitin. *Algorithmic Information Theory*. Cambridge University Press, 1987.

[23] M. Collins and N. Duffy. Convolution kernels for natural language. In T.G. Dietterich, S. Becker, and Z. Ghahramani, editors, *Advances in Neural Information Processing Systems 14*. MIT Press, 2002, pp. 625–632.

[24] T.H. Cormen, C.E. Leiserson, R.L. Rivest, and C. Stein. *Introduction to Algorithms*. MIT Press, 2001, 2nd edition.

[25] C. Cortes, P. Haffner, and M. Mohri. Positive definite rational kernels. In *Proceedings of The 16th Annual Conference on Computational Learning Theory (COLT 2003)*, volume 2777 of *Lecture Notes in Computer Science*. Springer-Verlag, 2003, pp. 41–56.

[26] C. Cortes, P. Haffner, and M. Mohri. Rational kernels. In Suzanna Becker, Sebastian Thrun, and Klaus Obermayer, editors, *Advances in Neural Information Processing Systems 15*. MIT Press, 2003.

[27] C. Cortes and V. Vapnik. Support vector networks. *Machine Learning*, **20** (1995): 273–297.

[28] T.M. Cover. Geometrical and statistical properties of systems of linear inequalities with applications in pattern recognition. *IEEE Trans. Elect. Comp.*, **14** (1965): 326–334.

[29] T.M. Cover and J.A. Thomas. *Elements of Information Theory*. Wiley-Interscience, 1991.

[30] K. Crammer and Y. Singer. Pranking with ranking. In T.G. Dietterich, S. Becker, and Z. Ghahramani, editors, *Advances in Neural Information Processing Systems 14*. MIT Press, 2002, pp. 641–647.

[31] N. Cristianini, H. Lodhi, and J. Shawe-Taylor. Latent semantic kernels. *Journal of Intelligent Information Systems*, **18** (2002): 127–152.

[32] N. Cristianini and J. Shawe-Taylor. *An Introduction to Support Vector Machines*. Cambridge: Cambridge University Press, 2000.

[33] N. Cristianini, J. Shawe-Taylor, A. Elisseeff, and J. Kandola. On kernel-target alignment. In T.G. Dietterich, S. Becker, and Z. Ghahramani, editors, *Advances in Neural Information Processing Systems 14*. MIT Press, 2002.

[34] N. Cristianini, J. Shawe-Taylor, and J. Kandola. Spectral kernel methods for clustering. In T.G. Dietterich, S. Becker, and Z. Ghahramani, editors, *Advances in Neural Information Processing Systems 14*. MIT Press, 2002, pp. 649–655.

[35] N. Cristianini, J. Shawe-Taylor, and H. Lodhi. Latent semantic kernels. In Carla Brodley and Andrea Dany In *Proceedings of the 18th International Conference on Machine Learning (ICML 2001)*. Morgan Kaufmann, 2001, pp. 66–73.

[36] M. Cuturi and J.-P. Vert. A covariance kernel for proteins. Technical report, 2003. http://arxiv.org/abs/q-bio.GN/0310022.

[37] S. Deerwester, S. Dumais, G. Furnas, T. Landauer, and R. Harshman. Indexing by latent semantic analysis. *Journal of the American Society for Information Science*, **41** (1990): 391–407

[38] L. Devroye, L. Györfi, and G. Lugosi. *A Probabilistic Theory of Pattern Recognition*. Number 31 in Applications of mathematics. Springer-Verlag, 1996.

[39] R.O. Duda and P.E. Hart. *Pattern Classification and Scene Analysis*. John Wiley & Sons, 1973.

[40] R.O. Duda, P.E. Hart, and D.G. Stork. *Pattern Classification*. Wiley-Interscience, 2000, 2nd edition.

[41] S.T. Dumais, J. Platt, D. Heckerman, and M. Sahami. Inductive learning algorithms and representations for text categorisation. In *Proceedings of the Seventh International Conference on Information and Knowledge Management*, 1998, pp. 148–155 (see www.csee.umbc.edu/cikm/1998#announce).

[42] R. Durbin, S. Eddy, A. Krogh, and G. Mitchison. *Biological Sequence Analysis: Probabilistic Models of Proteins and Nucleic Acids*. Cambridge University Press, 1998.

[43] T. Evgeniou, M. Pontil, and T. Poggio. Regularization networks and support vector machines. *Advances in Computational Mathematics*, **13**(1) (2000): 1–50.

[44] R.A. Fisher. The use of multiple measurements in taxonomic problems. *Annals of Eugenics*, **7**(2) (1986): 179–188.

[45] K.S. Fu. *Syntactic Methods in Pattern Recognition*. Academic Press, 1974.

[46] K. Fukunaga. *Introduction to Statistical Pattern Recognition*. Academic Press, 1990, 2nd edition.

[47] F. Girosi. An equivalence between sparse approximation and support vector machines. *Neural Computation*, **10**(6) (1998): 1455–1480.

[48] F. Girosi, M. Jones, and T. Poggio. Regularization theory and neural networks architectures. *Neural Computation*, **7**(2) 1995: 219–269.

[49]   G.H. Golub and C.F. Van Loan. *Matrix Computations*. Johns Hopkins University Press, 1996.

[50]   D. Gusfield. *Algorithms on Strings, Trees, and Sequences*. Cambridge University Press, 1997.

[51]   D.R. Hardoon, and J. Shawe-Taylor. KCCA for different level precision in content-based image retrieval. In *Proceedings of Third International Workshop on Content-Based Multimedia Indexing*, 2003, IRISA, Rennes, France.

[52]   D.R. Hardoon, S. Szedmak, and J. Shawe-Taylor. Canonical correlation analysis; an overview with application to learning methods. Technical Report CSD-TR-03-02, Royal Holloway University of London, 2003.

[53]   T. Hastie, R. Tibshirani, and J. Friedman. *The Elements of Statistical Learning – Data Mining, Inference and Prediction*. Springer-Verlag, 2001.

[54]   D. Haussler. Convolution kernels on discrete structures. Technical Report UCSC-CRL-99-10, University of California in Santa Cruz, Computer Science Department, July 1999.

[55]   R. Herbrich. *Learning Kernel Classifiers: Theory and Algorithms*. MIT Press, 2001.

[56]   R. Herbrich, T. Graepel, and K. Obermayer. Large margin rank boundaries for ordinal regression. In *Advances in Large Margin Classifiers*. MIT Press, 2000, pp. 115–132.

[57]   J. Hertz, A. Krogh, and R.G. Palmer. *Introduction to the Theory of Neural Computation*. Addison-Wesley, 1991.

[58]   A.E. Hoerl and R.W. Kennard. Ridge regression: Biased estimation for nonorthogonal problems. *Technometrics*, **12**(1) (1970): 55–67.

[59]   T. Hofmann. Learning the similarity of documents: an information-geometric approach to document retrieval and categorization. In *Proceedings of Advances in Neural Information Processing Systems (NIPS'99)*, volume 12. MIT Press, 2000.

[60]   A. Höskuldsson. Pls regression methods. *Journal of Chemometrics*, **2** (1998): 211–228.

[61]   H. Hotelling. Analysis of a complex of statistical variables into principal components. *Journal of Educational Psychology*, **24** (1933): 417–441 and 498–520.

[62]   H. Hotelling. Relations between two sets of variables. *Biometrika*, **28** (1936): 321–377.

[63]   T.S. Jaakkola and D. Haussler. Exploiting generative models in discriminative classifiers. In *Advances in Neural Information Processing Systems 11, 1998*. MIT Press, 1998.

[64]   T.S. Jaakkola and D. Haussler. Probabilistic kernel regression models. In *Proceedings of the 1999 Conference on AI and Statistics*. Morgan Kauffman, 1999.

[65]   T. Jebara and Risi Kondor. Bhattacharyya and expected likelihood kernels. In *Proceedings of the 16th Conference on Learning Theory (COLT)*. Association for computing Machinery (ACM), 2003.

[66]   F. Jiang and M. Littman. Approximate dimension equalization in vector-based information retrieval. In *Proceedings of XXVII International Conference on Machine Learning*. Morgan Kauffman, 2000.

[67] T. Joachims. Text categorization with support vector machines. In *European Conference on Machine Learning (ECML)*. Springer-Verlag, 1998.

[68] T. Joachims. *Learning to Classify Text using Support Vector Machines*. Kluwer, 2002.

[69] T. Joachims, N. Cristianini, and J. Shawe-Taylor. Composite kernels for hypertext categorisation. In *Proceedings of the International Conference on Machine Learning, ICML'01*. Morgan Kauffman, 2001.

[70] M.I. Jordan. *An Introduction to Probabilistic Graphical Models*. Forthcoming, 2004.

[71] J. Kandola, J. Shawe-Taylor, and N. Cristianini. Learning semantic similarity. In *Neural Information Processing Systems 15 (NIPS 15)*. MIT Press, 2002.

[72] J. Kandola, J. Shawe-Taylor, and N. Cristianini. On the extensions of kernel alignment. NeuroCOLT Technical Report NC-TR-2002-120, http://www.neurocolt.org, 2002.

[73] J. Kandola, J. Shawe-Taylor, and N. Cristianini. Optimizing kernel alignment over combinations of kernel. NeuroCOLT Technical Report NC-TR-2002-121, http://www.neurocolt.org, 2002.

[74] R. Kannan, S. Vempala, and A. Vetta. On clusterings: good, bad and spectral. In *Proc. of the 41st Foundations of Computer Science (FOCS '00)*. Morgan Kauffman, 2000.

[75] H. Kashima, K. Tsuda, and A. Inokuchi. Marginalized kernels between labeled graphs. In *Proceedings of the 20th International Conference on Machine Learning*. Morgan Kauffman, 2003.

[76] M. Kearns and U. Vazirani. *An Introduction to Computational Learning Theory*. MIT Press, 1994.

[77] T. Kin, K. Tsuda, and K. Asai. Marginalized kernels for RNA sequence data analysis. In R. H. Lathtop, K. Nakai, S. Miyano, T. Takagi, and M. Kanehisa, editors, *Genome Informatics 2002*. Universal Academic Press, 2002, pp. 112–132.

[78] A. Koestler. *The Sleepwalkers*. Penguin, 1979.

[79] V. Koltchinskii. Rademacher penalties and structural risk minimization. *IEEE Transactions on Information Theory*, **47**(5) (July 2001): 1902–1914.

[80] V. Koltchinskii and D. Panchenko. Rademacher processes and bounding the risk of function learning. *High Dimensional Probability II*, 2000, pp. 443–459.

[81] Vladimir I. Koltchinskii and Dmitry Panchenko. Empirical margin distributions and bounding the generalization error of combined classifiers. *Annals of Statistics*, **30**(1), (2002).

[82] R.I. Kondor and J. Lafferty. Diffusion kernels on graphs and other discrete structures. In *Proceedings of Intenational Conference on Machine Learning (ICML 2002)*. Morgan, Kauffman 2002.

[83] P.L. Lai and C. Fyfe. Kernel and nonlinear canonical correlation analysis. *International Journal of Neural Systems*, **10**(5) (2000): 365–377.

[84] J. Langford and J. Shawe-Taylor. PAC Bayes and margins. In *Advances in Neural Information Processing Systems 15*. MIT Press, 2003.

[85] M. Ledoux and M. Talagrand. *Probability in Banach Spaces: Isoperimetry and Processes*. Springer-Verlag, 1991.

[86] E. Leopold and J. Kinderman. Text categorization with support vector machines. How to represent texts in input space? *Machine Learning: Special Issue on Support Vector and Kernel Methods*, **46** (1–3) (2002): 423–444.

[87] C. Leslie, E. Eskin, A. Cohen, J. Weston, and William Stafford Noble. Mismatch string kernels for discriminative protein classification. *Bioinformatics*, 2003. to appear.

[88] C. Leslie, E. Eskin, and W.S. Noble. The spectrum kernel: A string kernel for SVM protein classification. In *Proceedings of the Pacific Symposium on Biocomputing (PSB-2002)*. World Scientific Publishing, 2002.

[89] C. Leslie, E. Eskin, J. Weston, and W.S. Noble. Mismatch string kernels for SVM protein classification. In *Advances in Neural Information Processing Systems 15*. MIT Press, 2003.

[90] C. Leslie and Rui Kuang. Fast kernels for inexact string matching. In *Proceedings of the 16th Conference on Learning Theory (COLT)*. ACM, 2003.

[91] M. Li and P. Vitanyi. *An Introduction to Kolmogorov Complexity and Its Applications*. Springer-Verlag, 1997.

[92] M.L. Littman, S.T. Dumais, and T.K. Landauer. Automatic cross-language information retrieval using latent semantic indexing. In G. Grefenstette, editor, *Cross Language Information Retrieval*. Kluwer, 1998.

[93] H. Lodhi, C. Saunders, J. Shawe-Taylor, N. Cristianini, and C. Watkins. Text classification using string kernels. *Journal of Machine Learning Research*, **2** (2002): 419–444.

[94] O.L. Mangasarian. *Nonlinear Programming*. SIAM, 1994.

[95] O.L. Mangasarian. Linear and nonlinear separation of patterns by linear programming. *Operations Research*, **13** (1965): 444–452.

[96] C. McDiarmid. On the method of bounded differences. In 141 London Mathematical Society Lecture Notes Series, editor, *Surveys in Combinatorics 1989*, Cambridge University Press, 1989, pp. 148–188.

[97] J. Mercer. Functions of positive and negative type and their connection with the theory of integral equations. *Philosophical Transactions of the Royal Society of London*, Series A **209** (1909): 415–446.

[98] C. Meyer. *Matrix Analysis and Applied Linear Algebra*. SIAM, 2000.

[99] C.A. Micchelli. Interpolation of scattered data: distance matrices and conditionally positive definite functions. *Constructive Approximation*, 2 (1986): 11–22.

[100] S. Mika, G. Rätsch, J. Weston, B. Schölkopf, and K.-R. Müller. Fisher discriminant analysis with kernels. In Y.-H. Hu, J. Larsen. E. Wilson, and S. Douglas, editors, *Neural Networks for Signal Processing IX*. IEEE, 1999, pp. 41–48.

[101] M. Minsky and S. Papert. *Perceptrons: An Introduction to Computational Geometry*. MIT Press, 1969.

[102] T. Mitchell. *Machine Learning*. McGraw-Hill, 1997.

[103] A. Ng, M.I. Jordan, and Y. Weiss. On spectral clustering: Analysis and an algorithm. In T.G. Dietterich, S. Becker, and Z. Ghahramani, editors, *Advances in Neural Information Processing Systems 14*. MIT Press, 2002.

[104] C.S. Ong, A. Smola, and Robert C. Williamson. Superkernels. In *Advances in Neural Information Processing Systems (NIPS 02)*. MIT Press, 2003.

[105] T. Pisanski and J. Shawe-Taylor. Characterising graph drawing with eigenvectors. *Journal of Chemical Information and Computer Sciences*, **40**(3) (2000): 567–571.

[106] T. Poggio. On optimal nonlinear associative recall. *Biological Cybernetics*, **19** (1975): 201–209.

[107] T. Poggio and F. Girosi. Regularization algorithms for learning that are equivalent to multilayer networks. *Science*, **247** (1990): 978–982.

[108] T. Poggio and S. Smale. The mathematics of learning: dealing with data. *American Mathematical Society*, **50**(5) (2003): 537–544.

[109] J.R. Quinlan. *C4.5: Programs for Machine Learning*. Morgan Kauffmann, 1993.

[110] B.D. Ripley. *Pattern Recognition and Neural Networks*. Cambridge University Press, 1996.

[111] F. Rosenblatt. The perceptron: A probabilistic model for information storage and organization in the brain. *Psychological Review*, **65**(6) (1958): 386–408.

[112] R. Rosipal and L.J. Trejo. Kernel partial least squares regression in reproducing kernel Hilbert space. *Journal of Machine Learning Research*, **2** (2001): 97–123.

[113] S. Saitoh. *Theory of Reproducing Kernels and its Applications*. Longman Scientific & Technical, 1988.

[114] G. Salton, A. Wang, and C. Yang. A vector space model for information retrieval. *Journal of the American Society for Information Science*, **18** (1975): 613–620.

[115] C. Saunders, A. Gammermann and V. Vovk. Ridge regression learning algorithm in dual variables. In J. Shavlik, editor, *Machine Learning: Proceedings of the Fifteenth International Conference(ICML '98)*. Morgan Kaufmann, 1998.

[116] C. Saunders, J. Shawe-Taylor, and A. Vinokourov. String kernels, Fisher kernels and finite state automata. In *Advances of Neural Information Processing Systems 15*. 2002.

[117] B. Schölkopf, C. Burges, and V. Vapnik. Extracting support data for a given task. In U.M. Fayyad and R. Uthurusamy, editors, *Proceedings, First International Conference on Knowledge Discovery & Data Mining*. AAAI Press, 1995.

[118] B. Schölkopf. *Support Vector Learning*. R. Oldenbourg Verlag, 1997.

[119] B. Schölkopf, J.C. Platt, J.S. Shawe-Taylor, A.J. Smola, and R.C. Williamson. Estimating the support of a high-dimensional distribution. *Neural Computation*, **13**(7) (2001): 1443–1471.

[120] B. Schölkopf and A. Smola. *Learning with Kernels*. MIT Press, 2002.

[121] B. Schölkopf, A. Smola, and K.-R. Müller. Nonlinear component analysis as a kernel eigenvalue problem. *Neural Computation*, **10** (1998): 1299–1319.

[122] B. Schölkopf, A. Smola, R. Williamson, and P. Bartlett. New support vector algorithms. *Neural Computation*, **12**(5) (2000): 1207–1245.

[123] A. Shashua. On the relationship between the support vector machine for classification and sparsified fisher's linear discriminant. *Neural Processing Letters*, **9**(2) (April 1999): 129-139.

[124] J. Shawe-Taylor, P.L. Bartlett, R.C. Williamson, and M. Anthony. Structural risk minimization over data-dependent hierarchies. *IEEE Transactions on Information Theory*, **44**(5) (1998): 1926–1940.

[125] J. Shawe-Taylor and N. Cristianini. On the generalisation of soft margin algorithms. *IEEE Transactions on Information Theory*, **48**(10) (2002): 2721–2735.

[126] J. Shawe-Taylor, N. Cristianini, and J. Kandola. On the concentration of spectral properties. In T.G. Dietterich, S. Becker, and Z. Ghahramani, editors, *Advances in Neural Information Processing Systems 14*. MIT Press, 2002, pp. 511–517.

[127] J. Shawe-Taylor, C. Williams, N. Cristianini, and J.S. Kandola. On the eigenspectrum of the Gram matrix and its relationship to the operator eigenspectrum. In *Proceedings of the 13th International Conference on Algorithmic Learning Theory (ALT2002)*, volume 2533, Springer-Verlag, 2002, pp. 23–40.

[128] G. Siolas and F. d'Alché Buc. Support vector machines based on a semantic kernel for text categorization. In *International Joint Conference on Neural Networks (1JCNN)*. Springer-Verlag, 2002.

[129] F.W. Smith. Pattern classifier design by linear programming. *IEEE Transactions on Computers*, **C-17** (1968): 367–372.

[130] A. Smola, B. Schölkopf, and K.-R. Müller. The connection between regularization operators and support vector kernels. *Neural Networks*, **11** (1998): 637–649.

[131] J.A.K. Suykens, T. Van Gestel, J. De Brabanter, B. De Moor, and J. Vandewalle. *Least Squares Support Vector Machines*. World Scientific Publishing Co., 2002.

[132] E. Takimoto and M. Warmuth. Path kernels and multiplicative updates. In *Proceedings of the 15th Conference on Learning Theory (COLT)*. ACM, 2002.

[133] E. Takimoto and M. Warmuth. Predicting nearly as well as the best pruning of a planar decision graph. *Theoretical Computer Science*, **288**(2) (2002): 217–235.

[134] M. Talagrand. Sharper bounds for Gaussian and empirical processes. *Annals of Probability*, **22** (1994): 28–76.

[135] M. Talagrand. The Glivenko–Cantelli problem, ten years later. *Journal of Theoretical Probability*, **9**(2) (1996): 371–384.

[136] D.M.J. Tax and R.P.W. Duin. Support vector domain description. *Pattern Recognition Letters*, pages **20**(11–13) (December 1999): 1191–1199.

[137] S. Theodoridis and K. Koutroumbas. *Pattern Recognition*. Academic Press, 2003.

[138] A.N. Tikhonov and V.Y. Arsenin. *Solutions of Ill-posed Problems*. W.H. Winston, 1977.

[139] K. Tsuda, T. Kin, and K. Asai. Marginalized kernels for biological sequences. *Bioinformatics*, **18** (2002): 268–275.

[140] V. Vapnik. *Estimation of Dependences Based on Empirical Data [in Russian]*. Nauka, Moscow, 1979. (English translation, Springer Verlag, 1982).

[141] V. Vapnik. *The Nature of Statistical Learning Theory*. Springer Verlag, 1995.

[142] V. Vapnik. *Statistical Learning Theory*. Wiley, 1998.

[143] V. Vapnik and A. Chervonenkis. A note on one class of perceptrons. *Automation and Remote Control*, **25** (1964).

[144] V. Vapnik and A. Chervonenkis. Uniform convergence of frequencies of occurence of events to their probabilities. *Doklady Akademii Nauk SSSR*, **181** (1968): 915–918.

[145] V. Vapnik and A. Chervonenkis. On the uniform convergence of relative frequencies of events to their probabilities. *Theory of Probability and its Applications*, **16**(2) (1971): 264–280.

[146] V. Vapnik and A. Lerner. Pattern recognition using generalized portrait method. *Automation and Remote Control*, **24** (1963).

[147] J.-P. Vert. Support vector machine prediction of signal peptide cleavage site using a new class of kernels for strings. In R.B. Altman, A.K. Dunker, L. Hunter, K. Lauerdale, and T.E. Klein, editors, *Proceedings of the Pacific Symposium on Biocomputing 2002*. World Scientific, 2002, pp. 649–660.

[148] J.-P. Vert. A tree kernel to analyze phylogenetic profiles. *Bioinformatics*, **18** (2002): 276–284.

[149] J.-P. Vert and M. Kanehisa. Graph-driven features extraction from microarray data using diffusion kernels and kernel CCA. In *Advances in Neural Information Processing Systems 15*. MIT Press, 2003.

[150] J.-P. Vert, H. Saigo, and T. Akutsu. Convolution and local alignment kernels. In B. Schölkopf, K. Tsuda, and J.-P. Vert, editors, *Kernel Methods in Computational Biology*. MIT Press, 2004.

[151] H.D. Vinod. Canonical ridge and econometrics of joint production. *J. Econometrics*, **4** (1976): 147–166.

[152] A. Vinokourov, D. Hardoon, J. Shawe-Taylor. Learning the semantics of multimedia content with application to web image retrieval and classification. In *Proceedings of Fourth International Symposium on Independent Component Analysis and Blind Source Separation*, Nara, 2003.

[153] A. Vinokourov, J. Shawe-Taylor, and N. Cristianini. Inferring a semantic representation of text via cross-language correlation analysis. In *Advances of Neural Information Processing Systems 15*. MIT Press, 2002.

[154] S.V.N. Vishwanathan and A.J. Smola. Fast kernels on strings and trees. In T.G. Dietterich, S. Becker, and Z. Ghahramani, editors, *Advances in Neural Information Processing Systems 14*. MIT Press, 2002.

[155] G. Wahba. *Spline Models for Observational Data*, volume 59 of *CBMS-NSF Regional Conference Series in Applied Mathematics*. SIAM, 1990.

[156] G. Wahba. Support vector machines, reproducing kernel Hilbert spaces and the randomized GACV. In B. Schölkopf, C.J.C. Burges, and A.J. Smola, editors, *Advances in Kernel Methods – Support Vector Learning*. MIT Press, pp. 69–88.

[157] C. Watkins. Kernels from matching operations. Technical Report CSD-TR-98-1?, Royal Holloway College, Computer Science Department, July 1999.

[158] C. Watkins. Dynamic alignment kernels. In A.J. Smola, P.L. Bartlett, B. Schölkopf, and D. Schuurmans, editors, *Advances in Large Margin Classifiers*. MIT Press, 2002, pp. 39–50.

[159] D.W. Wichern and R.A. Johnson. *Applied Multivariate Statistical Analysis*. Prentice Hall, 5th edition, 2002.

[160] B. Widrow and M. Hoff. Adaptive switching circuits. In *IRE WESCON Convention Record*, (1960), pp. 96–104.

[161] C.K.I. Williams. Prediction with Gaussian processes: From linear regression to linear prediction and beyond. In M.I. Jordan, editor, *Learning and Inference in Graphical Models*. Kluwer, 1998.

[162] H. Wold. Estimation of principal components and related models by iterative least squares. In P.R. Krishnaiah, editor, *Multivariate Analysis*. Academic Press, 1966, pp. 391–420.

[163] H. Wold. Path models with latent variables: the NIPALS approach. In H.M. Blalock *et al.*, editors, *Quantitative Sociology: International Perspectives on Mathematical and Statistical Model Building*. Academic Press, 1975, pp. 307–357.

[164] H. Wold. Soft modeling by latent variables; the nonlinear iterative partial least squares NIPALS approach. *Perspectives in Probability and Statistics*, **9** (1975): 117–142.

[165] H. Wold. Partial least squares. In S. Kotz and N.L. Johnson, editors, *Encyclopedia of the Statistical Sciences*, volume 6. John Wiley & Sons, 1985, pp. 581–591.

[166] H. Wolkowicz, R. Saigal, and editors L. Vandenberghe. *Handbook of Semidefinite Programming*. Kluwer, 2001.

[167] S.K.M. Wong, W. Ziarko, and P.C.N. Wong. Generalized vector space model in information retrieval. In *ACM SIGIR Conference on Research and Development in Information Retrieval (SIGIR'85)*. 1985, pp. 18–25.

[168] Y. Yamanishi, J.-P. Vert, A. Nakaya, and M. Kanehisa. Extraction of correlated gene clusters from multiple genomic data by generalized kernel canonical correlation analysis. *Bioinformatics*, 2003. to appear.

[169] H. Zha, X. He, C. Ding, M. Gu, and H. Simon. Spectral relaxation for k-means clustering. In T.G. Dietterich, S. Becker, and Z. Ghahramani, editors, *Advances in Neural Information Processing Systems 14*. MIT Press, 2002, pp. 1057–1064.

Index

Printed in the United States
By Bookmasters